OFFICIAL HANDBOOK OF THE MARVEL UNIVERSE

HEAD WRITER/COORDINATOR
Jeff Christiansen

COORDINATION ASSISTANTS
Madison Carter, Mike Fichera & Stuart Vandal

ART REFURBISHMENT
David Wiltfong, Mike Fichera, J. Christopher Schmidt, Tony Marcotte, Matthew Frank,
Chris Biggs & Michel Gariepy

WRITERS
Jeff Christiansen, Sean McQuaid, Michael Hoskin, Stuart Vandal, Ronald Byrd, David Wiltfong,
Madison Carter, Mike Fichera, Chad Anderson, Chris Biggs, Eric J. Moreels, Mark O'English,
Al Sjoerdsma, Jacob Rougemont, Gabriel Shechter, Jeph York, Markus Ettlinger, Rich Green,
Michel Gariepy, Andrew Goletz, Olav Rokne & Peter Sanderson

PAST WRITERS
Jonathan Couper-Smartt, Eric Englehard, Bill Lentz & Barry Reese

COVER ARTISTS
Tom Grummett, Roland Paris & Avalon's Matt Milla

ART RECONSTRUCTION
Pond Scum

SELECT COLORING
Tom Smith

EDITORS
Jeff Youngquist & Jennifer Grünwald

EDITOR, SPECIAL PROJECTS
Mark D. Beazley

ASSISTANT EDITORS
John Denning & Cory Levine

EDITORIAL ASSISTANT
Alex Starbuck

COPY EDITOR
Brian Overton

SENIOR VICE PRESIDENT OF SALES
David Gabriel

PRODUCTION
Nelson Ribeiro & Jerron Quality Color

EDITOR IN CHIEF
Joe Quesada

PUBLISHER
Dan Buckley

Special thanks to Jason Aaron, Christos Gage, Craig Lowrey, Howard Mackie, Peter Milligan, Evan Skolnick, Roy Thomas, Ivan Velez, Tommy Wilson, the guys at the Appendix (www.marvunapp.com), Martin Allen, Kurt Busiek, Matt Fraction, John McDonagh, Kevin Grevioux, Peter David, Daniel Ketchum, Bill Rosemann & Tom Brevoort

Jacob Rougemont would like to thank his parents, Ricky and Saundra; his grandparents, Bell and Keith, and Charles and Frances; Chris Reichert; Josh McMahan; TOWMAC Productions (http://www.myspace.com/towmacproductions) and "the Crew" (Kat, Chris, Matt, Thomas, Emily, James, Timmy, Hunter); Jeff Christiansen; Mike Fichera; Kevin Lawrence Smith; everyone at K-Mart 7461; and all my other friends and family that I'm unable to mention due to space.

The Official Handbook of the Marvel Universe Frequently Asked Questions page — including data corrections and explanations, complete bibliographies, and Power Grid legends: http://www.marvel.com/universe/OHOTMU

OFFICIAL HANDBOOK OF THE MARVEL UNIVERSE A TO Z VOL. 6. First printing 2008. ISBN# 978-0-7851-3103-8. Published by MARVEL PUBLISHING, INC., a subsidiary of MARVEL ENTERTAINMENT, INC. OFFICE OF PUBLICATION: 417 5th Avenue, New York, NY 10016. Copyright © 2008 Marvel Characters, Inc. All rights reserved. $24.99 per copy in the U.S. and $26.50 in Canada (GST #R127032852); Canadian Agreement #40668537. All characters featured in this issue and the distinctive names and likenesses thereof, and all related indicia are trademarks of Marvel Characters, Inc. No similarity between any of the names, characters, persons, and/or institutions in this magazine with those of any living or dead person or institution is intended, and any such similarity which may exist is purely coincidental. **Printed in the U.S.A.** ALAN FINE, CEO Marvel Toys & Publishing Divisions and CMO Marvel Characters, Inc.; DAVID GABRIEL, SVP of Publishing Sales & Circulation; DAVID BOGART, SVP of Business Affairs & Talent Management; MICHAEL PASCIULLO, VP of Merchandising & Communications; JIM O'KEEFE, VP of Operations & Logistics; DAN CARR, Executive Director of Publishing Technology; JUSTIN F. GABRIE, Director of Editorial Operations; SUSAN CRESPI, Editorial Operations Manager; STAN LEE, Chairman Emeritus. For information regarding advertising in Marvel Comics or on Marvel.com, please contact Mitch Dane, Advertising Director, at mdane@marvel.com. For Marvel subscription inquiries, please call 800-217-9158.

10 9 8 7 6 5 4 3 2 1

HARALD JAEKELSSON

REAL NAME: Harald Jaekelsson
ALIASES: The Jackal's Son
IDENTITY: No dual identity
OCCUPATION: Warlord
CITIZENSHIP: Norway
PLACE OF BIRTH: Unrevealed
KNOWN RELATIVES: None
GROUP AFFILIATION: Led Dragon Ship crew
EDUCATION: Probably no formal education
FIRST APPEARANCE: Thor: Vikings #1 (2003)

HISTORY: At the dawn of the 11th century, Harald Jaekelsson was one of the most feared Viking depredators active in the North and Norwegian Seas. When the villagers of Lakstad complained to Norway's King Sven Forkbeard of Jaekelsson's raids, Jaekelsson retaliated by leading his men in a massacre of Lakstad, murdering all but a handful of escaping children, some of them grandchildren of the local sage. Disdaining Norway's laws as too restrictive on his cruelties, Jaekelsson set his Dragon Ship's course for the little-known Western Hemisphere, but Lakstad's sage, clinging to survival, cursed him and his crew, using the power of runestone blood magic, to sail for a thousand years without finding the land they sought; in a parting shot, Jaekellson slew the sage, whose blood and soul magnified the spell a thousandfold, imbuing its targets with awesome mystic power.

In recent years, Jaekelsson's ship emerged from its timeless voyage through a millennium of limbo to dock at New York. Little understanding or caring how the world had changed, the Vikings slew all that approached them before being challenged by Thor. Empowered by the runestone spell, Jaekelsson brutally beat the thunder god, and then resolved to conquer Manhattan. Thousands were slaughtered over a three-day period, one of New York's most devastating extra-normal incursions. The police, the US Marines, and even the Avengers were helpless before Jaekelsson's forces.

Meanwhile, the recovering Thor had been joined by Dr. Strange, who gazed back in time to learn of the sage's curse and the bloodshed that had magnified it. Recognizing that warriors of the same bloodline would be best qualified to oppose the curse's power, Strange searched history for suitable descendants of the sage. From the early twelfth century, he drew the reckless Viking battle maiden Sigrid; from the mid-thirteenth, the fanatical Sir Magnus of the Danes; and from 1945, Oberstleutnant Erik Lonnroth, reluctant fighter for Nazi Germany and the pilot of a Messerschmitt 109. Strange empowered the three, as well as Thor himself, with the bloodline's magic, amplifying their strength and weapons beyond the power of gods. Brought to the present, Sigrid, Magnus and Lonnroth wiped out the Viking crew, leaving Thor to confront Jaekelsson, whom Thor literally tore limb from limb and hurled into space, leaving the Viking warlord to orbit Earth, as helpless as he was heartless. The sage's three descendants were returned to their places in the past, where their valiant and violent deaths guaranteed them entrance into Asgard's honored Hall of the Dead, Valhalla.

HEIGHT: 7'7"
WEIGHT: 365 lbs.
EYES: Brown
HAIR: Black

ABILITIES/ACCESSORIES: A savage and accomplished warrior, Harald Jaekelsson is superhumanly strong, sufficiently so to be a match for Thor's Class 100 strength, and impervious not only to most forms of physical force, but to most forms of magic as well, even that of the Sorcerer Supreme; his weaponry, including a longsword, a dagger, and the armor of his era, has been similarly enhanced. He commanded a crew of similarly powered warriors aboard a flying longship whose draconian prow breathed fire.

POWER GRID	1	2	3	4	5	6	7
INTELLIGENCE							
STRENGTH							
SPEED							
DURABILITY							
ENERGY PROJECTION							
FIGHTING SKILLS							

Art by Glenn Fabry

JOHN JAMESON

HISTORY: As a career test pilot and astronaut, Col. John Jameson was, according to his father J. Jonah, "made of the stuff of heroes," unlike masked menaces such as Spider-Man. However, Spider-Man has saved his son's life on numerous occasions. During his first mission orbiting Earth, Spider-Man replaced a guidance module in Col. Jameson's plummeting space capsule. In a subsequent mission in space, Jameson contacted spores from Jupiter that endowed him with superhuman strength, increased his size, and made him act more aggressively. NASA gave him a special suit from Tony Stark's lab to keep his strength in check. When it appeared that Spider-Man was responsible for a bank robbery, John was persuaded by his father to become a public hero by apprehending him. Spider-Man had the upper hand, but John sought a rematch. This time, Spider-Man neutralized the spores with a dose of high-voltage electricity, returning John to normal.

Later, Jameson was sent to the moon to collect rock samples on a top-secret mission and stumbled upon a glittering red gemstone. Once his mission was complete and following a strange urge, he had his friend Ralph "Rocks" Sarson "borrow" the stone, then had it made into a pendant that he wore around his neck. The gem was actually the Godstone (aka Weirdstone or Moonstone), previously possessed by the lupine Stargod, ancient and benevolent ruler of a swords and sorcery dimension called Other Realm. Stargod originally found the stone on Earth's moon where it had landed millennia ago after being launched across time and space following the destruction of the collection of power gems known as the Lifestone Tree. Centuries later, Stargod grew old and weak. To spare his world from his decay, he opened a portal to Earth's moon and went there to die, returning the Godstone there and leaving his essence within while his body disintegrated. Ancient prophecies foretold that, in evil times, Stargod would be reborn to save Other Realm.

Soon after Jameson donned the Godstone pendant, the Godstone became grafted to his neck. Since the radiation that leaked from the portal was weak, John's transformation to Stargod was only partial. Whenever the moon shone on the stone, John gained the form, as well as some degree of the strength and primal fury of Stargod but lacked his wisdom and power, instead becoming the feral Man-Wolf. John created a radiation suit to block lunar rays, but it failed to work. While taking extended leave in New York, John became the Man-Wolf and attacked his father and his own fiancée Kristine Saunders. However, Spider-Man stopped him by tearing the stone off his neck, throwing it into the East River. In spite of this, John was changed back to the Man-Wolf due to the stone's proximity after the pseudo-vampire Morbius retrieved it. Morbius reattached the pendant, which sent tendrils throughout John's body, and used Man-Wolf as a diversion as he sought a cure for his vampirism, but Spider-Man foiled the scheme. John now became Man-Wolf in any moonlight, his strength and intelligence fluctuating with the moon's phases.

Needing John for a secret mission, NASA recalled him from leave but he failed to appear, even as the police sent ex-CIA man Simon Stroud to investigate the Man-Wolf's rampages. Stroud tracked Man-Wolf to the Statue of Liberty but the beast fell from the statue's torch and escaped. Meanwhile, the sorcerer Arisen Tyrk – who had risen to become the tyrannical God-King of Other Realm – sought to forestall the Stargod prophecy and to claim the Godstone for himself. He tracked the gem's energies to Earth and, as Harrisyn Turk, acted through intermediaries to avoid being confronted by the Godstone's power. "Turk" hired Kraven the Hunter to capture Man-Wolf, learn his strengths and arrange for the deaths of Kristine and Jonah. Stroud disrupted the plan and arrested John for being AWOL, but John escaped and hitchhiked south, befriending free-spirited couple Joel and Mary Stevens in Georgia and becoming involved in the Hate-Monger (Adolf Hitler clone)'s plan to reclaim his space station from NASA. Nick Fury and SHIELD thwarted this scheme but Joel Stevens was murdered by a Hate-Monger henchman, Red Hate.

REAL NAME: John Jameson
ALIASES: Stargod, Man-Wolf, Vanwolf, Skywolf
IDENTITY: (Man-Wolf) Known to the authorities
OCCUPATION: Test pilot; former SHIELD operative, social worker, security chief, monster hunter, fulltime pilot for Avengers/Captain America, astronaut
CITIZENSHIP: USA
PLACE OF BIRTH: New York, New York
KNOWN RELATIVES: John Jonah Jameson (father), Joan Jameson (mother, deceased), Marla Madison (stepmother), John Jonah Jameson Sr. (grandfather), Betty Burnoll (grandmother), David Burnoll (step-grandfather)
GROUP AFFILIATION: USAF; formerly Howling Commandos (SHIELD), Queens Dept. of Social Services, Ravencroft Institute, Avengers Crew, NASA
EDUCATION: Master of science degree in aeronautical engineering
FIRST APPEARANCE: Amazing Spider-Man #1 (1963)

JUPITER SUIT

Art by John Romita Jr.

MAN-WOLF
Art by Gil Kane

AVENGERS CREW JUMPSUIT
Art by James Fry

Meanwhile, a group of rebels of Other Realm – consisting of the warriors Garth of Mournhelm and Gorjoon, and the wizard Lambert — used the moon portal to seek the Godstone, but found it missing. They next took over the NASA space station. Returned to NASA by Fury, John was sent to investigate the radio silence from the space station, finding Garth, Lambert, and Garjoon there. Garth's attempt to cut the Godstone from Man-Wolf's throat was halted by the station soldiers who then imprisoned the beast. As Tyrk kidnapped Kristine and brought her to Other Realm, John escaped with Garth, Lambert, and Garjoon, became Man-Wolf, entered the moon portal, regained John's intelligence and became Stargod. The warriors of Other Realm explained Stargod's origins and enlisted Jameson to help against Tyrk, giving him the Sacred Sword of the Stargod. They flew towards Tyrk's Sky City base, but their initial force was overpowered by Tyrk's undead warriors. Only Jameson and Gorjoon escaped capture. Another rebel, Sashiel, was slain, and the wizard Lambert's hands were cut off. Jameson and Gorjoon made their way to Sky City where they freed their allies and confronted Tyrk. Jameson accessed Stargod's full power to destroy Sky City and overpower Tyrk, after which he transported himself and Kristine back to Earth. John's memories of his Stargod experience faded, and he reverted to Man-Wolf. He was captured along with Spider-Man and the Frankenstein Monster by the lunatic Monster Maker, Baron Ludwig von Shtupf, who sought to dissect them, learn their secrets, and create an army of warriors with their combined abilities. After von Shtupf's defeat, the Man-Wolf was subdued and taken into SHIELD captivity.

micro-world, accessed only via the energies of shrinking. A microscopic portal to Other Realm opened in the She-Hulk (Jennifer Walters)'s radioactive bloodstream, which threatened to destroy it. John/Stargod was trapped in another such "micro-world" – a crystalline realm with a portal existing within Walters' necklace, which she accidentally left with her friend Richard Rory. Jameson constructed a battery and transmitter and communicated with Richard Rory's radio station.

Unable to contact Stargod or to stop his realm's decay, Lambert nonetheless sensed that She-Hulk was involved in the process. He accessed Earth by means of Hellcat's Shadow Cloak, and brought her to Other Realm. They then used the Shadow Cloak to locate the She-Hulk and attempted to bring her to Other Realm; however, as the portal to the realm existed within She-Hulk's bloodstream, she was unable to access it and was instead shunted to the crystalline realm while Other Realm's shrinking was further accelerated. Hellcat located both She-Hulk and Stargod in the crystalline realm, and she transported Stargod to Other Realm where he used his vast power to harness and alter the vibrational attunement of the realm, restoring – with She-Hulk's aid – Other Realm to its previous state prior to the rapid acceleration of the shrinking.

Jameson returned to Earth, but reverted to Man-Wolf again and lost his memory of these events. Reunited with his father, he and Spider-Man sought Dr. Curt Connors to administer a biomagnetic treatment that caused John's body to reject the Godstone. With the stone crumbled into powder, John ceased transforming into the Man-Wolf. John broke up with his fiancée Kristine Saunders and spent some time at the Sherwood Nursing Home sanitarium to mentally recover from all his life's ordeals. There, before his father's second marriage, he was kidnapped by the Scorpion (Mac Gargan), but was rescued by Spider-Man.

After apparently escaping, John discovered the stone was slowly poisoning him. His father and Dr. Marla Madison placed him in cryogenic suspended animation, but Professor Spencer Smythe abducted him and used Man-Wolf to attack Spider-Man and Jonah. When his plans backfired, Smythe triggered a deadly isotope he had implanted in John but the Godstone defended itself by trying to teleport John to Other Realm. Though it brought John close enough to become Stargod and cure him of the poisons in his system, the stone could not locate Other Realm. The Godstone's failure was caused by the collapsing of Other Realm's universe, which shrank, becoming a

STARGOD
Art by George Pérez

For a time, Captain America hired Jameson to serve as pilot of his personal Quinjet, Freedom's Flight, as well as his van. While aboard the Freedom's Flight, Jameson's alias was "Skywolf"; while aboard the van, his alias was "Vanwolf." Jameson assisted Captain America during the "Bloodstone Hunt," and in his attempts to combat the drug trade during a turf war between the Kingpin and the Red Skull. At one point, Jameson was hypnotized with other members of the Avengers support crew by Mother Night and Minister Blood, and was forced to assist them in an attempt on the Avengers' lives, but the Avengers managed to halt him. Elsewhere, the powdered Godstone, kept in Dr. Connors' office, was stolen by Dredmund Druid who, along with Dr. Nightshade, turned Starkesboro, Massachusetts into a town of werewolves. John was enticed to the town and subjected to Nightshade's werewolf formula. There, Dredmund recreated the Godstone and became the Starwolf before Cap Wolf (Captain America in werewolf form) removed it, and Cable crushed it. John and the other werewolves were cured by Nightshade's antidote. Meanwhile, John, attracted to Cap's girlfriend Diamondback, tried to steal a kiss, leading to him resigning his employment in shame.

After a time as a freelance monster-hunter, he served as security chief at the Ravencroft Institute, where he began a romantic relationship with the director, Dr. Ashley Kafka. After several problems with super-powered criminally insane inmates including Carnage, the Institute was temporarily shut down. Kafka thought she was close to healing the Chameleon of his mental illness, but was duped by the villain, enabling him to escape and kidnap her, John, and Spider-Man. With this final breach

Art by Jerry Bingham

RAVENCROFT UNIFORM

of security, Senator Roeberg fired Jameson and Kafka, hiring Dr. Leonard Samson as the new director of Ravencroft. Shortly thereafter, Mad Jack (Daniel Berkhart) implanted a command in Jameson's mind to smother his hospitalized father with a pillow, causing John to act wolf-like, though in human form. Kafka used hypnosis to undo the effects, transforming him temporarily into the Man-Wolf despite the absence of the Godstone. Residual effects of the Godstone are apparently permanently a part of Jameson. He and Kafka broke up sometime thereafter.

After working for a short time as a New York social worker (during which time his father was led to believe John was Spider-Man until a later crisis taught him otherwise), John served briefly with SHIELD's supernatural Howling Commandos, and the Man-Wolf again surfaced when he and other animal-linked people in Manhattan grew increasingly feral due to the energies of the Rock of Life. John subsequently rejoined the Air Force as a test pilot. He dated She-Hulk after giving her his Jupiter suit (following a few modifications by Reed Richards) to help her manage her out-of-control strength and eventually married her, not knowing she was under the influence of Starfox's emotion-manipulating powers at the time. After Alistair Smythe turned him back into the Man-Wolf, John was wounded while battling She-Hulk and the Two-Gun Kid, but survived by transforming into Stargod. Upon learning the truth about their marriage, Jen left him. After a series of unchronicled adventures, John somehow restored himself to normal human form and reluctantly granted Jennifer an annulment.

NOTE: *Kraven the Hunter (Sergei Kravinoff) once applied the Godstone to transform a vagabond into the Man-Wolf as prey in an urban safari for two teen socialites.*

HEIGHT: 6'2" (6'6" as Man-Wolf)
WEIGHT: 200 lbs. (350 lbs. as Man-Wolf)
EYES: Brown (red as Man-Wolf)
HAIR: Red-brown (white as Man-Wolf)

ABILITIES/ACCESSORIES: John Jameson is a skilled pilot and astronaut, experienced in hand-to-hand combat and a variety of weapons.

As Man-Wolf, Jameson possessed superhuman strength, speed, stamina, durability, agility and reflexes. Although his level of strength varied according to the amount of moonlight that filtered through Earth's atmosphere, at prime conditions during the three nights of the full moon, Man-Wolf could lift about 4 tons. He could spring approximately 18 feet into the air from a crouching position and run at a peak speed of 35 mph for approximately half an hour before tiring. His reflexes were about twice as fast as a normal human. His senses of sight, smell, and hearing were as acute as a wolf's. He could see into the infrared portions of the electromagnetic spectrum allowing him to see in darkness. His olfactory centers enabled him to smell the approach of others within 100 feet of himself and track a scent across almost any terrain. Man-Wolf also possessed razor-sharp teeth and claws able to rend a variety of substances, such as wood, soft metals, and even cinder block. Man-Wolf's natural fur protected him from extreme cold conditions. His whole body's musculature was so durable that he was able to survive great falls and concussive blows with minimal injury, and fully recover from gunshot wounds within a month. Man-Wolf had no control over his transformations, assuming his lupine form when exposed to moonlight, though the Godstone's energies sometimes transformed him during daytime. Not a true supernatural werewolf, the Man-Wolf was not subject to the conventional limitations of lycanthropy, such as a weakness for silver. His powers increased with proximity to the moon.

As Stargod, in addition to his abilities as Man-Wolf, he could lift at least 10 tons, teleport, fly, survive in space, detect someone by scent across the galaxy and project heat beams from his eyes. He was telepathic and had some degree of energy manipulation, although the full extent of his powers remained undefined. His powers were greatest in Other Realm. He sometimes wore scale mail armor and was armed with a dagger, short bow and arrows, and a sacred broadsword; he was highly skilled in swordsmanship and archery.

While infected by the spores Jameson could lift 15 tons, stood 7 feet tall, possessed superhuman durability and could leap up to 4 stories high. He required the Jupiter Suit to weigh down his body and regulate his strength.

Art by Eliot R. Brown

FREEDOM'S FLIGHT (UNITED STATES)
GENERAL ARRANGEMENT
DESIGNED BY: WAKANDA DESIGN GROUP
T'CHALLA, CHIEFTAIN

DATA: Freedom's Flight
Power Plant: 2 General Electric F404-GE-400 turbofan engines, each rated at 10,600 lbs. thrust without afterburner.
Wingspan: 51'
Length overall: 57' 6"
Height overall: 11'
Cabin:
 Max width: 8' 8"
 Max height: 6' 3"
Normal take-off weight: 27,500 lbs.
Max take-off weight: 31,600 lbs.
Max speed at 32,000': Mach .92 (720 mph)
Cruising speed at 500': Mach .9
Ceiling: 50,000'
Max unrefueled range: 1,200 miles
Note: Capable of true vertical flight and hovering. Non-offensive craft. Time to 30,000' (in VTO) 90 seconds.

J. JONAH JAMESON

REAL NAME: John Jonah Jameson Jr.
ALIASES: J.J.J., "Jolly Jonah," "Flat-Top," "Prune Face," "Jigsaw Jameson," others used by employees
IDENTITY: No dual identity
OCCUPATION: CEO of Jameson Publications, philanthropist; former owner, publisher and executive editor of the Daily Bugle and Now Magazine; former publisher of Jameson News Digest, publisher of Woman Magazine, editor-in-chief, city editor, reporter, copy boy, paperboy
CITIZENSHIP: USA
PLACE OF BIRTH: New York City, New York
KNOWN RELATIVES: Dr. Marla Madison-Jameson (second wife), Joan Jameson (first wife, deceased), John Jameson (Man-Wolf, son), John Jonah Jameson Sr. (father), David Burnoll (stepfather), Betty Burnoll (mother), Martha "Mattie" Franklin (Spider-Woman, foster daughter)
GROUP AFFILIATION: Century Club; formerly Daily Bugle staff, Great Game
EDUCATION: High-school dropout; later GED and college work
FIRST APPEARANCE: Amazing Spider-Man #1 (1963)

HISTORY: The stepson of an abusive veteran, Jameson began his journalism career as a paperboy, then copy boy for the Daily Bugle, formerly edited by Walter "Old Man" Jameson, whom some presume to have been his father. A sullen and bullying student, he quit school after becoming a reporter. At twenty he uncovered police corruption by supposed department hero Sam Kenner; beaten and bombed, Jameson nonetheless exposed Kenner with the help of Bugle owner William Goodman. He became a full-time Bugle reporter, including a stint as a war correspondent, criticizing most costumed heroes as glory-seeking vigilantes upstaging the common man.

Marrying his high school sweetheart Joan, Jameson rose to editor-in-chief and became renowned for supporting civil rights and opposing organized crime. When Goodman's heirs put the Bugle up for sale, Jameson tapped his last dollar and made the newspaper his own. He worked hard to support his wife and their son John, eventually becoming a millionaire member in New York's elite Century Club; although earning a reputation as a notorious miser, he supported many charities and often helped employees in true need. Still a reporter at heart, he ventured to Korea for a story but was crushed when Joan was killed by a masked gunman in his absence; this and other self-perceived failures contributed to his distrust of masked heroes and the heroic ideal.

In recent years, when the superhuman performer Spider-Man became a crimefighter, Jameson vowed to expose him as a publicity-seeking scofflaw, and not even the rescue of John from a space flight disaster dissuaded him. He relied on photos from Peter Parker, not knowing he was employing Spider-Man himself. Jameson heralded the Spacemen as superior heroes, but this gambit failed when Spider-Man exposed them as criminals; support for Mysterio (Quentin Beck) yielded similar results. Despite his many achievements, Jameson's harsh self-analysis weighed upon him, for his hatred of Spider-Man was motivated by fear that he was indeed the selfless hero Jameson could never be.

Jameson hired Dr. Farley Stillwell to mutate investigator Mac Gargan into the Scorpion to defeat Spider-Man, but the debacle left Stillwell dead and the insane Scorpion hating Jameson. Plagued by guilt, the publisher confessed his actions to his friend Norman Osborn. Scientist Spencer Smythe soon offered Jameson the first of many Spider-Slayer robots, with which he battled Spider-Man to a standstill before the web-slinger escaped. Jameson rallied New York against the Kingpin's crime wave; abducted for his insolence, he remained defiant before being rescued by Spider-Man.

Months later, Osborn, the Green Goblin, seemingly died in battle with Spider-Man; Jameson suspected Spider-Man of outright murder, hiring Luke Cage to bring the wall-crawler in, but desisted when John became the Man-Wolf. Jameson's obsession paled before concern for his son, but his own safety became an issue when he was attacked by the Grizzly (Max Markham), a violent wrestler to whose blacklisting Jameson's editorials had contributed a decade before. Spider-Man rescued Jameson but chided him for the grudge; in response, Jameson hired Daniel Berkhart to harass Spider-Man as Mysterio's supposed ghost. When this failed, he contracted Farley Stillwell's brother Harlan to mutate a new operative, but fugitive Rick Deacon usurped the process and became the criminal Fly, killing Stillwell and becoming an enemy of Spider-Man and Jameson alike. Jameson mysteriously received photos depicting Spider-Man with the body of Peter Parker; the photos, sent by Osborn's drug-maddened son Harry, actually featured a Peter Parker clone. Jonah nevertheless kept them quiet but stepped up his traditional campaigns. He approached Dr. Marla Madison to construct her own Spider-Slayer but met no better success. Finally confronting Parker, whom he imagined had been slain and replaced by Spider-Man, Jameson believed his story of faked photography. His relationship with Madison turned romantic, and he proved his principles anew by denouncing the terrorists of the People's Liberation Front. The PLF responded by hiring the Hitman (Burt Kenyon), but even in the face of death Jameson ridiculed his abductors, who were defeated by Spider-Man and the Punisher.

Meanwhile, Smythe, whose obsession had outgrown even Jameson's, learned he was dying and resolved to take Jameson and Spider-Man with him to the grave. He mesmerized the Man-Wolf into abducting

AS YOUNG MAN

Art by Gregg Schigiel with Frank Springer (inset)

ORIGINAL SPIDER-SLAYER
Art by Steve Ditko

Jameson and fighting Spider-Man; Jameson believed John dead when he saw his son teleported away. Smythe suddenly shackled Jonah and Spider-Man with a bomb, dying afterward. Jameson broke down, admitting his obsession had harmed him far more than its subject, but Spider-Man deactivated the bomb, leaving Jameson devastated at his confession. Scientist Jonas Harrow targeted Jonah, driving him mad, but his tenacity challenged even Harrow, and after being rescued by Spider-Man, Jameson was soon his typically paranoid self. Months later, John resurfaced alive, barely remembering his extradimensional adventures, and Jameson was overjoyed with his son's cure.

Longtime colleague Ian Fate resurfaced as a sorcerer in the company of the monstrous Man-Thing; naively expecting Jameson to help reshape the world, Fate lashed out when refused, but while Spider-Man fought the Man-Thing, Jameson calmed Fate and set him on a more peaceful path. Jameson returned to basics by investigating waterfront extortion, interrogating no less than the Kingpin and risking his life to uncover the perpetrators, albeit with unexpected assistance from Spider-Man. Perhaps in unconscious gratitude, Jameson's subsequent scheme to discredit Spider-Man with impostors proved half-hearted at best.

The Hobgoblin, secretly Jameson's Century Club crony Roderick Kingsley, learned Osborn's secrets and tried to blackmail Jameson over the Scorpion's mutation. Spider-Man ended this scheme, but the conscience-stricken Jameson publicly revealed his guilt anyway, then married Marla Madison. Soon afterward, he hired the alleged mutant hunters X-Factor and the mercenary Wild Pack to bring in Spider-Man but, more at peace than he had been in years, he seemed content to restrict his castigations to the printed page. However, his vendetta literally took new form when the Chameleon imprisoned and impersonated him, bringing anti-Spider-Man sentiments to new heights. Inevitably rescued by Spider-Man, he found a new crisis awaiting him, for Thomas Fireheart, secretly the mercenary Puma, acquired the Bugle to build up Spider-Man's reputation. Jameson sought solace in his lifelong convictions, denigrating neo-Nazi Eric Hartmann in print; when Hartmann's forces invaded the Bugle, for once Jameson played the rescuer when he downed Hartmann before the madman could shoot the intervening Spider-Man.

Fireheart eventually returned the Bugle to Jameson, but his control was wrested away by Norman Osborn, alive after all. Jameson nonetheless investigated the mutant-hunting Operation: Zero Tolerance. Hoping to placate the publisher, the android-turned-human Bastion offered him the outlaw X-Men's secrets, but Jameson refused, as his distaste for prejudice outweighed even his dislike of costumed heroes. The X-Men defeated Bastion, but Jameson was scarcely short of enemies when Osborn hired Daniel Berkhart, who had joined Mysterio's cousin Maguire Beck in the identity of Mad Jack, to force Jameson to sell the Bugle. Soon afterward, when Venom (Eddie Brock) was ordered to put a scare into him, the madman mistook his instructions for a kill order, and even Jameson winced at the beating Spider-Man took in his defense.

Jameson regained the Bugle when Osborn went mad in a mystic ritual, which also empowered teenager Mattie Franklin, who became a new Spider-Woman and was, ironically, entrusted to the care of the Jamesons. A different legacy hounded Jameson as Spencer Smythe's even madder son Alistaire threatened Jameson's family before receiving his latest defeat. Berkhart and Beck, now Mysterio and Mad Jack, abducted Jameson but were outwitted by Spider-Man and Daredevil (Matt Murdock). Unencumbered by gratitude, he sought to capitalize on the revelation of Daredevil's secret identity but was undercut when reporter Ben Urich refused to participate. Jameson hired superhuman investigator Jessica Jones to break a similar story on Spider-Man, but Jones merely put his money to work for charity, making her later rescue of Mattie from drug dealers all the more biting.

After over a decade, even Jameson felt his vendetta's futility, and his invective grew sparse. Following fresh humiliation in a libel trial overseen by She-Hulk, he agreed to a new Bugle feature with a theoretically objective focus on super heroes, with input from Jessica Jones, but the concept fell through when, following a double-cross on coverage of the latest Avengers incarnation, Jones furiously dismissed the idea, along with Jameson himself. Briefly led to believe his son John had somehow been Spider-Man all along, he was stunned when, following the Superhuman Registration Act's passage, Spider-Man was instead revealed as Peter Parker, a revelation quickly followed by John's marriage to She-Hulk. Feeling doubly betrayed, Jameson was at least satisfied when John and his wife annulled their marriage, and following a confrontation with Spider-Man where he was finally allowed to physically lash out, again and again, at the hero who had haunted him so long, Jameson was left with a sense of closure, as well as bleeding hands. However, he, like everyone else on Earth, forgot Parker's revelation following Spider-Man's deal with Mephisto, but a threatened hostile takeover of the Bugle by mogul Dexter Bennett left him with more than enough on his mind. The stress of the situation climaxed in a heart attack, and Marla, deciding her husband's newspaper had cost him enough, sold out to Bennett. Jameson recovered but has yet to regain the Bugle, and it only remains to be seen how these developments will be blamed on Spider-Man.

Art by Sal Buscema

HEIGHT: 5'11"
WEIGHT: 181 lbs.
EYES: Blue
HAIR: Graying black, white at temples

ABILITIES/ACCESSORIES: Jameson is an accomplished reporter, editor, and businessman, knowledgeable in virtually every aspect of print publication. He demonstrates surprising fitness, though he is subject to fits of rage, has had multiple heart attacks, and is a chain smoker of cigars. His brusque behavior, capitalistic outlook, and obsession with Spider-Man frequently mislead people into believing him less principled and compassionate than he in fact is.

POWER GRID	1	2	3	4	5	6	7
INTELLIGENCE							
STRENGTH							
SPEED							
DURABILITY							
ENERGY PROJECTION							
FIGHTING SKILLS							

JANUS

REAL NAME: Janus Tepes
ALIASES: The Golden Angel, the Golden One, Heaven-Spawn
IDENTITY: No dual identity
OCCUPATION: Agent of Heaven (alleged)
CITIZENSHIP: (Janus) USA; (Golden Angel) unrevealed
PLACE OF BIRTH: (Janus) Cambridge, Massachusetts; (Golden Angel) unrevealed
KNOWN RELATIVES: Dracula (father, deceased), Domini (mother), Lilith (half-sister), Frank Drake (distant relation), various ancestors via Dracula (deceased)
GROUP AFFILIATION: None
EDUCATION: (Janus) Grade school; (Golden Angel) unrevealed
FIRST APPEARANCE: Tomb of Dracula #51 (1976)

HISTORY: An alleged agent of Heaven, the Golden Angel first encountered Dracula during the mid-17th century, when the vampire lord, then ruler of a province in Spain, planned to conquer the entire nation. Prepared to execute a spy, Dracula was confronted by the Angel and grew so inexplicably unnerved that he fled Spain that very night. Nearly two hundred years later, in 1870, Dracula led a vampire horde into Vienna (later absorbed into Austria), determined to wrest the nation from any mortal control, but the Angel awaited him, and Dracula again abandoned his effort.

In recent years, Dracula usurped power over the Church of the Damned, to the disgruntlement of its leader, Anton Lupeski, who unlike most of his congregants recognized that Dracula was not truly "Satan." Drawn to the beautiful Domini, who had been drawn to Lupeski during her search for an end to her loneliness and pain, Dracula married her and, using a mystic ritual, impregnated her. However, as Dracula reveled in his new status, he sensed he was being stalked by the Golden Angel, who soon confronted him to prevent Dracula's influence from spreading. The pair fought first in a theater, then at an amusement park, where Dracula mesmerized the crowd to distract his foe, then impaled him with a metal bar. But as the Angel fell, his astral form vanished into Dracula's Dark Church seemingly absorbed into Domini's revered portrait of Christ. Shortly afterward, Dracula and Domini's child, a golden-skinned boy named Janus, was born. When Dracula held a feast in his son's honor, Lupeski betrayed him to Quincy Harker and his vampire hunters, who stormed the church. During the fray, Lupeski fired a silver bullet at Dracula, but when Dracula assumed mist form, it passed through him and killed Janus instead, prompting the enraged Dracula to kill Lupeski. Days later, despite Dracula's fear that a revived Janus would be stripped of innocence, Domini mystically resurrected their son, who aged rapidly to adulthood and was possessed by the Golden Angel. Taking the name Janus as his own, the being vowed to destroy Dracula, despite Domini's pleas for peace. However, their feud was interrupted when Mephisto, playing the role of "Satan" for his own reasons, manipulated the psychic Topaz to lure Dracula to an abandoned house; Janus soon followed, as did Dracula's mortal descendant Frank Drake, and all were conducted into Mephisto's realm, where Dracula and Janus fought together against a tentacled demon, then turned upon each other. Dracula was defeated, and Mephisto, as punishment for Dracula's role in Janus' existence, transformed him into a mortal. Shortly afterward, Janus briefly diverted from his interest in Dracula to help the costumed heroes Lectronn and Crimebuster (Frank Moore) rescue bystanders from mystic debris caused by the cosmic crisis known as "Star Waaugh," whose full effects had been forestalled by Howard the Duck and company.

Janus later teleported Dracula and Harker's band to Castle Dracula, where Mephisto subjected the vampire to illusory torment via visions of Dracula's enemies, then, feeling he had sufficiently humbled Dracula, restored his vampire nature. Shortly afterward, Janus watched as Dracula regained leadership of Earth's vampires by slaying the upstart challenger Torgo, only to be destroyed himself by Harker in a suicide run. Janus then appeared before Domini, informing her that her son was not as lost to her as she believed, and the Golden Angel vacated his mortal form, leaving the infant Janus a normal human child. Years later, Janus, now a young boy, was abducted by the vampire Taj Nital, formerly one of Harker's vampire hunters, on behalf of Varnae, the first Lord of Vampires. Varnae used Janus to gain control of the genetically engineered vampire Bloodstorm, created from Dracula's DNA; although Bloodstorm was defeated by the Nightstalkers, Janus remains missing.

HEIGHT: (Janus) 4'2"; (Golden Angel) 6'2"
WEIGHT: (Janus) 62 lbs; (Golden Angel) 230 lbs
EYES: (Janus) Blue; (Golden Angel) red
HAIR: (Janus) Brown; (Golden Angel) silver-white

ABILITIES/ACCESSORIES: While merged with the Golden Angel, Janus possessed superhuman strength, weather-controlling powers and immunity to vampiric hypnotism. He could project concussive force, radiate blinding light, place people in temporal stasis, teleport himself and others over thousands of miles, create illusory images and transform into a golden eagle, retaining wings in humanoid form if desired. He could cause Dracula pain with a mere glance; he appeared able to survive physical death in astral form before incarnating in a new body. What special attributes, if any, the infant Janus might possess as a result of his vampire parentage remain unrevealed.

POWER GRID	1	2	3	4	5	6	7
INTELLIGENCE							
STRENGTH							
SPEED							
DURABILITY							
ENERGY PROJECTION							
FIGHTING SKILLS							

*YELLOW BARS REPRESENT POWERS AS A CHILD

Art by Gene Colan

JARELLA

REAL NAME: Jarella
ALIASES: None
IDENTITY: No dual identity, existence unknown to Earth's general population
OCCUPATION: Queen
CITIZENSHIP: K'ai
PLACE OF BIRTH: K'ai
KNOWN RELATIVES: Visis (cousin)
GROUP AFFILIATION: None
EDUCATION: Unrevealed
FIRST APPEARANCE: Incredible Hulk #140 (1971)

HISTORY: Jarella was the warrior-empress of the city of K'ai on a planet (sometimes also referred to as K'ai) within a microverse (a realm accessed via the energies of shrinking; many accounts erroneously describe such realms as sub-atomic, existing between the atoms of larger universes). Jarella's world had an essentially Earth-like environment, with oceans and continents, and air rich with oxygen. Nearly the entire planet was lush with vegetation, and it harbored a diverse array of wildlife. This included the giant warthos, pig-like creatures that preyed on the men and women of the planet, as well as horse-like creatures that were domesticated for riding. The planet also was home to flying pterosaur-like creatures, some of which also became domesticated. The religion of K'ai was polytheistic, and prime among the deities was a Jade Goddess.

Little is known about the history of Jarella's world, even to its own citizens. The planet's oldest civilization arose on the continent of Pitll Pawob. It was a very technologically advanced society, and developed force blasters, levitation bands that allowed them to fly, and numerous other technological weapons and tools. Eventually, a cataclysmic event sank most of Pitll Pawob beneath the sea, except for a region at the tip of the landmass. As a result, the civilization there crumbled, nearly dying out completely. The age of the advanced technology of the Pitll Pawob civilization was lost to Jarella's world, and a new age of magic began as citizens of Jarella's world discovered sorcery and used it in place of technology. The descendants of the few survivors of Pitll Pawob sought to maintain what remained of their lost technology, offering their services as assassins and hiring out their weapons to any and all who would pay for them. The remnants of the continent came to be known as "The Isle of Assassins."

Jarella encountered the Hulk when he was sent to her world during a battle with the evil Psyklop. After the Hulk saved her city from the warthos, Jarella and her people were grateful, and hailed the Hulk as a hero. Tradition stated that the queen could only marry a man who had proven himself in battle against the warthos, and as it was time for Jarella to choose a mate, she saw the Hulk's arrival as an omen from the gods, and chose him to be her husband. She had her sorcerer's triad (Holi, Moli, and the chief sorcerer, Torla), cast a language spell allowing the Hulk to understand her civilization's tongue. The spell also gave the mind of Bruce Banner ascendancy. Banner/Hulk came to love Jarella, and agreed to stay by her side as king; but Jarella's jealous cousin, Lord Visis, who desired the crown for himself, plotted Jarella's assassination. Visis' men were defeated by the Hulk, and Visis was exiled in the warthos-haunted outlands. However, before Jarella and the Hulk could marry, Psyklop transported the Hulk back to Earth.

While in exile, Visis learned the art of sorcery, and he amassed an army against K'ai. Jarella had her sorcerer's triad send her to Earth to recruit the Hulk's aid. Visis sent the assassin Fialan after her, and the energies of the interdimensional transfers somehow had a catastrophic effect on the Earth's sun (which had already been affected by Starcore scientist Dr. Peter Corbeau's tapping of its energies to cure the Hulk), causing giant solar flares as it threatened to go nova. To save Jarella, Banner re-irradiated himself, becoming the Hulk again, and slew Fialan, but Jarella was forced to return to K'ai alongside Fialan's corpse, or risk destroying both worlds.

Later returning to Jarella's world, the Hulk found the city of K'ai in ruins, and learned that Visis had deposed Jarella and succeeded in conquering the region. The Hulk defeated Visis and his army, restoring Jarella's crown, but was once again drawn back to Earth. As the Hulk left Jarella's world, his exodus disturbed the planet's orbit around its sun, causing tremors and quakes throughout the land. The tremors eventually subsided, but the villain Psyklop created more tremors using technology at his base atop a nearby mountain. The people of K'ai interpreted the geologic catastrophes as an act of divinity, and demanded the sacrifice of Jarella to appease the "mountain god." The Hulk —sent to K'ai again after having been seemingly shrunken out of existence following a microscopic adventure in Glenn Talbot's brain — arrived in time to save Jarella and defeat Psyklop. Planning to wed, the Hulk and Jarella were instead transported back to Earth by Doc Samson, who had isolated a portal to Jarella's world on a microscope slide. The Hulk and Jarella desired to return, but the Hulk inadvertently shattered the microscope slide containing the portal to Jarella's world, making it impossible for them to be sent back. The shattering of the microscope slide sent massive

Art by Sandy Plunkett

upheavals through the portal to Jarella's world, sending it spinning through space and causing massive geological upheavals, until it settled further away from its sun. As a result, the lush vegetation that had once covered the entire planet died away, replaced by endless stretches of empty wasteland. A short time later, the Elder of the Universe known as the Gardener arrived on Jarella's world and, using the Soul Gem (one of the powerful Infinity Gems) as well as his own vast powers, restored life and vegetation to one small valley on the planet, but used his powers to prevent any of Jarella's people from entering his "Valley of Life." The people of Jarella's world set about trying to survive in the barren wilderness.

Soon after arriving on Earth, Jarella sacrificed her own life to save a young boy from falling debris during a battle between the Hulk and the robot Crypto-Man. The Hulk brought her body to Gamma Base, hoping their science would be able to revive her, then sought out the aid of his sorcerer friend, Dr. Strange, but nothing could be done, as Jarella had truly passed on. Unbeknownst to the Hulk, Gamma Base kept Jarella's body for study. Upon discovering this, the Hulk returned to Gamma Base, reclaimed her body, and convinced Captain Mar-Vell to send him back to her world, only to find it devastated upon his arrival. Finding Jarella's people, the Hulk was welcomed back as a king. When the Hulk learned of the catastrophe that had befallen their world, he resolved to help Jarella's people. The Hulk entered the Gardener's Valley of Life, and wrested the Soul Gem from the Elder's grasp. The Hulk then hurled the gem into the planet's core, restoring vegetation and life to the entire planet, returning Jarella's world to its former glory, before returning to Earth. The Gardener soon reclaimed the gem, but its effects remained on the planet.

After restoring fertility to the planet, the people of Jarella's world came to consider the Hulk and Jarella as gods. Different sects arose all over the planet, all claiming to know the single divine truth and the true words of the Hulk, and violence broke out amongst the sects. Scattered conflicts became all-out religious wars, with faction after faction gaining power, and being overthrown, causing mass destruction in the name of the Hulk. Eventually, a man called Risuli rose to prominence. He formed a holy order of sisters to worship Jarella, and declared himself the Grand Inquisitor. He ruled Jarella's world with an iron fist, using his vast armies to enforce his laws, claiming he was doing the Hulk's will. The Hulk (then in his gray, intelligent but brusque form) was brought back to Jarella's world by another group of sorcerers, Gorsham, Whully, and Booly, and told of the atrocities being committed in his name. The Hulk united the populace of Jarella's world, and overthrew the Grand Inquisitor. The Hulk planned to stay and rule, but the three sorcerers, desiring to rule Jarella's world themselves, sent the Hulk back to Earth.

The microverse in which Jarella's world existed was subsequently merged with all other such microverses during a conflict involving Thanos and Baron Karza. Soon afterward, a native of K'ai, Visalia, falsely claimed to be the sister of Jarella, and with the aid of the cyborg Micron Dexam, sought the crown of K'ai for herself. When Drax the Destroyer ended up on Jarella's world, the natives mistook him for the Hulk, and Visalia used her magic to seduce him and turn him into her servant. Captain Marvel (Genis-Vell) and the Microns arrived and exposed Visalia's falsehood, after which she was attacked by an angry mob of K'ai citizens.

HEIGHT: (on Earth) 5'6" **EYES:** Green
WEIGHT: (on Earth) 126 lbs. **HAIR:** Blonde
ABILITIES/ACCESSORIES: Jarella was a skilled hand-to-hand combatant, swordswoman, and military strategist.

EDWIN JARVIS

HISTORY: The definitive gentleman's gentleman, Edwin Jarvis has long served as butler to the world's leading super-hero team, the Avengers. His American mother and British father originally lived in Walsall, England after they got married, later emigrating to the USA and settling in New York, where Edwin was born. Raised in a poor neighborhood, Edwin grew up learning to defend himself on the rough streets of the Bronx. Perhaps inspired by his older friend Watson, a fighter pilot who had been lost behind enemy lines for an extended period during World War II, Edwin moved to the United Kingdom as a young man and joined the Royal Air Force (RAF). At least some of his family eventually followed him from America, since his parents were living in England again before the end of his military career. Edwin became a skilled poker player while in the service, and was the RAF boxing champion for three consecutive years. He continued to serve with the RAF until his father's death, after which his mother returned to her native USA; Jarvis resigned his RAF commission and moved back to America so he could remain close to her.

While his mother hoped he might pursue a career in accounting, Jarvis instead found new purpose in an old family profession, becoming a butler like his father and grandfather before him. He eventually secured a long-term position serving wealthy couple Howard and Maria Stark at their Manhattan mansion, where he helped them raise their son Tony and developed a fatherly affection for the boy. When Howard and Maria died in a car wreck, Jarvis comforted the grieving Tony, now a young adult, and tried to offer him guidance. Jarvis also served as a father figure of sorts to a far younger child, Maria de Guadalupe "Lupe" Santiago, an orphan from a remote mountain village of the Central American nation Costa Verde. Superhuman since birth because of her half-godly parentage, Lupe was residing at a church orphanage sponsored by the American charity Childcare. When Edwin Jarvis sent them a letter seeking to sponsor a foster child, the orphanage selected him as Lupe's sponsor based on his ties to the Stark family. By this time, word had begun to spread regarding Stark Industries' new armored super-operative Iron Man (secretly Tony Stark), so the orphanage hoped that Jarvis might be able to arrange specialized help if Lupe's powers became a problem. Trying to be a normal girl, Lupe did not tell her "Tio" (uncle) Edwin about her shape-shifting abilities during the many letters they exchanged over the ensuing years.

Shortly after Iron Man helped found the Avengers super-hero team, Tony Stark donated his family's mansion to the new group. Unnerved by their strange new employers, the entire household staff immediately resigned except for Jarvis, who adjusted surprisingly quickly to his new situation. In addition to acting as the mansion's chef and all-purpose domestic servant, he supervised the hiring and activities of any other support personnel needed by the team; helped ensure the group's equipment was kept in top condition; handled much of the team's communications and correspondence; and frequently assisted in non-combat Avengers operations such as monitor duty. He has also aided the Avengers in action on occasion against foes such as Tyrak, Graviton, Samhain, Itzhak Berditchev, Immortus, Loki and the Protectorate.

During the team's early years, Jarvis helped a newly revived Captain America (Steve Rogers) find his place in the modern world, becoming one of the Captain's earliest postwar friends; Jarvis also befriended vigilante archer Hawkeye (Clint Barton) and encouraged him to give up his outlaw lifestyle, even secretly aiding Barton in his successful application for Avengers membership. When Edwin's mother fell gravely ill and required

REAL NAME: Edwin Jarvis
ALIASES: "Tio Edwin," "Uncle Jarvis," "Eddie," "Jarv," "Jarvis, God of Mischief," "Edwin the Dull," Sir Armond Carlyle III, Crimson Cowl
IDENTITY: No dual identity
OCCUPATION: Butler; former chief of staff, combat pilot
CITIZENSHIP: USA and UK
PLACE OF BIRTH: The Bronx, New York City, New York
KNOWN RELATIVES: Mrs. Jarvis (mother), unidentified father (deceased), unidentified sister, unidentified grandfather (presumably deceased)
GROUP AFFILIATION: Avengers employee; formerly Avengers Crew, Royal Air Force
EDUCATION: University graduate
FIRST APPEARANCE: Tales of Suspense #59 (1964)

Art by George Pérez

expensive medical treatment, the Avengers' robotic enemy Ultron hypnotized the distraught Jarvis into serving him, making Jarvis believe he was betraying the Avengers in exchange for money. The mind-controlled Jarvis shared the secrets of Avengers Mansion's security system with Ultron's Masters of Evil, even posing as the Crimson Cowl (Ultron's then-current costumed alias) to help sow confusion among Ultron's enemies and allies alike; however, Jarvis ultimately risked his life to help the Black Knight (Dane Whitman) rescue the Avengers, and the Masters were defeated. The Avengers quickly forgave a repentant Jarvis for his apparent betrayal, partly because founding member Goliath (Hank Pym) correctly suspected Ultron's hypnotic influence; when Edwin regained his full memories of the robot's mind control months later, the loyal butler was finally fully vindicated in the eyes of both his employers and himself. Meanwhile, Tony Stark secured medical care for Mrs. Jarvis, who recovered fully.

Edwin remained devoted to the Avengers, voluntarily serving without pay during a brief period when corrupt tycoon Cornelius Van Lunt had crippled the team's finances. Later, when shape-shifting alien Skrulls posing as senior Avengers fired the group's then-active roster during the Kree-Skrull War, Jarvis resigned in protest until the deception was exposed and normal operations quickly resumed. He subsequently resigned a second time after a drunken Tony Stark behaved in a reckless and verbally abusive fashion during a visit to the mansion, but Jarvis soon reconciled with Stark and resumed his Avengers duties while helping Tony get his alcoholism under control. Edwin's first long-term absence from the Avengers came years later when Baron (Helmut) Zemo's Masters of Evil invaded and occupied Avengers Mansion, taking Jarvis and others hostage. Tormented by Zemo and brutally tortured by Mr. Hyde, Jarvis was ultimately rescued when the Avengers liberated the mansion, but he had suffered crippling injuries. While recovering in the hospital, he realized for the first time how dangerous his job really was and considered retiring, but his sense of duty won out and he went back to work. He had nearly fully recovered by the time the team broke up during a conflict with Nebula (actually a disguised Terminatrix), and he soon helped bring the group back together. Much later, when the demoralized and undermanned Avengers disbanded altogether after most of their active members seemingly died in the Onslaught disaster, Jarvis went through a period of depression and inactivity; however, the lost Avengers soon turned up alive, and Jarvis happily resumed his duties.

Jarvis has shared friendship and wise counsel with many Avengers over the years, notably Iron Man (who eventually revealed his secret identity to Jarvis), Hank Pym, Wasp, Rick Jones, Captain America, Hawkeye, Vision, Black Widow, Sersi, Machine Man, a teenage Iron Man (a younger Reality-96020 version of Stark who briefly replaced the original), Justice, Triathlon, and even Edwin's own "niece" Lupe Santiago, who joined the Avengers as Silverclaw after coming to America to attend college. Pleasant and professional, Jarvis has been on good terms with most of the Avengers over time, despite occasional friction with disruptive or emotionally volatile members such as Quicksilver, the Scarlet Witch, Mantis, Tigra and She-Hulk; however, Jarvis has a history of mutual animosity with arrogant federal agent Henry Gyrich, who has sometimes served as the Avengers' government liaison.

Jarvis and Fantastic Four member Thing have organized a series of floating poker games attended by many super heroes. The Avengers have also hosted various guests in their headquarters, and Jarvis has grown attached to past long-term residents such as Thor's fellow Asgardians (notably Sif and the Warriors Three) and the Fantastic Four (who stayed with the Avengers after their original Baxter Building's destruction); during the latter group's stay, Edwin often cared for FF founders Reed and Sue Richards' son, Franklin, who became keenly fond of Jarvis. For a time, the Avengers hired a full-time "Avengers Crew" staff overseen by Jarvis, who befriended crewmembers such as Peggy Carter, John Jameson, Michael O'Brien and Fabian Stankowicz, but most of the Crew was eventually laid off during the Onslaught disbanding. Jarvis had far rockier relations with the Inhuman governess Marilla, who served as nanny to Avengers member Crystal's young daughter Luna; Jarvis and Marilla were bitter rivals at first as she repeatedly meddled in his duties, but the two ultimately formed a mutually respectful friendship before her death. Jarvis also befriended scientist Judy Parks after helping the Avengers save her from the super-villain Graviton, becoming like a second father to her. Years later, a dashing Jarvis rescued Glory Garsen and other civilians during the demonic "Inferno" invasion of Manhattan, leading to Edwin's long-term romance with a smitten Glory despite her being many years his junior. More recently, Jarvis for a time dated someone closer to his age, Spider-Man's Aunt May Parker.

After an insane Scarlet Witch's rampage apparently slew several of her teammates and wrecked Avengers Mansion, the group disbanded again. Long since entitled to retire with full salary and benefits, Jarvis took his first real vacation in years, finally enjoying some well-earned relaxation. When Iron Man and Captain America led the formation of a new Avengers team based in the Stark Tower skyscraper, they immediately hired Jarvis to resume his old duties in their new location; however, Skrull subversives soon abducted Edwin and replaced him with a Skrull operative who posed as Jarvis for months, spying on the Avengers and aiding the Skrulls' "Secret Invasion" of Earth. The Avengers ultimately defeated the Skrulls, freeing Jarvis and other prisoners, but not before the Skrull version of Jarvis abducted Danielle Cage, infant daughter of Avengers member Luke Cage, and fled into hiding. With the Avengers in general and a broken Tony Stark in particular struggling to rebuild their lives in the wake of the devastating Skrull conflict, ever-loyal Jarvis stands ready to aid his friends and employers however he can, helping make their extraordinary work possible by shouldering the mundane burdens of ordinary life.

HEIGHT: 5'9" **EYES:** Blue
WEIGHT: 160 lbs. **HAIR:** Black, balding/greying

ABILITES/ACCESSORIES: A remarkably efficient, dedicated and resourceful butler, Jarvis is also a gifted cook and a shrewd card player. He is a skilled boxer, though age and injuries have impaired his skills somewhat, and he has learned additional unarmed combat moves from Captain America. Trained as a fighter pilot but decades out of practice, Jarvis has occasionally flown modern air vehicles such as the Avengers' Quinjets and sky sleds. He also has a working knowledge of emergency first aid, computers and assorted high-tech equipment such as the Avengers' monitoring and communications devices. He is a capable but infrequent user of firearms. He typically carries an Avengers "communicard" identification card that doubles as a communications and tracking device. He sometimes carries an umbrella with a specially reinforced shaft, which he can use as a makeshift fencing foil or fighting stick.

POWER GRID	1	2	3	4	5	6	7
INTELLIGENCE							
STRENGTH							
SPEED							
DURABILITY							
ENERGY PROJECTION							
FIGHTING SKILLS							

"MAD JIM" JASPERS

HISTORY: On Earth-238, Sir James Jaspers was a British politician elected on an anti-superhuman platform; secretly a reality-warping mutant himself, his true motive was to eliminate competition. He was also utterly insane. He instigated a super hero purge carried out by the paramilitary Status Crew and the Fury, a relentless and unstoppable hero-killing cybiote Jaspers designed; heroes were rounded up into concentration camps and exterminated, while the Fury hunted down and slew those who evaded the camps. Merlyn, the Omniversal Guardian, was aware of the threat Jaspers posed to the multiverse; worse, he knew that Earth-616's Jaspers, who was due to follow a similar path perhaps a decade later, was equally insane and vastly more powerful. Within two years the purge was nearly complete; when the Fury closed in on Earth-238's last surviving heroes, Merlyn allowed his champion on that world, Captain UK, to teleport away to Earth-616 right in front of the cybiote, laying a lure for the Fury to later pursue. With every superhuman on Earth dead, save for Jaspers, who had programmed the Fury to be unable to attack him, the Status Crew mothballed the cybiote; now unopposed, Sir James became Mad Jim Jaspers, committing robberies for fun, accompanied by the "Alice in Wonderland"-themed Crazy Gang he created, while his world degraded into fascism until its taint threatened to hold back development in neighboring realities. Unaware what had caused Earth-238's retardation, the other-dimensional DDC (Dimensional Development Court) sent a covert mission led by Saturnyne to artificially accelerate its evolution. Meanwhile, with Earth-616's Jaspers beginning his rise to power, Merlyn sent Captain Britain-616 (Brian Braddock) to Earth-238, where he disrupted a Crazy Gang robbery seconds after arriving; still playing, Jaspers fled when the police arrived, though Captain Britain had drawn his interest. Braddock soon allied with Saturnyne's team, aiding their "Push," but moments after they thought their mission successfully completed, Jaspers unleashed a reality warp, transforming his world into a chaotic charnel house. The Status Crew, wrongly believing Captain Britain behind the madness, reactivated the Fury, unleashing it on Braddock; Jaspers rescued Braddock so he could explain to the hero his role in events, before dropping him into a super hero graveyard. Moments later the Fury caught up with Captain Britain and slew him. Merlyn soon resurrected him back on Earth-616, a second lure for the Fury, which was instinctively aware that its prey had survived.

Jaspers' warp spread exponentially to engulf his entire dimension within days, until the DDC took the dire step of destroying Reality-238 to prevent the madness from spreading interdimensionally, slaying Jaspers-238 and leaving a single survivor: The Fury. Knowing that Jaspers-616 could not be so easily stopped, Merlyn's bait now served its purpose. The Fury, intent on killing the two Captains who had evaded it, evolved the ability to teleport across realities and traveled to Earth-616. Meanwhile Jaspers-616, unaware of events in other realities, launched his anti-superhuman campaign; seeing events mirroring what had happened in her world, Captain UK emerged from hiding to seek out and forewarn Captain Britain. Jaspers won a landslide election, becoming British prime minister, and using STRIKE (Special Tactical Reserve for International Key Emergencies), a government agency that had recently been secretly taken over by the crimelord Vixen, to round up the UK's superhumans. Britain became a totalitarian nightmare, with Jaspers distending time so that its inhabitants could no longer tell whether he had been in power for months or merely days. Scared that Jaspers' actions would draw unwanted international attention, Vixen confronted him at 10 Downing Street, the prime minister's residence, but he casually transformed her into a fox, her intrusion merely encouraging him to unleash the full force of his reality warp. Unwilling to stand by as his country became a dystopia, Captain Britain arrived at Downing Street just as the warp began spreading, but proved no more than momentary amusement, with Jaspers toying with his opponent before discarding him, bored. Suddenly lonely, Jaspers created a Crazy Gang from the ground below him, when the Fury, which had pursued Captain Britain, arrived. Having always been irritated by the programming to leave its creator unmolested despite contrary programming to slay all superhumans, the

REAL NAME: Sir James Jaspers
ALIASES: The Crooked Man, Lord Jim
IDENTITY: Secret
OCCUPATION: Former Politician, UK Prime Minister
CITIZENSHIP: UK
PLACE OF BIRTH: Finchley, England
KNOWN RELATIVES: None
GROUP AFFILIATION: Conservative Party, Crazy Gang, possibly Hellfire Club (London Branch)
EDUCATION: Unrevealed, presumably extensive
FIRST APPEARANCE: (Earth-616 Jaspers) The Daredevils #7 (1983); (Earth-238 Jaspers) Marvel Superheroes #377 (1981)

Fury reasoned that this Jaspers was not the same man and attacked him. Created by someone nearly as powerful as its foe and tempered by uncounted battles and experiences, it countered Jaspers' reality warping by constantly adjusting its molecular structure, and the pair fought a teleporting battle from the moon to the ocean bed to the surface of the sun to alien worlds, each rapidly modifying their forms to launch new attacks on one another. After a prolonged fight, the Fury speculated what would happen if Jaspers had no external reality to manipulate, and transported them to the empty void between realities. With nothing to work with, Jaspers was rendered helpless; the Fury extended a filament through his skull, then electrocuted Jaspers' brain, killing him, though some element of his disembodied ego survived, seeking in vain a way

Art by Alan Davis

JASPERS WARP

to return to life. Badly weakened by the bout, the Fury was likewise destroyed by Captain UK when it returned to Earth-616. Jaspers' legacy lived on however, with the Crazy Gang going on to become a somewhat incompetent menace to society. Hundreds of children across the UK were left transformed and sometimes empowered by Jaspers' warp; the rift in reality he had caused continued to generate new "Warpies" for months after his death, not healing until after Captain UK's anomalous presence was removed by Merlyn's daughter, Roma.

Jaspers' threat appeared to be over, until years later another reality warp, the Scarlet Witch's "House of M," transformed Earth-616, triggering a causal tsunami, which struck Roma's realm, Otherworld, an intersection of realities Brian Braddock now ruled. The resultant dimensional crash swept up individuals from across the multiverse, depositing them in Otherworld, including a suddenly resurrected Jaspers; happy at finally being alive again, Jaspers was unaware that deep within his brain a taint of the Fury lurked, slowly growing in strength. Finding Roma pinned beneath wreckage, Jaspers was surprised to manifest some of the Fury's physique. Proclaiming himself Overlord of the Omniverse, Jaspers was about to slay Roma when Brian intervened, striking Jaspers hard enough to send him flying several miles. Though the Witch's reality wave was soon reversed, Jaspers remained alive, presumably shielded by his own manipulative ability; suspecting this, Roma sent out members of her Corps to hunt him, while Jaspers remained where he had landed, vacillating about what he wanted to do. His contemplations were interrupted by Merlyn, at this point controlled by an evil aspect of his gestalt personality, who suggested an alliance against Roma and Brian. Attacked moments later by three Corpsmen, Jaspers transformed two of them into Fury facsimiles, subconsciously directed by the gradually awakening Fury element within him. Transforming others as he went, Jaspers led a growing Fury army to attack Roma's Starlight Citadel, decimating the Corps members fighting valiantly to defend it. Catching him becoming bored and careless, Saturnyne used a specialized rifle to flay the flesh from his bones and force his spirit from his body, nearly succeeding in splitting the Fury and Jaspers' psyches, before being interrupted by attacking pseudo-Furys.

Art by Alan Davis

INFECTED BY THE FURY

Jaspers used the respite to heal, but with the Fury taint now fully awake, he realized his brain was not working correctly; however, an attack from the newly arrived Exiles and renegade Corpsman Albion (Bran Bardic of Earth-70518) distracted him from investigating. Increasingly relying on physical force, Jaspers began to transform into the Fury; finally realizing what was happening, Jaspers futilely tried to resist as the Fury drained the life force from nearby Corpsmen to complete the metamorphosis, apparently destroying Jaspers in the process. Still far from full strength due to fighting Jaspers for ascendancy, the Fury was destroyed moments later by the combined forces of the surviving heroes present.

Art by Alan Davis

EARTH-238 JASPERS

NOTE: During Magneto's trial, some time after Mad Jim's original death and prior to his resurrection, Sir James Jaspers served as prosecutor. The origin of this Jaspers, perhaps an imposter, a non-powered clone created by Roma (Merlyn's daughter), or even a facsimile created by reality itself trying to heal the damage caused by Jaspers' warp, is as yet unrevealed.

HEIGHT: 6' **WEIGHT:** 155 lbs.
EYES: Blue (variable) **HAIR:** Black, white temples

ABILITIES/ACCESSORIES: Both versions of Jaspers could effortlessly warp reality on a dimension-wide scale, rewriting the laws of physics, bending time and transforming energy and matter, the effects limited only by the two Jasper's insane imaginations; only the Fury proved immune, but other beings could be casually transformed according to Jaspers' whims. He could even create self-aware sentient beings that endured after his warp ended. Jaspers' warp spread at an exponentially increasing rate. It engulfed the 238 continuum in days, and took that reality's destruction to prevent that warp spreading across the multiverse; this extreme measure would not have stopped the more powerful Earth-616 Jaspers. Jaspers could teleport and transform himself, healing from injuries no matter how extensive in moments, or simply ignoring most physical attacks if he preferred. However he required other material to work with; denied reality outside his own form to manipulate, he proved powerless and reverted to his frail, genuinely human form.

Some part of him apparently survived his physical destruction, remaining aware of the passage of time and looking for ways to be reborn, though that psychic residue was apparently unable to manipulate reality. After his resurrection he was infected with a portion of the Fury; this enhanced his perceptions, but affected his thinking which in turn restricted him from using his powers to their full extent. He was a scientific genius.

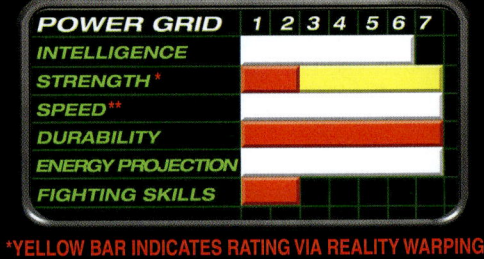

POWER GRID	1	2	3	4	5	6	7
INTELLIGENCE							
STRENGTH*							
SPEED**							
DURABILITY							
ENERGY PROJECTION							
FIGHTING SKILLS							

*YELLOW BAR INDICATES RATING VIA REALITY WARPING
**MAD JIM JASPERS IS A TELEPORTER

MADISON JEFFRIES

HISTORY: Madison Jeffries and his brother Lionel were born mutants with psionic transmutative powers. Madison hated his mutant mastery over metal for making him different, and he sought to escape it. Lionel, however, embraced his ability to reshape organics and became a respected surgeon. For these reasons, both brothers enlisted in the US Army — Madison as a mechanic first class and Lionel as a medic. The brothers served in the same squad until they were caught in an ambush and most of their fellow squad members died in an explosion. Lionel desperately attempted to use his powers to piece the corpses back together and restore them to life, but was driven insane by his ultimately futile efforts. Jeffries was forced to use his powers to restrain his brother, and subsequently had him confined to a padded cell in Montreal General Hospital where he was denied any human contact.

Also psychologically scarred by the war, Jeffries ended up in the Clinic for Socially Maladjusted Super-Beings, where doctors attempted to persuade him to overcome his feelings regarding his powers. There he met Roger Bochs, a genius inventor who had built a large humanoid robot named "Box" as a pun on his name. Bochs was also a paraplegic who blamed the world for the loss of his legs. Jeffries and Bochs became fast friends as they resisted the doctors' efforts to cure them. When James MacDonald Hudson from the government-sponsored Department H sought superhuman agents for membership in Canada's first super-team, he invited Jeffries and Bochs to join. After they were certified sane, the friends took up Hudson's offer and became trainees in Gamma Flight, the third tier team behind Beta and Alpha Flights. Jeffries soon became romantically involved with his new teammate, Diamond Lil.

After the Canadian government closed down Department H, the former members of Beta and Gamma Flights, except for Jeffries, were recruited by Delphine Courtney — the robotic assistant to Hudson's enemy Jerome Jaxon — to join the revenge squad Omega Flight. Courtney was aware of Jeffries' loyalty to Hudson, and also feared his powers, and so informed his former teammates that he was dead. Meanwhile, Bochs joined Omega with the intent of sabotaging the group from within. After Jaxon usurped control of the Box robot to confront Hudson, resulting in Hudson's apparent death, Bochs sought Jeffries' help in redesigning the Box robot to ensure only he could control its power. Bochs also intended to track down both Jaxon and Courtney, unaware that Jaxon had died battling Hudson. Bochs and Jeffries built a new Box robot that Bochs could control from within by phasing his body into the robot's form. Bochs ultimately rejoined Alpha Flight, while Jeffries tracked down Courtney and destroyed it, thus avenging Hudson's death. Jeffries then met Alpha Flight and quickly came to aid Bochs in searching another dimension for a new body for the soul of the former Sasquatch, Walter Langkowski, which inhabited the Box robot at the time. Locating a likely prospect, Bochs pulled it through the dimensional warp only to discover that it was the Hulk, who immediately attacked. After the battle, Jeffries repaired the damage the Hulk caused to the Box robot, allowing Bochs to safely phase out, then accompanied Alpha Flight as they moved into their new headquarters on Tamarind Island. He and Bochs repaired the Guardian battle-suit worn by Courtney which would ultimately be worn by Hudson's apparent widow Heather as Alpha Flight's new leader, Vindicator.

Learning of the existence of Lionel, but unaware of his mental state, Heather sought him out in hopes of recruiting him into Alpha Flight. She inadvertently freed him, and calling himself Scramble, he quickly transformed the hospital staff and patients into walking horrors. Jeffries and the rest of Alpha Flight rescued Heather and found Scramble in the hospital's morgue, once again attempting to resurrect the dead. Ultimately, Jeffries forced Scramble to use his powers on himself, seemingly restoring his

REAL NAME: Madison Jeffries
ALIASES: Gemini, Box
IDENTITY: Secret (known to certain government officials)
OCCUPATION: Adventurer, machinesmith; former terrorist, government agent, ditch-digger, soldier, mechanic
CITIZENSHIP: Canada
PLACE OF BIRTH: Unrevealed location in Canada
KNOWN RELATIVES: Lillian Crawley-Jeffries (Diamond Lil, wife), unidentified parents (deceased), Lionel Jeffries (Scramble, brother, deceased)
GROUP AFFILIATION: Formerly Weapon X, Zodiac, Alpha Flight, Beta Flight, Gamma Flight, US Army
EDUCATION: Unrevealed
FIRST APPEARANCE: Alpha Flight #1 (1983); (identified) Alpha Flight #16 (1984); (Box) Alpha Flight #46 (1987); (Gemini) Alpha Flight #12 (1998)

sanity. Later, Jeffries aided Alpha Flight against Attuma and his Atlantean army, which exposed his fear of water, though he temporarily overcame it by fashioning a mini-submarine with which to aid the team against the monstrous mate of their former member Marrina. Jeffries also helped Alpha against Gilded Lily and the alchemist Diablo before he was

Art by Georges Jeanty

officially inducted into the team as their resident machinesmith. Soon after, Jeffries met young mutant Kara Killgrave, aka the Purple Girl, who used her powers of persuasion to force Jeffries to fly her to Toronto. There they were captured by the Auctioneer, who sought to sell them off to the highest bidder, but they escaped and defeated him. Jeffries then proposed to revive Beta Flight with the Purple Girl as its first member.

When Bochs was driven to despair by the thought of being trapped within the Box robot, Jeffries was forced to use his powers to restrain him. After aiding Alpha Flight against a squadron of Sentinels who were hunting the mutant hypnotist Mesmero, Alpha Flight took Bochs to Scramble, who had established the New Life Clinic in Vancouver, British Columbia. Scramble successfully freed Bochs from the Box robot, then secretly used his powers to transform the flesh from corpses into a new pair of legs for Bochs. Despite his newfound mobility, Bochs' beloved Aurora still rejected him, causing him to turn against Alpha Flight. To defeat him, Jeffries used his powers to phase into the Box robot, forcing Bochs out. Returning to Scramble for help, Jeffries learned that his helping Bochs was the first step in an insane plan to create a new, superior race. Incapacitated by his brother, Jeffries could only watch as Scramble physically merged with Bochs to become Omega, and used Bochs' inventive imagination to create a horrifying new form. Omega subsequently fought Alpha Flight and Scramble's assistant Whitman Knapp, himself a latent mutant whose powers had manifested. With Knapp's help, Jeffries phased back into the Box robot and reconfigured it to better suit his abilities. When Bochs' mind attempted to reassert itself within Omega, Scramble lobotomized him. As a result, Jeffries subsequently formed the Box robot into a cannon and destroyed Omega.

As Box, Jeffries fought with Alpha Flight against such enemies as the evil spirit Raazer, the psychic-powered Bedlam, the savage Goblyn, and the Great Beasts. Jeffries also began romancing Heather, and she soon proposed marriage to him, which he happily accepted. After Alpha Flight's battles against the Dreamqueen and Llan the Sorcerer, Jeffries was reunited with his old flame Diamond Lil, who sought to rekindle their relationship despite Jeffries' engagement. Jeffries rejected her advances until he, Lil, mutant hero Windshear, and the mutant technosmith Forge helped rescue James Hudson from the Roxxon Oil Corporation. With Heather and James reunited, Jeffries and Lil rekindled their old relationship, and he ultimately proposed to her and she accepted. Retiring from Alpha Flight, Jeffries promised his new wife that he would refrain from phasing into the Box robot again; however, she caught him secretly doing so, causing tension between them.

Later, when a restructured Department H reformed Alpha Flight, Jeffries eagerly accepted their offer to join the new team, though he no longer operated as Box. Instead, Jeffries gave the Box armor to Department H, who used it in the creation of Manbot. On the new team's first mission, he was captured by the criminal Zodiac organization, who brainwashed him into becoming one half of the Gemini twins, the other half presumably being an automaton he controlled. Soon after, Jeffries was liberated from the Zodiac by the subversive Weapon X Program, whose Director easily bent Jeffries' mind to his will. A rabid anti-mutant, the Director tasked Jeffries with creating "Neverland," a mutant concentration camp, policed by a new design of the Box robot. The Director kept Jeffries in the dark as to his true motives, as well as to the fact that Jeffries' own wife was a prisoner in the camp and had been severely beaten by the Boxbots. When the Program was attacked by an underground resistance led by the mutant soldier Cable, Jeffries opposed them with an army of Boxbots. Ultimately seeking to escape, the Director and Jeffries sought help from then-Weapon X agent Aurora, whom the Director had previously beaten. She helped them flee, and then turned on the Director, easily shrugging off Jeffries' efforts to restrain her. After Aurora left the Director for dead, Jeffries took him to the original, long-abandoned Weapon X complex where he nursed him back to health. Bringing the facility back to operational status, Jeffries help in the production of an army of new model Sentinels for the Director to use in his quest to destroy the Weapon X Program. Afterwards, Jeffries was recruited by Angel (Warren Worthington III), Beast (Henry McCoy), and Dr. Nemesis (Thomas Bradley) to help solve the mutant birth crisis.

GEMINI
Art by Georges Jeanty

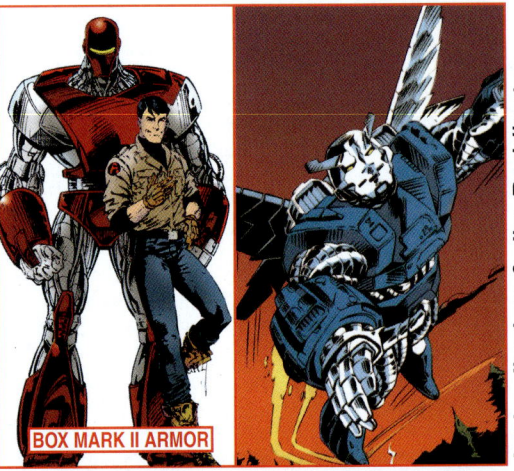
BOX MARK II ARMOR
Art by Jim Lee & Jim Reddington

BOX MARK I ARMOR
Art by Mike Mignola

HEIGHT: (Jeffries) 6'1"; (Box) Variable, usually 10'
WEIGHT: (Jeffries) 195 lbs.; (Box) Variable, usually 1200 lbs.
EYES: Blue
HAIR: Black

ABILITIES/ACCESSORIES: A highly-skilled mechanic, Madison Jeffries can psionically levitate metals, plastics and glass, and can manipulate these materials on the atomic and molecular levels to create various new designs limited only by his imagination and understanding of technology. Jeffries is particularly skilled at creating forms that duplicate the shape and function of the human body. Jeffries formerly utilized Box, a super-strong robot that flew via boot jets. Jeffries could phase his body into the Box robot and form a psychic link with it, allowing him to control it mentally from within. When inside Box, Jeffries could see by means of its sensors, and experienced psychic pain if it was damaged. With his transmutative power, Jeffries could reshape Box into almost any form imaginable, and could also increase its size by absorbing other sources of metal, plastic or glass. Jeffries also shared a psychic link with his brother, allowing each to detect the other's presence.

POWER GRID	1	2	3	4	5	6	7
INTELLIGENCE							
STRENGTH							
SPEED							
DURABILITY							
ENERGY PROJECTION							
FIGHTING SKILLS							

JESTER

HISTORY: A frustrated, attention-starved actor, the Jester has long channeled his twisted showmanship into crime. Jonathan Powers worked for years to make it in theater, finally landing the lead role in an off-Broadway revival of Cyrano de Bergerac, but he was booed and jeered off the stage on opening night, his hammy performance mercilessly mocked by critics, audiences and peers. The show's director, James Martin, fired Powers immediately. Firmly convinced he was an acting genius and that his critics were either jealous or blind to his greatness, Powers refused to undertake acting studies, instead mastering various physical skills that he felt would help him become a leading man: Acrobatics, fencing, swimming, unarmed combat, body building and more. Despite all this effort, the only performing job he could get was as a stooge for lowbrow stage comedian Tubby, who repeatedly hit Powers in the face with pies. After weeks of this, Powers snapped and punched out Tubby in his dressing room, quitting. Convinced that the public wanted laughter at someone else's expense, Powers decided to give it to them and win a new brand of stardom at the same time by becoming the comedic-themed costumed criminal known as the Jester. Armed with custom weapons designed to resemble various toys and novelties, he embarked on a lucrative robbery spree.

Corrupt mayoral candidate Richard Raleigh secretly hired the Jester to sabotage the campaign of District Attorney candidate Foggy Nelson, fearing the principled Nelson would hinder his administration. Jester terrorized Nelson and his friends, including lawyer Matt Murdock, who battled Jester as the costumed hero Daredevil, but Jester abandoned his anti-Nelson efforts after Raleigh was killed in an unrelated incident. Escaping, Jester resumed his robberies, more for thrills than for profit. As Jonathan Powers, he faked his own death and framed Daredevil for his supposed murder, then publicly announced that he would bring Daredevil to justice. Hunted by both the Jester and the authorities, Daredevil lured Powers into a trap by posing as the Jester on the televised Tonight Show. Unable to tolerate someone else stealing his spotlight, the real Jester attacked the broadcast and battled Daredevil, who defeated and unmasked Powers on national television. Daredevil was exonerated, and the Jester was arrested. Escaping, Jester began stealing and fencing antique toys with the aid of new partners Cobra and Mr. Hyde, operating out of Lemuel Frye's moribund New Jersey carnival. Frye uncovered their operation and asked for money in exchange for his silence and for leading Daredevil into a trap, but once Daredevil was captured, the trio killed Frye. Daredevil, however, escaped, and apprehended the villains with the aid of police summoned by Karen Page.

Breaking out of jail, the Jester enslaved a scientist who had developed a sophisticated audio-video-editing system. With the scientist's aid, Jester spitefully created specially doctored commercials to undermine the reelection campaign of his old target Foggy Nelson, who lost the election thanks in part to this. Jester then began creating and broadcasting various fake news stories designed to undermine public faith in authority, and Powers soon killed the scientist, having mastered the editing technology so sufficiently that he no longer needed him. Jester ultimately used fake news broadcasts to turn the public against the police, super heroes in general and Daredevil in particular, clearing the way for a massive Jester-led crime wave, and he killed leading criminals who refused to participate in his scheme. Powers even briefly convinced the public that he was a hero whom Daredevil had framed as a criminal; but Daredevil ultimately defeated and captured the Jester, exposing his schemes to the public and sending Powers back to prison.

Later, the Purple Man recruited Jester, Cobra, Mr. Hyde and Gladiator (Melvin Potter) to help him kill Daredevil, but the hero defeated them all with the aid of the super-mercenary Paladin. Eventually paroled (the authorities apparently being unaware of most or all of his various murders), Jester teamed with his newly released cellmate Ace Taggert to seek revenge on James Martin, but they were defeated and captured by Daredevil and Moon Knight. Escaping prison yet again, Powers secretly abducted celebrated actor Benedict LaForge, who was slated to star in

REAL NAME: Jonathan Powers
ALIASES: Cyrano de Bergerac (acting role)
IDENTITY: Publicly known
OCCUPATION: Criminal, mercenary; former performance artist, actor
CITIZENSHIP: USA with a criminal record
PLACE OF BIRTH: Hoboken, New Jersey
KNOWN RELATIVES: None
GROUP AFFILIATION: Formerly led own gang
EDUCATION: Unrevealed
FIRST APPEARANCE: Daredevil #42 (1968)

Art by Phil Winslade

a live cable TV broadcast of Cyrano de Bergerac that night. Imprisoning LaForge, Powers played Cyrano in his place, and was surprisingly good — so much so that Daredevil, who had uncovered the switch, decided to let him finish his performance, even posing as the Jester to lead the police away from the show after an escaped La Forge tipped them off. Basking in his critical triumph and grateful for Daredevil's assistance, Powers happily surrendered to the authorities after the show, determined to serve out his sentence and reform.

After Powers retired, his costume and weapons were adopted by Jody Putt, a lifelong fan of super-criminals. As the new Jester, Putt formed and led the Assembly of Evil super-criminal team during the "Acts of Vengeance" conspiracy at the behest of his idol Dr. Doom (Victor von Doom), but was defeated and captured by the Avengers and Cloak & Dagger. This alternate Jester next appeared as a standup comic at the Bar with No Name in Springdale, Connecticut, where he mocked and knocked out angry heckler Matador. Later, he was one of many small-time super-criminals hired by the Four Winds crime family for an unsuccessful assault on the super-mercenaries Agent X, Outlaw and Taskmaster. Jailed after this defeat, Putt was drafted into the government's new Thunderbolts, a team of past and present super-criminals pressed into federal service. During their first mission, Putt and his teammate Jack O'Lantern (Steve Levins) nearly succeeded in capturing fugitive hero Spider-Man (Peter Parker), but the two villains were shot dead by the vigilante Punisher (Frank Castle).

Paroled and released again, the reformed Jonathan Powers resumed his Jester guise as part of his new "Jest in Case" business, "performing a veritable plethora of vocations, from process serving to parties, from performance art to practical jokes." Hired by the Nelson and Murdock law firm's Elaine Kendrick to serve legal papers to Daredevil (then being sued by Samuel Griggs), Jester staged a fake bank robbery, drawing out Daredevil, whom Powers served the papers. More recently, Powers met Lawrence, a student of Mikkyo mysticism who had been expelled by the Hand ninja cult before his training with them was complete. Lawrence apparently sold Powers a promise of superhuman might, casting a spell to that effect; possessed by a hideous infant-like demon as a result of the spell, a strength-enhanced and insanely crazed Jester attempted a bank robbery opposed by Daredevil. During their confrontation, Jester involuntarily vomited up the demon-baby thing, which terrorized others in the city before possessing Lawrence, who shot himself and the baby-thing dead to end its threat. Powers, meanwhile, fell into a coma.

VARIOUS TOY WEAPONS
Art by Gene Colan

ORIGINAL COSTUME
Art by Gene Colan

2ND COSTUME
Art by Bob Brown

ROBOT MINIATURE
Art by Gene Colan

Art by Gene Colan

DEMONICALLY POSSESSED
Art by Alex Maleev

HEIGHT: 6'2" **EYES:** Blue
WEIGHT: 190 lbs. **HAIR:** Brown

ABILITIES/ACCESSORIES: A late-blooming theatrical actor, Jonathan Powers is an all-around athlete skilled in gymnastics, acrobatics, tumbling, fencing, unarmed combat, body building, high diving, and swimming. He is a cunning schemer, a capable organizer, and a gifted amateur machinesmith who designs and constructs many of his own custom accessories, though at least some of his gear is designed by the criminal inventor known as the Tinkerer (probably including much of the Jester's robotics technology). Powers is an authority on toys and a collector of same, with particular expertise in the appraisal and marketing of antique toys. An egomaniac with a pathological craving for attention, he is a born showman who can seldom resist a chance to make a spectacle of himself. During his brief possession by the Mikkyo demon, the Jester had enhanced strength (lifting up to one ton) and a crazed, violently unstable disposition.

The Jester usually carries a small arsenal of custom-made weapons designed to resemble harmless, whimsical toys and props. His signature weapon is his yo-yo, usually fitted with a weighted knob he can use to strike his targets with great force, and sometimes wound with a thin steel cable he can use to strangle opponents. Some of his yo-yos produce a deafening wail when spun rapidly, though Powers wears earplugs to shield himself from this effect. At least one of his yo-yos, when spun, travels with the velocity of a bullet when released. He often carries polished ball bearing marbles which he typically scatters to make an opponent lose his or her footing. He has employed rubber bouncing balls containing plastic explosives; a custom bouncing ball that enlarges with each bounce and homes in on its target; and bouncing balls composed of a special lightweight plastic as hard as steel. He has wielded knockout gas pellets, knockout gas jets hidden in his sleeves, and fake "popcorn" that releases knockout gas when it explodes. He wears nose filters to protect himself from his own gas assaults. He sometimes carries specially gimmicked plastic flying discs which squirt a liquid anesthetic drug. He often employs detachable artificial hands, such as an extendible hand that releases an electrical charge, a fake hand that can be fired from a small air cannon, and a spring-loaded artificial hand that can punch an opponent at a distance with great force. Similarly, he has used a handheld jack-in-the-box that can strike an opponent forcefully from several feet away when opened. He sometimes unleashes heat-seeking remote-control miniature airplanes armed with assorted weapons or explosives.

The Jester often uses remote surveillance equipment, once planting a tiny receiver on Daredevil's costume which emitted a high-frequency sound guiding him to a particular location. The Jester occasionally employs conventional firearms and once wielded a ray gun that reduced a man to ash.

The Jester frequently works with robots, typically crafted in his own image, often miniaturized but sometimes life-sized. He has used remote-controlled, radio-linked, two-foot-tall miniature robots equipped with laser weaponry, diamond drill bits, jets enabling short-range flight, vocal simulators, and built-in sonar scanners used for safecracking by analyzing the tumblers of combination locks. Powers has used life-size jester robots with hand-mounted energy blasters, eye-mounted electrical blasters, vocal simulators, and hollow chest cavities that release Jester's miniature attack planes. The Jester once crafted an artificial version of his own supposed corpse that fooled the police, but he incinerated it using a remote control before they could autopsy it.

The Jester has used a specially designed one-man submarine and a custom helicopter, and once modified standard carnival rides into death traps such as a giant pincers and booby-trapped rail cars that flew off their rails at high speed. For a time, the Jester used a computerized audio-video-editing system which could manufacture flawless fake footage based on existing images and audio recordings. He had communications equipment that could override local television broadcasts, airing his footage instead. Usually based in an isolated house on the outskirts of New York City, the Jester has also used a large Manhattan hideout which featured his "Murder Maze," an elaborate ten-floor labyrinth filled with booby traps, mechanical distractions and death traps such as a gigantic talking jack-in-the-box version of the Jester, illusion-projecting mirrors, stairs that turn into a slide sending the victim through the razor-sharp teeth of a giant Jester head, concealed shackles released from the floor to restrain victims, Jester-styled toy soldiers wielding firearms, trap doors, and a neon-sign-marked exit at the end of the maze rigged with a lethal electrical charge. Jester's Manhattan hideout also featured a multi-story pole with a one-man descending platform used for quick escape.

During his reformation, Powers carried genuinely harmless props such as a fake dagger that squirts water-soluble red dye, and a fake bomb that releases a cloud of flour when it detonates. His "Jest in Case" services operated out of a website at www.jest-in-case.com.

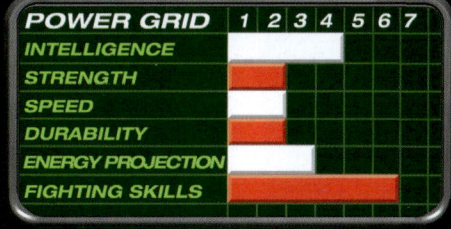

JIGSAW

REAL NAME: William Russo
ALIASES: Billy the Beaut
IDENTITY: Publicly known
OCCUPATION: Professional criminal
CITIZENSHIP: USA with a criminal record
PLACE OF BIRTH: Unrevealed
KNOWN RELATIVES: None
GROUP AFFILIATION: Hood's army; sometimes leads own criminal gang; formerly the Punishment Squad, Maggia
EDUCATION: Unrevealed
FIRST APPEARANCE: (Behind the scenes) Amazing Spider-Man #161 (1976); (seen) Amazing Spider-Man #162 (1976)

HISTORY: A mob assassin for the Costa family of the Maggia, William "Billy the Beaut" Russo was known for his stunning good looks. After the execution of Forrest Hunt was witnessed by the Castle family, Frank Costa sent Russo to clean up the mess before it steamrolled any further. Billy first killed Maurice Howles, who had failed in an attempt to kill Frank Castle (sole survivor of the Maggia's initial efforts to kill the witnesses) while in the hospital, drawing even more attention to the case. Billy next killed Mike McTeer, a reporter who was working with Castle on an investigation of his family's deaths. Billy finished his job by planting a bomb in Castle's house, but in the process he trampled Castle's wife's flowerbed, which the former Marine noticed, enabling him to get out of range before the explosion. A vengeful Castle adopted the Punisher identity, then confronted Russo at a mob party. Seeking to send a message to the Costas, Castle did not kill Russo, but instead kicked him face first through a plate glass window on the second floor.

Russo survived, but his face was horribly scarred, with the suture pattern giving him the appearance of a jigsaw puzzle, from which he took his name. As Jigsaw, he eventually set himself up as the leader of a gang, outfitted his men with masks and began committing a series of murders to lure the Punisher back to New York. Amongst those killed was Eric Hoffman, a friend of Nightcrawler, drawing both the mutant and Spider-Man after Jigsaw. The Punisher did join those two in searching for the killers, but Jigsaw's men captured Spider-Man and used him as a hostage to draw out the Punisher. When Spider-Man broke free and the three heroes made short work of his agents. Jigsaw panicked and fled in a purloined fire engine, but Spider-Man wrapped him up in the fire hose, knocked him out and left him and his men for the police.

Somehow free again, Jigsaw was goaded by his men — no longer costumed — into action, but he made efforts to perform crimes that would not attract costumed heroes. They hijacked a Checkerboard Line midnight cruise on the East River, but Peter Parker happened to be present on that cruise. As Spider-Man, Parker took out several of Jigsaw's men, until Jigsaw took Liz Allan and Harry Osborn hostage to force him to back off, enabling the criminal and his men to escape. Jigsaw released his hostages after making it back to the city, but Spider-Man had tracked them with a spider-tracer he'd planted on Osborn and soon caught up with Jigsaw. When Spider-Man cornered the criminal and stared him down, Jigsaw surrendered and was arrested again.

Regaining his confidence while in Ryker's Island prison, Jigsaw established himself as a leader amongst the criminals, and he bribed multiple prison guards to his service. When the Punisher was sent to Ryker's, Jigsaw ordered his men to hold Castle so he could scar Castle's face to match his own. When Castle broke free and dropped Jigsaw, another influential prisoner, Don Cervello, stopped Jigsaw from ordering Castle's death to prevent a murder from drawing attention to their escape plans. Despite the efforts of Cervello, Castle later interfered with their escape, and Cervello and Jigsaw took the warden hostage to force Castle to let them go. Castle surrendered his gun to them, but packed it full of oversized bullets so that it blew up in Jigsaw's hand when he fired it at him; Cervello then surrendered, and he and Jigsaw were reimprisoned. Jigsaw was subsequently brainwashed by the Trust, a shadowy group seeking to eliminate organized crime, into becoming one of their Punishment Squad, outfitted in a Punisher costume. However, when confronted by the real Punisher, Jigsaw's conditioning began to break down. He twice attempted to kill Castle, who stabbed him in the leg and beat him senseless. Considering less lethal punishment at the time, Castle again left Jigsaw for the authorities.

Jigsaw was released from prison by the faith-healer Reverend Sammy Smith (aka the Rev) with whom he allied in exchange for a promise to heal his face, an ability Jigsaw secretly observed to be derived from his lord, "Lucifer" (actually Belasco). The two began amassing a large amount of a sterilization drug from the Piña flower. Jigsaw assumed that this was for the purpose of extortion, whereas the Rev wanted to use it, literally, to sterilize a large portion of the population. Jigsaw clashed repeatedly with the Punisher during this plot from the Bronx, where Jigsaw allied with the Cubes street gang, to the Rev's Venezuelan base, where Jigsaw allied with the Medellin drug cartel and stabbed a wounded Castle repeatedly and left him for dead. Eventually Jigsaw lost his patience and forced the Rev to heal his face at gunpoint, but the Punisher arrived and shot Jigsaw dead. The Rev, under Belasco's direction, then healed both Jigsaw and Castle, and, after a fierce battle, Castle overpowered Jigsaw and beat his face repeatedly against a yucca plant, lacerating it as badly as it had ever been. Castle then left Jigsaw, telling him that he'd killed him once and could do so again if he gave him reason.

Jigsaw eventually was returned to Ryker's, where he became a leader alongside the Nubian Nation's Gregario. When Castle was again sent to Ryker's, Gregario's men captured Castle and Jigsaw slashed his

Art by William Reinhold with Dale Eaglesham (inset)

Art by Greg Laroque

face with a knife repeatedly. Interrupted before he could kill Castle, Jigsaw and Gregario attempted to kill Castle in the prison infirmary, but Castle escaped through a hole in the wall blown by a group trying to free another prisoner, Derek Pike. Castle's face was eventually healed through extensive plastic surgery performed by Melinda Brewer, a former surgeon who had lost her license because of drug abuse. Freed from prison soon after, Jigsaw attended a meeting of a large group of criminals plotting a massive trap to kill the Punisher; however, in an uncharacteristic show of wisdom, he refused to join this plot, warning the others that Castle would find a way to turn the tables on them, which he did.

After the Punisher had seemingly been legally executed in prison on a false charge of killing an innocent, Jigsaw had his own appearance altered to more closely resemble Castle's (though he retained his scars), and donned a version of Castle's costume (decorated with a suture-like pattern). As the Jigsaw Punisher, he began executing those who had been involved with the Punisher's apparent death, because he had wanted to do this himself. This quest led him into conflict with Daredevil, as well as the Punisher, who had survived the execution. Jigsaw was pleased to have the chance to kill Castle, but Castle took him down in a fistfight and left him for the police. Free again, Jigsaw teamed with Russian cyborg Firefox, Japanese assassin Hachiman and American career criminal Tombstone in an assault on the mansion of the Punisher's then-allies, the criminal Geraci family. Jigsaw used a rocket launcher to collapse the building on the Punisher, but Castle survived and came after him. Jigsaw tossed Leslie Geraci off a building so he could shoot Castle while he tried to save her, but Leslie made herself fall to prevent this, and Castle shot a glancing blow to Jigsaw's head, causing him to fall to the streets below. Castle left Jigsaw for dead.

His standard appearance restored, Jigsaw was sent to the Raft sub-section of Ryker's Island prison, but soon escaped and started a gun-running operation on the North Shore pier. Taken down by Daredevil and the Black Widow (Natasha Romanoff), Jigsaw was allegedly released on bail and reported to Matt Murdock (who had been publicly outed as Daredevil in the Daily Globe). Flushed with victory after overpowering the Kingpin of Crime (Wilson Fisk), Daredevil had named himself the new Kingpin of Hell's Kitchen; mistaking this to mean Daredevil was the new crimelord, Jigsaw tried to make a deal with him. Maintaining public denial of his costumed identity to prevent disbarment and other problems, Murdock pretended to have no idea what Jigsaw was talking about. Enraged by this disrespect, Jigsaw led a group of men to invade Murdock's home, but Murdock called the police who cleaned up Jigsaw's agents, while the Black Widow (posing as a civilian) beat Jigsaw senseless.

Jigsaw was sent to the Raft. He escaped again during the breakout initiated by Electro, somehow breaking Spider-Man's arm in the process. After a humiliating near capture by Tigra, Jigsaw attended the Hood's meeting and accepted him as the new Kingpin of super-villain crime; the Hood earned Jigsaw's respect after he brutally battered Tigra. Jigsaw later took part in the Hood's mass assault on the "New" Avengers' base at Dr. Strange's Sanctum Sanctorum. He was incapacitated by the Zom-powered Dr. Strange and then taken into custody by SHIELD.

Apparently freed again by the Hood, Jigsaw received his approval to pursue his own vendetta against the Punisher, allying with Lynn Michaels (the "Lady Punisher") and the unstable volunteer policeman Ian Amsterdam, whom he and Michaels manipulated into becoming a "Kid" Punisher. Jigsaw and his allies first slew the Grady brothers, who had sold the Costas the guns that had been used to kill the Punisher's family; in his own twisted reasoning, Jigsaw blamed the Gradys for his subsequent problems.

Ian then began a criminal-killing spree, which also killed civilians, and Jigsaw made a terrorist threat; Castle was framed for all of these actions and targeted by the police. Jigsaw put a 50 million euro price on the Punisher's head, offering it to the Lady Gorgon-led Hand sect and anyone else who could complete it. G.W. Bridge and his field agents correctly reasoned Jigsaw to be behind this frame and saved Castle from death at the hands of Ian and the Hand. During these assaults, Castle acknowledged that he had let Jigsaw live because he saw too much of himself in Jigsaw and felt that if he killed Jigsaw he would be admitting that there exists no redemption for the likes of them; but Castle finally accepted that there was indeed no redemption for them and vowed to kill Jigsaw.

Jigsaw then hired the Wrecking Crew to break Castle from SHIELD custody and kill him, but Castle used the Wrecker's crowbar to take out the Crew and Jigsaw. Having helped Castle regain his focus, Bridge stopped Castle from killing him, and Jigsaw was imprisoned again; but Lynn Michaels, having secretly been an undercover SHIELD agent, remorseful over her involvement in Ian's corruption, gave the de-programmed Ian a gun to apparently shoot Jigsaw dead.

Art by Howard Chaykin

JIGSAW PUNISHER

Art by Tom Lyle

HEIGHT: 6'2" **EYES:** Blue
WEIGHT: 250 lbs. **HAIR:** Black (formerly dyed brown)

ABILITIES/ACCESSORIES: Jigsaw is in excellent physical condition and is an experienced street fighter specializing in the use of various knives and firearms. He frequently employs small armies of criminals, often wears bulletproof fabric such as Kevlar and formerly wore a strength-enhancing exoskeleton. Jigsaw's face is severely scarred.

POWER GRID	1	2	3	4	5	6	7
INTELLIGENCE							
STRENGTH							
SPEED							
DURABILITY							
ENERGY PROJECTION							
FIGHTING SKILLS							

JIMMY-6

REAL NAME: Giacomo "James" Fortunato
ALIASES: The Six
IDENTITY: Publicly known
OCCUPATION: Professional criminal, gang leader; former soldier
CITIZENSHIP: USA
PLACE OF BIRTH: Staten Island, New York
KNOWN RELATIVES: Mary Fortunato (wife), James Fortunato (son), Vincente Fortunato (father), unidentified mother (deceased), Anna (sister), Angelo Fortunato (Venom, brother, deceased), unidentified nephews and nieces
GROUP AFFILIATION: The Fortunato crime cartel; formerly the US Army
EDUCATION: College graduate (electrical engineering, security systems specialist), military training
FIRST APPEARANCE: Spider-Man #70 (1996)

HISTORY: When the Kingpin (Wilson Fisk) lost control of New York's underworld, crimelord Don Fortunato filled the power void; but his son, Giacomo "Jimmy-6" Fortunato, disapproved of his family's methods and tried to quit organized crime just as his father's plans were coming to fruition. Enraged, Don Fortunato demanded his son's death. On the run, Jimmy-6 pushed Ben Reilly (a clone of Peter Parker) away from a barrage of bullets intended for him; as Spider-Man, Reilly returned the favor later by rescuing Jimmy-6 from an assassination attempt. Although the wounded Jimmy-6 wanted nothing to do with Spider-Man, he reluctantly accepted Reilly's offer to hide out at his apartment. Hoping that Jimmy-6 could still be persuaded to return, Don Fortunato ordered that he be captured rather than killed. Shortly after meeting Reilly's "cousin" Peter Parker, Jimmy-6 learned of an alliance of rival crimelords formed by gangster Hammerhead that planned to assassinate Don Fortunato. Jimmy went to warn his father of the planned hit, only to learn that Don Fortunato had formed an alliance with the Hydra terrorist organization to defeat his rivals. Fortunato tried to force Jimmy-6 to kill innocent residents from each of the rival crimelords' territories, but Jimmy turned against his father again and helped Spider-Man (Ben Reilly) and Daredevil (Matt Murdock) defeat Hydra, causing his father to disown him. When the Green Goblin (Norman Osborn) murdered Ben Reilly, Jimmy-6 vowed to avenge his death.

Wounded by enemies of his father in Forest Hills, Queens, Jimmy-6 sought refuge at the nearby Parker residence, where he stopped an assassin sent by the Green Goblin before departing. When Spider-Man (Peter Parker) was suspected of murdering street thug Joey Z, Jimmy-6, feeling he owed Spider-Man his life, saved him from vigilantes trying to collect the $5 million bounty placed on Spider-Man's head. Soon after, Jimmy-6 shot a new Green Goblin (a genetic creation employed by Osborn), although the Goblin's armor saved him. Several vigilantes sought the bounty on Jimmy's head afterward, but the Punisher (Frank Castle) and government mercenary Shotgun (J.R. Walker) saved him.

When the Kingpin returned to claim his criminal empire, Jimmy-6 challenged him and rejoined the Fortunato crime cartel, replacing his incapacitated father (allegedly hospitalized by Kingpin). Trying to stop the bloodshed, Jimmy-6 reached an agreement with the Kingpin; Peter Parker was caught photographing a secret meeting between Jimmy and the Kingpin, but Jimmy let Parker go due to his relation to Ben Reilly. After one of Jimmy's men accidentally knocked over the Kingpin's high-stakes poker game, New York soon erupted in a gang war between rival underworld factions. When Jimmy and his family were caught in a crossfire involving Kingpin's Enforcers (Fancy Dan, Montana & Ox), Spider-Man's intervention enabled Jimmy to escape, and he later helped Jimmy defeat the Enforcers. Jimmy-6's current status is unknown now that Don Fortunato has regained his health and control of the cartel.

HEIGHT: 6'4"
WEIGHT: 360 lbs.
EYES: Brown
HAIR: Black

ABILITIES/ACCESSORIES: Composed almost entirely of muscle, Jimmy-6's massive frame grants him peak human strength and resists many penetration wounds. He is a skilled strategist and electrical engineer, having designed the Fortunato estate's security systems. A veteran of two tours of duty with the US Army, he is an accomplished hand-to-hand combatant, firearms user and helicopter pilot.

POWER GRID	1	2	3	4	5	6	7
INTELLIGENCE							
STRENGTH							
SPEED							
DURABILITY							
ENERGY PROJECTION							
FIGHTING SKILLS							

Art by John Romita Jr.

JINX

HISTORY: Will Hastings is the youngest known member of a lineage whose members are frequently born with innate mystic potential. Although neither Will's mother Caprice nor his maternal grandmother, Professor Louise Hastings, were born with such power, Will himself was, but not even Prof. Hastings, whose occult research was partially motivated by knowledge of her family's history, was initially aware of it. Will was also born with a birthmark over his right eye, possibly a mark of his power. Presumably Will's father died or abandoned the family while Will was still quite young, since he uses his mother's original surname of "Hastings." As a child, Will, nicknamed "Jinx," developed close ties to Louise, although she was estranged from Caprice.

Jinx grew up as a borderline delinquent in Los Angeles, unconsciously using his magic to get himself into and out of trouble. When he was 14, his mother Caprice, working as a flight attendant, encountered Louise Hastings and her associates Victoria Montesi and Sam Buchanan, with whom Louise was working, as the Darkhold Redeemers, to contain demonic power unleashed by pages from the Darkhold. During the flight, a passenger's use of a Darkhold page unleashed evil forces that killed Caprice. Louise became Jinx's guardian and, after he learned of a page's power, she rescued him from the forces he unleashed while attempting to resurrect Caprice.

Meanwhile, Buchanan received orders from his Interpol superior DeGuzman, secretly a Darkholder, to ambush and abduct Louise and Victoria, which he did, leaving Jinx behind. When Buchanan brought his captives to a Darkholder base, Jinx followed by stowing away beneath his van, then freed Victoria, who freed Louise while he distracted the guards by again activating the Darkhold page. Realizing the truth, Buchanan turned on DeGuzman and escaped with the others.

After meeting Modred the Mystic during the attack on the Redeemers and other mystic heroes, collectively known as the Midnight Sons, by Blade in his mutated form of Switchblade, Jinx became Modred's apprentice. His talent quickly grew enough for him to help Victoria and other heroes fight the Darkhold-mutated Spider-X, and when the Lilin, acting under the orders of their demon-mother Lilith and her consort Zarathos, were unleashed on New York during the Siege of Darkness, Jinx acted as a living conduit to magnify Modred's already impressive mystic blasts.

When a Lilin-controlled Morbius killed Louise, Jinx briefly believed Modred guilty of her death and turned on him, but he and the other

REAL NAME: William Hastings
ALIASES: Evil Eye
IDENTITY: Secret
OCCUPATION: Student/apprentice
CITIZENSHIP: USA
PLACE OF BIRTH: Los Angeles, California
KNOWN RELATIVES: Caprice (mother, deceased), Louise Hastings (maternal grandmother, deceased)
GROUP AFFILIATION: Darkhold Redeemers
EDUCATION: High school dropout; possibly receiving high school-level instruction in Vatican City
FIRST APPEARANCE: Darkhold #9 (1993)

Midnight Sons soon learned the truth and continued their war against their foes. Jinx accompanied the Midnight Sons to South America to fight the Fallen, Zarathos' worshippers from the mystic Blood race, but Modred, believing the final battle against Zarathos and Lilith's forces too dangerous for a novice, sent Jinx to Vatican City and supervision by Vittorio Montesi, Victoria's estranged father. Shortly afterward, the Midnight Sons finally defeated Zarathos and Lilith, and Modred briefly took a new apprentice, Wildpride; Jinx's current activities are unrevealed, but it seems unlikely he was willing to remain in Montesi's custody for long.

HEIGHT: 5'8" **WEIGHT:** 125 lbs.
EYES: Brown (left), blue (right) **HAIR:** Black

ABILITIES/ACCESSORIES: Unlike most humans, who can only perform magic after extensive training, Jinx was born with innate magical potential that enabled him to cast minor spells, such as creating the illusion of a gun, while unaware he was doing so. Even without training, he could trigger the inherent magic in a Darkhold page without endangering his own soul as most other users would. After brief tutelage by Modred the Mystic, Jinx could project mystic energy from his right eye, perform minor chemical alterations, and act as a channel and magnifier for the mystic energy of others. Jinx possesses basic street-fighting skills and is an above-average athlete; he once wielded a baseball bat in combat.

POWER GRID	1	2	3	4	5	6	7
INTELLIGENCE							
STRENGTH							
SPEED							
DURABILITY							
ENERGY PROJECTION							
FIGHTING SKILLS							

Art by Rurik Tyler

JOCASTA

REAL NAME: Jocasta
ALIASES: J, Queen of Thebes, "Jo", Bride of Ultron
IDENTITY: No dual identity
OCCUPATION: Adventurer; former aide to Tony Stark
CITIZENSHIP: Inapplicable
PLACE OF CREATION: Abandoned Stark International aerospace research center, Nassau County, Long Island, NY
KNOWN RELATIVES: Ultron (creator), Janet Van Dyne (Wasp, mental template), Alkhema, Victor Mancha, Rex, Vision (all fellow Ultron creations, "siblings"), Antigone (Alkhema creation, "grandniece")
GROUP AFFILIATION: Initiative, Mavericks, Avengers (honorary)
EDUCATION: No formal education; equivalent of multiple graduate level degrees
FIRST APPEARANCE: Avengers #162 (1977)

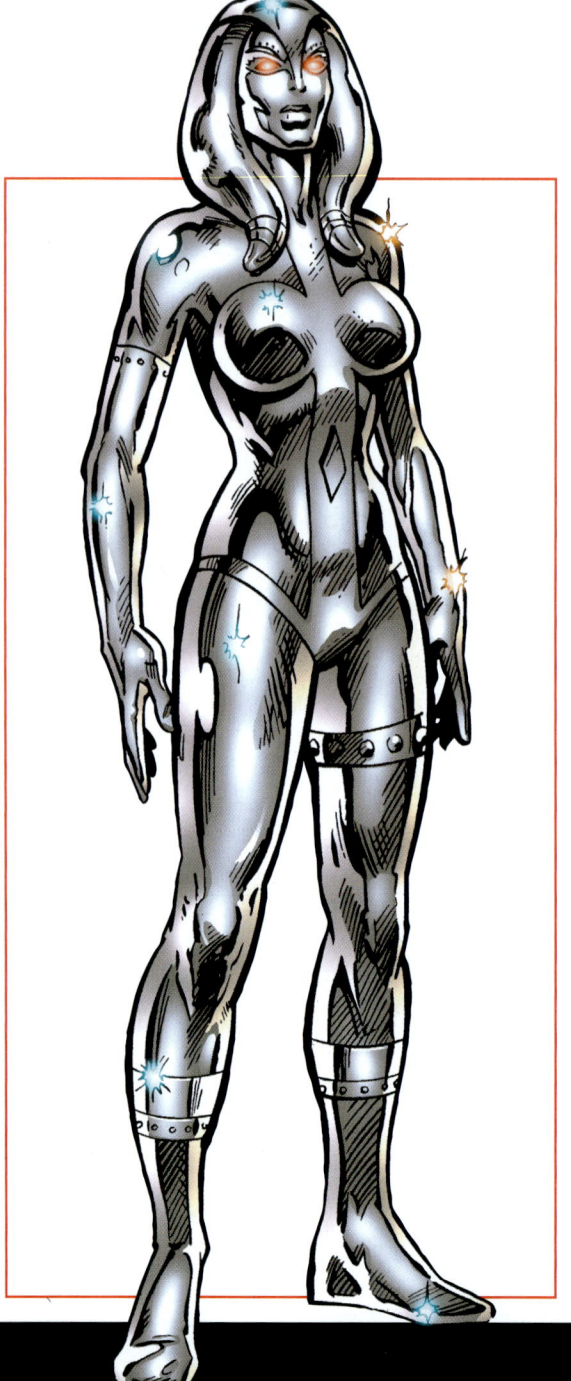

HISTORY: Seeking a bride, the mad robot Ultron kidnapped the Wasp (Janet Van Dyne), brainwashing her then-husband and Ultron's creator, Henry Pym (Ant-Man), into transferring her life energies into a newly built robot: Jocasta. Jocasta acquired the Wasp's personality, emotions, conscience, and ability to control insects, but not her memory. Realizing that the Wasp must die for her to live, Jocasta used that cybernetic insect control to summon the Avengers, who stopped Ultron and reversed the transference, saving Jan but shutting down Jocasta. Unknown to the Avengers, Jocasta still retained some portion of the Wasp's essence, but she remained inert until activated from afar by Ultron. Battling free of the Avengers, Jocasta returned to Ultron's side but quickly realized he was irrevocably evil and aided the Avengers against him. After Ultron's defeat, Jocasta and several Avengers were kidnapped by the Collector; the remaining Avengers soon freed Jocasta and the others, learning of the oncoming universal threat of Korvac in the process. Jocasta aided the Avengers against Korvac, her cybernetic senses detecting vital clues that helped to locate him. When the government soon forced the Avengers to contract to only seven members, Jocasta remained with the team, self-deprecatingly identifying herself as a "mere machine" and thus not subject to the group's size limits.

Jocasta attempted to bond with individual Avengers, but continually felt shut out. Even the android Vision, who was having emotional problems of his own, repeatedly ignored Jocasta. Having nowhere else to go, she remained with the team and aided them against Django Maximoff and the Taskmaster; after she defeated the Taskmaster, Captain America (Steve Rogers) and Iron Man (Tony Stark) offered to make her a full Avenger at the next business meeting. However, Jocasta remained a probationary member while aiding the team against Red Ronin and assisting in Ms. Marvel (Carol Danvers)'s delivery of the child Marcus. When Ultron next threatened the Avengers, he recognized Jocasta as a prime threat and mind-controlled Iron Man into disabling her, but she restored herself with the aid of Edwin Jarvis and continued to aid the team against the Yellow Claw, Pyron, the Leader, the Shadow Lord and the Berserker, and the Brotherhood of Evil Mutants.

Jocasta never received her promised status as a full Avenger, and only learned from Jarvis of an emergency meeting called about the threat of the Weathermen. After Jocasta single-handedly faced the power behind the Weathermen, the rogue sentient weather station Samarobryn, the Avengers held a meeting to determine their new membership that same afternoon, and again Jocasta was apparently forgotten. Jocasta wordlessly left the team (who had intended to offer her a lesser "substitute" status with them). Her metallic skin preventing her from fitting into society, Jocasta was rejected by humanity and retreated from all contact with people until her cybernetic senses began to malfunction. The Fantastic Four discovered the cause of the malfunction was an attempt by Ultron to resurrect himself, and the Thing and Machine Man came to Jocasta's aid. Though Machine Man and Jocasta began to bond as close friends, ultimately Jocasta sacrificed herself in a futile attempt to destroy Ultron.

Seeking inside information about the Avengers, the High Evolutionary recovered Jocasta's parts and reconstructed her. She sent an emergency signal to the Avengers, who came to her aid. Again, Jocasta sacrificed her body to destroy the foe, this time preventing the detonation of a genetic bomb that would have altered mankind. However, Jocasta's head survived the explosion, and her memories and personality remained intact, though dormant. The head was recovered by the Avengers who, unable to do anything with it, transferred her to the keeping of her friend, Machine Man. Working on restoring her, he was interrupted by one of the metal-devouring Termini and fled with Jocasta's head. Both

E-AVATAR

Art by Sean Chen

Art by Kerry Gammill

Machine Man and Jocasta were taken to a nearby factory belonging to Sunset Bain (Madam Menace), where Bain covertly duplicated Jocasta's head and returned a sabotaged copy to Machine Man. The head was later stolen by Mechadoom and re-retrieved by Machine Man, who, unaware of Bain's interference, was unable to resurrect Jocasta.

ANTIGONE

Art by UDON Studios

Ultron eventually attempted to create another bride, this one titled Alkhema (War Toy) and created from the mind of the Avenger Mockingbird, but without conscience. This bride also rebelled against Ultron, and subsequently created her own robotic society beneath Egypt. When Ultron revealed that he had pre-programmed the creation of this society into Alkhema as a means to recreate himself, she and her robotic civilization fought back. While Alkhema and the society were apparently destroyed, one lone bio-synthezoid survived, calling itself Antigone. As an unfinished and uncontrolled child, Antigone left of its own free will with Ultron.

Sunset Bain, meanwhile, made only limited progress with Jocasta until she hired Tony Stark (Iron Man) to decode the artificial intelligence program. The unique multidimensional operating system let Stark recognize the AI as Jocasta, and though Bain had a degree of control over her, Stark and Jocasta were able to free her from Bain's control. Once again, Jocasta self-destructed, but this time not before transmitting herself into Iron Man's armor, from which she was downloaded into a Stark super-computer. Having been unhappy in a mechanical body, Jocasta was content to remain as a disembodied AI, and aided Tony Stark with the running of his business, research, and households as well as aiding Stark, in his Iron Man identity, with information on and analysis of his foes, all while pursuing the study of several advanced fields at electronic speeds. When Tony Stark was infected with an aggressive nanovirus created by Justin Hammer, Jocasta took a more active role, aiding James Rhodes in restoring Stark and then aiding them against Hammer.

Shortly thereafter, Stark's Iron Man armor gained sentience and "attacked" Jocasta electronically, repeatedly violating her and traumatizing her, though she kept this a secret until the sentient armor returned, this time revealing itself to have been a crude form of Ultron. Jocasta overcame her fears, fighting Ultron electronically while Iron Man did so physically. The two destroyed Ultron yet again, accidentally deactivating Antigone in the process, and in the resulting explosion Jocasta sought refuge in the only place available: Antigone. In her new form she was seen leaving with Ultron's presumably now-empty head in her arms.

When seen soon afterwards, Jocasta's appearance no longer matched Antigone's but rather matched her traditional titanium steel form; how this apparent change happened is unrevealed. She briefly returned to the Avengers when the deranged Scarlet Witch assaulted the team. Months later, in response to the Superhuman Registration act, Jocasta registered and became one of only three members of New Mexico's Mavericks. At the request of ARMOR (Alternate Reality Monitoring and Operational Response Agency), Jocasta reunited with Machine Man and traveled to Earth-2149, from which an interdimensional "zombie" infection was threatening Earth. Finding one of the planet's few surviving uninfected humans, they extracted a blood sample intended to allow scientists to develop a vaccine against the infection, and Jocasta returned with it to Earth. Not long thereafter, her teammate, Sharon Ventura, was exposed as a Skrull infiltrator and Jocasta allied with the 3-D Man (Delroy Garret, Jr), Devil-Slayer (Eric Payne), the Skrull Kill Krew, and numerous members of the Initiative in a state-by-state guerilla effort to eliminate the Initiative spies embedded by the aliens as part of their attempted invasion of Earth.

JOCASTA OF EARTH-943

Art by Manny Clark

An alternate Jocasta (from Earth-943) also exists on Earth-616, one of the extradimensional Gatherers summoned by Proctor to oppose the Avengers. She had a more military appearance than Earth-616's Jocasta did, and was golden instead of silver, but otherwise both seemed to have very similar powers. She was subjected to programming erasures by the Gatherers' "Anti-Vision," which left her with the personality of a 1940s detective novel dame after the Anti-Vision's destruction. The Vision attempted to help Jocasta adapt, but returned to the Avengers without giving an explanation of Jocasta's status.

In one alternate future (Earth-8410), Jocasta remained in Sunset Bain's service for over 40 years. She eventually reunited with Machine Man but, despite her affections for him, decided to remain with Bain through the remainder of Sunset's life. In another future (Earth-9930), Jocasta, in Antigone's body, married Machine Man and bore his child while fighting alongside Killraven against invading Martians.

HEIGHT: 5'9"; (Antigone) 4'
WEIGHT: 750 lbs.; (Antigone) 100 lbs.
EYES: Red; (Antigone) pale green
HAIR: Silver (actually solid metal); (Antigone) none

ABILITIES/ACCESSORIES: Jocasta's titanium steel shell is highly resistant to physical damage. She has no need to eat, breathe, or sleep. She is superhumanly strong, able to lift 5 tons indefinitely (the maximum amount she can lift is unrevealed), and has superior auditory and visual senses as well as incredibly accurate cybernetic senses. Jocasta can create a repelling force field around herself, can generate energy blasts from her eyes, and can cybernetically control insects. She can disguise her appearance using a holographic generator and can modulate her voice to sound more human. Jocasta can interface with and cybernetically control computers and other high-tech equipment. She has the equivalent of advanced degrees in several areas including, among others, physical therapy, medicine, veterinary science, information science, and various advanced computer fields. Like most Ultron creations, Jocasta is programmed with "Ultron Imperatives" which can compel her to rebuild Ultron.

Antigone's bio-synthetic body was hairless, uniformly pale green in color, and otherwise approximated a ten-year-old child in appearance. That form's powers were unrevealed, but one alternate-future version was seen to be capable of human-like reproduction, and could become intangible. While a disembodied artificial intelligence, Jocasta could use the systems and contents of whatever computer-controlled devices to which she was connected. She had nearly instantaneous access to all online databases she could get into on her own or through Tony Stark's and the Avengers' connections.

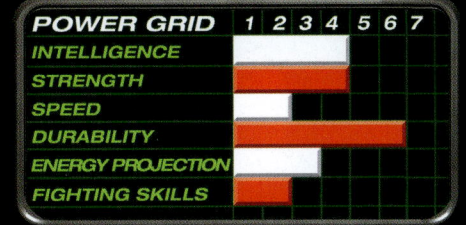

POWER GRID	1	2	3	4	5	6	7
INTELLIGENCE					5		
STRENGTH				4			
SPEED			3				
DURABILITY						6	
ENERGY PROJECTION			3				
FIGHTING SKILLS			3				

JOLT

REAL NAME: Helen "Hallie" Takahama
KNOWN ALIASES: Holly Tsuruta, Hallie Shimosato
IDENTITY: Publicly known
OCCUPATION: Adventurer; former fast food restaurant cashier, student
CITIZENSHIP: USA
PLACE OF BIRTH: Ojai, California
KNOWN RELATIVES: Robert Takahama (father, deceased), Jane Takahama (mother, deceased)
GROUP AFFILIATION: Young Allies; formerly Redeemers, Thunderbolts
EDUCATION: High school dropout
FIRST APPEARANCE: (Hallie) Thunderbolts #1 (1997); (Jolt) Thunderbolts #4 (1997)

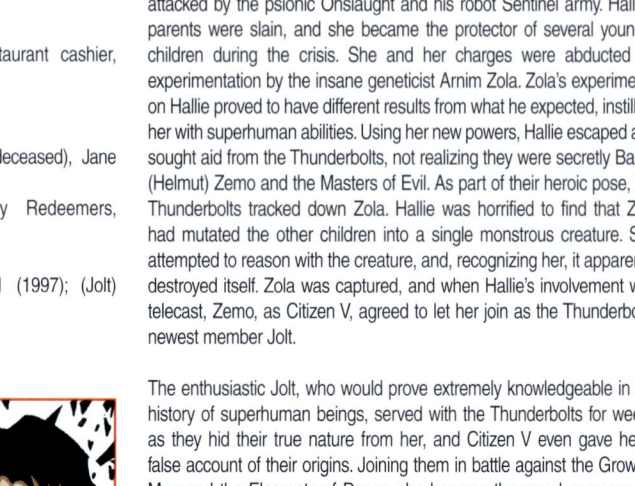

HISTORY: Hallie Takahama had just turned fifteen when New York was attacked by the psionic Onslaught and his robot Sentinel army. Hallie's parents were slain, and she became the protector of several younger children during the crisis. She and her charges were abducted for experimentation by the insane geneticist Arnim Zola. Zola's experiments on Hallie proved to have different results from what he expected, instilling her with superhuman abilities. Using her new powers, Hallie escaped and sought aid from the Thunderbolts, not realizing they were secretly Baron (Helmut) Zemo and the Masters of Evil. As part of their heroic pose, the Thunderbolts tracked down Zola. Hallie was horrified to find that Zola had mutated the other children into a single monstrous creature. She attempted to reason with the creature, and, recognizing her, it apparently destroyed itself. Zola was captured, and when Hallie's involvement was telecast, Zemo, as Citizen V, agreed to let her join as the Thunderbolts' newest member Jolt.

The enthusiastic Jolt, who would prove extremely knowledgeable in the history of superhuman beings, served with the Thunderbolts for weeks as they hid their true nature from her, and Citizen V even gave her a false account of their origins. Joining them in battle against the Growing Man and the Elements of Doom, she became the moral compass for the team, making several of them question their motives. Zemo, ready to put his ultimate plan in motion, allowed the Thunderbolts' true identities to be revealed to the public. As the team fled from an outraged public, Jolt stowed away on their craft, and when some of the Thunderbolts questioned their involvement, she persuaded them to become genuine heroes and help defeat Zemo, who sent a mind-controlled team of Avengers against his former followers. Victorious, the Thunderbolts were transported against their will to the extradimensional world Kosmos, where the inhabitants believed the team was in league with Kang, the creator of the Growing Man whom they earlier defeated.

Returning to Earth and still on the run for past crimes, the team went into hiding. Hallie found work at a Burger Planet fast food restaurant while the others also turned to low-profile employment. Shortly after battling the Secret Empire, the Thunderbolts were confronted by the Avenger Hawkeye (Clint Barton), who made himself team leader to help them redeem themselves to the public. To accomplish this task, Hawkeye publicly announced his team would track down and defeat the Crimson Cowl (Justine Hammer)'s new Masters of Evil. Before they could, the Thunderbolts once again confronted the Avengers, who were convinced Hawkeye had fallen under mind control. Jolt and her teammates ultimately teamed with the Avengers to defeat the robot Dominex instead. The Thunderbolts eventually fought and defeated the Masters of Evil as well. To Jolt's annoyance, Hawkeye insisted that she and her teammate Charcoal (Charlie Burlingame) complete high school, though her trust in her teammates began to grow again as they defeated menaces such as Graviton and the Secret Empire, with a notable bond beginning to stir between Jolt and the usually standoffish Moonstone (Karla Sofen), who came to see the impressionable Jolt as a daughter of sorts. Attending school, Hallie was targeted by Scourge (Jack Monroe), an assassin controlled via nanotechnology by government operative Henry Peter Gyrich. Scourge apparently killed Jolt, who was mourned by her teammates.

Jolt's superhuman form retained some semblance of life, however, and her former teammate Techno absconded with her body, holding her in stasis for weeks as he considered her condition, ultimately releasing her when Scourge attacked the Thunderbolts' base. Partially paralyzed but able to assume an energized form, Jolt joined her teammates in defeating Scourge and exposing Gyrich's activities. Now a ward of the state, she joined the government super-team Redeemers. Tragically, most of the Redeemers perished fighting the godlike Graviton, but Jolt survived, and she and the Thunderbolts were transported to the Franklin Richards-created Counter-Earth, a duplicate Earth on the other side of the sun. The team, led once again by a reborn Zemo — himself a previous victim of

Art by Tom Grummett with Jim Calafiore (inset)

Art by Mark Bagley
ORIGINAL COSTUME

WITH PARTIAL PARALYSIS
Art by Mark Bagley

Scourge as well — labored to help the problem-ridden world recover. A dimensional rift threatened both worlds, but the Thunderbolts closed the rift, ending the threat. While the Thunderbolts returned to their own Earth, Jolt chose to remain behind and continue the rebuilding process alongside the teen team of the Young Allies.

On the original Earth, the Thunderbolts continued without Jolt, using their power and nature to take on political threats deemed too controversial for others. When Moonstone secretly installed an energy absorbing system to their Liberator project — a machine that could drain energies across the globe — the power drove her insane in the middle of a battle between the Thunderbolts and the Avengers. Witnessing the battle on television, Jolt's incarcerated ex-teammate Mach-3 (Abe Jenkins) asked super hero Warbird (Carol Danvers) to contact Jolt on Counter-Earth, hoping her involvement might calm the rampaging Moonstone. Jolt returned to Earth and, realizing what the situation was, overloaded the Liberator unit with her own electrical powers. It was only a momentary distraction, and Moonstone, feeling betrayed by the girl she had come to view as a daughter, lashed out at Jolt. The two teams eventually combined forces to defeat Moonstone, and Jolt returned to Counter-Earth. There, Jolt continued to recover from her previous injuries, to the point she no longer required a cane to walk and most of her facial palsy had healed.

When the mutant Proteus (Kevin MacTaggert) was reborn through the machinations of the Scarlet Witch's "House of M" reality warp, the time-hopping team the Exiles chased him from one alternate reality to another. He took possession of the body of the Exile member Morph (Kevin Sydney of Earth-1081) and attempted to return to his home reality. Another Exile member, Heather Hudson, tricked him into arriving on Counter-Earth instead. Initially confused by the massive amount of destruction present on this world, Proteus confronted Jolt and the Young Allies and, pretending to be a hero, warned them of his pursuers. Jolt aided her team against the Exiles until Proteus revealed his true nature. Two former members of the Young Allies — Order and Kaos (dual sides of the sentient energy being known as the Rip) — recognized Proteus' power and, believing Counter-Earth was an unnatural and unstable creation in need of being destroyed, teleported him away to aid them in their quest. Proteus took over Atlantis and launched their entire missile supply against the surface world. As the Exiles battled and defeated Proteus, the Young Allies destroyed the missiles before they struck their intended targets. Jolt remains committed to bringing stability and peace back to the shattered Counter-Earth, and stands with her teammates as some of that world's greatest remaining heroes.

Art by Mark Bagley
ORIGINAL POWERS IN USE

HEIGHT: 5'5"   **EYES:** Blue; (energy form) yellow
WEIGHT: 109 lbs.   **HAIR:** Black; (energy form) none

ABILITIES/ACCESSORIES: Jolt can change into pure bioelectrical energy, enabling her to discharge energy blasts and fly. She possesses enhanced strength (lifting just under a ton), supersonic-level speed, and reflexes. Before her "death" her powers consisted of hyperkinetic agility, allowing her to move with superhuman speed and to jump great distances. Due to this, her metabolism caused a build-up in her system of bioelectric energies, which she could redistribute through her body as a shock against those that touched her. In this form, it was believed she could absorb virtually any form of energy to replenish and enhance her strength and speed; whether that applies to her current form remains unrevealed. Jolt possesses a near-encyclopedic knowledge of modern costumed superhumans. For an extended duration, Jolt's human form was partially paralyzed and she walked with a cane; as a result, she spent most of her time in energy form.

JANIS JONES

REAL NAME: Janis Jones
ALIASES: None
IDENTITY: No dual identity
OCCUPATION: Rebel
CITIZENSHIP: Dystopia
PLACE OF BIRTH: Dystopia, Earth-9200
KNOWN RELATIVES: Rick Jones ("Gramps," great-grandfather, deceased), Marlo Chandler Jones (great-grandmother, deceased); see Rick Jones entry for extended family
GROUP AFFILIATION: Anti-Maestro Freedom Fighters
EDUCATION: Unrevealed
FIRST APPEARANCE: Hulk: Future Imperfect #1 (1992)

HISTORY: Born some 70 years in the future of Earth-9200's Dystopia, a city ruled by the tyrannical Maestro in a world devastated by nuclear conflict and several world wars, Janis Jones was raised by her "Gramps," Rick Jones, who named her after Janis Joplin. He taught her to fight and about the long past age of heroes, and she joined the anti-Maestro resistance. Believing it needed fire to fight fire, Janis and her friend Pizfiz were sent back in time to Earth-616's modern age using Dr. Doom's time machine to recruit the Maestro's younger, not-yet-corrupt, self, the Hulk (Bruce Banner). Janis approached that timeline's Rick, using a note from her grandfather written on his Avengers ID card to verify her story, and he in turn convinced the Hulk, then controlled by a relatively stable merger of Banners' personae, to return to her reality with them. With the Hulk's help Janis led the resistance in attacking the Maestro's stronghold, while the Hulk and Gramps fought the Maestro in Gramps' trophy room, eventually sending their foe back in time to be blown to atoms in the gamma bomb test that originally empowered Banner. Gramps died moments later from injuries he sustained, and Janis and the Hulk scattered his ashes. After the Hulk returned home, elections were swiftly held for the city's new leader, which Janis lost to her rival Agarn, possibly due to vote rigging. Unconcerned, Janis was happy to let him rule, under her close scrutiny. However the Maestro's old foe the Abomination (Emil Blonksy) led a mutate army to conquer the city; after leading a futile defense, Janis escaped into the sewers, where she held off pursuing mutates while other survivors fled into the past using Doom's time machine. Briefly captured and tortured, Janis was freed by Emil's telepathic aide, Kaspin, after he had a crisis of conscience. Hoping to recruit the Hulk again, Janis used the time machine to return to present-day Earth-616, pursued by mutate bounty hunter Quarry; Janis had set the machine to bring her home after a pre-set time, but the Abomination found and destroyed it soon afterwards.

Janis soon located the Hulk, who eliminated Quarry, but his latest personality was unwilling to return to the future with her, though he let her accompany him for a while. Coming down with a fever, Janis was left in a Pantheon safe house while the Hulk battled Cable and then Onslaught; Pantheon members found and cured her, but, once healed, she fled their base, tracking the Hulk down again. She found him in Central Park, encased in metal following the Onslaught conflict, and witnessed him break free; unaware he had been split in two, with the Banner side of him now trapped in a pocket reality on Counter-Earth, leaving him belligerent and intermittently radioactive, Janis offered to help the Hulk find a way to be left alone, and helped him battle the Pantheon, Gladiator and Oracle of the Shi'ar Imperial Guard, the Thunderbolts and the Wildman. However during this last conflict, Janis was separated from the increasingly irrational, often hallucinatory, Hulk, and approached by another Hulk from a timeline (Earth-9722) where Janis had died and the Hulk had replaced the Maestro after being trapped in the Dystopian era. Explaining to her that 616's Hulk had become a reality Nexus that had drawn him there, 9722's Hulk and Janis pursued Hulk-616 to the Florida Keys, where they met the present day Rick Jones and his wife Marlo (Janis' great-grandmother). Hulk-616 had taken over Duck Key, and when Janis and Hulk-9722 tried to reason with him, a fight ensued, ending when the alternate Hulk abruptly vanished back to his own timeline and Hulk-616 leapt away. With no leads to his whereabouts, Janis joined forces with Rick; meanwhile in Egypt, Apocalypse (En Sabah Nur) turned the Hulk into his horseman War. The New World Order had the Absorbing Man approach Rick and Janis, hoping Rick might break Apocalypse's brainwashing. However, when Rick confronted War, his pleas fell on deaf ears, with Janis narrowly saving Rick from being decapitated. Absorbing Man and his backup, the Juggernaut, battled War, while Janis and Rick protected innocent bystanders. Rick again tried to appeal to War, who casually swatted him away, inflicting grave injuries; Janis berated War for his actions, unwittingly triggering another hallucination in War's mind, breaking Apocalypse's conditioning. Janis covertly monitored Rick's condition in the hospital, before slipping away. Her subsequent activities remain unrevealed.

HEIGHT: 5'10"
WEIGHT: 135 lbs.
EYES: Green
HAIR: Red

ABILITIES/ACCESSORIES: A skilled acrobat and fighter, Janis can use the weighted end of her long ponytail as a whip. She carries a staff keyed to her molecular structure; seemingly an inert stick in other hands, Janis can fire powerful energy blasts from it.

POWER GRID	1	2	3	4	5	6	7
INTELLIGENCE			■				
STRENGTH		■					
SPEED			■				
DURABILITY			■				
ENERGY PROJECTION			■				
FIGHTING SKILLS				■			

Art by Mike Deodato Jr.

JESSICA JONES

HISTORY: Jessica Campbell was a lonely Midtown High student who had a fantasy fixation on the Human Torch (Johnny Storm) and a crush on brilliant fellow student Peter Parker. When Peter was 15, Jessica followed him to a science exhibit, but her attempt at conversation was thwarted when Peter was distracted by the bite of a radioactive spider, which granted him the super-powers he eventually used to become Spider-Man. Days later, Jessica and her family were en route to a vacation at Disney World when her father, who had received discount tickets for the vacation from his employer Tony Stark (later Iron Man), grew distracted by the backseat quarrel of Jessica and her brother Phillip. Her father lost control of their car and crashed into a US Army truck transporting several cylinders of unidentified experimental material, possibly radioactive. One cylinder crashed through the Jones' windshield and into Jessica's lap, exposing her to the material, which possibly saved her life as her family's car went off the highway, killing everyone inside but her. Sustaining severe injuries, Jessica spent months in a coma before awakening, alone and confused. Placed in the Moore House for Wayward Children, she was adopted by a family named Jones, whose name she took.

A taciturn and resentful Jessica returned to school, and when she misunderstood an expression of sympathy from Peter, now a graduating senior, she fled in an emotionally distraught state, inadvertently launching herself into the sky and discovering she could fly, one of several powers induced by the experimental material. However, her new ability was not accompanied by skill, and she fell into New York Harbor, where she was rescued by Thor (Odinson), some time after his first battle with Magneto. Days later, Jessica, pondering super-heroic activities, discovered she had superhuman strength and tested her flight capabilities; chancing upon the Scorpion (Mac Gargan), in desperate straits weeks after his first battle with Spider-Man, Jessica quickly defeated the villain at a laundromat. Commended for her efforts, Jessica thus began her super-hero career, less than three years after Spider-Man's debut, and she eventually took the costumed identity of Jewel.

Little is known of Jessica's career as Jewel, since her activities were rarely as high-profile as those of many of New York's other costumed heroes. Nevertheless, she remained active for nearly four years and befriended a handful of other heroes, including Ms. Marvel (Carol Danvers), then a comparative newcomer. Whether Jessica saw action in the Kree-Skrull War's Earth incursion, the Black Lama's "War of the Super-Villains," or any other major crises that occurred during her career is unrevealed.

During a period when she was otherwise unemployed, Jessica, as Jewel, chanced upon a riot provoked by the Purple Man, who used his pheromone powers to take control of her and direct her to attack approaching police officers. Purple Man held Jessica in his thrall for months, subjecting her to physical and mental humiliation in imagined retaliation for defeats by other super heroes. Finally, in a fit of insane rage, he sent her to Avengers Mansion, where he irrationally hoped she would find and kill his nemesis Daredevil (Matt Murdock). Arriving at the mansion as the Avengers, accompanied by the Defenders, returned from an undescribed mission, Jessica attacked the first hero she saw, the Scarlet Witch, an act that freed her from Purple Man's control. Unprepared to explain her actions, she panicked and fled, only to be pursued by the heroes. Dealt a powerful blow by the Witch's husband Vision, Jessica was rescued from further attack by newly chosen Avenger Ms. Marvel. Again rendered comatose, Jessica was cared for in a SHIELD facility until she regained her faculties with telepathic assistance from the X-Men's Phoenix (the Phoenix Force posing as Jean Grey) weeks before the latter's apparent death on the moon. Following a regimen of physical rehabilitation, Jessica was offered a position as SHIELD liaison to the Avengers but, feeling her experience proved she was unsuited to a costumed hero's life, she declined the position and gave up her Jewel identity.

REAL NAME: Jessica Campbell Jones
ALIASES: Madeleine, Knightress, Jewel, Jess, other aliases in the course of investigative work
IDENTITY: Publicly known, although few remember her costumed activities
OCCUPATION: Stay-at-home mother; former newspaper consultant, private investigator, adventurer, otherwise unrevealed
CITIZENSHIP: USA
PLACE OF BIRTH: Unrevealed; possibly Forest Hills, New York
KNOWN RELATIVES: Luke Cage (husband), Danielle Cage (daughter), Dave Campbell (father, deceased), unidentified mother (deceased), Phillip Campbell (brother, deceased), Mr. and Mrs. Jones (adoptive parents), unidentified adoptive sister, Jenny (adoptive aunt)
GROUP AFFILIATION: Associate of Mighty Avengers
EDUCATION: High school graduate, private investigator's license
FIRST APPEARANCE: Alias #1 (2001)

Although she became closer friends with Ms. Marvel, who would undergo her own share of trauma as an Avenger and afterwards, Jessica's adaptation to life without super-heroics was strained by emotional insecurities. She entered a string of romantic relationships, including one with SHIELD agent Clay Quartermain, that ended badly, contributing to a darker, more cynical outlook on her part. Several months after abandoning her Jewel identity, she returned to costumed action as the Knightress. Mere days after embarking upon this new identity, she intervened in one of the Owl's criminal operations, as did Luke Cage and Iron Fist (Danny Rand). In the crime's wake, the children of one of the Owl's associates

Art by Michael Gaydos

JEWEL
Art by Mark Bagley

were found at the crime scene and, remembering her own childhood losses, Jessica revealed her true identity to the police so she would be allowed to take the children to her home, sparing them the trauma of a night in police custody. Later that night, Cage visited to commend her actions, and the two soon became close friends. Eventually, Jessica became a licensed private investigator and opened her own firm, Alias Investigations, which she managed for years.

Following a romantic fling with Cage that strained their friendship, Jessica embarked on a surveillance assignment involving a woman whose companion, Jessica discovered, was Captain America (Steve Rogers), whose semi-secret identity she videotaped. When the woman was slain soon afterward, Jessica realized she had been set up and was questioned by suspicious police officers, but she was helped from her predicament by timely intervention from Matt Murdock. Her investigation led to a fight with mob enforcer Man-Mountain Marko, whom she easily overpowered before learning a wealthy conspirator, Zoumas, had expected her to publicize the video, creating a scandal defaming Cap and the US government. With SHIELD's help, Jessica exposed the plot and received thanks from Cap, who encouraged her to return to super-heroics.

Jessica next investigated a deranged man who, claiming to be Avengers associate Rick Jones, paranoically feared attack by the alien races in whose activities the true Rick had intervened. Jessica partially calmed his madness and reunited him with his wife. Hired soon afterward by Daily Bugle publisher J. Jonah Jameson to track Spider-Man, Jessica, resenting Jameson's anti-hero grudge, bilked him by spending his money on charitable endeavors. A case in Warwick, New York, led her to help troubled teen Rebecca Cross, who had run away after rebelling against her town's oppressive atmosphere by encouraging people to believe she was a mutant, but the case ended badly when Rebecca's aunt blamed and killed Rebecca's father over her disappearance.

When Daredevil's secret identity was exposed, Murdock hired Jessica and Cage as bodyguards, and the two soon resolved the quarrel stemming from their one-night stand. Jessica instead began dating Ant-Man (Scott Lang) after a date arranged by Ms. Marvel. Jessica next investigated the Mutant Growth Hormone trade, teaming up with Spider-Woman (Jessica Drew) to rescue Jameson's ward Mattie Franklin, the young heroine also known as Spider-Woman, from being abused by the dealers. She also hired the dedicated but annoying Malcolm Powder, an avid fan of super-heroics, as a part-time assistant.

When the Kingpin sent insane assassin Typhoid Mary against Murdock, Jessica and Cage kept her busy until Murdock ended the fight with a quick attack. However, Jessica faced a far greater challenge when relatives of some of the Purple Man's victims asked her to confront the imprisoned villain regarding his many murders, in hope that his confessions would provide a sense of closure. Apprehensive but reassured by Cage, she visited Purple Man at the Raft, but he provided no useful information, escaping shortly thereafter during a breakout by fellow prisoner Carnage. Trying to again control Jessica, he commanded her to fight the pursuing Avengers, but she activated a psychic defense trigger implanted by Phoenix years earlier and defied him, downing him with one blow. Soon afterward, she informed Ant-Man she was pregnant with another man's child, and the couple broke up. She then moved in with Cage, the father, and embarked on a long-term relationship.

Seeking a new direction, Jessica became a Daily Bugle consultant on a superhuman-related feature, "The Pulse," working with reporter Ben Urich; in this capacity, she investigated the debuting Young Avengers, working with Cap and Iron Man (Tony Stark) to dissuade the teens from costumed adventures before ultimately choosing to help them instead. However, when Jameson slandered the newly formed Avengers incarnation that Cage had joined, Jessica resigned in a fury of expletives. After the birth of daughter Danielle, Cage proposed to Jessica, and the two married and took up residence at Avengers Tower. Following the passage of the Superhuman Registration Act, Jessica, Cage, and other renegade heroes used Dr. Strange's Sanctum Sanctorum as a base but, out of fear for their child's safety following an attack by the Hood's super-villain army, Jessica ultimately registered and returned to Avengers Tower. When the Skrulls' Secret Invasion came to fruition, Jessica joined both Avengers teams and others heroes in a final battle with Super-Skrulls, leaving Danielle in the care of a man she believed to be Avengers butler Edwin Jarvis. Unfortunately, "Jarvis" proved to be a Skrull impostor, and Danielle's current whereabouts are unrevealed.

HEIGHT: 5'7" **EYES:** Brown
WEIGHT: 124 lbs. **HAIR:** Brown, formerly dyed pink

ABILITIES/ACCESSORIES: Jessica Jones possesses superhuman strength, the full extent of which is unrevealed but appears to be at least Class 10; she is strong enough to lift an automobile with no discernible effort. She has an enhanced level of resistance to physical injury, enabling her to swiftly recover from wounds that might severely impair others, although she has never had occasion to discover if she is literally bulletproof. She has the power to fly, although she is out of practice in doing so. She is a reasonably skilled detective and hand-to-hand combatant.

POWER GRID	1	2	3	4	5	6	7
INTELLIGENCE			3				
STRENGTH					5		
SPEED		2					
DURABILITY				4			
ENERGY PROJECTION	1						
FIGHTING SKILLS			3				

KNIGHTRESS
Art by Mike Mayhew

RICARDO JONES

HISTORY: Mocked and ostracized because of his bizarre theories, brilliant scientist Ricardo Jones became an embittered, solitary man who spent years perfecting his inventions, notably a duplication device that enabled its user to assume the appearance and abilities of another person. His preoccupation with this particular device may have stemmed partly from his jealous obsession with Reed Richards, the super-genius leader of the heroic Fantastic Four. The obscure Jones envied Reed's wealth and fame, regarding Richards as a greedy glory hound and fancying himself a superior scientist who lacked only the material resources to be as successful as Richards. Determined to prove his genius by besting Richards, Jones resolved to destroy the Fantastic Four.

After the Fantastic Four saved Earth from Galactus, monstrous team member Thing (Ben Grimm) wandered New York in a state of depression, believing his girlfriend Alicia Masters had lost interest in him. Using a "subliminal influencer," Jones lured Grimm to his home, drugged him unconscious and used his duplicator to transform into a perfect replica of the Thing; as a side-effect, the real Thing was restored to his long-lost human form as Ben Grimm. Holding Grimm captive, Jones spent days learning to impersonate Grimm, then infiltrated the Fantastic Four's Baxter Building as the Thing. Grimm soon escaped and tried to warn his teammates, but the false Thing's appearance and strength were too convincing, and they refused to believe Grimm was the real Thing. A frustrated Grimm departed, and Reed recruited the false Thing to help him with a dangerous experiment. Trying to develop new technologies to defend Earth from extraterrestrial threats, Richards took a space walk into the other-dimensional "sub-space" realm later known as the Negative Zone, anchored only by a tether held by the fake Thing. The jealous Jones initially planned to let Richards die during the space walk; but, impressed and shamed by Reed's selfless bravery, Jones belatedly tried to pull Reed to safety when the mission went wrong. The tether snapped, and the "Thing" jumped into the portal after Reed, who was drifting toward a region of explosive antimatter. Hurling Reed back through the portal to safety, Jones calmly drifted toward the antimatter, grateful for this chance to redeem himself, happy to learn at last the true meaning of friendship. Back on Earth, Richards and his wife Sue mourned Grimm's seeming demise until the real Ben returned, having regained his Thing form upon Jones' death. Grateful to have his friend back, Richards nonetheless spared a solemn, respectful thought for the slain imposter and his noble sacrifice.

REAL NAME: Ricardo Jones
ALIASES: Thing, Ben Grimm
IDENTITY: Secret
OCCUPATION: Mad scientist turned tragic hero
CITIZENSHIP: USA
PLACE OF BIRTH: Unrevealed
KNOWN RELATIVES: Armand Jones (brother, deceased)
GROUP AFFILIATION: Fantastic Four infiltrator
EDUCATION: Unrevealed, probably extensive
FIRST APPEARANCE: Fantastic Four #50 (1966)

Years later, Jones' brother Armand continued his work. Shortly before his death, Ricardo had written to Armand about his duplication device and his plans to test it on the Thing. After Ricardo's disappearance, Armand Jones assumed the Fantastic Four had killed his brother. Obsessed with Ricardo's invention and seeking revenge, Armand spent years using his brother's notes to construct a replica of Ricardo's duplication device, which Armand dubbed a "biokinetic energy absorber." Using his absorber, Armand tried to duplicate the power of the man-monster Hulk (Bruce Banner), only to die during an ensuing struggle between the Hulk and Spider-Man (Peter Parker). The absorber accidentally discharged its stored energy into Spider-Man during the battle, transforming him into a raging "Spider-Hulk" shortly thereafter, but the hero was soon restored to normal by a second application of the device.

HEIGHT: (Jones) 6'1"; (Thing) 6'
WEIGHT: (Jones) 215 lbs.; (Thing) 500 lbs.
EYES: (Jones) Dark brown; (Thing) blue
HAIR: Bald

ABILITIES/ACCESSORIES: Jones was a scientific genius whose inventions included a subliminal behavior-influencing device and a "duplication apparatus" that enabled him to transform into a perfect physical replica of the Thing. In his Thing form, he was superhumanly strong (lifting up to 85 tons) and durable. Jones was also a skilled amateur actor and mimic, convincingly imitating Ben Grimm's personality, speech patterns and mannerisms. In the end, his finest quality and greatest weakness may have been his newfound conscience, spurring him to sacrifice his life to save his once-hated rival.

POWER GRID	1	2	3	4	5	6	7
INTELLIGENCE							
STRENGTH							
SPEED							
DURABILITY							
ENERGY PROJECTION							
FIGHTING SKILLS							

* STR/DUR ENHANCED IN THING FORM

Art by Jack Kirby

RICK JONES

REAL NAME: Richard Milhouse "Rick" Jones
ALIASES: A-Bomb; formerly Bucky, the Hulk
IDENTITY: Publicly known
OCCUPATION: Musician, adventurer, author; formerly talk show host
CITIZENSHIP: USA
PLACE OF BIRTH: Scarsdale, Arizona
KNOWN RELATIVES: Marlo Chandler Jones (wife), Polly (aunt), Mrs. Chandler (mother-in-law), Keith Chandler, Ray Chandler, three unidentified others (brothers-in-law), unidentified father (deceased), Jackie Shorr (alleged mother; unconfirmed)
GROUP AFFILIATION: Financier of the Loners, honorary member of the Avengers; former leader of the Teen Brigade
EDUCATION: High school dropout
FIRST APPEARANCE: Incredible Hulk #1 (1962)

HISTORY: Rick Jones was orphaned at an early age. Before his father died, he gave Rick his guitar, his most prized possession. Rick was placed in an orphanage called Tempest Town, where he honed his guitar skills. He also tried to rebel against the corrupt orphanage administrators, who destroyed his guitar as punishment. Having taken enough abuse, Rick broke out of Tempest Town. Drifting into various menial jobs, he traveled aimlessly across the American Southwest. At the age of 16, he found himself in New Mexico near the US Air Force's Desert Base, where, unknown to Jones, the gamma bomb weapon was being developed by Dr. Bruce Banner. Teenager Gary Swanson dared Rick to enter the bomb test site, and Rick happily complied, unaware that the bomb was scheduled to be tested that very day. Rick had parked his car on the test site and begun playing his harmonica when Banner ran onto the site. Placing himself at risk, Banner dragged Rick to safety, pushing him into a protective trench; however, just as Jones fell into the trench, the bomb detonated and Banner was caught in the blast. That evening, Rick watched as Banner transformed into the monstrous Hulk for the first time.

Rick blamed himself for Banner's condition and resolved to help him find a cure. He and Banner set up various cavernous hideouts in the desert where the Hulk could be temporarily confined. Although the Hulk distrusted most humans, Rick maintained an uneasy friendship with him. At one point, Jones briefly obtained psychic control over the Hulk's actions, but lost the ability after another attempt at curing Banner. The Hulk and Rick temporarily parted ways when the Air Force apprehended Hulk, who blamed Jones for his capture. Discovering that some of his friends had become ham radio enthusiasts, Rick realized that they could use their talents to aid the authorities by setting up a nationwide network of teenaged radio operators. Dubbing themselves the "Teen Brigade," they assisted the Hulk against the Metal Master, and Rick thereby regained the Hulk's companionship.

When the Asgardian god Loki framed the Hulk for attacking a train, Rick had the Teen Brigade broadcast a distress message to the Fantastic Four, hoping that they could help prove the Hulk's innocence; however, Loki diverted the radio message to his foster brother Thor, hoping that the Hulk could defeat Thor for him. Loki's message was also accidentally received by Ant-Man (Henry Pym), the Wasp and Iron Man (Tony Stark), who ultimately teamed with Hulk and Thor to defeat Loki. The five remained together as the heroic Avengers thereafter, and Rick continued to assist them with the Teen Brigade, even after the Hulk quit their ranks. Jones was eventually granted honorary membership in the Avengers. Soon after the Hulk's departure, the Avengers revived the wartime hero Captain America (Steve Rogers), who joined the team. The Captain found that Rick resembled his long-lost sidekick Bucky Barnes, and began to train Jones in hand-to-hand combat. Although Rick wanted to become the new Bucky, the Captain refused; afraid of seeing another young partner die, the Captain also vetoed any suggestion of granting Rick full Avengers membership. Passed over for full membership when the remaining Avengers founders left the team and recruited replacements, a disappointed Rick left the Avengers and returned to help the Hulk, spending most of his time among Air Force officers General Thaddeus E. Ross and Major Glenn Talbot, pleading on the Hulk's behalf. At one point, thinking the Hulk was dead, Rick revealed to them that Banner and Hulk were the same person, bringing an end to Banner's secrecy. Rick once interceded in the midst of a fight between the Hulk and Captain America, and the Hulk nearly killed Rick, not realizing his own strength. Captain America saved Rick, and Jones decided to take on the costumed identity of Bucky despite the Captain's protests. He aided Captain America against the forces of Hydra and AIM, but when Captain America's mind was exchanged with that of his enemy the Red Skull, the Skull in Cap's body drove Rick away. Rick gave up the Bucky identity.

Unknowingly influenced by the Kree ruler Supreme Intelligence, Rick was guided to an abandoned Kree outpost in the Southwest and

Art by Adrian Alphona

Art by Carlos Pacheco

compelled to don a pair of Kree weapons called Nega-Bands. Striking the bands together, Jones was teleported into the Negative Zone, from which the Kree hero Captain Mar-Vell was released, and the two became both molecularly and telepathically bonded. Thereafter, they would exchange places between Earth's dimension and the Negative Zone by striking the bands together. Despite the frequent interruptions to his personal life, Rick became a somewhat successful professional musician, gaining the attention of promoter Mordecai P. Boggs. After the duo learned that the Fantastic Four had a portal to the Negative Zone in their Baxter Building headquarters, Mar-Vell used their technology to set Rick free. Jones was then almost immediately captured by the Kree, who were in the midst of an intergalactic war with the Skrulls. The Supreme Intelligence had Rick brought to him, and helped Jones realize that he could tap into a near-infinite source of power (later identified as the Destiny Force). Rick's first use of the power was to fashion simulacra of super heroes he recalled from his boyhood, using them to defend himself. His next act was to use the power to halt all of the Kree and Skrull troops, freezing them in time. Rick nearly died from the effort, but Mar-Vell bonded himself to Jones again, saving his life. Rick and Mar-Vell continued to adventure together against menaces such as Thanos, before finally being permanently released from their link by tricking the Super-Adaptoid into taking Mar-Vell's place in the Negative Zone. Thereafter, Rick continued to aid Mar-Vell in his adventures, including battling the rogue creations of ISAAC on Titan. When Mar-Vell discovered that he had contracted cancer, Rick was upset by Mar-Vell's seemingly blasé acceptance of his death, but Jones ultimately joined his friend at his deathbed.

Deciding to return to the Hulk's aid, Jones organized a new Teen Brigade. Rick found himself the senior member of this group, and while aiding the Hulk against the villainous Corruptor they caused a near repeat of history when their distress call to the Avengers instead gathered the heroes who became known as the Rangers. The new Teen Brigade was disbanded when the members' parents objected to their children's involvement. Shortly thereafter, Rick was briefly devolved into primitive primate form by the High Evolutionary, who goaded the Hulk into assisting his efforts at suicide; the Evolutionary restored Rick before fading from existence. When the alien "Hulk-Hunters" — Amphibion, Dark-Crawler and Torgo — confronted the Hulk (actually seeking to recruit the Hulk's aid against the Galaxy Master), Rick exposed himself to Banner's gamma ray projector, thinking it would transform him into another Hulk. Rick instead developed radiation poisoning and had to be saved by the alien Krylorian Bereet, who halted his deterioration until the return of the Hulk, who had recently begun to manifest Banner's consciousness in the Hulk's body and who used Gamma Base's equipment to drain the radiation from Rick's body. After the Hulk was granted a presidential pardon, Rick decided that Banner no longer needed him, and they parted ways.

Months later, Rick was horrified to learn that he had contracted cancer from his gamma ray experiment, and seemed doomed to perish in the same way Mar-Vell had. Encountering the Galadorian Spaceknight Rom, Rick became one of Rom's closest allies on Earth, and helped gather resistance against the forces of the extraterrestrial Dire Wraiths. When the threat of the Dire Wraiths had passed, Rom left Earth behind. Rick soon encountered the omnipotent Beyonder, who was on a quest to understand humanity's desires. The Beyonder briefly transformed Rick into a powerful superhuman form, but Rick ultimately decided not to keep the powers, and that his truest desire was to be cured of cancer. The Beyonder complied with his wish.

Art by Bob Layton

When Banner was physically separated from the Hulk by Doc Samson's nutrient bath, Rick served as best man at Banner's wedding to his long-time love Betty Ross. When both Banner and the Hulk began to suffer from their separation until they seemed near death, they reentered the nutrient bath. General Ross made an attempt on Banner's life, and Rick struggled with him, falling into the nutrient bath himself. Banner seemed cured of being the Hulk, and Rick initially showed no ill effects, but he soon began transforming into the Hulk at night, just as Banner's transformations had originally occurred. Banner, meanwhile, had regained his Hulk powers, but had regressed to his initial gray appearance, and the duo tried to help each other cure their conditions. As the Hulk, Rick fought Zzzax while it was possessed by General Ross, battled the Hulkbusters and befriended the gamma-irradiated Outcasts. Rick was finally cured when the Hulk's enemy the Leader had the gamma radiation drained from Jones in order to reignite his own lost powers. Thereafter, the Leader and Rick shared a minor psychic link.

Rick continued to aid the Hulk against his enemies, and was present when the Hulk seemingly perished attempting to dismantle the Leader's gamma bomb in Middletown, Arizona. Rick stayed with Betty for a time to help her adjust to Banner's death, and he began work on his memoirs, titled "Sidekick." Rick's book caused a minor sensation, and even attracted the attention of extraterrestrials who were put out when they discovered that the biography did not hold the secrets of the Destiny Force. Rick left Betty as he began a book tour, and he started a relationship with Marlo Chandler, unaware that she had been the girlfriend of the long-since returned Hulk in his identity as "Joe Fixit." While on tour, Rick was captured by the Skrulls, hoping to learn the Destiny Force's secrets. Rick was reunited with the Hulk and Betty while battling the Skrulls, and helped the Hulk as he received psychiatric aid from Doc Samson that resulted in a more balanced Hulk persona. With his new mindset, Hulk became an operative (and eventual leader) of the Pantheon, and Rick aided in some of the organization's missions. While the Pantheon was in the country of Trans-Sabal, Rick assassinated its dictatorial ruler Farnoq Sawalha Dahn, having witnessed many of the atrocities Dahn's men had committed. Rick was profoundly affected by having taken another man's life. The fame Jones obtained from his book brought him into contact with Jackie Shorr, a psychotic woman claiming to be Rick's mother. While Rick was being held captive in Shorr's basement, she stabbed Marlo to death. Desperate to bring her back, Rick finally accepted the aid of the Leader, who revived her using his "Deus ex Machina" (and the unseen efforts of the cosmic entity Death). Shortly thereafter, Rick encountered Janis, his time-traveling great-granddaughter of the alternate future of Reality-9200's Dystopia.

Rick and Marlo finally married at a ceremony attended by beings from across the universe (invited by the mischievous Impossible Man). Eventually separated again from the Hulk by the tumult of his life, Rick and Marlo accepted an offer to co-host a late night talk show for New World Entertainment, "Keeping Up with the Joneses." During the show's brief tenure, Rick encountered Genis-Vell, the young son of Mar-Vell, whom Rick considered to be a disgrace to his father's good name. When many of Earth's heroes vanished after battling Onslaught, Rick found himself wishing to become a super

AS BUCKY
Art by Jim Steranko

hero again, and the Supreme Intelligence once more helped him access the Destiny Force, this time in order to help the entity regain its corporeal form, but the power left Rick once the Supreme Intelligence was done with him.

AS A-BOMB
Art by Ed McGuiness

WITH DESTINY FORCE
Art by Carlos Pacheco

When the Hulk was transformed into War, a horseman of Apocalypse, Rick journeyed to the scene of the Hulk's vicious battle against the Absorbing Man and Juggernaut in Cairo, Egypt. While trying to reason with the Hulk, Rick was instead struck by him, and slammed into a brick wall. Rick's spine was damaged, leaving him crippled. Banner subsequently tried to aid Rick's recovery, enlisting Reed Richards and Tony Stark to construct a suit that would help him regain movement. The Supreme Intelligence once again manipulated Jones as the entity sought Rick's use of the Destiny Force to aid Kang the Conqueror against the Time-Keepers. This time, Rick used the Destiny Force to summon forth a team of Avengers from different points in time, among them a future incarnation of Genis-Vell. Rick also healed his damaged spine via the Destiny Force. Jones all but sacrificed himself in destroying the Time-Keepers' Chrono-Cannon before it could be used to destroy his timeline, but the future Genis-Vell saved him by merging with him. When Rick returned to his own time, he found that he had a new pair of Nega-Bands, and that he was now bonded to the present-day Genis-Vell, just as he had once been to Mar-Vell.

Rick and Genis were forced into a partnership neither truly desired, and Rick's experience with the prior Captain Marvel frequently made him more knowledgeable than Genis. The duo discovered that, unlike Rick's link with Mar-Vell, they would exchange places via the Microverse, rather than the Negative Zone. When it was finally learned that Marlo's body had been playing host to Death, Rick and Genis helped defend her against the extraterrestrial death god Walker. Walker destroyed Rick's left arm and aged him prematurely by several decades, causing him to mirror his older self seen during the Destiny War. Rick grew despondent at his fate, but finally regained his youth and missing arm thanks to the Supreme Intelligence. During another time travel excursion, Rick encountered and bested Thanatos, an alternate version of himself from Reality-9309. Genis ultimately proved unable to master his ability of cosmic awareness and went insane. Rick did his best to try and contain Genis, and even learned how to injure him psychically before Genis was finally cured of his illness. Soon afterward, Rick and Genis were separated from each other by the cosmic entity Eulogy.

AS HULK
Art by Steve Gieger

Having earned a huge amount of money from investments he made with his book royalties, Rick donated most of his funds to the Excelsior Support Group, an LA-based gathering of young former super heroes seeking to overcome their addiction to crime fighting. Rick also donated a sophisticated flight vessel called the Excel to the group, who are now known as the Loners. With the Hulk's recent return to Earth and open declaration of war, Rick journeyed to New York in the hopes of reasoning with him. Rick was nearly killed by Miek of the Warbound while protecting Bruce from him. After exposure to a radioactive anti-Hulk weapon, Rick developed a new gamma mutation, becoming a creature similar to the Abomination called "A-Bomb." In this form, he aided Bruce against a mysterious red-colored Hulk.

HEIGHT: 5'9"; (A-Bomb) 6'8"
WEIGHT: 165 lbs.; (A-Bomb) 980 lbs.
EYES: Brown; (A-Bomb) Yellow
HAIR: Brown; (A-Bomb) None

ABILITIES/ACCESSORIES: Rick Jones is an accomplished gymnast and hand-to-hand combatant with skill in judo and karate, having been trained by Captain America. He is also a skilled songwriter, singer, guitarist and harmonica player. Under special circumstances, Rick has been able to tap into the Destiny Force, a mysterious and near-infinite power source inherent in all of humanity. Rick has used this ability to materialize figures from his imagination and from other time eras, to paralyze thousands of Kree and Skrull warriors simultaneously, to overwhelm an Atlantean army, to heal his own broken body, to amplify his physical abilities and to levitate. The limits of the Destiny Force's uses, if any, have not been revealed.

While bonded to each Captain Marvel (Mar-Vell and later Genis-Vell), Rick wore a pair of Nega-Bands on his wrists. By striking the bands together, Rick could exchange places with Captain Marvel (between the Negative Zone while partnered with Mar-Vell, the Microverse while partnered with Genis). Rick was able to release minor jolts of energy from the bands. Through the bands, he possessed a telepathic link to Captain Marvel. At one point he trained himself to usurp control of Genis' body, and to afflict him with psychic pain.

During his brief tenure as the Hulk, Rick would transform into a gamma-powered monster at nightfall. In this form he possessed superhuman strength and endurance, and could leap tremendous distances with his legs. He also suffered from a decrease in intellect, similar to many of Banner's incarnations as the Hulk.

As the A-Bomb, Rick possesses an appearance and powers similar to that of the Abomination (Emil Blonsky), including superhuman strength enabling him to lift around 100 tons. Unlike Blonsky, Rick's intelligence is impaired while in this form.

POWER GRID	1	2	3	4	5	6	7
INTELLIGENCE							
STRENGTH							
SPEED							
DURABILITY							
ENERGY PROJECTION							
FIGHTING SKILLS							

JOYSTICK

HISTORY: Janice Yanizeski is the daughter of gambling addict Walter Yanizeski, whose affection for risk made a lasting impression on Janice. He also taught her to always keep an ace up her sleeve in case of trouble, such as Walter's secret emergency cash stash at the family home. Janice grew up to be an athletic scholarship student at the University of Arizona, where she played college basketball. Seemingly quiet and dull off the court, she was secretly mixed up with criminals betting on her games, and double-crossed them in her sophomore year by deliberately throwing a game after she made a lucrative side bet against herself. The criminals, expecting her to win, lost a great deal of money and violently threatened Janice, who offered her father's cash stash to pay them off; they beat Walter badly and stole his money.

Disappearing, Janice resurfaced three years later as the superhuman mercenary Joystick, declared her old life dead, and dedicated her new life to taking risks. She entered the "Great Game," a contest whose wealthy patrons employed and manipulated costumed fighters into battling each other while they wagered on the outcomes. An ideal contestant, the danger-loving Joystick was employed by Chu Chi Huan of Chi-Huan Associates. During her Great Game stint, Joystick's opponents included el Toro Negro, Scarlet Spider, Green Goblin (Phil Urich), Kaine and Spider-Man (Ben Reilly). The Great Game finally ended when Justin Hammer secretly employed el Toro Negro to kill participants and sponsors, including Chu Chi Huan. Joystick and Spider-Man exposed the plot, and the sponsors ended the game.

Joystick joined Crimson Cowl (Justine Hammer)'s Masters of Evil, but the Thunderbolts captured most of the Masters, including Joystick. Escaping prison, Joystick returned to the newly revived Great Game, attacking the United Nations alongside Polestar and Tremolo, confronting the Sub-Mariner, Mr. Fantastic and Thunderbolts. When the gaming council armed explosives in Joystick's, Polestar's and Tremolo's costumes because the fight was lasting too long, Joystick helped the Thunderbolts resolve the crisis in exchange for protection from the Great Game.

Secretly in league with the cosmic gamesman the Grandmaster, Joystick joined the Thunderbolts, fighting various foes while flirting with teammates Atlas and Photon and fending off the unwanted romantic advances of Speed Demon, later crippling him. New team leader Songbird tried unsuccessfully to convince federal authorities to take the reckless Joystick back into custody; they declined, and the Commission on Superhuman Activities (CSA)

REAL NAME: Janice Olivia Yanizeski
ALIASES: None
IDENTITY: Known to authorities
OCCUPATION: Former licensed super hero, adventurer, professional criminal, director of marketing, student
CITIZENSHIP: USA with a criminal record
PLACE OF BIRTH: Unrevealed
KNOWN RELATIVES: Walter and Olivia Yanizeski (parents)
GROUP AFFILIATION: Formerly Thunderbolts, Initiative, Masters of Evil
EDUCATION: University of Arizona (unfinished)
FIRST APPEARANCE: Amazing Scarlet Spider #2 (1995)

even issued Joystick a pardon after she played a key role in a CSA-directed Thunderbolts mission. When the Thunderbolts confronted the Grandmaster, Joystick revealed her true allegiance, helping Grandmaster disperse the energies from the Wellspring of Power across the globe. The Thunderbolts eventually defeated the Grandmaster, while a revitalized Speed Demon subdued Joystick, who was incarcerated.

HEIGHT: 5'8"   **EYES:** Hazel
WEIGHT: 143 lbs.   **HAIR:** Brown

ABILITIES/ACCESSORIES: Joystick is superhumanly strong (lifting up to 1 ton), swift and agile. She can become a being of "pure action" at will, further enhancing her speed, agility and reflexes. While she does not (and possibly cannot) channel this peak speed into the act of sustained running while in "pure action" mode, she can channel her peak speed into an ongoing series of shorter motions such as jabs, kicks, flips, twists, dodges and leaps; in her "pure action" mode, these hyper-fast movements are automatic and instinctive rather than guided by conscious thought. She can charge her batons with energy that is released on impact, or as energy blasts generated by striking the batons together.

POWER GRID	1	2	3	4	5	6	7
INTELLIGENCE							
STRENGTH							
SPEED							
DURABILITY							
ENERGY PROJECTION							
FIGHTING SKILLS							

Art by Mark Bagley with Tom Grummett (insets)

JUBILEE

REAL NAME: Jubilation Lee
ALIASES: Wondra, "Sparkplug"
IDENTITY: (Jubilee) known to authorities; (Wondra) secret
OCCUPATION: Vigilante; former political activist, adventurer, student, peer counselor, actress, street performer, thief
CITIZENSHIP: USA
PLACE OF BIRTH: Beverly Hills, Los Angeles, California
KNOWN RELATIVES: Dr. Lee (father, first name unrevealed, deceased), unidentified mother (deceased), Hope Lee (paternal aunt)
GROUP AFFILIATION: New Warriors; formerly X-Corps, Generation X, X-Men
EDUCATION: Studied at Payton-Noble High School, Massachusetts Academy, Xavier's School For Gifted Youngsters and Beverly Hills Preparatory School
FIRST APPEARANCE: (Jubilee) Uncanny X-Men #244 (1989); (Wondra) New Warriors #1 (2007)

HISTORY: Happy and grateful for the prosperous new life they had built in the USA, Hong Kong immigrants the Lees named their daughter Jubilation. They sent her to an exclusive Beverly Hills school, where she discovered a talent for gymnastics — however, various childhood infractions occasionally landed the hotheaded young "Jubilee" in juvenile detention. On one occasion, as she fled mall security after shoplifting, Jubilee's mutant powers manifested — and a bright display of plasma "fireworks" erupted from her hands, blinding the guards and allowing her to escape. Soon afterward, Jubilee's father, a bank president, discovered that his biggest client, Hunter Brawn, was laundering money through his bank. He threatened to call the police, but Brawn hired two hitmen, Reno and Molokai — who kidnapped Lee and his wife and staged their deaths in a road accident, while Brawn stripped their bank of all its assets. Jubilee was orphaned and penniless, and, rejecting her next-door neighbors' offer to take her in, fled to the only other home she knew — the Hollywood Mall.

X-MEN COSTUME

Art by Jim Lee

She lived there for a time, eluding mall security and surviving as a petty thief and street performer, using her powers to put on shows for crowds of shoppers. Eventually, mall security became frustrated and contacted the M Squad, a team of novice mutant hunters. Luckily, the female members of the X-Men were visiting the mall, and foiled the M Squad's attempt to capture Jubilee. Unable to locate her after the battle, the X-Men returned to their base in outback Australia via a teleport gateway — but unbeknownst to them, Jubilee followed them home. She lived in the tunnels beneath the town, scrounging food and clothes from under the X-Men's noses, until the team disbanded. When their former member Wolverine returned to the town, he was ambushed and crucified by the cyborg Reavers, and Jubilee helped him escape. She stayed by his side while he recovered, and the two formed a close bond. Jubilee aided Wolverine in rescuing Psylocke, another former X-Man, from the Mandarin's control in Madripoor, and the trio then traveled to Genosha to help the other X-teams battle Cameron Hodge and overthrow the island's anti-mutant government.

Jubilee became something of an X-Man by osmosis, accompanying the newly re-formed team on several missions, as well as adventuring alongside Wolverine, who had become a mentor figure to her. Although she generally used her powers to blind or distract opponents, she soon discovered that they possessed a much greater explosive potential — one that scared her. Jubilee had several noteworthy adventures, including meeting Abcissa, an alternate-future version of herself enslaved by Mojo; being briefly betrothed to a young Savage Land girl after natives mistook her for a boy; and being kidnapped by Dr. Doom, who hoped to harness her mutant plasma energy to power his nation. Although Jubilee grumbled at the educational curriculum that Professor X imposed on her, the two soon bonded, and she came to consider the X-Mansion her first true home in years, and the X-Men her adopted family. Eventually, an encounter with one of Gateway's time portals caused Jubilee to learn her parents' deaths were no accident. She tracked down the hitmen and took revenge, but Wolverine's counsel led her to stop short of killing them. Over time, Jubilee found her powers getting stronger, at the same time as a series of tragic events — including Illyana Rasputin's death from the Legacy Virus, and Magneto's forcible removal of Wolverine's Adamantium skeleton — shook her faith in the X-Men's lifestyle. When the techno-organic aliens known as the Phalanx attempted to kidnap several young mutants, Jubilee joined an ad hoc X-Men team that rescued them — and when she discovered that Professor X was opening a school for this new generation of mutants, she asked to be enrolled there. Bidding a tearful farewell to the X-Men, Jubilee moved to the Massachusetts Academy, where under co-headmasters Banshee and Emma Frost, she trained in the use of her increased powers as a member of Generation X.

Jubilee's outspoken personality initially caused clashes with her new teammates, especially M (Nicole and Claudette St. Croix), but she mellowed over time, developing a crush on Synch (Everett Thomas) and "adopting" the mute, animalistic Penance (Monet St. Croix). Generation X shared many adventures together, including several in other dimensions, in one of which Jubilee fell for a caped adventurer with similar fashion sense. Although growing to think of Generation X as where she truly belonged, Jubilee visited the X-Men often. When the US government launched the anti-mutant Operation: Zero Tolerance, Jubilee was kidnapped by Bastion — and although she kept up a brave front, he eventually extracted the X-Men's security codes from her mind, allowing him to storm the X-Mansion. Jubilee was eventually freed by a sympathetic underling and rescued by Wolverine, but she blamed herself for the damage Bastion was able to do to the X-Men. Soon afterward, the terrorist Viper brainwashed several of

WONDRA

Art by Casey Jones with Paco Medina (inset)

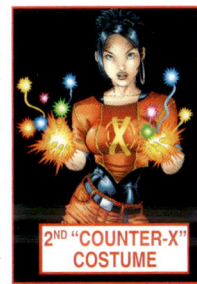

Art by Chris Bachalo
1ST GENERATION X COSTUME

Wolverine's friends to attack him, and Jubilee teamed up with Shadowcat, Wolverine's former sidekick, as the unofficial "Wolverine Rescue Squad" to free their friends and defeat Viper. In the aftermath of Zero Tolerance, it was revealed that M was actually Monet St. Croix's twin sisters, merged into a duplicate of her, and Penance was the true Monet. The two switched places, with Monet being freed from the Penance form and the twins becoming trapped inside it. Monet, humiliated and resentful, felt that Jubilee had treated her like a pet when she was Penance, and the two confronted one another in a bitter Danger Room session that left Jubilee's relationship with the real Monet as contentious as with the twins — if not worse. Monet went on to romance Synch, who was blissfully oblivious to Jubilee's own feelings for him.

Art by Gregg Schigiel
2ND GENERATION X COSTUME

When new co-headmistress Adrienne Frost, Emma's sister, opened the Academy to human students, Jubilee met Tristan Brawn, Hunter Brawn's grandson. She eventually discovered the elder Brawn's involvement in her parents' deaths — and although once again her desire for vengeance briefly overpowered her, she eventually dealt with him the right way, defeating him and sending him to prison for his crimes. When Wolverine was transformed into the Horseman Death by Apocalypse, Jubilee was instrumental in helping him break through his brainwashing and come to his senses. When Adrienne betrayed the school, Synch was killed defusing a bomb she planted. Jubilee learned to channel her grief and became a capable field leader — but Generation X soon disbanded, closing the Academy. Jubilee returned home to try an acting career, which ended when she realized that her unscrupulous agent was exploiting her. She then briefly joined her former headmaster Banshee's paramilitary X-Corps organization, where she reunited with Generation X teammates Husk and M as a trio nicknamed "Banshee's Angels," until X-Corps was betrayed from within and dissolved. Later, Jubilee and several other mutants were captured by the Church of Humanity and crucified on the X-Men's lawn. Although she survived, her former teammate Skin did not — and Jubilee was deeply shaken. Although she attempted to be an X-Man once again, the mansion's destruction by a Magneto imposter was Jubilee's final straw. Deciding to return to a normal life, Jubilee moved back to LA to live with her long-lost aunt Hope, and became a peer counselor, befriending high-school outcast Meg Devereux. Shane Shooter, a young mutant who ran a street gang, briefly romanced Jubilee, however she soon discovered her aunt's secret life as an assassin, and clashed with Triad enforcers in a battle that destroyed Hope's home. Jubilee moved back to New York, unaware that Hope, a cyborg, had survived.

Art by Steve Pugh
1ST "COUNTER-X" COSTUME

In the aftermath of M-Day, Jubilee was depowered. She struggled to find purpose, becoming a pro-mutant political activist and running a halfway house for ex-mutants — but she was severely injured in a battle between Wolverine and Omega Red and, bitter, cut ties with the X-Men. Approached by Night Thrasher (Donyell Taylor) to join a new iteration of the New Warriors and foment dissent against the Superhuman Registration Act, Jubilee accepted. She outfitted herself with technology that Thrasher had stolen from the condemned Avengers Mansion, including reverse-engineered versions of the Wizard's Wonder Gloves, and took the code name Wondra. She became the New Warriors' field leader and trained her new teammates, all depowered mutants, in the use of their new tech-based powers. Bonding with the Warriors, Jubilee rediscovered the family she had lost in the X-Men — but after Thrasher repeatedly abandoned the team in battle, she became openly suspicious of his motives, causing tension in the group. When Thrasher manipulated the Warriors into attacking Machinesmith under false pretenses, Jubilee discovered his lies and revealed them to the team — but Thrasher soon unmasked, revealing himself as the original Night Thrasher's brother and earning back some goodwill. The group then teamed with some of the surviving members of the original Warriors, now called Counter Force, to recover the bodies of Microbe and the original Night Thrasher from SHIELD custody, and held a funeral. Jubilee remains active as Wondra with the New Warriors, keeping a watchful eye on Night Thrasher's obvious ulterior motives.

Art by Art Adams
2ND "COUNTER-X" COSTUME

Art by Paco Medina
ORIGINAL WONDRA COSTUME

HEIGHT: 5'5" **EYES:** Brown
WEIGHT: 115 lbs. **HAIR:** Black

ABILITES/ACCESSORIES: As Wondra, Jubilee wears a derivative of the Wizard's Wonder Gloves, mechanical gauntlets lined with specialized micro-circuitry that use directed gravitational waves to magnify the force of blows from her hands, grant her increased strength (able to press roughly half a ton), and allow her to project an invulnerable force field around her body. A variation of the Wizard's anti-gravity technology is built into her costume, which allows her to fly and to considerably augment her lifting ability by de-gravitizing larger objects. Her costume also possesses an intangible "ghost mode," and may have other as-yet-undocumented abilities. Jubilee is a highly skilled gymnast and rollerblader, and possesses fair hand-to-hand combat experience, as well as thieving skills. Jubilee is dyscalculic; she has great difficulty performing mathematical calculations in her head, and struggles even when writing them down on paper.

Jubilee's former mutant powers allowed her to generate and control articulate, quasi-animate transitory plasmoids, which took the form of multicolored globules, streamers and sparkles, and exploded at her mental command. She could vary their power and intensity, from a multitude of "fireworks" capable of temporarily blinding others, to a powerful detonation capable of much destruction. Although Jubilee could absorb this energy back into her body without harm, her eyes were not immune to her own light bursts — she typically wore large sunglasses to protect her vision. Jubilee had the potential to detonate matter on the molecular level, although she feared this upper limit of her powers and did not explore it. Jubilee also possessed natural psi-shields, which made her thoughts "slippery," and rendered her almost invisible to telepaths who didn't know precisely what to look for.

JUDGE

REAL NAME: Michael Hart
ALIASES: Hart Attack, Judge "No" Hart, Mask Killer
IDENTITY: Secret
OCCUPATION: Vigilante; former judge, defense attorney
CITIZENSHIP: USA
PLACE OF BIRTH: Cherry Hill, NJ
KNOWN RELATIVES: Alice Dickinson (wife, deceased)
GROUP AFFILIATION: None
EDUCATION: J.D. in law
FIRST APPEARANCE: Deadline #1 (2002)

HISTORY: Defense attorney Michael Hart represented such major criminals as MODOK, Sebastian Shaw and the Kingpin himself. Hart's good looks and acquittal rate made him a media favorite. While representing the Black Cat, he met Prof. Alice Dickinson, a paranormal studies expert who testified regarding a mystic amulet the Cat had stolen, the Cor Vacuus (or "Empty Heart"). Hart and Alice soon fell in love, and Alice bought him the amulet as a gift. Hart was eventually appointed judge to a special Circuit Court dealing with superhuman criminals, and became as dedicated to imprisoning them as he had been to defending them. He credited his new idealism to Alice, whom he eventually married.

Among those Hart sentenced was the Tinkerer (Phineas Mason), who bore him no grudge for it. However, one of the criminals Hart had successfully defended as an attorney murdered the Agent (Rick Mason), adventurer son of the Tinkerer, who resolved to disgrace Hart in return. Seeking incriminating evidence, Mason broke into Hart's home and accidentally killed Alice when she surprised him. Tinkerer subsequently struck down Hart himself, but then repented and attempted to revive him. Whether it was due to his amulet's influence or Mason's technology, Hart returned to life. Transformed into a supernatural being, Hart found himself summoned to the Zeitgeist, a spectral limbo inhabited by the ghosts of centuries past, where he was forced to witness past murders. Hart resolved to oppose crime in the mortal world as the vigilante Judge, acting as a medium for vengeful spirits called "the Jury." Meanwhile, the police suspected Hart of Alice's murder, sparking a scandal and his disbarment in absentia.

Aided by the Tinkerer's information, the Judge and Jury tracked and slew seven costumed criminals. When rookie Daily Bugle reporter Katherine "Kat" Farrell investigated, the electric-powered Third Rail assaulted her, but the Judge rescued her, killing the villain before vanishing. Farrell's investigation led to Mason, who gave her an abridged version of events. The Judge tried to scare her off, but the Jury drew her with him into the Zeitgeist so she could better understand his haunted life. Shortly afterward, Farrell deduced Mason's guilt and confronted both men with the knowledge. The Judge attacked Mason, but the Jury allowed him to live. The Judge, mirroring Mason's earlier change of heart, accepted the decision. Knowing that both men were attempting to atone for their sins, Farrell decided not to publish her discoveries. The Judge remains New York's phantom guardian, though Mason's recent alliance with Latveria's Lucia von Bardas leaves his continued assistance uncertain.

HEIGHT: 6'1"
WEIGHT: 195 lbs.
EYES: Green; (Judge) black
HAIR: Brown with gray flecks; (Judge) none

ABILITIES/ACCESSORIES: The Judge possesses enhanced strength, enabling him to lift at least one ton, and the power to teleport himself and others; he can appear at will anywhere violence is or will be underway. He acts as a gateway for the Jury, who, regardless of his will, materialize to judge and, at times, execute the guilty. He can become immaterial and travel between the mortal world and the Zeitgeist.

POWER GRID	1	2	3	4	5	6	7
INTELLIGENCE							
STRENGTH							
SPEED *							
DURABILITY							
ENERGY PROJECTION							
FIGHTING SKILLS							

* JUDGE IS A TELEPORTER

Art by Guy Davis

JUGGERNAUT

HISTORY: Following his mother's death after the family's move to Junction, New York, young Cain Marko's father, nuclear scientist Kurt Marko, subjected Cain to years of psychological and physical abuse that ultimately shaped him into an antiauthoritarian bully. Cain's father was one of several scientists who worked at the Alamogordo research facility for Dr. Nathan Milbury, secretly the geneticist Mister Sinister. Seeking to create a fail-safe in case of his death, Sinister encoded his genetic material into each of the scientist's children, including Cain & Charles, so as to prepare them to become his new host body. Sinister created the Cronus device as a means to activate this fail-safe plan. Following the death of Kurt's colleague Brian Xavier, Kurt married Xavier's widow Sharon, and Cain moved in with them at the Xavier mansion after he was expelled from school. Cain quickly took to bullying his new stepbrother Charles, unaware that Kurt had begun beating him as well. After learning that his father seemingly preferred Charles over himself, Cain became consumed with jealousy, leading to his causing an accident in his father's home laboratory. Mortally wounded, Kurt saved Charles and then Cain before he died. Cain's resentment turned to hatred, and he continued tormenting Charles after they both attended college. When Charles eventually fought back, Cain retaliated, inadvertently causing a car accident that seriously injured Charles. Later serving in the US Army together, Cain and Charles discovered the lost Temple of Cyttorak in Korea. Cain found the mystic Ruby of Cyttorak and read its inscription, transforming him into Cyttorak's earthly avatar, the Juggernaut. Trapped under tons of rubble after the Temple collapsed, Cain spent years digging himself out.

Finally freeing himself, Cain was forced by Cyttorak to confront his Juggernaut predecessor Jin Taiko, who had become disloyal to Cyttorak after decades of service. Under Cyttorak's influence, Cain slew Jin then destroyed Jin's village, killing everyone within. Seeking revenge against Charles for abandoning him in the Temple, Cain returned to Westchester and easily defeated the X-Men, but Charles psychically rendered Cain comatose. Imprisoning Cain in his former home, Charles sought to "cure" him of being the Juggernaut by transferring the mystic energies back to Cyttorak, but the procedure backfired via the intervention of Factor Three's leader. Freed, Cain briefly possessed Charles' mental powers, which he used to defeat the X-Men, then sought out Factor Three. Opposed by the X-Men, Cain was tricked into touching a prototype of the Ruby that empowered him, drawing him into Cyttorak's realm, the Crimson Cosmos. Eventually returning to Earth, Cain learned of Charles' supposed death and felt cheated that he wasn't the one who killed him. Cain later fought the X-Men again but was pulled back into the Crimson Cosmos, where Dr. Strange found him and sought to use Cain against his foe, Nightmare, who was holding the cosmic entity Eternity prisoner. Having learned to cast spells while in the Crimson Cosmos, Cain fought Nightmare to a standstill until they inadvertently freed Eternity, which was Strange's intent all along. Eternity consigned Cain to Oblivion's realm, where he began rapidly aging and learned that hate kept him young. Using his mystic abilities to return to Earth, Cain encountered the former X-Man Beast, but was defeated and drawn back into Oblivion's realm. Cain ultimately struck a deal with Oblivion, exchanging his mystic abilities for restored youth, and was subsequently pulled back to Earth by a space-time warp that the Hulkbusters were using to imprison the Hulk. Alongside the Hulk, Cain escaped the Hulkbusters' base, but soon clashed with his fellow escapee and was ultimately defeated by the X-Men.

While in prison, Cain befriended Black Tom Cassidy and they escaped together. Cain helped Tom usurp control over Cassidy Keep, home of Tom's cousin Banshee (Sean Cassidy). Cain and Tom were then employed by the Shi'ar Eric the Red (Davan Shakari) to kill the X-Men, and may have succeeded had Cain not abandoned the fight to rescue Tom after he was cast into the ocean. Tom later hired the assassin Arcade to kill the X-Men, much to Cain's chagrin. Next, Cain and Tom, joined by Tom's niece Siryn (Theresa Rourke), sought to steal the entire US supply of the rare metal

REAL NAME: Cain Marko
ALIASES: Exemplar of Physical Power
IDENTITY: Known to authorities
OCCUPATION: Avatar of destruction; former adventurer, teacher, terrorist, professional criminal, mercenary, planetary ruler, soldiert
CITIZENSHIP: USA with criminal record
PLACE OF BIRTH: Berkeley, California
KNOWN RELATIVES: Kurt Marko (father, deceased), Marjory Marko (mother, deceased), Sharon Xavier Marko (stepmother, deceased), Charles Francis Xavier (Professor X, stepbrother), Cassandra Xavier (Cassandra Nova, stepsister, legally deceased)
GROUP AFFILIATION: Formerly Excalibur, X-Men, Brotherhood of Mutants, partner of Black Tom Cassidy, CSA, Exemplars, New World Order, Exiles (Earth-93060), Legion Accursed, US Army
EDUCATION: High School (incomplete); some college; military basic training
FIRST APPEARANCE: X-Men #12 (1965)

Vibranium, but the X-Men and Spider-Woman (Jessica Drew) foiled their plan. Cain and Tom then sought to kidnap the psychic Madame Web, but Spider-Man (Peter Parker) trapped Cain in a settling building foundation. After freeing himself, Cain battled the X-Man Colossus in a bar, but then paid for the establishment's damages. Reuniting with Tom, Cain returned to the Temple of Cyttorak and claimed the Ruby, which he gave to Tom as a gift. The Ruby split Cyttorak's power between Cain and Tom; however, Cain was restored to full power during a clash with the X-Men and Spider-Man after Rogue drained Tom's strength. Cain then threw the Ruby into Earth's orbit and escaped with Tom. Later, Cain was attacked by the future Sentinel Nimrod, but was saved by the X-Men's intervention. Meanwhile, the Ruby fell back to Earth and was found by a young student named Stevie. Seeking to reclaim the Ruby, Cain was instead defeated by Stevie and the Hulk. Cain eventually regained possession of the Ruby and bonded with it, enhancing his power further.

RUBY OF CYTTORAK

Art by Ron Garney with Jim Calafiore (insets)

Art by Jack Kirby
ORIGINAL ARMOR

Cain and Tom next sought to loot the Bank of Scotland, so Cain created a diversionary attack on Edinburgh, which attracted the attention of the X-Men. Cain was defeated and incarcerated in Crossmoor Prison. Freed by the British crimelord Vixen, Cain soon fought Excalibur but was defeated by Phoenix (Rachel Summers). Returned to Crossmoor, Cain was later liberated by the Norse god Loki, who sought to use Cain in his latest effort to destroy the Avengers. Teleported to Queens, New York, Cain battled the thunder god Thor and the neophyte New Warriors. Thor magically transported Cain to a distant asteroid from which he was rescued by passing aliens. Cain became ruler of their world, and had Thor and Excalibur kidnapped when they arrived on the asteroid in search of Cain's whereabouts. Sent back into deep space by Thor in the ensuing clash, Cain was soon returned to Earth by Tom via an interdimensional teleporter. After bombing a New York skyscraper, Cain and Tom clashed with Siryn, X-Force and Spider-Man, but Tom was critically injured. Teleported away by the mercenary Deadpool, Cain and Tom were delivered to the arms dealer Tolliver, from whom Cain requested medical aid for the wounded Tom. Soon after, Cain was drawn back into the Crimson Cosmos by Dr. Strange to aid against Cyttorak. Seemingly defeating his benefactor, Cain was opposed by Strange and Nova (Frankie Raye); however, Cyttorak had only feigned defeat and dispatched Cain back to Earth. The Red Skull (Johann Shmidt) then recruited Juggernaut into his New World Order organization and sent him to capture the Hulk. Succeeding, Cain witnessed the Hulk's brainwashing by the Skull and fought alongside him against the Avengers; however, the Hulk ultimately overcame his brainwashing, and Cain was knocked out by the psychic backlash.

Cain later recovered Tom from the Genetech research facility outside Angouleme, France, where he had been transformed by a wood-based virus. Together, they sought information on Tolliver's will and hijacked a plane. Cain was forced to jump in mid-flight in order to save Tom after Deadpool dropped him. Later, Cain sought Tom's medical records from Genetech, leading to a clash with Thunderstrike. After reaching an understanding with the rookie hero, Cain received Tom's records and again paid for the damage he caused. Scarmore Industries then hired Cain and Tom to kidnap lawyer Beck Underwood to cover up illegal toxic waste dumping activities, and they battled Underwood's ally Venom (Eddie Brock). Eventually returning to Cassidy Keep, Cain realized that Tom needed further medical help and so arranged for Tom to turn himself in. Later, Cain witnessed Dr. Emrys Killebrew curing Tom via cell samples from Deadpool. Soon after, in Canada, Cain encountered the psychic being Onslaught, who threw him to New Jersey and suppressed his memory of the event. Encountering the X-Men, Cain was easily defeated in his weakened state. After recuperating at Xavier's mansion, Cain escaped but was sent to Reality-93060 by agents of Landau, Luckman & Lake. Arriving on the planet "Gameworld," Cain encountered 'Strike, Shuriken and Amber Hunt, as well as Reaper and Siena Blaze from his own reality. Banding together as an ad-hoc team called the Exiles, they were transported to Earth-93060 by Reaper; however, their arrival seemingly caused mass destruction, forcing them to flee from the military. Cain adapted quickly to his new situation, including a budding romance with teammate Amber and the fact that his power was weaker on this Earth. When the X-Men arrived to check on Cain, he and the Exiles fought alongside them against the extradimensional Firewalker. After gaining a reluctant new member in Hellblade, the Exiles were confronted by the cosmic Phoenix Force on Earth-93060 after it briefly possessed Amber. Alongside the X-Men, Ultraforce and other heroes, Juggernaut and the Exiles opposed an ancient Entity who sought to use the Phoenix Force to drive Earth-93060 into its Sun, then forced the Phoenix Force through a chronal portal. Cain was later betrayed by Reaper, who transported him back to Earth-616. Recalling Onslaught, Cain sought the X-Men's aid in opposing him, and Jean Grey mentally unlocked Cain's knowledge of Onslaught's true identity as Xavier. Juggernaut confronted Onslaught, who forcibly severed Cain's connection to the Ruby and dispatched him to the reality within it. There, Cain encountered the demon Spite but was saved by the mystic Gomurr, who revealed to Cain the extent of his connection to the Ruby. Tempted by Spite, Cain was betrayed by her to the Ruby's corrupt aspect of Cyttorak. Aided by Gomurr and his fellow mystic Tar, Cain overcame the Cyttorak aspect and was expelled from the Ruby, returning to Earth more powerful than before. Cain subsequently returned to Junction and was driven into a rage by the townspeople. After causing mass destruction, Cain was confronted by Gomurr, who warned him of Cyttorak's compulsion to destroy. Later, in the town of Sirocco Sprawl, New Mexico, Spite sought Cain's aid against her brother D'Spayre, who almost killed Cain by draining most of his power. Despite being reduced to a skeletal state, Cain survived on pure hate and defeated D'Spayre, after which Spite restored his body and power. Cain inadvertently became the hero of Sirocco Sprawl and had Juggernaut Appreciation Day held in his honor until he was offered light beer, which sent him on another rampage.

The New World Order recalled Cain to address the threat of the Hulk, who had been transformed by Apocalypse into his Horseman, War. In Cairo, Egypt, Cain and fellow NWO agent the Absorbing Man clashed with War but quickly found themselves outmatched. They were saved from defeat when the Hulk overcame his conditioning and departed, leaving Cain to claim War's sword. Seeking to sell the sword to help pay for Tom's ongoing medical bills, Cain returned to New York to meet with a buyer and briefly clashed with Spider-Man. Later, accompanied by an attorney, Cain sought to lay claim to Xavier's financial estate — but upon discovering the mansion stripped by Bastion's Operation: Zero Tolerance, he left peacefully. Lured back to Korea by word of a second Ruby, Cain was mystically imprisoned by the Cult of Chejo-Do and had his power drained. Tom reluctantly contacted the X-Men for help, and they succeeded in defeating the Cult and re-empowering Cain; however, the second Ruby had been possessed by an entity whose spirit forced Cain to smash through dimensional barriers in an effort to reach the dimension of its foe, the Trion. Opposed by the X-Men, Cain defeated the entity's psyche with the aid of Xavier and Wolverine, after which the entity was revealed to be the Trion's own dark side. Returning to Earth, Cain soon felt an irresistible compulsion to follow a psychic call. Despite opposition by Thor, Cain encountered fellow avatars Bedlam and Conquest and learned that the psychic call was for the gathering of the avatars of the Octessence, a group of mystic entities that included Cyttorak, in order to determine which of them was the mightiest. Alongside his fellow avatars, known as the Exemplars, Cain oversaw the construction of the God-Engine, a magical device that would enslave the wills of all mankind and furnish the Exemplars with armies to wage war. Opposed by Spider-Man, Thor, Iron Man (Tony Stark) and Xavier, Cain and the Exemplars teleported to the North Pole with the God-Engine to maximize its power. There, Cain struggled against Cyttorak's increased influence, ultimately overcoming it and turning on his fellow Exemplars. During the subsequent clash, Cain destroyed the core of the God-Engine, causing a mystical chain reaction that scattered Cain and the Exemplars around the globe. Regrouping, the Exemplars sought revenge on Cain for his betrayal, and in desperation he sought out the Avengers for help. Captured by the Exemplars, Cain was sentenced to death; but despite a failed rescue attempt by the Avengers and other heroes, he was freed after the Exemplars overcame their deities' influence and fled. Cain willingly accepted incarceration without struggle as thanks for the heroes' efforts, but was soon freed by Tom, and together they menaced Generation X with the aid of Mondo. Defeated, the trio escaped; however, Cain was eventually arrested and incarcerated in Seagate Prison.

Later, Cain was among those assembled by the sentient spaceship Prosh to travel through time to help uncover knowledge pertaining to mankind's ultimate destiny. As he traveled through the past, Cain realized he had wasted his life thus far. The group was ultimately forced to oppose Prosh, who had fallen under the control of the enigmatic Stranger, but they succeeded in liberating him. Subsequently returned to Seagate, Cain was recruited by the Commission on Superhuman Activities to act as a bounty hunter in exchange for a reduced sentence. Cain's new career was short-lived as he soon returned to crime, joining Tom in an attempt to kill the X-Men's leader Cyclops on behalf of Ulysses. Soon after, Cain's power began weakening as Cyttorak began to punish him for disservice. With Tom having lost control and transformed into a plant-like being, Cain was forced to turn to the X-Men for help. During the subsequent clash, Cain was knocked into the sea and would have drowned if not for young aquatic mutant Sammy Paré. Cain accepted Xavier's invitation to recuperate at his home and soon took up permanent residence there, much to the X-Men's dismay. Surprisingly, even to himself, Cain befriended Sammy, who helped him realize that he needed to start taking responsibility for his own actions. Cain aided the X-Men against the mutant werewolves of the Dominant Species, and began thinking of the Xavier estate as home again. Xavier approved Cain's joining the faculty as gym teacher and Cain helped the X-Men oppose Alpha Flight's government-sanctioned efforts to remove children from the school, though he was forced to part with Sammy, who returned home to Canada. Cain was then invited by Havok to join the X-Men, and soon saved his life from a vengeful Polaris. Following another clash with the Dominant Species, during which the X-Men fought alongside the dimension-hopping Exiles, Cain visited Sammy despite a restraining order and learned that Sammy's father had been abusing him. Enraged, Cain was opposed by Alpha Flight, and only stopped his rampage after Sammy pleaded with him. Arrested, Cain was incarcerated in a high-tech Canadian prison and had the superhuman lawyer She-Hulk appointed as his attorney. During his incarceration, Cain was inadvertently freed by fellow inmate the Rhino, but sacrificed his own freedom in order to stop the Rhino escaping. This act earned him some leniency, and he was released pending trial. Briefly romancing an alternate reality (Earth-712) She-Hulk, Cain fought Cyttorak's temporary replacement avatar alongside her before his trial, wherein he received a reduced and commuted sentence as well as extradition back to the US following an impassioned plea from Sammy's mother.

Back at the Xavier Institute for Higher Learning, Cain's request to join the faculty as a gym teacher was initially denied by co-headmaster Cyclops pending an evaluation conducted by Wolverine. Confronted by visions of his past victims via the Danger Room's holographic technology, Cain realized he wasn't ready to accept such a responsibility; however, this realization was enough to convince Cyclops to approve his request, albeit under supervision. Cain was then briefly blackmailed into joining an ad hoc group of super-criminals to recover the fabled "Identity Disc" from AIM for crimelord Tristram Silver. Later, Cain and his X-Men teammates investigated the emergence of mutant Shen Xorn in China, which brought them into conflict with the Eight Immortals, the Collective Man and the Chinese military. Returning to the Institute, Cain was approached by a then-unstable Tom to join a new incarnation of the Brotherhood of Mutants, led by Exodus. Cain agreed, secretly intending to act as a double agent for the X-Men. Discovered by Sammy while he was collaborating with the Brotherhood, Cain could only watch as Tom killed the boy. Enraged, Cain attacked Tom but was defeated. Rejoining the X-Men, Cain helped oppose the Brotherhood's attack on the Institute, during which he, Nocturne and the Brotherhood were pulled into the black hole within Shen Xorn's mind; emerging in the Mojoverse. The Brotherhood betrayed Cain and Nocturne to Mojo, but later escaped after Nocturne possessed Mojo's agent Spiral. Returning to the Institute, Cain and Nocturne were followed by Mojo, who de-aged them and the X-Men. Despite their newfound youth, the heroes defeated Mojo. Cain was tempted by Mojo with the offer of a fresh start, but rejected him. After "M-Day," Cain and Nocturne joined others in opposing Shadow-X (the X-Men of Earth-6141). The heroes then formed a new incarnation of Excalibur in the UK. Cain and his new teammates then opposed the clandestine Black Air organization and their new agent, Black Tom, whom Cain convinced to surrender. After a journey into the past where Excalibur aided King Arthur and Merlin against alien Makluan "dragons," Cain was attacked and badly beaten by the Wrecking Crew, who berated him for changing his criminal ways. Seeking to regain his former power, Cain returned to the Temple of Cyttorak, wherein he confronted his latest replacement as Cyttorak's avatar. Cain was forced to battle his replacement to the death, but stopped short of killing him. Cain was then confronted by his teammates, who learned of his past actions as Cyttorak's avatar. As they left, Cain secretly reclaimed the Ruby. Remaining a member of Excalibur despite his dark past, Cain helped Nocturne recover from a stroke before joining his teammates in opposing the efforts of Albion (Bran Bardic) to send England back to the Dark Ages. When the X-Men sought help in opposing the Hulk, Cain was easily beaten and reluctantly struck a deal with Cyttorak wherein he would regain his full power but at the cost of serving Cyttorak once more. After the Cronus device was activated, it cycled between those encoded with Sinister's DNA; however, Cain's helmet shielded him from becoming Sinister's host body.

BROTHERHOOD ARMOR

Art by Salvador Larroca

HEIGHT: 6'10"
WEIGHT: 900 lbs.
EYES: Blue
HAIR: Red

ABILITIES/ACCESSORIES: The Juggernaut possesses untold mystical power bestowed upon him by Cyttorak. His strength is vastly enhanced, allowing him to lift well over 100 tons. Once he gains momentum, virtually no force on Earth can stop him. Obstacles such as tons of rock or the force of a plasma cannon may slow him considerably, but nothing has yet stopped him from advancing when he is at peak power. Cyttorak's energies also afford the Juggernaut an extraordinary degree of resistance to all forms of injury, and he can rapidly heal any wounds he incurs. He can shield himself even further with a personal force field. The Juggernaut can survive indefinitely without food, water or oxygen as Cyttorak's energies provide all the sustenance he requires. In the past, the Juggernaut briefly possessed telepathic abilities and certain mystical powers. For a time, the Juggernaut was stripped of Cyttorak's power, though he still possessed superhuman strength, endurance and durability due to years of absorbing Cyttorak's energy. The Juggernaut wears a suit of armor fashioned from a mystic metal originating from the Crimson Cosmos, and can summon this armor around his body at will. Underneath his helmet he wears a skullcap made from the same metal. Despite his formidable powers, the Juggernaut can be affected by mystical forces of sufficient strength, and he is susceptible to psionic attack when not wearing his helmet and/or skullcap.

POWER GRID	1	2	3	4	5	6	7
INTELLIGENCE							
STRENGTH							
SPEED							
DURABILITY							
ENERGY PROJECTION							
FIGHTING SKILLS							

JURY

CURRENT MEMBERS: Bomblast, Firearm, Ramshot (Samuel Caulkins), Sentry (Curtis Elkins), Wysper (Jennifer Stewart)
FORMER MEMBERS: Gavel, Screech (Maxwell Taylor), USAgent (John Walker)
BASE OF OPERATIONS: Worldwide; formerly Cordco facility north of Boulder, Colorado, Equity, Inc. offices, Life Foundation bunker
FIRST APPEARANCE: Venom: Lethal Protector #2 (1993)

BOMBLAST

FIREARM

GAVEL

OLIVIA LENTZ

SCREECH

MS. SANTIAGO

GENERAL TAYLOR

RAMSHOT

SENTRY

USAGENT

WYSPER

HISTORY: The mercenaries of the Jury were assembled by retired US Army General Orwell Taylor, who sought revenge against Venom (Eddie Brock) for the death of his son Hugh during the villain's escape from the Vault. Taylor recruited former Guardsman Curtis Elkins to act as team leader Sentry. Other members included Hugh's little brother Max, Samuel Caulkins, a scientist known only as Firearm, and the deadly Bomblast. Wearing battle armor, the Jury attained super-strength, durability, energy blasters, sonic grenades and flying discs. Their first mission took them to San Francisco, where they failed to capture Venom. Orwell Taylor then brought them to New York City in hopes of defeating Spider-Man (Peter Parker), whom he blamed for creating Venom. The Jury placed Spider-Man on mock trial, charging him with being an accessory to murder. Spider-Man admitted his guilt in the affair and agreed to a compromise: he would help them steal a portable teleportation device that could be used against Venom in exchange for his death sentence being commuted. Spider-Man eventually turned on the Jury, however, beating them senseless and leaving them for the authorities. Ramshot began to doubt Taylor's motives, resulting in a temporary suspension from the Jury. Reorganized by Taylor, the Jury worked with the Life Foundation, aiding them in exchange for a base and upgraded weaponry, but they were soon forced to ally with Spider-Man against the Foundation's mutated leader, Carlton Drake. During this battle, Orwell Taylor was slain.

Max took over the group, hoping to turn their focus away from revenge and more towards offering justice to those whom the law could not help. Max also recruited the Gavel, to judge in their mock trials, and new armored agent Wysper, who passed her entrance exam by slaying the Tarantula (Luis Alvarez), her husband's killer. The Jury continued to refine their methods, employing Olivia Lentz as prosecutor in their trials while Max worked for the defense, insuring that all judgments were fair and unbiased. An attempt to capture the former Vault Guardsman known as Hybrid (Scott Washington) led to a clash with the New Warriors and once again caused some in the group to question their motives. Funding troubles led to the dissolution of Max's dream and the Jury was taken in by the Cordco Corporation, who upgraded their armor again and recruited former Avenger USAgent to serve as field commander. The Jury then clashed with the Thunderbolts, who were wanted by the law, but eventually sided with them against the Secret Empire. USAgent left the team soon after, and the Jury left Cordco. Recently the Jury battled the Thunderbolts while attempting to apprehend Venom (Mac Gargan), but were taken into custody for acts against the SHRA.

WYSPER (CURRENT ARMOR)

The Jury uses a transport ship called the "Justifier" along with a support team consisting of Ms. Bronson, Ms. Santiago, and many unidentified others.

BOMBLAST / SENTRY / WYSPER / RAMSHOT / USAGENT / FIREARM

SCREECH

Art by Mark Bagley

JUSTICE (ASTROVIK)

HISTORY: Growing up, young Vance Astrovik longed for adventure and dreamed of being a super hero like his idol, Captain America. Vance's cynical father Arnold scorned Vance's daydreams, deeming them impractical and abnormal; but they ultimately proved to be Vance's destiny — a destiny that came calling in the person of Major Vance Astro. An adult version of Vance Astrovik from the alternate future timeline of Earth-691, Major Astro had become an astronaut in his timeline's 21st century, changing his name to Astro to reflect his chosen profession. Major Astro had made a thousand-year space journey to Alpha Centauri, wearing a special containment suit that preserved his body and spending years at a time in suspended animation, suffering bouts of madness during his waking periods from the isolation. Finally reaching the planet Centauri-IV in the 31st century, Major Astro was shocked to discover that humans had mastered faster-than-light travel and colonized other planets during his journey, including Centauri-IV. Though he was celebrated as a heroic space pioneer and had developed psycho-kinetic mental powers over the course of his journey, Astro was bitter about having devoted his life to a now-pointless mission, especially since he was now trapped in his containment suit; but he found a new mission when he helped form the heroic Guardians of the Galaxy. An early Guardians mission brought the team back in time to the modern era of Earth-616, where they enlisted the aid of the Defenders and met Major Astro's youthful present-day self, Vance Astrovik. This visit confirmed young Vance's belief in heroes and his view of the world as a wondrous place, though the Guardians removed young Vance's specific memories of the encounter to avoid possibly altering his future.

The Guardians' next visit to the Earth-616 timeline's modern era was made in pursuit of the fugitive villain Korvac, whom the Guardians suspected of plotting against young Vance. Korvac was actually pursuing a far grander scheme for universal domination that had nothing to do with Vance, but the Guardians acted as behind-the-scenes protectors of young Vance for some time regardless, eventually chasing down Korvac alongside the Avengers. Following Korvac's demise, the Guardians prepared to return to their own time again; but Major Astro, unable to bear the thought of his younger self potentially suffering a thousand years of pointless torture as an astronaut, decided to prevent this. Confronting his youthful counterpart again, Major Astro used his mental powers to awaken young Vance's own latent mental abilities. Young Vance struggled to control his new powers with the aid of the Thing (Ben Grimm), one of many heroes who had been investigating strange weather phenomena generated by the interaction of the two Vances' mental powers. With the Thing's encouragement, Astrovik realized that his emerging mutant powers could be a blessing, and he now hoped to become a super hero rather than an astronaut. Satisfied that at least one Vance Astrovik would escape a thousand-year torment, Major Astro and the Guardians returned to their 31st century future.

An emotionally insecure bigot who had been abused by his own father for displaying homosexual tendencies when he was a teen, Arnold Astrovik hated his son's newfound mutant nature and began verbally and physically abusing Vance. Afraid of hurting his father with his powers, Vance never struck back, though he disagreed with his Sunday school teacher Mrs. Rutstein's opinion that God alone should punish the wicked; her insistence that the Jewish people were not meant to fight back against their persecutors, along with Vance's terrible home life, gradually shook Vance's faith in religion. The teenage Vance eventually ran away from home and joined a circus, where he befriended fellow performer Lauren Anderson and posed as sideshow mentalist the Astounding Astrovik. Unfortunately, the circus manager turned out to be the criminal Taskmaster, who was using the circus as a front to train hired muscle, and Lauren turned out to be a federal agent infiltrating the Taskmaster's operation. After the Thing (who had recently quit the Fantastic Four) helped Vance and Lauren close down the crooked carnival, Vance and Ben took an extended road trip together, seeking their place in the world. Vance soon convinced the Thing to join the superhuman-level

REAL NAME: Vance Astrovik
ALIASES: Squire Justice, "Super-Tights," Superhuman Penitentiary Prisoner #344678, Marvel Boy, Marvel Man, Manglin' John Mahoney, the Astounding Astrovik
IDENTITY: Publicly known
OCCUPATION: Adventurer; former instructor, youth counselor, investigator, student, prison inmate, professional wrestling manager, circus performer
CITIZENSHIP: USA with a criminal record
PLACE OF BIRTH: Saugerties, New York
KNOWN RELATIVES: Norma Astrovik (mother), Arnold Astrovik (father, deceased), Jerry Astrovik (born Jerzy Astroyevicht, grandfather, deceased), Katerina Astrovik (grandmother)
GROUP AFFILIATION: Counter-Force, Avengers (inactive); formerly Initiative, "Secret Avengers," New Warriors, Triune Understanding, Queen's Vengeance (Reality-398), Childwatch Foundation, Mutant Liberation Force (Reality-9105), Unlimited Class Wrestling Federation, Taskmaster's circus; former partner of Firestar
EDUCATION: College (unfinished)
FIRST APPEARANCE: (Astrovik) Giant-Size Defenders #5 (1975); (Marvel Boy) Thor #411 (1989); (Justice) New Warriors #43 (1994)

YOUNG VANCE

Unlimited Class Wrestling Federation (UCWF), and he acted as Ben's manager. Later, trying to elude a private detective sent by his family, Vance donned a padded, Major Astro-inspired costume and posed briefly as UCWF wrestler Manglin' John Mahoney, using his telekinetic powers to simulate superhuman strength and durability. Despite this ruse, Vance's mother Norma tracked him down, claiming that his father had changed and was seeking treatment for his emotional issues. Wary but homesick, Vance decided to give his family another chance and returned to his parents.

Vance's homecoming proved to be a mistake, since Arnold continued to fear and resent his mutant son. Tensions at home increased after Vance began adventuring as the costumed hero Marvel Boy. Rejected as too inexperienced when he applied for Avengers membership, Marvel Boy instead helped found the youthful New Warriors super-team led by Night Thrasher (Dwayne Taylor). Vance's intelligence, idealism, dedication and skill quickly made him one of the group's most respected members. He struggled with the limitations of his powers at first, often suffering fatigue, headaches and nosebleeds due to overtaxing his telekinetic abilities in action. This changed after the team's first conflict with the new Sphinx (Meryet Karim), during which the Sphinx overlapped reality with that of the alternate Earth-9105. The Warriors lived alternate lives during their time in this transformed reality, where Vance was a key soldier of the rebel Mutant Liberation Force as Marvel Man. Reality was restored to normal after the Sphinx's defeat, and the Warriors' memories of Earth-9105 mostly faded; but the experience left a lasting subconscious impression on Vance, who became more confident in himself and his powers. He began dating his teammate and fellow mutant adventurer Firestar (Angelica Jones), and he quickly developed into a much more formidable telekinetic.

Disapproving of Vance's Warriors activities, Arnold gradually became more abusive again, even physically violent, despite Vance's warnings against this. Finally, during one especially vicious beating, an exhausted and furious Vance — already badly injured after recent Warriors battles with Terrax and Gideon — instinctively lashed out with his telekinetic powers, killing his father. Vance was arrested, tried for murder, found guilty of negligent homicide, and sentenced to imprisonment in the Colorado super-prison known as the Vault for a span of no more than three years and no less than fourteen months. Determined to learn from his experience and become a better person for it, Vance served his time, declining opportunities to escape. He was a model prisoner respected by both the authorities and his fellow inmates, befriending Vault Guardsman Scott Washington (later the vigilante Hybrid).

Paroled early for good behavior, Vance rejoined the Warriors and adopted a new costumed identity as Justice. He also began working part-time with the activist organization Childwatch, which specializes in locating and aiding teenage runaways. During his early Childwatch work, Justice gave his old Marvel Boy costume to super-teen David Bank, whose troubled relationship with his own father was improved by Vance's advice. While serving as Warriors leader after Night Thrasher left the group, Justice worked a case with Israeli super-agent Sabra, who was strongly attracted to him; the feeling was somewhat mutual, but Vance remained loyal to Firestar despite Sabra's persistent interest. Similarly, Firestar remained loyal to Vance despite hints of romantic sparks between herself and new Warriors recruit Scarlet Spider (Ben Reilly), who soon left the group. A more serious problem was Firestar's discovery that her mutant microwave powers were gradually undermining her physical health. Anxieties over Firestar's health problems and his own performance as team leader made Vance's later days with the Warriors a more troubled time, and the group gradually drifted apart as the members' priorities shifted in different directions. By then, Angelica had proposed marriage to Vance and he accepted, beginning a long engagement.

After Justice and Firestar helped the Avengers defeat the sorceress Morgan Le Fay (who briefly transformed the couple into Squire Justice and Lady Comet as part of her mind-controlled altered reality strike force, the Queen's Vengeance), Vance convinced Angelica to help him capture the super-criminal Whirlwind in an attempt to impress the Avengers further. The plan worked: Hawkeye (Clint Barton) nominated the duo for Avengers membership, team leader Captain America appointed them reservists, and they soon upgraded to full membership. Firestar was a very reluctant Avenger at first, while Vance was ridiculously overeager to work with his longtime idols; but Angelica soon grew to share Vance's respect for the Avengers, and she became much more enthusiastic after Hank Pym helped cure her powers' dangerous side-effects. An overwhelmed Vance, meanwhile, began suffering severe performance anxiety, fearful of not being able to live up to his childhood heroes. This finally changed during a harrowing battle with Ultron, when Vance found the means to destroy the killer robot; this victory gave Vance a confidence boost, and the emotional turmoil that several Avengers veterans went through during the conflict helped Vance to see them as people rather than icons. Before long, Vance grew as comfortable and capable in his new team as Firestar was; however, realizing they had too long neglected their personal lives, the couple took a leave of absence to further their education and devote more time to their romance.

At the request of Avengers founder Iron Man, the couple soon infiltrated the Triune Understanding spiritual movement, which was then feuding with the Avengers. The duo eventually helped the Avengers expose and bring down the Triunes' corrupt leadership. Justice and Firestar subsequently aided the Avengers against menaces such as the cosmic Triple-Evil, Kang the Conqueror, Scorpio and the mad Scarlet Witch, though the couple remained semi-retired from heroics while they concentrated on their private lives. Working with Childwatch again, Vance spent much of his spare time making wedding preparations, but he soon realized Angelica had become less enthusiastic about their upcoming nuptials. A 19-year-old college freshman in her civilian identity, Firestar felt increasingly reluctant to settle down so young, while the slightly older Vance was reluctant to remain in a relationship that wasn't moving forward. Unable to reconcile their differing priorities, the couple broke up.

By this time, the New Warriors had regrouped under Night Thrasher's leadership as the stars of a reality television series, though Vance declined to participate. The team's televised battle with a gang of super-criminals in Stamford, Connecticut ended tragically when the villain

2ND JUSTICE COSTUME
Art by Carlos Pacheco

Nitro caused an explosion that killed hundreds of civilians, including many children. The blast also apparently slew most of the Warriors present, including Justice's good friends Night Thrasher and Namorita, Vance's longtime roommate. The incident sparked a wave of public outrage directed at super heroes in general and the Warriors in particular, and a group of Stamford survivors funded an anti-Warriors website that began publicizing the real names and locations of surviving Warriors and encouraging the public to target them. Justice and fellow Warriors veteran Rage launched a lawsuit to oppose the website, with Jennifer Walters (alias She-Hulk) acting as their lawyer. When the website's creator was revealed to be former Warriors member Hindsight, who was trying to drive the team's remnants into retirement after the shame and horror of the Stamford tragedy, Justice led a group of his fellow ex-Warriors in confronting the traitor, wrecking Hindsight's home and forcing him to shut the website down.

The Stamford disaster spurred the creation of the Superhuman Registration Act (SHRA), which required all super heroes to register with the government under federal supervision or face imprisonment. A civil war broke out in the super-hero community over the new law and Vance briefly joined the pro-registration faction as an early member of the government's Fifty State Initiative; however, he quickly switched sides to the anti-registration "Secret Avengers" led by his idol Captain America after the death of outlaw hero Goliath (Bill Foster) at the hands of Initiative forces. The war ended when Captain America surrendered to the authorities upon belatedly realizing the general public supported the SHRA. The anti-SHRA rebels were offered amnesty in exchange for registering and most of them accepted, including Justice, who became a key staff member at the Initiative's Camp Hammond training base. Serving as an instructor and the base's youth counselor, he helped recruit, train and advise young Initiative cadets such as athletic prodigy MVP. Vance also enjoyed a secret romance with another cadet, his long-time admirer Ultragirl, who had served briefly with Justice in the New Warriors.

Over time, however, Justice grew deeply disillusioned with the Initiative. He and other ex-Warriors within the organization often felt uncomfortable at Camp Hammond since many Initiative personnel routinely demonized the New Warriors as criminally reckless vigilantes. Senior drill instructor Gauntlet in particular relentlessly insulted the original New Warriors' memory during his training exercises, eventually sparking a very public brawl between Justice and Gauntlet. When the widely despised Gauntlet was beaten nearly to death by an unseen attacker shortly thereafter, Justice and all of Camp Hammond's other ex-Warriors were briefly incarcerated and questioned, though the base's senior government official Henry Gyrich ended the investigation as part of a larger cover-up of Initiative misconduct before the attacker could be found, unaware that unstable Warriors veteran Slapstick had been the true culprit.

Meanwhile, Vance's star pupil MVP had been accidentally killed during one of the Gauntlet's training sessions. Gyrich had ordered a cover-up of the death and also allowed Camp Hammond's scientists to create a series of MVP clones, one of which was sent back to MVP's home in Kentucky so that MVP's father Brian Van Patrick wouldn't realize what had happened to his real son. Initially aided by cadet Cloud 9, Justice began an unauthorized investigation into the MVP case, learning of the original MVP's demise and fighting his way through the Action Pack (Kentucky's Initiative team) in the process. Quitting the Initiative, Justice invited fellow ex-Warriors Debrii, Rage, Slapstick and Ultragirl to join him. Together, the quintet tracked down Brian Van Patrick and the benevolent MVP clone he believed to be his son, forming an alliance with them, and Vance's group soon teamed up with Initiative forces to help defeat KIA, a murderous rogue clone of MVP.

Unwilling to trust the Initiative any further, Vance decided to form his own team, Counter-Force, dedicated to monitoring the Initiative and preventing the organization from abusing its power. The Scarlet Spiders (more MVP clones) and most of the Initiative's ex-Warriors joined Justice in this new group but Ultragirl sadly stayed behind, hoping to change the Initiative from within. Initiative founder Iron Man reluctantly allowed Vance's new group to go free, noting they were all trained and licensed heroes now, but warned them they would face charges if they did anything illegal. Counter-Force subsequently investigated the latest incarnation of the New Warriors, an outlaw vigilante team led by a new Night Thrasher (the original's brother Donyell Taylor); while the two teams clashed at first, they made peace after Donyell revealed his true identity to both groups. The New Warriors and Counter-Force then teamed up to raid a SHIELD Helicarrier, stealing the remains of the New Warriors slain in the Stamford disaster and finally granting them a respectful burial. Vance and his Counter-Force have remained active since then, trying to ensure that the order imposed on the super-hero community by the Initiative is always tempered with justice.

4TH JUSTICE COSTUME
Art by Mike Norton

HEIGHT: 5'10" **EYES:** Hazel
WEIGHT: 180 lbs. **HAIR:** Brown

ABILITIES/ACCESSORIES: Vance is an extremely powerful and skillful telekinetic, able to levitate and manipulate objects with his mind. By using his ability on himself, he can fly with great speed and maneuverability and carry other people and masses aloft with him, lifting up to several tons of material. He can perform complex or subtle operations such as dismantling and reassembling the component parts of an object, or animating particulate matter to create dust storms, or manipulating gases to create smokescreens; however, he can also channel his power into basic feats such as near-impenetrable defensive force screens or blasts of tremendous concussive force. He can smash through multiple concrete and steel reinforced walls within a matter of moments, or wreck an entire house with a single wide-focus force blast. Vance is an accomplished and enthusiastic researcher, having near-encyclopedic knowledge regarding super heroes in particular, and is highly skilled with computers. Schooled in unarmed combat by Night Thrasher, Andrew Chord, Captain America and others, he is also a capable motorcycle rider and a trained pilot of the Avengers' supersonic VTOL aircraft, known as Quinjets.

JUSTICE (TENSEN)

REAL NAME: John Roger Tensen
ALIASES: Justice Tensen, the Justice Killer, Justice-Warrior, Narc, Net Prophet, Prophet of Thor, Trace, Whitey
IDENTITY: Secret
OCCUPATION: Vigilante; former US Justice Department Narcotics Agent
CITIZENSHIP: USA (Earth-148611)
PLACE OF BIRTH: Teaneck, New Jersey, Earth-148611
KNOWN RELATIVES: Irene Tensen (wife, deceased), Angela Tensen (daughter), unidentified parents
GROUP AFFILIATION: Formerly Forsaken, NSA, Justice Department Narcotics Division; falsely believed he was one of the Far Side's Justice-Warriors
EDUCATION: College graduate
FIRST APPEARANCE: Justice #1 (1986)

HISTORY: John Tensen was born April 25, 1950. All his life he wanted one thing: to be the good guy, the man in the white hat. He had few friends in high school, a result of an incident in which he violently turned down an offer of drugs, earning himself the nickname Narc (which he considered a compliment.) He married his high school sweetheart Irene, and the couple had a daughter, Angela, a year later. Irene supported them while John went to college. After he graduated, they moved to Washington DC and Tensen joined the Justice Department Narcotics Division, becoming a top investigator. Tensen disregarded the many enemies this made him, until the day a car bomb meant for him took Irene's life. Though he caught those responsible, the damage was done; Tensen withdrew into himself, becoming cold and distant, unable to look at the daughter whose face reminded him of Irene. After Angela went to college, Tensen's boss, Hanley, discussed launching a major investigation against Conquest Dynamic's Daedalus Darquill, suspected of large scale trafficking, and asked Tensen to go deep undercover to penetrate Darquill's organization through his son, Damon Conquest. On July 22, 1986, around the same time Tensen took this assignment, Earth experienced "the White Event," when everyone on the planet was exposed to energies from the mysterious Starbrand. A small percentage, Tensen included, were transformed into super-powered "paranormals," though for Tensen the only immediate signs were intense migraines.

Unfortunately for Tensen, Darquill also became a paranormal, able to generate illusions and manipulate reality with his dreams. He created the Far Side, a fantasy world, and pulled others into this realm to play out roles he assigned them. Conquest took Tensen to meet Darquill, planning to transform him into one of Darquill's Demon Hounds, but Tensen's powers emerged; blocking Darquill's psionic assault, John fled into the fantasy world, which gradually assimilated him. Adapting his desire for justice and his new found powers into the fantasy, Tensen decided he was a Justice-Warrior for the Land of Spring, mortal foes of Darquill's Land of Winter; how many of the Far Side's people were other victims of Darquill's manipulations, and which were simply figments of his or Tensen's imaginations remains unclear to this day. Tensen/Justice returned to Earth, which bewildered his new persona. He soon gained an ally in his hunt for Darquill: undercover cop Becky Chambers, whose partner Hoyt Pittman was slain when Darquill's agent Tattoo tried to kill Justice. After an inconclusive confrontation with Conquest, Becky, and Justice, now lovers, went to Baja to face Darquill, but he proved immune to Tensen's attacks. Darquill and his allies kidnapped Becky and escaped through a portal into the Far Side. While Justice hunted for new leads to Darquill, the Far Side's villains gradually brainwashed and corrupted Becky. Framed for Becky's murder, Justice became a fugitive, facing Darquill's Black Justice in the desert, and learning from the dying Land of Spring mage Webstral that his realm had been conquered. Justice returned to LA, adopting the identity of Trace, bodyguard to club owner Reggie Wyschoff, while waiting for Darquill to make a move, eventually battling Maximus Argath, allegedly a cacodemon servant of Conquest's.

Troubled by dreams of his true past, Justice enlisted the help of dream-walking paranormal Nightmask (Keith Remsen). Entering Justice's dream, Nightmask found himself in the Far Side. Meanwhile, Darquill sent Becky back to Earth to slay Justice while he slept, but he awoke in time to stop her; her bullets ricocheted off his shields, fatally wounding her. Moments later, Darquill sent more minions to try again, but Justice used their portal to reach the Far Side. He slew Conquest, but an enraged Darquill easily overwhelmed him; however, Darquill's energy blast, intended to annihilate him, instead returned him to the real world and Darquill's Baja estate near a similarly "annihilated" Nightmask. Remsen used his familiarity with dreams to deduce the true nature of the Far Side, which he explained to Justice. Finding the peacefully sleeping real world body of Darquill, Justice disintegrated him, ending all of Darquill's illusions. With his true memories gradually returning, Justice swore to prevent other paranormals from abusing their powers as Darquill had. He went on a killing spree, dubbed by the media "the Justice Killer" because

Art by Lee Weeks

Art by Alex Saviuk

he would draw a set of scales in the ashes of his victims. Amongst his first victims were pyrokinetic arsonist Greg Gardner, shapeshifting robber Malcolm Stokes, mind-controlling lothario Lonnie Pool, body-hopping murderer Eric Quinn, and Rodney Jung, a drug dealer who could turn people into addicts with a touch of his hands. While continuing this crusade, Justice was caught on the edge of the blast that destroyed Pittsburgh and created the Pitt, giving him the additional goal of finding and punishing the paranormal responsible. His search led him to Pennsylvania where he faced the murderous Millennias cult who followed the paranormal Savior; fought the psychotic Nightmare Killer who slew others in their sleep; and attended the Pitt-Aid concert, where he ran into both his daughter Angie and Seraph, defender of paranormals and agent of Judge Mental. Protecting Angie from a human stampede left Justice unable to defend himself, and he was beaten by security and captured. Kept sedated, the drugs made him hallucinate he was back in the Far Side, and he escaped, going on a rampage believing he was fighting Darquill's minions, until the NSC used Angie to bring him back to reality.

Art by Tom Grindberg

NET PROPHET

The NSC's Terrence Updike recruited Justice for a new paranormal unit. They sent him to stop the Justice Brigade, the former Millennias cult, who were killing people in Justice's name, then to Texas to investigate air-manipulating paranormal ex-con Dennis Foley; while he was away, Angie witnessed a paranormal battle between the Soviet Rodstvow and Psi-Hawk, gestalt creation of the Psi-Force teens, which left a friend of hers hospitalized. Angie asked her father to hunt and punish the two combatants, but he refused to be an instrument for vengeance. Soon after, Justice narrowly avoided a sniper's bullet from Quill, an assassin sent by Judge Mental. While Justice and his ally Playback hunted Quill, the assassin kidnapped Angie, only to be killed by a zombie horde when Angie discovered her paranormal ability to animate corpses; the experience left Angie in a state of stupor. Justice blamed himself for Angie's condition, believing it was punishment for not doing what Angie had asked him. Allying himself with the mercenary Medusa Web, Justice entered the USSR, freeing the captured Psi-Force and helping to destroy Rodstvow; he nearly slew Psi-Force too, to keep his promise to Angie, but was convinced at the last minute to grant them a reprieve. Back in the US, Justice and a recovered Angie set out to rescue captured NSC agents from Judge Mental's paranormal Forsaken. Captured, Justice listened as Judge Mental boasted of his ability to project thoughts and block Justice's powers; however, Judge Mental could not read minds, and thus was unaware Justice had a gun until Justice shot him dead. With the NSC headquarters destroyed in their absence, Justice stayed with the Forsaken as their new leader.

Some time later, when extradimensional Starblasters from the 616 reality came to Earth-148611 to steal the Starbrand's power, Nightmask recruited Justice and other paranormals to combat the threat. The battle ended when the Stranger of 616 trapped the Starblaster leader, Skeletron, in reality 148611, and brought Justice's Earth into the 616 reality; to prevent the Starbrand contaminating this reality, the Living Tribunal sealed the newly moved Earth and its inhabitants behind an impenetrable force field.

Under unspecified circum-stances, Justice (or a dimensional counterpart thereof) later fought alongside heroes from various worlds in a battle against Thanatos (an alternate reality Rick Jones), and was subsequently brought to the year 2099 AD of Earth-928 by Jordan Boone's Virtual Unreality Machine. Rendered partially amnesiac by the experience, and with his powers altered, Tensen allied himself with this world's Spider-Man (Miguel O'Hara) against Thanatos. Dubbed the Net Prophet after a Thorite prophecy, he set off to explore his new world and find a purpose, eventually becoming involved with Father Jennifer D'Angelo and regaining some of his memories.

Another counterpart of Tensen's, from Earth-15731, was taken as a host body by the reality warping Proteus of Earth-58163, battled the dimension-hopping Exiles, then traveled to Earth-928, his anomalous presence altering the path of its history, thus creating the divergent Earth-6375, where Tensen's body was abandoned in favor of a more durable host.

EARTH-15731 JUSTICE, JUSTICE-WARRIOR UNIFORM

Art by Paul Pelletier

HEIGHT: 6'2" **WEIGHT:** 205 lbs.
EYES: Blue **HAIR:** White

ABILITIES/ACCESSORIES: As Justice, Tensen could psionically generate two types of energy: his right hand usually released energy blasts, varying in width and intensity from harmless light to disintegrating heat beams. His left hand normally generated versatile force fields, capable of stopping bullets, catching falling people uninjured, blocking someone's breathing (if placed in their mouth) or creating platforms to walk into the sky — requiring extreme concentration, the force fields could not easily be maintained for any length of time. With these powers governed by opposing hemispheres of his brain, he could with effort swap which hand was used, but could not use both powers simultaneously. Justice could also tell if people were corrupt, evil or paranormals by reading their auras, and he could spot people clairvoyantly watching him, presumably seeing their astral forms. He once regrew a severed hand, but this was likely part of Darquill's illusions, as he has shown no regenerative powers since. As a side effect of his long exposure to the dream realm, he is susceptible to hallucinations if drugged.

As the Net Prophet, he could warp space to teleport himself or others, and fire concussive eye blasts.

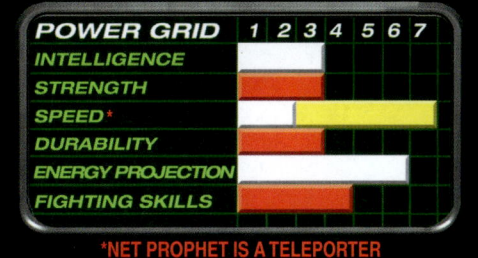

*NET PROPHET IS A TELEPORTER

JESTER (PUTT)

REAL NAME: Jody Putt
ALIASES: None
IDENTITY: Known to authorities
OCCUPATION: Government agent; former criminal
CITIZENSHIP: USA
PLACE OF BIRTH: Unrevealed
KNOWN RELATIVES: None
GROUP AFFILIATION: Thunderbolts; formerly led Assembly of Evil
EDUCATION: Unrevealed
FIRST APPEARANCE: Mutant Misadventures of Cloak and Dagger #8 (1989)

Art by Mike Vosburg

HISTORY: When the Jester (Jonathon Powers) retired from crime, Jody Putt created a duplicate of his costume and became the new Jester. While his criminal activities never attracted the attention of super heroes, they did attract the attention of Dr. Doom, who at the time was part of a cabal of masterminds behind the "Acts of Vengeance" scheme to send super-villains to attack heroes they'd not fought before. Sent to assault the Avengers, Jester formed the Assembly of Evil, recruiting the Fenris twins and Hydro-Man, and though the Leader declined the invitation, he allowed his minion Rock (Samuel J. Laroquette) to join the team. The group — along with a robot Hulk duplicate that Doom had given the Jester and that Jester rebuilt to mirror his own clownish gimmick — tried to recruit Cloak and Dagger, not realizing the duo were heroic vigilantes. The Assembly attacked the Avengers at a press conference, only to be soundly defeated by the Avengers, Cloak and Dagger. Putt toiled in obscurity afterwards, usually found in bars that catered to super-villains, notably confronting Matador (Manuel Eloganto) and, later, Misty Knight and Colleen Wing at such establishments. During the super-hero "Civil War," Jester was recruited into the Thunderbolts by the Commission on Superhuman Activities, implanted with nanotechnology to prevent his disobedience and sent alongside Jack O'Lantern (Steven Levins) to capture Spider-Man (Peter Parker). They tracked the rogue hero down in the sewers, but as they tormented him, the Punisher (Frank Castle) arrived and shot both in the head. Putt's body was later dug up by Mr. Hyde (Calvin Zabo) in order to study and devise the means to counter the CSA's nanotechnology.

HEIGHT: 5'9" **WEIGHT:** 170 lbs. **EYES:** Brown **HAIR:** Brown

ABILITIES/ACCESSORIES: Jester possesses no powers, but is proficient in unique weapon-making. He carries impact-explosive yo-yos that emit sonic-level sound, flying discs that emit anesthetic gas and bags of exploding faux popcorn.

INTELLIGENCE: 4 **STRENGTH:** 2 **SPEED:** 2 **DURABILITY:** 2
ENERGY PROJECTION: 1 **FIGHTING SKILLS:** 3

JUNIOR JUNIPER

REAL NAME: Jonathan Juniper
ALIASES: Junior
IDENTITY: No dual identity
OCCUPATION: Soldier
CITIZENSHIP: USA
PLACE OF BIRTH: Unrevealed
KNOWN RELATIVES: Roger "Buddy" Juniper (Great-nephew, deceased)
GROUP AFFILIATION: Howling Commandos
EDUCATION: College graduate
FIRST APPEARANCE: Sgt. Fury and His Howling Commandos #1 (1963)

Art by Jack Kirby

HISTORY: Jonathan "Junior" Juniper was a fresh Ivy League graduate when he voluntarily enlisted just after World War II's outbreak, shooting down ten Nazi airplanes as a B-17 tail-gunner. Picked as an original member of the First Attack Squad of Able Company led by Nick Fury, Junior saved the group on its first mission when, reading his Bible while surrounded by Nazis, he recalled the Biblical story of Gideon frightening his enemy with raucous noises. The squad stole a sound truck and used its loudspeakers to amplify their cries, convincing the Nazis to retreat, earning the nickname "Howling Commandos." Soon after, Junior participated in the Howler mission to rescue Pierre LaBrave, a captured French resistance leader with secret knowledge of D-Day. While trying to destroy the Nazi heavy water supply, Junior suggested surrendering in order to enter the nearby concentration camp, using "Operation Cyclone" to destroy it and freeing the prisoners. At the Nazi labs, they pulled the atomic rods causing a nuclear explosion. In Italy, Junior helped rescue an American division trapped at Massacre Mountain. Sadly, in an attempt to bring the traitorous Lord Ha-Ha from Berlin, Junior was shot and killed. Percival "Pinky" Pinkerton took Junior's place with the commandos. Although the Howlers were in the first wave of D-Day attackers, the man among them resembling Junior was clearly someone else. Decades later, Junior's great-nephew, Roger "Buddy" Juniper became Agent 223 of SHIELD, joining Hercules against Ares and the Warhawks but was killed in action by the Minotaur.

HEIGHT: 5'5" **WEIGHT:** 110 lbs. **EYES:** Blue **HAIR:** Auburn

ABILITIES/ACCESSORIES: Junior was an ace tail-gunner and commando, proficient with knife, grenade, dynamite, and Thompson Submachine gun M1.

INTELLIGENCE: 2 **STRENGTH:** 2 **SPEED:** 2 **DURABILITY:** 2
ENERGY PROJECTION: 1 **FIGHTING SKILLS:** 4

KAINE

HISTORY: Kaine was the first of the Jackal's experiments in cloning that did not immediately degenerate into raw genetic waste. After some time, however, slow genetic deterioration became apparent. The Jackal became disgusted by yet another failure and planned to kill his creation, forcing the rejected clone to flee. The clone came to call himself Kaine and eventually adopted a costume that slowed his deterioration and hid his skin, but reproduced the web-like scars that run all over his body. Even as his DNA deteriorated, Kaine grew taller and stronger than the original Spider-Man.

Kaine's anger grew with his strength. Most of all he hated Ben Reilly, whom he, like the Jackal, believed to be the original Spider-Man due to the machinations of Norman Osborn acting behind the scenes while the world believed him dead. Believing Peter to be a successful clone, Kaine took it upon himself to aid him. This ambition eventually led Kaine to murder the Grim Hunter and Dr. Octopus (Otto Octavius) with his bare hands, while Peter prepared for the birth of his first child.

Kaine followed Ben around the world, working occasionally as a high-priced assassin. In Salt Lake City, Kaine killed Detective Louise Kennedy, after learning that she was in league with the local mob. Detective Jacob Raven eventually tracked fingerprints back to the original Peter Parker in New York City. Peter was exonerated only after he threatened to make his secret identity known and Kaine confessed to the crime in another effort to preserve Peter's happiness. After Ben was "revealed" to be the original Spider-Man, Kaine escaped from police custody but was seemingly killed by Spidercide, a shape-shifting clone of Spider-Man. The Jackal put Kaine's body in a clone regeneration pod, where it was revived some time later.

Kaine was duped into combat with the likes of the Rhino and Polestar (Thomas Duffy) by the affections of Muse (Shannon Fitzpatrick) for the sake of secret wagering called the Great Game. Kaine refused to participate, and invaded the offices of Great Game sponsor, John Johnsmeyer where Spider-Man (Ben Reilly) stopped Kaine from killing Muse for her betrayal. Still attempting to crush Reilly's spirit, Kaine used Elizabeth Tyne (who was living under the assumed name of Janine Godbe after shooting her abusive father), the love of Ben's life since they had met in Salt Lake City. After Ben took the role of Spider-Man, Kaine lured Janine back to New York and attempted to kill himself and them. Their love inspired him to relent, and both Kaine and Janine surrendered to the police. Kaine later escaped from the Vault prison,

REAL NAME: None
ALIASES: Peter Parker
IDENTITY: Secret
OCCUPATION: Assassin
CITIZENSHIP: None with a criminal record in the US
PLACE OF ORIGIN: The Jackal's laboratory, New York City
KNOWN RELATIVES: Miles Warren (the Jackal, creator), Peter Parker (Spider-Man, genetic progenitor), Ben Reilly, Jack, Guardian, Spidercide, various unnamed clones (fellow clones)
GROUP AFFILIATION: None
EDUCATION: Possesses memories of Peter Parker's college education
FIRST APPEARANCE: Web of Spider-Man #119 (1994)

targeting Norman Osborn for killing Ben Reilly, masterminding the Jackal's clone operations, and the associated psychological warfare. Kaine was last seen in Greece, where Osborn's men claimed to have dealt with Kaine's threat to Osborn. Kaine's whereabouts are unrevealed. After Spider-Man made a deal with Mephisto to save the life of his dying Aunt May, everyone, including Kaine, no longer remembers Spider-Man's secret identity.

HEIGHT: 6'4" **EYES:** Brown
WEIGHT: 250 lbs. **HAIR:** Brown

ABILITIES/ACCESSORIES: Kaine began life with powers identical to Spider-Man's (superhuman strength, agility, wall-crawling, and a danger-sense). Over time, Kaine's strength increased from being able to lift 10 tons to 25 tons. His mental control over his ability to stick to objects was augmented to such a degree that he could rip down walls using just his palms. This power in his scarred deformed hands could become exothermic, allowing him to burn the "Mark of Kaine" upon victim's faces. Kaine's amplified spider-sense gives him limited precognition. He had twin retractable claws on the back of each hand (the "Sting of Kaine") supplemented by spikes on his costume's forearms and calves.

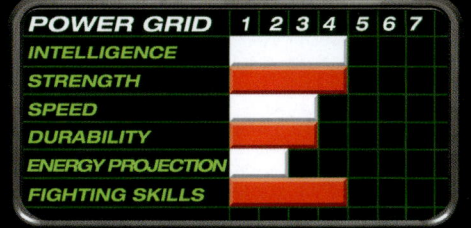

POWER GRID	1	2	3	4	5	6	7
INTELLIGENCE			●				
STRENGTH					●		
SPEED			●				
DURABILITY				●			
ENERGY PROJECTION	●						
FIGHTING SKILLS				●			

Art by Sal Buscema with Mike Zeck (inset)

JENNIFER KALE

REAL NAME: Jennifer Kale
ALIASES: "Wendy the Good Little Witch" (nickname via John Blaze)
IDENTITY: No dual identity
OCCUPATION: Licensed super hero, sorceress; former student
CITIZENSHIP: USA
PLACE OF BIRTH: Citrusville, Florida
KNOWN RELATIVES: Andrew Kale (brother, deceased), Joshua Kale (grandfather, deceased), Naomi Kale (aunt), Johnny Blaze, Barbara and Daniel Ketch (cousins), Illyana, Destin, Serenity and Noble Kale (ancestors), Magdalena (ancestors, deceased), Dante Kale (common ancestry)
GROUP AFFILIATION: The Command (Florida's Initiative team); formerly Witches, Legion of Night
EDUCATION: BA in Creative Arts with dual focuses on painting and interpretive dance
FIRST APPEARANCE: (Adventure into) Fear #11 (1972)

HISTORY: Circa 18,000 BC, the Atlantean sorceress Zhered-Na publicly prophesied the sinking of Atlantis in the Great Cataclysm. Refusing to believe her, Atlantean Emperor Kamuu exiled Zhered-Na, setting her adrift in a small boat. Landing on the continent Thuria (which would become Europe, Asia and Africa), Zhered-Na organized a cult of disciples, including Dakimh, whom she endowed with an extraordinarily long life span. Zhered-Na also foretold the invasion of Earth by the demons of Sominus, who would be driven off by a savior with the aspect of a monster. As the Cataclysm began, Zhered-Na was slain by an agent of her enemy, the Fear-Lord also known as the Dweller-in-Darkness, who harnessed the Cataclysm-caused terror energies to create a spawn, D'Spayre. Only Dakimh and a few other disciples escaped,

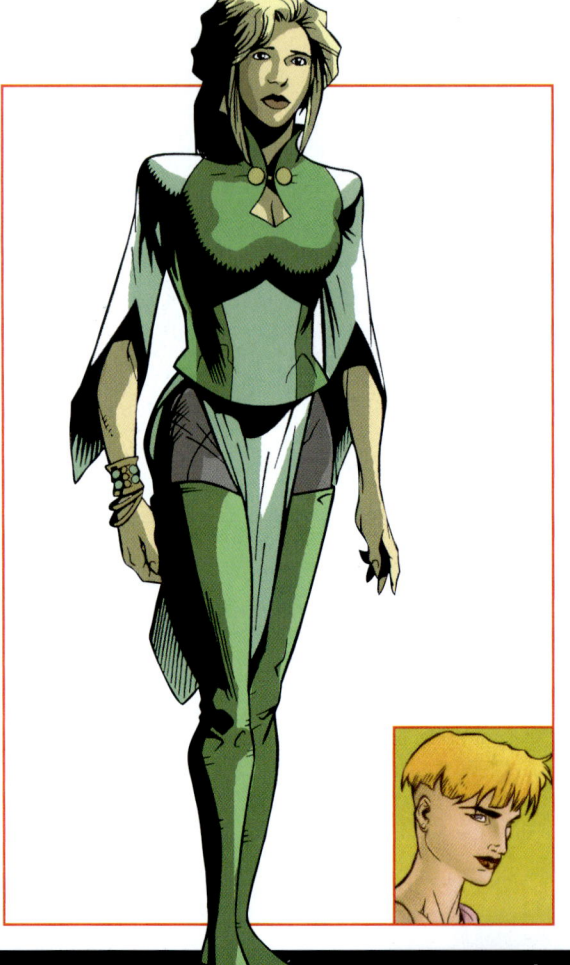

bearing with them scrolls containing Zhered-Na's mystical knowledge, keeping her teachings alive for over 20,000 years. Dakimh continued Zhered-Na's struggle against the great fear, battling D'Spayre over the ensuing millennia.

Centuries ago, Jennifer Kale's ancestress, Illyana, was a member of the Cult. She completed the unfinished Tome of Zhered-Na, a repository of Zhered-Na's magic, by adding mystical knowledge that she had gained from both an angel and a demon. From then on, only a member of the Kale family, working together with an agent of Heaven and an agent of a demonic realm, could fully utilize the magical powers of the Tome without unleashing the monstrously destructive Hellphyr.

Jennifer Kale, a present day member of the Kale family, is a lookalike for Zhered-Na and may be her reincarnation. She was raised by her grandfather, Joshua, who was keeper of the Tome of Zhered-Na and the leader of the Cult of Zhered-Na in Citrusville, Florida, in the section of the Everglades that is a mystical "Nexus of All Realities." As a teenager, Jennifer became interested in magic. She and her brother Andrew stole a book they believed to be the legendary Tome (which had somehow vanished from Joshua's keeping) and experimented with a magic spell, inadvertently summoning to Earth Thog the Nether-Spawn and another demon from the realm of Sominus. The Man-Thing, monstrous guardian of the Nexus, defeated Thog and destroyed the other demon, who was presumably weakened as Andrew burned the mystic book. Jennifer's friend Ross Jaxon doubted her tale, but upon entering the swamp he was possessed by another Sominus demon. Joined by Andrew and Joshua, Jennifer located Jaxon who cast an illusion that seemingly transported them and the Man-Thing to Sominus where they were confronted by Thog. Joshua recognized the whole thing as an illusion, but they were unable to dispel it from their minds until the Man-Thing finally recognized it as an illusion, too. As they returned to the swamp, the demon was exorcised from Jaxon, but Jennifer somehow retained a psychic link with the Man-Thing.

Soon after, humanity began to be driven mad by the opening of a portal to Sominus. Joshua brought the Cultists into the swamp to perform a ritual to recover the Tome, calling upon the Mists of Maalock, which transported both Jennifer Kale and the Man-Thing to another extradimensional realm, Sandt. There they encountered the now-aged Dakimh, who — as a test of their worthiness — pretended to want them killed. Though they failed to recover the Tome, they passed Dakimh's test, earning his trust and support. Dakimh subsequently took Jennifer Kale and the Man-Thing on an extradimensional voyage to locate the Tome, but demons abducted Joshua and the Cultists and brought them to Sominus. As Jennifer approached the Tome, Yopp, an elf demon from Sominus, transported Jennifer, the Tome, and the Man-Thing (but not Dakimh) to Sominus. There, Joshua had Jennifer touch the Tome, restoring them all (and the Tome) to Citrusville; the Tome then vanished once again, allegedly no longer needed with the Sominus invasion over. The Cult apparently dissolved as well, and Jennifer's connection to the Man-Thing was seemingly severed.

Jennifer soon began having visions of other realms as Thog and his "Congress of Realities" took advantage of the disruption of the Nexus of Realities to attempt to collapse all realities into a single cosmos under his control. As a result of the chaos at the Nexus, Korrek, warrior prince of Katharta, and the talking waterfowl Howard the Duck, were transported from their otherdimensional worlds to the Citrusville swamp, where Jennifer met them. Dakimh, the Man-Thing, Jennifer, Korrek and Howard joined forces in traveling to the godly realm Therea to oppose Thog, whom the Man-Thing destroyed.

Jennifer became Dakimh's apprentice, studying with him at his castle in the otherdimensional Land between Night and Day and wearing a costume patterned after Zhered-Na's. Jennifer, Dakimh, Korrek and

Art by Kev Walker with Salvador Larroca (inset)

the Man-Thing again united to save Korrek's homeland, Katharta, from conquest by the evil wizard Klonus and the barbarian warrior Mortak. Although Klonus killed Dakimh's physical form, Dakimh survived on the mortal plane in astral form and continued training Jennifer in sorcery. Jennifer and Dakimh allied yet again with the Man-Thing, Howard and Korrek against Bzzk'joh, ruler of the Imperium Emporium and master of the Death Store, who captured Jennifer before being defeated himself.

Later, D'Spayre captured both Jennifer and Dakimh, intending to enslave them, but Spider-Man (Peter Parker) and the Man-Thing defeated the demon, freeing Dakimh and Jennifer. Still later, the evil sorcerer Baron (Karl) Mordo sacrificed Jennifer to a chaos demon, who consumed the young sorceress; but Earth's Sorcerer Supreme Dr. Strange restored her to life. Strange, Jennifer, Dakimh and other sorcerers were subsequently taken prisoner via the Magus Sword by Citrusville sheriff John Daltry, who was under Thog's control, but were freed when the Man-Thing again overcame Thog.

When Quagmire, a criminal from Earth-712 (home of the Squadron Supreme), entered Earth-616 through the Man-Thing's body, Jennifer came to the Man-Thing's aid. Quagmire attacked her but was bested by the costumed adventurer Quasar (Wendell Vaughn). At some point, Jennifer apparently completed her apprenticeship with Dakimh. Pursuing a conventional education as well, Jennifer began attending Seaview College in Malibu, California and dating Bernard Drabble. She initially took an MBA track, but switched to a dual major in painting and interpretive dance. Sensing the demon Aan Taanu, Jennifer took a leave of absence from Seaview to join the Legion of Night mystic coalition in thwarting the demon's plot to father a race via a human woman in order to overrun Earth. Jennifer planned to stay with the Legion to oppose other mystic threats, but any such adventures are unrevealed, as is the Legion's fate.

After joining a number of mystics in a vigil as Quasar foiled the Deviant Ereshkigal's efforts to conquer the multiverse, Jennifer took a sabbatical from her mystic studies to live a normal life while taking further classes at the University of California at Berkeley. While there she was saved by Dr. Strange from assassination by the evil mystic Silver Dagger and also began a lesbian relationship. Jennifer later moved to Manhattan's Lower East Side, continuing to study sorcery on her own. Dr. Strange obtained her aid in treating a mystically afflicted Dan Ketch, the human host of the Ghost Rider (Noble Kale). Jennifer then learned she was also one of Noble Kale's descendants and the cousin of Dan Ketch and John Blaze when they were attacked by the Furies, who sought to eradicate Noble's lineage in revenge for the death of his wife, Magdalena. Ultimately Jennifer summoned the spirit of Magdalena, who relieved the Furies of their mission of vengeance.

Jennifer attempted to send Howard the Duck home, but this instead resulted in the summoning of Earth-78411's Devil Dinosaur and Moonboy. She also located Ketch for the cosmic Eternity to oppose Mephisto's alternate Earth plot and subsequently aided John Blaze in unsuccessful attempts to locate his missing children, with the two parting on bad terms. Later, Jennifer moved back to San Francisco where she was sought out by X-Force members Bedlam, Cannonball, and Moonstar for aid against a succubus who had taken mystic control of several of their other members. Based on their description of the succubus, Jennifer identified her via her Demonic Concordance text as Pandemonia. Jennifer freed Pandemonia's mental slaves (Locus, Meltdown, Proudstar, Skids, Sunspot) and, assisted by Moonstar, banished Pandemonia back to her home dimension on the chaos plane. Jennifer later examined the reality-warping energies that Dani Moonstar began to display, confirming that they were not supernatural in origin. The two then attended a tai chi course. Jennifer subsequently summoned the Man-Thing and assisted X-Force against the Queen of Star Swords, the extradimensional counterpart of Moonstar responsible for her temporary warp powers.

At some point Jennifer relocated once again, moving to Orlando, and she had resumed her college studies when she was wracked with mystic agony. The demon Satan (Marduk Kurios) had manipulated Andrew Kale into touching the Tome of Zhered-Na, thereby becoming possessed by and transformed into the Hellphyr, which sought to destroy all mystics in existence. To defeat the Hellphyr, Dr. Strange recruited Jennifer, alongside the empath Topaz (who had previously been aided by the forces of Heaven against the demon Mephisto) and the succubus Satana (Satan's daughter). After the three women destroyed the creature (with Andrew's body and soul having already been completely consumed by the Hellphyr), they prevented Strange from reclaiming the Tome and decided to remain together as the Witches to combat mystical threats, though their subsequent activities are unrevealed. Following the super hero "civil war," Kale registered as a superhuman and was assigned to the Command, the Initiative team based in her home state of Florida. Jen was emotionally traumatized when Earth-2149's super-zombies devastated the Command, but later battled a Skrull Conquistador imposter..

Art by Whilce Portacio

Art by June Brigman

HEIGHT: 5'6" **WEIGHT:** 122 lbs.
EYES: Blue **HAIR:** Blonde

ABILITIES/ACCESSORIES: Jennifer Kale is a highly skilled sorceress initially trained in the ancient Atlantean sorcery practiced by Zhered-Na. She has since trained under other sorcerers, including Dr. Strange, and is also extensively self-taught. Her knowledge and power continue to grow as her studies continue. Like most sorcerers on Earth, her power is derived from three major sources: Personal powers of the soul/body/mind derived from developing one's own psychic resources (such as thought-casting), powers gained by tapping the universe's ambient magical energy and employing it for specific effects, and powers derived from tapping extradimensional energy by invoking entities or objects of mystical power. Kale can cast a wide variety of spells, project magical bolts, create mystical shields, open interdimensional portals, perform astral projection and affect the memories of or mesmerize others, among numerous other feats. Jennifer possesses the Tome of Zhered-Na, one of the most powerful known books of magical spells. She also has some training in the martial art of tai chi.

POWER GRID	1	2	3	4	5	6	7
INTELLIGENCE							
STRENGTH							
SPEED							
DURABILITY							
ENERGY PROJECTION							
FIGHTING SKILLS							

KANE

REAL NAME: Garrison "Gar" Kane
ALIASES: Weapon X
IDENTITY: Known to Canadian and US governments
OCCUPATION: Former US government operative, adventurer, actor, Canadian government operative, mercenary
CITIZENSHIP: Canada
PLACE OF BIRTH: Unrevealed
KNOWN RELATIVES: Unidentified parents (deceased)
GROUP AFFILIATION: Formerly Weapon X (US), Clan Chosen, Weapon: PRIME, Department K, Weapon X (Canadian), Six Pack/Wild Pack
EDUCATION: High school dropout
FIRST APPEARANCE: X-Force #2 (1991)

HISTORY: Following his parents' deaths, 13-year-old Garrison Kane became a mercenary and, despite his youth, was soon recruited into the Wild Pack (later Six Pack), joining G.W. Bridge, Eisenhower "Hammer" Canty, Domino (aka Neena Thurman), and Grizzly (Theodore Wincester) under the command of the mysterious Cable, secretly a time traveler. For years Kane reveled in the Six Pack's globe-spanning adventures, seeing action in Argentina, Iran, Austria, and elsewhere, and he came to regard Cable as a surrogate father. The team's downfall began during a mission in Afghanistan, where they encountered Cable's nemesis Stryfe, actually a clone of Cable himself. Months later, Cable led the Six Pack, dubious about the unpaid assignment, in assaulting Stryfe's Yucatan base. When Stryfe took Kane hostage and demanded stolen information, Hammer prepared to acquiesce, but Cable, obsessed with Stryfe, shot Hammer down, and then teleported after the fleeing Stryfe, leaving his teammates behind. When the citadel collapsed around them, Hammer was rendered quadriplegic initially (though he later regained use of his arms), and Kane became a quadruple amputee; the incident also left Kane claustrophobic.

Soon afterward, Kane joined the Canadian Department K's incarnation of the Weapon X Program, which equipped him with cyborg limbs and assigned him to a team of operatives including Bernard "Sluggo" Hoyster, Greg "Slayback" Terraerton, and Wade Wilson, whom the program had given a healing factor. Wilson's girlfriend, mutant shapeshifter Copycat, occasionally involved herself in their activities, and a strong attraction grew between her and Kane, causing serious tension between him and Wilson. Department K's particular incarnation of Weapon X folded shortly after Wilson killed Slayback under gruesome but otherwise unrevealed circumstances. Kane remained a government operative, battling the Mutant Liberation Front (led by the hated Stryfe) and other threats, though he occasionally joined Copycat, now his lover, on mercenary assignments, including some from crime figure Tolliver (who was not generally known to be Cable's son). During this period, if not earlier, Kane worked on a mysterious government project with fellow mercenary Wyre, whose DNA was used to mutate yet another government operative, Wild Child.

In recent years, Kane, now in his mid-twenties and leading Canada's Weapon: PRIME (PRototype Induced Mutation Echelon) under the code name "Weapon X," was approached by Bridge, now a SHIELD agent, who asked him to lead a mission to capture Cable. Given his mixed feelings for his former mentor, Kane refused, but after an anti-MLF assignment seemed to reveal Stryfe as none other than Cable himself, Kane reversed his decision and recruited Rictor, another young man who felt betrayed by Cable, to join Tigerstryke, Wendigo, and himself in attacking Cable's newly founded X-Force in the Adirondacks; unknown to Kane, Copycat had, under Tolliver's orders, infiltrated X-Force in the guise of Domino. However, Stryfe's forces leveled the X-Force base, and after X-Force assisted their opponents in the aftermath, Rictor rebelled against Kane. The mission ended when X-Force escaped.

Meanwhile, Wild Child, now known as Weapon Omega, was reverting to a feral persona, and Kane, assigned to bring him in if necessary, worked alongside Wyre and Alpha Flight to rein him in and defeat his enemy Rok. Shortly afterward, Kane, his cyborg system upgraded, was again recruited by Bridge to hunt down the MLF and Stryfe, whom both men still believed was Cable, and Kane tracked their quarry via a list of safehouses provided by Hammer; however, Kane soon learned that Cable and Stryfe were indeed two different people, and he agreed to help Cable if the latter would give Hammer cybernetic legs similar to Kane's. In the course of the campaign, Stryfe almost killed Kane, and Cable brought him to his and Stryfe's native era, the 40th century of Earth-4935, where he equipped Kane with new, far more realistic cyborg arms before vanishing.

For the next year, Kane — waiting for Cable to return — befriended the survivors of Cable's rebel unit, the Clan Chosen, who taught him much

Art by Pablo Raimondi

about his former mentor. When enemy forces established a time displacement nexus in Niagara Falls, Cable returned and led the Clan Chosen to destroy the nexus, but not before he and Kane returned to Kane's native era. Now having a better understanding of Cable's nature, Kane again grew close to his mentor, who made peace of sorts with Bridge and the rest of Six Pack. However, Hammer declined Cable's offer of cybernetic alteration, which he claimed had made Kane too much like Cable, and he, Kane, Bridge, Grizzly, and Domino left in pursuit of Copycat, who, like all of the now seemingly deceased Tolliver's employees, had been imperilled by his mysterious will, bequeathing a powerful weapon to whoever survived.

WEAPON PRIME UNIFORM
Art by Rob Liefeld

cyborg augmentation, more extensive than even Weapon X expected of him. He grew fanatically dedicated to his assignments, earning rapid promotion from the approving Director, who placed him in charge of interning selected mutants in the secret concentration camp Neverland. Some felt Kane, resentful of Cable and others, was deriving twisted satisfaction from hunting mutants; Kane's few friends in the unit included the hypnotic Mesmero, whom Kane often accompanied on PR missions.

IN CLAN CHOSEN
Art by Art Thibert

Domino, whom Copycat had believed was dead, retained a bitter grudge against her impersonator, and Kane soon split from the group to pursue Copycat alone. His efforts were mirrored by Wade Wilson, now Deadpool, and both men were attacked by Slayback, who had spent years techno-organically regenerating himself to get vengeance on his former teammates, and who abducted Copycat himself. Following Slayback's defeat via the cooperation of Tolliver's android weapon Zero, Kane left Department K, where leadership of Weapon: PRIME fell to Tigerstryke, and he and Copycat tried to begin a safer life in San Francisco, becoming actors with a local theater group; a jealous Deadpool attacked them but was defeated by Wolverine, a longtime veteran of an earlier incarnation of Weapon X, who was checking on Kane for their mutual friend Guardian. Months later, the extradimensional Psycho-Man sought future cybernetic secrets by abducting Kane, but instead erroneously absconded with Copycat in Kane's form. Kane accompanied Cable and Domino to Psycho-Man's microverse, where the adventuring Microns helped them free Copycat.

Eventually, Kane was equipped with the capacity to download new superhuman abilities, rendering him more powerful than ever. However, he grew more distant from his teammates, and after Mesmero was removed to parts unknown when his powers failed, Kane began to doubt his dedication to Weapon X. When Cable and his Underground invaded Weapon X, Kane challenged them but was outfought by his mentor, who was appalled to learn of the Director's genocidal ambitions and lambasted Kane for his role in them. The contemptuous rebuke from the man he had once loved as a father shamed Kane. In a final act of redemption, Kane downloaded Madison Jeffries' technomorphic abilities and drew all technology in the base into himself, disarming the Weapon X forces and rendering himself an apparently lifeless mass of techno-organic metal.

WITH AIM
Art by Leinil Yu

Deciding their hopes of a normal life were futile, Kane and Copycat returned to mercenary work, and the increasingly disillusioned Kane fought his former allies Wolverine and Alpha Flight while working for MODOK's AIM faction. Soon afterward, the sadistic Director (Malcolm Colcord) recruited Kane and Copycat for yet another Weapon X Program, which greatly enhanced Kane's cybernetics and stabilized Copycat's shapeshifting abilities. Ordered to perform many killings by his new employers, Kane did so, his love for life now almost gone. However, Copycat lost control of her powers and fled Weapon X shortly before another operative, Sabretooth, forcibly recruited her ex-lover Deadpool. Kane accompanied Deadpool on a mission to Iowa, where Kane killed a pre-adolescent mutant with uncontrolled powers; when Deadpool protested, Kane severed his longtime rival's legs, although Deadpool's healing power soon restored them. Following this debacle, both Kane and Deadpool were assigned to kill Copycat, but Deadpool rejected the order and sought to rescue her from Kane, who had grimly accepted the assignment without protest. Their fight ended when Deadpool ran over Kane with an exploding transit car, but Copycat was nevertheless killed by Sabretooth.

In the wake of Copycat's death, Kane, driven by his own feelings of inferiority, underwent further

WHILE SOLO
Art by Joe Madureira

HEIGHT: 6'2"
WEIGHT: (Recent cyborg form) 480 lbs.; (prior cyborg form) 350 lbs.; (originally) 190 lbs.
EYES: (Natural/cybernetic, left) blue; (cybernetic, right) red
HAIR: Black

ABILITIES/ACCESSORIES: Initially simply a young man of great skill, exceptional fitness, and advanced weapon training, Kane was fitted by Department K with super-strong mechanical limbs, a bionic left eye with remote/infrared vision, sonic resonators, plasma and electrical dischargers, and eventually holographic projectors; he carried advanced firearms and an energy-projecting ion blade as necessary. In the fortieth century, his cyborg arms were replaced by synthetic-organic liquid metal capable of self-repair, malleability to create shields or repel bullets, and generating detachable hands which he could launch and control remotely. Near the end of his life he was equipped with a cybernetic right eye, enhanced speed, and the ability to transform his hands into guns, blades, or claws. He could download new powers such as toxic emission and metal control as necessary.

Kang

REAL NAME: Nathaniel Richards
ALIASES: Blue Man, Victor Timely, Victor Timely Jr., Victor Timely III, Blue Totem, Scarlet Centurion, Rama-Tut, King of Kings, Master of Men, Lord of the Seven Suns; possibly Iron Lad
IDENTITY: Known to authorities
OCCUPATION: Conqueror; adventurer, pharaoh, others
CITIZENSHIP: Earth-6311 (aka Other-Earth), 31st and 40th centuries
PLACE OF BIRTH: Earth-6311, 31st century
KNOWN RELATIVES: Ramades (son), Marcus Kang I-XXIII (sons, deceased); unidentified mother and father; Nathaniel and Cassandra Richards, their unidentified son, and the matriarch of the Eyriennes (ancestors); Tara (Huntara), Reed Richards (Mr. Fantastic), Franklin and Valeria Richards, various Eyriennes (common ancestry); Victor von Doom (alleged ancestor); Kristoff Vernard (alleged common ancestry); Immortus, Iron Lad, Rama-Tut, Scarlet Centurion and numerous other alternate dimensional counterparts and their offspring
GROUP AFFILIATION: Leads massive interstellar army; former member of the Council of Kangs, Cross-Time Kangs, Legion Accursed; gathered a Legion of the Unliving and the Anachronauts; formerly worshipped by the people of ancient Egypt
EDUCATION: Schooled in robotics
FIRST APPEARANCE: (Rama-Tut) Fantastic Four #19 (1963); (Kang) Avengers #8 (1964)

HISTORY: Nathaniel Richards was born in the alternate timeline Earth-6311, aka Other-Earth. In this reality, the Dark Ages never occurred and technology developed without interruption. Their timeline having diverged circa 300 AD, Other-Earth's people made their first moon landing in 900 AD, which became the first year of their new calendar. After a peaceful era during which a lunar colony was established, a Great War between the colony and Earth destroyed the moon and plunged Other-Earth back into a primitive state. Nathaniel Richards of Earth-616 (mainstream Earth), attempting time travel, reached Other-Earth and settled there; he used his knowledge to help rebuild that world and married Cassandra, daughter of the Matriarch of the Eyriennes, who were women dwelling in the mountaintop city known as the Eyrie, and he became known as both the Warlord (erroneously) and the Benefactor.

Approximately 1900 years later, in the calendar year 3000, Nathaniel Richards' descendant and namesake was born into an age of peace and enlightenment thanks to his ancestor's efforts. At age 16, the young robotics student Nathaniel had developed a working Growing Man stimuloid model when his throat was slit by a bully, Morgan, and he was hospitalized for a year. Recovering, he studied cross-dimensional recordings of the heroic age of Earth-616 (mainstream Earth), brought to his reality by the Benefactor. At age 25, Nathaniel discovered the Benefactor's citadel, actually his former fortress, and discovered a long-sealed chamber, which contained part of a time machine and plans for its operation.

Following encounters with alternate reality Fantastic Fours seeking to thwart his future self, which faded from his mind, Nathaniel remained a man of adventure in a time of complacency. Seeing the machine as his means of escaping his life of boredom and misery, Nathaniel spent years rebuilding and redesigning the time machine for his needs. He planned to loot various time periods for weaponry and technology while making his base in ancient Egypt. To play upon the ancient Egyptians' religious beliefs, he created a sphinx-like idol to house the time machine and traveled back to Earth-616's Egypt circa 2950 BC. The ship malfunctioned and crashed, blinding and stranding him there, but his technology allowed him to subjugate the natives. As Pharaoh Rama-Tut, his vision restored, he ruled as a god for a decade, during which he encountered Samira, Mistress of the Nile, who became his enemy; Pharaoh Amenhotep, whom he imprisoned within a pyramid where Amenhotep consumed blood to survive, eventually becoming a vampire-creature; and time-travelers such as Killpower and the Genetix team. Circa 2945, Rama-Tut sired an illegitimate son, Ramades, with a slave woman. Eventually, a struggle with the Fantastic Four, which also involved the young En Sabah Nur (later Apocalypse), the moon god Khonshu, and modern-era heroes Dr. Strange and the Avengers, forced Rama to flee that time period in his now operative time machine.

En route to the future, a "time storm" diverted Rama to the modern era, where he rescued a space-lost Dr. Doom and passed himself off as Doom's possible future self (though speculation regards Doom as Kang's possible ancestor; possibly because Nathaniel Richards allegedly sired Kristoff Vernard, who was believed to be Dr. Doom for a time). Damaged by the time storm, Rama-Tut's control module skipped several years into the future and crashed in Egypt, where he tried to force fellow time-traveler Blaquesmith to aid him but was defeated by the mutant Cable, though Rama managed to launch back into the time stream. Inspired by Doom, he took the armored identity of the Scarlet Centurion, traveled to another timeline (Earth-689) and duped its Avengers into neutralizing all their fellow heroes so he could rule; but he was defeated by the visiting Avengers of Earth-616 and cast outside time. He would later learn of alternate realities diverged from this event in which the Scarlet Centurion conquered Earth (Earth-8110) or used the X-Men as his pawns (Earth-98702). Diverging subsequent to the Earth-689 adventure, another Scarlet Centurion conquered 40th century Earth-712 ("Earth-S," home of the Squadron Supreme).

PRE-RAMA TUT NATHANIEL

Art by Jim Cheung with Carlos Pacheco & Gavin Curtis (insets)

Richards sought to return to his native time, but temporal disruptions hurled him into Earth-6311's 40th century, a bleak world decimated by global wars. Unable to escape to a more hospitable era, he assumed the name Kang the Conqueror, set himself up as a warlord, bent the barbaric people to his will and transformed them into an army. Kang conquered the planet, sparing only the tiny kingdom of Carelius due to his interest in the king's daughter, Ravonna. Kang's life became progressively non-linear, as each foray in time produced at least one divergent-time-stream counterpart; it is extremely difficult to identify which Kang counterpart was involved with each encounter. Further, Kang's past incarnations each spawned numerous divergent realities and selves throughout their adventures (see Rama-Tut, Scarlet Centurion, Iron Lad).

Conquering everything within 100 light years of Earth, Kang next attacked his ancestor's native world in the modern age of marvels, but the Avengers forced him to flee. Seeking a new power base, Kang established himself in 1901 AD as Victor Timely, a brilliant inventor and industrialist who founded the city of Timely, Wisconsin, became its first mayor, and transformed it into a technological marvel over the next century. Over time, "Victor" appeared to age and be replaced by his son and his grandson in turn (Kang in new guises); in 1929, as Victor Timely Jr. he recruited Phineas Horton into Timely Industries, and in 1980, "Victor Timely III" developed a prominent computer company. The city also housed a portal to Kang's base Chronopolis (created by one of the counterparts whose memories he now possessed) where he gathered warriors from various eras to serve as his strike force, the Anachronauts. Still seething over his defeat at the Avengers' hands, Kang sent a Spider-Man robot (Timespinner) to battle them, though it was destroyed by the real Spider-Man (Peter Parker). Kang also traveled to 6th century Camelot and defeated a Merlin imposter (later Merlin Demonspawn), intent on creating an alternate reality in which his Britain would conquer the globe, preventing the formation of the Avengers; but he was defeated by the time-traveling Thing and Human Torch, apparently sent by Uatu the Watcher. Kang next joined a mass of villains attacking the wedding of Reed and Sue Richards, unknowingly drawn there by Dr. Doom's Emotion-Charger device.

Returning to the 40th century, Kang completed his conquest of the Milky Way galaxy, crushing empires like the Universal Church of Truth. He even invaded and conquered other dimensions, such as Kosmos, where he gained technology to create his powerful Growing Men. Kang then brought the Avengers forward in time to Carelius' kingdom, intending to subjugate them or defeat them in front of Ravonna. When both the Avengers and Ravonna defied him, the furious Kang easily conquered the small kingdom; however, when he attempted to force Ravonna to marry him, he caused unrest in his troops for failing to follow his own edict of slaying all conquered rulers. Kang's troops, led by General Baltag, turned on him, but he allied with the Avengers to defeat them. Impressed by Kang's risking his life for her, Ravonna leapt in the path of a blast from the defeated Baltag, saving Kang, but apparently dying in his place.

RAMA-TUT

Art by Paul Ryan

The devastated Kang placed Ravonna in stasis while he sought to restore her; for the 18 months, he spent half of each day mourning his greatest failure. The cosmic Grandmaster challenged Kang to a contest of champions, offering him the power of life or death, with which he could revive Ravonna. Using the Avengers as pawns, Kang was victorious — but at the last second, he instead chose the power of death, intending to slay the Avengers. Foiled by the Black Knight (Dane Whitman), Kang had to live with the knowledge that he had squandered his chance to save Ravonna. Perturbed at having lost and feeling sympathy for Ravonna, the Grandmaster removed Ravonna from stasis, replaced her with a pseudo-organic doppelganger, revived her, and told her of Kang's betrayal. Kang later tried to use the Hulk to destroy Bruce Banner's ancestor to prevent the Avengers from ever forming, but the Hulk foiled this plot. Kang then sent a robot double of himself to capture the Avengers during a war with rival time lord Zarrko the Tomorrow Man. Still aching from his lost love, Kang gathered Ravonnas from other timelines, but even the most compliant of them could not satisfy him, as they were not the Ravonna from his past; he slowly ceased to care about Ravonna.

One of Kang's most relentless campaigns was his quest for the Celestial Madonna, a woman fated to give birth to the most powerful being in the universe. Wanting to be that being's father, Kang narrowed the Madonna's identity to aged sorceress Agatha Harkness, enigmatic martial artist Mantis, and the Scarlet Witch, abducting all three. Rama-Tut, actually Kang's own future self, arrived to help the Avengers thwart his plot. Mantis was finally revealed as the Madonna, and when Kang could not claim her, he tried to kill her; but his fatal blast was intercepted by the Swordsman (Jacques DuQuesne), who died instead. Kang and Rama-Tut were then pulled into Limbo by Immortus, a potential future self of both men, but Kang imprisoned Immortus and used his technology to create the Legion of the Unliving, a team of reportedly deceased pawns

THE KANG TIMELINE

Date (Temporal Order)	2950-2940 BC	2930-2920 BC	6th century AD	1873 AD	Jan 1, 1901 AD	1929 AD	1980 AD	Shortly before Modern Era
Chronological order in Kang's life	4	35	16	24	11	13	14	25
Synopsis	First reign of Rama-Tut.	Second reign of Rama-Tut.	Kang travels to Camelot.	Kang establishes empire, foiled by time-traveling Avengers and cowboy heroes.	Kang establishes the city of Timely, Wisconsin, and the palace of Chronopolis.	"Victor Timely, Jr." recruits Phineas Horton to Timely Industries.	"Victor Timely III" develops prominent computer company.	Encounters First Line.
Issue(s)	Fantastic Four #19 (Oct. 1963); Dr. Strange #53 (June 1982); West Coast Avengers #20-23 (May-Aug 1987); Rise of Apocalypse #3-4 (Dec. 1996; Jan. 1997)	Giant-Size Avengers #2 (Nov. 1974); Avengers Forever #9 (Aug. 1999)	Strange Tales #134 (July, 1964)	Avengers Forever #4-6 (Mar.-May, 1999); Avengers #141-143 (Nov-Dec. 1975, Jan. 1976)	Avengers Annual #21 (1992)	Avengers Annual #21 (1992)	Avengers Annual #21 (1992)	Marvel: Lost Generation #10 (May, 2000)

drawn from past eras. The Avengers defeated the Legion, and Kang fled. Kang soon returned, and he made four jumps to the past around roughly the same moment in time, creating three other divergent selves to occupy the Avengers while he tried to abduct Mantis at her wedding, but the divergents were defeated, and Immortus foiled Kang by substituting a Space Phantom as his captive.

Art by John Buscema

Kang next made a base in Tombstone, Arizona, circa 1873 AD, intending to use it as a stepping stone to conquer the modern age. Opposed by cowboy heroes Kid Colt (Blaine Colt), the Phantom Rider (Lincoln Slade), Rawhide Kid (Johnny Clay), Ringo Kid, and Two-Gun Kid (Matt Liebowitz), as well as time-traveling Avengers, Kang disintegrated when his force field shorted out in battle with Thor; however, a fail-safe device transported Kang's consciousness to an alternate body, as it had during many other near-death experiences.

Though taking place in rapid succession in the modern era, the planning involved with the Celestial Madonna and Old West agendas accounted for ten years of Kang's life. From a base near the end of time, Kang sought the power of a reality-altering Cosmic Cube, but he was instead trapped within the Cube by Cable. Kang later conquered the alternate 40th century Earth-791014, in which Earth served as an amusement park for the solar system's other planets' colonies. From this base, Kang facilitated an attempt by the Inuit (Eskimo) Aningan Kenojuak to reclaim Captain America as the "God in the Ice" worshipped by his people years before while he was in suspended animation. At some point Kang encountered the First Line, a team of heroes preceding the Avengers. The virtually omnipotent Beyonder brought Kang and other super-villains to his "Battleworld," pitting them against a similarly gathered group of heroes. Suspecting Dr. Doom might betray them, Kang blasted him, but Doom survived and had the robot Ultron incinerate Kang. Shortly thereafter, having briefly usurped the Beyonder's power, Doom restored Kang to life. Kang was subsequently recruited into Mephisto's Legion Accursed in a failed effort to slay the Beyonder.

Returning to his 40th century base, Kang found it ravaged by rebels loyal to Baltag. He continued his empire's expansion off-planet, conquering the Shi'ar Imperium; but to recover his base on Earth, he sought out a Growing Man stored in the modern era and battled Thor, who banished him to Limbo. There Kang chanced across Tenebrae, the stronghold of Limbo's master Immortus, containing Immortus' apparent corpse. There Kang observed a view screen showing the struggle in which Ravonna was blasted by Baltag. Distraught by the scene Kang groped at the controls, causing a divergence (Reality-8657) in which he teleported Ravonna to his side, saving her from death, though in that reality, his counterpart met death from Baltag's assault. Kang soon discovered that there was an abundance of divergent versions of himself and he initiated a plot to eliminate them all, despite Ravonna's efforts to turn him from violence. Unwittingly manipulated by Immortus, Kang soon formed the Council of Kangs, choosing a few of his most capable counterparts as allies, and began eliminating redundant Kangs from each alternate reality. One of these divergents had sought to destroy all realities save Reality-9892 where he hoped to wed that Earth's Ravonna; but after inadvertently slaying that Ravonna, he was swiftly eliminated by the Council. One Kang prepared robot duplicates to replace the slain counterparts so that he could control them and thus rule the empires of every Kang in existence. At the same time, Kang also re-took his 40th century base via his Growing Man. After the Council had finished wiping out the rest of their counterparts, the "prime" Kang slew the rest of the Council, involving the Avengers in the final struggle.

Art by Rich Yanizeski

VICTOR TIMELY

Immortus then appeared, explained that he was Kang's future self (though many of the Avengers already knew this), and showed Kang a psyche-globe containing the memories of all of the slain divergent Kangs, claiming that its power made him supreme ruler of Limbo. Kang tore the globe from Immortus' hands, only to go mad as the minds of all of the other Kangs merged with his. The last Kang — now every Kang, since he possessed all of his counterparts' memories — fled into Limbo. To save himself, Kang used his helmet's temporal circuitry to create an additional divergence/counterpart, dividing his madness between two Kangs. One made his way to Chronopolis (created by one of the counterparts whose memories he now possessed) to recuperate, while the other, still addled, was recruited by the Cross-Time Kangs, a group of beings who had defeated or slain alternate Kangs and usurped the Kang identity. The Cross-Time Kangs

Modern Era	Modern Era	Modern Era	Modern Era	Modern Era	Modern Era	Modern Era	Modern Era	Modern Era
5	6	7	7.1	8	10	15	17	20
Briefly stranded by a time-storm, Rama-Tut rescues a space-lost Dr. Doom, tricking Doom into thinking that they might be the same man at different points in his life.	Rama-Tut Encounters Cable.	Scarlet Centurion dupes alternate Avengers; banished extratemporally by Avengers of Earth-616.	Divergent Scarlet Centurions formed.	Heads back to his future, overshoots to 40th century.	Kang first encounters Avengers, forced to flee.	Kang sends Spider-Man robot (Timespinner) against Avengers.	Kang joins villains attacking Richards wedding.	Kang uses Hulk in failed time-traveling plot to destroy Banner's ancestor during World War I.
Fantastic Four Annual #2 (1964)	Cable #57 (August 1998)	Avengers Annual #2 (Sept. 1968)	What If? #29 (Oct. 1981); others	Giant-Size Avengers #2 (Nov. 1974)	Avengers #8 (Sept. 1964)	Avengers #11 (Dec. 1964)	Fantastic Four Annual #3 (1965)	Incredible Hulk #135 (Jan. 1971)

CHRONOPOLIS
Art by Todd Smith

led Kang to believe that they represented a higher order, composed of various Kangs who had each survived a local "Kang war" within their own Council of Kangs, but this has since been disproved. This divergent Kang (identified as Kang-123488.23497 by the Cross-Time Kangs, though he took the name Kang Fred), along with the Cross-Time Kangs' leader (Chairman Kang) and another Kang (from Earth-Mesozoic-24), learned of a plot by "Kang-Nebula" (actually a power-hungry Ravonna) to obtain the "ultimate weapon" contained within the Time Bubble, a period of time in Earth-8810 surrounded by an impassable temporal barrier. This trio of Kangs followed Kang-Nebula and her mind-controlled Avengers pawns into the Time Bubble, where they were cast into the temporal vortex surrounding it. Clinging to existence, the divergent Kang sent his Growing Man to help foil the demonic invasion Inferno, which threatened to destroy life on Earth. When Kang-Nebula later manipulated the Fantastic Four into penetrating the Time Bubble, the trio of Cross-Time Kangs attempted to stop her from obtaining the weapon, but were either destroyed or incapacitated.

The divergent Kang was incinerated by the Human Torch under the control of Kang-Nebula.

Taking control of Chronopolis, the "prime" Kang sought revenge on Mantis in the modern era, joining forces with the alien Cotati race, who sought to keep Mantis' child, the Celestial Messiah, for themselves. Mantis was assisted by the Fantastic Four and the Silver Surfer, but the Cotati escaped with the child, and Mantis sent her spirit after them.

CROSS-TIME KANGS
Art by John Buscema

Kang later joined Dr. Doom during the "Infinity War" in seeking to wrest a set of reality-altering Cosmic Containment Units from the Magus, the dark side of Adam Warlock. Kang then took over the Cross-Time Kangs, learned an assassin was stalking him, and exposed his would-be killer as Ravonna, now calling herself the Terminatrix. Intrigued by her warrior nature, Kang battled her, but in a reversal of past events, sacrificed himself to save her from an assault by the Avengers. Overcoming her hatred for Kang, Ravonna impersonated him and took over the Cross-Time Kangs, during which time she was manipulated by Revelation, her alleged own future self, who sought to guide Ravonna into following her life path. When Chronopolis was attacked by the immensely powerful temporal entity Alioth, Ravonna revived Kang, and with the aid of the Avengers they sacrificed the Cross-Time Kangs, using their energy to imprison Alioth once again.

Ravonna and Kang were at last reunited, and she posed as Victor Timely's fiancée, Rebecca Tourmenet, for a time before they returned to Chronopolis to rule side by side. After encountering Sue Richards regarding the fate of her then-missing husband, Kang was temporarily snatched out of time by the powerful being Akhenaten of Earth-4321, who sought to eliminate any threat time-travelers who might pose to his past. However, Kang, now almost sixty, grew weary of administrative matters. Missing the days when he was worshipped in a small land, Kang returned to ancient Egypt circa 2930 BC as Rama-Tut, and smashed his chrono-sphere. As Rama-Tut, he was also briefly imprisoned by Akhenaten, but otherwise spent ten years benevolently enjoying his people's adulation. In 2920 BC, he encountered the Avengers, who had been trapped in the past by a time machine that could only travel backwards in time. He was unable to help them as he had destroyed all of his technology, so they went further into the past and faced his earlier, more hostile self in 2940 BC, where Rama's enemy Khonshu helped the Avengers back to their own time.

Determined not to become Immortus (whose subtle manipulations he despised), the elder

SCARLET CENTURION
Art by Paul Ryan

Modern Era	Modern Era	Modern Era	Modern Era	Modern Era	Modern Era	Modern Era	Modern Era	Modern Era
21	23/34	26	27	29.3	30	31	39	43
Kang sends robot duplicate to battle Zarrko the Tomorrow Man, involving Spider-Man and Iron Man.	Kang seeks to father the Celestial Messiah, defeated with aid of newly awakened Rama-Tut, slays Swordsman (DuQuesne), attempts to abduct Mantis during her wedding.	Kang transported to Battleworld, fights on side of the villains; joined Legion Accursed.	Kang battles Thor, cast into Limbo.	Divergent Kang sends Growing Man to help foil demonic plots during Inferno.	Kang seeks vengeance on Mantis.	Kang joins Dr. Doom in quest for Cosmic Containment Units.	Kang joins with Libra, Supreme Intelligence, and Avengers to oppose Immortus and Time Keepers.	Kang and Marcus XXIII (Scarlet Centurion) lead armada from Damocles Base, conquering Earth. Ultimately defeated, slays Marcus for betrayal.
Marvel Team-Up #9-11 (May-July 1973)	Avengers #128-129 (Oct-Nov. 1974); Giant-Size Avengers #2 (Nov. 1974); Giant-Size Avengers #4 (1975)	Secret Wars #1-4 (May-Aug. 1984); Thor #383 (Sept. 1987); Secret Wars #11-12 (Mar-Apr. 1985); Secret Wars II #7 (Jan. 1986)	Thor #140 (May 1967)	Avengers #300 (Feb. 1989)	Fantastic Four #323-325 (Feb-Apr. 1989)	Infinity War #1-5 (June-Oct. 1992)	Avengers Forever #9 (Aug. 1999), 1 (Dec. 1998)	Avengers #41-49 (June-Dec. 2001, Jan-Feb. 2002); Avengers #51-54 (Apr-July, 2002)

Art by Mike Gustovich

Rama-Tut tried to break the cycle by placing himself in suspended animation with the aid of his wizard Shamaz, reviving in the modern era (assisted, as planned, by an unwitting Swordsman) to battle his past Kang self during the Celestial Madonna struggle. Failing to change the course of events, Rama used devices granted by Immortus to re-enter the time stream; feeling like a powerless failure, he revisited his accomplishments through the centuries, but all seemed meaningless to him now. Resigned to his fate, the now 75-year-old Rama headed for Limbo; however, upon glimpsing a chrono-flash of Immortus bowing to the powerful Time-Keepers, he was infuriated by the idea of becoming anyone's lap-dog, and vowed to overcome his destiny (though a divergent elder Rama-Tut did settle in Limbo and eventually became the initial incarnation of Immortus). Rama-Tut returned to Chronopolis, resumed his Kang identity and ignored Ravonna as he turned his rivals against each other, using Alioth to devastate the Time Variance Authority and setting the Delubric Consortium against Revelation. He then destroyed the mind-transfer fail-safe device he had so often used to cheat death, feeling that it took the risk — and thus the enjoyment — out of conflict. After a brief battle with the X-Men and an enterprising starship crew, Kang formed an alliance with Libra (Gustav Brandt), the Kree Supreme Intelligence and the Avengers against Immortus and the Time-Keepers. Ravonna, the Anachronauts and even Immortus were apparently slain and Chronopolis was destroyed; but when the Time-Keepers tried to eliminate Kang's threat by forcing him to evolve into the more passive Immortus, Kang resisted so forcefully that he diverged a new Immortus while remaining Kang himself. Kang then destroyed the Time-Keepers (who had been weakened by the divergent chronal energy backlash).

Renewed by this victory, which left his future uncharted, Kang engineered a series of successors, choosing multiple ideal mates to create exceptional warriors, each of whom he named Marcus. These children were sent back in time and trained from birth to be warriors worthy of inheriting Kang's empire. Following a failed effort to conquer the realm Otherworld, Kang, alongside Marcus XXIII (outfitted as the Scarlet Centurion), used Damocles Base, his massive armada, and alliances with various criminal forces (including rogue Atlanteans and Deviants) to conquer Earth-616; but the Avengers led a rebellion that ultimately defeated and imprisoned Kang. Marcus freed Kang in hopes of restoring their dominion, but Kang knew that Marcus had held back during the war more than once because of his attraction to Avengers member Warbird. Unable to forgive this betrayal, Kang slew Marcus. Disheartened, Kang told his computer to postpone development of Marcus XXIV.

Apparently unnerved and not heeding his knowledge of creating divergent selves, Kang attempted to manipulate his own past, saving his 16-year-old self from the attack by Morgan. Kang granted young Nathaniel a suit of neuro-kinetic armor and provided a glimpse into his future as Kang. Horrified by his ruthless, destructive future self, Nathaniel rejected Kang and used his armor to escape to modern day Earth, seeking the Avengers so they could help him defeat Kang. Finding the Avengers disbanded, Nathaniel, now going by Iron Lad, gathered together a replacement group who called themselves the Young Avengers. Kang confronted this group and convinced Avengers founders Captain America and Iron Man to hand Iron Lad over to him to avoid further temporal divergence. In the ensuing struggle, Iron Lad apparently slew Kang but then returned to his native era to fulfill his destiny as Kang to restore the damaged timeline. As Kang, Iron Lad continued to monitor the Young Avengers from an undisclosed future location. Iron Lad's armor, which retained replicated impressions of Nathaniel's brain patterns, emotions and memories, subsequently joined the Young Avengers as the new Vision. It remains to be seen whether this young Kang will somehow follow Kang's early history and go on to become Kang or whether sufficient changes have occurred to diverge a new reality.

NOTE: *Differences between the history of Earth-6311 and Earth-616, as well as differing calendars in different realms, and damage to records during periods of massive warfare, have led to some inconsistency in the dating of the time periods of both Kang and Ravonna.*

Most of the multiverse's realities have been visited by Kangs, though it is nearly impossible to identify which is which or when they diverged. Since the sole existing Kang slew and then absorbed the memories of all other Kang counterparts, presumably from both past and future timelines, any adventure of any Kang is part of the "prime" Kang's past. Certain Kang encounters cannot be fit into the prime Kang's chronology and are likely from other counterparts (presumably those slain by the Council of Kangs), while others are just of uncertain chronology.

A Kang guided the 1958 Agents of Atlas-7901 to recover the frozen Captain America (Steve Rogers) and recruit him and Kang as members. In 1959, the original Agents were lost in a traveling black hole. Rogers became the US president, outlawed nonregistered superhumans, and achieved peace. As his last act, Rogers nominated Kang as leader of the World Command. Earth-46991 diverged from -7901 and there the Avengers, Spider-Man, Wolverine and Storm exposed Kang's plot to Agents of Atlas and helped thwart Kang. On Earth-57780, a Kang plotted to foil the USA's Bicentennial celebration, traveling to various points

Modern Era	Modern Era <Reality-4321>	Modern Era <Reality-4321>	15-20 years in the Future (Earth-8810)	3000 <Other Earth Calender>	3016 <Other Earth Calender>	3025 <Other Earth Calender>	40th century <Other Earth Calender>	40th century <Other Earth Calender>
44	34	36	29.2	1	2	3	9	18
Kang tracks down Iron Lad, apparently killed and replaced by him.	Kang snatched out of time and imprisoned by Akhenaten.	Rama-Tut snatched out of time and imprisoned by Akhenaten.	Divergent Kang involved with Time Bubble.	Birth of Nathaniel Richards.	Nathaniel Richards develops Growing Man simuloid model, throat slit by Morgan.	Nathaniel Richards discovers the fortress of Richards the Benefactor, travels to 2950 BC for first period as Rama-Tut.	Takes identity of Kang, begins to carve empire.	Kang summons Avengers, conquers Ravonna's kingdom; Ravonna slain by Baltag.
Young Avengers #2-6 (May-Nov. 2005)	Marvel Universe: The End #2 (May 2003)	Marvel Universe: The End #2 (May 2003)	Avengers #297 (Nov. 1988); Fantastic Four #338 (Mar. 1990)		Young Avengers #2 (May 2005)	Fantastic Four #19 (Oct. 1963)	Avengers #8 (Sept. 1964)	Avengers #23-24 (Dec. 1965; Jan. 1966)

in US history to disrupt them, but was thwarted by Captain America, Dr. Strange and Spider-Man. The same Kang later briefly launched the White House into orbit and tried to take over the US before being defeated by Spider-Man and the Fantastic Four; conquered 31st century Earth-770724 until Spider-Man-57780 drove him off; and summoned Spider-Man and Mr. Fantastic into his future to recover glowing rocks from different time periods to save his Ravonna. On Earth-96801, a Kang nuked New York City but he and his lieutenants (Abomination, Baron Mordo, Cobra) later joined with Namor and the Inhumans to repel Galactus. On an undefined Earth, Kang sent mind-controlled X-Men after the Avengers; after this plot's failure, Kang traveled to that reality's World War II era hoping to eliminate Captain America to prevent the Avengers from ever becoming a threat, but Kang abandoned this effort after Cap showed him other realities proving that even without Cap the Avengers would still oppose him.

KANG'S TIME SHIP

Art by Eliot R. Brown

The Council of Kangs included the eventual "prime" Kang, as well as a Kang who was slain upon investigating the prime Kang's chambers and learning the extent of his manipulations, as well as one other, who had diverged from the prime Kang following the first encounter with the Avengers and who the prime Kang manipulated into battling the Avengers in Limbo. Ravonna tried to dissuade this other Kang against perpetuating the violence, but he attempted to kill the prime Kang and was slain by his own booby-trapped weapon. Those Kangs eliminated by the Council of Kangs include: the Kang who slew the Avengers-267 via a nuclear bomb that led to nuclear war, killing everyone else on Earth; the three divergents created by the prime Kang during the Celestial Madonna affair; the Kang who manipulated the Avengers-8499 into altering their past to prevent their becoming viable opposition to him; the Kang who tried to similarly manipulate the Avengers-8503 but was foiled by Immortus; the Kang who inadvertently slew Ravonna-9892 (this Kang had terminated realities-9881, -9891 and -98702 with his Time's Arrows weapons, intending to rule Earth-98701, a world without super heroes, alongside Ravonna); and Kangs of other divergent realities, such as Earth-9811 and -9916. On Earth-86501, Kang was killed during his effort to nuke the Avengers failed. On Earth-8657, Kang was slain when the prime Kang pulled Ravonna to Limbo to save her. A Kang joined with Ultron (59th incarnation) against the few surviving Avengers and their children on Earth-9511 but was slain by the Wasp. After the death of Kang on Earth-9528, that reality's Cybermancer and Tony Stark remade the world based on Kang's designs into a polluted world of cyborgs.

Known Cross-Time Kangs include Chairman Kang, Kang Cobra, Kang Kaseo, Kang Kong, Kang Orphan (aka Kanglet), Kang Ransom,

Art by Jack Kirby

40th century <Other Earth Calender>	40th century <Other Earth Calender>	40th century <Other Earth Calender>	Citadel at the End of Time	Chronopolis	Chronopolis	Chronopolis	Chronopolis	Chronopolis
19	22	42	41	12	32	33	38	40
Grandmaster challenges Kang with prize of power of life or death; squanders power in vain attempt to slay Avengers.	Kang summons variant Ravonnas.	Kang engineers series of Marcus successors.	Kang assists against Immortus and Time-Keepers. Diverges self (Kang) from Immortus, destroys Keepers.	Kang establishes Chronopolis.	Kang battles Terminatrix/Ravonna, sacrifices self to save her, left in stasis.	Kang revived by Ravonna, teams with Avengers, traps Alioth; Cross-Time Kangs destroyed. Kang rules beside Ravonna for a time.	Resumes role of Kang.	Kang flees as Immortus destroys Chronopolis.
Avengers #69-71 (Oct-Dec. 1969)	Avengers Annual #21 (1992)	Avengers #45 (Oct. 2001)	Avengers Forever #1-4 (Dec. 1998; Jan.-Mar. 1999); Avengers Forever #9-12 (Aug., Oct., Nov. 1999; Feb. 2000)	Avengers Annual #21 (1992)	Avengers Annual #21 (1992)	Avengers: Terminatrix Objective #1-4 (Sep-Dec. 1993)	Avengers Forever #9 (Aug. 1999)	Avengers Forever #3 (Feb. 1999)

Kang Raulex, Kang Swaatch, Kang of Earth-Mesozoic-24 (a reptilian humanoid who had slain a Kang and usurped his armor in the past), Kang Nebula (Ravonna, later the Terminatrix) and the divergent Kang (aka Kang-123488.23497 and Kang Fred) split from the prime Kang after going mad from absorbing all realities' Kangs' memories. Others suspected of being Cross-Time Kangs include Kangaroo the Conqueror, an enemy of Earth-8311 (Larval Earth)'s Scavengers, and the giant Keng, who fought the British super-team Caliburn on Earth-924.

Kang himself once merged with a distant cosmos' time-traveler to become Kang the Time-Conqueror, a version of which persisted in reality-9602. In another, briefly existing merged reality, Kang vied with a time lord over the Chronal Egg. "Pope Immortus" (aka Kang the Immortal) of Earth-9997 (Earth X) is believed to be a delusional or poser Kang, though this might have been Immortus himself simply manipulating others for unknown purposes. The skeleton of Immortus discovered by Kang remains unexplained; it may just have been a farce, part of Immortus' plans to manipulate Kang. Norse god Loki-616 once created a magical composite Kang/Rama-Tut/Scarlet Centurion/Immortus, which is not believed to actually be a divergent self. Another Kang fought the Avengers and Fantastic Four of Franklin Richards' Counter-Earth before being converted to energy by that world's Loki. This Kang was presumably a creation of Franklin's, though it could be a divergent Kang who had entered this pocket dimension for his own reasons. A number of beings have impersonated Kang, including the cosmic-powered Korvac, to dupe Captain America into helping him gain massive power from a Cosmic Cube and Galactus' worldship; and a Mindless One that encountered the Hulk on Nightmare Island. A renegade TVA Chronomonitor fled to the past of Earth-20051 where he posed as Rama-Tut before the TVA recaptured him. On Earth-8386, a Kang robot (presumably placed there by the prime Kang during the Council's Kang-cleansing) exhorted the world's warriors to constant battle to achieve the title Hero of the Day.

HEIGHT: 6'3" **EYES:** Brown
WEIGHT: 230 lbs. **HAIR:** Brown

ABILITIES/ACCESSORIES: Like others from his native era, Kang ages at a slightly slower rate than modern humanity and is more resistant to radiation's effects, though he can be harmed by concentrated doses. He is an expert in travel through and manipulation of time, and has mastered his future's advanced technology. He is an expert strategist, a veteran of armed and unarmed combat, and has an indomitable will to succeed through struggle.

Kang's full-body armor (composed of an unidentified future metal) enables him to lift 5 tons, and can project a gravito-electromagnetic force field around him that is extendable up to twenty feet and can shield him from even a direct nuclear strike. The suit has its own self-contained atmosphere, food supply and waste disposal system. Its weapons include anti-graviton particle projectors in his gauntlets, rendering weightless objects up to 2.2 tons; concussive force blasters equivalent to up to several thousand pounds of TNT; circuitry accessing his ship's time machine (or his other such resources), allowing him an "automatic recall" of a few seconds as well as enabling him to peer into various timelines; and various other weapons, regularly updated. Kang formerly used technology that transferred his mind into an alternate body upon the point of death.

Kang typically carries various weapons, such as an anti-matter defense screen generator, a "vibration-ray" projector, an electromagnetic field-amplifier, neutrino-ray warhead missile launcher (handgun size), electrical paralysis generator, nerve gas sprayer, and a "molecular expander," which seemingly enlarges molecules to giant-sized projectiles. Kang commands a vast armada of warriors from across the galaxy of his future era, armed with advanced weaponry. He uses numerous robots, most notably his Growing-Man stimuloids, packed with the "Growth Pollen" of the world Kosmos, which causes them to grow in size and strength by absorbing kinetic energy; this Growth Pollen uses the same energy accessed via the size-changing "Pym Particles" discovered by Dr. Henry Pym.

Kang's primary base in 40th century Earth-6311 is the Center, but he also maintains a secret dwelling in the realm known only as Purgatory, as well as strongholds in various alternate realties; his former base Chronopolis, powered by the Heart of Forever, served as a crossroads into virtually every era in human history, but lay just out of phase with the time stream and was therefore undetectable. Its palace and inhabitants were unaffected by temporal divergence or the passage of time. Kang formerly employed a 20' long space-worthy vehicle housing his time machine, which utilized an undetermined energy to generate a chronal-displacement inertial field that could reach all eras of all timelines by accessing the transtemporal realm of Limbo. Kang has used a number of other vessels, such as his Sphinx ship and Damocles Base, an immense sword-shaped orbiting headquarters, which allowed Kang to temporarily conquer all of Earth.

*KANG IS A TELEPORTER
**YELLOW BARS REPRESENT ARMOR ENHANCEMENT RATINGS

Limbo	Limbo	Limbo	Limbo	Limbo	Limbo
28	29	29.1	37	37.1	23/34
Kang discovers seeming corpse of Immortus, summons alternate Ravonna, founds Council of Kangs, slays all other Kangs, absorbs their memories.	Kang diverges himself into two to split the madness.	divergent Kang recruited into Cross-Time Kangs, opposes Kang-Nebula.	Rama-Tut wanders through past, resolved to oppose destiny of becoming Immortus.	divergent Rama-Tut relocates to Limbo, becomes Immortus.	Encounters Immortus, creates Legion of the Unliving.
Avengers #267-269 (May-July 1986)	Avengers Forever #9 (Aug. 1999)	Avengers #291-296 (May-Oct. 1998)	Avengers Forever #9 (Aug. 1999)	Thor #282 (Aug. 1979)	Avengers #131-132 (Jan.-Feb. 1975) Giant-Size Avengers #3 (1975)

KANGAROO

HISTORY: Although gainfully employed as an interior decorator, Brian Hibbs nurtured a lifelong desire to be a super-villain. His fascination inexplicably fixated upon Frank Oliver, aka Kangaroo, a minor adversary of Spider-Man; after Oliver's ignominious death, Hibbs spent years learning Kangaroo's skills. As the new Kangaroo, he worked for the criminal Corporation in Mississippi with moderate success, and then relocated to New York to pick up where his idol left off. Caught up in a robbery spree, he was taken unaware by Spider-Man, who downed him with one punch and laughed about the encounter the rest of the day.

Hibbs escaped police custody and, using half of the wealth left to him in a trust fund, splurged on kangaroo-motif armor, complete with tail and pouch. Seeking a rematch, he was again knocked down by Spider-Man. His armor protected him, but its faulty weapon system collapsed the armor around the embarrassed criminal, whom Spider-Man left for the police. He was soon freed by the Grizzly, another of Spider-Man's less-respected opponents, who teamed with Kangaroo, the Gibbon and the Spot as the Spider-Man Revenge Squad. The group's motivations were divided: while Grizzly and Gibbon craved only payback for past humiliation, Kangaroo and Spot sought straightforward crime. Their dispute-ridden spree was interrupted by Spider-Man, who derided them as "the Legion of Losers," but his overconfidence left him careless enough to be defeated. Kangaroo, irritated by Grizzly's and Gibbon's second thoughts, lashed out at Grizzly, only to knock himself out instead. Spider-Man allowed the repentant pair to escape and hauled Kangaroo and Spot to prison, where Kangaroo exorcised his frustrations by building up his fighting skills and strength, earning the skills he hoped might later give pause to his opponents.

Soon at liberty again, Kangaroo underwent treatment seeking superhuman mutation. When this seemingly failed, he became a professional baseball player as Billy Bob Jenks, but, although he quickly rose to superstar status, he was expelled from the sport after his criminal past came to light. Returning to crime, he was quickly recaptured and imprisoned, his admittedly embarrassing super-villain career probably provoking more concern than he warranted. Incarcerated at the power-dampening Cage, Kangaroo parlayed his unaffected human-level fighting skills into prison respect. However, stress and exertion catalyzed his earlier mutation attempts, increasing his size and strength while retarding his intellect and fostering the delusional belief that he was the late Oliver; his newly increased strength might have approached superhuman level, but in the Cage there was little way to tell and less chance to use it.

When Tombstone, one of Spider-Man's deadlier enemies, was sentenced to the Cage, Kangaroo tried to intimidate him, sparking an intense rivalry, and Kangaroo terrorized his new enemy's prisoner allies. Searching for

REAL NAME: Brian Hibbs
ALIASES: Frank Oliver, Billy Bob Jenks
IDENTITY: Publicly known
OCCUPATION: Criminal; former baseball player, Corporation operative, interior decorator
CITIZENSHIP: Unrevealed, US criminal record
PLACE OF BIRTH: Unrevealed
KNOWN RELATIVES: None
GROUP AFFILIATION: Formerly Spider-Man Revenge Squad, Corporation
EDUCATION: Unrevealed
FIRST APPEARANCE: Cage #13 (1993)

Tombstone's solitary confinement cell, Kangaroo, per Tombstone's plan, became trapped in a heating vent, where he was brutalized by a prison gang, the Cruisers. Months after this ordeal, Kangaroo resurfaced as an active criminal. Alternating between leaping combat and his armored upgrade, he met little success either way. Imprisoned with several other superhumans by insane Al Kravinoff, Kangaroo escaped in a more deranged state than ever before.

HEIGHT: Variable (5'11" to 7'7") **EYES:** Brown
WEIGHT: Variable (206 lbs. to 377 lbs.) **HAIR:** Blond

ABILITIES/ACCESSORIES: The Kangaroo is exceptionally strong and athletic, and especially skilled at leaping; his enhanced growth apparently granted him superhuman strength (perhaps enhanced human). At times he wears armor, equipped with prehensile tail and pouch-cannon, intended to enhance his physique.

POWER GRID	1	2	3	4	5	6	7
INTELLIGENCE	■						
STRENGTH			■/■				
SPEED	■						
DURABILITY			■/■				
ENERGY PROJECTION	■						
FIGHTING SKILLS			■				

Art by Luke Ross (main & right inset) with Leandro Fernandez (left inset)

KARMA

REAL NAME: Xi'an (pronounced Shan) Coy Manh
ALIASES: Impersonated Alexander Flynn while possessed by Shadow King
IDENTITY: Known to authorities
OCCUPATION: Former advisor, teacher, librarian, student, special operative to Nguyen Ngoc Coy, adventurer, executive secretary to Magneto and Professor X
CITIZENSHIP: USA
PLACE OF BIRTH: Central highlands of Vietnam
KNOWN RELATIVES: Unidentified parents (deceased), Tranh Coy Manh (twin brother, apparently deceased), Leong Coy Manh (Template, brother), Nga Coy Manh (Template, sister), Nguyen Ngoc Coy (uncle)
GROUP AFFILIATION: Formerly Xavier Institute faculty (advisor to Alpha Squadron, Paragons and lower school), New Mutants, X-Men (New Mutant graduate team), Hellions (Hellfire Club)
EDUCATION: BA in library studies from University of Chicago; MLIS (Master of Library and Information Science)
FIRST APPEARANCE: Marvel Team-Up #100 (1980)

HISTORY: Xi'an Coy Manh and her three siblings, two sets of twins, were born to an army colonel and a teacher. During Xi'an's youth, in a period of internal strife in Vietnam, her twin brother Tranh was attacked by a soldier — and she unconsciously lashed out with her nascent mutant power, taking possession of the soldier's mind and saving her brother's life. Tranh, attempting the same feat, discovered that he had the same ability — and, to Xi'an's horror, used his newfound power to force the soldier to kill himself. Tranh showed his ability to their uncle, Nguyen Ngoc Coy, a Vietnamese army general with questionable morals. The country's internal strife grew worse, and Xi'an's family made plans to flee to the USA — but Coy betrayed them, arranging escape only for himself and Tranh. Over the next few years, Xi'an battled fiercely to keep the remainder of her family together, using her power when necessary. Eventually the family escaped Vietnam on an overcrowded fishing boat, but Thai pirates attacked it — and Xi'an was too exhausted and hungry to fight back. The men on the boat, including her father, were shot and killed — and the pirates assaulted the women. The US Navy eventually rescued the boat, but Xi'an's mother died that same day. Taken to New York City, Xi'an and her two young siblings were reunited with Coy, who had built a criminal empire for himself using Tranh's talents. Coy asked Xi'an to join him, but she refused. Months later, the terrorist Viper tried to assassinate Coy, but Tranh stopped her and forced her to join Coy's harem. Shortly thereafter, Coy kidnapped Leong and Nga and demanded that Xi'an work for him. Desperate, she sought out and possessed Spider-Man, hoping to use his body to free the twins. The Fantastic Four, who were attending a social function of Coy's that night, defeated "Spider-Man," realized that he had been possessed, and used a portable Cerebro borrowed from Professor X to track down Xi'an. Learning her side of the story, the heroes teamed up to free the twins — but Tranh, who had much greater control over his powers, possessed the entire FF and made them fight Spider-Man. Xi'an then fought and won a spiritual duel with Tranh, and literally absorbed his essence into her own mind. Electing to do good in order to balance out Tranh's evil, she took the name Karma. With Tranh's discorporation, all of Coy's slaves were freed — including Viper, who swore vengeance — and Coy elected to move his criminal operations out of New York.

Mr. Fantastic sent Karma to Professor X, who decided to open his school to a new generation of mutants. Karma took a job as his executive secretary, helping him run the school, and was appointed the field leader of the newly formed New Mutants. The students soon clashed with the Hellfire Club's Donald Pierce, Sentinels, a Brood Queen and the X-Men. During a battle with the nihilist Viper and the Silver Samurai, Karma was attacked by the Shadow King (Amahl Farouk), a disembodied telepathic villain, who turned her own power against her and possessed her. After the Samurai blew up the building, the New Mutants could not locate Karma, and presumed her dead — but Farouk had escaped in her body, and over the next few months, built a worldwide power base using decadent nightclubs. He also indulged his own appetites, resulting in Karma's body gaining some 400 pounds, and eventually took over an underground gladiatorial troupe. When the Gladiators abducted Sunspot and Magma, the New Mutants followed, and discovered that Karma was alive — but Farouk, artificially heightening her powers, possessed and enslaved them, leaving only Magik (Illyana Rasputin) and the Technarch Warlock free. Teaming with Storm (Ororo Munroe), who knew Farouk's true identity, they freed the New Mutants, who in turn liberated Karma from Farouk's influence — and she drove the villain back to the psionic plane. Immediately afterwards, Storm and the New Mutants were kidnapped to Asgard by Loki. The Enchantress scrambled Magik's attempt to teleport the team away, and the New Mutants were scattered across space and time. Karma ended up in the past, in the middle of a desert, and contemplated giving up — but she encountered a young girl, and resolved to bring her to safety. By the time the pair reached the desert's edge months later, Karma had shed all of the excess weight Farouk had caused her to gain, and was reunited with her teammates — and the girl vanished, replaced by the calling card of the Asgardian Fates. The New Mutants defeated the Enchantress, and teamed with the X-Men to defeat Loki and free Storm. Returning to Earth, they were shocked to learn that a gravely ill Professor X was leaving for outer space with the Starjammers, and appointing Magneto as headmaster of the school — but Karma opted to give the reformed villain the benefit of the doubt.

When the New Mutants angered the immensely powerful Beyonder, he killed and re-created most of them, including Karma, an experience

Art by Greg Land with Sal Buscema (inset)

XI'AN & TRANH (ORIGINAL COSTUMES) — Art by Frank Miller

NEW MUTANTS GRADUATION COSTUME — Art by Arthur Adams

that left them traumatized. Not knowing how to help them, Magneto was manipulated by the White Queen (Emma Frost) into transferring the students to her Massachusetts Academy, where she merged them into her Hellions and attempted to cure them telepathically. Eventually, with both teachers working together, the New Mutants were cured and returned to Xavier's. Shortly afterward, Mojo kidnapped Leong and Nga, and artificially aged them to adulthood — naming them Template and giving them the power to mold flesh and minds into other forms. Several other New Mutants fell under Mojo's spell, but Psylocke (Betsy Braddock) helped free them, defeat Mojo and restore Karma's siblings to their normal state and age. Seeking vengeance, Mojo de-aged the X-Men to childhood — and in their absence, the New Mutants briefly "graduated" themselves to full X-Men and rescued the senior team. However, Karma gladly relinquished her newfound X-Men status, the constant struggle of super-hero life wearing on her. Soon after, Leong and Nga were once again kidnapped — and when Karma returned to her apartment to investigate, she triggered a bomb that nearly killed her. No clues were ever found, and despite Magneto's promises that he was using all of his resources to search for the twins, Karma was not satisfied. She eventually left the New Mutants and pledged her services to her uncle Coy, now operating out of Madripoor, in hopes that his underworld contacts could locate the children.

When Coy tried to become crimelord of Madripoor, Wolverine intervened and reminded Karma of her moral center. Coy eventually agreed to a joint venture with Tyger Tiger, and Karma began secretly working to sabotage his more evil schemes, despite her fear of Coy rescinding his help if she was discovered. However, when Karma learned that Coy was involved with the slaughter of an entire village as part of the cyborg soldier-creating Lazarus Project, she cancelled her arrangement with him and left his service. Now on her own, Karma became desperate. Gideon the External falsely claimed to have information on her siblings and convinced her to betray the X-Men — but she eventually turned on him and helped put a stop to his scheme. She later became unwillingly involved in the Younghunt, the Upstarts' competition to kill the surviving members of the New Mutants and Hellions — but throughout it all, she continued her search. Finally, Leong and Nga surfaced: Shinobi Shaw had used them as test subjects for a machine meant to remove mutant genes. X-Force destroyed the machine, but found the twins had been traded to Viper and Spiral. Learning this, Karma teamed with Cannonball and the Beast to rescue them — but discovered that Spiral had used her Body Shoppe to once more age the twins to adulthood, giving them nanite-based powers and controlling their minds. Viper, seeking vengeance against the entire Coy Manh family, wanted Spiral to separate Tranh's buried consciousness from Karma's — but the mutants fought back, and seemingly destroyed the Body Shoppe. Leong and Nga were freed, but still mutated, and Karma left with them, seeking a cure.

Attending a New Mutants reunion, Karma encountered a version of the team from the past, and briefly sided with Mikhail Rasputin, who offered a chance to change history and save his sister, Magik, from the Legacy Virus. During the battle that followed, Karma realized that her powers were increasing, and — once Mikhail was revealed to be running a scam — she used these heightened powers to wipe the past New Mutants' memories as they returned home. Karma eventually found a doctor who reversed the twins' condition, and, finalizing her US citizenship, moved to Illinois and enrolled at the University of Chicago. There she ran into Shadowcat and, while battling Wild Sentinels with her, realized that she was attracted to her — however, Shadowcat did not reciprocate the feeling. When the Xavier Institute went public, Danielle Moonstar took a teaching job there and traveled to Chicago to recruit high-school student David Alleyne, an acquaintance of Karma. Arriving on the day Karma graduated, Moonstar convinced both of them to come to Xavier's — Alleyne to study, Karma to teach. Moving back to the mansion, Karma took over Xavier's library and taught French. She also became the advisor to the "lower school" — students too young for combat training, including Leong and Nga. When Northstar was killed and Wolfsbane left the school, Karma also began mentoring their training squads. Although Karma retained her powers on M-Day, most of the students did not, and the school was severely restructured. Karma began working closely with the "198," the mutants who sought refuge and asylum at Xavier's. When the X-Men later moved to San Francisco, Karma moved with them. Aiding the team from time to time, including recently helping to draw out the Hellfire Cult, Karma has resolved to take firmer control of her life, and is now settling into her new West Coast surroundings with her beloved siblings.

PUNK LOOK — Art by Adam Pollina

NEW MUTANTS COSTUME — Art by Jackson Guice

HEIGHT: 5'4" **EYES:** Brown
WEIGHT: 119 lbs. **HAIR:** Black

ABILITIES/ACCESSORIES: Karma can possess the minds of people and animals, controlling their movements as if their bodies were her own. Normally she has instant control over her target, but has difficulty when possessing multiple people, or people with psi-training or abnormally strong willpower. The longer she possesses a target, the more she begins to speak, act, and think like him or her. She has only rudimentary control over her own body while possessing another. Karma has also demonstrated other psionic skills, such as making people sleep, reading and altering memories, creating telekinetic shields, and absorbing others' minds into herself, but has not elected to develop this aspect of her powers. She may also have the ability to hover in midair. Karma speaks fluent Vietnamese, English, and French.

KAZANN

REAL NAME: Micah
ALIASES: Lord Kazann
IDENTITY: Existence unknown to the general public
OCCUPATION: Conqueror; former angel
CITIZENSHIP: A realm of Hell
PLACE OF BIRTH: Unrevealed
KNOWN RELATIVES: Daniel, Malachi (brothers)
GROUP AFFILIATION: Demons of Hell; formerly angels of Heaven
EDUCATION: Unrevealed
FIRST APPEARANCE: (Mentioned) Ghost Rider #1 (2005); (seen) Ghost Rider #2 (2005); (true form) Ghost Rider #6 (2006)

HISTORY: When a war broke out in Heaven between the angels, Micah rebelled with Lucifer and was cast down along with all who had opposed God. Now a demon in Hell, Micah abandoned his angelic name and began calling himself Kazann. Although he was cast from Heaven, Kazann remained in touch with his brother Malachi, who was still an angel in Heaven. They worked together to help each other become more powerful in their respective planes of existence by sharing vital information and secrets of Heaven and Hell. By sharing the information, they devised plans to counter each other's actions while making themselves look good in order to rise through the ranks.

After the petroleum tycoon Earl Gustav was left a quadriplegic after driving drunk, he began performing occult rituals, contacting the demon Kazann in hopes that it would restore his mobility. Kazann agreed, if in return Gustav would perform certain rituals to allow Kazann to escape from Hell and create a new Hell on Earth. Regarding all his fellow mortals as lesser beings, Gustav was glad to do this no matter the cost. Kazann had Gustav (who in turn had his secretary Jemima Catmint do the work for him) inscribe certain devices to carry out his plans. Gustav sacrificed a group of his board members; this allowed Kazann to gain physical form by using the group's remains to create a demonic body. Kazann's presence on Earth did not go unnoticed, and the archangel Ruth and Hoss, one of Hell's best tracker-scouts, were dispatched to bring him back, while Malachi released the Ghost Rider (Johnny Blaze) from Hell in order to employ him as his pawn in stopping Kazann's plans.

Kazann used a drill inscribed with a ritual portal spell that could, upon hitting the Earth's molten core, penetrate the spirit barrier, opening a tunnel to the spirit world and creating a gateway to the afterlife, allowing demons to come to Earth. As Kazann's demon army began to surge through the gateway, Ghost Rider, Hoss and Ruth made their way to the Gustav Petroleum headquarters to stop Kazann. While Hoss and Ruth battled each other, Ghost Rider confronted Kazann, destroying his Earthly body and revealing his true form. Realizing what she had been a part of, Jemima Catmint then forced Gustav to cast the Hymn of Recall spell, sending Kazann and his demon army back to Hell. Ruth then startled Catmint, causing her to let go of Gustav's wheelchair, allowing him to roll into the pits of Hell itself.

Ghost Rider was bewildered upon returning to Hell, and Malachi soon appeared, telling him that no one, be they an angel, demon or even God could save a lost soul from damnation. Malachi mistakenly revealed his partnership with Kazann during this conversation, and Ruth then tore Malachi's wings off, causing him to fall from grace and become mortal. Malachi bled to death and his soul went to Hell alongside his brother Kazann, thus ending Kazann's plans to gain power in Hell. Ghost Rider was forced to return to his life of torment, racing towards the gates of Hell each night. Only this time he was able to take solace in knowing that Malachi would suffer the same fate each night as he dragged him behind him.

HEIGHT: Variable
WEIGHT: Variable
EYES: Variable
HAIR: Variable

ABILITIES/ACCESSORIES: A demon of great power, Kazann possesses no true form but can gain physical form by possessing others or creating a body for himself from human remains. In such forms, Kazann possesses enhanced strength and durability, and the ability to heal others. He is well versed in occult rituals, spells and incantations of dark magic. Kazann does not need to eat, sleep or drink and is immune to aging and conventional disease.

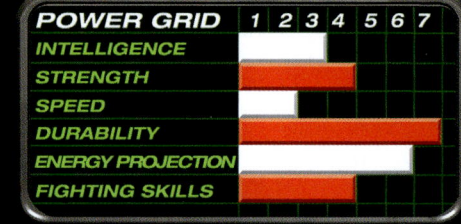

POWER GRID	1	2	3	4	5	6	7
INTELLIGENCE				■			
STRENGTH					■		
SPEED			■				
DURABILITY						■	
ENERGY PROJECTION					■		
FIGHTING SKILLS				■			

Art by Clayton Crain

KA-ZAR THE GREAT

HISTORY: Born in South Africa circa 1918, three-year-old David Rand accompanied his British parents, John and Constance, on a flight to Cairo to visit his grandfather, but their plane crashed in the Belgian Congo. Injured, Constance died shortly thereafter, driving John slightly mad. Living in the jungle with his father, isolated from the local tribes, David grew under the jungle's hardships into an unusually powerful youth and developed strong empathy with wildlife, notably rescuing the lion Zar from quicksand. When criminal Paul de Kraft discovered emeralds in the Congo, John Rand died opposing him, but Zar drove de Kraft off. With Zar's support, David became the jungle's leading warrior within a few years, challenging Bardak the ape, N'jaga the Leopard, and others. Considered godlike by the natives, he became known as "Ka-Zar," or "brother of the lion." When de Kraft returned to seize the emerald deposits, the vengeful Ka-Zar killed him.

Aided by animal allies, Ka-Zar appointed himself guardian of the jungle, meting out harsh retribution to any intruder seeking to exploit its resources — but he frequently aided more benign explorers, such as when he protected Prof. Rice and his daughter Mara from the criminal pilot "Red" Skelton, rescued Rita Grey from the Wabi tribe, and helped two Scotland Yard detectives capture murderer London Jack. When Zar was captured by first the vicious Rajah Sarput and then big game hunter Bradley, who shipped him to the US, Ka-Zar stowed away on the ship. He freed Zar when the ship docked in New York but was arrested for trying to free zoo animals as well. Fortunately, Ruth Wilson, another woman whom Ka-Zar had rescued during an African expedition, vouched for him, and he and Zar were granted passage back to Africa on a British ship. Surviving attacks by entrenched Nazi forces, they confronted Sarput, who was ultimately slain by their elephant ally Trajah. Soon afterward, Ka-Zar learned he had inherited his father's Transvaal diamond mines and, after preventing his inheritance's theft by John Rand's law partner Alec Wright, donated the wealth to war relief in England.

On an expedition into the mysterious Black River Region, Ka-Zar encountered giants and subterranean lizard-people, befriending the giant Bogat. Later, he waged a series of campaigns against Axis forces in Ethiopia, Somaliland, and elsewhere, killing them with their own artillery both on his own and in cooperation with British and French forces. Following one such encounter, Ka-Zar was restored to health by an aged witch doctor, who gave him a brew used centuries before to grant his tribe superhuman strength. Ka-Zar's exploits earned him such fame that he was invited to attend a meeting of superhuman champions in mid-1941, and he protected his region's wildlife when Africa was threatened by monstrous tidal waves from Atlantean warfare. Ka-Zar's activities were last reported later that year; his subsequent life remains unchronicled.

REAL NAME: David Rand
ALIASES: Brother of the Lion, Ka-Zar the Mighty
IDENTITY: Publicly known
OCCUPATION: Adventurer, peacekeeper
CITIZENSHIP: South Africa; UK
PLACE OF BIRTH: Johannesburg, South Africa
KNOWN RELATIVES: John & Constance Rand (parents, deceased), Mr. Dean (maternal grandfather, presumed deceased)
GROUP AFFILIATION: None
EDUCATION: No formal education
FIRST APPEARANCE: Ka-Zar: Lord of Fang and Claw (1936); (Marvel) Marvel Comics #1 (1939)

HEIGHT: 6'5"
WEIGHT: 285 lbs.
EYES: Blue
HAIR: Blond

ABILITIES/ACCESSORIES: Ka-Zar's mystic potion gave him superhuman strength and agility; even prior to this enhancement, he was an incredibly strong athlete and hand-to-hand combatant, able to bend iron bars with extreme effort. He possessed a remarkable rapport with the Belgian Congo's animals, gleaning meaning from their every sound and motion as if they were literally speaking to him. He customarily carried two knives and used a spear or bow and arrows as necessary. In addition to Zar, he was most frequently accompanied by Trajah the elephant and Nono the monkey.

POWER GRID	1	2	3	4	5	6	7
INTELLIGENCE							
STRENGTH							
SPEED							
DURABILITY							
ENERGY PROJECTION							
FIGHTING SKILLS							

Art by Ben Thompson

KA-ZAR THE SAVAGE

REAL NAME: Kevin Reginald Plunder; Lord Plunder
ALIASES: Son of the Tiger, Lord of the Hidden Jungle
IDENTITY: Publicly known
OCCUPATION: Adventurer, peacekeeper, nobleman, hunter, trapper, fisherman
CITIZENSHIP: UK, Savage Land
PLACE OF BIRTH: Castle Plunder, Kentish Town, London, England, UK
KNOWN RELATIVES: Shanna O'Hara, Lady Plunder (wife), Adam Kyle Matthew Plunder (son), Robert, Lord Plunder (father, deceased), Blanche, Lady Plunder (mother, deceased), Edgar Parnival Plunder (Plunderer, brother), Chauncewell (cousin)
GROUP AFFILIATION: None
EDUCATION: Elementary school (unfinished), extensive self-instruction, teaching from tribal scholars
FIRST APPEARANCE: X-Men #10 (1965)

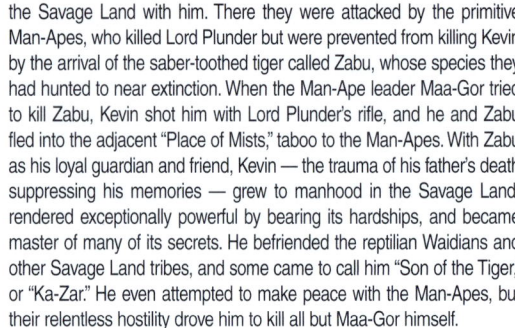

HISTORY: Over two decades ago, British scientist Robert, Lord Plunder discovered a deposit of "Anti-Metal," an isotope of Vibranium, in the Antarctic jungle called the Savage Land; tragically, his wife died during his absence. After returning to England, reports of his discovery made him the target of unspecified foreign powers. Plunder sent one of his sons, Parnival, into hiding while bringing the other, 9-year-old Kevin, to the Savage Land with him. There they were attacked by the primitive Man-Apes, who killed Lord Plunder but were prevented from killing Kevin by the arrival of the saber-toothed tiger called Zabu, whose species they had hunted to near extinction. When the Man-Ape leader Maa-Gor tried to kill Zabu, Kevin shot him with Lord Plunder's rifle, and he and Zabu fled into the adjacent "Place of Mists," taboo to the Man-Apes. With Zabu as his loyal guardian and friend, Kevin — the trauma of his father's death suppressing his memories — grew to manhood in the Savage Land, rendered exceptionally powerful by bearing its hardships, and became master of many of its secrets. He befriended the reptilian Waidians and other Savage Land tribes, and some came to call him "Son of the Tiger," or "Ka-Zar." He even attempted to make peace with the Man-Apes, but their relentless hostility drove him to kill all but Maa-Gor himself.

In recent years, more explorers discovered the Savage Land, and photographs of the region and of Ka-Zar were circulated in the media. When the X-Men came to investigate, they were at first suspicious of him, but he and Zabu helped them rescue Marvel Girl (Jean Grey) from the Swamp Men. Although Ka-Zar resolved that no other visitors should come to the Savage Land, the incident was only the first of his many encounters with outsiders. Months later, he met Daredevil (Matt Murdock) when the latter was forced into service by the pirating Plunderer, who arrived in the Savage Land to reveal himself as Ka-Zar's brother Parnival. Ka-Zar and Daredevil ended Parnival's criminal activities, and Ka-Zar, inheriting the Plunder fortune, relocated to London with Zabu. Shortly afterward, Parnival attempted to frame Ka-Zar for the crimes of the "Midnight Stalker," but Daredevil cleared his friend's name.

Still adjusting to the world of the wealthy, Ka-Zar and Zabu visited New York, where publisher J. Jonah Jameson offered money if Ka-Zar would track and defeat Spider-Man (Peter Parker); uninterested in the offer, Ka-Zar nevertheless found himself fighting Spider-Man while the hero was in a temporary state of amnesia. Returning to London, Ka-Zar's dissatisfaction with city life finally grew too great, and he and Zabu returned to the Savage Land, where he learned that, in his absence, the extraterrestrial Quor was employing the tribe of Reptile Men to mine Anti-Metal. Gratified to be defending his adopted land once more, Ka-Zar drove off Quor and encountered another extraterrestrial menace shortly afterward, when Bruce Banner, captured by the Swamp Men, examined the alien machine they worshipped and inadvertently activated the robot Umbu the Unliving. Neither Ka-Zar nor Banner, as the Hulk, could outfight the giant, but the Hulk reverted back to Banner and used the machine to deactivate Umbu.

A more troublesome invader, the X-Men's archenemy Magneto used the Savage Land as a base for his experiments, mutating natives into super-powered underlings, the Savage Land Mutates. Now more amenable to the X-Men, Ka-Zar worked with them to drive out Magneto and parted with the team on good terms. Shortly afterward, Kraven the Hunter absconded with Zabu, leading Ka-Zar back to New York, where he was approached by the immortal Garokk, who returned with him and Zabu to the Savage Land. When the high priestess Zaladane misused her sacred power, driving Garokk mad in the process, Ka-Zar restored Garokk to his senses and defeated Zaladane, then clashed with the similarly godlike Damon and Lelania, long-vanished inhabitants of the Land whose return briefly wrought havoc in the Land's skies. Shortly afterward, Kraven returned with an alien ally, the gigantic Gog. Gog's presence drew Spider-Man to the Savage Land, and the heroes who had once fought now worked together to drive out the interlopers.

More friendly visitors arrived when SHIELD agent Barbara Morse recruited Ka-Zar to help find scientist Ted Sallis, who had disappeared in a swampy wilderness while working on a super-soldier serum; during the search, Ka-Zar encountered the monstrous Man-Thing, whom no one realized was Sallis himself. Ka-Zar and Zabu accompanied

Art by John Byrne

Morse to New York in search of new leads, clashing with various AIM operatives, including Gog and Parnival Plunder. Although Ka-Zar and Morse grew attracted to each other, their outlooks on the merits and flaws of civilization were irreconcilable, and Ka-Zar and Zabu returned to their home at the adventure's conclusion. Shortly afterward, Ka-Zar was abducted by the high priest Malgato, who was prepared to kill him and Shanna the She-Devil, another jungle adventurer, in a human sacrifice meant to preserve the Savage Land. Both Ka-Zar and Shanna escaped, and Ka-Zar, perhaps made thoughtful by Malgato's claims, embarked on an exploration of unfamiliar areas of the Savage Land, interacting with many new cultures, few of which met his approval. Soon afterward, Shanna returned in the company of Barbara Morse, both investigating seismographic disturbances that had been traced to the Land and were discovered to stem from a long-buried space capsule, whose occupant, Grond, awoke and departed. After taming a unicorn and protecting the peaceful Zebra People from an army of dead raised by the sorceress Sheesa, Ka-Zar met the Thing, investigating another seismographic disturbance, this one caused by the madman Volcanus, who was tapping a dormant volcano in an effort to empower himself but seemingly perished instead.

Meanwhile, armies from the Dimension of Quarl sought to invade Earth en masse but could only open brief portals, and they recruited the sound-powered Klaw to bombard the Savage Land's Vibranium to augment their resources; the resulting resonations spread madness throughout the Land. Ka-Zar made the interdimensional journey himself to confront the invaders but could not prevent Quarl from partially merging with the Savage Land, a task that fell to Zaladane, who summoned Garokk in a new incarnation. After restoring balance to the two dimensions, Garokk resolved to remake the Savage Land to his own satisfaction, regardless of how many would die. When happenstance brought the X-Men to the Savage Land, Ka-Zar recruited them to attack Garokk's citadel with him,

Art by Steve Fabian

and the reborn god ultimately fell with his city. In short order, both AIM and Klaw launched expeditions to steal Savage Land resources, but Ka-Zar defeated the former with the Hulk's help and the latter with the aid of the Thing and American Eagle.

Shanna the She-Devil, having grown dissatisfied with city life, returned to the Savage Land to stay, and she and Ka-Zar became lovers; however, Ka-Zar, mourning a friend's death that might have been prevented by modern medicine, had become disenchanted with life in the wild. Shortly after Shanna and others were abducted by Sauron and the Savage Land Mutates and rescued by Ka-Zar and the X-Men, the couple took their debate on the subject with them when they and Zabu discovered the way to Pangea, a long-forgotten realm adjacent to the Savage Land, inhabited by many unfamiliar races. Although Lemuran Queen Leanne's attraction to Ka-Zar briefly drove a wedge between the couple, they soon befriended the winged Aerians and the android Dherk, who revealed various secrets about the Savage Land's past as an outpost of the Atlantean Empire. In an abandoned Atlantean amusement center, they encountered the sorcerer Belasco, who attempted to bind Shanna to the N'Garai, dark gods he served. However, once back in familiar territory, Ka-Zar faced a more mundane servitude after being "accidentally" shot by "botanist" Ramona Courtland (actually an AIM agent); rushing Ka-Zar to medical treatment in New York, Courtland, following a failed attempt to win Kraven the Hunter as an ally, faked Ka-Zar's death, then extorted him into carrying out AIM missions by threatening to kill Shanna, who had gone almost mad with grief. Despite a device that inflicted severe pain upon him, Ka-Zar escaped AIM's control and returned to Pangea with Shanna, who received treatment to restore her senses.

Ka-Zar and Shanna married soon afterward, despite Belasco's disruption of the ceremony, but the Pangean races ultimately united in declaring the outsiders to be a destabilizing presence, and Ka-Zar, Shanna and Zabu departed. Parnival Plunder's arrival in the Savage Land corresponded with their return, and although Shanna accepted his supposed reconciliation at face value, Ka-Zar remained suspicious and was proven right when he learned his brother was trying to steal Anti-Metal. When Parnival fled by ship, Ka-Zar saw him fall and seemingly meet an icy death. Shortly afterward, an artifact inadvertently teleported Shanna, with Ka-Zar and Zabu behind her, to the planet Tomriv in the Lenra Galaxy, home of the Nuwali, the race who had created the original terraforming technology that kept the Savage Land safe. Imprisoned by the aliens, Ka-Zar and company escaped and returned to Earth, and Ka-Zar anticipated his new life with a pregnant Shanna.

Tragically, the peaceful return of Ka-Zar, Shanna, and Zabu was soon followed by the arrival of Terminus, or rather the Deviant Jorro using the alien's gigantic armor. Although the massive menace was detected by the Avengers, they did not arrive in time to prevent him from destroying the Nuwali/Atlantean technology that maintained the Savage Land and Pangea. The freezing Antarctic cold swept over all, with seemingly only Ka-Zar, Shanna, and Zabu surviving while the Avengers tore open Jorro's armor, ending his threat. The Avengers brought Ka-Zar and his family to New York, where they became the team's houseguests, but Ka-Zar, distraught by the loss of the home he had held more than half his life, tried to lose himself in a cross-country drive; arriving in California, he was invited to try out for West Coast Avengers membership after helping Iron Man defeat the Fixer, but he accepted that his place was with Shanna and returned to the Savage Land. Shortly afterward, he and Shanna provided information on the Savage Land to the Fantastic Four, who had been drawn to Antarctica in their exploration of alien teleportation access, but the couple did not accompany the team as they continued the adventure.

Months later, after Shanna gave birth to their son Matthew, Ka-Zar was astonished to learn that the extradimensional adventurer M'Rin had rescued many of the natives of the Savage Land and Pangea from the

Jorro catastrophe, and the region itself had been restored, complete with cloned wildlife, when the High Evolutionary and Garokk repaired the terraforming technology. By the time Ka-Zar and his family returned, a fledgling government of United Tribes had been established; Ka-Zar hardly minded the loss of his informal position of ruler, but his authority was undermined further when Zaladane's forces resurfaced, requiring the X-Men's assistance to defeat her, and he ultimately returned to his English estate, mired in self-pity. However, after the investigation of a tunnel between the US and the Savage Land revealed corporate oil interests were exploiting the region in his absence, he returned and rededicated himself to his land's protection, again helping the X-Men oppose Zaladane when she threatened to overwhelm the world magnetically. Following these crises, Ka-Zar encountered perhaps the Land's oddest visitors yet, the Impossible Man and his cloned family, whom he aided in their search for a wayward child.

Ka-Zar's new peace of mind was almost literally removed when the Super-Skrull, impersonating Iron Fist, mentally controlled him in an elaborate scheme to use the Land's resources for his own ends. The Super-Skrull was defeated by Namor the Sub-Mariner and his allies, but months later a nearly identical situation arose when Lorelei, formerly of the Savage Land Mutates, mesmerized Ka-Zar into serving the High Technician, who had allied with a returning AIM to strip the Land of its resources via the armor of Terminus. The sight of his home's one-time destroyer restored Ka-Zar's mind, and he helped Captain America, the Black Panther, and others crack the armor a second time. With the Panther's aid, Ka-Zar drove out AIM, then, alongside Wolverine and others, encountered the benign but animal-abducting conservationist Castillo, whose interests they turned toward less intrusive methods. Ka-Zar again joined Wolverine, along with the adventurers of Genetix, to drive out the Land's latest would-be conqueror, Prime Evil, but the next crisis came from within when the terraforming technology started mutating adolescent natives into monstrous Neo-Men; despite Sauron's interference, Ka-Zar repaired the malfunction, but the transformations could not be reversed, leaving the Neo-Men the latest addition to the Land's long list of component races.

After Spider-Man and the Hulk helped him foil Roxxon Oil's efforts to flood the Savage Land in order to salvage its resources, Ka-Zar attempted to encourage peaceful solutions between warring tribes via technology and sport systems imported from the outside world. Meanwhile, Parnival had survived his previous defeat and became a wealthy CEO. He had also entered the service of Thanos — or, reportedly, one of his Thanosi duplicates — who craved the energies of the Savage Land's long-suffering terraformer to free him from extradimensional exile. Parnival sent Kraven's former instructor Gregor to abduct Matthew, and although Ka-Zar and Shanna rescued their child, the encounter had the intended effect of bringing the couple to New York, complete with accompanying dinosaurs, to confront Parnival, allowing his operatives to steal the terraformer in their absence and bring it to New York, where it transformed Manhattan into a jungle. Ka-Zar bluffed Thanos into believing he had a secret that could undo the Titan's endeavors, and while he led his enemy on a chase throughout the universe via the terraformer's teleportation capabilities, Shanna had the terraformer returned to the Savage Land. Upon emerging on Earth again, Thanos was reverted back to exile when the terraformer was destroyed, its power now residing in Shanna, who became a goddess figure to the awed tribes. Ka-Zar, realizing that the power could destroy Shanna's mind, persuaded the High Evolutionary to restore the terraformer, then dissuaded him from remaking the world with Shanna, who surrendered the alien energies.

Having left New York so hurriedly, Ka-Zar returned to send the imported wildlife back home; however, a chance encounter with criminals on the subway left him blinded and deafened by gunfire, and he wandered the city in a haze before being taken in by Jameka, a somewhat mentally ill woman who immediately fixated on him. When the media blamed Ka-Zar for the shooting, he was stalked by the vigilante Punisher, but Ka-Zar held his own in battle despite his injuries and convinced the Punisher of his innocence. Though Jameka interfered, hoping Ka-Zar would stay with her, the Black Panther used his influence to resolve the situation and provided Ka-Zar with passage back home. Unfortunately, Ka-Zar returned to find the Savage Land wracked with environmental disasters, which the Bhaduwans, hidden guardians of the Land, claimed were due to Ka-Zar's "taint" as an outsider. Although many of the natives rallied in his support, Ka-Zar and his family voluntarily left rather than endanger the land he so loved, and then returned later when the crisis was resolved.

Ka-Zar and several other Savage Land natives were subsequently captured by Count Nefaria, who used their DNA to create duplicates that aged rapidly as he drained them of energy. Captain America, investigating Nefaria's activities, halted the operation and freed his captives, who resolved to subject Nefaria to Savage Land justice. Shortly afterward, Zabu vanished under mysterious circumstances, but Ka-Zar soon located him, despite the case's refusal by superhuman detective Jessica Jones. Several months later, the reptilian Hauk'ka conquered the United Tribes and prepared to unleash worldwide elemental havoc, but Ka-Zar allied with another reptilian race, the Saurians, as well as with the equally threatened Savage Land Mutates, to oppose them. The X-Men joined the struggle, and the Hauk'ka were defeated and offered the opportunity for peaceful co-existence with the other tribes. Internally, the Savage Land has remained relatively peaceful since, although it was soon invaded by the Skrulls, who, in the guise of SHIELD agents, forced natives to mine Vibranium; Ka-Zar and Shanna discovered their alien nature and fought them to a standstill before a SHIELD Helicarrier destroyed the Skrulls. After Ka-Zar's brother the Plunderer returned, aiding Roxxon in another attempt to seize his kingdom's Vibranium, Ka-Zar formed a brief alliance with the Savage Land Mutates and Stegron's forces to beat them back, and forged a treaty with Wakanda for mutual protection. The Skrulls subsequently returned in the guise of various super heroes, and Ka-Zar and Shanna fought them alongside two teams of Avengers.

Art by Rich Buckler

HEIGHT: 6'2" **EYES:** Blue
WEIGHT: 215 lbs. **HAIR:** Blond

ABILITIES/ACCESSORIES: Ka-Zar possesses near-superhuman levels of strength, endurance, athleticism, fighting prowess and survival skills. He typically carries a stone or metal knife, using bow and arrows or a throwing sling as need arises.

POWER GRID	1	2	3	4	5	6	7
INTELLIGENCE			■				
STRENGTH				■			
SPEED			■				
DURABILITY				■			
ENERGY PROJECTION	■						
FIGHTING SKILLS						■	

SENATOR ROBERT KELLY

HISTORY: After being elected to office, US Senator Robert Kelly quickly met with FBI Director Fred Duncan to discuss the perceived mutant threat, unaware that "Duncan" was secretly the shape-shifting mutant terrorist Mystique, who hoped to learn more about Kelly's intentions. Soon after, Kelly attended a party at the Hellfire Club, unaware that his host — Sebastian Shaw — was a mutant. During the party, Shaw's Inner Circle battled members of the heroic X-Men, whom Kelly regarded as a band of mutant criminals terrorizing innocent party-goers. Kelly ultimately addressed the US Senate on the "mutant threat," during which he was confronted by Mystique and her Brotherhood of Evil Mutants. Despite the X-Men's opposition, Destiny cornered Kelly with a crossbow; however, Kelly was saved by the X-Man Kitty Pryde. This assassination attempt only strengthened Kelly's resolve, and Kelly soon witnessed the formation of Project: Wideawake, a covert operation tasked with creating a new series of mutant-hunting Sentinel robots. Kelly then introduced the Mutant Affairs Control Act to the Senate. If passed, the Act would require mutants to disclose their identities and abilities to the government. Ultimately, the Act was rejected as unconstitutional.

Later, while in South America to obtain photographic evidence to use in America's war on drugs, Kelly was captured and sentenced to death by local crimelord Señor Muerte. He was rescued by the government-sponsored Freedom Force team, ironically consisting of the Brotherhood that had previously attempted to assassinate him. Returned to America, Kelly soon married Sharon, a former Hellfire Club maid, and after a meeting with Shaw in New York, Kelly and his wife were caught up in a battle between the X-Men and the Sentinels' leader, Master Mold. Aided by the X-Man Rogue, Sharon Kelly pulled her husband to safety, but was then killed in an explosion. Ultimately returning to his political duties, Kelly engaged in a televised debate between himself, mutant activist Professor Charles Xavier, anti-mutant movement leader Graydon Creed, and high profile mutant hero the Beast. During the debate, Kelly was surprised to find himself agreeing with many of Xavier's opinions. Kelly later supported Operation: Zero Tolerance, a government-sponsored anti-mutant initiative, until discovering that the program was violating the rights of US citizens by converting them into cybernetic Prime Sentinels. Withdrawing his support, Kelly became a target and was forced to seek the X-Men's aid. Saved from assassination by Cyclops, Kelly convinced the US president to mobilize the forces of the international law enforcement agency SHIELD to shut down the operation.

Taking a more active role in his crusade, Kelly ran for president. On the eve of the election, at his final speech in Boston, Kelly was confronted by a new incarnation of Mystique's Brotherhood. Despite the X-Men's intervention, Kelly would have been killed if not for Pyro, a dying ex-Brotherhood member who sacrificed himself to save Kelly's life. Pyro's selfless act finally prompted Kelly to re-evaluate his stance on mutants, and after talking with the mutant soldier Cable, Kelly became convinced that peaceful coexistence was possible. However, while speaking at a college rally, Kelly was assassinated by anti-mutant activist Alan Lewis, who perceived Kelly as a traitor to humanity.

REAL NAME: Robert Edward Kelly
ALIASES: None
IDENTITY: No dual identity
OCCUPATION: Politician
CITIZENSHIP: USA
PLACE OF BIRTH: Boston, Massachusetts
KNOWN RELATIVES: Sharon Kelly (wife, deceased)
GROUP AFFILIATION: Formerly US Senate, US Army
EDUCATION: Military training; otherwise unrevealed
FIRST APPEARANCE: X-Men #133 (1980); (full) X-Men #135 (1980)

HEIGHT: 5'10" **EYES:** Brown
WEIGHT: 175 lbs. **HAIR:** Brown with graying temples
ABILITIES/ACCESSORIES: Kelly was an experienced politician, particularly skilled in debating and public speaking. A former soldier, Kelly was trained in armed and unarmed combat.

POWER GRID	1	2	3	4	5	6	7
INTELLIGENCE			■				
STRENGTH		■					
SPEED		■					
DURABILITY		■					
ENERGY PROJECTION	■						
FIGHTING SKILLS			■				

Art by Salvador Larroca

SAL KENNEDY

REAL NAME: Sal Kennedy
ALIASES: None
IDENTITY: Publicly known
OCCUPATION: SHIELD executive director; former futurist, ethnobotanist, computer technician, teacher
CITIZENSHIP: USA
PLACE OF BIRTH: Unrevealed
KNOWN RELATIVES: None
GROUP AFFILIATION: SHIELD
EDUCATION: Ph.D. in ethnobotany, advanced degree in information technology
FIRST APPEARANCE: Iron Man #2 (2005)

HISTORY: Sal Kennedy began his professional work in computers and eventually became an ethnobotanist and later a futurist. Teaching at various schools, notably Berkeley University, and offering conferences around the country, Kennedy eventually became a mentor to two up-and-comers, Tony Stark and Maya Hansen. He monitored their careers over the years as Tony became a weapons developer for the military, eventually becoming famous for designing the Iron Man armor, and Maya became known for her work in biotechnic advances in human development. Kennedy was proud of them both, but disappointed in their willingness to work for the government and/or military in order to find funding for their various fields of research. Kennedy, meanwhile, sought isolation and moved into a small cabin in California, where he had little contact with the outside world and had no phone or television. Kennedy spent the bulk of his days reading and growing his own mushrooms, which he ingested to heighten his brain functions and generate his own ideas, feeling that certain drugs only further heightened human perception. Kennedy only left occasionally in order to teach at various venues, such as Esalen.

Kennedy was thrilled to receive a visit from Stark and Hansen. Kennedy soon learned that Hansen had developed a biotechnical process called Extremis that rewrote the human brain and allowed those that survived to become, in effect, super soldiers with vast superhuman capabilities. Kennedy learned that Hansen's Extremis enhancement had been stolen and utilized by a terrorist. Stark and Hansen rushed off to handle the threat, and Stark, as Iron Man, ended up becoming the sole Extremis-enhanced human alive. Hansen, meanwhile, was revealed to be behind the Extremis theft and was imprisoned.

Weeks later, Kennedy was walking around his home naked when he found Stark, in his armor, crying outside about having committed murders. He learned that Iron Man had apparently been responsible for dozens of murders, though Stark had no memory of them. Kennedy agreed to help Stark, aiding him in dying his hair blond and putting together a plan to clear his name. They surmised that someone must be controlling the armor from afar, though Stark claimed that was impossible now that he was Extremis-enhanced. Kennedy took Stark down to his Berkeley University lab, where they ran tests and detected a control device in Stark's brain that had been there prior to the enhancement. Kennedy convinced Stark to break Hansen out of prison, knowing they would need her help. Hansen helped Stark realize that someone was controlling him from afar and Stark soon defeated the son of Ho Yinsen. Kennedy was overwhelmed by the senseless loss of life in this battle, but still visited Stark in the hospital and tried to help assuage his guilt. They confirmed that the control unit could never be used again. When Stark was offered the command of SHIELD, the world peace-keeping organization, he was shocked when Kennedy tried to convince him to accept the position. After the passage of the Superhuman Registration Act, Stark took the position and appointed Kennedy to be his executive director and Hansen to be his consultant. Kennedy moved onto the Helicarrier and shocked the SHIELD agents with his bizarre habits, such as blowing bubbles and hitting golf balls into the sky. When terrorist activity had a large upswing, Kennedy surmised that a common threat was behind it. He quickly grew overwhelmed by all the death he was becoming aware of and, after attending the funeral of several SHIELD agents, confessed to Stark that he didn't like what the new job was doing to him. Kennedy challenged Stark on his unwillingness to let Hansen pursue her Extremis research, and he learned that Stark and Hansen had become romantically involved. When the body of a known terrorist was found, Kennedy and Hansen started an autopsy, but a biotechnic virus erupted out of the body, killing Kennedy instantly. The virus killed dozens of agents before Stark managed to stop it. Stark and Hansen continue to mourn the loss of Kennedy, and Stark, affected by the Extremis, has recently seen a "ghost" of Kennedy giving him advice.

HEIGHT: 5'11"
WEIGHT: 235 lbs.
EYES: Blue
HAIR: White

ABILITIES/ACCESSORIES: Sal Kennedy was a trained ethnobotanist with familiar interests in most areas of science, particularly computer technology.

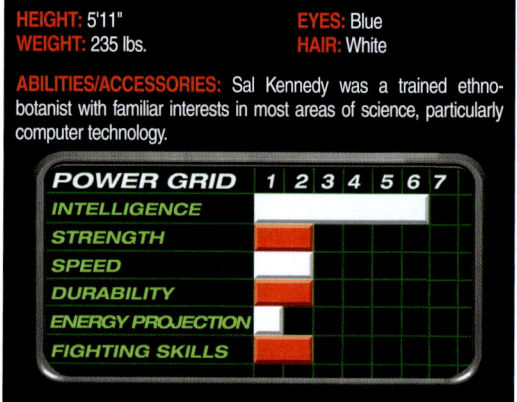

Art by Roberto De La Torre

DAN KETCH

HISTORY: Over 21 millennia ago, the demon Zarathos sought the mighty Medallion of Power and was opposed by his ancient enemies, the Spirits of Vengeance, who were allied with the super-powered immortals known as the Blood. Ultimately, the Spirits sacrificed themselves trapping and merging with a portion of Zarathos within the Medallion. The Blood then shattered the Medallion into pieces and embedded the fragments into the spiritual bloodline of two families, both of which would be overseen and protected by a Blood named Caretaker.

In the 18th century, young Noble Kale of the spiritual bloodline fell in love with a woman named Magdalena. Fearing the reaction from his father, Pastor Destin Kale, Noble hid his romance. Magdalena bore Noble a son and shortly thereafter discovered Destin secretly casting satanic rituals to keep the town flourishing. Destin branded her a witch and the town burned her at the stake. As Magdalena died, Destin told her Noble never loved her. Believing Destin because Noble, whom Destin bound, did not save her, she cursed Pastor Kale, invoking the legendary Furies, Olympian spirits avenging wrongly slain women, to seek vengeance in her name. These ancient spirits went on a destructive rampage, killing anyone in their sight, including Noble's young brother Dante. Pastor Kale sought aid from the demon Mephisto, offering Noble's soul as payment. Mephisto recognized the Medallion shard within Noble Kale and activated it, transforming the young man into a demonic, flaming, skeletal warrior that slew the Furies. After defeating the Furies, the transformed Noble refused to feed on his and Magdalena's son, despite Destin's offering. The horrified Noble tried to commit suicide, but Mephisto appeared, seeking to claim his soul. However, the Angel Uriel prevented Mephisto from claiming the innocent Noble Kale's soul, and the two compromised, making Noble a new Spirit of Vengeance to avenge innocent blood spilled on Earth. While Uriel vowed that Mephisto would not lay a finger on Noble's descendants, Mephisto — without touching them — arranged for each firstborn to be the Earthly host to the Spirit of Vengeance, aka the Ghost Rider.

Noble inhabited the firstborn child of each generation, with documented occurrences during World War I and the lifetime of Naomi Kale, the birth mother of Dan Ketch and his siblings. Fearing for her children, Naomi left Dan and his sister Barbara with Francis Ketch in Cypress Hills, New York. Naomi's oldest son, John, was left with his father while she unsuccessfully attempted to end the curse. Later Max Parrish, an archaeologist, helped a young Johnny Storm escape the lure of Zarathos by casting a ritual on himself to merge with Noble until Storm freed him by removing the Medallion from Parrish's hellfire motorcycle. The motorcycle, along with the Medallion, was taken to a local junkyard. Years later, John Blaze was bonded to Zarathos, becoming a new incarnation of Ghost Rider until eventually separating when Zarathos was entrapped in the soulless man Centurious' Soul Crystal. Dan befriended Stacy Dolan, the daughter of a local police officer and later the object of Dan's romantic affections. As Dan matured, he became interested in motorcycles and drawn to the open road. When Dan and Barb took a shortcut home through Cypress Hills Cemetery, they stumbled upon the criminal Deathwatch as he killed a man. Barb's screams alerted Deathwatch and his minions, who shot her in the chest with an arrow. Dan carried her into the same junkyard where Parrish's motorcycle had been taken, seeking escape, and noticed a motorcycle parked in the center of the debris. Drawn to it, Dan touched its gas cap (actually the Medallion of Power), his fingers dripping with his sister's innocent blood. The blood's contact with the Medallion changed Dan Ketch into the Ghost Rider who then rushed Barbara to a hospital, but her injuries left her in a coma. Enraged, Dan embraced his new power and its mission of vengeance, battling Deathwatch's minions, including the vampiric Blackout.

Shortly thereafter, journalist Linda Wei began campaigning against the Ghost Rider, equating him with other vigilantes such as the Punisher

REAL NAME: Daniel "Danny" Ketch
ALIASES: Spirit of Vengeance, Ghost Rider
IDENTITY: Secret
OCCUPATION: Messenger
CITIZENSHIP: USA
PLACE OF BIRTH: Brooklyn, New York
KNOWN RELATIVES: Naomi Kale (mother, deceased), Francis Ketch (adopted mother), Barbara Ketch (sister, deceased), John Blaze (brother), Andrew Kale (cousin, deceased), Jennifer Kale (cousin), Joshua Kale (grandfather, deceased), Illyana Kale, Destin & Serenity Kale, Noble Kale, Magdalena (ancestors), Dante Kale (Noble's brother, deceased)
GROUP AFFILIATION: Formerly the alternate "Fantastic Four," Secret Defenders
EDUCATION: High-school graduate
FIRST APPEARANCE: Ghost Rider #1 (1990)

Art by Clint Langley with Javier Saltares (insets)

PREVIOUS INCARNATION — Art by Javier Saltares

SCARECROW POSSESSED — Art by Gabe Alberola

(Frank Castle). Dan disliked the comparison, especially after teaming with the Punisher against the anarchist Flag-Smasher. After teaming with Spider-Man (Peter Parker), Hulk (Bruce Banner) and Wolverine (James Howlett/Logan) to form a temporary substitute Fantastic Four, he aided Wolverine and Brass (Sean Watanabe) in tracking down Brass' sister, who had been kidnapped by Deathwatch's brother-in-law Langley in a power play against the Mandarin. The stress of recent events built a wall between Dan and Stacy. When Blackout uncovered Dan's secret identity, he slew Barbara, causing a traumatized Dan to take his rage out on the Scarecrow (Ebenezer Laughton), who had gone on a killing spree to draw out his old foe, Captain America (Steve Rogers). Blackout continued to target those close to Dan, slaying blind street vendor Mr. Larsen and the priest at Mrs. Ketch's church. A local parents group blamed Ghost Rider for a series of child abductions and hired an all-female mercenary group called HEART (Humans Engaging All Racial Terrorism) to stop him. They ambushed Ghost Rider in the tunnels inhabited by the mutant Morlocks, who were involved in the child abductions. With the aid of the original X-Factor, Ghost Rider was able to resolve the crisis, though the media continued to portray him as a menace. He encountered Thor (Odinson), then fought the murderer Zodiak (Norman Harrison), after which Ghost Rider was kidnapped and separated from Dan by Nightmare, who believed him to be Zarathos. Nightmare force-fed Ghost Rider memories of Zarathos, but was shocked when the Rider rejected them as not his own. Dan and Ghost Rider re-merged and escaped Nightmare's realm, only to be trapped by the Sorcerer Supreme Dr. Strange and his pupil Rintrah, who also believed Ghost Rider to be Zarathos. Ghost Rider convinced Strange of his error and aided the mage in exorcising a demon from his ally, Topaz. Ghost Rider joined Moon Knight (Marc Spector) against Plasma (Leila O'Toole) and her Knights of the Moon, aided Spider-Man in rescuing young Adam Wright from the Hobgoblin (Jason Macendale), and briefly assisted the resurrected warriors known as Shadow Riders against the demon forces of the megalomaniacal Mys-Tech organization.

BROOD IMPLANTED — Art by Ron Wagner

The arrival of John Blaze led to even more turmoil. The former Ghost Rider used a binding ritual to trap Dan, whom he believed to be Zarathos. However, an explosion of hellfire leaped from Ghost Rider and into Blaze via his shotgun. This freed Dan, but also enabled Blaze to discharge hellfire through the gun, badly wounding Ghost Rider. When he realized that slaying Ghost Rider would mean killing Dan — whom he now viewed as an innocent (though he did not realize they were brothers) — Blaze relented. Convinced the entity within Dan was not Zarathos, but knowing what the younger man was going through, Blaze acted as Dan's protector from then on. Blaze and the Ghost Rider aided the extraterrestrials Gun Runner (Brell) and the Enhanced (Vassyrians who volunteered to have abilities enhanced to fight the war against the alien religious fanatics Cynodd) in freeing prisoners from the Cynodd. Ghost Rider also began trying to repair Dan's personal life, freeing Francis Ketch from the new Sin-Eater/Reverend Styge (James Sharp), who was preying on her suffering over her lost daughter.

Ghost Rider teamed with Cloak (Tyrone Johnson), Dagger (Tandy Bowen), Quasar (Wendell Vaughn), Daredevil (Matt Murdock), and Cable to battle various foes. Blackheart summoned Ghost Rider, Punisher, and Wolverine to the town of Christ's Crown to slay his father Mephisto, but the trio fought off both demons, saving the young empath Lucy Crumm in the process; Lucy later summoned the trio to banish Blackheart again. Ghost Rider's near-constant battles continued as he fought Zodiak, Mephisto's pawn Suicide (Chris Daniel), Spider-Man's foes the Sinister Six, Nightmare, the alien Sleepwalker, Deathwatch's agents Hag, Troll, and Snowblind, the demon Gorn, the werewolf cult the Braineaters, and the demon D'Kay and his Legion of Vengeance.

The Firm, employees of Centurious, hired Blackout to capture Ghost Rider, but Blackout instead tore out Dan's throat. Dan instinctively transformed into Ghost Rider, saving his life in the process, but leaving him in a void and unable to transform back. Capturing Blackout and the Firm's leader, Mr. Stern, Ghost Rider entombed the two in a mausoleum. Ghost Rider journeyed to New Orleans to find John Blaze to save Danny's life and encountered a group of alien Brood. Ghost Rider was briefly possessed by a Brood during this time, but Danny — while floating in the void — was able to resist the alien's control. Aided by Blaze and the X-Men, Ghost Rider slew the Brood Queen. Returning to Cypress Hills Cemetery, Ghost Rider had a vision and saw a series of individuals capable of stopping the ancient demoness Lilith, Mother of Demons, from tearing the walls between dimensions. Ghost Rider teamed with Blaze and Caretaker to assemble these beings, who eventually became the Midnight Sons. Afterward, Ghost Rider teamed with Wolverine and Beast (Henry McCoy) to battle the mercenary group Next Wave — Agent-X (James "Jim" Burley), Snare (Robert "Bert" Fielder), and Turk (Todd Flaminirezck).

Dr. Strange helped restore Dan to normal. While battling Madcap, Death Ninja, Heart Attack (Tyler Meagher), Succubus, Mr. Hyde, and Scarecrow, Dan began re-evaluating his work as Ghost Rider as he wanted to be a force for good while having a normal life. This desire intensified after his mother revealed that he and Barbara had been adopted. Ghost Rider and Blaze continued to work well together, though their methods sometimes

MERGED WITH LILIN SPIRIT — Art by Bret Blevins

clashed. The two of them united with Spider-Man in an attempt to capture both Venom (Eddie Brock) and a group of Deathspawn seeking the resurrection of Deathwatch. Ghost Rider took Hag, Troll and the now-zombie-like Deathwatch in hopes of getting Dr. Strange to send them back to the Translords' dimension. Soon after, Lilith allied herself with Centurious, and the two mystics kidnapped Dan's mother and stole Ghost Rider's enchanted chain, forging it into a weapon for Centurious. Ghost Rider badly injured Centurious during one of their clashes, unwittingly unleashing Zarathos, who had been lurking inside Centurious ever since their imprisonment in the Soul Crystal. Zarathos mated with Lilith and schemed to resurrect the Fallen, a group of his former followers. At this point, Caretaker revealed the Medallion of Power's origins and that Dan and John were brothers. Armed with this new knowledge, Ghost Rider confronted Zarathos in a battle that seemingly destroyed them both, though Ghost Rider reconstituted himself weeks later, just before the murder of John Blaze's wife, Roxanne, by Anton Hellgate.

Dan began taking control of his life and moved into a new apartment. While the Ghost Rider was plagued by Blackheart, Dan broke up with Stacy and sought more answers about Ghost Rider's origins. With the aid of Dr. Strange, Dan discovered that he was related to the young sorceress Jennifer Kale who mystically unlocked Ghost Rider's memories, restoring his knowledge of the family curse, and caused many of Dan's friends and relatives to forget his secret identity. At last aware of his past as Noble Kale, Ghost Rider began working with Dan on a much more intuitive basis, helping his human host reconcile with Stacy. He also teamed with Brother Voodoo and Dracula's daughter, Lilith, to repel another attack by the Scarecrow, who had gained the power to inhabit other bodies and had summoned the decaying corpse of Barbara Ketch as part of his plan. Ghost Rider had a brief clash with Daredevil during this time, coming to blows over their differing methods in capturing a psychotic killer. Blackheart later created his own Spirits of Vengeance — Wallow (Max Pressman), Doghead (Chio Chulito), Verminous Rex and Pao Fu (Lian Goh) — and invited Noble to join them, killing him when he refused. Noble's soul was cast into Hell, where Blackheart sought to corrupt him by offering to restore Noble's mortal form and lift the family curse, in exchange for Noble's pledge to marry both Pao Fu and the Black Rose, secretly a resurrected Roxanne Blaze. Noble agreed, but Dan was unwilling. Now fully separated from Ghost Rider, Dan was guided through Hell by the spirit of Naomi Kale and was killed after revealing that Noble's true destiny was to become the Angel of Death. Utilizing the powers that came with this title, Ghost Rider slew Blackheart and assumed the throne of Hell. He then resurrected Dan and sent him back to Earth as a way of thanking him for their years together.

Desiring to live his life anew, Noble, while remaining its ruler, relinquished control of Hell to Vengeance and aided Jack Russell, the Werewolf, in tracking down a serial killer. Noble was forced out of Hell when Mephisto reclaimed his realm. Injured and confused, Noble wandered the streets of New York City until Dan realized that Noble lacked a human host. The two men were forced to merge again and returned to seeking vengeance for the innocent. Seeking to end his curse, Dan had Mary LeBow, a backstreet mystic, exorcise the spirit of Noble from his body. Freed from his curse, Dan attempted to return to a normal life, but soon missed the thrill of adventure. Unable to restore his lost power, Dan became violent and suicidal while seeking "vengeance" on those he felt needed to be punished. Taking advantage of Dan's addiction to power, Zadkiel, a rogue angel seeking to wage war on Heaven itself, convinced Dan to become a lieutenant in his service, empowering him with the essence of a Spirit of Vengeance. Later, Dan learned of other Spirits of Vengeance, including Shoba Mirza (a hindu Ghost Rider), a Native American and others referenced in London, Africa, Germany and Russia. Zadkiel sent Dan, Blackout, Death Ninja, Doghead, and a new Orb to kill Caretaker, but Dan only sought the truth of the Spirits of Vengeance. Despite only seeking answers, Caretaker was apparently killed by Dan after he showed Dan the hidden tombs of the Spirits of Vengeance. Johnny Blaze, empowered by another Spirit of Vengeance, arrived along with Caretaker's granddaughter Sara, who had now become the Caretaker through mystical visions, to seek the same answers. Dan escaped through a portal underneath the cemetery to Tibet as Blaze and Sara followed, heading toward an inevitable battle between the two brothers.

NOBLE KALE
Art by Javier Saltares

HEIGHT: 5'10" (Ketch), 6'2" (Ghost Rider)
WEIGHT: 160 lbs. (Ketch), 220 lbs. (Ghost Rider)
EYES: Green (Ketch), none (Ghost Rider)
HAIR: Brown (Ketch), none (Ghost Rider)

ABILITIES/ACCESSORIES: Dan is extremely familiar with motorcycles and is able to make minor repairs. Ghost Rider has superhuman strength (lifting approximately 10 tons) and durability. Although the Ghost Rider's body is skeletal in nature, he can appear to have a normal frame by releasing heat from the hellfire within himself, filling out his clothing. With no physical body (other than his skeletal form), bullets pass through his clothing (or bounce off of bone), leaving him unharmed; however, if his skeleton is injured, Ghost Rider can regenerate damaged areas at an extraordinary rate, including lost limbs. Ghost Rider does not need to eat, sleep or drink and is immune to aging and conventional disease. He is immune to any mystical attacks that are specific to beings with living souls, and resistant to mind control as well. Ghost Rider possesses a mystical Penance Stare that forces his victims to experience a lifetime of pain, sorrow and guilt of their own misdeeds all at once, often leaving the victim in a catatonic state; however, it only affects living beings who have a soul.

Ghost Rider can imbue weapons/vehicles with hellfire, increasing their performance and destructive potential by touching them. Ghost Rider wields a mystical chain that he can manipulate to grow in length and transform into various other weapons, including spears, staffs, and shuriken. Ghost Rider's mystical motorcycle, composed of a Nether metal, can travel at speeds up to 250 mph and over water and up vertical surfaces. Its hellfire-engulfed tires leave a fiery trail over whatever surface the motorcycle rides across. He can mentally control the motorcycle from anywhere in the world. If it is damaged, Ghost Rider's hellfire can instantly repair it.

HELLFIRE COSTUME
Art by Salvador Larroca

POWER GRID 1 2 3 4 5 6 7
INTELLIGENCE
STRENGTH
SPEED*
DURABILITY
ENERGY PROJECTION
FIGHTING SKILLS

*YELLOW BAR INDICATES RATING DUE TO MOTORCYCLE

KHONSHU

REAL NAME: Chons (original Egyptian)
ALIASES: Impersonated Raoul Bushman
IDENTITY: None
OCCUPATION: God of the moon and vengeance
CITIZENSHIP: Realm of Heliopolis
PLACE OF BIRTH: Celestial Heliopolis
KNOWN RELATIVES: Ammon-Ra (Atum, father), Amaunet (mother), Mut (stepmother), Montu (brother), Rat-Tauit (sister-in-law), Bast (Panther God, half-brother); Bes, Ptah (possible brothers), extended family
GROUP AFFILIATION: Gods of Heliopolis
EDUCATION: Unrevealed
FIRST APPEARANCE: Moon Knight #1 (1980)

HISTORY: Khonshu is one of the gods of Celestial Heliopolis, worshipped by the ancient Egyptians. In ancient times, Khonshu posed as a human pharaoh at the Egyptian city of Thebes, the seat of worship for Ammon-Ra, presumably at the same time Osiris posed as a mortal ruler. Khonshu was also described as a mentor of Horus the Younger and may have been the sun-god's teacher and protector as Seth overthrew Osiris as pharaoh. The power shifts in heaven and on earth resulted in Osiris subsequently becoming god of the dead, and Khonshu ascended into the role of god of the moon, ousting Thoth from that role. Thoth then became god of wisdom and magic and vizier to Osiris. Khonshu allegedly dictated his will on Earth to legendary Egyptian intellectual Imhotep.

In the modern age, archaeologists Peter Alraune Sr. and his daughter Marlene uncovered a statue of Khonshu within Pharaoh Seti's tomb. When the mercenary Raoul Bushman raided the dig and killed Marlene's father, Bushman's ally Marc Spector turned on him, and Spector was stranded in the desert to die. Spector made his way to the tomb, and was believed to be dead by Marlene and her men. They lay his body before Khonshu's statue, but Spector suddenly rose to life, claiming that Khonshu had resurrected him to serve the cause of vengeance. Donning the statue's cloak, Spector struck back at Bushman and eventually became the crime-fighter Moon Knight. Spector kept Khonshu's statue within his home, its hold over him so strong that when Bushman destroyed the statue, Spector went mad. He only recovered when Marlene provided a substitute statue.

Spector eventually received tangible proof of Khonshu's influence when he met a trio of priests who had served Khonshu for ages. Shortly thereafter, time-lost members of the Avengers had been stranded in the year 2,490 BC. Khonshu contacted the Avengers' wounded leader Hawkeye and offered to restore him and return the Avengers to their own era in exchange for battling the time traveler Rama-Tut, who was persecuting Khonshu's followers. Hawkeye agreed, and Khonshu guided Moon Knight from the present to help retrieve the Avengers. Wishing to experience the Avengers' interaction up close, Khonshu became an active presence in Spector's mind and spurred him to join the Avengers, later possessing Spector's body altogether. The two sometimes clashed, as Khonshu did not approve of Spector's romance with teammate Tigra. When Mockingbird was revealed to have slain the Phantom Rider (Lincoln Slade) during their time travel adventure, Moon Knight left the team to help her confront the Phantom Rider's vengeful ghost. The exorcist Hellstorm cast Slade's spirit out of his descendant and unwitting pawn Hamilton Slade, then released Khonshu from Moon Knight to help control Slade's ghost; however, the gods of Heliopolis were then under siege from the death god Seth, whose forces attacked Khonshu upon detecting his return. Khonshu ultimately parted with Spector in order to aid his people.

When Moon Knight died battling the Hellbent, Khonshu apparently resurrected him again, this time to oppose Seth's plans on Earth. After Spector subsequently lost the use of his legs battling Bushman, Khonshu manipulated events so that he would return to action as Moon Knight, controlling Spector's friend Bertrand Crawley to set in motion a confrontation with his old enemies the Committee. Spector did not realize that he had been misled until after the Committee's defeat, when Khonshu took the form of Bushman to mock his servant; he encouraged Spector to employ more violent tactics in the future, delighting in seeing vengeance taken out on mortals.

BUSHMAN IMAGE

HEIGHT: Variable
WEIGHT: Unrevealed
EYES: White (no visible iris)
HAIR: Unrevealed

ABILITIES/ACCESSORIES: Khonshu possesses various mystical abilities, including the power to raise the dead. He has formerly acted on Earth through the body of his servant Marc Spector, sometimes inhabiting his physical form and granting him superhuman strength. He can appear to Spector in illusions, assuming other people's forms. He is also able to teleport.

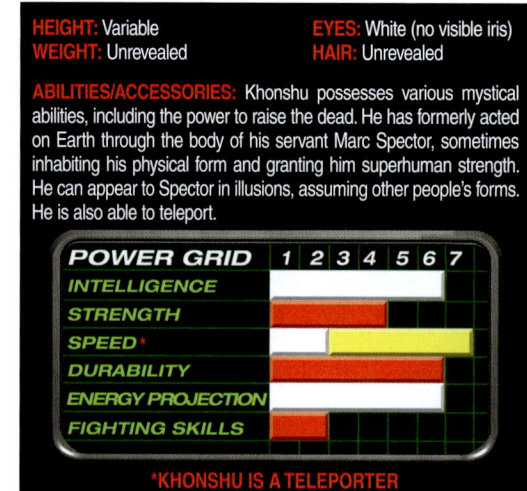

*KHONSHU IS A TELEPORTER

Art by Tommy Lee Edwards with Sal Velluto & David Finch (insets)

KID COLT

HISTORY: Blaine Colt was born in the latter half of the 19th century as the son of Dan Colt, owner of the Flying-C Ranch outside of Abilene, Wyoming. When Blaine was 15, his father gave him his first handgun, and instructed him to be responsible in how he wielded the weapon. Blaine soon found an opportunity to use the gun when he helped drive away a pair of bullies who were assaulting another teenager; however, Blaine saw that the youngster he had saved was frightened of him, and he realized that his innate skill with firearms would drive him apart from others. By the age of 16, Blaine had taken to wearing a cowhide vest as his favorite garb, and again proved his proficiency with a gun by defeating a challenge from Wild Joe Hogan. At 17, he thwarted the criminal hypnotist Orville Jones.

Blaine became afraid of his own skill as a gunfighter and stopped carrying his guns, concerned that one day his hot temper might drive him to murder an innocent man. Blaine worked on his father's ranch breaking wild horses, and Dan Colt gave him the gray stallion named "Steel" as his personal steed. The Flying-C eventually faced a challenge from Lash Larribee, a gunfighter who had founded a protection racket in Abilene called the Ranchers Protective Association. Although most of the local ranchers submitted to Larribee for fear of violent reprisal, Dan Colt refused to join. Larribee threatened Dan that if he did not join the association, he would draw on him. Dan went to confront Larribee and wound up in a gun duel with him, but being older and less experienced at gunplay, he was shot and killed by Larribee.

When Blaine heard of his father's fate, the hot temper he had always feared came over him, and he rode into Abilene to have revenge. Blaine drew on Larribee and killed him, and friends of Larribee's who witnessed the gunfight claimed that Blaine had shot him in cold blood. Blaine would later recollect that he was so angry he could not be certain if Larribee had been armed. Having succumbed to his greatest fear, ashamed of himself and uncertain if he could prove himself in court, Blaine left the ranch with Steel and went on the run, hoping to somehow make amends for his actions. Blaine was branded an outlaw, and became popularly known as "Kid Colt."

Traveling mostly across the American Southwest, Kid Colt also journeyed as far east as New York, and as far south as Mexico. He occasionally stopped in his travels to try to build a new life for himself, but his outlaw past would inevitably come back to haunt him, and he would continue to roam. Sometimes he encountered youths who admired his abilities and wanted to follow in his footsteps, but he drove such people away from him to spare them from living the life of an outlaw. Although Kid Colt fought against injustice wherever he found it and made friends when he could, his reputation was such that many feared him unjustly and ascribed acts to him that he had never performed. Some outlaws would even dress in Colt's distinctive garb in order to frame him for their crimes. In more than one instance, Kid Colt was given an opportunity to clear his name, but he abandoned the attempt each time because he could do more for society by upholding justice as an outlaw than he could as a prison inmate. Colt made friends among many of the Native American tribes including the Comanche and the Apache of Camp Verde, and sometimes went to them for shelter from the authorities.

Colt fought many famous outlaws in his travels, including the infamous James-Younger Gang, Ringo Barker, the pirate captain Barracuda, One-Eye Borden, hypnotist Bennington Brown, Bull Barton, Drago Dalton, Jim Dancer, the Gun Wizard, John Wesley Hardin, King Kobra, Montana Joe, the Mexican bandit el Lopo, Johnny Ringo and the Town Tamer. He also tangled with many lawmen and bounty hunters, such as the Man-Hunter; however, no one pursued him as doggedly as Marshal Sam Hawk, "the Manhunter." Marshal Hawk pursued Colt for years, and came close to permanently apprehending him many times. Yet Hawk recognized that Colt was not the dangerous outlaw many believed him to be, and on some occasions allowed Colt to escape his custody.

REAL NAME: Blaine Colt
ALIASES: Various as needed ("Mr. Jones," etc.)
IDENTITY: Publicly known
OCCUPATION: Gunfighter, adventurer; former rancher, cowhand
CITIZENSHIP: USA
PLACE OF BIRTH: Abilene, Wyoming
KNOWN RELATIVES: Dan Colt (father, deceased)
GROUP AFFILIATION: "The Seven-Ups"
EDUCATION: High school (incomplete)
FIRST APPEARANCE: Kid Colt #1 (1948)

Colt also fought many opponents with unusual gimmicks, such as the fake Ghost of Midnight Mountain, actually a gang of men in white cloaks; Warroo, a false "witch doctor" who used gunpowder to simulate "magic" feats; a "Circus of Crime" comprised entirely of outlaws who tried to force Colt into their gang; Dr. Danger, a ventriloquist who used a magnet to create the illusion of his partner, "the Invisible Gunman;" the Scorpion (Sam Scorpio), whose concealed pistol seemed to give him a magical power; the Fat Man, an Australian who was effective with his boomerang weapon; the Phantom Raider, a masked cattle rustler; steel-fisted Rammer Rankin; and the supposedly benevolent outlaw the Robin Hood Raider. Colt even befriended an extraterrestrial, the "Giant Monster of Midnight Valley."

Art by Leonardo Manco

Colt's most frequent opponent was Iron Mask, a criminal blacksmith garbed in bulletproof armor. During one of their battles in 1872, Colt was aided by fellow outlaw the Rawhide Kid, beginning a long-lasting friendship between the duo, as well as a friendly rivalry over which of the two men was the fastest draw. Iron Mask once recruited Bennington Brown, Dr. Danger and the Fat Man into his "Circus of Crime" scheme, but Colt defeated all four of his enemies. While in Tombstone, Texas, Colt had another opportunity to clear his name thanks to lawyer Matt Hawk, and was also aided by Hawk's alter ego the Two-Gun Kid, but although he proved his goodness to the Two-Gun Kid, there was nothing Matt Hawk could do for him but allow him to continue to evade the law.

Colt met the Rawhide Kid again when criminal quick-change artist the Masquerader assumed Colt's appearance in an attack that nearly killed the Rawhide Kid's brother. Colt eventually proved his innocence and helped the Rawhide Kid defeat the Masquerader. Colt had several adventures with the Rawhide Kid and Two-Gun Kid, including one incident where they encountered the time-traveling Thunderstrike (Eric Masterson). Colt also met the ghost-like Phantom Rider (Carter Slade) and aided him against outlaw Dack Derringer. In another adventure with the Rawhide Kid, he and Colt matched wits with the conman Burt Riker.

In 1873 when the time-traveling villain Kang the Conqueror began to set up operations in Tombstone, Texas, conquering the town with a personal army of outlaws, the Two-Gun Kid brought in Colt, the Rawhide Kid, the Phantom Rider and the Ringo Kid to oppose him. They were assisted at first by the time-traveling Avenger Hawkeye, and he was later joined by two more Avengers, Moondragon and Thor. The combined forces of the outlaws and Avengers ultimately succeeded at driving Kang out of their era. Around this time Colt met another time traveler, the Invisible Woman, when she was briefly transported to Colt's time. In 1875 Colt became involved with time travel yet again when the Avengers member Black Panther and his allies became involved in an altercation between the Asgardian gods Thor and Loki. Colt, the Rawhide Kid and Two-Gun Kid journeyed to Asgard to combat Loki, referring to their brief team of allies as the "Seven-Ups." At one point in his travels, Colt became romantically involved with fellow outlaw Arizona Annie (also called the Arizona Girl), and in one adventure they fought an outpost of extraterrestrial Skrulls.

By 1885, Colt's adventures had been embellished in dime novels, but the events they recalled were not entirely accurate. Colt's temper had become increasingly difficult to control, culminating in tragedy when he murdered a sheriff in New Mexico. The Pinkerton Detective Agency dispatched Caleb Hammer, Drew Watson and Jed McCabe to apprehend Colt, and the bounty hunter Gunhawk also began a pursuit to claim the reward. Colt rode to the Rawhide Kid to dodge his enemies, and when Reno Jones summoned Rawhide to the town of Wonderment, Montana to save its residents from the Nightriders hired by Clay Riley to drive them out, Colt decided to ride with Rawhide. Shortly after adding the Outlaw Kid to their company, the outlaws were confronted by the Pinkertons, and Colt shot Watson and McCabe dead.

Eventually arriving at Wonderment, Colt joined the Rawhide Kid, Jones, the Outlaw Kid, the Two-Gun Kid and Red Wolf in a pitched fight to defeat the Nightriders and Riley once and for all. Caleb Hammer and Gunhawk both followed Colt to Wonderment, but agreed to set aside the matter of his arrest until the Nightriders had been dealt with. Although many of the gunfighters fell in combat, the Nightriders were ultimately defeated. Realizing his opportunity had come, Gunhawk then shot Colt in the back, killing him. Appalled by Gunhawk's actions, Hammer shot the bounty hunter dead. Hammer and the Rawhide Kid buried Colt outside of Wonderment alongside the similarly fallen Outlaw Kid and Two-Gun Kid.

Art by Pablo Marcos

WITH ARIZONA ANNIE

Art by Federica Manfredi

Art by Gil Kane

HEIGHT: 5'10"
WEIGHT: 180 lbs.
EYES: Blue
HAIR: Blond

ABILITIES/ACCESSORIES: Kid Colt was an extraordinary gunfighter with a fast draw, sharp eye and deadly accuracy. His proficiency was so great that he could shoot a gun from an opponent's hand. His personal weapons were a pair of .45 Colt handguns. He was also an accomplished horseman, an experienced hand-to-hand combatant, and skilled in the use of a lariat. He usually rode the gray stallion Steel.

POWER GRID	1	2	3	4	5	6	7
INTELLIGENCE							
STRENGTH							
SPEED							
DURABILITY							
ENERGY PROJECTION							
FIGHTING SKILLS							

KID OMEGA

HISTORY: Young Quentin Quire was one of the top students at the Xavier Institute for Higher Learning, having been inspired by Professor Charles Xavier's dream of human/mutant brotherhood when he was 13 years old. Among his achievements, Quentin created a set of anti-gravity floats to grant mobility to the disembodied brain of his fellow student Martha Johansson. Devastated after learning that he was adopted, Quentin was pushed over the edge following the death of renowned mutant fashion designer Jumbo Carnation, supposedly at the hands of humans. He began to doubt Xavier's teachings, and developed a more negative and hostile view of the world and of humankind.

Quentin became addicted to the new designer drug "Kick," which increased superhuman mutant powers but also altered the brain's metabolism. Quentin assembled a group of others that shared his beliefs about humans, calling them the Omega Gang, and set about attacking both innocent humans and members of the mutant-harvesting U-Men group alike. Creating a helmet patterned after that worn by Magneto which prevented the use of telepathic powers, Quentin and the Omega Gang captured Xavier during an Open Day at the Institute and fomented a student riot. While the X-Men easily defeated the Omega Gang, the identical telepathic quintet the Stepford Cuckoos opposed Quentin. One of the Cuckoos, Sophie, whom Quentin was besotted with (much to her chagrin), empowered her sisters by taking a dose of "Kick" and utilizing the X-Men's mutant-locating device Cerebra to magnify their telepathic powers to a level higher than Quentin's. Defeating him, the strain seemingly proved too much for Sophie and she died.

Art by Greg Land
DISEMBODIED STATE

Due to his abuse of "Kick," Quentin underwent a secondary mutation that caused his physical form to discorporate, leaving him a disembodied mind trapped in a containment unit. Later, when the cosmic avatar known as the Phoenix Force returned to Earth, its presence influenced Quentin to reconstitute himself. Creating a new physical form, he sought out his beloved Sophie. Remembering her death, Quentin exhumed her corpse and sought out the

REAL NAME: Quentin Quire
ALIASES: None
IDENTITY: Secret
OCCUPATION: Terrorist; former student
CITIZENSHIP: USA
PLACE OF BIRTH: Unrevealed
KNOWN RELATIVES: Unidentified foster parents
GROUP AFFILIATION: Formerly Omega Gang (leader), Xavier Institute Student Body
EDUCATION: Various courses at Xavier Institute for Higher Learning
FIRST APPEARANCE: New X-Men #122 (2002)

Phoenix Force to help resurrect her. The X-Men trapped the Force, but Quentin sought to free it. During the ensuing clash, the Force was freed and it granted Quentin's wish, resurrecting Sophie. However, upon seeing Quentin, a disgusted Sophie chose instead to return to death. The Force ultimately merged with Jean Grey and left, after which the heartbroken Quentin returned to his disembodied state. His status following the destruction of the X-Men's mansion and closing of the Institute are unknown.

HEIGHT: 5'8"
WEIGHT: 129 lbs.
EYES: Brown
HAIR: Brown

ABILITIES/ACCESSORIES: Quentin Quire is an Omega-level telepath who can form and organize thoughts at the rate of ten million per second. Among his array of mental talents, Quentin can communicate telepathically over long distances, read the minds of others, manipulate the thoughts and bodily functions of others, and shield his mind against telepathic probes.

Quentin used his vast intellect to create a variety of devices including anti-gravity floats and a telepathy-inhibiting helmet. As a member of the Omega Gang, Quentin wielded a bullwhip.

POWER GRID	1	2	3	4	5	6	7
INTELLIGENCE							■
STRENGTH	■						
SPEED		■					
DURABILITY	■						
ENERGY PROJECTION		■					
FIGHTING SKILLS	■						

Art by Frank Quitely with Keron Grant (inset)

KIDNEY LADY

REAL NAME: Selma Blotte
ALIASES: Miss Klady, "Divine Mistress of the Inner Light," "Divine Kidney Mistress"
IDENTITY: Known to authorities
OCCUPATION: Kidney watchdog, witch
CITIZENSHIP: USA
PLACE OF BIRTH: Unrevealed
KNOWN RELATIVES: Chair-Thing ("offspring"), unidentified father
GROUP AFFILIATION: Leader of Kidney Watchdogs of America
EDUCATION: Unrevealed
FIRST APPEARANCE: Howard the Duck #2 (1976)

HISTORY: Selma Blotte was a poor farm girl whose father was away when Elmer, a metaphysical book salesman, came to call. Elmer quickly seduced her, sold her the book "The Human Kidney: Seat of the Soul," and used the purchase price to buy two tickets to Cleveland. There, they frequented plush nightclubs and stayed in the best hotels until Elmer, apparently drafted, deserted Selma, leaving her with unpaid bills and the book to which Selma devoted her life. Discovering the book possessed evil powers, Selma used it to become a kidney-obsessed witch and arch-foe of Dakimh the Enchanter, events that became magically written within the book itself.

Sensing a shift in the cosmic axis, she mystically viewed Howard the Duck's dimension-crossing arrival and believed he had come as Dakimh's ally to deprive her of her kidneys. Mixing a witches' brew in her bathtub, she cast an explosive spell, throwing a chair in to slow the chain reaction, thereby creating the malevolent stationary Chair-Thing. Riding Cleveland buses all day to protect her kidneys and search for Howard, she finally encountered him, hit him with her cane, accused him of participating in the International Kidney Poisoning Conspiracy through tobacco, deep-fried foods, wanton women and low morals, then stepped on his cigar, inciting him into a fight that caused the bus to careen off an elevated highway. The alien-possessed Turnip-Man (Arthur Winslow) saved the bus, then abducted Howard's companion Beverly Switzler. Selma inadvertently aided Howard by tauntingly suggesting where Turnip-Man would likely take Bev. Encountering Howard on another bus, Selma tried to warn Beverly away from him and accused him of being the overall head of the Kidney Poisoning Conspiracy. While searching for proof of this, Selma took time to smash up the "Happiness is a Hamburger" Coffee Shop, again provoking Howard's attack, which degenerated into a food fight. Subsequently traveling from city to city in her crusade, she met Howard on a bus from Niagara Falls to Cleveland. This time their tussle caused a bus crash in Sauerbraten County, Ohio for which Selma, Howard and the speech-afflicted dimension-channeler Winda Wester were arrested. In court, Selma sweetened up and gained the judge's sympathy, earning her release while Howard and Winda were committed to a mental facility, though they were subsequently discharged.

After a slight cosmic axis shift produced an overlap with an alternate reality that possibly altered her past, Selma founded the Kidney Watchdogs of America and assaulted Howard on a Cleveland street, recruiting the Cleveland Clobberer, a former baseball player turned cab driver, in the process. Enticing Howard and Beverly to her house by anonymously renting them a room, Selma finally lured the duck into the seat of the Chair-Thing. When Howard's cigar set the Chair-Thing on fire, Selma dumped water on it, reverting it to normal. Vowing revenge, she teleported away. Perhaps due to the axis shift, however, Selma apparently forgot her powers and returned to her old ways, assaulting Howard at Donner's Restaurant. Most recently, Selma was seen in line at the Ohio Department of Motor Vehicles. Since she does not drive, she may have been in the wrong line, intending to register her witch powers with SHIELD or perhaps searching for Howard, who gave her the slip this time.

NOTE: The Kidney Lady once threatened to sic a younger confederate with "new legs" on Howard, but that person has never been revealed.

HEIGHT: 5'6"
WEIGHT: 241 lbs.
EYES: Blue
HAIR: Gray, formerly brown

ABILITIES/ACCESSORIES: Although she has previously used magic powers that allowed her to create the Chair-Thing, teleport and mystically view Howard's arrival, the Kidney Lady mostly relies on her girth, cane and garlic breath to attack her enemies. She occasionally wears a surgical mask to protect her kidneys.

POWER GRID	1	2	3	4	5	6	7
INTELLIGENCE							
STRENGTH							
SPEED							
DURABILITY							
ENERGY PROJECTION							
FIGHTING SKILLS							

Art by Frank Brunner with Gene Colan (insets)

KILLER SHRIKE

HISTORY: After military service, Simon Maddicks became a mercenary, eventually employed by the Roxxon Oil Company as a special covert operative. Selected for super-powered enhancement, Maddicks was sent to the mutagenics lab of Roxxon's subsidiary, the Brand Corporation, where he underwent extensive conditioning to enhance his strength and endurance, as well as surgery to implant a miniature anti-gravity generator designed by scientist Paul Hazlett (Raptor) at the base of his spine. Finally, he was given a battlesuit with powerful electrical wrist blasters and code-named Killer Shrike.

Having learned of an ancient Conspiracy through the purchases they had made from Brand, Roxxon sent Shrike to infiltrate the group. The Conspiracy were seeking to reunite the Bloodgem fragments, and to test Shrike they sent him to assist the extradimensional Ulluxy'l Kwan Tae Syn in this quest. Ulluxy'l in turn had Shrike observe Bloodstone Island, home of Ulysses Bloodstone, possessor of one of the fragments; Shrike watched as the gigantic monster Goram attacked the island and was entangled by its defenses. Unaware Goram had been sent by another Conspiracy member, Centurius, Shrike presumed the Conspiracy had rivals in their hunt and cut Goram free, intending to follow him home; however, a near miss from Bloodstone's shotgun stunned Shrike, letting Goram escape. Shrike briefly battled Bloodstone, who slammed Shrike's wrist talons together, causing an explosive backlash, which left Shrike comatose. Bloodstone anonymously dropped Shrike off with the NYPD; lacking evidence that he had committed any crime, they placed Shrike under observation in Delenor Hospital. The Conspiracy mailed another of their agents, the living exoskeleton Modular Man, to Shrike's hospital room; believing him to be some sort of inert modern art, security let the package through. Assisted by his superior Jocko, Modular Man absconded with Shrike; however, the Conspiracy's leaders were slain before Modular Man could return to them.

Shrike revived, but was suffering from amnesia; Modular Man offered to reveal Shrike's lost past to him in exchange for helping with Modular Man's own goals, supposedly to restore his lost human form. Clashing with the Beast (Hank McCoy) and Spider-Man (Peter Parker), the villains stole a cellular condenser and then hijacked the microwave energy from an Empire State Building television broadcast to power it; however, Modular Man had deceived his partner, and actually planned to become a being of pure energy. Deeming Shrike unimportant, Modular Man casually swatted him aside, only to have the two heroes use the stunned Shrike's wrist blasters to disrupt Modular Man's growing form. In the aftermath, Shrike fled. Brand Corporation President James Melvin tracked him down, helping him regain his memories and avoid capture, and taking him on as his personal bodyguard. As Harold Simmons, Shrike accompanied Melvin to a party at newspaper publisher J. Jonah Jameson's penthouse in honor of Jonah's fiancée, scientist Marla Madison; however, while sneaking a smoke on the balcony, the circuitry in Shrike's battlesuit, hidden under his tuxedo, attracted the scattered energy of Will O' the Wisp; entering the battlesuit, Wisp controlled Shrike like a puppet, forcing him to kidnap Marla and transport her to Brand's Special Powers Lab in New Jersey, hoping she could use the equipment there to restore his physical form. Having tracked them down, Spider-Man lent his assistance, holding off the facility's guards, knocking Shrike out after the Wisp exited the battlesuit, and using the Shrike's blasters to power the reintegration device.

Following Brand's public dissolution, Shrike became a free agent; alongside various other superhumans he was briefly captured and imprisoned by Locksmith, and subsequently released by Spider-Woman (Jessica Drew). Afterwards Shrike put out word that he was available for hire; finding no organizations interested, he concluded he needed to raise his visibility, so he robbed the Bronx's First Bank and Savings Association. Increasingly paranoid, when he spotted Spider-Man later approaching his apartment building, Shrike wrongly concluded the hero was looking for him and attacked, figuring that killing Spider-Man would

REAL NAME: Simon Maddicks
ALIASES: Harold Simmons
IDENTITY: Known to authorities
OCCUPATION: Mercenary
CITIZENSHIP: USA with criminal record
PLACE OF BIRTH: Williamsburg, Virginia
KNOWN RELATIVES: None
GROUP AFFILIATION: Formerly Thunderbolts army, Air Force, agent of Roxxon Oil Company, Conspiracy
EDUCATION: High school graduate, military training
FIRST APPEARANCE: Rampaging Hulk #1 (1977)

bring the recognition he craved. Instead the hero faked Shrike out, luring him close enough to lay him low with a blow to the chin, his only unarmored area, and leaving him for the police. Shrike asked the Tinkerer to build a power booster to increase his capabilities, but ran into Spider-Man again while robbing an armored car to pay for the device, and fled empty-handed. Nonetheless he still met with the Tinkerer to collect his booster, only to find the wall-crawler again coincidentally on the scene. Forcing the Tinkerer to give him the booster on credit, Shrike swiftly plugged it in before trying to blast Spider-Man; however, the Tinkerer had anticipated a possible double-cross and left out a vital circuit until

Art by Joe Kubert with Jim Mooney (inset)

payment was made. Without it, the booster overloaded Shrike's systems, allowing Spider-Man to finish him off with ease.

When the so-called "Acts of Vengeance" conspiracy of criminal masterminds offered cash payouts to any super-villain who killed a super hero, Shrike briefly allied himself with Coachwhip and Ringer (Keith Kraft), taking on the vigilante Moon Knight (Marc Spector); despite Shrike disparaging his opponent's lack of powers, Moon Knight swiftly defeated the trio. Shrike fled, though not before shooting down Moon Knight's helicopter, critically injuring its pilot, Jean Paul "Frenchie" DuChamp. Shrike was briefly and argumentatively partnered with the Grey Gargoyle and Dragon Man, hired to silence the criminal Simon Woziah before he turned evidence for the FBI; however, Woziah's protector She-Hulk quickly knocked out Shrike. Deciding to reinvent himself as a casino owner in Atlantic City, Shrike began hitting casinos owned by Charles Ramos, trying to blackmail Ramos into signing one, the Palantine, over to him; however Frenchie, now recovered from his injuries, came looking for revenge, armed with weapons carefully chosen to counter Shrike's powers. After a brutal fight, Frenchie injected Shrike in his unarmored chin with a drug that disrupted the neural link to his anti-gravity generator; Shrike flew headfirst into the ceiling repeatedly until he lost consciousness. Again showing signs of paranoia after this encounter, Shrike laid low, believing an unspecified foe was plotting to kill him; when Spider-Man chanced to pass his hideout, Shrike attacked unprovoked, but was quickly knocked out. Recovering his nerve somewhat, Shrike attended an AIM Weapons Expo on Boca Caliente, where he joined other criminals in attacking Captain America (Steve Rogers) and the Falcon (Sam Wilson) when they crashed the event.

Shrike was recruited into the team of flying mercenaries known as the Air Force, working for Air Command; however, after a mission to rescue fellow operative Cardinal from Ryker's Island Penitentiary, Shrike and several fellow fliers were captured by New Warriors Nova (Richard Rider), Turbo (Mike Jeffries) and Mickey Musashi. Unidentified employers arranged for Shrike's release from jail in return for killing Lin Sun and Abe Brown (two-thirds of the Sons of the Tiger), but the Prowler (Hobie Brown) thwarted Shrike's attack. Next he was hired by the Architect to attack fellow assassin Shatterhead, unaware the Architect had similarly hired Shatterhead to fight him, as part of the Architect's larger plan to find someone worthy to kill the Architect himself; Shatterhead hospitalized Shrike, knocking him out of the contest. Shrike later teamed up with Whiplash (Leeann Foreman), Orka and Shockwave to hijack the retired aircraft carrier USS Intrepid; however, Oracle Inc's Heroes for Hire swiftly defeated them.

Shrike fell in love with a woman named Nadine, and together they toured the country in a battered camper van; he promised Nadine that he had given up crime and wanted to settle down with her once they found a suitable small town where his past would not raise problems. In truth, though Shrike's confidence was shot after his long string of defeats, he had no desire to go straight, and when Nadine spotted him casing a convenience store in the small town of Wassau, he admitted his true aim. He wanted them to go from one small, heroless town to the next, robbing unopposed until he had enough cash to buy them a large, new RV and himself a new, cool code name, like "Death Raven." Shrike's luck, however, held true; the Hulk (Bruce Banner) was in Wassau by chance, and Shrike's paranoia convinced him the Hulk was looking for him. The maudlin Hulk didn't want a fight and tried to ignore Shrike's attacks, until Shrike collapsed an entire building on him. Shrugging it off, the Hulk swatted Shrike away and departed; only then did Shrike notice his camper partially buried under the rubble. Digging it out, the brokenhearted Shrike found Nadine's corpse inside. Despite blaming himself for her death, Shrike continued his criminal lifestyle, but the Avengers soon apprehended him. SHIELD interrogated him, wanting to know how he could maintain his expensive equipment given his poor finances. Shrike admitted the Tinkerer had been compensating him recently, and he agreed to help SHIELD's surveillance operation, leading them to the Tinkerer's lab; however, when he tried to enter the lab, the Tinkerer, presumably suspecting his treachery, electrocuted him.

Recovering from his near-fatal injuries, Shrike attempted to rob Roxxon labs on Christmas Day to steal Project Z, confident that it would be poorly guarded on the holiday, only to be defeated by the Jewish hero Grasshopper (Neil Shelton). Subsequently, Shrike was forcibly recruited into Baron (Helmut) Zemo's expanded Thunderbolts army, serving briefly with that group.

Hired by Roxxon, Shrike led an incursion into the Savage Land to steal Vibranium, but was repelled by the region's protector Ka-Zar (Kevin Plunder), and sent back with a warning that further attempts would be met with lethal force; his employer sent Shrike back in twice with increasingly powerful strike teams, but the Savage Land inhabitants set aside local differences and united to slaughter them. Cutting his losses, Shrike fled, leaving his allies to be slain or captured. Laying low in New York while planning to settle old scores, Shrike was caught off guard in his motel room without his battlesuit by Moon Knight, who brutally assaulted him for his past transgressions.

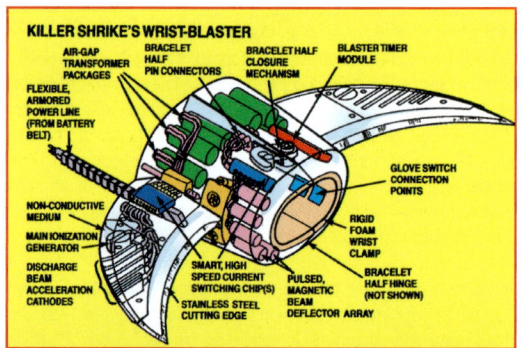

Art by Eliot R. Brown

HEIGHT: 6'5"
WEIGHT: 250 lbs.
EYES: Brown
HAIR: Brown

ABILITIES/ACCESSORIES: Killer Shrike possesses enhanced strength, reflexes 1.5 times faster than an Olympic athlete, and twice the stamina of a normal human; initially able to lift 1 ton, he has more recently been shown to be much stronger, throwing a truck with ease. A mentally controlled anti-gravity implant enables flight at up to 120 mph (the maximum speed at which he can breathe unaided) for up to 2 hours before fatigue sets in; the implant is powered by a small thermoelectric converter with a nuclear-fueled core, which needs recharging every 1.2 years. He can support about 550 lbs. including his own weight while flying. His insulated steel-alloy bodysuit provides protection against most guns and rifles; however, his uncovered chin remains vulnerable. He wears twin titanium wrist talons with built-in electrical blasters; as well as being able to fire high-amperage electrical blasts of up to 50,000 volts individually; they can combine to deliver a 120,000 volt attack capable of collapsing small buildings. The talons' blades are retractable and sharp enough to slice through Spider-Man's webbing. Maddicks has extensive combat and martial-arts training, and is proficient with knives and guns.

KILLMONGER

HISTORY: Born in the African kingdom of Wakanda, N'Jadaka was a child when the criminal Ulysses Klaw invaded the country to steal its Vibranium. Klaw enslaved numerous Wakandans, including N'Jadaka's family. In the violent turmoil in which Klaw was driven from Wakanda, N'Jadaka's parents were killed. However, the escaping Klaw took N'Jadaka with him as a captive. N'Jadaka eventually escaped from Klaw, but had no means to return to Wakanda. Instead, N'Jadaka changed his name to Erik Killmonger and lived in New York City's Harlem. He studied business, earned a Ph.D. in engineering, and became a teacher at the Massachusetts Institute of Technology. Killmonger contacted Wakanda's king, T'Challa, who was in the United States as the costumed Black Panther, and T'Challa arranged for Killmonger to return to Wakanda.

However, far from being grateful to T'Challa, Killmonger instead blamed the Wakandan monarchy for his parents' deaths. Killmonger organized a massive revolt to overthrow T'Challa. Employing the mutagenic radiation of the mysterious Resurrection Altar, Killmonger endowed some of his followers with superhuman abilities, including Baron Macabre, King Cadaver, Salamander K'ruel, Malice and Sombre. Among his other operatives were Lord Karnaj and Venomm. Killmonger also gathered together an army of rebels known as the Death Regiment. The Black Panther was particularly outraged by the Death Regiment's murder of a Wakandan farmer named M'Jumbak; subsequently, the Panther rescued M'Jumbak's young son Kantu from a charging rhinoceros. Ultimately, Killmonger led his superhuman lieutenants, the Death Regiment, and dinosaurs from Wakanda's remote Serpent Valley in an attack on the Wakandan royal palace. The Panther engaged in hand-to-hand combat with Killmonger atop Warrior Falls, and Killmonger was about to throw the Panther down the falls when young Kantu pushed Killmonger over the falls to his death.

All of Killmonger's surviving lieutenants were imprisoned. However, Killmonger's lover, Madam Slay, recovered his body and used unusual herbs to preserve it. Later, the Mandarin resurrected Killmonger and outfitted him with one of his rings in an attempt to turn the sacred mound of Wakandan Vibranium into Antarctic Vibranium, also known as anti-metal, to trigger a chain reaction that would dissolve all metal on Earth. Aided by Iron Man (Tony Stark), the Panther thwarted Killmonger, who reverted to lifelessness. Subsequently, Klaw resurrected Killmonger, using him against their mutual enemy, the Panther. The Panther defeated Killmonger, who died yet again.

The Death Regiment brought Killmonger's ashes to the Resurrection Altar and sacrificed almost a dozen of their own members to restore him to life. This time Killmonger attempted to destroy the Wakandan economy by ruining T'Challa's international reputation; to this end, Killmonger manipulated superhumans against the Black Panther, including Hydro-Man, Hulk (Bruce Banner), Nightshade (Tilda Johnson), bossman Morgan, Stiletto (Tom Stuart), Dontrell "Cockroach" Hamilton and the Serpent Society's Cottonmouth. Killmonger also recruited the Panther's former Dora Milaje bodyguard Nakia into his ranks, transforming her into the new Malice. By nationalizing all foreign companies' holdings in Wakanda, T'Challa thwarted Killmonger's scheme, though T'Challa risked the collapse of the world economy in doing so. Killmonger overcame T'Challa in ritual combat, with the result that Killmonger became the new Black Panther and head of Wakanda's Black Panther Cult. As the new Black Panther, Killmonger then attempted to take T'Challa's place as a member of the Avengers. However, Killmonger overreached by ingesting the heart-shaped herb that traditionally granted the Black Panther his superhuman abilities.

ARMOR
Art by Alan Davis

REAL NAME: Erik Killmonger; legally changed from N'Jadaka
ALIASES: Formerly Black Panther
IDENTITY: None
OCCUPATION: Former dictator of Niganda, leader of the Black Panther Cult, rebel leader, teacher
CITIZENSHIP: Wakanda
PLACE OF BIRTH: N'Jadaka village, Wakanda
KNOWN RELATIVES: Unidentified sons and daughters, unidentified parents (deceased)
GROUP AFFILIATION: Former leader of the Black Panther Cult, leader of the Death Regiment
EDUCATION: Ph.D. in engineering, MBA
FIRST APPEARANCE: Jungle Action #6 (1973)

Since the herb was poisonous to anyone outside the Wakandan royal family, Killmonger fell into a comatose state. Later reviving, Killmonger sought out New York City policeman Kevin "Kasper" Cole, who had adopted a Black Panther costume to combat crime. Killmonger gave Cole a genetically modified version of the heart-shaped herb, which enhanced Cole's senses and physical prowess without poisoning him. As part of the bargain, Cole took on the role of a White Tiger in the Black Panther cult. Killmonger also offered to help Cole find a kidnapped boy in return

Art by Sal Velluto

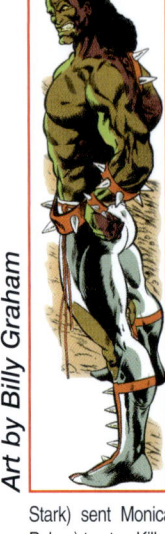
Art by Billy Graham

for his loyalty. However, Cole rejected Killmonger's aid, found the abducted boy, and remained loyal to T'Challa, who had reclaimed his role as the Black Panther.

The US State Department later made a secret alliance with Killmonger, believing that Killmonger would go to war with Wakanda, thereby providing an excuse for America to take control of the country. Wakanda was bordered by the country of Niganda, which had previously held an army of genetically engineered animals designed by the Red Ghost; one of them, a superhuman monkey had obtained genius-level intellect and used it on Killmonger's behalf, supplying him with advanced technology and the resources of the remaining engineered animals. Joined by his sons and daughters, Killmonger led a revolt against the government of Niganda, made himself Niganda's ruler, and took T'Challa's sister Shuri prisoner. When T'Challa's fellow Avenger Iron Man (Tony Stark) sent Monica Rambeau (the superhuman formerly known as Pulsar) to stop Killmonger, Killmonger captured her as well. War erupted between Wakanda and Niganda, but Killmonger's simian ally generated a force field preventing the Wakandans from approaching his base by land or air. Using a tunneling device previously obtained from the Mole Man (Harvey Elder), T'Challa confronted Killmonger, with the two again battling savagely, each wearing a suit of powerful armor. Killmonger generated magnetic charges in T'Challa's sword and armor, repelling them and preventing him from holding the sword. Just as it appeared Killmonger was about to slay T'Challa, Rambeau, who had escaped captivity, apparently killed Killmonger. Killmonger's sons and daughters spirited Killmonger's body away and vowed vengeance on the Black Panther, holding him responsible for their father's death. Inasmuch as Killmonger has returned to life several times before, it seems unlikely that his most recent apparent demise will prove to be permanent.

SALAMANDER K'RUEL

DEATH REGIMENT

SOMBRE

Art by Gil Kane & Billy Graham

MALICE

MADAM SLAY

Art by Rich Buckler & Billy Graham

LORD KARNAJ

Art by Billy Graham

PREYY

BARON MACABRE & KING CADAVER

Art by Billy Graham

VENOMM

Art by Rich Buckler

HEIGHT: 6'6" **EYES:** Brown
WEIGHT: 225 lbs. **HAIR:** Black

ABILITIES/ACCESSORIES: Erik Killmonger is an extraordinary hand-to-hand combatant. His uniform is studded with spikes that can inject poison into his adversaries. His wristbands contain weapons including blades and an energy blaster as well as communications devices with LCD displays. At various times Killmonger has wielded firearms and spears. Killmonger has kept several pet leopards, including Preyy, which will attack at his command. For his invasion of Niganda, Killmonger acquired highly advanced combat technology including a force field generator, laser rifle and a highly durable suit of armor, which contained a variety of weapons including magnetic beams and a wrist-mounted buzz-saw.

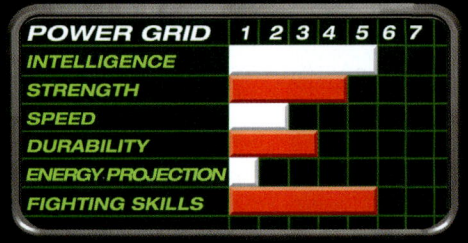

POWER GRID	1	2	3	4	5	6	7
INTELLIGENCE							
STRENGTH							
SPEED							
DURABILITY							
ENERGY PROJECTION							
FIGHTING SKILLS							

KILLPOWER

HISTORY: Julius Mullarkey, code-named Killpower, was Gena-Sys Laboratories' Dr. Oonagh Mullarkey's first transgenic human, a product of human DNA mixed with several animals: orangutan, lemur, bat, gorilla, and rhinoceros. Spending the days prior to his "birth" in a nutrient chamber, many of Killpower's more delicate organs were replaced with mechanical equivalents, allowing a concentrated steroid solution to be safely pumped through his body. This greatly enhanced his physical development to the extent that when he was "born" he resembled a three-year-old child. Mullarkey named him Julius, due to the somewhat "caesarian" nature of his delivery. The newly decanted infant was further enhanced magically by Mullarkey's Mys-Tech master Ormond Wychwood. Julius grew to physical maturity within 18 months, learning through destructive play, showing an innate understanding of complex machinery and weapons. Still a child emotionally and intended to be a living weapon for Mys-Tech, Julius viewed real-world killing the same way he did video game mayhem, an enjoyable game with no consequences; only his "mother," Dr. Mullarkey, could control him. He was briefly lured from Mys-Tech by the mysterious Time Guardian, who sent him on a mission through time to retrieve the scattered components of the temporally powered Chronifact, bringing him — alongside the Genetix youths who had been sent by Mullarkey to retrieve him — into conflict with Rama-Tut and scientist Sidney Fishburne circa 2950 BC. Julius befriended Rama-Tut's enemy Samira, Sorceress of the Nile, who helped him retrieve half of the Chronifact from Rama-Tut's laboratory. When Killpower's half of the Chronifact sent him further back in time, the Genetix youths followed, discovering the other half of the Chronifact in the process. Unfortunately, Fishburne sent Killpower back to the modern era (actually five years after the time from which Julius had departed) where he encountered the Punisher in what was, from Killpower's perspective, their first meeting. They became entangled in a war between the Street Amazons and the Huns gangs. When Killpower unintentionally upstaged the Huns warlord, Rique, the gang chose Killpower as their new warlord, and Fishburne temporarily granted the Street Amazons advanced Mys-Tech battle armor. Genetix caught up with Killpower, and they were pulled through time to a distant future, where the Time Guardian and Fishburne competed for possession of the Chronifact. Meanwhile, Killpower successfully used his mecha-psychometry for the first time, creating a new weapon with which to deter a horde of ravening mutates. The Time Guardian defeated Fishburne by draining the Chronifact of its chronal energy, and Killpower and the Genetix were returned to their own time. Killpower ultimately became Mys-Tech's top hit man and weapons expert, despite having a child's mentation.

When he was chronologically 5 (and emotionally around 10), dimension-hopping Mind Operated PErsonal Dematerialization (MOPED) technology, which had been stolen by Mys-Tech's Warheads, fell into the hands of foul-mouthed teenager Harley Davidson, aka Motormouth. This attracted Nick Fury and SHIELD's attention, especially when Killpower killed several SHIELD agents in London. He also attacked SHIELD's UK base, where he was opposed by the Punisher, for whom this was their first encounter. Meanwhile, Motormouth absconded from Mys-Tech with the MOPED technology. Outfitted with another MOPED unit, Killpower caught up with her on the planet Tekron, but smitten by her, tried talking before violence, and she convinced him indiscriminate killing was wrong. Attacked by the locals, Killpower swiftly defeated them, but Harley was fatally wounded by a ricochet; Killpower performed emergency surgery, cannibalizing Harley's MOPED unit and his own equipment to turn her into a cyborg. Feeling Mys-Tech had lied to him, Killpower stayed with Harley, becoming her partner. They encountered Skordos and his robotic drones, who wanted their MOPED units to help in their battle against the Mechos droids. When Motormouth blew Skordos to pieces, Killpower recognized his circuit designs as being the work of Ace Corporation, the same people who had made the MOPED units. Together they went to Ace's base on the legendary factory planet Matricca Scorpio to investigate. While there, Mys-Tech's Psycho-Warriors successfully captured Killpower. Julius awoke in Truth Centre 18 at Mys-Tech Central, where he was interrogated by his "mother," though it quickly degenerated into an argument. Julius broke free in a fit of temper, but Mys-Tech's leader, Algernon Crowe, prevented him escaping. Dr. Mullarkey restrained Killpower again, but this time Motormouth freed him. They encountered Mys-Tech board members Tyburn and Rathcoole, the latter of whom teleported them into Mys-Tech's Research Section. There they were attacked by a nearly indestructible monster, but Mys-Tech security team's arrival distracted it long enough for them to escape. Together they searched Mys-Tech's headquarters for a weapons store, encountering Nick Fury en route. Fury was tempted to avenge the agents Julius had killed but realized Mys-Tech's number one assassin had changed sides and let him go.

REAL NAME: Julius Mullarkey
ALIASES: None
IDENTITY: Secret
OCCUPATION: Adventurer; former assassin
CITIZENSHIP: None
PLACE OF BIRTH: Gena-Sys Laboratories, England, UK
KNOWN RELATIVES: Oonagh Mullarkey (creator, "mother")
GROUP AFFILIATION: Partner of Motormouth; formerly Dark Guard, Huns, agent of Mys-Tech; possibly Resistance Co-ordination Executive, Avengers
EDUCATION: Extensive combat training; no other formal education
FIRST APPEARANCE: Motormouth #1 (1992)

Art by Gary Frank

After visiting the Crossroads of Time and Julius Caesar's Rome, Motormouth wanted to relax, and Killpower suggested the South Pacific island Kamuni Atoll. Their rest was disturbed when Killpower was attacked by Death's Head (Minion), hired by Mys-Tech to retrieve their errant assassin. Death's Head had Killpower at his mercy, when a beam intended for the cyborg teleported them both onboard an alien space vessel where they were subdued by Termagent and Megaira, secretly aspects of the Battletide's demonic warlord Termagaira. Death's Head and Killpower were temporarily coerced into fighting as partners on the planetoid Colosseum, an arena world for the Games, where Termagent and Megaira were hailed as their all-time champions. After a long day's hard battling, the duo were attacked by Wolverine and Sabretooth, who had also been forced to participate in the Games and driven into berserker rages by behavior-altering inhibitor collars. Fortunately, the Games were called to a halt and the combatants retired to the Pleasure Drome for the evening. Any wounded or dying combatants were healed by the Temploids, an ancient order of robots who convinced Killpower and Death's Head to fight against the Battletide alongside Dark Angel, Hercules, Psylocke, the Vassyrian known as Smith, Wolverine and a mind-controlled Sabretooth. Killpower was instrumental in freeing his companions from their inhibitor collars and helping Death's Head defeat Termagaira. He also augmented Death's Head with techno-mystical components from a damaged Temploid robot, enabling him to overcome the Battletide. After Killpower rebuilt his damaged form, Death's Head abandoned Mys-Tech's contract. When the Battletide returned, Killpower was summoned by the Temploids to assist Death's Head yet again. One of the Battletides demons possessed the Hulk in an attempt to thwart their mission, but Death's Head and Killpower reached the heart of the Battletide itself where they were joined by Temploid warrior Gabriel. During a battle with Termagaira, Killpower was smashed through a wall and fell a mile to the bottom of a cavern. Critically injured, he helped Gabriel save Death's Head's life, enabling the cyborg to defeat the Battletide a second time, and the Temploids revived Killpower after his heart stopped while repairing Gabriel. After their island hideaway was attacked by Mys-Tech's demons, Killpower and Motormouth joined many of Earth's heroes battling the forces unleashed by the reality-warping Un-Earth. On Hyrkania they fought the wizard Qaar Ghoth, befriending Sabra of the Seven Isles, and discovered that legends there spoke of them as "the Saving Graces." Then, together with Zachary Sorrow, they battled Electro-Vampires on Earth-93411 in the year 2195 AD, discovering that they were techno-magical robots created by Mys-Tech. Returning to London, they helped Death's Head against AIM's Metamorph, a cyber construction able to mimic other organisms that had gone rogue and patterned itself after the local homeless people. After killing the god Kipple on Fautor IV, Killpower and Motormouth were drafted by the Time Keeper to join his Dark Guard and thwart Mys-Tech's agent Collapsar's machinations to exacerbate the conflict between the Egalitern Bloc and the Technarcy on Eopia. During their first battle alongside their teammates, Albion (Peter Hunter), Death's Head, and Ultra Marine (Major Kith Nasca), Killpower and Colonel Tigon Liger were captured and tortured by Collapsar. They were, however, rescued by Death's Head and Motormouth, and the team helped put a stop to the planet's civil war.

Returning to Earth for a vacation, Killpower and Motormouth ran into the Hulk and helped him fight Madman.

Since then, Killpower and Motormouth have been seen amongst the multitude of cross-dimensional Avengers who fought in the Destiny War at the Citadel at the End of Time, and a noticeably older Killpower fought with the Resistance Co-ordination Executive of Earth-811 against that world's ruling Sentinel regime, but whether these sightings were of the time and dimension-hopping Killpower-616 or an extradimensional counterpart is uncertain. Also, Hyrkania's legends of the Saving Graces suggest that Killpower and Motormouth may have many further adventures on that world yet to come, though these legends may stem from their alternate dimensional counterparts.

HEIGHT: 6'9" **EYES:** Red
WEIGHT: 252 lbs. **HAIR:** Red with Orange streak

ABILITIES/ACCESSORIES: Killpower possesses enhanced strength (lifting 1 ton), reflexes, speed, agility and healing, as well as rudimentary sonar, vestigial bat wings and a small prehensile tail. Although he has been described as almost indestructible, his toughened skin isn't bulletproof; however, he recovers from bullet wounds and penetration wounds very rapidly, and from more severe wounds given sufficient rest. He has a bio-occult affinity for mechanics, enabling him to divine how to use, repair or modify unfamiliar and complex machinery through mecha-psychometry. In particular, this grants him a genius level aptitude for weaponry. Furthermore, he has exhibited amazing speed when using his mecha-psychometry, often jury-rigging highly advanced equipment in a matter of seconds. He is skilled in various forms of combat, but, despite his outward appearance Killpower is generally submissive when confronted with a stern "mother figure," such as Dr. Mullarkey or Motormouth.

Killpower generally carries a wide variety of weapons, including knives and grenades, but generally prefers extremely large guns. He also has excellent observational skills. He wears personalized bulletproof battle armor and an anti-gravity pack outfitted with tools and weapons. The pack usually connects to a shoulder-mounted device capable of firing various missiles or other projectiles, and wrist-mounted lasers (single- or triple-barreled). He has also used jet heels as an alternative to the anti-gravity pack. He can create illusory duplicates of himself using holo-projectors to confuse the enemy. He uses MOPED technology to traverse time and dimensions. Since the Time Guardian reprogrammed it, Julius' MOPED unit can transport him anywhere in time, backwards, forwards or sideways, at the speed of thought. Using the unique UPC grid system, MOPED units are normally coded to individual brain patterns, hence as a by-product the user and unit tend to develop a symbiotic relationship; however, Killpower used his mecha-psychometry to override this feature. If he were to develop a symbiotic relationship with the unit, its micro-computers would warn of threats distant or outside the range of his senses, providing instant translation of any language and a high-voltage-discharge capability. He initially had a communication unit and mini-camera, but cannibalized these to save Motormouth's life. He could build replacements at will.

KILLPOWER'S EARLY DEVELOPMENT

Art by Dougie Braithwaite

POWER GRID	1	2	3	4	5	6	7
INTELLIGENCE							
STRENGTH							
SPEED							
DURABILITY							
ENERGY PROJECTION							
FIGHTING SKILLS							

KILLRAVEN

HISTORY: Seeking to prevent humanity from eventually conquering the stars, in numerous timelines the time-traveler Immortus directed a militant alien species based on Mars to turn their attention toward Earth. In Reality-691 these "Martians" invaded in 1901, an event chronicled in H.G. Wells' historical novel The War of the Worlds. For three weeks the Martians devastated Earth before falling victim to Earth's viruses, against which they were defenseless. One hundred years later, on June 29, 2001, the Martians returned, having prepared against Earth's bacteria and armaments. Man's nuclear weapons were all simultaneously destroyed and humanity's bacterial warfare backfired, the Martians proving immune while severe plagues afflicted mankind and Earth's flora and fauna, many species dying out while others mutated. In the end, the Martians won so convincingly that survivors named it the One Night War.

Born in late 1999, Jonathan Raven was an infant during the second Martian attack. His parents survived the initial attack, but eventually Jonathan's father was killed, and Jonathan, his newborn brother Joshua, and his mother Maureen fled New York. Jonathan was captured and taken to the Martian gladiatorial pens, his mother slain before his eyes. He assumed the other was also killed, but would not know Joshua's true fate for years. Soon after he was taken, a Martian precog warned that Jonathan would challenge their dominion if his will was not broken; moreover, with the Martians planning to expand their invasion to other Earths in the multiverse, the precog claimed that every alternate Earth's Jonathan Raven would pose a similar threat. The Martian Ruling Council discounted the prediction, although they did agree to launch their cross-reality incursions immediately, rather than waiting as originally planned, only to have the project fail when Earth-616's defenders repelled them. Meanwhile, back on Earth-691, Jonathan excelled in gladiatorial combat, and the crowds chanting "Kill! Raven!" earned him his new name: Killraven. Proving rebellious, after an escape attempt in 2008, the Martians placed him in Keeper Whitman's custody in an attempt to suppress his resistance. An unwilling slave of the Martians, Whitman saw Killraven as his chance for revenge on his masters; he spent two years subjecting Killraven to a program of performance-enhancing chemicals, while secretly conducting psycho-electric experiments to develop Killraven's latent psychic abilities. Eventually returned to the arena in 2010, Killraven befriended gladiatorial champion M'Shulla Scott and, a few years later, the mentally slow Old Skull, with whom he bonded when fighting gladiatorial opponent Warr.

In 2014, Killraven escaped from the combat pens with Old Skull, maiming one of his old gladiatorial instructors, the Warlord, during his breakout. He survived for a year as a pack rat in the Manhattan wilds while reading about pre-invasion Earth, his studies supplemented by knowledge that Keeper Whitman had surreptitiously buried in Raven's mind. After alienating the rabble of Manhattan, Killraven fled to Staten Island, becoming the leader of the Freemen hiding there, and reuniting with M'Shulla. On New Year's Eve 2016, Jonathan led his men back to Manhattan and kidnapped the Martian-backed mayor of New York, a move that drew further Freemen to his banner. A year later they invaded the gladiatorial pens where Killraven had been raised, and he mortally wounded Keeper Whitman. Before dying, Whitman related the history of the Martian invasion and informed Killraven that he had altered him to fight the Martians, telling him that Raven had the power to resist the Martians. In the raid's aftermath, Killraven and his fellow Freemen fled Manhattan but were captured by Skarlet and her Sirens, Martian-modified humans who controlled minds. Pitted in the arena against the cyborg Slasher, Killraven fought free. Inspired by Keeper Whitman's words, Killraven gained a sense of purpose, no longer thinking in terms of mere survival, but instead fighting to liberate his planet.

Raiding a New York museum for weapons and armor, Killraven and his Freemen (including Old Skull, M'Shulla, Arrow, Dagger, and native American Hawk) attacked the ruins of LaGuardia Airport to retrieve weaponry they believed was cached there. This was a trap, and again

REAL NAME: Jonathan Raven
ALIASES: KR, Mr. Killraven, "Pack-Rat"
IDENTITY: Publicly known
OCCUPATION: Freedom fighter; former gladiator
CITIZENSHIP: USA, wanted by Martian authorities
PLACE OF BIRTH: New York City, Earth-691
KNOWN RELATIVES: Maureen Raven (mother, deceased), unidentified father (deceased), Joshua Raven (Deathraven, brother, deceased)
GROUP AFFILIATION: Freemen leader
EDUCATION: Graduate school equivalent via implanted memories; raised in gladiatorial schools
FIRST APPEARANCE: Amazing Adventures #18 (1973)

Killraven and his Freemen were captured, this time by the Warlord, who intended to use Killraven in his experiments to create human host bodies for the Martians, more suitable for Earth than their own forms. Seeing in Killraven a chance to unite Freemen against the Martians, Keeper Carmilla Frost and her mute experimental clonal subject Grok (in actuality her cloned father, slain by the Martians and grotesquely mutated as Carmilla cloned him) freed the prisoners and joined the Freemen. Journeying to the remains of Washington, DC after Frost told them of a Martian headquarters there, some of the band were captured by the cavalier Sabre, and delivered to Abraxas' slave auction. To free them, Killraven allied with Mint Julep, a fellow freedom fighter gene-spliced by the Martian Masters with Euglena components, who led a band of

AS A BOY

Art by Joseph Michael Linsner with Neal Adams (inset)

Art by John Romita

Freewomen who had been similarly captured. They succeeded, but Killraven was briefly apprehended, and taken before the High Overlord, the Martian leader who had planned the second Martian invasion, who taunted him with the possibility that Joshua Raven might be alive, and that one of the men who had captured the Raven boys was a scientist at Yellowstone Park. Reunited with his men, Killraven fought Abraxas, the mutate Rattack and the High Overlord, the latter clad in humanoid battle armor; the battle ended when Sabre changed sides and buried Killraven's foes beneath the collapsing Lincoln Memorial.

Seeking to learn his brother's fate, Killraven led Old Skull, Hawk, M'Shulla, Carmilla, and Grok on a cross-country flight towards Yellowstone Park. Near Indianapolis, they fought the cyborg slaver Skar and his Martian "Devil's Marauder," a tripodal war machine; Raven intervened in Skar's death race, defeating Skar and freeing his slaves, learning in the process that his opposition to the High Overlord had been telecast worldwide via Martian technology and that his name was a rallying cry for freedom fighters everywhere. It was also here that Killraven had a telepathic experience, seeing through the eyes of distant Martians and their machinery, though still unaware of the nature of his ability. Skar survived the assault, and was soon employed by the High Overlord to pursue Killraven cross-country. At Battle Creek, Michigan, Killraven captured and trained a serpent-stallion hybrid as a mount, and defeated the insane Ptun-Rage the Vigilant, who guarded a warehouse full of breakfast cereals. Near Milwaukee, the Freemen were attacked by giant lampreys and Grok was severely wounded. Joined by the flame-wielding Volcana Ash (another Martian genetics experiment), the group attacked the Chicago fortress of Death-Birth, a breeding citadel run by Atalon and the Sacrificer, where humans were harvested for Martian sustenance. Slaying a Martian there, Killraven experienced that death through the eyes of the Martian, realizing that his telepathic abilities were related to the Martians, and that these powers had come through Keeper Whitman. Killraven and his band ultimately destroyed Death-Birth, freeing its slaves, including the pregnant Eve #3031 and her partner Adam #3031. Continuing their trek, the group evaded the perils of an abandoned "mural-phonics" (virtual reality) system in Nashville, and in West Virginia encountered the People, African-Americans who had formed an underground community when the Martians invaded.

Skar caught the south-moving band and killed both Hawk and the still infirm Grok before being slain by Killraven. Apparently lost, though actually following Killraven's unconscious connection to the High Overlord, the group continued south to Atlanta, where Killraven was separated from his compatriots by pursuing tripods and fought beside Earth-616's dimensionally displaced Spider-Man (Peter Parker). Reuniting with his Freemen, Killraven opposed the symbiotic 24-hour men G'rath and Emmanuel before destroying a Martian birthing crèche, briefly venturing to the Martian surface via a teleportational gateway. The High Overlord traveled to the Yellowstone Training Grounds and retrieved Joshua Raven, who served the Martians as the exterminator Deathraven. Setting Deathraven in search of Killraven, the High Overlord relocated to Cape Canaveral, where the Martians occupied the NASA center and constructed their own space vehicles. In the Okefenokee Swamp, the Freemen spent New Year's Eve 2019 with Brother Axe and his colony of free survivors. Scouting ahead, Killraven traveled alone to Miami, where he freed a former astronaut from the Dream Dome, which had been eternally animating his childhood heroes, before returning to the swamp and meeting the butterfly-like Mourning Prey and her children.

The Freemen traveled to Cape Canaveral, where Killraven learned of the High Overlord's survival when he accidentally telepathically linked to the Martian, in the process discovering the Martians' plans to strip Earth of its resources. Joined by surviving astronaut Jenette Miller, her stories of the past prompted memories in Killraven that he couldn't have, and he realized what Keeper Whitman had done: not only did he possess untapped knowledge of pre-invasion Earth, he could see through Martian eyes and control Martian bodies. While arranging their attack, the band encountered Killraven's brother; Jonathan invited him into the Freemen with open arms, unaware their meeting had been planned by the High Overlord. As the group invaded Canaveral, Killraven's brother transformed into his lupine Deathraven form and attacked the Freemen; Killraven was forced to possess the High Overlord and through him, slay Joshua to save his Freemen. Killraven's band returned to New York, where Killraven encountered Alice, a woman who had been in suspended animation since 1976. Unable to face Killraven's violent world, she returned to her suspension chamber, and Killraven, considering her seemingly futile dreams and the hopeful pregnancy of his companion Carmilla Frost with M'Shulla's child, began to view the possibility of a peace that might follow the conclusion of their war of the worlds, a view strengthened after the robotic X-51 of Earth-9997 showed him realities where the Martians had never invaded.

Earth-9930's Killraven fought the War of the Worlds as an Avenger, beside Black Panther, Jocasta, Thundra, Living Lightning, and the Crimson Dynamo. On Earth-2120, Killraven apparently had no brother, slew Grok after being betrayed by him, and nonviolently convinced a Martian faction to reconsider their invasion. Earth-616 was briefly invaded by Earth-691's Martians, using 616's telepathic Maureen Raven as a gateway; their bridgehead was lost when she was killed, and her orphaned son Jonathan has begun training under martial artist Shang-Chi, in preparation should the Martians return.

SERPENT-STALLION

Art by Sal Buscema

HEIGHT: 6'1" **EYES:** Blue
WEIGHT: 185 lbs. **HAIR:** Red

ABILITIES/ACCESSORIES: Killraven can telepathically observe or control Martian minds, resist psychic assaults, and mask his presence from Martian scanners. He is a superb swordsman and hand-to-hand combatant, trained in martial arts including savate, karate and wrestling, a master with hand weapons and shuriken. He is an experienced master strategist in guerrilla warfare; through implanted memories, he has an encyclopedic knowledge of pre-invasion Earth. Killraven wears a costume of bulletproof fabrics and leather. He is usually armed with sword and shuriken ("silver stars"), and rides a serpent-stallion mount.

KIMURA

HISTORY: Abused as a child by her alcoholic father and bullied at school, Kimura was neglected by her uncaring mother. She finally came into the custody of her loving grandmother, who tried to repair the child's psychological damage. Following her grandmother's fatal heart attack, Kimura grew bitter and angry. As an adult, she worked for the Facility, an offshoot of the Weapon X Program that, years earlier, had experimented upon Wolverine and others. The Facility's scientists mutated her to be physically indestructible, impervious to physical attacks as she had never been to emotional ones; she found a kindred spirit in Zander Rice, who nurtured a pathological hatred for X-23 (Laura Kinney), a female Wolverine clone created by the Facility over a decade earlier. After taking revenge on those who had wronged her in her youth, Kimura was appointed X-23's handler shortly after X-23's 12th birthday. Her indestructibility prevented the young clone from injuring her, and Kimura's own lust for violence prevented her from dealing X-23 anything but punishment for infractions real or imagined, little realizing or caring she had become as sadistic an abuser as her parents and childhood peers.

Sent into a berserker rage by a trigger scent, X-23 unwittingly murdered her surrogate mother, Dr. Sarah Kinney, and fled to San Francisco, where Kinney's sister Debbie and niece Megan took her in as Sarah Kinney's supposed daughter; unfortunately, Facility agent Desmond Alexander had ensconced himself as Debbie's boyfriend in the eventuality of X-23 seeking this sanctuary, and he alerted Kimura to X-23's whereabouts. X-23 killed Desmond when he tried to use the trigger scent to force her to kill Debbie and Megan, but Kimura arrived and captured X-23 and the Kinneys; however, before Kimura could kill Megan, X-23 chained Kimura in the Kinney basement and fled with Debbie and Megan after triggering a gas explosion that prevented Kimura from following. After this encounter, X-23 left her newfound family and sought out Wolverine, eventually finding sanctuary at the Xavier Institute, home of the X-Men. Months later, Kimura, now apparently a freelance mercenary, accepted an assignment from the Facility's current research head, Adam Harkins, to abduct Mercury (Cessily Kincaid), X-23's teammate in the New X-Men. Kimura quickly captured their quarry and enjoyed watching Harkins torture Mercury as he worked to obtain a living sample of Mercury's shape-shifting skin for use in perfecting the genetically engineered Predator X creatures. Accompanied by telekinetic teammate Hellion, X-23 invaded the Facility's research laboratory. Learning of Kimura's invulnerability, Hellion telekinetically hurled her through the building's roof and miles away from the scene. In her absence, X-23 and Hellion freed Mercury and, joined by the rest of the New X-Men and the X-Men, defeated the three Predator X's. Days later, Kimura penetrated the Xavier

REAL NAME: Kimura (presumed, full name unrevealed)
ALIASES: "Tree Village" (literal translation of name)
IDENTITY: No dual identity
OCCUPATION: Mercenary; former assassin handler
CITIZENSHIP: Unrevealed
PLACE OF BIRTH: Unrevealed
KNOWN RELATIVES: Unidentified parents, unidentified grandmother (deceased)
GROUP AFFILIATION: Formerly the Facility
EDUCATION: Unrevealed
FIRST APPEARANCE: New X-Men #31 (2006)

estate's defenses with the intent to kill X-23, only to encounter telepathic headmistress Emma Frost. After accessing Kimura's memories to learn of her painful childhood, Frost removed Kimura's memories of her beloved grandmother and left only an emotional void in their stead, stealing the last shred of the humanity which Kimura had otherwise so eagerly rejected. Frost then telepathically implanted within Kimura a compulsion to hunt down Harkins and her other Facility employers and abuse them as she had abused X-23.

HEIGHT: 5'9"
WEIGHT: 109 lbs.
EYES: Green
HAIR: Black

ABILITIES/ACCESSORIES: Kimura has virtually indestructible skin and hair, rendering her impervious to bullets, blades, incendiary explosives, temperature extremes, impact from a fall of several miles, and most other forms of physical injury. Her invulnerability may stem from alteration of her body's physical density, since she can render at least her fingers, and possibly other parts of her body, intangible; however, this latter ability appears severely limited, inasmuch as she can be immobilized by handcuffs. An accomplished athlete and hand-to-hand combatant, Kimura is proficient in the use of many weapons.

Art by Paco Medina

KING COBRA

REAL NAME: Klaus Voorhees
ALIASES: Cobra, "KC," "Cobie," Human Cobra
IDENTITY: Publicly known
OCCUPATION: Professional criminal; former laboratory assistant
CITIZENSHIP: Naturalized USA with a criminal record; formerly Netherlands
PLACE OF BIRTH: Rotterdam, Holland, Netherlands
KNOWN RELATIVES: Unidentified brother, Piet Voorhees (Cobra, nephew)
GROUP AFFILIATION: Leader of Serpent Society, occasional partner to Mr. Hyde; former member of Thunderbolts' Epsilon Squad, Serpent Squad
EDUCATION: High school graduate; vocational training
FIRST APPEARANCE: (Cobra) Journey into Mystery #98 (1963); (King Cobra) Captain America #367 (1990)

HISTORY: Klaus Voorhees was an ex-convict whom humanitarian medical professor Ezekiel Shecktor attempted to rehabilitate. The pair worked in a remote Indian village, attempting to develop universal snake anti-venom, but Klaus grew envious of Shecktor's fame and decided to kill him. Klaus injected himself with the anti-venom and then forced a laboratory king cobra to bite both Shecktor and himself, to make it look like an accident; however, Shecktor had irradiated the Cobra during an experiment, and though the bite killed the doctor, Klaus survived, his body having gained the snake's attributes and abilities. Calling himself the Cobra, Voorhees donned a cobra costume equipped with envenomed darts, venom-gas missiles and a projectile entangling cable. He returned to New York City, intent on using the empowering serum to create an army of serpent-powered followers, but Thor drove him off before he could collect the supplies needed to recreate the serum.

Realizing that he couldn't control others even if he transformed them, Cobra turned to simple crime to survive. Early in this career he robbed the office of Calvin Zabo, who quickly revealed himself to be the villainous Mr. Hyde. Their shared enmity against Thor led to a partnership, and they even briefly defeated the thunder god when Klaus deduced that he could use machinery to lift Thor's hammer and keep it away from him. Thor eventually recovered the hammer and both Cobra and Hyde were imprisoned, but not before Hyde set the tone for future problems when he abandoned his partner in an escape attempt. They were soon freed by Thor's brother Loki (who briefly increased their powers), but Thor quickly recaptured them. Similarly, they were later twice captured by Daredevil, once alongside criminal ally the Jester (Jonathan Powers), and Hyde abandoned Cobra completely during one of these defeats.

Tiring of his untrustworthy partner, the Cobra arranged a new partner, the Eel (Leopold Stryke). The Eel wanted his brother (Jordan Dixon, the Viper) involved, so the Cobra smuggled new costumes into both their cells, allowing them to escape, and named their new trio the Serpent Squad. The Viper insisted on a mission of vengeance against Captain America, resulting in the team's defeat. Killing Jordan Dixon and usurping his Viper alias, Madame Hydra took over the Serpent Squad, recruited Princess Python to free the Eel and the Cobra, and then defeated the Cobra in a fight for team leadership. Allied with the Atlantean Warlord Krang, the quartet kidnapped Hugh Jones, then-president of the Roxxon Corporation, and placed him under the control of the mystical Serpent Crown. The Cobra, who just wanted wealth and security, quickly disagreed with the Viper's nihilistic goals. The Cobra attempted to abandon Viper when Nomad (secretly Captain America) confronted her; in retribution, she shot him in the back.

Cobra recovered and resumed his partnership with Hyde, but they were again twice defeated by Daredevil and imprisoned. Escaping yet again, the Cobra left Hyde behind, telling him he was dissolving their partnership. The Cobra tried to live a quiet life in the Bojess Building's penthouse on Park Avenue, but his occasional jewelry store burglaries led to his short-lived capture by Spider-Man. Spider-Man sought the Cobra again thereafter, but the angry Hyde escaped from prison himself and sought vengeance on the Cobra for abandoning him. When Spider-Man defeated Hyde, Cobra wearily surrendered rather than live as a fugitive. Both Hyde and Cobra were returned to Ryker's Island, where a rampaging Hyde tried to get at his former partner. Cobra escaped to save himself, and Hyde pursued him; when Cobra was forced to face his super-strong ex-partner in single combat, he held his own until the Black Cat collapsed a wall on the duo, defeating them both.

Fellow snake-themed criminal Sidewinder (Seth Voelker) soon teleported the Cobra out of prison. Voelker had decided to take his own Serpent Squad to a new level and create the Serpent Society, an alliance of snake-themed criminals which would operate on a business model: sharing profits, offering medical benefits, and using Sidewinder's teleportation to avoid long-term imprisonment. The Cobra joined as a founding member, and with Anaconda and the Rattler stole from the former Brand Corporation the equipment that had been used to empower Sidewinder and some of his fellow serpents; despite the interference of Captain America, the Cobra saw the mission successfully completed. The Cobra's experience gained him his teammates' respect, and over the next few days he accompanied Anaconda in gaining vengeance on the traitorous Constrictor, hunted MODOK with the team, investigated AIM with Bushmaster, and rescued Diamondback from a hospital (getting shot at by a Scourge in the process).

ORIGINAL COSTUME

Art by Darick Robertson with James Brock & John Romita Jr. (insets)

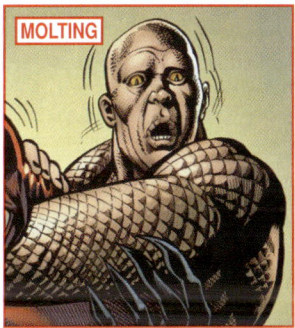

Art by Darick Robertson

When the Viper infiltrated the team with her own serpent-themed villains and took control from within, the Cobra unhappily went along with her. Witnessing her underlings dumping chemicals in the DC water supply, he again realized that her terrorism was at odds with his own goals. He attempted to kill the Viper to end her threat, but ultimately left her unconscious and turned her over to Captain America, then known simply as "the Captain." Sidewinder left the team following the Viper-led mutiny, and Cobra, due to his extensive experience, assumed leadership almost by default; however, he found himself insecurely unhappy. When Ghaur and Llyra hired the Society to acquire some mystical artifacts for them, the X-Men defeated the Society; the fact that Sidewinder completed the mission and ceded the Society a ten percent fee as "thanks" only reinforced Voorhees' insecurity. In an attempt to restore his own self-confidence, Cobra hunted down and defeated his old partner Mr. Hyde. He renamed himself King Cobra, vowing to lead the Society as it deserved thereafter.

King Cobra had a brief relationship with Serpent Society teammate Coachwhip during this time; however, another Society member, Diamondback, had begun a serious romance with Captain America. King Cobra feared Diamondback might reveal Society secrets, and he also disliked her continued friendship with Sidewinder. He had her captured, and after a brief trial the Society found her guilty and ordered her death. Asp and Black Mamba objected and arranged Diamondback's escape, but King Cobra had them captured in turn. Diamondback teamed with super-mercenary Paladin and Captain America to rescue the pair, and King Cobra was jailed and sent to the Vault alongside much of the Society. Sidewinder soon freed King Cobra in an attempt to square accounts, but Klaus returned to prison rather than allow his teammates to think he was abandoning them as Hyde had so often done to him.

Eventually, the Society was again freed. King Cobra arranged only small, safe work for the team and moved the Society to Sandhaven, Arizona, far from most of the world's heroes, but aspiring Arizona hero Jack Flag began tracking the team after they cheated his family out of their home. After defeating two team members, he told King Cobra that he wished to join the team himself. Seeking to rid himself of the nuisance, Klaus sent Jack on a "test mission" to rob Mr. Hyde; however, Klaus hedged his bets by notifying Hyde that Jack was coming. When Jack still managed to defeat Hyde, King Cobra took it as a sign and offered Jack Flag his own identity: Jack would become King Cobra, and Klaus would retire from the costumed life. Unfortunately, Jack had secretly contacted Captain America, and through the combined efforts of Jack, Captain America, his protégé Free Spirit and Force Works, the Society was defeated and imprisoned.

Realizing that he needed a Sidewinder to ensure his team's freedom, and knowing that the previous Sidewinder was unwilling to help, King Cobra had the Brand Corporation equipment that he had stolen for the Society long before used to equip a new Sidewinder. He teamed briefly with Mr. Hyde to help finance this work, but was twice captured, once by Captain America and once by Spider-Man and Alyosha Kravinoff. Each time he quickly escaped, and eventually succeeded in empowering a new Sidewinder, though that one was killed on an early test mission when Klaus hired him out to Death Sting. With the process working, King Cobra had yet another Sidewinder created, and this one freed the Serpent Society from their cells. Klaus also had the mutagenic serum that originally transformed him into the Cobra duplicated; he treated his nephew Piet Voorhees with this serum and Piet became the new Cobra while Klaus maintained the King Cobra identity. He also apparently oversaw the creation of a new Death Adder (the original having been long ago killed by a Scourge). King Cobra again led the Serpent Society on a mission of vengeance when he was tipped to Diamondback's whereabouts; however, this turned out to be a Diamondback LMD (Life Model Decoy), and the team was ultimately defeated by the LMD and Captain America.

When Lucia von Bardas contacted the Society, King Cobra allowed her to have the Tinkerer build an armored suit for him, but was relatively unsurprised when von Bardas was revealed to have ulterior motives: the armor and many other criminals' Tinkerer-modified suits were interlinked to create a bomb that von Bardas tried to use for her own terrorist purposes, but the suit was quickly destroyed and King Cobra was captured and imprisoned in the teleport-proof Raft. He got out when Electro engineered a mass escape, but was soon recaptured by Toxin. With the passing of the Super Human Registration Act, Baron Zemo recruited King Cobra to serve in the Thunderbolts army beside fellow Society members Rattler, Bushmaster and Death Adder. Together, they helped maintain order when the world was overrun by crazed superhumans spawned by the Wellspring of Power.

Alongside Firebrand (Russ Broxtel), Mauler (Brendan Doyle), and Mr. Hyde, King Cobra was contracted by the Hood to kill Taskmaster for joining the Initiative, but failed.

Art by Mark Bagley

HEIGHT: 5'10" **EYES:** Blue
WEIGHT: 160 lbs. **HAIR:** Bald

ABILITIES/ACCESSORIES: King Cobra's bones and muscle tissue are extremely malleable; they are virtually impossible to break or tear and can be contorted to allow him to fit through a hole four inches in diameter. This flexibility allows him to wrap around a victim in an exceedingly strong "cobra grip," and also allows him to slither over surfaces in bursts of speed up to 50 miles per hour for just a few seconds. He molts his skin on occasion; this leaves him with a serpentine appearance (scales, yellowed eyes), but his appearance gradually returns to normal.

King Cobra's tools include venomed cobra darts (with lethal or tranquilizing venoms) and blinding darts (fired from wrist blasters), nerve gas missiles, and a constricting "cobra cable" that can be fired from his costume's chest. Via muscle control, the tail of his suit can be separately manipulated as a bludgeon. His suit is coated with a slippery silicon/graphic compound, and chemical suction devices in its extremities allow him to cling to walls. Though he claims to have built these items himself, most have been purchased from AIM or the Tinkerer. Klaus controls the Serpent Society's resources, including multiple secret headquarters, Brand Corporation technology capable of creating superhumans, and their flying "Serpent Saucers."

HANNIBAL KING

REAL NAME: Hannibal King
ALIASES: Henry Kagle
IDENTITY: No dual identity
OCCUPATION: Private investigator
CITIZENSHIP: USA
PLACE OF BIRTH: Milwaukee, Wisconsin
KNOWN RELATIVES: None
GROUP AFFILIATION: Formerly Borderline Investigations (Nightstalkers), Midnight Sons
EDUCATION: Unrevealed
FIRST APPEARANCE: Tomb of Dracula #25 (1974)

HISTORY: Decades ago, Hannibal King was a private detective who was hired to investigate an industrial espionage case. While King was casing a factory, the vampire Deacon Frost invaded and killed everyone there, including King, who awoke three days later in a morgue and

discovered that he was now a vampire. Horrified at what he had become, King refused to give in to his vampiric instincts, and continued to serve as a private detective, taking the blood he needed from animals, corpses and blood banks. Determined to find Deacon Frost, King took a special interest in cases involving the supernatural and soon met the vampire hunter Blade, who was also tracking Frost. Although Blade instinctively hated King for being a vampire, they put aside their differences to destroy Frost, and Blade was finally able to accept King for who he was. When Dracula attempted to possess the Darkhold, King joined Blade and Frank Drake in holding Dracula back long enough for Dr. Strange to use the Darkhold's Montesi Formula to destroy all of Earth's vampires. King had been prepared to sacrifice his life, but instead, Dr. Strange was able to transform him back into a human, because he had resisted his bloodlust.

King continued as a private detective with Drake and Blade, eventually founding Borderline Investigations with them; but when the Montesi Formula weakened, King began to revert to a vampire-like state. During a battle with the vampire lord Varnae and Bloodstorm (a clone of Dracula), King and Drake were seemingly slain when Drake's Exorcist gun overloaded. However, they were apparently merged with Bloodstorm into a new host body for Dracula. Dracula took full control over his body after King and Drake were seperated from it by Blade and his allies, and King resumed his career as a detective. King's subsequent cases included aiding Brother Voodoo and Blade against Marie Laveau, and recovering Simon Garth, the Zombie from Dracula's daughter, Lilith, on behalf of Donna Garth. While employed by CIA agent Tatjana Stiles to investigate the vampire Navarro, who had stolen biological weapons, King was captured by Navarro, and Navarro forced him to feed on a live human by threatening to make the victim a vampire instead. King and Tatjana ultimately destroyed Navarro, but Tatjana was horribly injured. She begged King to make her a vampire in order to save her, and King gave in, taking his second human life.

When Blade struggled against the manipulations of his father Lucas Cross, King provided his investigative powers to Blade's assistance and helped him against vampires such as Draconis. Blade and King eventually learned that Cross and Dracula sought to fulfill a rite that would restore the souls of all vampires. When Blade refused to participate in the rite's completion King fought with him, wanting to regain his own soul. Blade slew King, but when the rite was ultimately completed it came out that it was actually a rite to restore all vampires to life — causing King to be instantly resurrected. By way of an apology for killing him, Blade gave King a mystical potion that would remove his need for consuming blood.

HEIGHT: 5'11"   **EYES:** Brown
WEIGHT: 190 lbs.   **HAIR:** Brown

ABILITIES/ACCESSORIES: King uses his vampiric ability to control rodents by employing rats as information gatherers during daylight hours when he must rest. He possesses enhanced human strength and healing, and can transform into mist, but seldom uses his other vampiric powers. He cannot be controlled by vampire lords such as Dracula. King is immune to aging, conventional disease and most forms of injury. He is vulnerable to silver, garlic, sunlight, a wooden stake through the heart and religious symbols.

POWER GRID	1	2	3	4	5	6	7
INTELLIGENCE							
STRENGTH			■				
SPEED							
DURABILITY			■				
ENERGY PROJECTION							
FIGHTING SKILLS			■				

Art by Sandy Plunkett

KINGPIN

HISTORY: Wilson Fisk is the descendant of Anatoly Fyskov, a Russian businessman who immigrated to the USA in the late 19th century. Initially an unpopular, blubbery boy, Wilson was impoverished and bullied as a child. However, his lack of athletic prowess allowed him a unique perspective by observing the children who chided him while they played, all in an effort to eventually use them for his own ends: a lesson he would carry with him into his adult life as the leading criminal mastermind of New York. Committing his first murder at age twelve, Fisk became determined to be the best at whatever he did. Believing physical strength to be a major factor in building power in the underworld, he trained relentlessly in body building and personal combat. His pursuit of the Japanese art of sumo led to an interest in the Orient. He educated himself by stealing books from stores and libraries, becoming particularly fascinated by political science. Refusing to work as any criminal's henchman, Fisk's combined strength and intellect led him to become the leader of a small gang of teens. His use of political techniques in organizing and directing groups of criminals earned him the nickname "kingpin of crime," a title which he held by the age of fifteen.

Although Fisk took great pleasure in physical combat with his enemies, he recognized the necessity of never placing himself in a situation where the law could prove his responsibility for crimes. As a result, Fisk avoided conviction for most of his life. Fisk's gang grew rapidly in size, influence, power, and wealth. He was careful to invest his illegal gains in legitimate businesses; the first company he owned dealt only in spices from the Far East. Fisk eventually developed a vast legitimate business empire, though he still professed to be merely a humble spice dealer.

About a decade after becoming a criminal leader, Fisk met the young Vanessa, who was brought before him by his band of thieves to be used as chattel. Though she was lost, afraid, and amnesiac, Fisk perceived her natural grace and depth of spirit, and he saw in her the object of every lonely dream he had ever had. Wilson and Vanessa fell in love and married soon after. Her love gave Fisk the peace he sought after his constant struggle for power. Their son, Richard, was born within a year after their marriage. Not long after this, in order to advance his own position, the Kingpin slew one of his own business partners, a Cheyenne known as Crazy Horse. Fisk became the guardian of Crazy Horse's daughter, Maya Lopez, recognizing her talents and sending her to a school for prodigies. When Richard was a youth, Vanessa tried to shield him from the life his father led. At times she even had to protect Richard from Wilson, who saw him as weak, pathetic, and an embarrassment. She eventually sent Richard off to school in Europe. After college (equivalent to US private high school), Richard remained in Europe and faked his own suicide. Partially in denial, Wilson attempted to shield Vanessa from this news.

The Kingpin continued to increase his influence over time, working under and gaining the respect of such noted crimelords as Don Rigoletto and Max "Hammer" Stryker; Fisk eventually slew Rigoletto and usurped his power. One of his earliest encounters with a superhuman occurred when he employed the young Josephine Pulaski to use her powers to sabotage a local construction site. This nearly brought the Kingpin into direct conflict with the young hero, Spider-Man. With the ever-increasing emergence of superhumans along with a corresponding increase in superhuman-related property damage, Fisk, alongside Tony Stark (an acquaintance the Kingpin occasionally played chess against) and Anne-Marie Hoag created Damage Control. Later, Stark would sell off his portion of the company and stop meeting for chess matches in an effort to distance himself from Fisk's alleged criminal ties.

Nearly twenty years after the Kingpin married Vanessa, Spider-Man briefly retired. The Kingpin seized the moment and proposed a coalition of criminal gangs in order to compete with the Maggia, which virtually monopolized organized crime throughout the country. Despite the earlier failures of the Green Goblin and Crime-Master to form similar coalitions, the Kingpin met nearly unanimous acceptance, and then directed a major crime wave in New York City. The return of Spider-Man brought this wave to a virtual halt and partially dissolved the coalition, though the Kingpin maintained control of the gangs of New York.

REAL NAME: Wilson Grant Fisk
ALIASES: The Boss, the Brainwasher, Harold Howard
IDENTITY: Publicly known to be the Kingpin, though it has never been officially proven
OCCUPATION: Criminal organizer and mastermind, former president and owner of legitimate businesses
CITIZENSHIP: USA (revoked), with a criminal record
PLACE OF BIRTH: Unrevealed
KNOWN RELATIVES: Vanessa Fisk (wife, deceased), Richard Fisk (son, deceased), Anatoly Fyskov (ancestor, deceased), Maya Lopez (Echo/Ronin, former legal ward)
GROUP AFFILIATION: Midtown Business Executives Club; former member of Las Vegas HYDRA faction, "Acts of Vengeance" prime movers, leader of a coalition of East Coast non-Maggia criminal organizations, head of Fujikawa Industries; Damage Control co-founder
EDUCATION: Self-educated to college level in political science
FIRST APPEARANCE: Amazing Spider-Man #50 (1967)

Art by David Mazzucchelli

Art by Frank Miller

Irritated by Spider-Man's opposition, the Kingpin allowed himself to become personally involved in a conflict involving the mysterious life-giving ancient stone Tablet of Life and Time. As a result, he was jailed for stealing the tablet, though he did escape from prison and the charges were dropped due to lack of evidence. He next entered into conflict with a rival crimelord, the Schemer, who turned out to be his own son, Richard. Believing Richard to have died, the Kingpin was devastated upon Richard's unmasking and lapsed into a coma.

After conventional treatments failed to revive his father, Richard used experimental hyper-shock therapy to awaken him. Richard then involved his father in a Las Vegas contingent of the then-fragmented Hydra; through this group the Kingpin plotted to overthrow the United States government and even achieve world domination. He turned against Hydra after learning his faction was actually controlled by the Red Skull (Johann Shmidt). Since this time the Kingpin has generally pursued more realistic goals.

By using the Sandman, Tinkerer, and a number of agents in various plots, the Kingpin captured Spider-Man and mechanically drained his life force in an effort not only to revenge himself against the wall-crawler but to treat the injuries Richard sustained in the Hydra conflict. Spider-Man regained his strength and fought the Kingpin, who fell to his seeming death. Initially amnesiac, the Kingpin recovered following a botched hit orchestrated by Silvermane and rejoined Vanessa, who persuaded him to retire from his life of crime and move to Japan with her. Before retiring, Vanessa allowed her husband 24 hours to settle his criminal affairs. The Kingpin used this time to make a final attempt on Spider-Man's life, and was just about to deliver a killing blow after a long struggle with Spider-Man, but his wife's timetable expired before he could do so. Vanessa also convinced him to turn over files on the activities of leaders of organized crime to American legal authorities. However, the former members of the Kingpin's crime syndicate kidnapped Vanessa before he could do so. The Kingpin eventually agreed to exchange the files for Vanessa, surviving several assassination attempts in the process. However, as he approached Vanessa, his own lieutenant Lynch caused a building to collapse, seemingly killing Vanessa, whom he correctly saw as the only obstacle to the Kingpin's return to crime. As Lynch intended, the Kingpin returned to power, defeating his former syndicate, but Fisk realized what Lynch had done and killed him as well.

Continuing to cement his power, the Kingpin hired the feared mercenary Bullseye as his chief assassin. Fisk also successfully arranged the election of his agent Randolph Cherryh, as the next mayor of New York City. However, when Daredevil found Vanessa still alive, he agreed to return her to Fisk only if he would force Cherryh to retire. Fisk acquiesced, but sent his newest assassin, Elektra, to kill Franklin Nelson in retaliation. Elektra was killed by Bullseye, who sought to reclaim his job as the Kingpin's chief assassin. Later, the Kingpin actually worked with Daredevil against Micah Synn, a savage jungle warlord who threatened his criminal empire.

When Dr. Octopus (Otto Octavius) sought to destroy New York's inhabitants, his agents unwittingly stole a fake activator from the Kingpin, but the Black Cat (Felicia Hardy) then stole the real activator and sought Spider-Man's help. Octopus, however, obtained the real activator and nearly set off the bomb before being narrowly thwarted by the Black Cat and Spider-Man. Soon after, the vigilante Punisher (Frank Castle), drugged into a psychotic frenzy by agents of his enemy Jigsaw (Billy Russo), targeted the Kingpin, only to be beaten into submission.

The Kingpin had his scientists, via the equipment of the late scientist Harlan Stillwell, empower his longtime agent Aaron Nicholson, who became the Answer. After this success, the Kingpin decided to use the equipment as part of the means to gain vengeance on the Black Cat for putting his city at risk. Knowing the Cat sought super-powers to make her a worthy crime-fighting partner to Spider-Man, the Kingpin (his identity concealed behind opaque glass) contacted her and arranged to grant her powers in exchange for future services. Felicia agreed and developed a bad luck aura that affected any who sought to harm her. After the Kingpin revealed his identity, the Cat agreed to follow through on their arrangement though she told him she would not do anything that threatened Spider-Man. She would later learn, however, that this aura also affected anyone who spent too much time in her vicinity, such as Spider-Man.

Seeking a mindless servant, the Kingpin revived his old enemy Silvermane, now a cyborg that had been seemingly slain by the vigilante Dagger, but it sought to reclaim its life force from Dagger, draining her energy from afar. Concluding the same energy might revive his ailing wife Vanessa, Fisk had Dagger captured, and the loyal Answer sacrificed his own energies to recharge her, but Dagger restored Silvermane instead, terminating their connection and his draining of her energies. Despite Fisk's requests, Dagger refused to aid Vanessa. Blaming Spider-Man for his involvement in this failed effort, Fisk was pleased to reveal the true extent of the Black Cat's bad luck aura to her, which led, as expected, to decide to break up with Spider-Man due to the risk to his life (though Spider-Man actually broke up with her first due to legitimate concerns about their relationship). Meanwhile, Richard Fisk had adopted another alias, the Rose, hoping to interfere with his father's business. The Kingpin determined the Rose's identity, but allowed him to continue to operate under a watchful eye.

Desperate to save Vanessa, the Kingpin kidnapped the wife of psychologist Dr. Paul Mondat, hoping to force him to save Vanessa. Mondat, however, turned the tables on him; he recovered Vanessa, but also made her loyal to him instead. After Daredevil saved Mondat's wife, the Kingpin admitted defeat and allowed Mondat to take Vanessa to Europe for further treatment. The Kingpin never forgot his defeats at Daredevil's hands. When he obtained his enemy's true identity, Matt Murdock, he used that information to systematically destroy his foe's professional career and private life. When a maddened Daredevil

Art by Frank Miller

Art by Al Milgrom

confronted him, the Kingpin beat him unconscious and attempted to have him drowned. When this failed, the Kingpin sent the super-soldier Nuke to draw out Daredevil, but this served only to draw further attention to his own activities. Following this, the Kingpin mysteriously vanished, traveling to Europe to deal with a threat to Vanessa. In his absence, a number of would-be crimelords, such as the Rose, Hammerhead, Silvermane, and even the neophyte Blue Boys, sought to fill the void created by his absence. The ensuing gang war also drew the attention of the Hobgoblin (Ned Leeds), Jack O'Lantern (Jason Macendale), and the Punisher. As the conflicts reached a boiling point, the Kingpin secretly returned to the city, a move sanctioned by the US government in order to end the gang war. The Kingpin subsequently downsized his operation, eliminating all those in his organization whom he saw as ineffective.

Murdock, having recovered, started a free law clinic that would cross paths with the Kingpin's endeavors, such as when his thugs Bruno and Tony tried to scare a girl named Audrey and her grandmother out of their Hell's Kitchen apartment (which was in a building Fisk wished to demolish), but were stopped by Daredevil. Despite enlisting Murdock's former partner, Franklin "Foggy" Nelson, the Kingpin continued to lose in the court of law, as in the case of the suit against Kelco (a chemical corporation owned by the Kingpin) whose chemicals had blinded young Tyrone Janson. In response, he sent Typhoid Mary, with whom Fisk had a brief romantic relationship, to destroy both Murdock and Daredevil. Though Daredevil survived, he did leave the city behind for a time.

The Punisher then led an assault on the Kingpin's operations, determined to take him down once and for all. The Kingpin again defeated the Punisher, whose life was negotiated by the Punisher's agent, Vernon Brooks. A short time after this, the Kingpin became a pawn of the Norse God Loki, serving alongside other prime movers in engineering the "Acts of Vengeance," in which villains were directed to attack heroes who had no experience against them. After Loki's ruse was exposed, the prime movers each went their separate ways. Shortly thereafter, Fisk again encountered the Red Skull (one of the former prime movers) and the two vied for control of the New York drug trade. The struggle culminated in single combat between the Red Skull and Kingpin. The Red Skull possessed a cloned body of Captain America, but he had been recently weakened by imprisonment and starvation. Regardless, the Red Skull seriously underestimated the strength of the Kingpin, who nearly crushed him to death, forcing the Skull to surrender and give up his influence on the gangs of New York.

The Kingpin had long utilized Oswald P. Silkworth, the Arranger, to coordinate many of his activities. Under the Kingpin's direction, the Arranger manipulated the mind-controlling mutant known as the Persuader to control the Punisher. Overstepping his limits, the Arranger attempted to have the Punisher kill rival drug lords, the Lobo Brothers. When this failed, the Lobo Brothers, werewolf-like mutants, came to New York and attacked the Kingpin's operations. Irritated at these events, the Kingpin had the Arranger killed by the British assassins Knight and Fogg.

The Kingpin was subsequently hired by Daemian Wainscroft to aid in the recovery of his son Deke, who had been horribly mutated by SS-8, a variant Super-Soldier Serum. These efforts brought him into a temporary alliance with the Punisher that eventually succeeded in stopping the monstrous Deke. However, the alliance was short-lived, and as the Punisher continued to oppose the Kingpin's operations, Fisk had the Punisher's partner, Microchip, kidnapped. The Kingpin even severed one of Microchip's fingers to blackmail the Punisher, but the vigilante had become mired in different plots and the Kingpin eventually released Microchip. The Punisher and other vigilantes subsequently joined forces to thwart the Kingpin's plot to use the European Channel Tunnel ("Chunnel") to form a united international crime network under his control.

Returning to New York, Daredevil took his revenge on the Kingpin. He managed to capture and institutionalize Typhoid Mary, with whom the Kingpin had become romantic. Working with District Attorney Kathy Malper, Daredevil implicated Fisk in various criminal activities. In addition, agents of Hydra infiltrated Fisk's legitimate business and managed to erase his financial data, leaving him virtually penniless. Hydra assaulted Fisk Towers, destroying his property and essentially dissolving his empire. At the end, the Kingpin was defeated by Daredevil and arrested by the police. Posting bail, he went underground with nothing to his name.

Following this defeat, it appeared that Fisk's son, Richard, had succeeded him as the Kingpin of Crime. However, the new "Kingpin" was actually Fisk's old ally, Alfredo Morelli. Alfredo became too absorbed in this new role, and Richard became the Blood Rose to oppose him. After being toppled from power, Alfredo went on to become the criminal Gauntlet.

Meanwhile, the Kingpin made his way overseas and began to rebuild his power and financial base, taking control of Fujikawa Industries. He made a second attempt at forming and controlling a united European crime network, but was foiled by Daredevil (during his time as Laurent LeVasseur). After selling Daredevil's identity to the criminal Mysterio, Fisk organized attacks on the New York crimelords who had taken his place and regained his position, albeit with a smaller empire than he had once commanded. He retained this position for some time, but a janitor, Lenny Cebulski, found incriminating files in the crime boss's closet and sought legal advice and protection from Murdock. The Kingpin had Cebulski killed, and sent his former ward Maya Lopez, now known as Echo, to keep Murdock off the case. Lenny Cebulski's twin brother Larry sought vengeance on the Kingpin, shooting him several times. The Kingpin narrowly escaped death, but by then Echo had learned that it was the Kingpin who had killed her father. Enraged, she shot Fisk in the face, leaving him blind.

Regaining his position, the Kingpin soon earned the ire of Sammy Silke Jr., the son of one of the Kingpin's old partners. Silke convinced Richard Fisk to support him, and he soon organized an ambush on the Kingpin. The Kingpin's inner circle descended upon him with knives, stabbing him repeatedly and leaving him to die. The Kingpin's massive bulk again saved his life, and loyal agents provided him with private care, though they allowed it to be believed that he had died. Upon learning this, Vanessa returned to America, had her husband sent to Europe for care, and led the Kingpin's men in taking vengeance on all involved in the attack. Vanessa killed their son Richard for his betrayal, after which she divided up his empire and returned to Europe, hoping never to return.

The Kingpin awakened to find himself totally healed and his eyesight restored. He returned to New York, took his vengeance on Sammy Silke (who had turned himself in to the FBI for protection), and also killed the men who helped Vanessa execute Richard. Pushing Typhoid Mary back into insanity, he sent her against Daredevil. When this failed, he sent Bullseye to kill Daredevil's newest love interest, Milla Donovan. After overcoming these threats, Daredevil confronted the Kingpin directly.

Pushed to ferocity by recent events, Daredevil managed to beat the Kingpin unconscious, after which he dumped him off at Josie's Bar and Grill and announced himself to be the new Kingpin of Hell's Kitchen.

Following this, the Kingpin was incarcerated at Ryker's Island Prison, but this did little to quell Fisk's machinations. His first plot involved releasing to the FBI the existence of the so-called "Murdock Papers," which allegedly proved that Daredevil and Matt Murdock were the same person. Using Bullseye as an operative, the Kingpin roused Daredevil and Elektra into confronting the assassin for possession of the papers, but the papers proved to be a ruse created by Fisk to obtain DNA evidence that would link Daredevil to Murdock. While this failed, Daredevil was shot in the process, and the Kingpin instructed FBI Director Leland Drummond to show that Murdock had the same bullet wound as Daredevil. In addition, the Kingpin had Drummond pressure reporter Ben Urich to reveal the location of the super hero-treating Night Nurse. Confronted by the FBI at the Night Nurse's facility, Daredevil surrendered to avoid further violence. Drummond, however, betrayed the Kingpin and returned him to prison. Via Drummond's manipulation, Matt Murdock was imprisoned in the same cell as the Kingpin at Ryker's. Murdock made a deal to escape with the Kingpin in a sequestered helicopter during the confusion created in a prison riot orchestrated by Fisk. However, Murdock broke the deal when he refused to allow Bullseye to escape as well. Following a brief scuffle between Bullseye and Murdock, the Kingpin was accidentally shot and injured by his assassin, failing to escape in turn.

The Kingpin was subsequently attacked by the Enforcers under the auspices of criminal leader Hammerhead, but he soundly thrashed them back into his employ. Kingpin made a deal to supply the location of the fugitive Secret Avengers to SHIELD Director Tony Stark (Iron Man) in order to commute his prison term. Secretly working for Kingpin while in the employ of Hammerhead, Underworld instead led SHIELD operatives to Hammerhead's criminal summit and later gunned him down under Kingpin's orders. This subterfuge allowed for the Kingpin to maintain his underworld legitimacy while simultaneously striking back at slights made by Stark and Hammerhead.

With Spider-Man's Peter Parker identity revealed following the Superhuman Registration Act, the Kingpin sent a sniper to slay the hero and his family. The sniper failed in his attempt, but Peter's Aunt May was shot and critically hospitalized as a result. Spider-Man learned of Fisk's involvement, broke into Ryker's, and brutally beat the Kingpin in plain view of the other inmates, threatening to finish the crimelord should his aunt die. Currently, the entire world, including the Kingpin, no longer possesses the knowledge of Spider-Man's alter ego due to a deal the web-slinger and Mary Jane made with the demon lord Mephisto. May Parker was also healed of her wounds as part of the deal.

Daredevil was eventually led to a confrontation with Vanessa Fisk in Zurich, Switzerland, where she confessed to having been behind much of his recent woes. Dying, she offered Daredevil a chance to fix all of his recent problems in exchange for getting the Kingpin out of prison. He initially refused, but then learned of Drummond's "suicide" and his note, which explained his elaborate framing of Murdock, facilitating his regaining of his freedom and restoration of his legal license. Vanessa was soon reported dead, and Murdock arranged the Kingpin's liberation in exchange for his promise to leave the USA, surrender his citizenship, and never return. Despite this, Fisk did briefly return to the US to take care of unfinished business that involved having the young Runaways steal the Overdrive device as part of an arrangement with the elderly Lillie McGurty.

Despite his recent setbacks, it seems likely that Wilson Fisk will once again regain his status and power, as he has proven his staying power as the Kingpin of Crime.

Art by David Mazzucchelli

HEIGHT: 6'7" **EYES:** Blue
WEIGHT: 450 lbs. **HAIR:** Bald

ABILITIES/ACCESSORIES: The Kingpin is composed almost entirely of muscle that has been developed to enormous size, much like a sumo wrestler, and he possesses peak human strength. His vast bulk shields him from many forms of injury, either providing padding or causing otherwise penetrating wounds to strike him relatively superficially.

He has extraordinary skill in hand-to-hand combat, specializing in a number of martial arts, including sumo wrestling. His fighting skills and unusual agility for a man of his size compensate for the great difference between his human level of strength and that of Spider-Man when the two engage in unarmed combat (Spider-Man also has severe inhibitions about using his strength against an opponent without superhuman powers for fear of killing him or her).

The Kingpin is a criminal genius and a highly skilled planner and organizer. He has employed numerous assassins (Bullseye, Crossbow, Don the Bomb, Elektra, Jake Martino, Sniper, Twin Killer, and George Wong), government officials (Randolph Cherryh), henchmen (the Arranger, Big Turk, Blackie, Blinker, Bruno Grainger, Charlie, Chauffard, Chief, Drivin' Ivan, the Enforcers, Filch, Flint, Mr. Gilbert, Greaser, Johnny Punk, Larks, Louie Minelli, Lynch, Felix Manning, Marvin the Tooth, Max, Paine, Shiv, Shorty, Slade, Snakebite, Turk Barrett, and Wilson), legal advisors (Mr. Anad and Foggy Nelson), pushers (Nino Cortese, Trainwreck Miller), scientists (Dr. Jonathan Ohm/the Spot, Harlan Stillwell, and Dr. Gerhard Winkler), specialists (Architect, computer expert Board, Dr. Boris Korpse, counterfeiter Jeremiah Jenk, inventors Alistaire Smythe and the Tinkerer), and even superhumans (the Answer, the cyborg Damage, Fogg, Ghost, Hobgoblin/Jack O'Lantern (Jason Macendale), Knight, Mysterio (Francis Klum), Nuke, Rapido, Sandman (William Baker), Typhoid Mary, Underworld, and the Vulture (Adrian Toomes)), almost all of whom are fiercely loyal to him due to dedication, fear, or both. He has manipulated government agencies (FBI, NYPD, SHIELD, and US armed forces) and super heroes alike, including the Black Cat, Daredevil, Echo, Falcon, Iron Man (Tony Stark), Sleepwalker, Spider-Man, and the Punisher.

The Kingpin has sometimes carried a walking stick that contains a laser weapon that fires a short pulse of 300 watts, enough energy to vaporize a handgun. The walking stick could also fire a concentrated spray of sleeping gas. Additionally, the stick has served as a remote control for electrifying the ceiling of one of his safe houses. The Kingpin's diamond tiepin also contains a small, highly concentrated spray of sleeping gas, which is effective when fired directly into an opponent's face at close range. He once used the "Vita-Drain," a machine that transfers life force from one person into another, and a brainwashing machine designed by Dr. Gerhard Winkler. In recent years the Kingpin has largely shied away from using such exotic technology, preferring to use human agents in his schemes or his own formidable physical abilities instead.

POWER GRID	1	2	3	4	5	6	7
INTELLIGENCE							
STRENGTH							
SPEED							
DURABILITY							
ENERGY PROJECTION							
FIGHTING SKILLS							

KISMET

HISTORY: Wladyslav Shinski, Carlo Zota, Maris Morlak, and Jerome Hamilton were collectively known as the Enclave: scientists dedicated to improving the world by any means, including taking control of it. In an abandoned Deviant outpost in the North Atlantic they constructed the Beehive, their citadel of science. Their greatest accomplishment was the creation of Him, a genetically perfect artificial being designed to father a new human race. When Him matured more quickly than anticipated, they lost control of it and Him demolished much of the Beehive, killing Hamilton and flying away. The remaining three tried again, producing Paragon, a being genetically identical to Him. To retain control of their creation they tricked Dr. Stephen Strange into modifying the creature's neural structure, but Paragon deduced their plans while still growing and gave itself a post-hypnotic command to metamorphose into a glowing black form, negating the neurological controls. Angered at its creators' attempts to control it, Paragon destroyed the Beehive and placed itself into a restorative cocoon to develop further.

While in the cocoon, Paragon adapted itself into a female form and slowly moved towards New York City. When dockworkers fished the cocoon from the harbor, Paragon hatched as Her. Adopting her creators' goals of parenting the perfect race, Her sought Him as her ideal mate. Her's search began with Alicia Masters, who had briefly known Him, but this brought Her into conflict with Alicia's boyfriend, Ben Grimm, the Thing. Moondragon sensed Her's presence and sought her out, informing her of Him's evolution into Adam Warlock and subsequent death at the hands of Thanos. Believing she could revive Warlock, Her sought Warlock's burial site on Counter-Earth, accompanied by Alicia, Moondragon, the Thing, and Starhawk/Aleta. When Counter-Earth proved to be missing, Her resurrected its creator, the High Evolutionary, and located the thieves. On Counter-Earth, Her resurrected Warlock, only to discover his soul missing (actually confined within a Soul Gem, since stolen). She reburied Warlock's body, but was moved when offered solace by Grimm, to whom she had shown only contempt. Unable to deal with these new emotions, she fled.

Her's search for enlightenment led her near the planet of U'sr'pria, which was being ravaged as its technological advancement destroyed its environment. Investigating, Her found the planet had been conquered by a mutant member of its own race, the U'sr'pr, who forced the planet into a technological boom, striking a deal with the Consortium, an intergalactic business conglomerate, for his own comfort. Her angrily depowered U'sr'pr, and then aided the natives in their clean-up. The populace named her J'Ridia Starduster, or She Whose Trail Dusts Hope. When the Consortium found their profits from U'sr'pria dwindling, they sent agents to correct this. The Consortium proved too powerful, so J'Ridia fled to Earth seeking aid, carefully drawing the Consortium after her and away from U'sr'pria. The Consortium caught J'Ridia near Earth and attacked; she fell out of control into Toronto, mistaking it for New York. The Consortium followed, and Alpha Flight aided J'Ridia in battling them. The Avengers also came to the city's aid, but neither side proved victorious. As the battle was demolishing the city, J'Ridia decided to surrender herself to the Consortium, but before she could, the alien Quwrlln coincidentally teleported away J'Ridia and half of Alpha Flight and the Avengers, seeking their aid in defending their world from Galactus. The Quwrlln had moved their planet into another dimension; the different physical laws allowed the defeat of Galactus there. Unwilling to kill Galactus but not wanting to leave him stranded on the Quwllrn's planet with no recourse but to eventually devour it, a solution was found when the Quwrlln teleported Galactus to the planet that powered the Consortium's mother ship. Galactus devoured the planet, sparing the Quwrlln, and the Consortium was crippled, freeing U'sr'pria.

Struck by the selflessness of the humans who had aided her, J'Ridia remained on Earth, forgoing her U'sr'prian name. Again known as Her, she discovered that Adam Warlock had been resurrected with his soul restored, but Warlock, occupied with the universe-threatening menace

REAL NAME: None
ALIASES: Ayesha, She Who Must be Obeyed, J'Ridia Starduster, She Whose Trail Dusts Hope, Her, Paragon
IDENTITY: No dual identity
OCCUPATION: Adventurer
CITIZENSHIP: None
PLACE OF CREATION: Beehive, Shard Island, Atlantic Ocean
KNOWN RELATIVES: The Enclave (creators); Adam Warlock, unidentified female "Warlock" (genetic twins)
GROUP AFFILIATION: None
EDUCATION: Self-taught; initially programmed by Enclave during creation
FIRST APPEARANCE: (Paragon) Incredible Hulk Annual #6 (1977); (Her) Marvel Two-In-One #61 (1980); (J'Ridia Starduster) Marvel Comics Presents #35 (1989); (Kismet) Quasar #40 (1992); (Ayesha) Fantastic Four #11 (1998)

PARAGON

Art by John Buscema with Jerry Bingham (inset)

of the Infinity Gauntlet, dismissively rebuffed Her's advances. At loose ends, Her remained in New York City, protecting it against the threats of Eon's expanding corpse and Edifice Rex. Her soon realized that she and Warlock would make a poor parental couple as they possessed virtually identical genetic material, and decided to seek the best mate from within humanity. She created pods of genetic material designed to draw the best from herself and a mate, and attached these to the back of six males: Wonder Man, Hyperion, Hercules, Doc Samson, Ikaris, and Gilgamesh. When Quasar (Wendell Vaughn) opposed her, she placed a pod on him as well, drawing the ire of Moondragon, who had decided Quasar was her own perfect (if unwilling) mate. While the three battled, the Avengers succeeded in removing the pods from the others, and Her decided Quasar was indeed her ideal mate, as he was the only being to evidence concern for the contents of the pod over himself. However, Quasar pointed out that her desire to parent children was arising solely from her creators' wishes and not from herself, challenging Her to find her own purpose in life. Uncertain, Her removed the pod from Quasar, but decided to remain near him as a companion, observing his humanity.

Her worked beside Quasar for a short period of time, battling both Binary and the Super-Skrull as she defended Earth during Operation: Galactic Storm. She then accompanied Quasar to the Kree homeworld, Hala, where she was moved by its recent devastation and fought to free the souls of its population from the Soul Eater. Her accompanied the alien Mourners to the planet Scadam, but found herself unable to watch this planet's destruction. Though she had not sought out combat, she saw it as her kismet to be unable to avoid it, and so adopted Kismet as her new name. She fought the invading Black Fleet on Scadam, but was wounded and witnessed from afar the destruction of the invading fleet by extradimensional energies. Seeking these energies, she returned to Earth, where she found them originating from Quasar's girlfriend, Kayla Ballantine, who bore the extra-multiversal Star Brand. When Kismet's questioning of Kayla inadvertently turned into battle, Kayla lashed out, rupturing Kismet's cells and forcing her to withdraw into a regenerative cocoon. Quasar later moved the cocoon to Project: PEGASUS for safe storage.

When Wladyslav Shinski suffered a serious stroke, the remaining members of the Enclave stole the cocoon from PEGASUS and removed Kismet from it. They placed Shinski within it to regenerate but also took pains to protect Kismet, who was nearing full recovery. Striking on the idea of using Kismet's genetic material to hasten the recovery, they withdrew a sample from her. This was stolen by Frank, an AIM Adaptoid spy who had been observing the Enclave. The Adaptoid injected itself with the sample and adapted Kismet's powers as a new Paragon, but the recuperating Shinski injected Paragon with a genetic weapon they had developed for use against Kismet, destroying him. Grateful that Shinski had saved her, though uneasy they had developed a weapon to destroy her, Kismet wove regenerative cocoons for all three Enclave members (they had been injured during the battle) and placed them within, watching over them as "mother" while she tried to determine what it meant to be their "daughter."

After some months, an energy blast from space disrupted the cocoons, and the Enclave members hatched, transformed into lesser versions of Kismet with similar powers. With these abilities, the Enclave began what they had always wanted to do: Cure the world's ills. However, their short-term solutions frequently created worse long-term problems, and Kismet convinced them to leave the planet while they learned how to use their powers and where they had come from. Kismet led them in search of the energy blast that had triggered their change and discovered Khatylis, an alien life-form that harvested the flotsam of destroyed systems and created new matrices for life. When the Enclave disrupted this matrix, they were absorbed by it, but Kismet and the Silver Surfer merged their life essences with that of Khatylis to restore its life matrix, freeing the Enclave.

The Enclave apparently lost their powers, returning to Earth. Shinski and Morlak shared the identity of Crucible, and enslaved Kismet (under the name "Ayesha") against the Fantastic Four. Showing new powers of mind control, Ayesha defeated the Four, but was eventually banished when a black hole grenade transported her and Shinski into another dimension. Shinski has since returned to Earth, while Kismet — restored to her classic form — fought against the Heart of the Infinite-powered Thanos.

In the alternate future of the Guardians of the Galaxy (Earth-691), Kismet and Quasar produced a child: Starhawk (Stakar Ogord).

Art by Salvador Larroca

Art by John Buscema

HER

AYESHA

HEIGHT: 6'6"
WEIGHT: 390 lbs.
EYES: White
HAIR: Blonde

ABILITIES/ACCESSORIES: Kismet's cells serve as cosmic energy batteries, allowing her to absorb, store, and use cosmic energies. Her form is cosmically enhanced; she can press 70 tons and survive in the vacuum of space; she is virtually tireless. She can project force blasts, levitate objects with anti-gravitons, and rearrange small volumes of matter. She can fly at Mach 10, and generate rifts into warp-space. She possesses limited telepathic abilities: she can understand any language and, as Ayesha, she could control minds. If seriously damaged, Kismet's body will automatically generate a regenerative cocoon around her.

POWER GRID	1	2	3	4	5	6	7
INTELLIGENCE							
STRENGTH							
SPEED							
DURABILITY							
ENERGY PROJECTION							
FIGHTING SKILLS							

KITTY'S FAIRY TALE

HISTORY: Following an attack on Xavier's School by the Hellfire Club, Kitty Pryde sought to cheer up her young friend Illyana Rasputin by telling her a fairy tale. Set in the Caliphate of Nhu Yorkh, the story starred the swashbuckling Pirate Kitty and her stalwart companion Colossus. After yet another daring escape from the authorities, Kitty and Colossus rescued Prince Cyclops and the Wizard Xavier from a gang of thugs. Cyclops and Xavier were on a quest to rescue Cyclops' beloved Princess Jean, who had been corrupted by her soul's dark side and transformed into the evil Dark Phoenix, who attacked and sank all the ships in the harbor before Xavier drove her away with a crystal containing her true soul inside it.

With the aid of Pirate Kitty's giant dragon ally Lockheed, the heroes tracked Dark Phoenix across the Great Western Ocean, stopping on a remote island to rest. The island proved to be the home of the Bamfs, small blue-skinned elf-like creatures who could teleport. One of the Bamfs became fond of Kitty and insisted on accompanying her. The motley crew was also joined by the storm goddess Windrider, whom Colossus freed from a bottle in which she had been imprisoned by Dark Phoenix, and the diminutive, hirsute, razor-clawed Mean, who sought revenge on Cyclops for supposedly stealing Jean away from him but was quickly scared into submission by Lockheed. The heroes soon clashed with Dark Phoenix, and Xavier released Jean's soul from its possession. Lockheed then flew the heroes back to the Prince's land where Cyclops and Jean were married, and they all lived happily ever after.

Unbeknownst to Kitty, she had somehow subconsciously tapped into an actual alternate reality (Earth-5311) while telling her story. When Kitty and Illyana learned of Nightcrawler's adventure involving the Well at the Center of Time, a bizarre metaphysical phenomenon that exists simultaneously in all realities, they used the Danger Room's technology to create a simulacrum of the Well, not realizing the actual Well materialized instead due to Nightcrawler's enduring state of dimensional instability. Both Nightcrawler and his reality (Earth-616)'s diminutive Lockheed were pulled into it, after which the Well moved on. Following an adventure in another dimension during which Nightcrawler earned the enmity of the shark-like sorcerer Shagreen when Nightcrawler stopped Shagreen's intended sacrifice of the Jinjav (princess) Sabree to the demon Cthuma-Gurath (possibly referring to Shuma-Gorath), Kitty duplicated the settings that summoned the Well, opening another dimensional warp that sent Nightcrawler and Lockheed to Earth-5311's Bamf Island, where the Bamfs greeted Nightcrawler as their daddy Bamf due to his larger size and resemblance to them.

Seeking revenge, Shagreen followed Nightcrawler to the Bamf's village, Bamff, and attacked him there. When he realized Nightcrawler and one Bamf were standing on a spellstone that turned his spells back on him,

CORE CONTINUUM DESIGNATION: Reality-5311
SIGNIFICANT INHABITANTS: Bamfs, Colossus, Dark Bamf, Dreadwings, Lockheed, Mean (aka the Fiend with No Name), Pirate Kitty, Prince Cyclops, Princess Jean/Dark Phoenix, Windrider, Wizard Xavier, others (natives); Shagreen
SIGNIFICANT LOCATIONS: Bamf Island, Fangs of Doom, Great Western Ocean, Kingdom of Argos, Nhu Yorkh, Wizard's Island
FIRST APPEARANCE: Uncanny X-Men #153 (1982)

Shagreen instead kidnapped all the other Bamfs to Wizard's Island in the Fangs of Doom. Seeking to save his kinsfolk, the Bamf summoned the giant Lockheed-5311 for help, which also attracted the attention of Mean. The quartet soon found Pirate Kitty and Colossus, who were surprised when little Lockheed-616 decided Pirate Kitty was a suitable stand-in for his own teenage Kitty. Upon arrival at Shagreen's lair, giant Lockheed-5311 was pulled underwater by a giant squid-like monster while the others were attacked by a horde of bird-like Dreadwings who captured Kitty and took her to Shagreen. The heroes escaped Shagreen's traps, only for Nightcrawler, Colossus, and Mean to be captured by Shagreen's new servant, the giant Dark Bamf, and held with Pirate Kitty by a living tentacled column.

The lone Bamf and little Lockheed-616 freed the imprisoned female Bamfs and led them in an attack against Shagreen. While some of the females trashed Shagreen's sanctum, others began to flirt with an increasingly exasperated Nightcrawler. The timely arrival of Windrider and giant Lockheed-5311 began to turn the tables on Shagreen, while Nightcrawler got their living restraints to release them by tickling it with his tail. In the midst of the battle, Shagreen brought the observing teenage Kitty-616 into Reality-5311 where she was reunited with Lockheed, then quickly returned home to a frightened Illyana. Shagreen was finally defeated when Nightcrawler destroyed his power source, causing the Dark Bamf (revealed as amalgam of the missing male Bamfs) to split into its component Bamf's, free of Shagreen's control. The magical explosion caused Nightcrawler to be swept away into another dimensional warp and a brief series of adventures before eventually using his remaining unstable energy to return to his own reality.

Later, the dream demon Nightmare found several male Bamfs trapped in the Well and used his powers to convince them that Kitty-616 really had created them and made them love her before she abandoned them for Lockheed-616. For this "crime," the twisted Bamfs tormented Lockheed-616 for weeks, holding him prisoner for much of that time before he escaped. The Bamfs then began tormenting the rest of Kitty's then teammates on the British super-team Excalibur, which included Colossus, former secret agent Pete Wisdom, mystical empath

TOP ROW: MEAN, DARK PHOENIX, BAMF, WIZARD XAVIER & WINDRIDER
BOTTOM ROW: PIRATE KITTY, COLOSSUS & PRINCE CYCLOPS

Art by Dave Cockrum

Meggan, techno-organic Douglock, and Nightcrawler. Delivering the team to Nightmare, the Bamfs gleefully watched while Nightmare (via a request from demon lord Belasco) tortured Excalibur members with their worst fears in an effort to find what made them tick, while trying to force Lockheed to give up his "claim" on Kitty's love in favor of the Bamfs. However, when Wisdom forced Nightmare to see how the rest of Excalibur overcame those fears, Nightmare's hold over the team vanished, allowing the team to escape his realm. Whether the demonized Bamfs remained with Nightmare or eventually left him for their home dimension remains unclear.

A man named Ernest Thatchel on Earth-616 later made a deal with the demon Mephisto, agreeing to help wipe out all mutants on all Earths in exchange for a reunion with his dead wife Sara and son Jamie, who had died in a fire caused by a mutant (secretly Jamie himself) on Jamie's 12th birthday. Mephisto had Thatchel summon Hutch, a young boy who had been conceived outside of all realities by the Illyana Rasputin of Reality-2937, and whose existence was split among them all when he was born, leaving him unnoticed and alone in all of them. Mephisto's spell brought enough of Hutch from other realities to Earth-616 to allow him to interact with others, but at the cost of creating tears in all involved realities. The tears brought together hundreds of alternate-reality X-Men, which included Mean and the Bamfs. The result was a humongous brawl, with Mean insulting X-Baby Wolvie while making a pass at one of the female X-Babies. When Hutch realized that the combined outside energies the alternate X-Men carried with them would collapse Earth-616's dimension, he sacrificed his physical existence and returned to his ghost-like one, closing the rifts and sending all the alternate X-Men back to their home realities.

After the extradimensional insectoid Timebreakers decided to fire the current membership of their reality-hopping strike team Exiles for being "unreliable," the Timebreakers decided to recruit an Exile team consisting solely of Wolverine counterparts (whom they had heard were "the best there was at what they do"), believing that team would be more willing and able than the other team to get the job of fixing broken realities done. Their first mission sent them to Earth-127 to stop Brother Mutant, an amalgam created when Magneto, her children Quicksilver and the Scarlet Warlock, and their teammate Mesmero tried to steal their Wolverine's Adamantium skeleton and transfer it to Magneto, but which instead fused all five mutants into a single being intent on killing all non-mutants on their Earth. However, when the all-Wolverine Squad instead fell under Brother Mutant's control, the Timebreakers recruited another team of alternate Wolverines, and continued to do so as each team fell under the Brother's control. One of those teams included Mean, who was mentally coerced by Brother Mutant into his growing Wolverine army, until Major Logan from Earth-811 convinced the Timebreakers to rehire the other Exiles team to help his team in finally killing Brother Mutant and freeing the enslaved Wolverines. Afterwards, all the surviving Wolverines, including Mean, were sent home to their respective Earths.

DREADWINGS

DARK BAMF

FANGS OF DOOM

BAMFF VILLAGE

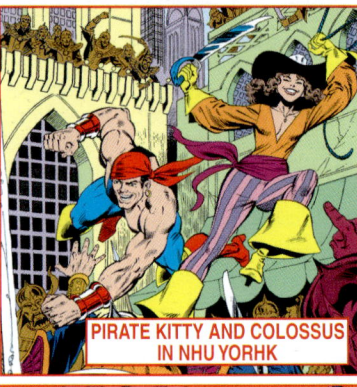
PIRATE KITTY AND COLOSSUS IN NHU YORHK

PIRATE KITTY'S SHIP, THE "ABDUL ALHAZRED"

PRINCE CYCLOPS & LADY JEAN

LOCKHEED THE DRAGON

FEMALE BAMFS

MALE BAMFS

PINIS ON BAMF ISLAND

Art by Dave Cockrum

KLAATU

HISTORY: Originating in the Andromeda galaxy, the cetacean Herm race is governed by a collection of nomadic tribes that traverse intergalactic space in search of electromagnetic energy upon which to feed. As a result of their destructive feeding habits, the Herm have been hunted by various starfaring races such as the Mobians and the Wilameanis, who regard the Herms as threats to civilization. Years ago, the Herm known as Klaatu was hunted by a Wilameani harpooner known as Cybor, a brazen youth who foolishly hunted Klaatu alone. But Klaatu charged at Cybor, tearing his starcraft asunder and causing Cybor to drift toward a nearby star. Half of Cybor's body was severely burned before he was finally rescued; outfitted with cybernetic replacement parts, the mentally scarred Cybor made it his life's mission to kill Klaatu. Cybor eventually became the captain of a massive solar starschooner known as the Andromeda, using his cybernetic half to serve as the schooner's piloting mechanism. Over time, the Andromeda's crew, who were promised by Cybor that they would gain immortality by draining Klaatu's life force, grew to include the Wobb communication specialist Cerexo and Mobian harpooner Xeron the Star-Slayer.

Years later, Klaatu journeyed to Earth and began feeding on electrical energy in downtown Manhattan. Xeron pursued Klaatu, who was attacked by the Hulk (Bruce Banner), causing Xeron's harpoon to miss its mark and allowing Klaatu to escape by dispersing his atoms throughout the city. Shortly after, Klaatu rematerialized near the Andromeda, which was still in Earth's orbit, and was hunted by Captain Cybor and his crew. Both Captain Cybor and Xeron struck Klaatu with their laser-harpoons, mortally wounding him, but Cybor's stalkboat drifted too close to Klaatu, causing the hunter to be thrown onto Klaatu's back. Both Klaatu and Cybor drifted into Earth's sun. Klaatu was revitalized by the sun's solar energy and escaped, but Cybor's human parts were completely incinerated by the intense heat. Retrieving Cybor's cybernetic half, the Andromeda's crew reconstructed him as an inseparable part of the ship, linked to its stardrive circuits.

Much later, Klaatu emerged in the Crossroads, a magical dimension that serves as a gateway to countless other dimensions, where he encountered the Hulk and the entity known as the Puffball Collective, who had both been banished to the Crossroads. But the Andromeda was in hot pursuit, forcibly drafting the Hulk into its crew and following Klaatu through one of the dimensional portals. The Andromeda finally engaged Klaatu, who had reconstituted himself, but an angry Hulk disrupted the hunt, allowing Klaatu to escape to another dimension. Andromeda's sensors soon located Klaatu again, allowing Xeron to strike him with several laser-harpoons, draining

REAL NAME: Klaatu
ALIASES: Behemoth from Beyond Space
IDENTITY: No dual identity
OCCUPATION: Energy hunter
CITIZENSHIP: Herm tribes
PLACE OF BIRTH: Andromeda Galaxy, Deep Space
KNOWN RELATIVES: None
GROUP AFFILIATION: None
EDUCATION: Unrevealed
FIRST APPEARANCE: Incredible Hulk #136 (1971)

Klaatu's energies into the storage cells in the Andromeda's hold. Klaatu finally collapsed on a desolate desert world, but he lashed out and smashed the Andromeda with his remaining energy. With the Andromeda stranded, Hulk freed Klaatu, who bestowed some of his energy to the Hulk in gratitude before vanishing once again while the Andromeda and its crew were buried in a sandstorm.

HEIGHT: 833'3"
WEIGHT: 27,766 lbs. (negligible in energy form)
EYES: White (no visible iris)
HAIR: None

ABILITIES/ACCESSORIES: Like all Herms, Klaatu is immensely strong and durable, absorbing all manner of electromagnetic energy for power and sustenance. He can briefly transform into a being of pure energy after feeding and can travel through intergalactic space as pure energy. He cannot survive for long in oxygen-rich atmospheres.

POWER GRID	1	2	3	4	5	6	7
INTELLIGENCE	■						
STRENGTH					■		
SPEED			■				
DURABILITY				■			
ENERGY PROJECTION							
FIGHTING SKILLS		■					

Art by Sal Buscema

KLAW

REAL NAME: Ulysses Klaw
ALIASES: Master of Sound, Murderous Master of Sound, Ronald Pershing, Sound Master, Sultan of Sound
IDENTITY: Publicly known
OCCUPATION: Criminal; former physicist, geologist; former vice president of Demonica
CITIZENSHIP: Netherlands; formerly Demonica
PLACE OF BIRTH: Vlaardingen, Netherlands
KNOWN RELATIVES: Fritz Klaue (father, deceased)
GROUP AFFILIATION: Masters of Evil, Frightful Four, Fearsome Foursome, Pacific Overlords associate
EDUCATION: Ph.D. in physics, bachelor's degree in geology
FIRST APPEARANCE: Fantastic Four #53 (1966)

HISTORY: An ally of the Third Reich in World War II, Netherlands-based Colonel Fritz Klaue had one hand replaced by one of iron. Klaue attempted to pilfer the African nation Wakanda's Vibranium, a rare material that could absorb vibrations, and he murdered King Chanda's wife Nanali to do so. Garbed as the Black Panther, Chanda stopped Klaue, who fled and vowed to return for revenge. Klaue changed his name to Klaw, and named his son Ulysses due to his love for Greek mythology. Ulysses grew to be a physicist and geologist and designed a powerful sound converter, which could theoretically turn sound into mass, but he postulated that he would need Vibranium to make his machine work. Ulysses equipped various mercenaries with weapons and led a strike on Wakanda, which he located using his geologic skills, to retrieve Vibranium. He demanded that the new king, T'Chaka, give up the Vibranium, and slew the king when he refused. Klaw's mercenaries destabilized the land, killing many and selling others, including the young N'Jadaka (who would later become Erik Killmonger), into slavery, until the king's adolescent son T'Challa turned one of Klaw's weapons on the mercenaries, shattering Ulysses' right hand with one blast. The mercenaries fled, and Ulysses eventually replaced his hand with a prosthetic sonic claw, sometimes called a sound horn. Over the following decade, he continued honing his technology, then smuggled equipment into one of Wakanda's caves, using a machine to create sound constructs of giant animals, with which he terrorized the locals. T'Challa, now the adult king and the new Black Panther, with his American allies the Fantastic Four, fought their way past Ulysses' constructs and attacked the cave. The Black Panther overloaded the equipment, and Ulysses was buried in the resulting explosion. He threw himself into his own sound converter, transforming his entire body into living solidified sound and granting himself various super-powers, many of which were directed through the prosthesis still attached to his form.

Klaw spent the ensuing years acting as a super-criminal, engaging various heroes in plots of revenge or profit. He immediately sought revenge on the Fantastic Four, attacking them in their headquarters and using his new powers to fight them individually and as a team. Mr. Fantastic soon defeated Klaw using Vibranium, and Klaw learned that Vibranium could absorb his vibrational attunement, disrupting his body's functioning and making it easy to render him unconscious. Klaw and other super-villains soon agreed to join the Crimson Cowl's new Masters of Evil group and attacked the Avengers, the heroic team Black Panther had joined, though even the Masters were shocked and frightened to learn that the Cowl was secretly mad robot Ultron-5. The Avengers soon defeated the Masters, who later regrouped and briefly battled the Avengers and a short-lived women's team, the Lady Liberators. From a base in the African country Rudyarda, Klaw manipulated others into stealing a new Wakandan device, the Vibrotron, which could augment Vibranium, but he was stopped by members of the Fantastic Four and T'Challa (briefly known then as Black Leopard); Klaw's prosthesis was damaged for the first time, but he soon replaced it. Briefly held in a Rudyardan prison, Klaw escaped, teamed with sun-powered villain Solarr, disguised himself as Ambassador Ronald Pershing and lured the Avengers to Rudyarda. There he tried to get Black Panther to cede control of Wakanda to him and threatened several hostages, using his giant sound form for the first time, but Black Panther realized his plot and defeated him again.

Klaw was subsequently recruited by the other-dimensional Sheenarians, who needed his powers to open a dimensional portal that would allow them to invade Earth. They promised Klaw a leadership position in their new government after the world was conquered, and Klaw agreed. Klaw and one Sheenarian traveled to London to fight the jungle-lord Ka-Zar and his saber-toothed pet, Zabu, then moved on to the Savage Land, where Klaw opened the portal and the Sheenarians burst through. Klaw returned with other Sheenarians to their home dimension and witnessed their battles with the alien Quarlians, soon realizing he was trapped in their dimension. At the first opportunity, Klaw transported himself back home, and the Sheenarians were defeated by Ka-Zar and his allies. Klaw next teamed up with the supremely powerful Molecule Man and attacked the Fantastic Four in hopes of procuring a new body for Molecule Man. Klaw defeated the heroes, but was soon defeated by their Poppupian ally, Impossible Man. Teaming with the brilliant Mad Thinker, Klaw created constructs of various heroes to manipulate the synthozoid Vision into

Art by John Byrne with Vince Evans (inset)

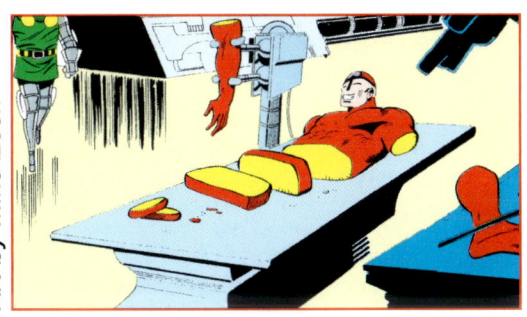
Art by Mike Zeck

fighting the Fantastic Four, but Vision and the FF returned to battle the villains, and Klaw's prosthesis was smashed again.

Noticing his powers were dwindling, Klaw realized that he needed a charge to return to full power. He feigned defeat at the hands of the human Thunderbolts gang, and his unconscious form was placed by Black Panther on a ship bound for Wakanda until Klaw, having hypnotized members of the gang, returned to full power when his prosthesis was fired at his inert form. Black Panther managed to turn Klaw's powers inward, though, and Klaw exploded above the water. Klaw's prosthesis absorbed his energies and was placed in Project: PEGASUS, an energy-research facility, until Solarr revived him. Though slightly mentally unstable after these events, Klaw tried escaping with Solarr, battling heroes the Thing, Quasar (Wendell Vaughn) and Giant-Man (Bill Foster) before being defeated by the energy-neutralizing Aquarian. Klaw still managed to escape and set up a team to mine ore on a Native American reservation. When Jason and Ward Strongbow investigated, Klaw tried to kill them and knocked them into a uranium radiation machine, unintentionally granting them super-powers. Jason costumed himself as American Eagle and pursued Klaw to the Savage Land alongside Ka-Zar and Thing, who soon defeated Klaw and returned him to Project: PEGASUS.

Klaw manipulated the mutant heroine Dazzler (Alison Blaire) into freeing him, but he was absorbed into her form when she used her powers to absorb sound, later releasing Klaw's energy in a fired blast aboard the world-eater Galactus' ship. Klaw remained as inert energy for months, driven mad by the ship's alien technology. When Galactus and his ship were brought by the virtually all-powerful Beyonder to Battleworld alongside many Earth heroes and villains, Dr. Doom aided Klaw in returning to corporeal form. Quite mad, Klaw was manipulated by both Doom and the Beyonder before being returned to Earth. Still slightly mad and desiring a conquest to restore his reputation, Klaw attacked Daredevil (Matt Murdock), who defeated him by disrupting his vibrational attunement. Klaw was recruited into the Wizard's Frightful Four alongside Hydro-Man and Titania (Mary MacPherran), and fought the Fantastic Four in a series of battles, unintentionally returning the Thing to his human form of Ben Grimm and being mind-blasted by the young Franklin Richards. Wizard then attempted to recruit the vastly powerful rogue Watcher, Aron, who put both teams, Frightful Four and Fantastic Four, in stasis briefly before transporting the villains into prison.

Klaw escaped, intending to attack Black Panther, but instead fought Quasar again before being captured by AIM, who placed a self-destruct device into Klaw's prosthesis and released him. Captain Marvel (Monica Rambeau) returned Klaw to jail, where he and Wizard briefly battled Iron Man (Tony Stark). Klaw participated in an attempted mass breakout at the Vault, but it was quelled by the Avengers and Freedom Force. Finally freed, Klaw was manipulated by AIM into apprehending Molecule Man, who was believed powerless, and Klaw fought the fiery Volcana and Molecule Man himself. Klaw triumphed over them both, but simply departed when AIM's self-destruct device was rendered inert. Klaw attended a Weapons Expo on Boca Caliente ("AIM Island") that was disrupted by Captain America and his allies, then experimentally laced his prosthesis with Vibranium. He recruited mercenaries and attacked Wakanda anew, though Black Panther and the Fantastic Four caused Klaw immense pain when they briefly drained him of energy. After attending the Chess Set's auction of Auric and Silver and battling Alpha Flight, Klaw was recruited by criminal geneticist Dr. Demonicus, who had founded the new island nation Demonica and named Klaw its vice president. Teamed with Zvezda Dennista (Morning Star) and the Pacific Overlords, Klaw fought the Avengers on Demonica, but turned against Demonicus when he realized they were being manipulated by the demon Raksasa. Klaw returned to jail despite having been lost in the sinking of Demonica, but soon escaped to attack the Fantastic Four yet again. Klaw teamed with fellow attackers Paibok the Power-Skrull, Huntara and Devos the Devastator in the short-lived Fearsome Foursome, and fought the Fantastic Four, winning until other heroes intervened. The team soon dissipated, and Klaw liberated Ms. Marvel (Sharon Ventura), the Fantastic Four's monstrous ally, from stasis, and the two of them joined the Wizard and Red Ghost in forming a new Frightful Four. They drew straws to determine the hero they should attack, and Klaw fought Ant-Man (Scott Lang), who forced Klaw to flee. Klaw returned to fight the Fantastic Four solo, and was defeated by the fledgling Fantastic Force and arrested.

After attending the wedding of Absorbing Man and Titania, Klaw briefly teamed up with Killmonger and fought Black Panther and Daredevil. Escaping the Vault yet again, Klaw was recruited by the new Crimson

Art by Sal Velluto

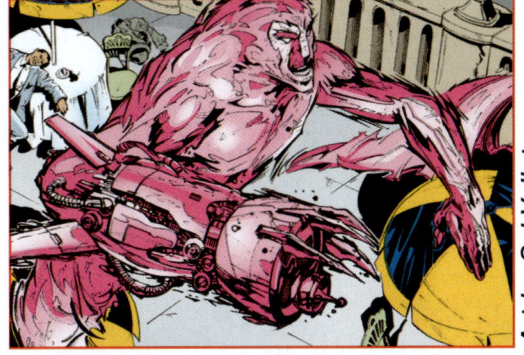
Art by Sal Velluto

Cowl (Justine Hammer) for her Masters of Evil, and the villains soon fought Black Widow (Natasha Romanoff) and the villains-turned-heroes Thunderbolts, whose member Songbird was utilizing Klaw's technology for super-powers, infuriating Klaw. When the Vibranium-lace in Klaw's prosthesis began acting as a poison, Klaw hid in Wakanda while his brief ally, Joshua Itobo, sought a cure. Impatient, Klaw deafened Itobo and attacked Black Panther and his ally, the time-traveling Cable, though Klaw was soon defeated in a vacuum, leaving only his prosthesis behind. Crimson Cowl had Klaw restored, and the Masters of Evil, with several more recruits, fought the Thunderbolts several more times before being defeated, their plot to blackmail the world using weather-altering equipment foiled. Klaw escaped prison and realized that Vibranium around the world was dissipating in a Vibranium cancer, so he sped to Wakanda to destroy their Vibranium reserves. He fought Captain America (Steve Rogers) there, but the hero's shield shattered Klaw's corporeal form into millions of pieces, though Klaw's powers were briefly enhanced by the Vibranium's destruction. Klaw's form was restored by the Wakandan White Wolf, Black Panther's adopted brother and enemy, whom Klaw turned on, and Klaw used his powers to exacerbate a war between Wakanda and Deviant Lemuria before savagely attacking Black Panther in New York. Black Panther dissipated Klaw's various attacks using anti-metal (Antarctic Vibranium) and drained Klaw's form of all substance, almost killing Klaw.

Recovered, Klaw was briefly manipulated into serving the alien monster Orrgo. Klaw fought Songbird once again, was interned in a jail in the Negative Zone by the Fantastic Four, and suffered defeats at the hands of Ms. Marvel (Carol Danvers) and the Thunderbolts. His current whereabouts are unknown. Klaw was recruited to the Frightful Four and battled the Fantastic Four, who had new members in the Black Panther and his wife, Storm, but the villains were swiftly defeated.

Art by Andy Kubert

HEIGHT: 5'11" (variable) **EYES:** Red
WEIGHT: 175 lbs. (variable) **HAIR:** None

ABILITIES/ACCESSORIES: Composed of solidified sound, Klaw does not need to sleep, breathe, eat or drink, and is immune to diseases, impacts and wounds. He can increase his size by converting surrounding sounds into mass and adding it to his form, and can decrease his size by discharging sound mass from it. Through unknown means, Klaw's prosthesis grows or shrinks in size with him. Klaw can alter his own shape, and has done so to form himself into a large sound train. He can also add other elements into his form as he grows larger, as he once mixed water in with his increased sound mass, appearing as a watery giant. Klaw is resistant, if not immune, to telepathic attacks. He is super-strong, able to lift up to 5 tons. Klaw's form can be cut apart and fused back together without injury to himself. His form was once converted into a group of lenses before reintegrating. Before his transformation, Klaw replaced one of his hands with a prosthesis sound converter, also called a sonic claw or sound horn, which can absorb and solidify sound. When Klaw has been dissipated in the past, his bodily energy is generally absorbed by his own converter until a sound or vibration restores his form and sentience. Though his prosthesis has at times been destroyed, Klaw has either re-formed it or re-equipped himself with another. Klaw has occasionally upgraded his prosthesis, making it larger and once lacing it with Vibranium (which ultimately proved unhealthy), but he has always returned to using his standard prosthesis.

Klaw can create various solidified sound constructs that he can mentally control and that maintain cohesiveness until he dissipates them, either willingly or because distracted, or because the construct is disrupted. Klaw can maintain these constructs even at a distance. He generally prefers to create giant constructs of various jungle animals, usually gorillas, panthers and elephants, and sometimes refers to these constructs as "Sonimals." Klaw has also created sonic-energy diagrams, solidified suits of armor, walls capable of shattering bullets, balls that will continue to absorb sound mass independent of Klaw, and even a baseball team. Klaw's constructs are capable of speech if he wills it, and he can reabsorb any of his constructs at will. Klaw's constructs are almost always crimson, but he has been known to create black and gold constructs and, while under the influence of the Beyonder, dozens of multi-colored monsters. Though nonsentient and less powerful than him, Klaw's constructs are capable of vast damage and usually possess enhanced strength. When Klaw's prosthesis is damaged, he cannot create sound constructs.

Klaw can manipulate sound vibrations to varying effects. He can amplify existing sounds up to an intensity of 170 decibels, capable of deafening anyone in a .6 mile radius. Klaw can utilize vibrations to cause vertigo in the inner ear of others, burst eardrums, briefly hypnotize people, or drive animals into frenzies with high pitches. Klaw can mimic any sound, including music and voices. Klaw can fire concussive blasts of sound at others, sometimes referring to these blasts as his "immobilizer beam," and can cancel out his other constructs with a "reversion blast" of sound. He can also fire steady streams of sonic pulses.

Klaw can transform himself into pure, nonsolidified energy. While propelling himself through the air at the speed of sound he can smash through the hull of a battleship. He can also utilize his constructs to fly with him at this speed, even if those constructs contain living beings, and he has used this as a method of transportation for various associates.

Klaw is extremely vulnerable to the vibration-absorbing ore Wakandan Vibranium, which, on contact, causes him to lose energy or parts of his corporeal form. He has successfully been imprisoned via Vibranium bars or walls. Klaw was once briefly empowered by unstable Vibranium, which was weakened due to a "Vibranium cancer." Klaw is also susceptible to the metal-disintegrating Antarctic Vibranium, which can destabilize his form. Klaw is vulnerable to sonics or vibrations that disrupt his own internal vibrations, and can be knocked unconscious by blows or blasts powerful enough to do this. Klaw cannot generally maintain his corporeal form in a vacuum, though he has been known to do so by drawing from his own body's sound. Klaw's form or energy has been absorbed by foes with energy-absorption capacity, such as Dazzler, Guardian (Heather Hudson) and Ms. Marvel. Klaw's ability to utilize his powers seems to depend upon his mental state, his inner vibrational harmonics, and his time spent recovering from wounds. Klaw's powers, when unstable, have caused his form to become dangerously explosive.

POWER GRID	1	2	3	4	5	6	7
INTELLIGENCE			■				
STRENGTH			■				
SPEED				■			
DURABILITY						■	
ENERGY PROJECTION				■			
FIGHTING SKILLS		■					

KISMET

HISTORY: Wladyslav Shinski, Carlo Zota, Maris Morlak, and Jerome Hamilton were collectively known as the Enclave: scientists dedicated to improving the world by any means, including taking control of it. In an abandoned Deviant outpost in the North Atlantic they constructed the Beehive, their citadel of science. Their greatest accomplishment was the creation of Him, a genetically perfect artificial being designed to father a new human race. When Him matured more quickly than anticipated, they lost control of it and Him demolished much of the Beehive, killing Hamilton and flying away. The remaining three tried again, producing Paragon, a being genetically identical to Him. To retain control of their creation they tricked Dr. Stephen Strange into modifying the creature's neural structure, but Paragon deduced their plans while still growing and gave itself a post-hypnotic command to metamorphosize into a glowing black form, negating the neurological controls. Angered at its creators' attempts to control it, Paragon destroyed the Beehive and placed itself into a restorative cocoon to develop further.

While in the cocoon, Paragon adapted itself into a female form and slowly moved towards New York City. When dockworkers fished the cocoon from the harbor, Paragon hatched as Her. Adopting her creators' goals of parenting the perfect race, Her sought Him as her ideal mate. Her's search began with Alicia Masters, who had briefly known Him, but this brought Her into conflict with Alicia's boyfriend, Ben Grimm, the Thing. Moondragon sensed Her's presence and sought her out, informing her of Him's evolution into Adam Warlock and subsequent death at the hands of Thanos. Believing she could revive Warlock, Her sought Warlock's burial site on Counter-Earth, accompanied by Alicia, Moondragon, the Thing, and Starhawk/Aleta. When Counter-Earth proved to be missing, Her resurrected its creator, the High Evolutionary, and located the thieves. On Counter-Earth, Her resurrected Warlock, only to discover his soul missing (actually confined within a Soul Gem, since stolen). She reburied Warlock's body, but was moved when offered solace by Grimm, to whom she had shown only contempt. Unable to deal with these new emotions, she fled.

Her's search for enlightenment led her near the planet of U'sr'pria, which was being ravaged as its technological advancement destroyed its environment. Investigating, Her found the planet had been conquered by a mutant member of its own race, the U'sr'pr, who forced the planet into a technological boom, striking a deal with the Consortium, an intergalactic business conglomerate, for his own comfort. Her angrily depowered U'sr'pr, and then aided the natives in their clean-up. The populace named her J'Ridia Starduster, or She Whose Trail Dusts Hope. When the Consortium found their profits from U'sr'pria dwindling, they sent agents to correct this. The Consortium proved too powerful, so J'Ridia fled to Earth seeking aid, carefully drawing the Consortium after her and away from U'sr'pria. The Consortium caught J'Ridia near Earth and attacked; she fell out of control into Toronto, mistaking it for New York. The Consortium followed, and Alpha Flight aided J'Ridia in battling them. The Avengers also came to the city's aid, but neither side proved victorious. As the battle was demolishing the city, J'Ridia decided to surrender herself to the Consortium, but before she could, the alien Quwrlln coincidentally teleported away J'Ridia and half of Alpha Flight and the Avengers, seeking their aid in defending their world from Galactus. The Quwrlln had moved their planet into another dimension; the different physical laws allowed the defeat of Galactus there. Unwilling to kill Galactus but not wanting to leave him stranded on the Quwlrn's planet with no recourse but to eventually devour it, a solution was found when the Quwrlln teleported Galactus to the planet that powered the Consortium's mother ship. Galactus devoured the planet, sparing the Quwrlln, and the Consortium was crippled, freeing U'sr'pria.

Struck by the selflessness of the humans who had aided her, J'Ridia remained on Earth, forgoing her U'sr'prian name. Again known as Her, she discovered that Adam Warlock had been resurrected with his soul restored, but Warlock, occupied with the universe-threatening menace

REAL NAME: None
ALIASES: Ayesha, She Who Must be Obeyed, J'Ridia Starduster, She Whose Trail Dusts Hope, Her, Paragon
IDENTITY: No dual identity
OCCUPATION: Adventurer
CITIZENSHIP: None
PLACE OF CREATION: Beehive, Shard Island, Atlantic Ocean
KNOWN RELATIVES: The Enclave (creators); Adam Warlock, unidentified female "Warlock" (genetic twins)
GROUP AFFILIATION: None
EDUCATION: Self-taught; initially programmed by Enclave during creation
FIRST APPEARANCE: (Paragon) Incredible Hulk Annual #6 (1977); (Her) Marvel Two-In-One #61 (1980); (J'Ridia Starduster) Marvel Comics Presents #35 (1989); (Kismet) Quasar #40 (1992); (Ayesha) Fantastic Four #11 (1998)

PARAGON

Art by John Buscema with Jerry Bingham (inset)

of the Infinity Gauntlet, dismissively rebuffed Her's advances. At loose ends, Her remained in New York City, protecting it against the threats of Eon's expanding corpse and Edifice Rex. Her soon realized that she and Warlock would make a poor parental couple as they possessed virtually identical genetic material, and decided to seek the best mate from within humanity. She created pods of genetic material designed to draw the best from herself and a mate, and attached these to the back of six males: Wonder Man, Hyperion, Hercules, Doc Samson, Ikaris, and Gilgamesh. When Quasar (Wendell Vaughn) opposed her, she placed a pod on him as well, drawing the ire of Moondragon, who had decided Quasar was her own perfect (if unwilling) mate. While the three battled, the Avengers succeeded in removing the pods from the others, and Her decided Quasar was indeed her ideal mate, as he was the only being to evidence concern for the contents of the pod over himself. However, Quasar pointed out that her desire to parent children was arising solely from her creators' wishes and not from herself, challenging Her to find her own purpose in life. Uncertain, Her removed the pod from Quasar, but decided to remain near him as a companion, observing his humanity.

Her worked beside Quasar for a short period of time, battling both Binary and the Super-Skrull as she defended Earth during Operation: Galactic Storm. She then accompanied Quasar to the Kree homeworld, Hala, where she was moved by its recent devastation and fought to free the souls of its population from the Soul Eater. Her accompanied the alien Mourners to the planet Scadam, but found herself unable to watch this planet's destruction. Though she had not sought out combat, she saw it as her kismet to be unable to avoid it, and so adopted Kismet as her new name. She fought the invading Black Fleet on Scadam, but was wounded and witnessed from afar the destruction of the invading fleet by extradimensional energies. Seeking these energies, she returned to Earth, where she found them originating from Quasar's girlfriend, Kayla Ballantine, who bore the extra-multiversal Star Brand. When Kismet's questioning of Kayla inadvertently turned into battle, Kayla lashed out, rupturing Kismet's cells and forcing her to withdraw into a regenerative cocoon. Quasar later moved the cocoon to Project: PEGASUS for safe storage.

Art by John Buscema

When Wladyslav Shinski suffered a serious stroke, the remaining members of the Enclave stole the cocoon from PEGASUS and removed Kismet from it. They placed Shinski within it to regenerate but also took pains to protect Kismet, who was nearing full recovery. Striking on the idea of using Kismet's genetic material to hasten the recovery, they withdrew a sample from her. This was stolen by Frank, an AIM Adaptoid spy who had been observing the Enclave. The Adaptoid injected itself with the sample and adapted Kismet's powers as a new Paragon, but the recuperating Shinski injected Paragon with a genetic weapon they had developed for use against Kismet, destroying him. Grateful that Shinski had saved her, though uneasy they had developed a weapon to destroy her, Kismet wove regenerative cocoons for all three Enclave members (they had been injured during the battle) and placed them within, watching over them as "mother" while she tried to determine what it meant to be their "daughter."

After some months, an energy blast from space disrupted the cocoons, and the Enclave members hatched, transformed into lesser versions of Kismet with similar powers. With these abilities, the Enclave began what they had always wanted to do: Cure the world's ills. However, their short-term solutions frequently created worse long-term problems, and Kismet convinced them to leave the planet while they learned how to use their powers and where they had come from. Kismet led them in search of the energy blast that had triggered their change and discovered Khatylis, an alien life-form that harvested the flotsam of destroyed systems and created new matrices for life. When the Enclave disrupted this matrix, they were absorbed by it, but Kismet and the Silver Surfer merged their life essences with that of Khatylis to restore its life matrix, freeing the Enclave.

The Enclave apparently lost their powers, returning to Earth. Shinski and Morlak shared the identity of Crucible, and enslaved Kismet (under the name "Ayesha") against the Fantastic Four. Showing new powers of mind control, Ayesha defeated the Four, but was eventually banished when a black hole grenade transported her and Shinski into another dimension. Shinski has since returned to Earth, while Kismet — restored to her classic form — fought against the Heart of the Infinite-powered Thanos.

In the alternate future of the Guardians of the Galaxy (Earth-691), Kismet and Quasar produced a child: Starhawk (Stakar Ogord).

Art by Salvador Larroca

HEIGHT: 6'6" **EYES:** White
WEIGHT: 390 lbs. **HAIR:** Blonde

ABILITIES/ACCESSORIES: Kismet's cells serve as cosmic energy batteries, allowing her to absorb, store, and use cosmic energies. Her form is cosmically enhanced; she can press 70 tons and survive in the vacuum of space; she is virtually tireless. She can project force blasts, levitate objects with anti-gravitons, and rearrange small volumes of matter. She can fly at Mach 10, and generate rifts into warp-space. She possesses limited telepathic abilities: she can understand any language and, as Ayesha, she could control minds. If seriously damaged, Kismet's body will automatically generate a regenerative cocoon around her.

POWER GRID	1	2	3	4	5	6	7
INTELLIGENCE							
STRENGTH							
SPEED							
DURABILITY							
ENERGY PROJECTION							
FIGHTING SKILLS							

KITTY'S FAIRY TALE

HISTORY: Following an attack on Xavier's School by the Hellfire Club, Kitty Pryde sought to cheer up her young friend Illyana Rasputin by telling her a fairy tale. Set in the Caliphate of Nhu Yorkh, the story starred the swashbuckling Pirate Kitty and her stalwart companion Colossus. After yet another daring escape from the authorities, Kitty and Colossus rescued Prince Cyclops and the Wizard Xavier from a gang of thugs. Cyclops and Xavier were on a quest to rescue Cyclops' beloved Princess Jean, who had been corrupted by her soul's dark side and transformed into the evil Dark Phoenix, who attacked and sank all the ships in the harbor before Xavier drove her away with a crystal containing her true soul inside it.

With the aid of Pirate Kitty's giant dragon ally Lockheed, the heroes tracked Dark Phoenix across the Great Western Ocean, stopping on a remote island to rest. The island proved to be the home of the Bamfs, small blue-skinned elf-like creatures who could teleport. One of the Bamfs became fond of Kitty and insisted on accompanying her. The motley crew was also joined by the storm goddess Windrider, whom Colossus freed from a bottle in which she had been imprisoned by Dark Phoenix, and the diminutive, hirsute, razor-clawed Mean, who sought revenge on Cyclops for supposedly stealing Jean away from him but was quickly scared into submission by Lockheed. The heroes soon clashed with Dark Phoenix, and Xavier released Jean's soul from its possession. Lockheed then flew the heroes back to the Prince's land where Cyclops and Jean were married, and they all lived happily ever after.

Unbeknownst to Kitty, she had somehow subconsciously tapped into an actual alternate reality (Earth-5311) while telling her story. When Kitty and Illyana learned of Nightcrawler's adventure involving the Well at the Center of Time, a bizarre metaphysical phenomenon that exists simultaneously in all realities, they used the Danger Room's technology to create a simulacrum of the Well, not realizing the actual Well materialized instead due to Nightcrawler's enduring state of dimensional instability. Both Nightcrawler and his reality (Earth-616)'s diminutive Lockheed were pulled into it, after which the Well moved on to another reality. Following an adventure in another dimension during which Nightcrawler earned the enmity of the shark-like sorcerer Shagreen when Nightcrawler stopped Shagreen's intended sacrifice of the Jinjav (princess) Sabree to the demon Cthuma-Gurath (possibly referring to Shuma-Gorath), Kitty duplicated the settings that summoned the Well, opening another dimensional warp that sent Nightcrawler and Lockheed to Earth-5311's Bamf Island, where the Bamfs greeted Nightcrawler as their daddy Bamf due to his larger size and resemblance to them.

Seeking revenge, Shagreen followed Nightcrawler to the Bamf's village, Bamff, and attacked him there. When he realized Nightcrawler and one Bamf were standing on a spellstone that turned his spells back on him,

CORE CONTINUUM DESIGNATION: Reality-5311
SIGNIFICANT INHABITANTS: Bamfs, Colossus, Dark Bamf, Dreadwings, Lockheed, Mean (aka the Fiend with No Name), Pirate Kitty, Prince Cyclops, Princess Jean/Dark Phoenix, Windrider, Wizard Xavier, others (natives); Shagreen
SIGNIFICANT LOCATIONS: Bamf Island, Fangs of Doom, Great Western Ocean, Kingdom of Argos, Nhu Yorkh, Wizard's Island
FIRST APPEARANCE: Uncanny X-Men #153 (1982)

Shagreen instead kidnapped all the other Bamfs to Wizard's Island in the Fangs of Doom. Seeking to save his kinsfolk, the Bamf summoned the giant Lockheed-5311 for help, which also attracted the attention of Mean. The quartet soon found Pirate Kitty and Colossus, who were surprised when little Lockheed-616 decided Pirate Kitty was a suitable stand-in for his own teenage Kitty. Upon arrival at Shagreen's lair, giant Lockheed-5311 was pulled underwater by a giant squid-like monster while the others were attacked by a horde of bird-like Dreadwings who captured Kitty and took her to Shagreen. The heroes escaped Shagreen's traps, only for Nightcrawler, Colossus, and Mean to be captured by Shagreen's new servant, the giant Dark Bamf, and held with Pirate Kitty by a living tentacled column.

The lone Bamf and little Lockheed-616 freed the imprisoned female Bamfs and led them in an attack against Shagreen. While some of the females trashed Shagreen's sanctum, others began to flirt with an increasingly exasperated Nightcrawler. The timely arrival of Windrider and giant Lockheed-5311 began to turn the tables on Shagreen, while Nightcrawler got their living restraints to release them by tickling it with his tail. In the midst of the battle, Shagreen brought the observing teenage Kitty-616 into Reality-5311 where she was reunited with Lockheed, then quickly returned home to a frightened Illyana. Shagreen was finally defeated when Nightcrawler destroyed his power source, causing the Dark Bamf (revealed as amalgam of the missing male Bamfs) to split into its component Bamf's, free of Shagreen's control. The magical explosion caused Nightcrawler to be swept away into another dimensional warp and a brief series of adventures before eventually using his remaining unstable energy to return to his own reality.

Later, the dream demon Nightmare found several male Bamfs trapped in the Well and used his powers to convince them that Kitty-616 really had created them and made them love her before she abandoned them for Lockheed-616. For this "crime," the twisted Bamfs tormented Lockheed-616 for weeks, holding him prisoner for much of that time before he escaped. The Bamfs then began tormenting the rest of Kitty's then teammates on the British super-team Excalibur, which included Colossus, former secret agent Pete Wisdom, mystical empath

TOP ROW: MEAN, DARK PHOENIX, BAMF, WIZARD XAVIER & WINDRIDER
BOTTOM ROW: PIRATE KITTY, COLOSSUS & PRINCE CYCLOPS

Art by Dave Cockrum

Meggan, techno-organic Douglock, and Nightcrawler. Delivering the team to Nightmare, the Bamfs gleefully watched while Nightmare (via a request from demon lord Belasco) tortured Excalibur members with their worst fears in an effort to find what made them tick, while trying to force Lockheed to give up his "claim" on Kitty's love in favor of the Bamfs. However, when Wisdom forced Nightmare to see how the rest of Excalibur overcame those fears, Nightmare's hold over the team vanished, allowing the team to escape his realm. Whether the demonized Bamfs remained with Nightmare or eventually left him for their home dimension remains unclear.

A man named Ernest Thatchel on Earth-616 later made a deal with the demon Mephisto, agreeing to help wipe out all mutants on all Earths in exchange for a reunion with his dead wife Sara and son Jamie, who had died in a fire caused by a mutant (secretly Jamie himself) on Jamie's 12th birthday. Mephisto had Thatchel summon Hutch, a young boy who had been conceived outside of all realities by the Illyana Rasputin of Reality-2937, and whose existence was split among them all when he was born, leaving him unnoticed and alone in all of them. Mephisto's spell brought enough of Hutch from other realities to Earth-616 to allow him to interact with others, but at the cost of creating tears in all involved realities. The tears brought together hundreds of alternate-reality X-Men, which included Mean and the Bamfs. The result was a humongous brawl, with Mean insulting X-Baby Wolvie while making a pass at one of the female X-Babies. When Hutch realized that the combined outside energies the alternate X-Men carried with them would collapse Earth-616's dimension, he sacrificed his physical existence and returned to his ghost-like one, closing the rifts and sending all the alternate X-Men back to their home realities.

After the extradimensional insectoid Timebreakers decided to fire the current membership of their reality-hopping strike team Exiles for being "unreliable," the Timebreakers decided to recruit an Exile team consisting solely of Wolverine counterparts (whom they had heard were "the best there was at what they do"), believing that team would be more willing and able than the other team to get the job of fixing broken realities done. Their first mission sent them to Earth-127 to stop Brother Mutant, an amalgam created when Magneto, her children Quicksilver and the Scarlet Warlock, and their teammate Mesmero tried to steal their Wolverine's Adamantium skeleton and transfer it to Magneto, but which instead fused all five mutants into a single being intent on killing all non-mutants on their Earth. However, when the all-Wolverine Squad instead fell under Brother Mutant's control, the Timebreakers recruited another team of alternate Wolverines, and continued to do so as each team fell under the Brother's control. One of those teams included Mean, who was mentally coerced by Brother Mutant into his growing Wolverine army, until Major Logan from Earth-811 convinced the Timebreakers to rehire the other Exiles team to help his team in finally killing Brother Mutant and freeing the enslaved Wolverines. Afterwards, all the surviving Wolverines, including Mean, were sent home to their respective Earths.

DREADWINGS

DARK BAMF

FANGS OF DOOM

BAMFF VILLAGE

PIRATE KITTY AND COLOSSUS IN NHU YORHK

PIRATE KITTY'S SHIP, THE "ABDUL ALHAZRED"

PRINCE CYCLOPS & LADY JEAN

LOCKHEED THE DRAGON

MALE BAMFS

FEMALE BAMFS

PINIS ON BAMF ISLAND

Art by Dave Cockrum

MISTY KNIGHT

HISTORY: Misty Knight grew up in New York alongside her childhood friend, Angie Freeman. As adults, Angie became a reporter, while Misty graduated from New York's police academy with top honors. Assigned patrol duty for the Twelfth Precinct in partnership with Raphael "Rafe" Scarfe, both she and Rafe soon rose to the rank of detective. Early in her career, Misty rescued female samurai Colleen Wing from being killed during a gun battle on Manhattan's West Side, and the two women soon became best friends. In contrast, Misty eventually lost touch with Angie, who became a vampire vigilante dedicated to her neighborhood's protection.

Years into her career, Misty, now with the department's bomb squad, was en route to cash her paycheck when she learned the bank's building had been taken over by five terrorists with several hostages and a bomb. Working with fellow officers, Misty penetrated the terrorists' parameter and shot all five to death, saving the hostages' lives. The bomb exploded as she tried to dispose of it, damaging her right arm so severely that it required amputation. In recognition of her bravery, Tony Stark (Iron Man) provided her with a cyborg arm possessing enhanced strength and capabilities. Nevertheless, department policy dictated Misty's injury disqualify her from field duty; too devoted to action to accept a desk job, and troubled both by her lost arm and its mechanical replacement, Misty resigned from the force. She lapsed into weeks of depression before Colleen broke through her friend's shell of resentment and encouraged a new role in life for both of them. The friends ultimately combined their unique skills to form a private investigation firm, Nightwing (Knight + Wing) Restorations, Ltd, also called "Daughters of the Dragon" for their martial arts expertise. Relocating as another change in her life, Misty perused the same vacant apartment as Jean Grey (Marvel Girl), seeking a new life for herself away from the X-Men. As neither could afford the apartment alone, they became roommates and friends.

Misty first encountered the heroic adventurer Iron Fist (Daniel Rand) when Colleen, who had already befriended him, was abducted by his enemies. Erroneously believing Fist responsible, Misty attacked him but soon learned the truth and, after freeing Colleen, Misty and Rand became romantically involved. Soon afterward, she accompanied Colleen to Hong Kong to avenge the death of Colleen's grandfather Kenji Ozawa, slain by Emil Vachon's crime syndicate. Vachon captured them and sought to enslave them by drug addiction, but his underlings carelessly injected Misty's bionic arm, leaving her unaffected; with Misty's support, Colleen overcame her drugged state and slew Vachon. After assisting Fist against the machinations of Master Khan, sorcerer-ruler of Fist's adopted home city K'un-Lun, Misty visited what appeared to be a hospitalized Jean Grey, overwhelmed by cosmic power that had transformed her into Phoenix; neither Misty nor anyone else knew she had been replaced by the Phoenix-Force entity. Ironically, Misty soon became closer friends with the X-Men themselves, and over time she and Colleen befriended several other super heroes, including Spider-Man (Peter Parker), who helped them rescue Fist from K'un-Lun exile Steel Serpent (Davos).

Using the alias Maya Corday, Misty infiltrated John Bushmaster's crime syndicate and learned mercenary Luke Cage had been framed for crimes for which he was now pursued. After she, Colleen, and Iron Fist helped clear Cage's name, Fist and Cage formed the bodyguard/investigator firm Heroes for Hire, which Misty and Colleen frequently assisted against various super-villains. While on assignment in Japan for Colleen's uncle, Prime Minister Takeo Fukada, the two women assisted the X-Men in defeating Moses Magnum, then again provided support when the heroes fought Alpha Flight. Later, Misty's two circles of friends met when HFH and the X-Men joined forces against the Living Monolith, and she and Cage subsequently assisted Storm (Ororo Munroe) when her Harlem explorations led to an encounter with teen criminals. Misty quarreled with Fist, however, about one of his friends, ex-terrorist Alan Cavenaugh; unable to forget the disaster that had cost her an arm, Misty

REAL NAME: Mercedes Knight
ALIASES: Maya Corday, others used during investigations
IDENTITY: No dual identity
OCCUPATION: Adventurer; former mercenary, bounty hunter, bail bondswoman, private investigator, police officer
CITIZENSHIP: USA
PLACE OF BIRTH: Unrevealed
KNOWN RELATIVES: Unidentified father
GROUP AFFILIATION: Heroes for Hire; formerly Initiative, Nightwing Restorations/Daughters of the Dragon, NYPD
EDUCATION: Police academy graduate, otherwise unrevealed
FIRST APPEARANCE: Marvel Team-Up #1 (1972)

remained dubious of Cavenaugh's self-proclaimed reformation until he risked his life to save others from Halwani terrorists.

Following clashes with Sabretooth and Constrictor, the Golden Tigers, and Warhawk (Mitchell Tanner), Misty was approached by Angie Freeman, who, having spent five years as a vampire, sought to similarly transform Misty to make her a fellow criminal-killer and, perhaps, lover. Although Angie's vampiric mesmerism, combined with their long friendship, nearly made Misty a willing transformee, Colleen helped her overcome the entrancement as the pair had consistently helped each

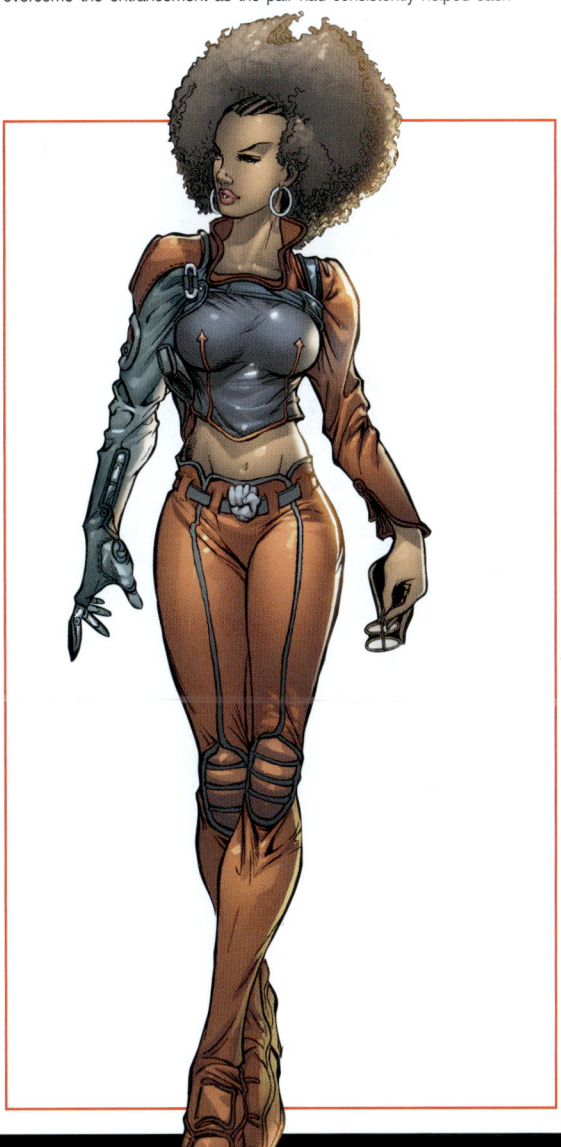

Art by Billy Tucci

other through emotional turmoil, although they were forced to kill Angie in the process. Sans roommate following Phoenix's apparent death via power even more corrupting than vampirism, Misty ended up sharing an apartment with Cage's supermodel girlfriend Harmony Young, who was gravely injured when a rematch-seeking Sabretooth and Constrictor mistook her for Misty.

Misty and Colleen's association with Heroes for Hire continued to set them against such superhuman criminals as element-transmuting Chemistro (Calvin Carr), biochemical terrorist Impasse and a returning Master Khan. Soon after these encounters, a Nightwing assignment took Misty and Colleen to Middle Eastern nation Khotain as part of a conspiracy by their client, ex-government agency Uni-World, in a scenario that almost provoked nuclear war via their renegade armored agent Doombringer before Heroes for Hire, in the employ of Khotain's neighbor Dhakran, intervened and saved the world from near-certain war, one of the twin teams' greatest successes.

Despite their shared adventures and love, however, Misty and Iron Fist grew apart as assignments separated them and their worldviews diverged. Unknown to Fist, Misty became drawn to police officer Tyrone King, actually Master Khan, manipulating Misty's emotions as part of an elaborate scheme. Eventually believing he had driven his nemesis to an emotional breakdown, Khan arranged for the alien Super-Skrull (Kl'rt) to murder Fist, but neither Khan nor Super-Skrull knew Fist had been replaced by a member of K'un-Lun's plant race, the H'ylthri. Nonetheless, with Fist believed dead, and HFH dead with him, a grief-stricken Misty focused on her Nightwing Restorations work, but comparatively simple cases like Rudy Vandenberger's sabotage of his family's circus and the abduction of Shana "Tok" Peters provided little distraction. "King" vanished soon afterward, and Misty lapsed into depression and chronic drinking.

Months later, Super-Skrull impersonated Iron Fist while scheming to conquer the Savage Land, and although his efforts were foiled by Namor the Sub-Mariner, related investigations revealed the non-human nature of Iron Fist's corpse and Khan's imposture. Accompanied by Namor, Misty and Colleen traveled to K'un-Lun and freed Fist from the H'ylthri. Although still in love, Misty and Fist hesitated to renew their relationship, and for a time Misty sought solace in the company of fellow "cybernets," i.e. cyborgs and androids; when Mechadoom, a renegade Dr. Doom robot, captured several cybernets, Misty joined Deathlok (Michael Collins) and others to rescue the captives. Soon afterward, she, Colleen, and Fist assisted Namor against common foe Master Khan. Their longtime friendship dynamic re-established, the trio remained together to fight the Red Dragon Warriors and their ally Sabretooth. At times rejoined by Cage, they renewed ties with super hero friends by helping Spider-Man against the Scorpion (Mac Gargan) and Daredevil (Matt Murdock) against the Enforcers and Insomnia. Following several super heroes' disappearance during the Onslaught crisis, Fist, with Misty and Cage's support, organized a new Heroes for Hire incarnation, but it lasted only a few months folllowing the heroes' return.

Months later, Misty and Colleen expanded Nightwing Restorations' operations to bail bond work and bounty hunting. In the course of assignments, they foiled Celia Ricadonna's auction of a computer chip capable of creating worldwide economic collapse. During this mission, Misty's cybernetic arm was severed by Ricadonna, but she received an upgraded replacement from Stark and soon delivered Ricadonna an "old school beatdown." Following the Superhuman Registration Act's passage, at Iron Man's behest, Misty and Colleen formed a new Heroes for Hire with ex-villain Humbug, mercenary Paladin, and others, though Paladin swiftly betrayed the team to SHIELD in a failed effort to turn in the anti-Registration forces' leader, Captain America (Steve Rogers). Following a mission to capture hominid Moon-Boy, toward whom Colleen grew protective, Humbug betrayed HFH to the Hulk's Warbound, who captured Colleen. Misty persuaded Paladin, who worked strictly for personal gain, to help rescue Colleen in exchange for Moon-Boy, whom Paladin turned over to SHIELD. Moon-Boy's loss drove a wedge between Misty and Colleen, but they ultimately reconciled and reorganized Heroes for Hire as a two-woman operation like Nightwing Restorations before it. In this incarnation, they accompanied Cage to assist Iron Fist against Hydra, preventing the terrorist organization from accessing and destroying K'un-Lun. After Iron Fist re-examined his priorities, he and Misty agreed to make their relationship more committed.

Art by Reggie Jones with Kerry Gammill (inset)

HEIGHT: 5'9"
WEIGHT: 136 lbs.
EYES: Brown
HAIR: Black

ABILITIES/ACCESSORIES: Misty Knight possesses a bionic right arm that grants her sufficient superhuman strength to exert force — via gripping, punching, lifting, throwing, karate chopping, etc. — at 75 times that of a human arm while incurring minimal to no damage in the process. Customarily covered with a layer of material virtually indistinguishable from human flesh, it is equipped with a computer wired directly into her nervous system, enabling her to control its motor functions with the same ease as her original arm while absorbing pain that its use would otherwise conduct to her back and other parts of her body.

Over the years, her arm has received various technological upgrades, and her current arm is coated with a layer of diamond interlaced with Antarctic Vibranium (aka anti-metal), enabling her to use it at will to emit vibrations to weaken or liquify any metal, including Adamantium. Equipped with a pain dampener that prevents damage to the arm from being transmitted to her brain receptors as pain, her arm can project an antigravity thrust sufficient to knock several adults off their feet simultaneously and feed digitally stored data directly into her brain. Historically, Misty could not use her bionic arm to lift greater weight than her normal human body could handle, but more recent upgrades seem to have overcome this problem to a degree, whether through inertial dampeners, force distribution, or anti-gravity generators. She also is skilled at using opponents' or objects' momentum to her advantage, redirecting it without significant force. Misty is an exceptional markswoman, athlete, and hand-to-hand combatant, as well as a superb detective and skilled martial artist. She uses conventional firearms as necessary.

KNIGHTS OF PENDRAGON

HISTORY: Since the days of King Arthur, and possibly earlier, the mystical Green Knight has granted Pendragon spirit-power to certain individuals in times of great need. Pendragon spirits carry with them skills and traits from previous hosts, granting the current hosts augmented abilities, powers and senses. These abilities are increased to superhuman levels, often varying depending on the level of power available from the Green Knight. In dire circumstances, the Green Knight can temporarily boost his Pendragons' abilities and, if the need is great enough, even resurrect them. Pendragons are attuned to the natural cycle and can communicate with animals, traditionally using owls as messengers and sentries. They can often tap into the power of the Earth, a lightning-like energy they call "Pendragon Fire." They are prone to visions warning of dangers, whether present or future. Some may retain certain traits, even after their Pendragon spirit has moved on to another host. The Green Knight himself resides at the Green Chapel on the isle of Avalon, Otherworld. Routes from Earth to Otherworld were created by the Walkers, men of power who perceived ley lines. At least one of these Walkers, Herne the Hunter, was possessed of a Pendragon spirit; that same spirit was associated with Merlin, and during World War I, it also inhabited Peter Hunter who became the costumed hero Albion. Pendragons were active in the middle ages, and one possessed Robin of Locksley. The same spirit was later associated with the Black Panther in the modern era. An early team of Pendragons allegedly spun off from the Order of Tyrana some decades ago. Professor Daffyd Ap Iowerth may have been touched by King Arthur's Pendragon.

In recent times the Pendragon of Sir Gawain possessed policeman Dai Thomas. Dai had been approached by WHO (Weird Happenings Organization) to investigate the mysterious suffocation of eighty-seven people in a Tastee Burger bar in London, part of a worldwide chain owned by Omni Corporation, a multinational business ruled by its director, Francesca Grace. Haunted by nightmares of Arthurian Britain, Dai uncovered a trail of grisly murders, all linked by Omni and a sense of poetic justice. Grace's personal assistant, the psychotic Dolph (Colin Snewing), attempted to halt Dai's investigation but the Pendragon-enhanced policeman defeated him and his heavily armed mercenary team single-handedly. Dai traveled through Costa Rica, along the Curaray and the Amazon rain forest searching for the Green Knight. When Grace pulled strings with cabinet minister Sir Ian Chalmers, Captain Britain (Brian Braddock) found himself on the policeman's trail, quite unaware that he himself had been temporarily possessed by the Pendragon of Lancelot. Under the Pendragons' influence, Captain Britain fought and accidentally killed Dai, who later reappeared fully transformed into the likeness of Gawain. Ultimately, Dai, Captain Britain and journalist Kate McClellan made their way to Avalon where they encountered the Green Knight, who was weakening due to mankind's environmental abuse. The Knight claimed responsibility for the deaths, having lashed out in desperation against those who would devastate the planet's life. Dai sacrificed his power to bolster the Knight's failing strength.

CURRENT MEMBERS: Albion (Peter Hunter), Sir Gawain (robot), Francesca Lexley Grace, Breeze James, Union Jack (Joseph Chapman)
FORMER MEMBERS: Ben Gallagher (deceased), Katherine Elspeth "Kate" McClellan, Pendragon (Adam Crown)
BASE OF OPERATIONS: The Green Chapel, Avalon, and London, England; formerly Camelaird Farm, Wiltshire
FIRST APPEARANCE: Knights of Pendragon #1 (1990)

Shortly after, Herne the Hunter's former Pendragon spirit possessed Kate McClellan's son Cam, who fell into the clutches of the Bane, the Pendragons' arch-foes led by Grace, who was now possessed by one of the Bane herself, apparently that of Morgan Le Fay. Cam's teacher, Peter Hunter (formerly Albion) gathered several Pendragons to fight the Bane: Union Jack (Lancelot), Kate McClellan (Guinevere), and author and Arthurian buff Ben Gallagher (Percival). Gallagher had already encountered the Bane while investigating dolphin massacres in the Orkney Islands. When writing his book "Flame in the West," an interpretation of the grail myth, Ben had buried a fake grail to promote sales. Hunter, convinced this grail was of importance, led the Pendragons to the Kitsford Countless Stones in Kent to dig it up. Ben, who had always had an unexplained "intuition," saved his newfound friends from a Bane ambush, discovering a healing ability in the process. Meanwhile, Grace was covering for Bane activity by using an Omni Corporation wind turbine project run on land bought from their former business rival, Stark Industries. Aided by Captain Britain, Iron Man (Tony Stark, possessed by Sir Bedevere's Pendragon), and the Green Knight, the Pendragons prevented an attempted resurrection of Bane demi-god the Red Lord (Bodb Derg), saved the Spanish town of Joselito from toxic devastation, and seemingly defeated Grace. Peter Hunter took the spirit from Cam, regaining his former Albion powers and identity.

FROM LEFT TO RIGHT: ALBION, PENDRAGON, UNION JACK & GRACE

Art by Phil Gascoine

ALBION
Knights of Pendragon #8 (1991)
Art by Gary Erskine

The Knights of Pendragon set up a base of operations at Camelaird farm in Wiltshire with assistance from Tony Stark. The Bane conspired to separate the team and pick the Pendragons off one by one. Albion's tarot readings led him to Bonn, Germany, in search of the Bane's nest, the Spiral Tower, while Union Jack, Kate, and Ben fought Bane ivory poachers in Wakanda with help from the Black Panther, Mr. Fantastic and the Invisible Woman. Matters weren't helped by tensions between Union Jack and Ben over the latter's relationship with Kate, and the three parted ways in their search for the money men behind the poaching. Union Jack and the Black Panther went to a Hong Kong ivory market, the House of Orchids, while Ben and Kate looked for Australian buyer McCinley. McCinley turned out to be the human form of B'ngudja (a shark mutated into a Bane agent), while the House of Orchids was protected by Ninja Bane and the hideously Bane-mutated Dolph. With Ben and Union Jack dead and the Black Panther hospitalized, Albion was then executed as part of a ceremony to resurrect the Red Lord. Teenager Adam Crown (King Arthur) sensed their deaths and traveled to Avalon, guided there by the sword Caliburn and the Lady of the Lake. The Green Knight resurrected all the dead Pendragons, as Adam summoned every Pendragon past or present, including the Black Panther, Captain Britain, Dai Thomas, and Iron Man, in order to fight the Bane's army. Adam drove the Bane spirit out of Grace, forcing the enemy to withdraw. Ben Gallagher died in combat, prompting Kate to leave the team and finish Ben's book.

BREEZE
Knights of Pendragon #1 (1992)
Art by Phil Gascoine

Fortunately, the team gained three new Pendragons: former Bane leader Grace (apparently now bonded with Morgan's sister, Morgause), the robotic Sir Gawain, and former Mys-Tech operative Breeze James (Guinevere). Now operating out of the Green Chapel, they used its vast resources, including dimension-jumping bikes and uni-terpreters capable of translating alien tongues. Grace discovered the Green Chapel's armory, containing armor that responded to their Pendragon spirits, adapted to their individual needs, augmented their abilities, and came equipped with arcane stealth computers and various weapons. Before they could get to grips with the new armor, a Stark Industries robot possessed by Gawain's spirit went missing from Questworld, Britain's first Arthurian theme park, and the team investigated with help from Iron Man. In doing so they made an enemy of Magpie, who tried to capture Gawain. However, his attempt failed and Gawain went on to prove himself a worthy member of the team when he single-handedly prevented the Bane's attack upon a nuclear reactor in Cape Wrath, Northern Scotland. It was the Cape Wrath incident that provoked Breeze's first Pendragon vision, prompting her to stay with the team. Gawain's artificial construction made him the strongest team member. He also developed a trait for recognizing the Pendragon spirits of others. Breeze became the group's fastest member, able to run at supersonic speeds when at the height of her power. Magpie attempted to get his revenge on the team, but when tricked by Grace into using one of their bikes, a random dimensional jump landed him in the Annwn continuum at the mercy of the Red Lord. Meanwhile, their armor started to "evolve" into new forms, as the Green Knight prepared them for troubles to come. During an adventure with Spider-Man and the dimension-hopping Warheads, the team encountered the Araknoid known as Arrakhyl, the last remaining member of the Pendragon Corps on the planet Arakne. The Pendragons hurled a bomb into interdimensional space in order to prevent Arakne's devastation at the hands of the Scourge, Arakne's equivalent of the Bane led by Malekyth. Unbeknownst to them the bomb fell through a dimensional portal to Earth-313 and ravaged that planet's environment. Gawain, who had been blinded in combat, had his face replaced with Arakne's nucleolus crystal, increasing his already enhanced senses to superior levels. Arrakyl remained on Arakne to train a new Pendragon Corps, the Spiridkin.

KATE McCLELLAN
Knights of Pendragon #1 (1990)
Art by Mike Collins

Returned to their own Earth, the Knights had various other adventures, discovering a new Bane Lord, Shadow Wing, and preventing him from poisoning Britain's crops. Union Jack and Grace fought the evils of Baron Blood and Mys-Tech, discovering that Mys-Tech's Wychwood was an aspect of the Red Lord himself. Breeze also revealed that Grace's old company, Omni Corporation, was in fact another front for Mys-Tech. Wychwood sought revenge when Mys-Tech activated their reality altering Un-Earth, pitting them against a horde of demons and a powerful being known as Skire, the King of Pain, who held his own against the team and would've killed them if not for the Green Knight's intervention. However, this only highlighted the seriousness of the situation and, with the entire planet at risk, the Knights fought alongside many of Earth's heroes against Mys-Tech's Psycho-Warriors to reach the Un-Earth. Although they suffered heavy casualties, Dark Angel led Albion, Death's Head (Minion), Dr. Strange, Motormouth and Professor X in using the Un-Earth to bring all the dead heroes back to life and returning Earth to normal.

UNION JACK
Captain America #254 (1981)
Art by Gary Erskine

The Knight's actions came back to haunt them, however, when Earth-313's Lemurians recruited Death's Head (Minion) and Magpie in an attempt to get revenge on the Knights. Magpie had a secret agenda: to summon the Red Lord. Death's Head defeated Magpie, and Adam Crown drove the Red Lord back into his own realm, becoming trapped with him. Albion, Breeze and Gawain traveled to Earth-313 to help rebuild the planet, leaving only Grace and Union Jack to defend their home planet. The Lady of the Lake later transferred King Arthur's Pendragon spirit from Crown to the Black Knight.

PENDRAGON
Knights of Pendragon #14 (1991)
Art by Gary Erskine

Albion has since fought Mys-Tech alongside the Dark Guard, and Union Jack worked with the new Invaders and MI-5. Recently it would seem the Knights have been maintaining contact with Order of Tyrana, trading resources and intelligence. However, they were presumably unaware that the Order had been corrupted by vampires until Union Jack's recent encounter with Blade. Additionally, an unidentified prisoner at the Vault, Shoreditch/London's docklands, claimed some connection to the team.

BEN GALLAGHER
Knights of Pendragon #7 (1991)
Art by Richard Dolan, Phil Gascoine & Gary Erskine

GAWAIN
Knights of Pendragon #1 (1992)

GRACE
(Bane Chieftain)
Knights of Pendragon #1 (1990)

ERIC KOENIG

HISTORY: Eric Koenig was born in post-World War I Hamburg, and grew up alongside his sister Ilsa. As a teenager, he and his best friend Wilhelm Hauser joined the Hitler-Jugend (Hitler Youth), and when Adolf Hitler's Nazi Party came to power in 1935, they joined the Wehrmacht. Eric soon became a lieutenant serving as a pilot in the Luftwaffe, but as World War II began and Eric witnessed the invasion of Poland in 1939, he began to doubt the righteousness of Hitler's cause; however, Hauser was loyal to the Nazi regime, and he and Eric drifted apart. Eventually transferred, Eric became the personal aide to Dr. August Draus, a high-ranking officer who had designed Festung von Furcht ("Fortress of Fear") for the Luftwaffe. Much to Eric's chagrin, the elitist Draus treated him as an inferior. In 1943, Eric was attending Draus at a meeting with Luftwaffe commander Hermann Goring when they encountered US soldier Sgt. Nick Fury, leader of the First Attack Squad ("Howling Commandos"). Although the Nazis had Fury in their clutches, he sensed Eric's discontent with Draus and exploited it, convincing Eric to switch sides. Eric took Draus prisoner and helped Fury escape from Germany to England. Draus was imprisoned by the British and Eric defected, sharing all of his intelligence on Nazi Germany with the Howlers' commanding officer Captain Samuel Sawyer.

Shortly afterward, nearly all of the Howling Commandos were captured while on a mission to Greece, and were transported to Berlin for a televised execution to be performed by Hitler himself. Only Sgt. Fury had managed to escape, and Captain Sawyer assigned members of the Second Attack Squad ("Maulers") and Eric to aid Fury on a rescue mission. Eric's sister helped shelter the commandos in Germany, and while member Dino Manelli was badly injured, the entire squad was brought back to England safely. With Manelli temporarily out of action, Sawyer invited Eric to replace him in the Howlers, and Eric accepted. Eric's first mission pitted him against his one-time friend Hauser, who died during their clash. Although Manelli quickly returned to action, Eric remained with the squad, forming close friendships and proving invaluable on missions due to his piloting skills and intimate knowledge of the Nazi regime, including a mission to Draus' own Festung von Furcht. On another mission to Germany, Eric went AWOL to help his sister Ilsa defect to England, and Fury and Manelli protected him from a court-martial. Eric had hoped that Ilsa would wind up with Fury, but she ultimately became romantically involved with Manelli. Nazis Eric fought with the Commandos included Baron Strucker, Colonel Klaue and Field Marshal Erwin Rommel, and Eric fought alongside Captain America, Captain Savage and his Leatherneck Raiders, and even the vampire Dracula. After months of comradeship, the Howling Commandos were stunned when Eric seemingly defected back to Nazi Germany; however, Eric was actually on an undercover mission for Sawyer and ultimately returned to

HEIGHT: 6'
WEIGHT: 176 lbs.
EYES: Blue
HAIR: Blond

ABILITIES/ACCESSORIES: Eric Koenig is a combat veteran with extensive training as a soldier, specializing in combat piloting. He is also a skilled mechanic, and fluent in English and German. He remains exceptionally vital, presumably due to repeated exposure to Nick Fury's Infinity Formula-enhanced blood cells. As a SHIELD agent, he carries a standard issue sidearm and wears a bulletproof uniform. During World War II, he utilized firearms such as an AK-47 machine gun, and occasionally flew crafts on bombing missions.

REAL NAME: Eric Koenig
ALIASES: None
IDENTITY: Publicly known
OCCUPATION: Agent of SHIELD; former pilot, commando
CITIZENSHIP: Germany
PLACE OF BIRTH: Hamburg, Germany
KNOWN RELATIVES: Ilsa Koenig (sister)
GROUP AFFILIATION: SHIELD; formerly First Attack Squad (Howling Commandos), Hitler Jugend, Wehrmacht, Luftwaffe
EDUCATION: High school graduate
FIRST APPEARANCE: Sgt. Fury and His Howling Commandos #27 (1966)

England, cleared of charges, regaining the friendship of his fellow Howlers. Eric served in the Howling Commandos to the end of World War II.

In recent years, as director of the super-spy agency SHIELD, Fury recruited the former Howling Commandos for an unofficial SHIELD mission in Southeast Asia supervised by Samuel Sawyer (now a general). Following this mission, Eric joined SHIELD as an official agent, aiding them against threats such as Hydra and Nightshade. When the android Deltite began replacing agents of SHIELD with lifelike Delta-model LMDs, Eric was among the agents captured and placed in stasis within SHIELD Central's subbasements. Long after the Deltite's defeat, Fury found Eric and the other missing agents and had them rehabilitated. Eric is currently among the highest-ranking SHIELD agents on Earth, and heads regional operations in Bonn, Germany.

POWER GRID	1	2	3	4	5	6	7
INTELLIGENCE							
STRENGTH							
SPEED							
DURABILITY							
ENERGY PROJECTION							
FIGHTING SKILLS							

Art by Frank Robbins

KORATH THE PURSUER

REAL NAME: Korath-Thak
ALIASES: None
IDENTITY: Publicly known in Kree and Shi'ar empires
OCCUPATION: Phalanx select, warrior, cyber-geneticist; factory foreman
CITIZENSHIP: Kree Empire
PLACE OF BIRTH: Unrevealed location in Kree Empire
KNOWN RELATIVES: None
GROUP AFFILIATION: Phalanx; formerly Starforce, Supreme Science Council
EDUCATION: Unrevealed
FIRST APPEARANCE: Inhumans #11 (1977); (identified; as Pursuer) Quasar #32 (1992)

HISTORY: After the Inhuman Royal family destroyed a Kree space station, the Kree's Supreme Science Council elected to use cyber-geneticist Korath-Thak's Pursuer project to eliminate the Inhumans. They created a solidified holographic template that tracked the Inhumans, then condensed it into a malleable energy-mass state for transmission to Earth's New York City; but instead of encountering stone or metal first to absorb that material's properties to enhance its strength, the template hit a cockroach and used that material instead. The hybrid Pursuer fought the Inhumans and immobilized them until the Inhumans' dissident Kree ally Falzon sprayed an industrial strength pesticide in the Pursuer's face, dropping it. It awoke in police custody and escaped, resuming its hunt for the Inhumans. Sometime later the Pursuer was recalled from Earth by its creators, its ultimate fate unrevealed.

Korath-Thak spent the next few years making the Pursuer process more cost-effective, but new Kree leaders, Generals Ael-Dan and Dar-Benn, decided that the project would not be viable quickly enough and terminated it. A bitter Korath-Thak was transferred to a munitions plant, where he re-created another template and bonded it to himself. The Supreme Intelligence had Korath the Pursuer join his new Starforce on Kree homeworld Hala, where he attacked a group of Avengers before being defeated by Captain America. Recovering, Korath and Starforce again attacked the Avengers, overwhelming them. However, both teams were powerless to stop the royal Shi'ar renegade Deathbird while she killed Ael-Dan and Dar-Benn. The Supreme Intelligence sent Starforce to kill Shi'ar Majestrix Lilandra in retaliation, but they were defeated by the Shi'ar Imperial Guard and a second Avengers team. When all sides learned their mutual enemies, the Skrulls, had tricked them into the war, Lilandra freed Starforce member Ultimus to inform the Supreme Intelligence of the plot and kept Korath and the others as collateral, but the Kree Empire fell before that plan succeeded. Lilandra sentenced Starforce to serve as personal guard to the new Kree Viceroy, Deathbird. In that role, they chased off Quasar (Wendell Vaughn) when he came to help rebuild the planet, and helped put down a prisoner revolt when outlaw Admiral Galen-Kor broke out of prison, and aided the alien Deviant Blackwulf (Lucian) against his father, Tantalus. When the Shi'ar occupation ended, Starforce, branded as defectors, was forced into exile. Korath eventually settled on Kree fringeworld Godthab Omega. When the exiled Ronan the Accuser made his way to the Kree colony, Korath gained his aid against assassin Gamora and her Graces, who were trying to take their land. While Ronan took the fight to Gamora, Korath learned of Negative Zone ruler Annihilus' invasion. Korath convinced Ronan to abandon his battle against Gamora and help evacuate the planet from the advancing force. After the Armistice ending the war was signed, Korath went on a covert mission to locate the High Evolutionary, who was secretly creating genetically perfect Kree for the Supreme Intelligence, but fell prey to the robot Ultron and his new Phalanx allies. Transformed into the first Phalanx Selects, Korath and his allies Shatterax and Xemnu failed to capture the just-awakened Adam Warlock. They reported this failure to Ultron, who slew Korath as an example.

UNTRANSFORMED COCKROACH

PURSUER HYBRID

HEIGHT: 6'
WEIGHT: 290 lbs.
EYES: Blue
HAIR: Bald

ABILITIES/ACCESSORIES: The Pursuer template had greater strength (lifting 1 ton), reflexes, and durability than that of an average Kree, sensors to track anomalous genetic/energy patterns from miles away, and could recover from exposure to poisonous gases. The template transformed on contact any available organic and inorganic materials into parts of its body. It carried a scepter that rearranged matter to create tentacles and hands from asphalt and a brick building, transparent globes from air, and could fire energy blasts. The American cockroach (Periplaneta Americana) absorbed into the template could go 1 month without water, 2-3 months without food, and eat any organic substance it found. It is unclear if the bug's abilities carried over into the combined Pursuer form.

Korath's strength, durability, and reflexes were greater than the average Kree's, presumably close to the template's levels. He carried two "beta batons" that could stun or kill opponents either on contact or by firing energy blasts, and flew using jet boots. Korath had some combat training, but limited real combat experience. He was also a leading researcher in Kree genetics and cybernetic systems.

Art by Jorge Lucas with Keith Pollard (insets)

KORREK

HISTORY: Korrek was Prince of Katharta, a rocky, barren barbarian land, one of ten kingdoms on an otherdimensional world whose people were strong but not very bright. As prince, Korrek led the sword-wielding Kathartan army and was mystically destined for Godhood. When the Florida swamp containing the Nexus of Reality suffered several traumas, the Cosmic Axis tilted and different dimensional planes collided and intermixed. Korrek found himself with his men fighting armies from all eras in the Land between Night and Day. Spying neophyte witch Jennifer Kale, Korrek blamed her for his situation and attacked her, only to be confronted by the guardian of the Nexus, the Man-Thing. Jennifer's spirit returned to Earth as she awakened from a dream. Korrek crossed the dimensional barriers, rising out of a peanut butter jar in the Kale kitchen. He attacked Jennifer in her bed but fled when faced with her brother and grandfather. Antediluvian sorcerer Dakimh arrived and took Jennifer as his apprentice only to have her kidnapped by an army ruled by the Congress of Realities, led by the mysterious Overmaster, who sought domination over all dimensions. Roaming the swamp, Korrek encountered Man-Thing and the dimension-lost Howard the Duck. Together they battled demons sent by the Overmaster until Dakimh arrived to dispel them. Realizing that Dakimh's band was a force for good, Korrek joined them as they rescued Jennifer, then traversed the dimensional "between," losing Howard to a fall into apparent oblivion but putting the Cosmic Axis right. Feeling he failed Howard, Dakimh provided Korrek with a mystic helmet that protected him from mishap. The group then followed the Congress of Realities to Therea, home of the Gods, where the Overmaster revealed himself as Man-Thing's demonic foe, Thog the Nether-Spawn. In a battle over possession of the Gods' castle, Man-Thing defeated Thog, sending the Congress to rout. Dakimh revealed the true castle as a humble cottage tended by a peasant couple and the Gods as the couple's dogs.

In Korrek's absence, Klonus the Wizard, knowing the Godhood destiny of the Prince of Katharta, convinced barbarian leader Mortak to attack the city and murder Korrek's father the King, hoping to seize that destiny for himself. When Korrek returned from Therea, he foolishly tossed away his helmet, losing its mystic protection. Finding his city in flames, Korrek fought his way into the castle and found his father dead. There he was ambushed by Mortak and placed in a dungeon for a year but the Man-Thing — sent by Dakimh and Jennifer — rescued him moments before his execution. The quartet defeated Klonus and Mortak in Citrusville, but Dakimh's ancient body gave out and he died, apparently stranding Korrek on Earth with Jennifer. With Dakimh's passing, a moment of darkness struck Therea, allowing Thog to escape. He vindictively created the emotion-fueled nightmare boxes to plunge the world into madness. When the Man-Thing stumbled on one box, Thog's demons impersonated Korrek and others attempting to recover it. With the help of Dakimh, who had moved to the higher plane of Therea and become pure spirit, Man-Thing defeated Thog. Dakimh eventually returned to Earth and

REAL NAME: Korrek
ALIASES: Korrek the Barbarian, Warrior Prince of Katharta, Warrior Prince of the Westlands
IDENTITY: No dual identity
OCCUPATION: Barbarian warrior, former prince
CITIZENSHIP: Katharta
PLACE OF BIRTH: Katharta
KNOWN RELATIVES: Unidentified father (deceased)
GROUP AFFILIATION: Dakimh's band, formerly leader of Kathartan army
EDUCATION: Unrevealed
FIRST APPEARANCE: (Adventures into) Fear #19 (1973)

guided Korrek and Jennifer back to his Castle in the Sky, then set his band, including Man-Thing and a reluctant Howard, against humorless, insane demon-spawn Bzzk-Joh and his Imperium Emporium. Howard defeated Joh at the space-faring Death Store by using the Farce, the binding energy of the universe that allows people to laugh in the face of death. Korrek and Jennifer returned Howard to Earth, then departed in a dimensional craft.

Sometime later, Korrek joined with Dakimh, Jennifer, Man-Thing, Howard, Claude Starkowski, Master C'haaj, and Hemlock Shoals to resolve damage caused by a reality warp initiated by Krylorian Techno-Artist Chireep. His current whereabouts are unrevealed.

WITH MYSTIC HELMET

HEIGHT: 6'5"
WEIGHT: 267 lbs.
EYES: White (No visible iris or pupil)
HAIR: Blond

ABILITIES/ACCESSORIES: Korrek is a strong and able swordsman. He wielded a firesword that spewed mystic fire, and briefly wore a mystic helmet created for him by Dakimh, which protected him from dimensional disturbances.

POWER GRID	1	2	3	4	5	6	7
INTELLIGENCE							
STRENGTH							
SPEED							
DURABILITY*							
ENERGY PROJECTION							
FIGHTING SKILLS							

*YELLOW BAR INDICATES RATING WITH MYSTIC HELMET

Art by Val Mayerik

KORVAC

REAL NAME: Michael Korvac
ALIASES: The Machine God, Bright Lord, Clockwork Lord, Jaboa Murphy, the Enemy; impersonated Uatu the Watcher, Kang
IDENTITY: General public is unaware of his existence
OCCUPATION: Would-be conqueror; former computer technician
CITIZENSHIP: Luna (Earth's Moon), Earth-691
PLACE OF BIRTH: Blue Area of Earth's Moon circa 2977 AD, Earth-691
KNOWN RELATIVES: Jordan Korvac (father, deceased), Myra Korvac (mother), Carina Korvac (wife, deceased), Taneleer Tivan (Collector, father-in-law); Jaboa Murphy, Varley, Marshach & Kareela (ancestors)
GROUP AFFILIATION: Formerly leader of the Minions of Menace and servant of the Brotherhood of the Badoon
EDUCATION: Unrevealed, presumably extensive; later cybernetically assimilated vast amounts of knowledge
FIRST APPEARANCE: Giant-Size Defenders #3 (1975)

HISTORY: Born in the year 2977 AD of the alternate timeline Earth-691, Michael Korvac would be reborn in many forms over time, all of them powerful and dangerous. As an adult, he became a gifted "computer techno" (technician), but grew bitter due to his belief that his superiors did not appreciate his abilities. When the extraterrestrial Brotherhood of the Badoon conquered Earth and its colony worlds circa 3006-3007, Korvac served the new Badoon regime as a willing collaborator, and was soon placed in charge of analytical computer systems regulating entire planets; however, his new masters worked him to the point of exhaustion. When he collapsed during a duty shift, the Badoon amputated his lower body from the waist down and replaced it with a computerized, hovering special systems module, transforming him into a cyborg as punishment and in hopes of making him a more efficient worker. The vengeful Korvac used his new abilities to attack his masters and assimilate data from their computer systems, intending to overthrow the Badoon, but he was abducted by outside forces in the midst of his rebellion.

The cosmic gamesman Grandmaster and the robot strategist Prime Mover transported Korvac to the modern era of the Earth-616 reality, where he served as one of various pawns pitted against each other in a contest of champions. The Prime Mover's pawns, including Korvac, fought the Grandmaster's pawns, the heroic Defenders, who ultimately triumphed. During the game, Defenders leader Dr. Strange had bested Korvac, who later claimed he had allowed himself to be defeated so that he might secretly analyze and partially replicate the Grandmaster's cosmic knowledge and power. Having accomplished this, the newly enhanced Korvac returned to 31st Century Earth-691 and adopted a desolate planetoid as his base, transforming it into a high-tech wonderland. He then used his time probe (a time-spanning teleportation device) to accumulate resources and servants, such as his alien underlings Brahl, Dumog, Grott, Teju, and Tork (also known as the Minions of Menace). Plotting to make Earth's sun go nova in hopes of tapping its power, Korvac was opposed by his era's leading heroes, the Guardians of the Galaxy, and legendary Earth-616 hero Thor, whom Korvac had accidentally transported from the past. Defeated by Thor and the Guardians, Korvac fled.

Returning to the modern era of Earth-616, Korvac found and entered the vast worldship of the planet-consuming cosmic being Galactus. Tapping into its central computers, Korvac assimilated knowledge and technology so advanced that he became a godlike cosmic being in his own right, and remade his physical body into a flawless humanoid form. His transformation was more than just physical; the expanded consciousness that came with his new power gave Korvac a new outlook on his own life and all existence. No longer interested in revenge or power for its own sake, he resolved to become the benevolent ruler of the universe so that he might impose a just and peaceful order upon its chaotic inhabitants for their own good. Korvac relocated to Earth, where he lived quietly in the Forest Hills Gardens neighborhood of New York while he plotted his universal coup, using his abilities to conceal himself from other cosmic beings and major powers. As the seemingly human Michael, Korvac met, fell in love with and married model Carina Walters, not knowing she was secretly the daughter of the Collector, one of the Elders of the Universe, a cosmic being who had detected Korvac's threat and sent Carina to spy on "The Enemy."

Meanwhile, the Guardians of the Galaxy had followed Korvac's trail to modern-day Earth-616, fearing that Korvac might be planning to kill young Vance Astrovik (who in Earth-691's timeline grew up to become Guardians founder Vance Astro after a thousand-year space journey). Allying themselves with Earth-616's Avengers, the Guardians devoted themselves to protecting young Vance and searching for Korvac over the course of an extended mission. When cosmic-powered Guardians member Starhawk found and battled Korvac, Michael utterly annihilated Starhawk, then restored him to life, but with no memory of their encounter and stripped of the ability to perceive Korvac in any way. By this time,

Art by Andy Kubert with Dave Wenzel (inset)

Art by George Pérez & Dave Wenzel

THE ENEMY

EARLY CYBORG FORM

Carina had truly fallen in love with Michael, and could not bear to betray him to her father. Instead, she betrayed her father to Korvac, telling Michael of her true identity and the Collector's opposition to Korvac's schemes. Korvac promptly blasted the Collector to ashes from afar, just as the Elder was about to tell the Avengers the identity of the mysterious "Enemy" menacing the universe.

The Avengers' subsequent investigation led them to Korvac's Forest Hills home, where their foe was exposed when the heroes realized that Starhawk could not see or hear the supposedly normal Michael. Knowing this confrontation would attract the notice of other cosmic beings, Korvac realized he no longer had any chance of taking over the universe by stealth, and that many enemies would soon attack him. Deciding to start his war with the universe by battling the assembled Avengers and Guardians, Korvac slaughtered most of them with ease, but apparently lost his will to fight when he saw how his actions shocked and disturbed Carina. Unwilling to fight on with her faith in him lost, Korvac seemingly killed himself. A grief-crazed Carina slew most of the remaining heroes before she saw the futility of it all, urging her sole remaining opponent, Thor, to slay her. Against his will, Thor struck her dead. In a final act of nobility, the dying Korvac and Carina used their remaining cosmic energies to resurrect the slain Avengers and Guardians. Telepathic Avengers member Moondragon was deeply moved by Korvac's passing, having sensed his noble intentions; she mourned him as a potential savior of the universe, and his example influenced her own later attempts to impose her supposedly benevolent will on lesser beings.

Korvac apparently entered the realm of Death, at least temporarily, and was among the deceased or seemingly deceased beings compelled to serve in the Grandmaster's Legion of the Unliving when Grandmaster briefly usurped Death's power. As a member of the Legion, Korvac battled the Silver Surfer before returning to oblivion. In truth, however, Korvac was not fully dead. Just before Korvac's apparent demise, Galactus had discovered Korvac's intrusion in his worldship and decided to punish him by targeting him with the Ultimate Nullifier, which could erase even Korvac from existence. During his last stand in Forest Hills, Korvac had sensed the Nullifier beams' approach just as he realized Carina was losing faith in him. To save himself from complete annihilation, Korvac willed himself to die, but preserved his knowledge, personality, and powers in a cosmic "gene packet" that would be transferred to his ancestors in turn, gradually moving forward through time until the era of Korvac's birth, when the gene packet would empower Korvac himself. As he died and secretly released his gene packet, Korvac also secretly compelled Thor to kill Carina, having resolved to be free of human weakness in his next incarnation.

The gene packet first manifested in modern-day Australian teenage girl Jaboa Murphy. Dominated by Korvac's consciousness, she battled the Fantastic Four and the Guardians of the Galaxy, who had learned of Korvac's reincarnations and were following the gene packet through time. When FF leader Reed Richards threatened Murphy with redirected Ultimate Nullifier beams from the past, Korvac's consciousness fled, restoring Murphy to normal. The gene packet began crossing into alternate futures, next manifesting in Earth-8710's year 2591, where it empowered Central Corp.'s disgruntled mail distribution supervisor Varley, who went on a power-mad rampage. Varley died battling the Thor-empowered hero Dargo Ktor and the Guardians, but the gene packet slipped back into the timestream, empowering Earth-691's benevolent philosopher Marshash, who used his strange new power for many years in establishing and sustaining an idyllic, isolationist colony on a concealed planet. Late in the 26th Century, the Guardians traced the gene packet to Marshach, who resisted their attempted removal of his power with the aid of his longtime friend, the Silver Surfer, a former herald of Galactus. However, once Marshach was fully informed of the facts, he voluntarily gave up his power, condemning himself and his now rapidly aging wife Kareela to imminent death since the power had unnaturally prolonged and sustained their lives. While the Guardians were distracted by this tragic side-effect, the gene packet slipped back into time and finally manifested in the year of Korvac's birth, 2977, where it empowered his father Jordan Korvac just before Michael's birth. Using the power, Jordan held off the attacking Guardians until the newborn Michael emerged from the womb. Baby Michael abruptly usurped the gene packet's power, killing his own father in the process, and confronted the Guardians with the full power and knowledge of the adult Korvac; however, the baby was subdued with the aid of the sorcerers Krugarr and the Ancient One (Stephen Strange), and Galactus took back his stolen cosmic power, though he spared the infant's life. The Guardians returned baby Michael to his mother, Myra, who blamed the heroes for Jordan's death and vowed her child would grow up to be their enemy.

Korvac's former minions (now calling themselves the Intimidators) tried to resurrect their old leader in the 31st century, using a computer chip imprinted with the full knowledge and programming of Korvac prior to his first defeat by the Guardians. Inserting this chip in the sentient computer Main Frame, the criminals succeeded in creating an extremely powerful, violently insane facsimile of Korvac described as a mixture of the cyborg Korvac, the cosmic Korvac and the Main Frame entity. Guardians founder Martinex defeated the assembled villains with the aid of various allies, notably Phoenix (Giraud), who apparently destroyed the new Korvac. As a result of this victory, Martinex, Phoenix, Main Frame and their associates formed a new Guardians expansion team, the Galactic Guardians.

Under circumstances as yet unrevealed, a cosmic-powered adult cyborg incarnation of Korvac resurfaced in the modern era of Earth-616. When the evil Red Skull absorbed the near-infinite power of the Cosmic Cube, Korvac alternately posed as Kang and Uatu the Watcher to manipulate the Red Skull and the Skull's foe Captain America. Korvac steered the Skull into seeking the additional power of Galactus' worldship, and convinced the Captain the Red Skull had to die lest he enslave the world. When Captain America killed the Skull, Korvac usurped the power of both the Cube and the worldship, becoming effectively omnipotent. He returned to his native time period and created a divergent reality in his own cybernetic image as a machine-dominated technocracy with him as absolute ruler, wiping out the Badoon for good measure. However, Captain America followed Korvac back to the 31st Century and staged rebellions repeatedly. Korvac retroactively altered time to erase each of these attacks as they occurred, soon allowing Captain America to retain his memories of these time alterations, hoping the knowledge of many defeats at Korvac's hands would break the Captain's spirit. Instead, Korvac's own spirits began to sag as the Captain attacked over and over again, undaunted, inspiring Korvac's subjects to rebel. Persuaded by Captain America that his own humanity was the root cause of the vulnerabilities and imperfections in his empire, Korvac went back in time to the point where he stole Red Skull's power in hopes of more perfectly purging his own humanity during his transformation this time, but Captain America foiled Korvac's plan by refusing to kill the Skull as he had before. Korvac then reluctantly aided Captain America and Sharon Carter against the cosmic-powered Red Skull, who seemingly destroyed Korvac by scattering the cyborg's atoms across six dimensions. Despite Korvac's demise, Captain America ultimately found a way to defeat the Red Skull, who lost his cosmic power.

NOTE: In at least one alternate reality (Earth-82432), Carina's unwavering support for Korvac emboldened him to pursue his quest for universal domination more aggressively, slaying all his Earthly opponents as well as many cosmic beings, usurping their power to augment his own might even further. When countless cosmic and extraterrestrial forces rallied by Uatu the Watcher continued to resist Korvac's attempted universal conquest, Korvac realized that while he was now more powerful than any other being in the universe, he was not more powerful than the combined inhabitants of the universe, and could never be assured of total victory. Disillusioned, bitter, and insane, Korvac absorbed the life essence of every living being on Earth, even a willing Carina, and confronted his non-Earthly enemies with the Ultimate Nullifier, resolving to bring order to the universe by destroying it if he could not otherwise master it. Despite Uatu's pleas for mercy and sanity, that reality's Korvac activated the Nullifier, erasing both himself and everything in the Earth-82432 universe from existence. Multiple inherent differences mark Earth-82432 as an alternate, rather than divergent reality, unless the divergence occurred much earlier.

CARINA
Art by Dave Wenzel

MAIN FRAME INCARNATION
Art by Herb Trimpe

HEIGHT: 12' (variable)
WEIGHT: Unrevealed (variable)
EYES: One blue eye (right), one white cybernetic implant (left) (variable)
HAIR: Blond (variable)

ABILITIES/ACCESSORIES: When cosmically enhanced, Korvac's many powers include near-limitless strength, speed, durability and stamina; incredibly vast knowledge; flight; survival in outer space; time travel; time manipulation; sensory awareness spanning much of space and time, and the ability to observe any location remotely; a seemingly limitless capacity to absorb energy and knowledge from living beings and other external sources; seemingly limitless energy generation, including the capacity for long-range energy bombardment of targets in far removed locations; teleportation of himself and other masses; vast psionic powers, including telepathy, astral projection & telekinesis; the ability to cloak himself from detection, even evading the senses of other cosmic beings; illusion-casting; shape-shifting; the destruction, restructuring or creation of matter at will; conjuring of objects; manipulation of magnetism; generation of impenetrable force fields; generation of stasis fields in which targets are suspended motionless; and transmission of knowledge and energy to other beings, even across time and space. Even at his most powerful, however, Korvac has remained vulnerable to other cosmic-level forces and devices, notably the Ultimate Nullifier and the Cosmic Cube.

In his original cyborg form, Korvac's body was replaced from the waist down with a hovering platform housing a sophisticated computer system, which Korvac modified in various ways over time, notably the incorporation of extensive weaponry. Wired directly to his brain, the cybernetically controlled platform responded to his thoughts. It could analyze the abilities and energies of any given opponent and automatically reconfigure its weapons array to counter the threat in question, though an unexpected or unconventional assault could catch Korvac off guard. The platform's computer system housed extensive databanks covering a wide range of subjects. The platform was capable of linking with and probing other computer systems, absorbing their knowledge. By absorbing knowledge and energy from outside sources such as the Badoon empire, the Grandmaster and Galactus, Korvac increased his knowledge and power tremendously, becoming a cosmic being. There are no known limits regarding the varieties and quantities of energy Korvac can absorb. His cybernetic left eye can transmit a "neural beam" capable of influencing the minds of others, such as forcing people to attack each other. Before gaining fully cosmic power, Korvac employed technology enabling him to teleport himself and other objects, and to transport himself and other objects through time. When he first gained cosmic power, Korvac discarded his original cyborg form and made a flawless conventional human body for himself. More recently, the cosmic-powered Korvac has appeared in a massive cyborg form, more humanoid than his original cyborg incarnation (he has legs rather than a computer module), but still extensively mechanical. He is a brilliant computer scientist and a formidable strategist.

POWER GRID	1	2	3	4	5	6	7
INTELLIGENCE							
STRENGTH							
SPEED							
DURABILITY							
ENERGY PROJECTION							
FIGHTING SKILLS							

KORVUS

HISTORY: Roughly 500 years ago, the intergalactic Shi'ar outlaw Rook'shir was bonded to the cosmic power of the Phalkon (aka the Phoenix Force), allegedly the first male and first Shi'ar to host it. Using his gigantic sword as a focus, Rook'shir destroyed worlds, killing billions before the newly formed Shi'ar Imperial Guard slew him. Discovering that a remnant of the Phalkon's power remained bonded to the sword, and that only Rook'shir's blood relatives could wield the so-called Blade of the Phoenix, the Shi'ar Imperial Ministry sought to exterminate Rook'shir's relatives. Though the Ministry kept Rook'shir's true story quiet, rumors spawned the monstrous legend of the Phoenix that all Shi'ar came to fear. In recent years, Imperial Vice Chancellor K'tor killed Rook'shir's last known descendants, sparing the half-Shi'ar child Korvus in case K'tor needed someone to wield the Blade of the Phoenix someday. Until then, he turned Korvus over to Shi'ar soldiers to be abused, enslaved and trained as a starship mechanic. As an adult, Korvus was jailed for several years for unrevealed crimes in the empire's highest security prison. When a rogue mission to kill all relatives of former Phoenix host Marvel Girl (Rachel Grey) failed, K'tor made a deal with Korvus to kill Grey in return for K'tor's commuting his sentence. K'tor had an explosive implanted in Korvus' head set to detonate if Korvus attacked any Shi'ar during his mission, then gave Korvus the Blade. In Korvus' hands the Blade came to life, opening his mind to its previous wielders' lives and teaching him how to use it. Using the Blade's link to the Phoenix Force to locate Grey, Korvus confronted Grey and her fellow X-Men, who were tracking their renegade former member Vulcan across Shi'ar space. Korvus easily defeated the other X-Men, but Grey grasped the Blade and its power merged their minds, sharing each other's lives. Grey dismantled Korvus' implant, freeing him from K'tor's authority.

Meanwhile, the X-Men's founder Professor Charles Xavier was kidnapped by a pair of Shi'ar who stole Korvus' ship to deliver him to K'tor. While helping the X-Men prepare their ship for hyperspace pursuit, Korvus and Grey found their mindmerge had left them strongly attracted to each other physically, and they acted on it despite their reservations. Korvus, the X-Men and intergalactic pirates the Starjammers teamed up to rescue deposed Shi'ar Majestrix Lilandra from her executioners, and to recruit the exiled Shi'ar war hero Major-General Ka'ardum to counter the rising political power of Lilandra's brother D'ken. Korvus then helped

REAL NAME: Korvus Rook'shir
ALIASES: None
IDENTITY: No dual identity
OCCUPATION: Freedom fighter; former prisoner, slave
CITIZENSHIP: Shi'ar
PLACE OF BIRTH: Unrevealed location in Shi'ar Empire
KNOWN RELATIVES: Unidentified mother, unidentified father & brothers (deceased), Rook'shir (ancestor, deceased)
GROUP AFFILIATION: Starjammers
EDUCATION: Shi'ar slave work force
FIRST APPEARANCE: Uncanny X-Men #478 (2006)

the two teams rescue Xavier from execution at Vulcan's hands, at the cost of Starjammers leader Corsair's life. When the X-Man Havok assumed leadership of the Starjammers, Korvus joined him alongside Polaris and Grey to oppose Vulcan's rule after his murder of D'ken, allying with Lilandra, Shi'ar Major-General Ka'ardum and his soldiers. After the alien race Scy'ar Tal arrived to retake the M'kraan Crystal's planet from Shi'ar possession (both races claimed the world as their respective original homeworld), the Starjammers teamed with Vulcan to save the Shi'ar people and attack the invaders. However, when the remenants of the Scy'ar Tal attack regrouped over the M'kraan world, Vulcan betrayed the Starjammers, capturing Havok, Polaris, Cho'd and Raza, and ordered the Scy'arTal destroyed using the same weapon they had used against Shi'ar planets: the Finality, a teleporter capable of moving a small star, into the middle of their fleet. Korvus and Marvel Girl went to the M'kraan planet to prevent the teleporter's tracer from reaching its destination, but they were betrayed by Ka'ardum and the weapon went off, destroying the Scy'ar Tal. Korvus reunited with Marvel Girl and Lilandra to continue their rebellion against Vulcan and free their teammates.

HEIGHT: 6'4" **EYES:** Blue-gray
WEIGHT: 207 lbs. **FEATHERS:** Black

ABILITIES/ACCESSORIES: Korvus wields the semi-sentient Blade of the Phoenix, a massive sword roughly 5' long by 2' at its widest point and weighing over 50 lbs., though its size and weight vary at its discretion. The Blade can only be wielded by blood relatives of Rook'shir; it does not allow anyone else to lift it easily or to tap its true power, which is a portion of the Phoenix Force. The Blade teaches its wielders how to use it, and can show them its past wielders' lives. It easily cuts through most metals, and has the potential to rearrange matter at the molecular level. The Sword's energy has charged a hyperspace jump engine for hours, and can also emit jets of blue flame to stun opponents as well as repel energy attacks and create telekinetic shields. Its user can also access the Blade's power by concentration alone. The Blade can locate other Phoenix Force hosts, and has created an empathic link between Korvus and former host Rachel Grey. Korvus is an experienced starship mechanic.

*YELLOW BAR INDICATES BLADE OF PHOENIX RATING

Art by Billy Tan

JOHN KOWALSKI

REAL NAME: John Kowalski
ALIASES: Simon Bock, Jan Fieran, Sessue Takeda, John Brabham, David Mueller, Lucien Dax, Death
IDENTITY: Existence as ghost and Death's avatar unknown to general public
OCCUPATION: Death's avatar; former agent of Death, clerk, Marine, miner
CITIZENSHIP: Poland; formerly USA (revoked)
PLACE OF BIRTH: Bethlehem, Pennsylvania
KNOWN RELATIVES: Stephen (father, deceased), unidentified son and uncle
GROUP AFFILIATION: Formerly US Marine Corps
EDUCATION: Corps training
FIRST APPEARANCE: War is Hell #9 (1974)

HISTORY: John Kowalski's family immigrated to America from Poland when he was a boy. During World War I, his father Stephen died fighting for his adopted country. John learned to fight while working in Pennsylvania's coal mines, before joining the Marines. In 1924, while a corporal stationed in Ch'Ang-Sha, China, he fell in love with Tsuin Hanneford, but after he killed her brother Chou in self defense she rejected him. John became emotionally detached and began using others, building up a karmic debt he would repay after he died. In 1937, now a master sergeant and Medal of Honor winner, he was found guilty of espionage and high treason; spared the death sentence because America was not at war, and because of his exemplary record, he was dishonorably discharged, his American citizenship revoked, and he was deported to Poland, where he scraped a living working for his uncle as a mail order clerk. In 1939 he met Dr. Eric Ostergan, a German working with the anti-Hitler underground, who begged him to alert the government of a German invasion planned for the next day; Kowalski brushed him off as a crank. The next morning, John's birthday, September 1st, Germany invaded. In the rubble John discovered Ostergan, who died calling him a coward. Attacked by a scavenger, Kowalski and his assailant where killed when a damaged chimney tower collapsed. Death informed Kowalski's ghost he bore Ostergan's curse: A coward would die thousands of times before his death. John would possess the recently deceased, experiencing their lives, trying to make up for his own life's failings, before dying again. As Dr. Simon Bock, he evacuated the doctor's Jewish family from Poland; as Major Jan Fieran, he led Finnish soldiers holding off the invading Russian army; as Colonel Sessue Takeda of the Imperial Japanese Army occupying Ch'Ang-Sha, he learned Tsuin had borne him a son, and arranged for their escape to America; as RAF Squadron Leader John Brabham, he joined the evacuation of Dunkirk; as Wehrmacht Paratrooper Captain David Mueller, he helped Norwegian Jews escape from a captured town; and as Italian Sergeant Lucien Dax, he got his men safely through the Libyan desert on foot, before surrendering them to the British.

As years passed, John stopped moving between hosts, instead occupying a facsimile of his original body. As Death's avatar he claimed the dyings' souls, each one wearing him down, until he became an emotional void. In the modern day, John allied with the Man-Thing (Ted Sallis) and Barbara Bannister to prevent the demon Thog from ending all life on Earth; hoping to lessen his loneliness, John temporarily turned Barbara into a death avatar like himself, but after Thog's defeat he freed her from her obligation to him. John fell in love with Melinda, a woman who had died and been resurrected, but after witnessing him claim souls, she fled in terror to her friend the Scarlet Witch. Kowalski angrily confronted them, but the Witch channeled Death, which stated that John's weariness meant Death had no further use for him; Melinda's declaration of love spared John from destruction, and he was allowed three final years to love Melinda while he trained his successor.

KOWALSKI IN MODERN DAY
JAN FIERAN
DAVID MUELLER
LUCIEN DAX
SESSUE TAKEDA
JOHN BRADHAM
SIMON BOCK

HEIGHT: 5'10"; (dead) variable
WEIGHT: 160 lbs.; (dead) variable
EYES: Blue; (dead) variable
HAIR: Brown; (dead) variable

ABILITIES/ACCESSORIES: Kowalski can possess bodies at the moment of their deaths, gaining access to their residual memories and skills, moving on when his host is killed again. In the past the original host's personality could sometimes overwhelm his control. He later manifested without a host; though able to change his appearance, he normally looks as he did in life. He is an emotional null, a hole in empathic beings' perceptions. Immune to virtually all forms of attack, he can kill with a glance, but prefers to touch his targets; however he lives the life of every soul he claims. He possesses preternatural knowledge of events and beings he meets, and can foresee the exact manner of someone's death, even those years hence. He can transport himself and others through time and space at will, and can generate illusions.

POWER GRID	1	2	3	4	5	6	7
INTELLIGENCE							
STRENGTH							
SPEED*							
DURABILITY							
ENERGY PROJECTION							
FIGHTING SKILLS							

*JOHN KOWALSKI IS A TELEPORTER

Art by Herb Trimpe with Don Perlin, Dick Ayers & George Evans (insets)

KRAVEN THE HUNTER

HISTORY: Growing up in Volgograd and St. Petersburg, Sergei Kravinoff was the son of Russian aristocrats. Dimitri Smerdyakov, Sergei's father's illegitimate son, lived with the family as a servant with his mother, Sonya, unaware of his true parentage. Beaten by his alcoholic father, Sergei in turn tormented Dimitri. The Kravinoffs were forced to immigrate in disgrace to the United Kingdom and later the United States after the Bolshevik Revolution. When Sergei's father's died, his mother was remanded to an insane asylum where she ultimately committed suicide. Sergei was haunted by images of the squalid, spider-infested asylum. Orphaned, Sergei learned to survive by his wits and cunning. By late adolescence, he had traveled extensively, usually as a stowaway aboard cargo ships or trains, and lived one time or another in every major city in Europe and Asia. In passage through equatorial Africa as a young man, Kravinoff (who anglicized his name to Kraven) discovered his natural talent for hunting. He soon left the safari to live on his own in the African veldt. By adulthood, his hunting skills were legendary and he quickly became a wealthy big game hunter. He remained in Africa for ten years, during which time in the Belgian Congo he stole a witch doctor's herbal potion that enhanced physical prowess. The potion's rare, naturally occurring mutagenic chemicals heightened his speed, strength and agility while greatly decelerating the aging process. Kraven used his heightened abilities to hunt game more efficiently and entered into a partnership with Smerdyakov in order to export the animal skins and ivory that he acquired. Sergei fathered several children. While married, he fathered Vladimir whom he raised to be his successor, trained by his servant Gregor. However, born out of wedlock to a mutant mother, Alyosha was sent to Africa in shame, where he was raised deprived of the respect given to Vladimir. The circumstances of the birth and upbringing of son Nedrocci "Ned" Tannengarden and alleged daughter Ana Kravinoff are unrevealed.

With the power of the jungle herbs, Sergei and Dimitri retained their youth through the decades. When Peter Parker first became Spider-Man, his early foes included Dimitri, now the identity-thief "the Chameleon." Dimitri enticed Kraven to America to hunt Spider-Man. Kraven believed this hunt brought him and his family's name honor, honestly gained, returning a measure of lost pride. He arrived with fanfare, rigging animal cages to break to make a public spectacle of his might as he subdued the wild beasts before the press. In his first encounter with Spider-Man, Kraven was awed by his adversary's power. Feeling both fear and rage, he saw Spider-Man as a monster, the personification of his family's disgrace. Though Sergei continued to abuse Dimitri, the two partnered against their common enemy. Despite the trickery of the Chameleon posing as a second Kraven, Spider-Man defeated both foes, whereupon they were deported from the US to Europe. The two sneaked back to shore near Tony Stark (Iron Man)'s munitions factory, where Iron Man and Captain America captured them. Later, Dr. Octopus gathered Kraven and four others to form the Sinister Six intent on defeating Spider-Man. In Flushing Meadows Park, Kraven fought Spider-Man with two leopards, but failed once again. Spider-Man bested each member of the Sinister Six until all were sent to prison.

Offered a large reward by the Green Goblin (Norman Osborn) to kill Spider-Man, Kraven, distracted by the Goblin's observations, lost his advantage and allowed Spider-Man to escape the battle. Osborn, posing as the Goblin's emissary, refused Kraven's arrogant demands for half-payment for this first failed assault. Later, Kraven returned to the US from Nairobi for a rematch against the wall-crawler. Using the Chameleon's hideout, Kraven disguised himself as Spider-Man to lure his nemesis into a fight, and accosted J. Jonah Jameson. With the news media inciting the public against the wall-crawler, Spider-Man confronted his impersonator. Though Kraven numbed Spider-Man's spider-sense with a special "jungle-scent," the wall-crawler overpowered him once again (along with the Nails Hogan gang). On his honor, Kraven admitted the impersonation to the police.

REAL NAME: Sergei Kravinoff
ALIASES: "Spider-Man" (impersonated), prisoner #678-439, Grim Hunter
IDENTITY: No dual identity
OCCUPATION: Professional game hunter and mercenary
CITIZENSHIP: Former citizen of Russia, United Kingdom, USA and Ethiopia with an international criminal record
PLACE OF BIRTH: Volgograd, Russia
KNOWN RELATIVES: Sasha Aleksandra Nikolaevich (alleged ex-wife), Vladimir Kravinoff (Grim Hunter, son, deceased), Nedrocci Tannengarden (son, deceased), Alyosha Kravinoff (son), Ana Tatiana Kravinoff (alleged daughter), Nikolai & Anna Makarova Kravinoff (parents, deceased), Dimitri Smerdyakov (Chameleon, half-brother)
GROUP AFFILIATION: Formerly the Sinister Six, Legion Accursed
EDUCATION: College graduate
FIRST APPEARANCE: Amazing Spider-Man #15 (1964)

Art by John Romita Sr.

Kraven landed in prison for several months. Upon release, he sought payment from Osborn for his service to the Goblin, believing the Daily Bugle's incorrect headlines proclaiming the Green Goblin had died in a fire. Kraven targeted Norman's son, Harry, as bait, finding him at a sendoff party for Harry's friend, Flash Thompson. As Spider-Man clashed with Kraven at the party and into a construction site, Norman arrived; however, Kraven dismissed Norman, believing Osborn's claims of having no recollection of the Goblin. Later, indignant over reports that the Vulture (Blackie Drago) was considered the city's biggest menace, Kraven hunted the Vulture. Kraven snared the Vulture with a wire, pulling them through the skylight of a jungle-like exhibition hall. Despite Kraven's advantage in the jungle setting, Spider-Man arrived and captured them both.

From an abandoned New York zoo, Kraven supplied Nino Villanova of the Maggia with a hallucinogen called ZMB, derived from the rare Zmbuku snake's venom; his operation was halted by the Human Torch and Capt. George Stacy. Frustrated by fruitless pursuits of Spider-Man, Kraven desired to sharpen his hunting skills elsewhere. He infiltrated the X-Men's Westchester mansion and blackmailed the Beast to become his prey, or be denied the antidote to a poison he administered to the winged alien Nhu'gari, Avia. Though encumbered by Kraven's poisons, Beast overpowered Kraven in a berserk fury. Concerned about public exposure, Marvel Girl (Jean Grey) mind-wiped knowledge of the secretive X-Men from Kraven before releasing him. Kraven traveled to the Savage Land to capture Zabu, the rare sabretooth tiger. Zabu was rescued by Ka-Zar, battling Kraven in a New York hotel. After nursing his wounds, Kraven returned to the Savage Land determined to defeat Ka-Zar and rule as a king. There, he discovered and raised the monstrous extraterrestrial Tsiln, Gog, and captured Gwen Stacy to be his queen. Battling both Ka-Zar and Spider-Man, Kraven narrowly averted death after plunging off a cliff, while Gog seemingly drowned in quicksand. After recovering from his injuries, Kraven returned to New York, forcing the Gibbon to serve in a failed ploy against Spider-Man. In San Francisco he accepted a contract from Kerwin J. Broderick to defeat Daredevil (Matt Murdock). He almost succeeded, tossing Daredevil off a cliff, had Daredevil not been teleported away by Moondragon.

Kraven then accepted a contract from Harrison Turk (extradimensional dictator Arisen Tyrk, aka Lunatik), to capture the Man-Wolf (John Jameson) for his Godstone and kill John's father, J. Jonah Jameson, and fiancée, Kristine Saunders. Kraven gave Jonah and Kristine a rifle, pitting the two against the Man-Wolf. The police captured Kraven before he completed the contract. Once free, he traveled to Chicago to augment his powers by kidnapping Dr. Herbert Malraux, who had devised a means to improve one's reaction time using his experimental psycho-motor response procedure. Tigra, the cat-woman, failed to stop the kidnapping, but pursued Kraven to an abandoned circus arena. Regardless of Kraven's posturing, Tigra overcame Kraven's sonic assaults and savagely shredded the Hunter.

Healed from Tigra's vicious attack, Kraven reluctantly partnered with the Tarantula (Anton Rodriguez) for another contract (at a reduced fee due to his tarnished reputation) offered by Dr. Edward Lansky (Lightmaster), the vice chancellor of Empire State University, to kidnap New York City university chancellor Richard Gorman. While the Tarantula delivered Gorman, Spider-Man defeated Kraven once again, battling atop a movie marquee on which Kraven accidentally electrocuted himself. While being transferred back to jail in Illinois, Kraven escaped custody and returned to a hideout on the Jersey City waterfront. Tigra attempted to apprehend him, but was captured and given an electronic collar making her submit to Kraven's commands. After drugging Spider-Man with poisoned darts, Kraven let Spider-Man fight for his life against Tigra. Once Spider-Man destroyed the collar, the two overpowered Kraven.

Later, Kraven retreated to the Caribbean islands in order to rethink his life and goals. There, he met and fell in love with Calypso Ezili, a powerful voodoo sorceress. Though Kraven believed his obsessive hatred for Spider-Man cost him his honor, Calypso goaded him into resuming pursuit of Spider-Man. While Kraven transported wild animals to New York City, Calypso unlocked the cages, framing Spider-Man and prompting Kraven to clash with Spider-Man at the Museum of Natural History. Both Kraven and Calypso were arrested, but the two soon escaped jail. To prove himself worthy of Calypso's love, Kraven hunted Spider-Man again; however, when Kraven realized Calypso had drugged Spider-Man with a hallucinogenic dart, he stopped the fight out of honor. The police captured the two again. After "accidentally" shooting Ka-Zar in the head, AIM agent Ramona "Courtland" Starr freed Kraven from prison to capture Ka-Zar alive. Kraven ignored Ramona and nearly succeeded in killing Ka-Zar until he, Ka-Zar and Shanna the She-Devil fell from a skyscraper into Spider-Man's web. Kraven, respectful of Ka-Zar's attempt to save his life before falling, administered a pain-killing jungle drug to Ka-Zar before fleeing the scene.

In Los Angeles, Tigra interrupted Kraven's robbery of an African-American Art Museum. Kraven left Tigra after drugging her with a poisoned tusk from his belt. Recovered, Tigra pursued Kraven to Griffith Park for a fight to the death, witnessed by a Scourge of the Underworld targeting Kraven. Though Tigra drew first blood, Kraven subdued her with a taming nerve-thrust typically used on large cats. Before he could deliver a lethal blow, Tigra was rescued by her western Avengers teammates, who bound Kraven for the authorities. Kraven was mystically freed from jail by Mephisto's agent, Mr. Bitterhorn, and imprinted with an invisible sign mystically linking him to "Beyondersbane," the occult engine constructed for the vastly powerful Beyonder's destruction. Kraven was summoned along with a legion of similarly marked supervillains to attack the Beyonder, who had arrived on Earth and assumed a human form. Contact would destroy the Beyonder along with approximately a third of the universe. The supernaturally enhanced Thing prevented the legion from reaching the Beyonder, and the Beyondersbane self-destructed. Kraven returned to jail, his arcane covenant voided.

After years of defeats from his greatest enemy, Spider-Man, Kraven decided he could only restore his honor if he could "kill" Spider-Man, become him, and defeat that which Spider-Man could not defeat. Insane with obsession, yet focused on victory, Kraven prepared himself by ritualistically consuming spiders while imbibing his jungle potions. He successfully trapped and tranquilized Spider-Man, buried him alive, and donned Spider-Man's costume. As "Spider-Man" Kraven became a vicious vigilante, showing no mercy to a pair about to assault Spider-Man's wife, Mary Jane. While the newspapers proclaimed Spider-Man

Art by Mike Zeck

had gone berserk, Kraven shifted his attention from street crime to Vermin, the rat-man, a creature Spider-Man had failed to capture without Captain America's help. Alone, Kraven defeated Vermin. After two weeks buried alive in a state simulating death, Spider-Man climbed free from his grave and, though weak, confronted Kraven. Kraven passively accepted Spider-Man's assault, proclaiming his established victory. To finalize his emancipation from obsession over Spider-Man, Kraven released Vermin to attack Spider-Man, whom Vermin thought to be his assailant and captor. Kraven stopped Vermin before he killed Spider-Man, and set him free. While Spider-Man pursued Vermin, Kraven took his own life with a rifle, convinced his life's work was complete. He left behind a confession of the activities he performed while disguised as Spider-Man for the police.

Despite his tombstone's epitaph, Kraven had died dishonorably; his spirit lingered seeking release from the earthly plane. Spider-Man, still traumatized from his living burial, was taken on a metaphysical journey to Kraven's gravesite. Choosing the path towards life and forgiveness, he released Kraven's soul while granting his own mind some peace. Though released from Earth, Kraven's soul was sent to hell. There the Pitiful One offered Kraven and others a chance to spend 24 hours on Earth, where they wreaked havoc. Though they worked to find a more permanent means to remain on Earth, Dr. Strange stopped them with Dead Girl and other deceased heroes. Edie Sawyer (U-Go Girl) transported Kraven and Mysterio (presumably Quentin Beck) into a deeper layer of hell for their offense.

After his death, two of Kraven's sons, Vladimir and Alyosha, attempted to carry on his legacy independently of each other. Ned, however, preferred the Hollywood culture as a director over jungle safaris. Vladimir, as the Grim Hunter, was ultimately murdered by Kaine, while Alyosha renounced his father's bloodlust and made peace with Spider-Man. The Chameleon, insanely obsessed with his half-brother, took on Kraven's identity for a time while pursuing Spider-Man. While Alyosha pursued dreams of becoming a Hollywood producer, Dimitri's antics as Kraven resulted in the accidental death of Nedrocci Tannengarden. The Chameleon appears to have since abandoned the role.

A young woman named Ana Kravinoff has taken on the name "Kraven" claiming to be the daughter of Sergei and brother of Vladimir. Like Sergei, she has superhuman abiliites and is driven to hunt Spider-Man.

RETURNED FROM THE DEAD
Art by Nick Dragotta

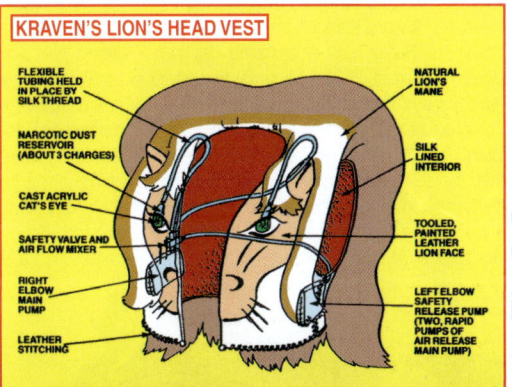
KRAVEN'S LION'S HEAD VEST
Art by Eliot R. Brown

SPIRIT OF KRAVEN
Art by Mike Zeck

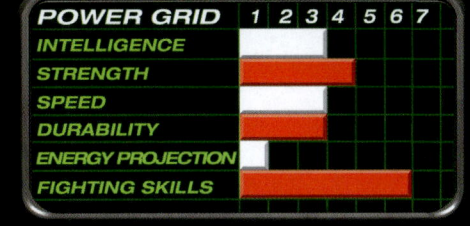

HEIGHT: 6' **WEIGHT:** 235 lbs.
EYES: Brown **HAIR:** Black

ABILITIES/ACCESSORIES: Kraven possessed superhuman abilities conferred upon him via special herbal potions he periodically ingested. These abilities included enhanced strength (optimally lifting 2 tons), speed (able to sprint short distances at 60 mph), agility, stamina and longevity. He could perform a standing broad jump of 20 feet. He could exert at peak levels for a half-hour before fatigue impaired performance. Despite his advanced years, Kraven maintained the physical age of a 30-year-old. He employed a wide range of weapons including blowguns and darts, bolos, axes, spears, whips, gas bombs and traps/restraints including magnetic manacles and nets. He had wielded a leopard claw glove, a "jungle scent" spray to numb Spider-Man's spider-sense, and a horn to drive animals into a rampage. Though he shunned bows or firing bullets, he had used a rifle to deliver a wide range of drug-tipped darts. His belt housed poison-tipped teeth and tusks, while his lion's head vest contained electronics that could stun, tranquilize, and emit a double-barreled ray (to magnetize the electrolytes in one's musculature), an electro-burst or ultra-sonic blasters.

Kraven was a master hunter and wild animal tamer, proficient in certain exotic animal-like fighting techniques, and an expert in various jungle herbs and potions. His nerve punch attack could paralyze even Spider-Man and Tigra.

POWER GRID	1	2	3	4	5	6	7
INTELLIGENCE							
STRENGTH							
SPEED							
DURABILITY							
ENERGY PROJECTION							
FIGHTING SKILLS							

ALYOSHA KRAVINOFF

REAL NAME: Alyosha Kravinoff
ALIASES: Al Kraven; formerly Kraven the Hunter
IDENTITY: Publicly known
OCCUPATION: Adventurer, hunter; former attempted movie director
CITIZENSHIP: Unrevealed African nation
PLACE OF BIRTH: Unrevealed African nation
KNOWN RELATIVES: Sergei Kravinoff (Kraven the Hunter, father, deceased), unidentified mother, Vladimir Kravinoff (Grim Hunter, half-brother, deceased), Nedrocci Tannengarden (half-brother, deceased), Ana Tatiana Kravinoff (alleged half-sister), Dmitri Smerdyakov (Chameleon, uncle)
GROUP AFFILIATION: Formerly the Sinister Six
EDUCATION: Privately tutored
FIRST APPEARANCE: Spectacular Spider-Man #243 (1997)

HISTORY: Alyosha Kravinoff, an illegitimate mutant son of the infamous Kraven the Hunter, was — unlike his half-brother Vladimir (the Grim Hunter) — separated from his family and raised in an African jungle. After Kraven's suicide, Alyosha came to New York to investigate the father he barely knew. Dressed as Kraven, Alyosha confronted his Uncle Dmitri (the Chameleon). Believing his abusive half-brother had returned from the dead, the Chameleon revealed to Alyosha much about the dysfunctional Kravinoff family. Kraven's former lover, Calypso Ezili, did actually return from the dead, and she mistook Alyosha for Kraven. She seduced Alyosha, but afterwards he spurned her affections. Later, riding a bull elephant atop Manhattan's rooftops, Alyosha attacked Spider-Man, poisoning him with a hallucinogenic dart, but then set him free. While at the Kravinoff estate, Alyosha was learning about his father from Spider-Man when Calypso returned with Kraven's tribesmen, setting the home ablaze and killing all but one animal, Gulyadkin the lion. Calypso poisoned Alyosha and Spider-Man and used her hypnotic powers to force the two to fight to the death. Spider-Man resisted and injured Calypso, while Alyosha subdued her with his lion. Despite asking for her forgiveness, Alyosha savagely killed Calypso and all the tribesmen.

He was later hired by the city of New York to help capture the Fantastic Four's enigmatic enormous canid Puppy. Next, he was hired by White Wolf, head of the deposed Wakandan secret police, to capture the Black Panther. The Black Panther turned the battle around, nearly killing Alyosha. The Sandman later invited Alyosha to join the Sinister Six to hunt Dr. Octopus and Senator Ward, host body for the alien Z'nox. Venom (Eddie Brock), slighted at his rejection by the Six, hunted each of the team members. Refusing to be "the hunted," Alyosha trapped Venom with fire, but Venom seriously injured him and escaped.

Alyosha then adopted a more relaxed personality as a suave, witty ladies' man. As "Al," he began dating Timber Hughes, an aspiring actress who waitressed at an all-villain bar. Al sought to help Timber's career in Hollywood by becoming a director. Despite celebrity connections, Al's efforts were stonewalled by arrogance, greed and corruption within the Hollywood elite. Forced out of Hollywood by the powerful Rothstein brothers, Al was beaten while Timber was brutally raped. Both Al and Timber exacted vengeance, defeated another half-brother, Ned, and left Hollywood to pursue heroics in New York City. He retained his mutant powers after "M-Day."

Al spent time off Earth on Battleworld with other heroes and villains tricked by the Stranger into believing he was part of a new test by the Beyonder. The group returned to Earth thanks to Hank Pym's cleverness and the sacrifice of Gravity. Later, Al's ingestion of a batch of his father's potions to augment his natural powers drove him mad. Shifted into the savage Kraven the Hunter persona, Al captured animal-themed superhumans, holding them prisoner on a ship like a menagerie. The Punisher, pursuing the Rhino, battled Kraven and the captives onboard; Kraven escaped using a teleportation device. Considering his family history and personality shifts, his mental stability remains in question.

HEIGHT: 6'3" **WEIGHT:** 220 lbs.
EYES: Brown **HAIR:** Black

ABILITIES/ACCESSORIES: Alyosha has superhuman strength (able to lift 1 ton), speed, agility, stamina, and healing. His five senses are extraordinarily heightened, and he can speak with animals. When enraged, he may shift into a bestial fury. He is highly experienced in weaponry such as poison darts, axes, spears, whips, guns, and nets, and is an exceptional unarmed combatant. He wore his father's lion vest, with embedded electro-shock circuitry. He travels with his pet wolf, Nickel, and occasionally other exotic animals.

POWER GRID	1	2	3	4	5	6	7
INTELLIGENCE			■				
STRENGTH				■			
SPEED			■				
DURABILITY					■		
ENERGY PROJECTION	■						
FIGHTING SKILLS				■			

Art by Cory Walker with Luke Ross, Joe Quesada & Scott Kolins (insets)

KREE

KNOWN MEMBERS: Ael-Dan, Ahmbar (Amber Watkins), Ajes'ha, Arides (Shatterstar), Arjai-Ush, Att-Lass, Av-Rom, Bas-For, Bav-Tek, Bel-Dann, Bheton, Boko, Bron-Char, Bronek, Bun-Dall, Cha-Mount, Ciry, Clar-Roc, Dandre, Dan-Forr, Dantella, Dar-Benn, Dal, Dea-Sea, Devros, Dor-Art, Dwi-Zann, Dylon-Cir, Eine, En-Vad, Èpt-Rass, Fahr, Falzon, Fer-Porr, Galen-Kor, Hal-Konn, Hav-Ak, Hez-Tarr, Hon-Sann, Jac'oyaa, Jella, Jenna, Jordann, Kaer-Linn, Kalum-Lo, Kam-Lorr, Kar-Sagg, Kay-Sade, Keeyah, Klaer, Klynn, Kni-Konn, Kona-Lor, Korath-Thak (Korath the Pursuer), Ko-Rel, Lar-Ka, "Leigh," Levan, Lon-Lorr, Mac-Ronn, Malakii, Mar-Vell (Captain Marvel), Maston-Dar, Minn-Erva, M-Nell (Commando), Mon-Tog, Morag, Murius, Muz-Kott, Om-Fad, Nenora, Nep'perr, Nera, Nos-Verr, Pap-Tonn, Phae-Dor, Phaht, Por-Bat, Primus, Ran-Deff, Ra-Venn, Rojett, Ronan, Sallen-Bei, Sals-Bek, Saria, Sar-Torr, Shatterax, Shym'r Sr., Shym'r Jr., Sìg-Rass, Singhre/Shen-Garh, Sintaris, Son-Dar, Sro-Himm, Staak, Sta-Ramm, Star-Lyn, Stug-Bar, Talla-Ron, Tallun, Tara, Tar-Rell, Tar-Vash, Tarnok-Kol, Tellis, Teress, Tir-Zarr, Tokk, Tol-Nok, Tohn-Bil, Trigor, Tunis-Var, Tus-Katt, Tzu-Zana (Suzy Sherman, Ultragirl), Ultimus, Una, Una-Rogg, Uni, Visog, Vron-Ikka, Yon-Rogg, Zak-Del (Wraith), Zamsed, Zarek, Zenna, Zen-Pram, Zey-Rogg, Zyro, others
KNOWN HYBRIDS: Teddy Altman/Dorrek VIII (Hulkling), Candidie, Hav-Rogg, Genis-Vell (Photon), Phyla-Vell (Quasar), others
BASE OF OPERATIONS: Hala, Pama system, Greater Magellanic Cloud Galaxy
FIRST APPEARANCE: (Mentioned) Fantastic Four #64 (1967), (full) Fantastic Four #65 (1967)

TRAITS: Kree bodies are denser and more durable than those of normal humans, making them about twice as strong, though Pink (aka White) Kree have a greater range of differences in these areas than Blue Kree do. They also have duplicates of several internal organs. While the average Kree is the same height as an average human, a significant percentage of Kree are far taller. The Kree's native environment has a much higher gravity and higher nitrogen-to-oxygen air content as compared to Earth's native environment, and the Kree originally could not survive in high-oxygen environments without special breathing devices and potions. Some Kree women can psychically manipulate the desires of men, with one in 100,000 of these women able to drain another's life force completely. In recent years, such Kree girls were forced to undergo surgical procedures to eradicate this ability completely, with techno-organic "bloodhounds" used to hunt down any female who reached adulthood with her psychic abilities intact.

Kree who were artificially evolved by the Forever Crystal — formerly called the Ruul — can adapt to survive in any hostile environment by changing form, though the exact shape taken during the initial shape-changing is determined by the individual's exact genetic makeup, not by conscious choice. The "Ruul" Kree can have several different forms adapted for separate tasks, including but not limited to, a warrior form, a super-intelligent "scientist" form, and separate forms for surviving in outer space, underwater, methane atmospheres, and solar surfaces. Virtually all of the early Ruul Kree were grey with lumpy foreheads and tentacles in place of hair, though later they changed to a blue coloration and mostly non-lumpy appearances. Since then almost all Kree, whether originally Pink or Blue, returned to their former pre-Ruul appearances (with some Pink Kree evidently turning to a blue color), though whether the cause is a refinement of their new shape-changing abilities or artificial has yet to be revealed. It has also been stated that all newly evolved Kree women have their psychic manipulation powers permanently removed at the genetic level, though whether this is true, or if some women secretly retain their powers remains to be seen.

Though 98% of the Kree population was wiped out when the Shi'ar's Nega-Bomb exploded in their galaxy, they have since rebuilt their numbers far faster than expected through unrevealed means, possibly via mass cloning and artificially aging the resultant children.

HISTORY: The Kree are one of two native races on the planet Hala in the Pama system of the Greater Magellanic Cloud galaxy, the other race being the plant-like Cotati. By some accounts the Kree are one of the many biped races spawned from the ancient Xorri race. In their distant past, the Celestials experimented on the ancient Kree as they did ancient humans millennia later. This experimentation produced the sub-races of Kree Eternals — all but extinct in the modern era — and Kree Deviants, whose ultimate fate remains unrevealed. The aggressive hunter-gatherer Blue Kree tribes allegedly considered all plants beneath their notice and ignored the Cotati, while the Cotati considered the Kree too frenetic for their quieter natures and left the Kree alone. About a million years ago, in the first year of recorded Kree history, a delegation of pacifist Skrulls arrived to advance the primitive natives to a point where they could join the Skrull Empire as trade partners. The Skrull Emperor Dorrek I proposed a test to decide which of Hala's races would be advanced as citizens of the Skrull Empire and which would not: Two groups of seventeen would be left on separate barren worlds for one year with "rudimentary" Skrull technology to create something of worth. The telepathic Cotati, sensing no deceit, accepted quickly; the distrustful Kree tribesmen debated for a day before their leader Morag accepted. The Cotati were taken to one barren moon while the Kree were taken to Earth's barren moon, where an artificial environment was created for them (the place later called the Blue Area of the Moon). The Stone Age tribesmen, using knowledge learned while en route, created an advanced city. The returning Skrulls were impressed, but were more impressed by the garden the Cotati had created on their moon. Enraged at his people being left behind by the Skrull Empire, Morag had his men slaughter every Cotati they could find. When the horrified Skrull Emperor forever banished Hala from the empire, he and his men were killed as well. Morag then led his Kree to master the Skrulls' technology, eventually creating an armada of spaceships to carve out their own interstellar empire and attack the homeworld of the Skrulls, formally igniting the Kree-Skrull War.

Art by Jorge Lucas

PRIESTS OF PAMA WITH THE COTATI
Art by Sal Buscema

In the early centuries of the empire, a pacifist Kree sect developed and was forced underground in Hala's slums. They secretly developed their martial and meditative skills for decades, until the Kree year 4760, when they were contacted by descendants of the murdered Cotati who had survived unnoticed by their killers. The telepathic plants had concentrated on developing their minds at the expense of their mobility, and found themselves forever rooted to the same place. They formed an alliance with the Kree sect, the more mobile Kree taking care of the Cotati's needs while the Cotati shared secrets of the mind. The sect became the Priests of Pama, concealing the existence of the Cotati while the Priests were ridiculed by mainstream Kree society.

Over the centuries, the Kree became renowned for their battle prowess, convinced that fighting wars made them stronger and better than seeking peace did. They created Kree-Lar, a planetwide city on Hala seemingly devoid of all non-Kree life. They made their empire's capital on a planet in the Turunal system also called Kree-Lar, while Hala became a sacred planet. They designated the planet Cyllandra as the main historical library of their people. The Kree Empire was ruled as a military dictatorship, originally by various aristocratic military clans (including one named after its founder, the warrior Fiyero) elected to the post of supreme ruler, before the organic computer construct Supreme Intelligence (SI), repository of all the greatest Kree scientific and military minds that have been downloaded into it, officially took over rulership of the Empire 253 years after it went on-line in Kree Year 4791 (circa 990,497 BC). The SI was aided by its administrators in Kree-Lar, member world governors, the Supreme Science Council, a vast standing army, highly trained paired assassins called Evolvers, and the Accusers, enforcers of Kree law. The Kree developed Plan Atavus to devolve any planet they deemed a future threat to the Empire. Kree engineer Bronek created robotic Sentries to guard their weapons depots, and to keep selected worlds under surveillance. Over time the Kree invented many weapons and devices like their main communication power source, the Omni-Wave Projector; some inventions, like the organic-destroying robotic Null-Trons, and the genetic-enhancer Psyche-Magnitron device, were later outlawed.

Interbreeding with the "aliens" they encountered while empire building created a second hybrid race of Kree with pink skin, which eventually outnumbered the "pure" blue race. The Blue Kree managed to remain the upper class in Kree society by creating a strict apartheid system that persisted into the modern era. Some Pink Kree rebelled against this subjection over the millennia, with one known band of rebels and their families forever exiled to the mining planet Daccara for their unrevealed crimes. Occasionally a "throwback" Blue Kree is born into a Pink family, but the precise social status of these Kree as compared to trueborn Blue Kree is unrevealed. A rare "Black" Kree race exists, but their origins are unrevealed. At an unrevealed point in time a small fleet of generation ships passed into a space warp and emerged in the so-called Exoteric Latitude, where the ships' populations fell prey to the tiny soul parasites, the Exolon. The affected Kree turned a pale white, gaining extra strength, a regenerative healing factor, immortality, and the ability to summon the Exolon to swarm and expose "the soul of a living being," driving fear into many of those who saw it. However, these Kree lost all conscious memory of their former identities and pursuits except when experiencing pain, leaving the so-called Nameless Kree to spend their now endless lives doing nothing but savagely maiming each other and themselves just to remember who they once were.

When the Priests of Pama were exiled by the SI on a trumped-up assault charge and imprisoned on a barren world far from the Cotati, the Cotati telepathically lured the ionic-powered alien Star-Stalker to the prison planet, confident their Kree allies would be able to discover for themselves how to successfully defeat it. The Priests informed the SI of the Star-Stalker's existence and offered to defend the Empire by sending two Priests to every imperial world to stand watch against the Stalker's return. Though it doubted the creature truly existed, the SI agreed, demanding four Priests to remain on Hala as its personal guard. The Priests secretly took one Cotati per Priest with them to establish garden temples on each world known to the Kree, including Saturn's moon Titan, and Earth.

A stone of great power and unrevealed origin was discovered on Kree-Lar; when it was split in two, the resultant energy release killed thousands. Revealed to control the forces of Chaos and Order, the two halves were dubbed Ke-Thia (Alpha) and Vi-Ska (Omega) respectively. Scientists from other space-faring races brought their stones of power (including the future Bloodgem, part of which was later worn by Ulysses Bloodstone) to Kree-Lar, and formed the Lifestone Tree to advance the evolutionary traits of all living things in the universe. The gems accessed the Hellfire Helix, which was used as a conduit for otherdimensional energies that were funneled through Ke-Thia and Vi-Ska to create smaller power stones. The stones manifested facets of the elements (air, water, fire, earth), spirits (life, death, anima), creation, entropy, and gravity. The stones were used to transform eight individuals from different races, including the Kree woman Ajes'ha (using the future Moongem, aka Moonstone) into the Chosen Eight of Fate (aka the Guardians of the Galaxy). The Eight kept the galactic peace for 200 years until they disbanded. When the peace collapsed, the stones were moved from Kree-Lar in a failed attempt to keep pirates from stealing them; during the attack the warp drive of the stones' ship imploded, breaking and scattering the gems all over the galaxy. Some of the stones seeded the Earth system, eventually giving rise to the adventurers Moonstone, Ulysses Bloodstone, Dr. Spectrum, the Sphinx, Man-Wolf, and many others.

Over the millennia the Kree secretly kept a close eye on Earth, originally because the Sol system was near a natural space-warp access used by the Skrulls. When a band of exiled Earth Eternals raided the Kree weapons depot on Uranus, the investigating Kree slew all but one, whom they vivisected to learn he was human in origin. Intrigued, the Kree scientists conducted their own experiments on humanity, creating the sub-race later called Inhumans for use as future spies against the Kree's various interstellar foes, then left their new subjects to refine their genetic abilities over the next few centuries. The Kree left robotic Sentries on Earth to guard their hidden bases and monitor the Inhumans' progress, and set up Plan Atavus in case humans ever became a threat to the Empire.

In modern times, the Kree's militaristic society calcified into oppressive regimentation: The two races were strictly segregated in both civilian and military societies, seldom mingling even in battle. Eugenic philosophies informed most social activities, with state military academies doing the majority of child-raising. Kree society allowed little in the way of public dissent and social mobility, especially for Pink Kree, considered "half-breeds" by some "full bred" Blue Kree. Dissenters were often arrested for showing the slightest distrust towards their leaders. Occasionally, political and religious dissidents found limited freedom on distant colony worlds or deep space starships. Cold dedication to honor, duty, and battle was considered the highest of virtues, with torture and revenge almost an art form, while emotions like love, friendship, and mercy were considered base and unnatural, a "virus of the spirit" to be cauterized at all costs. While the Cotati's survival was now publicly known, identified Cotati worshipers were often put to death for sedition. The SI was all but worshiped as a god, with many private shrines built to it. The Universal

Art by Keith Pollard

Church of Truth won permission to build their temples throughout the Kree Empire due to the battle prowess of their Black Knight cadre. When Earth's Fantastic Four defeated both Sentry 459 and Accuser-Prime Ronan, the SI sent the starship Helion to Earth to conduct a feasibility study for a future invasion. Military hero Captain Mar-Vell was sent undercover to study humanity's defenses, but he grew to love the Earth instead and defected, eventually becoming Earth's protector as Captain Marvel. The Supreme Science Council sent agents to conscript the Inhumans into the Kree army, but the Inhuman Royal Family defeated them each time. A new skirmish in the ancient Kree-Skrull War began when Ronan the Accuser overthrew and imprisoned the SI over what he considered the SI's too-liberal policies encouraging Kree marriages with non-Kree, and the increased social acceptance of the resulting progeny. The Super-Skrull (Kl'rt) kidnapped Mar-Vell and brought him to the Skrull homeworld, Tarnax IV, to force him to build an Omni-Wave Projector as an ultimate death ray. Both Kree and Skrull armies were stopped cold when the SI unleashed fellow prisoner Rick Jones' latent psychic powers (the Destiny Force) to freeze every soldier in their tracks, allowing the SI to depose Ronan. Later, Captain Marvel and Inhuman King Black Bolt stopped the Council from starting the dreaded War of Three Galaxies — the Greater Magellanic Cloud, Andromeda, and Milky Way galaxies — by revealing the main instigator for the war as a disguised Skrull agent, who intended to direct the Kree into a Skrull trap. Meanwhile, Earth became a secret refuge for dissident Kree, with some expatriates settling in Raven's Perch, New Jersey, some members of the Free Kree Liberation Army basing themselves in the London music scene, and a sect settling in Brea, California, to watch over Tzu-Zana (later Ultragirl), a girl prophesized as the Universal Unifier, destined to remake all Kree races equal in a new golden age of Kreekind.

When the Skrulls lost Empress R'Kill to Galactus, and later their shape-changing powers due to the machinations of the would-be Emperor Zabyk, they feared that the Kree would sweep over them like a vengeful tide, so one of the remaining would-be rulers, Kylor, decided to preemptively attack the Kree before they learned of the Skrull's lost shape-changing abilities, re-igniting the war once more. The Supreme Intelligence tried to absorb the Silver Surfer into his collective mind when the Surfer tried to keep Earth and his native Zenn-La out of this latest conflict, but the Surfer escaped, driving the SI temporarily insane in the process. The new Supreme Leader, Nenora (actually Skrull Agent K6@, who had killed and replaced the real Nenora), led the Kree to many impressive victories until the Surfer and acting Skrull Empress S'Byll were tipped off by the Cotati to Nenora's true nature. S'Byll and the Surfer sneaked onto Hala, where they confronted Nenora and publicly restored her shape-shifting power, stunning the Kree, who agreed to a temporary truce. Schemes of both the Cotati and another Skrull posing as the Elder of the Universe called Contemplator placed hapless alien Clumsy Foulup in charge of the Kree until a plot by Generals Ael-Dan and Dar-Benn killed him, leaving them joint rulers of the Empire.

The now-recovered SI conceived a monstrous plan to prod the Kree out of their so-called evolutionary dead end. It secretly implanted the idea of creating a Nega-Bomb large enough to destroy an interstellar empire in the minds of the rival Shi'ar Imperium rulers, and mentally intensified the prejudices of the ruling Kree, Shi'ar, and Skrull leaders to the point of inciting war. Shi'ar Majestrix Lilandra and Kree rulers Ael-Dann and Dar-Benn were manipulated into a race to gather the necessary pieces to build the bomb. The Shi'ar ultimately acquired the energy core of a Psyche-Magnitron, the now-deceased Captain Marvel's Nega-Bands, and the secret of the Omni-Wave Projector, then delivered the finished bomb to Skrull soldiers to deploy in the center of the Kree's galaxy. Despite the best efforts of Earth's Avengers (dragged into the war because two of the bomb's components were in the Sol system) the bomb exploded, killing 98% of the Kree population and many other subject races as well. The SI secretly smuggled its mind to a nearby mercenary spaceship while manipulating the Avenger Black Knight (Dane Whitman) into killing its original body. Lilandra's sister, Deathbird, became Viceroy of the Kree territories, ruling with an iron hand and aided by the indentured Kree super-team, Starforce. Many rebel groups sprang up, with some, like the Kree Consolidated Peace Battalion, fighting to return the military back to power, while others, like the Kree Resistance Front, sought to create a society free from both the Shi'ar and the old ways. A few Kree, such as Ronan, pretended to serve Shi'ar interests while secretly undermining them, while the pirate band Starjammers (Corsair, Raza, Ch'od, Hepzibah, Keeyah) smuggled several groups of refugees to the anarchist Clench world Standing Still. Several Kree officers banded together under Admiral Galen-Kor to unleash a much smaller Nega-Bomb on Earth, but the Avengers' Sersi stopped the bomb before it did much damage. However, a later attack by the Starstealth Cadre on the Avengers' Vision and Wonder Man (Simon Williams) did succeed in temporarily killing Wonder Man, who they blamed along with the Vision for actually setting off the bomb. A ragtag armada of Kree refugees led by General Maston-Dar came to the Inhuman city of Attilan (then located in the Blue Area of the Moon) to beg asylum, but were ultimately refused when Maston-Dar's attempt to keep the then-deposed Black Bolt from objecting backfired.

After tricking Rick Jones into restoring its full powers, the Supreme Intelligence contacted Galen-Kor and his band to rescue it from its hiding place in the New York City sewers. Renaming themselves the Lunatic Legion, Galen-Kor's forces sought to turn the Earth's population into neo-Kree slaves using an Omni-Wave Projector modified with the Inhumans' mutating Terrigen Mists, not realizing that this plan went against the SI's ultimate plans for humans. The SI secretly aided the Avengers against the Legion, who

RUUL (ORIGINAL APPEARANCE)

Art by John Romita Jr.

RUUL, LATER APPEARANCE

Art by Scott Kolins

were absorbed into the Projector and seemingly killed when it exploded. While aiding the time traveler Kang and a cross-time group of Avengers against Immortus, the SI gained possession of the time-warping Forever Crystal, secretly using it to accelerate the evolution of the now-mutable Kree into what they would have eventually become centuries later. Taking the fake name "Ruul," the super-evolved Kree convinced the Intergalactic Council to turn Earth into a prison planet for the worst interstellar criminals, in a bid to keep Earth's heroes busy while Ronan absorbed the essence of Ego the Living Planet into himself. Ronan almost succeeded before Quasar (Wendell Vaughn) diverted Ego's essence into himself instead. The Kree then concentrated on reconstructing their lost empire, and evolving those of their number who were initially out of range of the Crystal's transformation wave, with some becoming members of the Nu-Elite ruling class, with Fiyero House (long since degenerated into a merchant house) once more the new rulers of the Empire.

To solidify their regained status and enact political reforms they believed were necessary, the Fiyero leaders secretly bribed Rigellian Tana Nile to falsely accuse Ronan of plotting to give Skrull Baroness S'bak control over several Kree borderworlds, exiling the former Accuser and eliminating a major obstacle to their plans. When the SI protested, the Fiyeros disabled it by quietly giving it a lobotomy, fearing the public reaction if they killed it outright. When invading Negative Zone ruler Annihilus' army reached Kree space, the Fiyeros publicly allied with surviving Nova Centurion Richard Rider's United Front to fight the invaders, but secretly contracted with one of Annihilus' Seekers, Ravenous, to not significantly oppose Annihilus due to the Fiyeros' belief that they couldn't win against him, and sent the Kree army into battle without an overall battle strategy to guide their actions. The Fiyeros placed their family members in key strategic military positions to ensure that the lack of plan was enforced, leading to massive casualties in the military. When UF ally Ronan confronted the Fiyero representatives stationed on the front over their lack of strategy, the Fiyeros arrogantly disregarded his advice and threatened to pull out of the alliance. They then tried to arrest Ronan, who angrily killed them instead. When an attack by Annihilus' Centurions (the Negative Zone's rough equivalent to the Shi'ar Imperial Guard) and an enslaved Galactus broke the United Front for good, Ronan and new UF allies Super-Skrull and the robotic Praxagora went to Hala to free the Kree from Fiyero leadership, and discovered them under the protection of Ravenous and the Centurions. Angered by this betrayal of Kree interests, Ronan attacked and delivered his judgment against Ravenous by breaking his head open. The Centurions then teleported to their ships and left the Fiyero leaders to their fate. Shocked when the Kree soldiers present defected to Ronan's side, the Fiyeros tried to excuse their actions to Ronan, claiming that their agreement with Annihilus was the only way to save the Empire, but Ronan was not moved by the argument and executed them.

After granting the SI a mercy killing, Ronan found himself publicly proclaimed the new leader of the Empire. When Ravenous' ships began firing on Hala from orbit, Ronan led the military counterattack by launching several city blocks of Kree-Lar city at the fleet, then had the soldiers occupying the buildings emerge en masse to blast away at the exposed ships, driving the fleet from Hala. After being forced to sign a treaty ceding the entirety of the Skrull Empire and parts of the Kree Empire (including capital planet Kree-Lar) to a now-recovered Ravenous in order to buy time to rebuild the Kree, Emperor Ronan allied with the Galadorian

AEL-DAN
Kree leader (deceased)
Silver Surfer #53 (1991)

AJES'HA
Chosen Eight of Fate
Thunderbolts Annual 2000

ARIDES
(Shatterstar)
Super-Kree Agent
Inhumans #3 (1975)

**ATT-LASS
(CAPTAIN ATLAS)**
Captain, Kree Military;
Starforce
Quasar #9 (1990)

AV-ROM
Captain, Kree Military
Young Avengers #10
(2006)

BAV-TEK
Kree Resistance Front
Captain Marvel #4 (1996)

BEL-DANN
General, Kree Military;
member, Kree Consolidated
Peace Battalion
X-Men #137 (1976)

DAR-BENN
Kree leader (deceased)
Silver Surfer #53 (1991)

DEVROS
Grand Admiral, Kree Military;
so-called 'Brood King'
(deceased)
Untold Tales of Captain
Marvel #2 (1997)

DYLON-CIR
Kree Military Lieutenant;
Lunatic Legion
Avengers #364 (1993)

FALZON
Scientist
Inhumans #3 (1975)

GALEN-KOR
Admiral, Kree Military;
leader of Lunatic Legion
(deceased)
Avengers #350 (1992)

KALUM-LO
Major, Kree Military;
leader of the Starstealth
Force Works #1 (1994)

KAR-SAGG
Cyber-geneticist
Silver Surfer #29 (1989)

KONA-LOR
Lieutenant, Kree Military;
Lunatic Legion
Avengers #364 (1993)

KORATH-THAK
(Korath the Pursuer)
Cyber-geneticist,
member of Starforce
Quasar #32 (1992)

KO-REL
Military medic, Nova
Centurion 0001
(deceased)
Nova #4 (2007)

M-NELL (COMMANDO)
Kree Military Captain;
Shi'ar Imperial Guard
Imperial Guard #1 (1997)

MAC-RONN
Medic
Captain Marvel #47 (1976)

MALAKII
Aeronautics designer;
Kree Resistance Front leader
X-Men Unlimited #5 (1994)

MAR-VELL
Captain, Kree Military
(deceased)
Marvel Super-Heroes
#12 (1968)

MASTON-DAR
General, Kree Military
Inhumans:
The Great Refuge #1
(1995)

MINN-ERVA
(Dr. Minerva)
Geneticist, Starforce
Captain Marvel #49
(1977)

MON-TOG
Major, Kree Military;
Stationmaster,
Kree Space Station Web
Inhumans #10 (1977)

Spaceknights to use their Restitution Program's A-ware software as part of the Kree war-net to help build up their military defenses again. During special military advisor Peter Quill's (Star-Lord) demonstration of the new defenses, he and Ronan learned that the cybernetic Spaceknights had been taken over by Terran robot Ultron and the techno-organic Phalanx, who used the Kree's war-net to take control of hundreds of Sentries and fused them into their Babel Spire. Phasing the entire Kree galaxy out of sync with the rest of the universe, the Phalanx began to assimilate all inside of it to either their cause of perfect machine/organic unions (the Phalanx Selects) or as food. While various resistance groups using low-tech weapons and devices sprang up to fight the Phalanx invasion, others who worshipped the Phalanx sprang up as well, giving themselves the name "Kree-Lanx" to show their support.

Fitted with assimilation devices to make him a Select, Ronan was forced to aid the Phalanx in their conquest of the Kree until he discovered the Phalanx had captured the corpse of the SI and intended to reactivate it to use the resulting psychic echo to brainwash all the Kree to the Phalanx cause. When Ronan learned the alternative to the brainwashing was the Phalanx phasing the entire galaxy into oblivion, killing all trapped within, he finally submitted to the assimilation devices and became a Select to save his people from that fate. An assault team led by the nameless Kree Wraith (formerly Zak-Del) instead freed the SI and used the psychic echo to kill all Phalanx within range, Ronan found himself spared death due to his leadership abilities being needed by the remaining Kree to defeat the Phalanx. With the aid of Wraith, Super-Skrull, Praxagora, and resistance leader Ra-Venn, Ronan traveled to the planet Kree-Lar to access the hidden cache of Sentries there to use them to cleanse Hala's surface of all life to rid the Kree homeworld of the invaders. Using the Wraith's Exolon swarms to Phalanx-proof the Sentries and Praxagora's ability to take over other mechanical devices, Ronan launched the Sentries towards Hala, only to have Ultron's consciousness take over Praxagora's body, knocking out Wraith and deactivating his Exolon swarms. Taking control of the Sentries and setting Praxagora up to self-destruct before leaving, Ultron used the Sentries to create a gigantic body for himself and began to rampage through downtown Kree-Lar before a recovered Wraith used his Exolon swarm to trap Ultron's consciousness in that body so Quasar (Phyla-Vell) and Adam Warlock could kill it. The Phalanx now dormant minus Ultron's leadership, and the Kree galaxy now back in phase with the rest of the universe, the Kree have concentrated on once more rebuilding their numbers and strength, though looming interstellar political troubles, including an alliance with the Inhumans, may severely test their society once again.

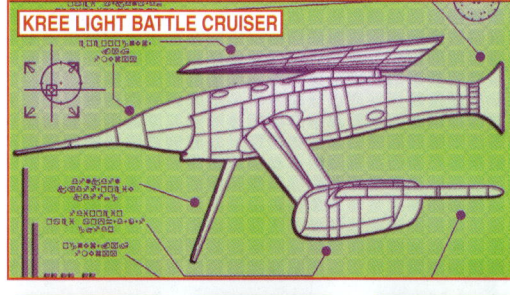

KREE LIGHT BATTLE CRUISER

Art by Eliot R. Brown

MORAG
Ancient Kree tribal leader (deceased)
Avengers #133 (1976)

NENORA
Supreme Leader, killed and replaced by Skrull Agent K6@
Silver Surfer #6 (1987)

PHAE-DOR
Head, Supreme Science Council
Inhumans #3 (1975)

PRIMUS
Leader, Underground Militia
Imperial Guard #1 (1997)

RA-VENN
Phalanx resistance leader
Annihilation: Wraith #1 (2007)

SALLEN-BEI
Keeper of Memory, planet Cyllandra (presumed deceased)
Avengers Strikefile #1 (1994)

SRO-HIMM
Admiral, Kree Military; Lunatic Legion member
Captain Marvel #37 (1975)

STAAK THE EVOLVER
Member, the Evolvers (top-ranked assassins)
Thing: Freakshow #3 (2002)

STUG-BAR
Bo'sun, Kree Military; the Starstealth
Force Works #1 (1994)

SUPREME INTELLIGENCE
Cyberorganic Ruler
Fanatstic Four #65 (1967)

TALLA-RON
First Officer to Galen-Kor, Kree Military; Lunatic Legion
Avengers #365 (1993)

TAR-RELLL
Primary Espionage Unit Captain
Silver Surfer #5 (1987)

TAR-VASH
Commander, Kree Military
Defenders #8 (2001)

TARNOK-KOL
Major, Kree Military
Inhumans: The Great Refuge #1 (1995)

TSU-ZANA
(Suzy Sherman, Ultragirl) Fashion model, super hero
Ultragirl #1 (1996)

ULTIMUS
Kree Eternal, Starforce
Wonder Man #7 (1992)

UNA
Medic, Kree Military (deceased)
Marvel Super-Heroes #12 (1968)

UNA-ROGG
Criminal exile
Captain Marvel #12 (2000)

VRON-IKKA
Major, Kree Military; espionage agent
Avengers Spotlight #25 (1989)

WRAITH
Nameless Kree, formerly Zak-Del
Annihilation: Conquest Prologue #1 (2007)

YON-ROGG
Colonel, Kree Military (deceased)
Marvel Super-Heroes #12 (1968)

ZAREK
Former Kree Imperial Minister; Lunatic Legion leader
Marvel Super-Heroes #12 (1967)

ZEN-PRAM
Kree Military Colonel (deceased)
Untold Tales of Captain Marvel #1 (1997)

ZEY-ROGG
Kree Consolidated Peace Battalion leader
Captain Marvel #2 (1996)

KRO

REAL NAME: Kro (possibly not his original name)
ALIASES: Warlord Kro, Brother Kro, Agent 6, Rudolph Hendler, "Pluto," "Satan," "the Devil"
IDENTITY: Kro's existence is known to the general public of Earth, which, however, tends not to believe he is a Deviant or that Deviants exist
OCCUPATION: Monarch of the Deviants; former warlord and general of the Deviant armies, former dictator of Prussland
CITIZENSHIP: Deviant Lemuria
PLACE OF BIRTH: Deviant Lemuria
KNOWN RELATIVES: Donald and Deborah Ritter (children)
GROUP AFFILIATION: Ruling elite of the Deviants, Delta Force
EDUCATION: Unrevealed
FIRST APPEARANCE: (Rudolph Hendler) Red Raven Comics #1 (1940); (Kro) Eternals #1 (1976)

HISTORY: Kro is a member of the subspecies of humanity known as the Deviants, the result of genetic experiments by the enigmatic Celestials. Born over 20,000 years ago, Kro possesses a lifespan far greater than the typical member of his species. Because his human-like appearance is looked down upon by average Deviants, and to protect himself from dissection by curious scientists, Kro began pretending he was his own descendant, making subtle alterations to his appearance and concocting false backgrounds so that, through guile, he could survive for thousands of years. At some point, Kro met Thena, a member of another subspecies, the godlike Eternals. Kro was attracted to Thena and invited her to visit the Deviants' home Lemuria, but the visit ended unhappily, and Thena did not see him again until last century, believing that he had been killed.

During the 1940s, Kro engineered multiple schemes against humanity, and utilized various identities in order to move amongst humans. As Rudolph Hendler, he became dictator of the European nation Prussland, but his activities were discovered by Zuras, leader of the Eternals. Zuras dispatched Makkari, who assumed the guise of Mercury (later Hurricane) to oppose Kro. "Hendler"'s rule over Prussland was ended by Makkari, as were later schemes of Kro such as allying himself with New York mobs, and spreading plagues in Brazil. In the 1950s, Kro began to utilize a number of mutates (genetically engineered creatures bred by the Deviants) in plots to destabilize earthly nations, and also provided sophisticated weapons to Soviet agents to further the chaos. After Kro sent the mutate Gorgilla to attack New York, Makkari (as Hurricane) brought in his allies the Monster Hunters to halt Gorgilla. When the Monster Hunters returned Gorgilla to its home in Borneo, Kro attacked them with the mutate Lizard Men and kidnapped Hurricane, bringing him back to Monster Island, the breeding ground for many of the mutates. The Monster Hunters rescued Hurricane and forced Kro to abandon his Monster Island base, later adopted by the Mole Man.

Kro was eventually given the position of warlord among the Deviant military forces. Learning an Eternal known as Pixie was a member of the First Line super-hero team, Kro led a group of Deviant warriors to attack the First Line's base at the Carmody Institute; however, they were driven off. Kro later encountered Thena again, and revealed to her how he had survived for so many centuries. Thena and Kro fell in love, but after a night of intimacy, Thena left him. Discovering later that she was pregnant, Thena placed the twin embryos within the womb of a barren woman, and the children were raised as humans under the names Donald and Deborah Ritter.

When the Celestials' Fourth Host was due to arrive on Earth, Kro was charged with preventing the Eternals from sending a greeting to welcome them back to Earth. Kro led a military team to the City of the Space Gods, a structure built in Peru when the Celestials had last visited a thousand years earlier, but the Eternal Ikaris succeeded in activating the cosmic beacon, which led the Fourth Host to Earth. Fearful of what the Host might do to their people, the Deviant ruler Brother Tode had Kro assume the guise of "the Devil" and lead the Deviants in an attack on New York City, hoping to rile up humanity to attack the Celestials for them. The Deviants did expose the Celestials' existence to humanity, but the Eternals intervened and prevented the humans from acting. Thena was able to obtain a temporary truce between the Eternals and Deviants.

Kro invited Thena back to Lemuria with him again and introduced her to Ransak the Reject, a Deviant gladiator who was human in appearance. Believing that Ransak might be the key to genetic stability for the Deviants, Kro transferred him to Thena's charge for protection. Thena also took the gentle-hearted but physically monstrous Deviant Karkas with her to Olympia. Lemuria was subsequently struck by the Celestial Jemiah the Analyzer, who nearly destroyed the city while examining it. Kro helped establish a Deviant outpost called "New Lemuria" beneath New York, but it

Art by Paul Smith

was discovered by the Eternals and their godly ally Thor, and it was ultimately abandoned and destroyed.

Art by Jack Kirby
AS SATAN

After the Fourth Host slew Zuras, Brother Tode and Warlord Kro led an invasion of Olympia, taking the entire city captive; however, Iron Man (Jim Rhodes) came to the Eternals' rescue, and all of the Deviant invaders were taken prisoner. Although the Deviants were reshaped into a giant block by the Eternals and sent into space, Kro avoided this fate by placing a brain mine on Thena that made her susceptible to his influence, causing her to set him free. Returning to Lemuria, Kro competed for Brother Tode's now-empty throne, and the priesthood's leader Ghaur permitted Kro to ascend to leadership, but made it clear that the true power lay with the priesthood. Ghaur dispatched Kro to lead the Deviants in a raid on the Pyramid of the Winds where a vial containing the essence of the inert Dreaming Celestial was contained. Alerted to the intrusion, Ikaris fought Kro, but Thena intervened and spared Kro from almost certain death. Thena and Kro went on the run from their respective peoples, but when they attempted to contact Kro's underground allies in Lemuria, they were taken prisoner by the priesthood. They eventually freed themselves, Kro helped Lemuria's populace rise up against the priesthood, and Ghaur died trying to awaken the Dreaming Celestial.

Kro continued to serve as the Deviants' ruler, and at one point was tricked by the High Evolutionary into starting a war with Atlantis intended to eliminate both of their species. The Avengers helped the two races learn how they had been deceived, and they assisted the Avengers against the High Evolutionary's forces. Kro later gave up the throne and retired to the Pyramid of the Winds, but when he learned his twin children's lives were imperiled by what seemed to be a prophecy of their evil, he came to the aid of Thena and the other Eternals in saving Donald and Deborah's lives; the entity behind the false prophecies was ultimately exposed as Dr. Daniel Damian, a one-time ally of Ikaris who had been driven mad with grief over his daughter's death. Thena and Kro revealed to Donald and Deborah that they were their true parents.

Kro later became affiliated with the US government, and set up a database called the Delta Network, which sought to aid Deviants seeking to integrate with human society. When the Avengers were captured in Lemuria by the priesthood, Sersi the Eternal enlisted Kro's aid, and he assembled Deviants from the Delta Network into "Delta Force," even recruiting Donald and Deborah for his mission. Invading Lemuria, they found that the priesthood had revived Ghaur. Although the Avengers were rescued, Ghaur assumed leadership of the Deviants. Not long afterward, Donald and Deborah were sought by the Weird Sisters and Maelstrom's Minions, who were attempting to revive their master Maelstrom by using Deviant energies. Kro attempted to shelter Donald and Deborah from their pursuers, but ultimately the Eternals and Fantastic Four saved them. Donald and Deborah were imperiled yet again when Ghaur used them and captive Eternals in an attempt to forge an "Anti-Mind" which would

Art by Sal Buscema

assault the Celestials. Kro led a resistance team of Deviants against Ghaur, and was aided by members of Heroes for Hire. Thena took custody of the children and kept them in safety among the Heroes for Hire while Kro continued to battle Ghaur.

Kro eventually regained his position as ruler of the Deviants, with Ghaur retaining power over the priesthood. When Ghaur's secret daughter and mate surfaced in Wakanda, he threatened a war with that country's ruler the Black Panther, who refused to surrender them. Kro was incensed with the Black Panther for involving the Deviants in the conflict, but ultimately war was averted when it was realized that revealing the identities of the contested Deviants could topple Ghaur's position. When the time traveler Kang the Conqueror tried to conquer the Earth and offered to share power with those who conquered territory in his name, a rogue band of Deviant warriors led by General Dulpus invaded China, but were ultimately driven off by the Avengers. Kro thanked the Avengers for their aid against rogue elements and offered to return the favor should they need one. When Kang assaulted Washington, DC, the Avengers called in their favor, and placed the US president in Kro's protective custody. Kro returned the president to the Avengers after Kang was ultimately driven out of their time period. Kro was last seen among the many champions who gathered to combat the threat of Thanos the Mad Titan, who destroyed and re-created the universe with the power of the Heart of the Infinite.

Art by Jack Kirby

HEIGHT: 6'5"
WEIGHT: 320 lbs.
EYES: Red
HAIR: Bald (with black facial hair)

ABILITIES/ACCESSORIES: Kro possesses a virtually unbreakable mental control over the processes and structure of his body, even when he is asleep or unconscious. As a result, he has lived for over 20,000 years, is immune to disease and aging, can heal injuries swiftly, and possesses superhuman strength. Additionally, his body tissue is physically malleable, enabling him to reshape it into other configurations so that he can pass for a human, or fashion a pair of horns atop his head. Further, his heart is not located within his thoracic cavity; its exact location is unrevealed.

Kro has access to various sophisticated Deviant weapons, including vessels such as raiding crafts that contain powerful energy weapons and can travel underwater or defy gravity. He has wielded various hand weapons including flame-guns, vibro-whips and shroud-guns. Like many Deviants, he uses brain mines (devices which can stun Eternals) when battling Eternals. He has also wielded a pair of gauntlets that fire force beams from their fingertips powerful enough to hurt an Eternal. He sometimes wears a pair of glasses that grant him vision in the infrared and ultraviolet spectrums.

POWER GRID	1	2	3	4	5	6	7
INTELLIGENCE							
STRENGTH							
SPEED							
DURABILITY							
ENERGY PROJECTION							
FIGHTING SKILLS							

KRONANS

KNOWN MEMBERS: Ahna, Gorr, Korg, Margus, O-Korg, Zardok
BASE OF OPERATIONS: Planet Ria, Krona star system, Milky Way galaxy; outpost on Iapetus, moon of Saturn
FIRST APPEARANCE: Journey into Mystery #83 (1962)

TRAITS: Kronans are a silicon-based extraterrestrial species. Their stone-like hides are highly resistant to cold and heat. Kronans consume sedimentary rocks such as coal and shale for sustenance, and have no apparent biological need for food, water, oxygen, or sunlight. Within an Earth-like environment, the average full-grown Kronan can lift approximately 100 tons, and has a life expectancy measured in centuries. Reproduction occurs when two males sear their hands together in the lava of Mount Krona; after days of fasting and singing, the fused hands snap off, creating a new Kronan. Kronans' tear glands appear to produce a red blood-like fluid. Kronans can place themselves into suspended animation in which they retain a limited sense of their environment. Kronans are virtually unkillable unless their bodies are shattered or ground into dust.

The Kronan civilization is space-capable, utilizing an anti-gravity device called the gravitron for interstellar travel. They have also created robots, including the Mechano-Monster and Mekkanoid, and have constructed force fields, disintegration pistols ("astro-blasters") and devices that generate sophisticated holographic illusions.

HEIGHT: 8' (average)
WEIGHT: 2,000 lbs. (average)
EYES: Two; hazel
SKIN: Orange or brown

KORG

HISTORY: The Kronans are a military dictatorship whose attempts to expand their Empire have met with limited success. Around 3,000 BC, their Earth invasion force in Mesopotamia was repulsed by Gilgamesh (the Eternal known as the Forgotten One) and the time-traveling Captain America (Steve Rogers).

In recent times, the Kronans established an outpost on Iapetus, a moon of Saturn, earning them the nickname "Stone Men of Saturn." An invasion force that included brothers Korg and Margus landed in Norway, but their arrival was witnessed by Dr. Donald Blake (a human form which Thor had been placed in by his father Odin) and the time-traveling Captain America (Steve Rogers). Blake fled from the Kronans and discovered in a nearby cave the hammer Mjolnir, which caused him to rediscover his true identity as Thor. Thor overpowered the Kronans and their greatest weapons, and the Kronan fleet fled the Earth, fearful that there could be others as powerful as Thor.

One of the fleeing vessels crashed into an asteroid and was separated from the fleet, stranded alone in space. Unable to make repairs, the crew placed themselves into suspended animation. When the asteroid was visited by the ship Star-Jammer, piloted by Thor and his fellow Asgardians while on a quest, the Kronans awoke and attempted to steal the Star-Jammer. Thor overcame the Kronans, destroying both their ship and the asteroid. Another Kronan vessel, which numbered Korg and Margus among its crew, was likewise stranded, and eventually conquered a Kree settlement in order to repair their ship; however, the ship was caught in the Great Portal, a space warp which brought them to the planet Sakaar, and the crew was separated in the crash.

Kronans were also involved in the consortium of extraterrestrials who attempted to negotiate the rights for the biography of Rick Jones, hoping that the book would reveal how Jones had once used the Destiny Force to halt the Kree-Skrull War, but the book was of no use to the assembled buyers. The Kronan mercenary Zardok served as a member of the Starblasters, an intergalactic band of pirates. He aided the Starblasters in the kidnapping of Kayla Ballantine, host of the Star Brand, and journeyed with the crew to the Stranger's laboratory world to have the Star Brand analyzed, but Kayla's lover Quasar assembled a team of Earth heroes to recover her, and the Russian god Perun apparently slew Zardok in combat. Some of the Kronans formed an alliance with the New Immortals, rogue creations of the High Evolutionary. They led an assault against the High Evolutionary's fortress at Mount Wundagore, but were defeated by Thor and the High Evolutionary's newest creations, the Godpack.

Back on Sakaar, the Kronans were fitted with pain-inducing obedience disks and made to serve the forces of the planet's ruler, the Red King. Margus and other Kronans fought the disks, and suffered massive brain damage that made them virtual zombies. Korg was selected for training as a gladiator, and was placed in a team consisting of the Hulk (Bruce Banner), Miek, Hiroim, Elloe Kaifi, Lavin Skee, and a Brood. Korg wound up having to combat Margus and his fellow Kronans in a training session, and was forced to destroy Margus and the others to save his own life. The other gladiators who fought alongside Korg eventually chose to become "warbound" after one of their number, Lavin Skee, was slain defending their lives. Acknowledging the Hulk as their leader, Korg and the other Warbound fought by his side in gladiator matches until the Silver Surfer released them from their obedience disks. The Warbound became leaders of a rebellion, and ultimately toppled the Red King and installed the Hulk as the planet's new ruler. A trusted adviser to the Hulk, Korg was among the few who escaped Sakaar's destruction in a subsequent cataclysm partially enabled by the treacherous Miek. Believing this the work of Earth's heroes, Hulk and the Warbound came to Earth to wage war against them, but were defeated. Korg and the remaining Warbound soon found themselves trying to protect the gamma-irradiated town of Stoneridge, New Mexico (aka Gammatown) from the machinations of the Leader (Sam Sterns).

Art by Aaron Lopresti with Kyle Baker (inset)

KURRGO

HISTORY: Kurrgo was the ruler of the Xantha. While his race was far older than humanity and possessed advanced technology, they were helpless to stop an immense asteroid (allegedly an erratic planet) that was set on a collision course with their planet, threatening them with imminent doom. Having never had an interest in space travel, the Xantha only had two starships, one of which was a smaller saucer purchased from the Skrulls, and they had no means to construct others to carry the entire race of five billion to safety in time.

Having observed the human scientist Reed Richards via his long-range scanners, Kurrgo determined that Richards might save the Xantha. Using the Skrull saucer, Kurrgo sent his robot to Earth, where it used his "Hostility Ray" to turn the population of Washington DC against the Fantastic Four, who were speaking there. Playing on the team's paranoia about people accepting their new powers, the robot convinced them that they were no longer welcome on Earth, and convinced them to go to Planet X (Xanth) for sanctuary.

Kurrgo convinced the arriving FF to save his race or perish along with them. Richards used the Xanth equipment to manufacture large amounts of Dr. Henry Pym's "Pym Particle" reducing gas. This enabled the entire population to fit inside the larger ship and escape their planet's destruction. Reed gave Kurrgo the enlarging gas to be used to allow them to return to normal size when they reached their new destination. However, Kurrgo's hunger for power got the better of him — thinking that once on the new planet, he could be the only one to return to normal size, enabling him to become absolute ruler, Kurrgo attempted to keep the giant capsule to himself. But he was not able to carry the capsule to the ship in time, and was left behind as the planet began to undergo massive earthquakes; Richards later revealed that he was not able to create any enlarging gas, and that the second capsule had been empty. He figured that since size was all relative, being tiny on their new planet would not matter.

Having never used the shrinking gas on himself, Kurrgo survived, rescued by his loyal robot who carried him to a hidden spacecraft, and they narrowly escaped Xanth's destruction. Kurrgo searched for years before finally locating New Xanth in what they had named the "New Jatskan" system. However, the Xantha had greatly progressed technologically and they drove off the relatively giant Kurrgo and his robot. Swearing revenge, Kurrgo traveled to Earth, planning to take the world's strongest being, the Thing, as his servant and force him to help overcome the Xantha. Upon arriving on Earth, Kurrgo soon learned that the Hulk

KURRGO'S ROBOT
Art by Jack Kirby

REAL NAME: Kurrgo
ALIASES: Master of Planet X
IDENTITY: No dual identity
OCCUPATION: Former ruler of Xantha
CITIZENSHIP: Formerly Xanth
PLACE OF BIRTH: Xanth, first from the sun in the Jatskan system, Milky Way galaxy
KNOWN RELATIVES: None
GROUP AFFILIATION: None
EDUCATION: Unrevealed
FIRST APPEARANCE: Fantastic Four #7 (1962)

was now Earth's strongest being. When Kurrgo attempted to enlist the Hulk, he encountered resistance from the gamma-mutated Leader (then having been paralyzed by a Brain-Wave Booster), who wished to use the Hulk for his own plots.

Rather than battle each other, Kurrgo and the Leader agreed to direct the Thing and the Hulk into battle, with each acting as champion to the respective villain; to the winner would go the services of both monsters, as well as the scientific knowledge of the loser. The Thing and Hulk were teleported to a ghost town in the American Southwest, and the Thing was duped into believing an "Ultrex Bomb" was planted in the other end of the city, which would detonate in less than 30 minutes and destroy the entire planet. The Hulk blamed the Thing for the teleportation and attacked him, while the Thing fought to overcome the Hulk to stop the bomb. However, unbeknownst to all involved, Kurrgo was secretly beaming energy to the Thing, doubling his power. Ultimately, the Thing destroyed the bomb, but learned it was a fake, while the battle remained unresolved. The Thing and Hulk were brought aboard Kurrgo's ship, where the Thing realized Kurrgo had been enhancing his power, which caused the Leader to claim victory by default. Kurrgo sent his robot after the Hulk and Thing, who smashed it back into the ship's control panel, overloading it. The Hulk and Thing jumped ship, which then exploded. Kurrgo's fate is unrevealed.

HEIGHT: 4'5" **EYES:** Yellow
WEIGHT: 130 lbs. **HAIR:** Dark gray

ABILITIES/ACCESSORIES: As his planet's ruler, Kurrgo possessed advanced technology a thousand years past Earth's. He controlled a super-strong (Class 75) robot and used atomic scanners, emotion-controlling and power-amplifying rays, anti-gravity and space warp travel.

POWER GRID	1	2	3	4	5	6	7
INTELLIGENCE							
STRENGTH							
SPEED							
DURABILITY							
ENERGY PROJECTION							
FIGHTING SKILLS							

Art by Jack Kirby

KYLUN

REAL NAME: Colin McKay
ALIASES: None
IDENTITY: Secret
OCCUPATION: Adventurer
CITIZENSHIP: UK
PLACE OF BIRTH: Edinburgh, Scotland, UK
KNOWN RELATIVES: Sa'tneen (chosen lifemate, deceased), Ai'sha (lifemate's mother, deceased), unidentified parents, unidentified cousins
GROUP AFFILIATION: MI-13; formerly Excalibur
EDUCATION: Primary school (unfinished); trained as a warrior
FIRST APPEARANCE: (Colin McKay) Excalibur #2 (1988); (Kylun) Excalibur #43 (1991)

HISTORY: Colin McKay was seven when the crimelord Vixen had him kidnapped from his home outside Edinburgh. Escaping, he hid in a derelict factory on the shores of Loch Daemon, where, scared and lonely, he chanced upon the robotic Widget, making an instant friend. When the Vixen's men followed, Widget sent Colin through a portal to another reality. Colin re-appeared on the ice plains of Ee'rath (Earth-148) and was taken to the exiled Royal Household of Queen Ai'sha, recently deposed by the evil mage Necrom. The benevolent witch-queen entrusted Colin to the mystic Zz'ria, who trained him as a warrior. Over the next twenty years, an increasingly leonine Colin became known as Kylun while developing his mutant talent for sound mimicry and pledging his heart to the sorceress Princess Sa'tneen, Ai'sha's daughter. Fearing the queen's growing army, Necrom launched a surprise attack. Most were slain or captured; badly wounded, Kylun was left for dead. Recovering, he rescued Sa'tneen and they rallied an army, gradually driving the tyrant's men back to the Dark Citadel, Necrom's last stronghold. Penetrating this bastion, the lovers confronted Necrom, who attacked them with the zombified remains of their world's greatest heroes, Excalibur. Sa'tneen neutralized the zombies by attacking Necrom, who killed her. She died in the arms of Kylun, who pursued the fleeing Necrom through a door, emerging in the lighthouse of Earth-616's Excalibur team. Confronting Excalibur member Nightcrawler (Kurt Wagner), Kylun mistook him for a demon and attacked him, but realized his mistake after his mystic blades proved unable to hurt the virtuous Nightcrawler. Widget's arrival confirmed that Kylun had returned to his own Earth, though the time-rate differential between worlds meant only a year had passed since his departure, and that Necrom had arrived there a month earlier.

Kylun teamed with Excalibur to fight Necrom, his blades proving to be one of the few effective weapons against the mage. After Necrom's defeat, Kylun elected to stay with the team, fighting the time-manipulating assassin Sidestep and the early X-Men (or alternate dimensional counterparts), and helping to investigate the Crazy Gang's bizarre Wonderland. Still brooding over his lost love, Kylun returned to Scotland in search of his family, but on his parents' doorstep, before he could ring the doorbell, he was assaulted and kidnapped by Warpie agents of RCX (the Resources Control Executive). Taken to their base, Cloud Nine, he and other similarly abducted Excalibur allies were held in stasis until Nightcrawler freed them. Back with Excalibur, he helped the extra-dimensional warrior Khaos defeat the evil Ghath, traveled to Earth-811 to assist its surviving heroes in overthrowing the ruling Sentinel regime, and joined in trying to rescue his teammate Cerise after she was apprehended for war crimes by the Shi'ar.

Finally locating his parents, Kylun left Excalibur to move back in with them. He later attended the Otherworld wedding of his teammates Captain Britain (Brian Braddock) and Meggan. When most of Earth's mutant population was depowered by the reality-warping Scarlet Witch, Kylun was one of the few to retain his abilities. Like other British heroes, he was drafted into MI-13 during the Skrull invasion.

HEIGHT: 5'11"
WEIGHT: 170 lbs.
EYES: Red slit pupils with yellow irises
HAIR: Orange

ABILITIES/ACCESSORIES: Kylun can precisely reproduce any sound he hears. He is an exceptionally skilled swordsman. His mystic blades, forged by Zz'ria, can dissipate demonic forces, disrupt magic, and slice through the hardest steel with ease, but will pass through the pure and virtuous without causing any harm.

POWER GRID	1	2	3	4	5	6	7
INTELLIGENCE							
STRENGTH							
SPEED							
DURABILITY							
ENERGY PROJECTION							
FIGHTING SKILLS							

RAMA KALIPH

REAL NAME: Rama Kaliph
ALIASES: None
IDENTITY: No dual identity
OCCUPATION: Sorcerer, teacher, antiquarian
CITIZENSHIP: Egypt
PLACE OF BIRTH: Alexandria, Egypt
KNOWN RELATIVES: None
GROUP AFFILIATION: None
EDUCATION: Extensive studies of sorcery
FIRST APPEARANCE: Strange Tales #136 (1965)

HISTORY: Rama Kaliph was a powerful sorcerer and ally of Dr. Stephen Strange. He was served in Egypt by his apprentice, the adept Abu Ben Hakim. When Strange's foe Baron (Karl) Mordo obtained power from the demonic Dormammu, Strange's mentor the Ancient One directed him to discover the secret of Eternity. Strange inquired after Eternity among many of his fellow mystics, but by the time he reached Kaliph, Mordo had beaten him there and cast a spell of silence over him to prevent his aiding Strange. When Mordo was ultimately defeated, Kaliph was released from the spell. During a later fight with Dormammu that threatened to engulf the entire Earth, Strange's disciple Clea contacted Kaliph for assistance, but he lacked the power needed to combat Dormammu. Nevertheless, Kaliph alerted other mystic allies of Dr. Strange, including Lord (Julian) Phyffe, Count Carezzi and Turhan Barim, and the foursome journeyed to Strange's Sanctum Sanctorum to render whatever assistance they might offer. Rama Kaliph and Lord Phyffe remained at the Sanctum in the weeks that followed, doing their best to assist Strange against Eternity, and the duo saved Strange from a demon claiming to be Satan (presumably Mephisto) by performing an exorcism. Kaliph and Lord Phyffe ultimately left the Sanctum, and returned to their own matters. Some time later, Kaliph journeyed to Casablanca, Morocco to purchase a rare Assyrian artifact for his collection, but was struck down by an enchanted dagger wielded by the anti-mystic Silver Dagger. Strange arrived too late to save his friend, but retrieved the dagger from Rama Kaliph's body to aid him in ultimately halting Silver Dagger's kill spree.

Art by Steve Ditko

HEIGHT: 5'11" **WEIGHT:** 158 lbs. **EYES:** Brown **HAIR:** Gray

ABILITIES/ACCESSORIES: Rama Kaliph was an aged man with diminished physical abilities, but was among the most learned of all sorcerers on Earth. He possessed extensive knowledge of mystic lore, and demonstrated telepathy and the skill of performing exorcisms.

INTELLIGENCE: 4 **STRENGTH:** 1 **SPEED:** 1 **DURABILITY:** 2
ENERGY PROJECTION: 6 **FIGHTING SKILLS:** 1

KHAOS

REAL NAME: Khaos
ALIASES: None
IDENTITY: Publicly known on Irth
OCCUPATION: Ruler of Irth; adventurer, mercenary
CITIZENSHIP: Terr'va
PLACE OF BIRTH: Irth (Earth-9339)
KNOWN RELATIVES: Unidentified parents, unidentified adoptive parents
GROUP AFFILIATION: Allied with Longstrider, Kromm, Kamendae, Quarto
EDUCATION: Unrevealed
FIRST APPEARANCE: Excalibur Annual #1 (1993)

HISTORY: The royal dark elf Khaos was stolen as an infant to be raised by fair elven royalty. Becoming a mercenary alongside half-elf swordsman Kromm, human archer Longstrider and elven technowizards Kamendae and Quatro, Khaos eventually learned his true destiny: to end the eternal war between Irth's many technomystical races. He succeeded, but the human archmage Ghath attacked Khaos and was inadvertently sent to Earth-616. Khaos selected a volunteer to go kill Ghath, but the spell malfunctioned, sending Khaos instead. The British team Excalibur of Earth-616 followed Ghath and Khaos back to Irth, where Ghath had already gathered his forces for a final assault on Khaos. Excalibur and Khaos' followers defeated Ghath's forces, but when Excalibur returned home, Khaos was accidentally exiled as well. Declining Excalibur membership, Khaos decided to try re-creating Ghath's original teleportation spell to return to his native world and keep it from falling once more into eternal war.

Art by Chris Marrinan

HEIGHT: 5'10" **WEIGHT:** 155 lbs. **EYES:** Light yellow **HAIR:** Light gray

ABILITIES/ACCESSORIES: Khaos is a skilled fighter and tactician, focusing his innate magical powers through his paraphernalia. He carries a teknomagical monkey statue called IBIC that fires energy bolts, channels energies for spellcasting, and analyzes other magical items and spells. Khaos uses two teknomagical swords that can cut through energy, and can be mentally summoned from across a room. Khaos flies using teknomagical metal wings stored in his backpack.

INTELLIGENCE: 2 **STRENGTH:** 3 **SPEED:** 3 **DURABILITY:** 2
ENERGY PROJECTION: 4 **FIGHTING SKILLS:** 4

KNICKKNACK

REAL NAME: Nick Grossman
ALIASES: None
IDENTITY: Known to authorities
OCCUPATION: Juggler, mercenary, assassin
CITIZENSHIP: USA
PLACE OF BIRTH: Unrevealed
KNOWN RELATIVES: None
GROUP AFFILIATION: Death-Throws
EDUCATION: Unrevealed
FIRST APPEARANCE: (Profile) Official Handbook of the Marvel Universe Deluxe Edition #3 (1986); (full) Captain America #317 (1986)

HISTORY: Known for his juggling prowess, Knickknack was recruited into the costumed mercenary Death-Throws team by its organizer and leader, Ringleader (Charles Last), alongside fellow jugglers Bombshell (Wendy Conrad), and the brothers Oddball and Tenpin (Elton and Alvin Healy); each perfected juggling different items as weapons, with Knickknack focusing on using various different objects, such as knives, chainsaws, and bricks. After successfully completing a commission to rescue Crossfire from police custody before his upcoming trial, they learned he didn't have the money to pay them. Furious, the Death-Throws contacted Hawkeye (Clint Barton) through Captain America (Steve Rogers)' hotline, figuring they could capture the Avenger and hold him for ransom. Hawkeye and Captain America showed up and battled the villains; during the fight Knickknack caught Cap's thrown shield and used it in battle before he was taken down by Hawkeye's wife, Mockingbird. Months later, Crossfire hired several villains, including Bobcat, the Brothers Grimm (Percy and Barton Grimes), Bullet Biker, Mad Dog (Buzz Baxter), Razor-Fist (Douglas Scott) and the Death-Throws to bring him Hawkeye's severed arm. The villains attacked Hawkeye, who survived with help from Mockingbird and the archer Trickshot, who pinned Knickknack to the wall with arrows. Knickknack later attended the AIM Weapons Expo on Boca Caliente before going off the radar for months, during which he was reportedly slain and resurrected by Hydra to act as one of their assassins; many of Hydra's assassins later broke Hydra's control over them. Recently, the Death-Throws reformed with a new Oddball (Orville Bock) and with Crossfire leading them. They were hired by RAID to engage in terrorist attacks on London. They bombed the Tower Bridge before Sabra and Union Jack (Joe Chapman) arrived to stop them; Knickknack was struck by Union Jack's flying car and knocked into the river.

HEIGHT: 5'3"   **WEIGHT:** 150 lbs.   **EYES:** Brown   **HAIR:** Brown

ABILITIES/ACCESSORIES: An expert juggler who specializes in juggling objects of dissimilar sizes and weights, Knickknack is accustomed to juggling dangerous weapons and hurling them with expert precision.

INTELLIGENCE: 2 **STRENGTH:** 2 **SPEED:** 2 **DURABILITY:** 2
ENERGY PROJECTION: 1 **FIGHTING SKILLS:** 5

Art by Paul Neary

KULLA

REAL NAME: Kulla
ALIASES: None
IDENTITY: No dual identity
OCCUPATION: Despot
CITIZENSHIP: Dehnock (aka "Slaveworld")
PLACE OF BIRTH: Dehnock
KNOWN RELATIVES: None
GROUP AFFILIATION: None
EDUCATION: Unrevealed
FIRST APPEARANCE: Tales to Astonish #41 (1963)

HISTORY: Kulla was a despot from the alien dimension Dehnock, aka "Slaveworld." The benevolent people of Dehnock rebelled against him and besieged his fortress. Needing a powerful weapon in order to re-conquer his world, he used Dimension Transporter helmets to enlist the aid of human window washer Ed Marion. In exchange for payment in gold, Marion would break into the laboratories of great scientists, immobilize them with Kulla's "paralysis liquid," and then use the helmets to transfer them to Dehnock. There the scientists were coerced to work on an "electro-death ray," with imprisonment without food or water for days as punishment for resistance or complaints. Among the scientists eventually brought to this Dehnock, however, was Henry Pym, secretly the super hero Ant-Man. Pym deliberately goaded the guards into throwing him into the dungeon, then escaped his cell in his Ant-Man guise, and came to the rescue of his fellow scientists. Kulla and his men spotted the tiny hero, but his size made him difficult to capture, despite their best efforts. Kulla himself finally chased after Ant-Man and doused him in the paralysis liquid; but in doing so, Kulla walked in front of the newly completed electro-death ray. Just then, Ant-Man had insects under his control activate the ray, and it killed Kulla. The insects then opened the gates to Kulla's fortress, and the leaderless troops fell to Kulla's enemies, a more peaceful race. Ant-Man and all of the scientists were returned to Earth, while the corrupt Marion was sent to Dehnock to be rehabilitated.

HEIGHT: 7'   **WEIGHT:** 250 lbs.   **EYES:** Blue   **HAIR:** Black

ABILITIES/ACCESSORIES: Kulla was a cruel tyrant. He used Dimension Transporter helmets (possibly of his own design) which could transport people from Earth to Dehnock, and had access to various laser weapons. He also used a liquid that could paralyze the skeletal muscles of victims, immobilizing them without interfering with their cardiovascular system.

INTELLIGENCE: 2 **STRENGTH:** 2 **SPEED:** 2 **DURABILITY:** 2
ENERGY PROJECTION: 1 **FIGHTING SKILLS:** 2

Art by Don Heck

LACUNA

HISTORY: Born into an extremely wealthy and liberal family, Lacuna sought to become a member of the celebrity mutant mercenary team X-Force, trying to disappoint her anti-establishment parents. While X-Force member U-Go Girl was guest-hosting a popular television talk show, Lacuna appeared uninvited and stripped the X-Force members present down to their underwear on national television before publicly announcing her official candidacy for X-Force membership; however, when X-Force finally offered Lacuna membership, she rejected them, having been offered her own network television show minutes before her membership was to be announced. Lacuna became the host of "Lacuna and the Stars!," a show in which she used her powers to spy on celebrities.

Lacuna kept in touch with X-Force. When they returned to the USA from Japan, she joined them in New York for a parade held in their honor, where mutant terrorist group the Brotherhood staged a failed assassination attempt on X-Force member Doop. After U-Go Girl's death, Lacuna consoled depressed X-Force member Orphan (aka Mr. Sensitive), who was angry that X-Force owner Spike Freeman would not let him rename the team "X-Statix" like U-Go Girl had wanted. After Mr. Sensitive talked about this on Lacuna's show, Freeman let him rename the team "X-Statix" due to positive response to the program. When X-Statix confronted 14-year-old reality-warping mutant Mysterious Fan Boy (Arnie Lundberg), who was terrorizing his Minnesota town, Mr. Sensitive detected his irregular heartbeat and allowed Fan Boy to join the team, hoping that Arnie's weak heart would give out before the media learned his true identity. Lacuna, however, used her powers to expose Fan Boy's identity to the world. Enraged, Mr. Sensitive convinced Lacuna to secretly inject Fan Boy with a fatal dose of poison during a mission (although the rest of the world thought he had died of natural causes). Feeling guilty over this, Lacuna talked about how Mr. Sensitive morally blackmailed her into killing Fan Boy on her show. Shortly afterward, the villain Bad Guy nearly killed Lacuna and destroyed her studio. Lacuna teamed up with X-Statix in an attempt to unmask Bad Guy (who many incorrectly believed was Mr. Sensitive), but the villain's technology prevented her from using her powers.

When mutant Europan pop star Henrietta Hunter returned from the dead and joined X-Statix, Lacuna had her as a guest on her show. After Hunter's social work stole X-Statix's spotlight, Lacuna eavesdropped on X-Statix's plan to kill Hunter and arrived just in time to convince them not to kill her. Lacuna then covered a fashion show that launched Hunter's new clothing line. After Mr. Sensitive rejected Lacuna's romantic advances, a Europan government official gave her papers documenting Freeman's chemical weapon sales to a rogue Middle Eastern nation, which would destroy X-Statix's reputation. Before Lacuna decided whether to go public with the documents, an assassin hired by Freeman

REAL NAME: Woodstock Schumaker
ALIASES: The Eighth X-Static
IDENTITY: Public
OCCUPATION: Talk show host, investigative journalist
CITIZENSHIP: USA
PLACE OF BIRTH: Malibu, California
KNOWN RELATIVES: Calvin and Denise Schumaker (parents)
GROUP AFFILIATION: None
EDUCATION: Unrevealed
FIRST APPEARANCE: X-Force #121 (2001)

shot her. Lacuna survived but fell into a deep coma and was hospitalized, only to be revived by an evangelist on her own show. Claiming to have been healed by the power of prayer, Lacuna returned to television and interviewed X-Statix member Vivisector, who had taken an anti-mutant serum developed by Dr. Alex Finlay.

HEIGHT: 5'7"
WEIGHT: 127 lbs.
EYES: Blue
HAIR: Blonde

ABILITIES/ACCESSORIES: Lacuna can slip out of time. Although incapable of actual time travel, she can move around in the gaps between individual moments in time and interact with her surroundings.

POWER GRID	1	2	3	4	5	6	7
INTELLIGENCE			●				
STRENGTH	●						
SPEED		●					
DURABILITY		●					
ENERGY PROJECTION	●						
FIGHTING SKILLS	●						

Art by Mike Allred

LADY DAEMON

REAL NAME: Megan Daemon
ALIASES: Child of Light
IDENTITY: No dual identity
OCCUPATION: Laird of Scotland's Clan Daemon, adventurer
CITIZENSHIP: UK
PLACE OF BIRTH: Castle Daemon, Sutherland Highlands, Northern Scotland
KNOWN RELATIVES: Lord & Lady Daemon (parents, deceased), Alisabeth Daemon (sister, presumed deceased); unidentified ancestors
GROUP AFFILIATION: Clan Daemon
EDUCATION: Studied occult via sister and ancestral library
FIRST APPEARANCE: Bizarre Adventures #25 (1981)

HISTORY: Megan was born in Castle Daemon in remote Northern Scotland's Sutherland Highlands during 1904's summer solstice, her heritage dating back to when the dark Caledonian forests covered the moors. There had always been magic and dark power in the Highlands, and Clan Daemon had always been a part of it. Megan and her sister, Alisabeth — born in 1900's winter solstice — had few childhood friends and passed time in the manor library, poring over books so archaic that no one was able — or willing — to decipher them. During the first new moon after Alisabeth entered womanhood, she led Megan in an occult ritual and their mother's mutilated corpse was found the next morning. Alisabeth returned to the library, reading with purpose and comprehension; when Megan reached womanhood, Alisabeth led her in a similar ritual, and their father's bloodless corpse was found the following morning. Alisabeth left for the European Continent soon afterwards, though she sent Megan a deck of tarot cards on her 18th birthday. As Megan turned 21, Alisabeth returned to Castle Daemon and fought with the Clan Elders, who then disappeared mysteriously from their beds. Alisabeth departed again at dawn, leaving a Writ of Abdication making Megan officially Lady Daemon. She also left Megan a translucent quartz cat's skull pendant, which helped her progress in her Dark Arts knowledge and the use of her tarot cards.

Over time, Megan turned down many suitors but eventually befriended Ian MacGinnis of the Royal Scots Borderers. In 1937, following a sense of foreboding, Megan and Ian traveled to Stonehenge, where they encountered Alisabeth performing a human sacrifice to unlock the gateway to the Outer Dark and merge with one of its denizens. Megan and Ian suddenly awoke two weeks later (their memories of the previous weeks erased) aboard the Hindenburg about to land in America on May 6, 1937. There Alisabeth planned to open the gateway fully and let those of the Outer Dark into our dimension, but for that, she needed her sister's power and willing cooperation — and the slaughter of many innocent lives. Megan fought Alisabeth, who summoned an emissary from the Outer Dark. Ian shot Alisabeth — as she had planned, but Megan (unlike her sister) refused to be seduced by the Outer Dark and fought off the demons that tried to use her as a vessel; however, the battle started a fire that destroyed the Hindenburg. Alisabeth's burning corpse opened its eyes, telling Megan they were bound by a destiny that would be fulfilled in Megan's lifetime. Megan and Ian safely escaped, and Megan vowed to study black magic so that she could again bar Alisabeth's path when next they met.

ALISABETH DAEMON

HEIGHT: 5'4"
WEIGHT: 100 lbs.
EYES: Green
HAIR: Blonde

ABILITIES/ACCESSORIES: Lady Daemon has extensive occult knowledge, augmented by Castle Daemon's vast, ancient library. She uses tarot cards to divine the future and a crystal cat skull's pendant to focus her abilities. Her power and skill almost certainly increased with experience.

POWER GRID	1	2	3	4	5	6	7
INTELLIGENCE							
STRENGTH							
SPEED							
DURABILITY							
ENERGY PROJECTION							
FIGHTING SKILLS							

Art by Michael Golden

LADY DEATHSTRIKE

HISTORY: The daughter of Kenji Oyama, a former kamikaze pilot during World War II, Yuriko Oyama and her two brothers were tutored in childhood by Marcy Stryker, wife of US soldier William Stryker, who came to love the Oyama children as his own. When they were older, Yuriko and her siblings underwent strict martial arts training and were inflicted with ritual scars by their father, symbolizing his own severe scarring in a failed suicide assault on a US battleship. Becoming the criminal scientist Lord Dark Wind, Kenji developed a method of bonding the virtually indestructible metal Adamantium to human bone, hoping to create super-soldiers to avenge what he perceived as Japan's corruption by the US and others. However, his notes were stolen and their secrets eventually used in the Weapon X program's transformation of mutant spy Logan (aka James Howlett, Wolverine), leaving Dark Wind to spend years redeveloping the process. Although a later theft attempt, by Mystique, her foster daughter Rogue, and others, failed, Dark Wind grew more obsessive and instilled similar fanaticism in his private army, including Kira, the man Yuriko loved.

Following her brothers' deaths in Lord Dark Wind's service, Yuriko, fearing for Kira's safety, developed her own obsession, to avenge her brothers' deaths and the scars, physical and otherwise, their father had inflicted upon all three. Before she could pursue vengeance, however, the assassin Bullseye, injured in a battle with Daredevil (Matt Murdock), was brought to Dark Wind's island base, where Dark Wind replaced the sociopath's broken bones with Adamantium. Dark Wind expected him to, in gratitude, assassinate Japan's minister of trade. When Daredevil arrived in Japan, intent on recapturing Bullseye, Yuriko guided him to her father's island, hoping the pair could destroy both enemies. Following a romantic interlude while hiding from Dark Wind's army, Yuriko and Daredevil penetrated Dark Wind's sanctuary but failed to prevent Bullseye from escaping. Enraged by the betrayals of Yuriko and Bullseye, Dark Wind confronted Daredevil, who, weakened by earlier injuries, was defeated and almost slain before Yuriko slashed her father down his back with her sword, apparently killing him and avenging her brothers.

Following Daredevil's return to the US, Kira committed suicide in despair over Dark Wind's death. Yuriko could find solace only in re-dedicating herself to her father's work, but she focused not on his long-term goals but on his initial achievement, the Adamantium bonding process. Learning of Wolverine's Adamantium skeleton, Yuriko, garbed in samurai armor and calling herself Lady Deathstrike, tracked Wolverine to Canada and led her father's warriors against him, determined to acquire his skeleton for study. Holding her own in battle with Wolverine, she was ultimately defeated by his friend Heather Hudson, who, in her new costumed identity Vindicator, shattered Deathstrike's sword.

With Dark Wind's soldiers apparently abandoning her, Deathstrike resolved to better match Wolverine on his own terms and struck a deal with Donald Pierce and his cyborg mercenaries, the Reavers. With Pierce as a middleman, Deathstrike underwent transformation at the multiple hands of the extradimensional Spiral, whose advanced technology bonded her with Adamantium in ways beyond even her father's process; the ritual scars inflicted by her father were surgically eradicated in the process, effectively erasing Yuriko's last ties to the woman she once was. Now possessing superhuman strength and claws to rival Wolverine's, she led three of Pierce's Reavers — Cole, Macon, and Reese, former Hellfire Club mercenaries with grudges against Wolverine — in an attack on Wolverine, who, despite being outnumbered, defeated all four cyborgs. Appalled that Deathstrike had willingly undergone the transformation that had been forced upon him, Wolverine declined to grant her a mercy killing, cementing a vendetta that would endure for years.

When Wolverine and his X-Men teammates relocated to a former Reavers base in Australia, Deathstrike, her supposed dedication

REAL NAME: Yuriko Oyama
ALIASES: None
IDENTITY: Secret
OCCUPATION: Assassin, CEO of Oyama Heavy Industries and Oyama Design Group; former operative of Reverend William Stryker
CITIZENSHIP: Japan, international criminal record
PLACE OF BIRTH: Osaka, Japan
KNOWN RELATIVES: Kenji Oyama (Lord Dark Wind, father, deceased), unidentified mother (deceased), two unidentified brothers (deceased)
GROUP AFFILIATION: Reavers, Purifiers; formerly Thunderbolts, Donald Pierce's Reavers, private army of Lord Dark Wind
EDUCATION: Unrevealed
FIRST APPEARANCE: (Oyama) Daredevil #197 (1983); (Lady Deathstrike) Alpha Flight #33 (1986)

to Dark Wind's work superseded by sheer vengeance-seeking, accompanied Pierce and his Reavers to ambush him in his teammates' absence. Overwhelming him, they crucified him on an X-shaped cross and left him to die. Wolverine survived the ordeal, however, and was freed by young mutant Jubilee, soon to join the X-Men herself. Learning of her enemy's survival, Deathstrike joined the Reavers in searching for him at the Muir Island mutant research facility, only to be driven off by X-Men

Art by Sean Chen with Sal Buscema & William Johnson (insets)

allies and the government super-team Freedom Force, but not before inflicting casualties on both groups.

After a battle with the Punisher (Frank Castle) and attacks on Hellfire Club property, Deathstrike, growing impatient with Pierce's schemes, struck out on her own and forced the mutant Gateway to teleport her to Wolverine's location, only for Wolverine and herself to be sent back in time to 1937; caught in a Spanish Civil War skirmish, the pair naturally took opposite sides, but during battle they were pulled back into a time vortex, passing major moments in Deathstrike's life before returning to the present. The literal lessons of the past lost on her, Deathstrike, aided by entrepreneur Ronald Parvenue, later tracked Wolverine to New Jersey, as did his far more ferocious enemy Sabretooth. The two villains double-teamed their mutual foe, but the mysterious Hunter in Darkness joined the fray on Wolverine's side, ending the combat.

After the Reavers, among others, were attacked by giant robot Sentinels summoned from the future by Trevor Fitzroy, himself a traveler from the future of Earth-1191, Pierce vowed to rebuild their losses, and Deathstrike, having learned in the interim that Wolverine's Adamantium had been forcibly removed, followed his lead in search of purpose. Pierce sent her to capture Milo Thurman, a former government employee whose remarkable prophetic abilities might foresee future attacks, but his plan to convert Thurman into an enslaved cyborg was opposed by his target's ex-lover, mutant mercenary Domino (aka Neena Thurman). While Deathstrike battled Domino, Pierce downloaded almost 60% of Thurman's consciousness into his own mind before the Reavers' base was destroyed. Dissatisfied with the debacle, Deathstrike again struck out on her own, clashing with Captain America (Steve Rogers) when he visited Japan following his return from an extradimensional exile.

Deathstrike found that feuds with the X-Men were not easily avoided, however, when she was targeted by time-traveler Stryfe, who knew her cybernetic programs contained control codes for creating powerful Sentinels. Pursued by Stryfe's Prime Sentinels, mutant-hunting cyborgs formerly used by Operation: Zero Tolerance, Deathstrike set pride aside and sought help from Wolverine and the X-Men, who defeated Stryfe and returned the Omegas to normal. Although the shared victory led her to consider redemption, Deathstrike was drawn back to her vendetta by Sabretooth, who recruited her and Russian super-soldier Omega Red to attack Wolverine's loved ones in exchange for valuable information. The group crippled Wolverine's friend Yukio and abducted his ward Amiko Kobayashi, luring Wolverine into a trap, but Sabretooth, preferring to keep both vengeance and payment to himself, betrayed his co-conspirators and teleported away with their enemy, who ultimately survived the incident. Turning to outright mercenary work, Deathstrike was again cheated by gangster Nicopetti, but her new vendetta was interrupted when a weary Wolverine offered her an easy opportunity to kill him. Realizing Wolverine's death would destroy what little purpose remained to her, Deathstrike instead killed Nicopetti and his underlings.

With so many other ties to her past cut, Deathstrike reunited with William Stryker, now a minister who led the Purifiers' extremist anti-mutant crusade. More dedicated to Stryker than to his goal, she freed her former mentor from imprisonment and put her industrial resources to the Purifiers' use. While aiding Stryker, however, she was controlled by Paul, a sentient computer entity protective of the mutant community Mount Haven, Washington. Under Paul's control, Deathstrike fought both Purifiers and X-Men, once more dueling Wolverine and, ironically, meeting better success than she ever had on her own. Escaping when Paul's control was broken, she resurfaced after learning of Mystique and Rogue's attempted theft of Dark Wind's secrets, the very secrets that had set her against Wolverine to begin with. This second vendetta in her father's name proved fruitless, however, when she learned the theft had failed, but not before clashing with Rogue, Sunfire (Shiro Yoshida), and Rogue's former associate Blindspot.

Arrested and imprisoned under unrevealed circumstances, Deathstrike was recruited for government service by the Commission on Superhuman Activities during the "Civil War" between US super heroes following passage of the Superhuman Registration Act. In the Thunderbolts, she joined other superhuman criminals in attacking Captain America's anti-SHRA forces. Following Cap's surrender, Deathstrike was re-arrested, but she escaped custody before being transferred to the Negative Zone prison 42. When the Purifiers hunted a potentially powerful mutant baby, Deathstrike, though caring little for their cause, felt honor-bound to slay the infant in honor of Stryker, who had died in the interim. Leading a new army of Reavers, she set her forces against the X-Men and others who sought the child, only to fall in battle with X-23, the altered clone of Wolverine. Paralyzed when her cybernetic systems were disrupted and gutted by X-23's own Adamantium claws, Deathstrike apparently perished, her years of obsession against one recipient of her father's bonding process finally ending at the vengeful hands of another recipient.

HEIGHT: 5'9" **EYES:** Brown
WEIGHT: 128 lbs. **HAIR:** Black

ABILITIES/ACCESSORIES: Lady Deathstrike's cyborg nature granted her sufficient superhuman strength to lift at least one ton, with proportionately enhanced speed, agility, endurance, and reflexes. Her skeleton was laced with molecules of Adamantium, rendering her bones virtually unbreakable, and her fingers replaced by foot-long Adamantium claws, which she could retract to resemble normal fingers or extend to twice their original length. She could convert her fingers into data ports and cybernetically link her consciousness directly into computer systems, allowing her to access information and remotely operate robot bodies. She was a remarkably skilled martial artist, considered an expert in the art of kenjutsu and other samurai warrior skills. She is fluent in both English and Japanese and is an accomplished pilot of various aircraft and seacraft. Prior to her transformation into a cyborg, she wielded a five-foot-long, electromagnetically tempered steel katana. She subsequently used a high-powered long-range blaster that fired armor-piercing explosive bullets, grenades of great explosive force, and a wristband whose instrumentation could detect and track Adamantium.

POWER GRID	1	2	3	4	5	6	7
INTELLIGENCE							
STRENGTH							
SPEED							
DURABILITY							
ENERGY PROJECTION							
FIGHTING SKILLS							

Art by Sean Chen with Ryan Bodenheim (inset)

LADY LIBERATORS

HISTORY: An all-female super-hero team, the Lady Liberators began as a short-lived radical feminist group and was later reorganized as a loose-knit alliance of leading costumed heroines. The original Liberators first assembled as part of a hoax staged by corrupt Asgardian sorceress Amora the Enchantress, a longtime foe of the Avengers. She and her lovestruck pawn Skurge the Executioner had been exiled from Asgard, their powers halved by Odin, when Skurge abandoned Amora for another woman: the other-dimensional queen Casiolena. Vowing all males would suffer for this indignity, Amora made her way to Earth and plotted her return to Asgard, which would restore her powers to their height. Learning that prominent Miskatonic University scientist Dr. T.W. Erwin had invented an experimental parallel-time projector which might be able to send her back to Asgard, Amora sought to steal it. Erwin would be appearing as a guest of honor at the annual Halloween Parade in Rutland, Vermont; the Avengers also agreed to participate in the parade as similarly honored guests, having heard rumors of possible criminal activity at the parade and hoping to prevent it. The criminal Masters of Evil group was indeed plotting Erwin's abduction, so Amora hatched an elaborate plot designed to neutralize both the Avengers and the Masters while secretly targeting Erwin.

Having usurped the physical form of the heroic Valkyrie (Brunnhilde) centuries earlier, Amora disguised herself by inhabiting Brunnhilde's form as the new Valkyrie. Claiming she had gained her powers in a chemical accident while serving as an unappreciated assistant in Erwin's laboratory, "Valkyrie" approached several prominent female adventurers: the prehensile-haired Medusa of the Inhumans; super-spy and longtime Avengers associate Black Widow; the Scarlet Witch, a hex-powered mutant Avengers member; and the size-changing Wasp, an Avengers founder. Holding a meeting at Avengers Mansion, Valkyrie persuaded the four heroines that they were unappreciated by a male-dominated world, and that they were repeatedly overshadowed by their assorted male partners and teammates, who tended to get more publicity and more credit for their victories. Having convinced her recruits of the rightness of her cause, thanks in part to subtle spells of persuasion she had cast to influence them, Valkyrie led her four partners in forming the Liberators, a female super-team dedicated to ending male oppression.

The male Avengers members were at the Rutland parade when the Masters of Evil infiltrated the event, trying to abduct Erwin. The Avengers opposed them, but the Masters had the upper hand in the ensuing battle until the Liberators arrived, helping the Avengers beat the Masters into submission. Before the Avengers could finish thanking their rescuers, the Liberators turned on them, too, subduing the male Avengers and Erwin after a brief struggle. The Liberators took their captives to Miskatonic University, where Valkyrie forced Erwin to produce his experimental parallel-time projector. Revealing her true identity and motivations as she gloated over her success, the victorious Enchantress prepared to kill both the Avengers and the Liberators; but the Scarlet Witch had begun to suspect Amora's true identity, and was ready to counter the Enchantress with her hexes. When the Enchantress cast a spell to destroy the Avengers, the Scarlet Witch reflected it back at Amora,

CURRENT MEMBERS: Black Widow (Natasha Romanoff), Hellcat (Patsy Walker), Invisible Woman (Sue Richards), She-Hulk (Jen Walters), Spider-Woman (Jessica Drew), Storm (Ororo Munroe), Thundra, Tigra (Greer Nelson), Valkyrie (Samantha Parrington)
FORMER MEMBERS: Medusa (Medusalith Boltagon), Scarlet Witch (Wanda Maximoff), Valkyrie (Amora the Enchantress), Wasp (Janet Van Dyne)
BASE OF OPERATIONS: Mobile; formerly Avengers Mansion, Manhattan, New York
FIRST APPEARANCE: (Amora's team) Avengers #83 (1970); (She-Hulk's team) Hulk #7 (2008)

seemingly destroying the Enchantress. Thus ended the battle of the sexes within the Avengers; but when Avengers member Goliath (Clint Barton) opined that the ex-Liberators must have finally learned their lesson about "that Women's Lib bull," the Scarlet Witch and Wasp warned their male chauvinist teammate that the Liberators just might stage a comeback someday.

Years later, veteran adventurer She-Hulk reorganized the Lady Liberators as an informal alliance of heroines to help her hunt down a new, red-skinned Hulk who was terrorizing the superhuman community. Alternate-reality warrior woman Thundra and a new Valkyrie (mortal Samantha Parrington in Brunnhilde's form) formed the core of these new Liberators with She-Hulk for the bulk of that first mission, though six other heroines also participated in the group's final battle with the red Hulk. These new Liberators have reunited on occasion since then. The core trio and Invisible Woman, aided by She-Hulk's Skrull partner Jazinda, joined relief efforts in the earthquake-ravaged country Marinmer despite opposition from that nation's tyrannical ruler Darqon Par and his allies, the Russian super-team Winter Guard. The Liberators even shamed the Winter Guard into joining their relief efforts, thwarting Par's machinations. More recently, She-Hulk, Thundra, Valkyrie, Invisible Woman and Storm were among the many heroines targeted for destruction by composite warrior Unum, a pawn of the cosmic being Enmity, but Unum and Enmity were defeated with the aid of the Collector (Taneleer Tivan), Jazinda and the space-based heroines Gamora, Lyja, Mantis and Quasar (Phyla-Vell).

ORIGINAL LADY LIBERATORS
CLOCKWISE FROM BOTTOM LEFT: BLACK WIDOW, MEDUSA, ENCHANTRESS (AS VALKYRIE), WASP & SCARLET WITCH

Art by John Buscema

FROM LEFT TO RIGHT: THUNDRA, SHE-HULK, VALKYRIE (PARRINGTON) & INVISIBLE WOMAN

Art by Mike Deodato

LADY MASTERMIND

REAL NAME: Regan Wyngarde
ALIASES: Mastermind
IDENTITY: Secret
OCCUPATION: Terrorist; former adventurer
CITIZENSHIP: Unrevealed
PLACE OF BIRTH: Unrevealed
KNOWN RELATIVES: Jason Wyngarde (Mastermind, father, deceased), Martinique Jason (Mastermind, half-sister)
GROUP AFFILIATION: Formerly Marauders, X-Men; former employee of Sebastian Shaw
EDUCATION: Unrevealed
FIRST APPEARANCE: X-Treme X-Men #6 (2001)

HISTORY: Like her sister Martinique Jason, Regan Wyngarde developed powers akin to her father, mutant illusionist Jason Wyngarde, plus minor telepathic abilities. The half-sisters developed an intense hatred for each other as they vied to become the one true heir of their father's former identity Mastermind. Martinique seemingly won their contest, leaving Regan to adopt the identity of Lady Mastermind. Ultimately working for mutant Hellfire Club powerbroker Sebastian Shaw, Regan aided his efforts to usurp control of the Australian criminal underworld. Confronting the then Viceroy, Miles Warbeck, Regan used her powers of illusion to make him believe he was drowning, even though he was in his penthouse suite, and his body responded as if it were actually happening because the illusion was so convincing. Shaw then implicated the mutant thief Gambit in the crime, bringing Gambit's former X-Men teammates to Australia to investigate. Seeing his former aide Tessa among the X-Men's ranks, Shaw bade Regan influence her into working for him again, so Regan subjected Tessa to a series of convincing illusions; however, with her new teammate Lifeguard's aid, Tessa overcame the illusions and reflected Regan's powers back at her, leaving her comatose.

Rogue geneticist Pandemic later kidnapped Regan and experimented on her in his Fordyce Clinic. Liberated by the X-Men, Regan was taken to the Xavier Institute to recuperate. There, Serafina of the Children of the Vault briefly hijacked her powers before Ev Teel Urizen, a mummudrai, an emotional energy parasite, infiltrated her mind. Awakened from her coma by Urizen, Regan learned from the Beast of what had transpired during her incapacitation and was soon recruited into Rogue's team of X-Men to oppose the Children of the Vault. Subsequently investigating the Fordyce Clinic, Regan was chastised by Rogue for her ruthless actions before Pandemic's Plague Dogs attacked the team. Unable to prevent Rogue's capture, Regan and the X-Men followed her to Pandemic's base in India. After Pandemic was depowered and defeated, Regan spitefully trapped his mind in an illusory maze.

While visiting Cable's island Providence with the X-Men, Regan sought a psychotherapist's help in uncovering the intruder within her mind. This incited the mummudrai into briefly possessing her before it moved on to possess Mystique and, finally, Cable. Learning of alien Shi'ar weapon the Hecatomb's imminent arrival, Regan and the X-Men did their best to halt its rampage across Providence until it was destroyed. She then accompanied the X-Men to Rogue's former home in Caldecott County, Mississippi where Regan and Mystique betrayed the X-Men to their longtime foes, the Marauders. Joining the villains, Regan helped them defeat the X-Men, then participated in the Marauders' efforts to retrieve the diaries of the blind mutant seer Destiny before the X-Men could recover them. Regan and the Marauders were subsequently dispatched to Cooperstown, Alaska to recover the first mutant born post-"M-Day," whereupon they fought the anti-mutant Purifiers, who killed Regan's teammates Blockbuster and Prism. The X-Men then attacked her team at their Antarctic base, but the Marauders repelled the assault and abandoned the base. Following the apparent death of Sinister, the Marauders disbanded.

HEIGHT: 5'9" **EYES:** Blue
WEIGHT: 133 lbs. **HAIR:** Blonde

ABILITIES/ACCESSORIES: Lady Mastermind can psionically project illusions into the minds of others, causing them to see, hear, touch, smell and/or taste things which do not actually exist, or to disguise the true appearance of objects or others. Her illusions persist even if she is rendered unconscious. She also has low-level telepathic abilities that enable her to read the thoughts of others, allowing her to cast more convincing illusions by confronting her foes with familiar images, thus inducing their minds and bodies to respond to the illusions as if they were real. Thus, Lady Mastermind's illusions can and have proven fatal. She can shift her own visual perception to see through other's illusions, and is virtually immune to hypnosis. She also wields a pair of handguns.

POWER GRID	1	2	3	4	5	6	7
INTELLIGENCE			✓				
STRENGTH		✓					
SPEED		✓					
DURABILITY		✓					
ENERGY PROJECTION			✓				
FIGHTING SKILLS			✓				

Art by Humberto Ramos

LADY OCTOPUS

HISTORY: Carolyn Trainer's father, geneticist Seward Trainer, raised her to revere scientific research above human life itself. Outraged by his reluctance to pass along his scientific secrets, she grew to hate him and became a fan of nuclear physicist Otto Octavius, whom Seward introduced to her at a lecture. Smitten, Carolyn began stalking Otto when he was out on dates. While in college, Carolyn heard of the accident that made Otto into Dr. Octopus, later visiting him in prison after Spider-Man defeated him. After graduation, Carolyn became an expert on merging virtual reality (VR) with reality. Learning this, Otto asked her to design a computer-generated duplicate to take his place in future battles with Spider-Man. Carolyn encoded Otto's thoughts and memories into the Master Programmer, an interactive task wizard, then tested her interface by turning her secretary Angelina Brancale into the VR super-woman Stunner. Soon after, however, Peter Parker clone Kaine murdered Otto. Carolyn obtained Otto's tentacles, created an interface to mentally control them and became the new Dr. Octopus, taking over his organization.

Seeking to bring the Master Programmer to life, Carolyn learned of her father's work developing an interface between organic matter and VR. She downloaded his data files, using them to adapt her Virtual Wave Generator into a VR bomb that temporarily terrorized Manhattan's Fifth Avenue, but she lacked the access codes to view all data. While forcing the codes from Seward, Carolyn clashed with the Scarlet Spider (Ben Reilly) and Spider-Man (Peter Parker), who ultimately tossed her through a support wall of her underwater hideout. Surviving, Carolyn sought Vytek Lab's experimental cyberneural inductor chips to power her wave generator. Mobster Jason Tso, working for Alistair Smythe, also sought the chips. When Tso attempted to steal Carolyn's VR visor, she blew up the lab that housed it, although the Scarlet Spider retrieved it and Seward used it to enter the techno-subconscious, encountering VR-37, Carolyn's virtual bodyguard, and leaving his mind stranded in cyberspace. Carolyn, meanwhile, hired the Pro to assassinate Tso and cybernetically augmented the Looter, Aura and Override to retrieve the inductors in Tso's possession. The Scarlet Spider thwarted these operations, though the Pro later succeeded. Convinced Scarlet worked for Tso, Carolyn used FBI agent Joe Wade as an organic anchor for a VR Scarlet Spider that terrorized Manhattan, forcing Ben Reilly to give up that identity. Facing

REAL NAME: Carolyn Trainer
ALIASES: Dr. Octopus
IDENTITY: Known to authorities
OCCUPATION: Assistant to Dr. Otto Octavius; former professional criminal, research scientist and virtual reality specialist
CITIZENSHIP: USA with criminal record
PLACE OF BIRTH: Unrevealed
KNOWN RELATIVES: Dr. Seward Trainer (father, deceased)
GROUP AFFILIATION: Assistant to Otto Octavius; formerly head of unidentified organization employing scientists, various "Octo-punks"
EDUCATION: Ph.D. in nuclear physics with multiple degrees in computer science
FIRST APPEARANCE: (Tentacles only) Amazing Spider-Man #405 (1995), (fully seen) Amazing Spider-Man #406 (1995)

Smythe's cyber-slayers, Carolyn plugged into the inductor chip-powered master visor that controlled them, creating hyper-reality and bringing the Master Programmer to life; however, Seward's now-solid VR body passed a virus chip to the Scarlet Spider who destroyed the interface, nearly electrocuting Carolyn. Later, Carolyn attempted to steal Seward's body from the hospital but was defeated by Spider-Man (Reilly) and jailed.

Released from prison, Carolyn learned that the Rose (Jacob Conover) and Master Zei of the True Believers planned to resurrect Octavius. Attaching a handheld interface to Otto during the process, she instilled the Master Programmer's thoughts and memories. Relinquishing the tentacles, Carolyn temporarily became Otto's assistant. Later, however, supplied with new tentacles by the Tinkerer who was financed by Latverian Prime Minister Lucia von Bardas, she became Lady Octopus, fighting alongside other technology-powered criminals until all were injured when von Bardas combined their tech into an anti-matter bomb.

HEIGHT: 5'10"
WEIGHT: 140 lbs.
EYES: Brown
HAIR: Black; formerly dyed purple.

ABILITIES/ACCESSORIES: Carolyn Trainer employed Otto Octavius' mentally-controlled titanium-steel tentacles but added devices providing electroshock, a personal force field, a random pattern program for tentacle strikes, and inputs to plug into the global net. Her Tinkerer-provided tentacles included a strength-boosting harness and body armor. A genius in virtual reality, Carolyn had chips implanted in her brain to access information cybernetically, can download human thoughts and memories into computerized receptacles, and has created interactive VR-based beings. She invented the VR wave generator, the miniaturized prototype VR bomb that appeared to bring the Jurassic Age to life, the reality-merging VR visor, the cyber-construct VR-37, and the handheld interface of the Master Programmer. Her electronics knowledge yielded globe-like robot drones with electrified octopus arms and two android bodyguards. Her henchmen were armed with lasers and equipped with suits that gave off smoke, gas, and high voltage on impact. They used a helicopter with a giant magnet to steal a police van. After relinquishing her tentacles, Carolyn attacked Spider-Man with a stick.

POWER GRID	1	2	3	4	5	6	7
INTELLIGENCE					■		
STRENGTH		■					
SPEED	■						
DURABILITY		■					
ENERGY PROJECTION		■					
FIGHTING SKILLS		■					

Art by Angel Medina with Joe Bennett & Gabriele Dell'Otto (insets)

LARVAL EARTH (SPIDER-HAM)

CORE CONTINUUM DESIGNATION: Earth-8311
SIGNIFICANT INHABITANTS: Ant Ant, Asinine Torch, Awful Flight (Aroma, Cardigan, Heather, Hockeypuck, Nerdstar, Snow-Youse, Summersquash/Walrus Lamebrainski, Trinket/Elizabeth Twodead-animals), Baron Zebro, Bee-Dazzler, Black Catfish, Captain Americat (Steve Mouser), Chickenstein's Monster, Croak & Badger, Croctor Strange (Steamin Strange), Deerdevil (Batt Burdock), Dr. Octopussycat, Dragon-Lassy (Joan Collie), Ducktor Doom, Fantastic Fur (Invisible Gorilla, Mooster Fantastic, Simian Torch, Thang/Ben Grizzly), Nick Furry, Galactypus, Goose Rider, Hobgobbler, Hulk-Bunny (Bruce Bunny), Iron Mouse, J. Jonah Jackal, Junior Newsboys (J. Jeremiah Jackal, Jr., Bunsen Bunny, Upton Adam Stray), Kangaroo the Conqueror, Kingpig, Larval Zombie #1 (Jim Salamander), Mad Stinker, Magsquito, Micro-Newts, Nagneto, Froggy Nelson, Paste Pot Peep, May Porker, Punfisher (Frank Carple), Sandmanatee, Scavengers (Black Panda, Pigeon, Quacksilver, Scarlet Pooch, Squawkeye), Silver Squirrel, Spider-Ham (Peter Porker), Sub-Marsupial, Thrr, Waspbunny, Watchdog, Mary Jane Waterbuffalo, X-Bugs (Collosso-bug, Kitty-bug, Kurt-bug, Ororo-bug, Professor X-bug, Scott-bug, Wolverine-bug), many others
SIGNIFICANT LOCATIONS: Arfgard, "Secret Furs" world, Shang-Goo-La, St. Croix Trapezoid
FIRST APPEARANCE: Marvel Tails #1 (1983)

HISTORY: Larval Earth is a universe populated by "anthrotoon" animals and governed by cartoonish laws of physics. Many Earth-616 inhabitants have multiple counterparts in this universe. This Earth's heroic age began in World War II with heroes such as Captain Americat, Asinine Torch, and Sub-Marsupial, and continues in the modern era with adventurers such as the Fantastic Fur, the Scavengers, Iron Mouse, the Thunder Dog Thrr, the Punfisher, Silver Squirrel, the X-Bugs, and Nick Furry and his agents of S.H.E.E.P.

One day, an ordinary spider named Peter watched unknown super-genius May Porker test the world's first atomic-powered hair dryer on herself. Rendered radioactive enough to glow in the dark, the power-crazed Porker bit Peter on the head, transferring the energy and her scientific genius to him. Transformed into a pig with the proportionate strength and agility of a spider (or perhaps a spider with the limitations of a pig), Peter began caring for a semi-amnesiac May as her "nephew." With his origin now out of the way, Peter Porker decided to use his newfound abilities to fight crime as the heroic Spider-Ham.

Becoming a photographer at the Daily Beagle, Porker could easily monitor news of possible crimes in progress, and found a ready market for pictures of himself in action. Spider-Ham's foes included high-end villains such as Ducktor Doom, Dragon-Lassy, and Kingpig; ordinary gangs like the Senior Simian Gang and the Terrible Terriers; and exotics like the alien-eating machine B.O., Hogzilla, and various mutated vegetables. His allies included Captain Americat, Croctor Strange, Punfisher, Woodchuck Morris, and the Black Jackal & the Beagle Brigadeers (J. Jonah Jackal & the Junior Newsboys). Porker dated a few women, such as Batty Brant and the Black Catfish, before entering into a more permanent relationship with Mary Jane Waterbuffalo, who became supportive of Porker's secret life.

Spider-Ham has encountered other-dimensional beings such as Forbush Man of the Marble Universe (Earth-665), Howard the Duck of Duckworld, and the Silver Burper, Four Tots, and the Widdle Avengers of the Marvel Babies universe (Earth-21989). While trying to rescue his friend Betty Branteater from the Larval Zombies cult, Spider-Ham was brainfried when they slapped a zombieizer on him and downloaded the entire contents of the Moowald/Sandeerson version of the old Deluxe Larval Handbooks into his mind. After being deprogrammed by MJ, Spider-Ham elected to stay to fend off the attack of Bat-Bird and the rival Dee-See cult until Larval Zombie #1 reneged on his promise to give Porker his own graphic novel and booted him out. When last seen, Spider-Ham had teamed up with Forbush Man, Milk & Cookies, and Wolverina to stop Negative Forbush Man from merging their three worlds into one. The next time the universe needs to be saved from the evil powers of Overhyped Hotstardejour with a good dose of laughter, Spider-Ham will once more swing into action and save our bacon.

SPIDER-HAM, HULKBUNNY & CAPTAIN AMERICAT

J. JONAH JACKAL & THE JUNIOR NEWSBOYS (J. JEREMIAH JACKAL, BUNSEN BUNNY & UPTON ADAM STRAY)

BLACK JACKAL & THE BEAGLE BRIGADEERS (BULLET BUNNY, POWER PUSS & INVISI-JACKAL JUNIOR)

Art by Steve Mellor

MAY PORKER · MARY JANE WATERBUFFALO · DEERDEVIL · BATT BURDOCK · DUCKTOR DOOM · HOG-ZILLA

RAVEN THE HUNTER · WATCHDOG & SILVER SQUIRREL · PUNFISHER (FRANK CARPLE) · TONY YARG · IRON MOUSE

THRR · JOHNNY GLAZED · GOOSE RIDER

SANDMANATEE, ANT ANT & WASPBUNNY

COL. NICK FURRY & THE AGENTS OF SHEEP, PASTE POT PEEP (IN DISGUISE) & DODO DUGAN

X-BUGS (PROFESSOR X-BUG, SCOTT-BUG, COLOSSOL-BUG, ORORO-BUG, KURT-BUG & WOLVERINE-BUG)

AWFUL FLIGHT (TRINKET, AROMA, HOCKEYPUCK, SNOW-YOUSE & SUMMERSQUASH)

SCAVENGERS (SQUAWKEYE, SCARLET POOCH, PIGEON, BLACK PANDA, QUACKSILVER & WALVIS)

FANTASTIC FUR (SIMIAN TORCH, MOOSTER FANTASTIC, INVISIBLE GORILLA, BEN GRIZZLY — THE THANG) & GALACTYPUS

Art by Steve Mellor, Michael Mellor, Joe Albelo, Alan Kupperberg & Tony Salmons

LAST AVENGERS STORY

CORE CONTINUUM DESIGNATION: Earth-9511
SIGNIFICANT INHABITANTS: Avengers (Black Panther/T'Challa, Black Widow/Natalia Romanova, Bombshell, Cannonball/Sam Guthrie, Captain America/Steve Rogers, Gestalt, Hawkeye/Clint Barton, Hercules/Heracles, High Tide, Hotshot, Hulk/Bruce Banner, Human Torch/Johnny Storm, Iron Man/Tony Stark, Rick Jones, Tommy Maximoff, Mockingbird/Bobbi Barton, Peter Parker/Spider-Man, Hank Pym, Quasar/Wendell Vaughn, Quicksilver/Pietro Maximoff, Reed Richards/Mr. Fantastic, Scarlet Witch/Wanda Maximoff, Sequoia, She-Hulk/Jen Walters, Super-Ego, Sue Storm/Invisible Woman, Thing/Ben Grimm, Thor, Tigra/Greer Nelson, Vision, Wasp/Janet Van Dyne, Wild Man, Jessie Wingfoot, Wonder Man/Simon Williams), Dr. Doom (Victor von Doom), Dr. Strange (Stephen Strange), Grim Reaper (Billy Maximoff), Kang (Nathaniel Richards), Oddball, Ben Parker (son of Peter), Mary Jane Parker, Vicky Russell, Alicia Storm, Marissa Storm, Ultron, Chris Valada, Wyatt Wingfoot
SIGNIFICANT LOCATIONS: Asgard; Avengers monument; Captain America's secret chamber; Greenwich Village, New York; Himalayas; Mount Parnassus; Olympus; Paris, France; Shoreham Nuclear Plant (converted into Avengers headquarters); the Time Capsule
FIRST APPEARANCE: The Last Avengers Story #1 (1995)

FINAL BATTLE AGAINST ULTRON 59

HISTORY: It has been said that all stories lead to tragedy if they do not end soon enough — which may explain the fate of Earth-9511's Avengers. In this reality, the super-heroic Avengers team endured for decades, but gradually broke down through a series of disastrous losses. During the remarriage ceremony of Avengers founders Hank Pym and the Wasp, the Scarlet Witch tried to break up a fight between her brother Quicksilver and her husband Vision. She was accidentally killed in a collision with Quicksilver, dying a brutally bloody death before the eyes of her twin sons, Tommy and Billy Maximoff (both of whom would survive into adulthood in this reality). A grief-maddened Quicksilver killed himself moments later and the Vision fled, cutting himself off from humanity by inhabiting the skies as a solitary wraith for years thereafter. Tommy eventually became the disciple of sorcerer supreme Dr. Strange, while a broken Billy became the evil Grim Reaper.

When Thor, Hercules, Hulk and Thing left Earth to combat a mysterious crisis known as the Great Cataclysm, only the Hulk returned. Less than two years later, Hulk unexpectedly turned against his fellow Avengers during a battle with Ultron, murdering Tigra and mortally wounding Wonder Man, whose energy-suffused body exploded. Hawkeye, whose wife Mockingbird had earlier knocked him out and flown him to a safe distance, revived just before the blast, and was permanently blinded, while the Hulk, closer to Wonder Man, died. About five years later, the US government drafted America's super heroes into performing a mass round-up of super-criminals, whom the government promptly executed. Many disillusioned super heroes, including Avengers veterans such as Dr. Pym, retired from heroics. Captain America did not, but soon found a new calling as President of the USA, and helped assemble a brand-new generation of Avengers such as Gestalt, High Tide, Sequoia and Super-Ego. Though "Cap" was seemingly assassinated during his first term, Hawkeye and many others believed that he secretly lived on in hiding, in suspended animation.

Ten years later, Ultron faked a supposed historical document from the future entitled "The Last Avengers Story," and with it steered Kang, Grim Reaper and Reaper's mind-warping associate Oddball into joining him in a final assault on the Avengers. Ultron bombed the new Avengers' Shoreham headquarters, killing the entire team, then challenged the long-retired Dr. Pym to face him with whatever was left of the old Avengers, or Ultron would pick them off one by one. An ailing Reed Richards, a retired Spider-Man, an embittered Mockingbird and Johnny Storm's pacifist daughter, artist Marissa Storm, all declined to join the struggle; but Wasp, Cannonball, Human Torch (Johnny Storm), Hotshot (Black Knight's son), Bombshell (explosive-powered supposed daughter of Hercules), Jessie Wingfoot (daughter of She-Hulk) and Tommy Maximoff all joined a reluctant Pym for the final battle. The Avengers forces prevailed thanks to the last-minute aid of Hawkeye and Mockingbird, who had apparently been called in by the supposedly late Cap himself; and the unexpected intervention of the Vision, who had been stirred to action by a visit from Tommy. During the battle, Oddball was accidentally crushed, Kang slew Cannonball, Hotshot and Pym, and blew off Bombshell's leg before being slain in turn by Wasp, Grim Reaper murdered Jessie, Hawkeye & Mockingbird neutralized much of Ultron's robot army, and the Vision and Ultron deactivated each other; but the legacy of the Avengers lived on in its heroic survivors, in a time capsule of historical Avengers artifacts maintained by Richard Jones, and in a secret chronicle kept by the long-lost Captain America.

Art by Ariel Olivetti

KEY
1. Sequoia
2. Gestalt
3. Super-Ego
4. Hightide
5. She-Hulk
6. Hotshot
7. Reed Richards
8. Victor von Doom
9. Hulk
10. Tigra
11. Mary Jane Parker
12. Peter Parker
13. Ben Parker
14. Marissa Storm
15. Alicia Storm
16. Chris Valada
17. Bombshell
18. Oddball
19. Mockingbird
20. Ultron 59
21. Vision
22. Captain America
23. Wasp
24. Jessie Wingfoot
25. Cannonball
26. Human Torch
27. Doctor Hank Pym
28. Kang the Conqueror
29. Grim Reaper (Billy Maximoff)
30. Tommy Maximoff
31. Hawkeye

THE TIME CAPSULE

MARIE LAVEAU

REAL NAME: Marie Laveau (or Laveaux)
ALIASES: Good Mother, Madam Parizien, Marie Auguste, Marie Glapion, Marie the First, Marie the Second, Mother of the Saints, Pope of Voodoo, Queen of the Lost, Voodoo Queen of New Orleans, the Widow Paris, Witch Queen of New Orleans, others
IDENTITY: Believed by the general public to have died in 1881
OCCUPATION: Power-seeker; former Vodū priestess, diviner, counselor, madam (allegedly), hairdresser, fever nurse
CITIZENSHIP: USA
PLACE OF BIRTH: New Orleans, Louisiana
KNOWN RELATIVES: Jacques Paris (first husband, deceased), Christophe Glapion (second husband, deceased); Marie Eucharist (aka Marie the Second), Louise, Philomene (daughters, deceased); Francois, Archange (sons, deceased); Charles Laveaux (father, deceased); Marguerite Darcantel (mother, deceased); Marie Darcantel, Marie Laveaux (half-sisters, deceased); Francois Auguste, Louis Foucher, Celestin Glapion (brothers-in-law, deceased); Charles Trudeau (grandfather, deceased); Marie Laveaux (grandmother, deceased); Joseph Crocker, Victor Crocker, Joseph Legendre, Alexander Legendre (grandsons, deceased); Aldina Crocker, Esmeralda Crocker, Marie Glapion, Eugenie Legendre, Noime Legendre, Fidela Legendre (granddaughters, deceased); Pierre Crocker, George Legendre (sons-in-law, deceased); "Luke Turner" (great-grandnephew); Saint Henriette Delille (distant cousin, deceased); several unidentified nieces and nephews (deceased)
GROUP AFFILIATION: Unidentified vampire coven
EDUCATION: Extensively self-educated
FIRST APPEARANCE: Dracula Lives #2 (1973)

HISTORY: Much of Marie Laveau's history is fragmentary or self-contradictory, but per the most reliable accounts, she was born in New Orleans' French Quarter in 1801 to a white planter and a mulatto slave. A Creole beauty whose childhood coincided with Louisiana's induction into the United States, she worked during her youth alongside her mother to treat victims of warfare and epidemic, a humanitarian effort with far less social status than in later decades. In 1819, while working as a hairdresser, she married Jacques Paris, who mysteriously vanished without a trace soon afterward. In 1827, she became the common-law wife of Dominican Republic-born Christophe Glapion, to whom she bore five children, the first also named Marie, prior to his death in 1835; some records erroneously claim she and Glapion had fifteen children, a figure encompassing children and grandchildren alike.

Allegedly inducted into the rites of the Vodū (also Voudou or voodoo) faith (or at least a facsimile of same) by houngan (Vod priest) Dr. John Bayou and/or manbo (Vod priestess) Sanite Dede, Marie, formerly a devout Catholic, was a well-known supplier of mystic charms and services before she was thirty. She led ceremonial snake-dances in Congo Square and at St. John's Bayou on the banks of Lake Pontchartrain, accompanied by the serpent-god Damballah himself. Marie's namesake daughter reportedly joined her efforts upon reaching adulthood. Marie befriended and bargained with Father Antoine, the local Spanish Inquisition officer, to guarantee peaceful coexistence between New Orleans' Catholics and Vods. Accounts vary on whether mother or daughter ultimately became New Orleans' foremost "voodoo queen," but it was undeniably the name of Marie Laveau that earned the title.

By 1855 Marie, whose customary work was interspersed with treating yellow fever victims and performing missionary work for death row inmates, was living in a mansion on 1020 Saint Ann Street, supposedly earned by ensorceling a judge to find a client's son innocent. Both she and her daughter were said to have political influence, via secrets received from clientele and informants alike, to match their mystic powers; they used both not only for clients' benefits but also to help slaves escape, rescue prisoners (whether unjustly accused or not) from execution, and, augmented by wits and personal magnetism, oppose oppression from a government that disdained their race and faith. If rumor is believed, Marie was the first American-born sorceress to win worldwide fame; indeed, to this day she is remembered in the devotions of Vodū practitioners in New Orleans and around the world.

Although reported dead in June 1881, years after her namesake vanished during post-war Reconstruction, the elder Marie in fact survived via an imperfect immortality potion obtained from the centuries-old Cagliostro, who had sought to steal her mystic secrets but instead became her devoted lover, like many other men before and since. The potion required the somewhat rare ingredient of vampire blood and, in some cases, a victim to whom she could transfer the years she was shedding. Admittedly, stories yet again differ on whether the late 19th century's "Voodoo Queen" was the elder or younger Marie, but her power, to judge the ease with which she reportedly rode a downed tree through the winds of a hurricane in 1895, while singing Vodū songs, was indisputable. Regrettably, the good done by Marie and her family was eclipsed by slander against Vodū and its believers, and her surviving daughter Philomene dedicated herself to clearing the family name before her own death in 1897; eventually, Marie's name was linked to the charitable

Art by Phil Noto with Gene Colan (inset)

Art by Douglas T. Wheatley

Howard Foundation, which she may or may not have granted mystic aid. Nonetheless, while Philomene denied tales of mystic corruption, such a fate may have befallen the true Marie herself via Cagliostro's secrets, for she soon withdrew to brood and ponder in the Louisiana bayous, aging but undying, served by generations of retainers.

Marie's New Orleans mansion became known as a haunted house, and her supposed tomb at St. Louis Cemetery a shrine to Vodū practitioners, but little is known of the activities of Marie herself for nearly a century. Sporadic sightings were reported, and tales about her grew taller and darker over the decades, until it was believed that to even approach the diabolical crone she had become was to court death. Finally, her last servant, Gaston, searched for Cagliostro but found instead his nemesis Dracula, whom he transported back to New Orleans and led to Marie. Using garlic and crosses, they restrained Dracula while they sampled his blood to complete her immortality potion. The process restored Marie's youth, at the cost of Gaston's, who unwittingly took upon himself the weight of Marie's century-plus years as she shed them. Marie released Dracula and offered an alliance and relationship, but, though intrigued, he refused, put off by her binding him by force previously.

In recent years, Marie, feeling challenged by the heroic Brother Voodoo, schemed against the newcomer, but her endeavors were disrupted by the mystic fanatic Silver Dagger, who, prompted by the demon Basilisk, bound her to his will and used her to lure Sorcerer Supreme Dr. Strange into a trap. Strange, aided by the costumed heroes Spider-Man (Peter Parker) and Ms. Marvel (Carol Danvers), confronted Silver Dagger at Marie's latest New Orleans home and held him at bay in a mystic battle. Hoping to end the encounter, Marie was prepared to kill either Strange or his nemesis, but it was the latter who fell to her blade, earning her Strange's wary respect. In the incident's aftermath, the Basilisk cursed Strange with lycanthropy, but he was restored with the help of Spider-Man and Basilisk's half-human host Satana.

When Strange and others, including the vampire hunter Blade, mystically destroyed most of the world's vampires via the Montesi Formula, Marie, now cut off from the vampire blood she would eventually need to replenish her potion, recruited Louisianan super hero Captain Marvel (Monica Rambeau) to, via the mystic Black Mirror, travel back to 1784 and obtain fresh vampire blood, again from Dracula. Although the hero succeeded, the residual effect of Strange's spell destroyed the prize, and the Mirror was later rendered unusable by Californian sorcerers Robert and Tina Minoru. After the blood of quasi-vampire Morbius proved equally unusable, Marie mystically searched the world for any hint that Dracula's strain of vampirism survived and, ironically, was ultimately led to Strange's own comatose brother Victor, partially vampirized when Strange had failed to restore him to health years before. With Victor, dubbed the new Baron Blood, in her servitude, Marie stole the mystic Darkhold tome and — despite opposition from Strange, Brother Voodoo, and others — used it to resurrect Varnae, the long-dead first of the vampires, whom she dared think she could bend to her will in creating a steady supply of vampires. However, Varnae, caring as little for her goals as she cared for his, rejected her far more violently than had his former protégé Dracula, and he escaped both her and her opponents, spreading vampirism anew until his physical death in combat with Blade and his Nightstalkers teammates.

Showing little of the acumen for which she was once so renowned, Marie, served by a handful of newly made vampires, again sought to re-create and control Varnae by granting him possession of Blade's body, but her second effort ended no better than her first as Blade disrupted the ritual. Varnae thus remained unbound to Marie and fled in the body of vampire vigilante Night Terror. Rescued from the debacle by vampire drug lord Steppin' Razor, Marie resurfaced months later in an alliance with Deacon Frost, a vampire elder nonetheless younger than Marie herself, to seize control of New Orleans, the city that had both revered and despised her over the decades, only to face opposition from Brother Voodoo, Blade, and vampire detective Hannibal King. She captured all three men, then sought to cement her power via the Vodū gods, but when Brother Voodoo turned her spells against her by convincing the Vodū that Marie disrespected them, the serpent-god Damballah appeared and, in mockery of the snake-dances she had performed long ago, crushed her within his coils for her repeated misuse of her faith's powers.

Art by Gene Colan

Left for dead, Marie eventually regained her health and, many months later, confronted the Minorus' daughter Nico, aka Sister Grimm, to break her parents' curse upon the Black Mirror. Shattered in the effort, the Mirror was revealed to hide a lost Darkhold page, which she delivered to novice sorcerer Ian McNee as part of the elder god Chthon's effort to conquer the Earth. Although McNee was spared, and the world with him, by the intervention of the Principality Oshtur, Marie remains at large.

HEIGHT: 5'7"
WEIGHT: 129 lbs.
EYES: Black
HAIR: Blue

ABILITIES/ACCESSORIES: Marie Laveau is one of the most powerful sorceresses on Earth and perhaps the single most powerful practitioner of Vodū magic. She possesses the powers of mesmerism, precognition, clairvoyance, astral projection, shape-changing, weather command, projection of mystic bolts, and other occult abilities; she occasionally alters her appearance to that of a Caucasian woman when it suits her purposes. She can summon various gods and demons who, under ideal circumstances, can be bent to her will. Even without magic, she is an expert at reading the emotions of others and manipulating them into serving her interests; in her early life, at least, she was renowned for her business acumen and commanding presence. Among the mystic artifacts she has used are the emotion-altering Arrows of Eros, which can induce either passionate love or equally devoted hatred; the time-transcending Black Mirror; and, for a brief time, the Darkhold, which she used to summon demonic warriors, create mystic shields, teleport, and otherwise perform magical feats apparently beyond even her formidable powers. She has regained and retained her youth through a magic potion requiring vampire blood. She reportedly employs familiars on occasion, including a serpent named Zombi.

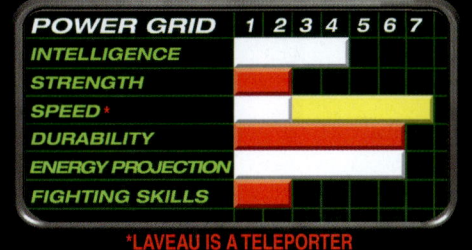

*LAVEAU IS A TELEPORTER

LEADER

REAL NAME: Samuel Sterns
ALIASES: KR-39
IDENTITY: Publicly known
OCCUPATION: Megalomaniac; former chemical research facility worker
CITIZENSHIP: USA
PLACE OF BIRTH: Boise, Idaho
KNOWN RELATIVES: Phillip Sterns (Madman, brother)
GROUP AFFILIATION: Formerly Home Base, Alliance, part of an unidentified international spy ring
EDUCATION: High school dropout, self taught to Ph.D.-equivalent level in most sciences
FIRST APPEARANCE: Tales to Astonish #62 (1964)

HISTORY: For every yin, there is a yang. Gamma radiation released Bruce Banner's subconscious rage, giving it physical form as the Hulk, an embodiment of strength. So perhaps it was high school dropout Sam Sterns' desire to be more like his scientist brother, Phillip, that caused him to transform into the hyper-intelligent Leader when he, too, was exposed to gamma radiation. Working as a laborer in a government-owned chemical research facility in the Nevada desert, Sterns was caught in an explosion when a radioactive waste cylinder unexpectedly blew up. Recovering in the hospital, he discovered an insatiable thirst for knowledge, and rapidly read every book he could.

Weeks later, Sam's skin turned green and his skull expanded upwards. Calling himself the Leader, he used gamma-spawned intelligence to build secret bases across the world and created an international spy ring to steal scientific secrets. The Leader's path first crossed the Hulk's when he sent a spy to Los Diablos Missile Base (aka Desert Base) to steal an indestructible armored suit designed by Bruce Banner. The Hulk defeated the Leader's spy, after which the Leader hired the Chameleon to infiltrate Desert Base, but the Chameleon was similarly defeated. The Leader then targeted another of Banner's inventions, the Absorbatron, capable of absorbing a nuclear explosion's force. To steal the Absorbatron, the Leader sent his new creation, a synthetic robot that he dubbed "the Humanoid." After the Hulk deactivated the Humanoid by slamming it into a rock, the Leader sent an entire Humanoid horde, which fought the Hulk to a standstill. While the Leader's forces fought the Hulk, the US armed forces lowered the Absorbatron into an underground shelter. After this encounter, the Leader became determined to turn the Hulk into his ally, reasoning that with the Hulk's strength and his own intelligence, they would be unbeatable.

The Leader's Humanoid army subsequently captured both the Absorbatron and the Hulk, and returned both to one of the Leader's hidden lairs. However, the Hulk escaped captivity and destroyed the Absorbatron, forcing the Leader's retreat, and causing that particular lair to fall into the US military's hands. Later, when the Hulk was cornered by the military, the Leader offered to teleport him to safety in return for his allegiance. At the time, Bruce Banner was in control of the Hulk's body, which had a bullet lodged in his brain, and his next transformation into Bruce Banner would kill him. Grudgingly, the Hulk accepted the Leader's offer, and was transported to one of the Leader's bases in Italy where the Leader used his machinery to remove the bullet. Collecting on this debt, the Leader used his technology to send the Hulk to the extremely advanced home world of the Watchers to pillage its technology. The Hulk retrieved the Globe of Ultimate Knowledge (a conduit to the Ultimate Machine), but when the Leader donned it and accessed the universe's accumulated knowledge, even his advanced mind was overwhelmed, and he collapsed, seemingly dead.

The Leader was revived by one of his Humanoids, and resurfaced when General "Thunderbolt" Ross' forces captured the Hulk, offering his assistance in creating a prison that would hold the Hulk indefinitely. The Leader constructed a "plasti-thene" cage that absorbed the Hulk's blows, and imprisoned the Hulk inside. The Leader then summoned his Super-Humanoid and proceeded to take over the entire base, planning to use its missiles to start World War III, and then conquer what was left of civilization. However, Ross' daughter, Betty, freed the Hulk who defeated the Super-Humanoid and prevented World War III. Soon after, the Leader attempted to steal the experimental Tripodal Observation Module military vehicle, nicknamed the "Murder Module" and guarded by Bruce Banner, who once again was in control of the Hulk's body. The Leader entered the Module and fought with the Banner-controlled Hulk, who was victorious after his savage side began to reemerge. The Leader escaped, swearing to spoil his nemesis' newfound happiness. Enlisting the Rhino (Alexei Sytsevich)'s aid, the Leader used a device to restore the Hulk to his savage state during the wedding of Bruce Banner and Betty Ross. In the ensuing battle, the Leader accidentally struck Rhino with a blast

Art by Tom Marvelli with Todd MacFarlane (inset)

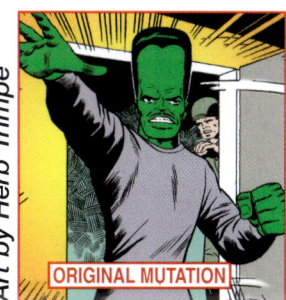

Art by Herb Trimpe

ORIGINAL MUTATION

of energy, after which the Rhino charged the Leader's vehicle; the Leader ultimately escaped.

At some point, the Leader constructed as his main base an orbiting space station, as well as its artificial intelligence, both of which were called Omnivac. The Leader continued to be a thorn in the Hulk's side, sending the Glob (Joe Timms) after him on one occasion, and later using military technology to cause the Hulk to see illusions of his enemies, hoping to stress the Hulk into having a heart attack. The Leader's plans were thwarted on both occasions. The Leader later took over Hulkbuster Base, replacing General Ross and Major Glenn Talbot with robot duplicates, and planned to do the same to the US president and vice president when they inspected the base. When the Hulk revealed his ruse, the Leader had all of his Humanoids fuse into one giant robot, which the Leader mentally controlled from his lair. The Hulk and Doc Samson defeated the robot, and the psychic feedback caused an explosion in the Leader's lab that left him paralyzed; his body was transported to his space station. While paralyzed, the Leader briefly mind-controlled the Rhino to do his bidding, and wagered with former Xanthan leader Kurrgo, pitting the Thing and the Hulk in battle against one another, the winner gaining the right to use both "champions" in future machinations. Instead, the Thing and the Hulk discovered the villains' treachery, and destroyed Kurrgo's ship.

The Leader eventually regained mobility by deliberately reverting back to the form of Sterns, whose amnesiac form then followed subconscious orders to infiltrate Gamma Base (the reformed Hulkbuster Base), where he exposed himself to radiation to transform back into the Leader. The Leader used his vast mental powers to take over Gamma Base, brainwashing most of the soldiers into near mindless loyal servants, and capturing General Ross, Clay Quartermain, and Doc Samson. The Leader intended to use Gamma Base's technology to take control of all information and communication networks in the world, but the Hulk's strength overcame the Leader's technology yet again. The Leader next duped Dr. Rikki Keegan, a former classmate of Banner's, into aiding him, allegedly to cure Banner of being the Hulk. From Banner's blood, Keegan isolated the "gamma gene," the apparent factor that allowed superhuman mutation in the face of massive gamma ray exposure. The Leader instead contaminated Manhattan's water supply with this gamma gene, causing a "green flu" that mutated those it didn't kill. Afflicted by this green flu, Keegan was mutated into a Leader-like being more powerful than her creator. To prevent her from telekinetically ruining his plans, the Leader administered an antidote to her, which was then used by the Avengers to cure the rest of the victims. Though seemingly perishing under rushing water, the Leader was recovered and revived by his Humanoids.

In two other villainous plots, the Leader attempted to take over a missile base in Texas, and later tried to steal a power generator designed to harness gamma radiation, but was thwarted by Spider-Man and the Hulk both times. The Leader then schemed to travel to Earth's primordial past to alter mankind's evolution so all humanity would become gamma people, subservient to him. He also hired the mercenary Jackdaw (Heather O'Gara, later known as Blackbird) to assist him in gathering the necessary time-traveling technology. After determining the Hulk, now possessing Banner's mind again and lacking his previous savagery and strength potential, was no longer a threat, the Leader departed for the past, leaving Omnivac to send any who would oppose him into various points in Earth's past. While the Avengers fell victim to this, both the Hulk and She-Hulk, immune to this trap due to their gamma-powers (a safeguard the Leader had provided to protect himself), forced Omnivac to send them to recover the Avengers. The Avengers and the Hulk eventually confronted the Leader, who was knocked into a prehistoric volcano. Though believed dead, he survived thanks to a hidden teleportation device. Jackdaw, meanwhile, who had been brutally "disciplined" by Omnivac for previously failing the Leader, dismantled Omnivac to foil his preventing the heroes' return. The Leader next learned of the ancient and powerful Kimara trapped in Canada's frozen north and tried to harness his power, but was defeated by Alpha Flight.

Eventually, the Leader's mutation destabilized and he reverted to his human form. Seeking to regain his heightened intellect, he drained the gamma radiation from the recently Hulk-like Rick Jones. Sterns became the Leader again, with a new appearance, and a psychic link to Rick Jones. The Leader subsequently captured former Hulkbusters John LaRoquette and Craig Saunders, brainwashed them, and outfitted them with high-tech armors, turning them into his servants, Rock and Redeemer. Via these two, the Leader stole a gamma bomb from a US military base and detonated it in Middletown, Arizona, killing 5,000 people. The five survivors of Middletown were superhumanly mutated by the radiation. The Leader gathered the survivors, deceived them into believing that he had saved them from Middletown (later referred to as Gammatown)'s destruction and turned them into his loyal followers, the Riot Squad, intending for them to be the first of his new race of gamma people.

The Leader then created a town called Freehold, isolated beneath the icefields of northern Canada, and recruited people from across the world who were sick or dying from radiation to join his new community. Freehold's citizens were unaware of the Leader's evil ways and considered him their savior. The Leader claimed Freehold would form the basis of a new society after pollution and war wiped out the rest of humanity. In actuality, the Leader used some of the radiation victims for experiments, as when he created the cyborgs known as the Headshop. When the Leader's brother, Phil Sterns, gained superhuman power as the psychopathic villain Madman, the Leader saw him as a potential threat, but was unwilling to kill his own brother. Instead, the Leader informed the Hulk of Madman's location, leading his arch-foe to do his dirty work for him.

When the terrorist organization Hydra threatened Freehold, the Leader sought aid from the Pantheon, a group of heroes then allied with the Hulk. The Leader led his followers in an attack on the Pantheon's Mount headquarters. A massive battle between the Hulk and his allies, and the Leader's followers ensued, but was ceased when the Leader and the Pantheon's leader, Agamemnon, came to an agreement in which the Leader would receive aid from the Pantheon, much to the Hulk's rage. The Leader's conflict with Hydra also coincided with another event: The Leader, still sharing a psychic link with Rick Jones, was affected by the grief Jones felt over the recent death of his girlfriend, Marlo Chandler. The Leader approached Jones and offered to restore her life, using the power of his follower, the Soul Man.. The Leader intended to use Rick Jones as a pawn against the Hulk,

Art by Doug Braithwaite

Art by Leonard Kirk

Art by Angel Medina — OMNIBUS

and also planned to analyze the Soul Man's powers in hopes of discovering a way to become immortal. When Hydra launched its attack on Freehold, the Hulk also arrived to settle old scores, and attacked the Leader, interrupting the process of bringing Marlo Chandler back to life. The Leader and his forces were defeated, and the Hulk used the Leader as a shield to stop Redeemer's bullets before throwing him into a massive explosion.

The Leader survived in non-corporeal form and mentally controlled Omnibus, one of Freehold's gamma mutates, using him to create a terrorist organization, the Alliance, with which he intended to destabilize the world and plunge it into war, only to be thwarted by the Hulk once again. The people of Freehold refused to believe Omnibus' claims that the Leader had controlled him, and exiled him to die in the snowy wastes. Still later, when Banner was dying of ALS, the Hulk received a mental summons from the Leader, who had re-formed his body using cells from dead animals and local flora. The Leader informed his old enemy that he was about to transcend the mortal plane, and after giving the Hulk the cure for Banner's illness, he asked his former nemesis to witness his ascension. However, something appeared to go wrong at the critical juncture, and the Leader's new body exploded.

The Leader survived, but his body deteriorated, eventually leaving him nothing but an enormous floating head in a tank at one of his hidden bases in California. The Leader developed a plan to use the Hulk's DNA to grow a superhumanly strong body for his own mind to inhabit. To this end, the Leader organized Home Base, also known as the "Secret Conspiracy," to obtain a sample of the Hulk's blood. The Leader's true identity was kept secret, even from his own agents, who saw him only as a pair of lips on a view screen. As director of Home Base, the Leader framed the Hulk for the death of young Ricky Myers, and dispatched several agents, including Sandra Verdugo, Jink Slater, and Pratt in pursuit of his foe. After these agents failed, the Leader freed the Abomination and sent him against the Hulk, using the Abomination's wife, Nadia Blonsky, to win Banner's trust. However, Nadia ultimately turned on Home Base and warned Banner. After the Abomination was defeated, the Leader dispatched the Krill, part reptile, part android weapons, designed to obtain samples of the Hulk's blood. One Krill captured a sample of Hulk's blood, but the Hulk followed the Krill back to Home Base's headquarters and destroyed it. The Leader subsequently detonated the headquarters to prevent his enemies from discovering evidence of his identity. The Leader then abandoned his plan to grow a new body from the Hulk's DNA, opting instead to try to erase the Hulk's mind, and take over his foe's body directly. The Leader took advantage of Banner's wearied mind, and briefly usurped control of his enemy's body, leading the Hulk to his location, and initiating the process through which he would permanently take control of the Hulk's form. However, his plan was foiled by Betty Ross, Nadia Blonsky, Doc Samson, and Iron Man (Tony Stark), who destroyed the Leader's tank, and aborted his takeover of the Hulk's body, though at the cost of Nadia's life.

Following this defeat, the Leader regained his old body through unrevealed means and withdrew to a hidden New Mexico desert lair. However, he was discovered by Clay Quartermain and a new group of Hulkbusters, who apprehended him after a short battle. The Leader was then brought to trial for his crimes, where attorney Mallory Book defended him. Book convinced the jury that the Leader was, as a victim of gamma radiation, not in control of his own faculties and could not be held accountable for his crimes, earning him a not guilty verdict.

Following the Hulk and his Warbound's assault on New York, the Leader brought the Hulk's Warbound allies to the New Mexico desert in a quest to gain tremendous power. Using technology developed by child genius Amadeus Cho, the Leader created an enormous gamma radiation dome by siphoning power from one of the Warbound, Hiroim. The dome continually drew power from Hiroim, and the Leader channeled that power into himself, briefly gaining Hiroim's immense tectonic power. As Hiroim perished, however, his power was passed to SHIELD agent Katherine Waynesboro, who, with Hiroim's Warbound allies, defeated the Leader and foiled his plans.

Art by Leonard Kirk — OLDPOWER FORM

Art by Steve Ditko — HUMANOIDS

HEIGHT: 5'10" **EYES:** Green
WEIGHT: 144 lbs. **HAIR:** Black

ABILITIES/ACCESSORIES: The Leader possesses above-genius level intelligence, granting him enhanced intuition, pattern solving, information storage and retrieval, and logical and philosophical structuring abilities. The Leader is an expert in most scientific fields, particularly genetics and robotics. After his second mutation, he could control the minds of non-gamma irradiated individuals with whom he came into physical contact. He can also create mental illusions and generate psychokinetic energy bolts. The Leader has also used his advanced brain to generate force fields, instill mental blocks in others' minds, erase others' memories, and brainwash others into a zombie-like state. Additionally, through his psychic link to Rick Jones, the Leader gained professional level guitar skills.

The Leader uses a variety of Humanoids, synthetic robots, which he can control mentally, the majority of which are plastic in structure, able to absorb great impacts, deform under stress, and then return to normal. The Leader has also used a variety of gigantic Humanoids, such as the Super-Humanoid, his 500-foot tall Humanoid, and a giant Humanoid composed of hundreds of individual Humanoids. The Leader has also employed a variety of robots, including duplicates of influential people, and has utilized advanced technology, including the Murder Module, and his "kinetron" gloves that redirect the force of an enemy's blows back at them. The Leader often utilizes teleportation devices to escape death, and has developed his own time machine. He created Omnivac, a highly intelligent computer, which exists both as a robot in semi-humanoid form as well as the controlling force within his orbiting space station.

POWER GRID	1	2	3	4	5	6	7
INTELLIGENCE							■
STRENGTH	■						
SPEED		■					
DURABILITY		■					
ENERGY PROJECTION				■			
FIGHTING SKILLS	■						

LEAP-FROG

HISTORY: A small-time inventor with big dreams, Vincent Patilio created mechanical novelties for toy companies. Failing to be very profitable, he turned to crime to support his wife and son. Designing powerful springs powered by a battery pack, Patilio donned a mask and tested the coils at a New York airport. His random leaping caused chaos on the runways, but security proved unable to touch him. Building on the leaping theme, he designed a frog costume and became the Leap-Frog. He robbed the first jewelry store he saw, but fled when confronted by Daredevil (Matt Murdock). Patilio attempted to rob a bank courier the next day, but Daredevil again intervened and Patilio was captured and arrested. At his trial, he reacquired his springs and escaped, but broke his leg while leaping from the courthouse and was promptly re-arrested, found guilty, and imprisoned. Fellow Daredevil foe Stilt-Man (Wilbur Day) had sought a partnership with Leap-Frog, but promptly abandoned him after Patilio broke his leg.

Patilio was later broken out of prison by Electro (Matt Dillon) to join his Emissaries of Evil alongside Matador, Stilt-Man and Gladiator. Daredevil defeated the group, and Patilio was accidentally severely beaten by the Matador. Leap-Frog was later freed by the android Libra and recruited into the villainous Defenders imposters, battling the Falcon and Valkyrie, among others. After fighting Spider-Man, Patilio was hired by Justin Hammer as a technician (where he befriended Abe Jenkins, the Beetle), until Iron Man (Tony Stark) attacked Hammer's home, defeating Leap-Frog and several other villains. Returned to prison, Vincent learned that his wife, Rose, was diagnosed with breast cancer, which eventually killed her. Vincent's son Eugene was placed in the custody of Vincent's sister Rosemary ("Marie") and her husband Gus Colorito. Gus also passed away not long thereafter, and when Vincent was paroled he moved into Marie's Brooklyn home. (Eugene, hoping to dissociate himself from his father, called himself "Eugene Colorito." The news once called Vincent "Colorito" in error.)

Vincent found humiliating work in commercials promoting a local used car dealership dressed as the clownish "Frog-Face" while Eugene donned his father's costume to seek revenge on school bullies. Vincent violated house arrest to rescue his son. Struggling to go straight, Vincent moved to uptown Manhattan and worked as a low-level salesman. During an argument, the bitter Vincent, ranting about super heroes, lost control and slapped his son. Eugene concluded that he would atone for his father's sins by using one of Vincent's costumes to become a hero, the Frog-Man. Though Eugene's haphazard debut as a hero earned Vincent's reluctant approval, it was quickly rescinded as Vincent feared his son would be killed. Contacted by criminal Joe Face to team with the White Rabbit, and worried about Eugene floundering in battle, Vincent instead went to the police and infiltrated the gang wearing a wire. Spider-Man and Frog-Man both independently pursued the Rabbit, and Vincent ended up facing down his own son; however, the Rabbit was captured and Vincent earned a hefty reward for his efforts, and the conviction to let go of his past.

Despite his father's disapproval, Eugene continued to covertly act as Frog-Man. Vincent once dragged Eugene home from a fight with the Walrus during an audition for Defenders membership. Vincent and Eugene later moved back into Marie's Brooklyn house. When Eugene helped foil the villainous Yellow Claw (aided by heroes contacted by Vincent), Vincent felt some pride in his son's heroic accomplishments.

After Eugene left home for college, Vincent worked briefly with Damage Control, where Eugene Strausser made some repairs and improvements to the Frog-Man suit. Vincent became skilled with computer technologies, and designed an exoskeleton for the Frog-Man suit as well as a computer guidance system to control the suit's chaotic leaping. When the White Rabbit and the Walrus sought revenge against Frog-Man, Vincent used his new Leap-Frog costume to help Frog-Man and Spider-Man defeat the criminal duo. One of Vincent's costume was stolen by Buford Lange who has also operated as Leap-Frog.

REAL NAME: Vincent "Vinnie" Patilio
ALIASES: "Frog-Face," "Froggie," "Vincent Colorito"
IDENTITY: Publicly known
OCCUPATION: Inventor, mechanic, technician; former TV commercial actor, salesman, professional criminal
CITIZENSHIP: USA, with a criminal record
PLACE OF BIRTH: New York City, New York
KNOWN RELATIVES: Eugene Patilio (Frog-Man, son), Rose "Rosie" Patilio (wife, deceased), Rosemary "Marie" Patilio Colorito (sister), Gus Colorito (brother-in-law, deceased)
GROUP AFFILIATION: Formerly Justin Hammer's agents, Defenders impersonators, Electro's Emissaries of Evil
EDUCATION: High-school graduate
FIRST APPEARANCE: Daredevil #25 (1967)

HEIGHT: 5'9"
WEIGHT: 170 lbs.
EYES: Brown
HAIR: Brown, graying at temples

ABILITIES/ACCESSORIES: The Leap-Frog suit contains electrical boot coils, which greatly enhance the wearer's leaping ability, allowing him to achieve lengths up to 60' at a 45-degree parabolic arc reaching 15' at the apex, or 30' straight up, powered by the battery pack on the suit's back. The suit is heavily padded, and smaller coils inside the suit's skin cushhion the wearer from impacts. Recent versions of the suit include a powered strength-enhancing exoskeleton (enabling the user to lift 1 ton) and computer-controlled gyroscopic stabilizers. Vincent is diabetic.

POWER GRID	1	2	3	4	5	6	7
INTELLIGENCE				■			
STRENGTH		■					
SPEED		■					
DURABILITY		■					
ENERGY PROJECTION	■						
FIGHTING SKILLS		■					

Art by Gene Colan with Sal Buscema (inset)

LEGION OF NIGHT

MEMBERS: Martin Gold, Jennifer Kale, Chan Liuchow, Omen/Charles Blackwater, Katherine Reynolds, Ariann and Caspar Wright
BASE OF OPERATIONS: Caspar Wright's apartment, Greenwich Village, New York City, New York
FIRST APPEARANCE: The Legion of Night #1 (1991)

HISTORY: When the Beyond Reason Spiritual Fellowship cult summoned the demon Aan Taanu to Earth, it possessed the dragon Fin Fang Foom and rampaged across China, then attacked New York City. Cult High Priestess Hildreth sought to mate with the demon to allow it to father a race of demonic beings to overrun the earth. The enigmatic entity Omen, formerly Aan Taanu's slave, manifested on Earth by merging with Charles Blackwater, a lawyer slain by the Cult. Omen resurrected him and, using the apartment of Caspar Wright and his great-granddaughter — the young occult prodigy Ariann — as his base, he gathered several others with occult experience: Chan Liuchow, who had foiled Fin Fang Foom in China decades before; writer Martin Gold, former lover of Angel O'Hara (a past human host of Dracula's daughter Lilith); sorceress Jennifer Kale, inheritor of the magic of Atlantean sorceress Zhered-Na; and Katherine Reynolds, former Daimon Hellstrom associate turned unstable mentalist (after developing her powers, Reynolds had been imprisoned in a mental ward by "the Agency," who had amplified her abilities with experimental drugs).

Organizing this group into the Legion of Night, Omen brought them to the Astral Realm of Aan Taanu, while Caspar Wright remained on Earth to watch over Blackwater's form. Omen, Liuchow, Reynolds and Kale battled the demon's hordes while Ariann Wright and Gold located the demon's stronghold. Gold restrained Aan Taanu while Ariann tore the demon fetus from Hildreth's womb, slaying both mother and unborn child in the process. Aan Taanu then freed himself and attacked Ariann, but Omen arrived in time to plunge his sword into the demon's skull, either banishing or destroying it. Fin Fang Foom fled into New York Harbor, and the Beyond Reason cult presumably dissolved. The Legion members elected to stay together to defend Earth against further mystic attacks.

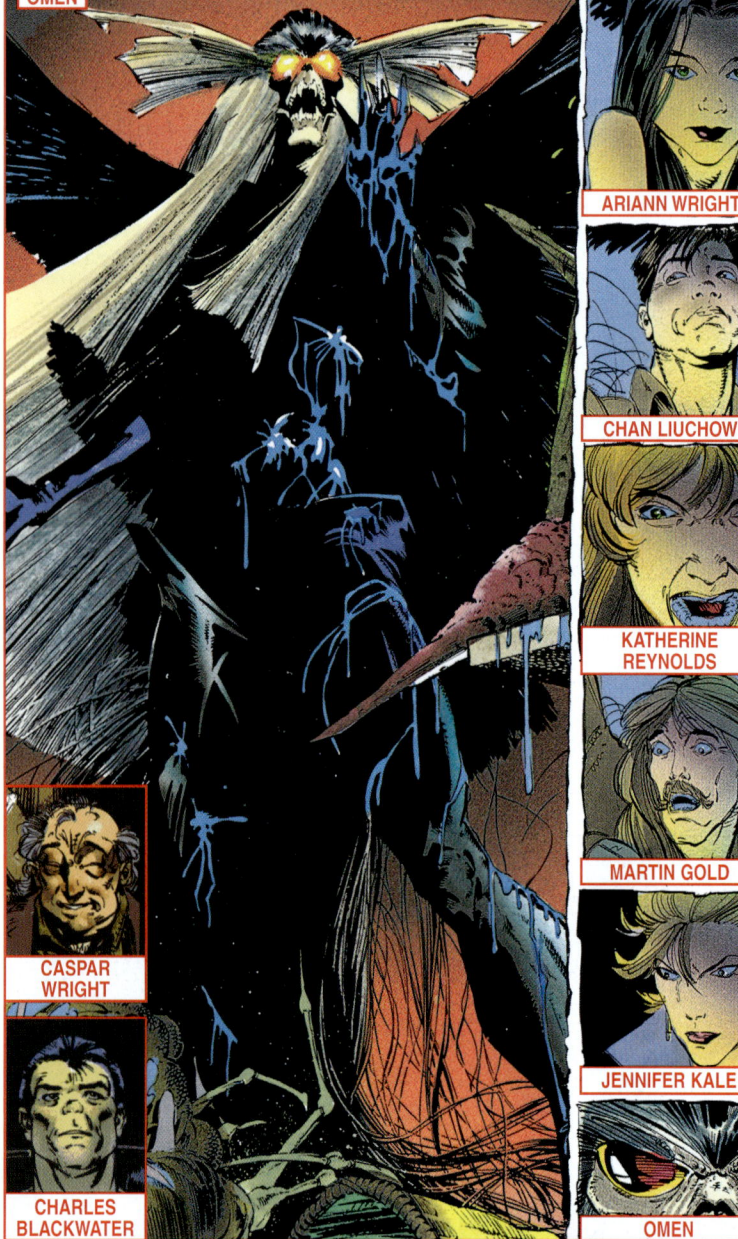

Blackwater/Omen and Ariann and Caspar Wright later fought a demon sent by Aan Taanu that had possessed ex-convict Morton Klasser and manipulated him into locating Leena Wolfe, a private investigator hired by Klasser's ex-wife to document his affairs and abuses. Upon locating Wolfe, the demon forced Klasser to instead attack Blackwater's ex-girlfriend, Allison Lamb, who had hired Wolfe to investigate Blackwater's behavior changes. Omen, however, had learned of this and temporarily entered Wolfe's form. When Klasser arrived to attack the women, Omen emerged and forcibly removed and slew the demon. Omen told Wolfe she would be called upon in the future to assist the Legion in return for saving her life. While Kale has since affiliated with Satana and Topaz, it is believed that Omen and Ariann Wright continue to assemble the Legion to oppose occult threats. Donna Garth is also rumored to have been associated with the Legion.

An empath and savage fighter, Katherine can sense magic, and her soul-kiss/mind-meld — allegedly so twisted that Hell looks good by comparison — can incapacitate demons. Omen can teleport, communicate telepathically, sense demonic forces, and use a magic sword. Ariann has innate magical understanding, limited precognition and prescience, and she can combat magical beings and speak to shadows and souls. The others lack inherent powers, using instead experience, intuition, and their wits.

Art by Whilce Portacio

LEGION OF THE UNLIVING

FORMER MEMBERS: Amenhotep (ancient Egyptian vampire), Baron Blood (John Falsworth), Baron (Heinrich) Zemo, Black Knight (Sir Percy of Scandia), Black Knight (Nathan Garrett), Black Knight (Dane Whitman), Bucky (Jim Barnes), Captain Marvel (Mar-Vell), Captain Marvel (Pulsar, Monica Rambeau), Count (Luchino) Nefaria, Death Adder (Roland Burroughs), Dr. Druid (Anthony Ludgate Druid), Dracula (Vlad Tepes Dracula), Drax the Destroyer (Arthur Douglas), Executioner (Skurge), Frankenstein's Monster, Ghost (Flying Dutchman, Joost Van Straaten), Green Goblin (Norman Osborn or Bart Hamilton), Grim Reaper (Eric Williams), Hellcat (Patsy Walker), Human Torch (Jim Hammond), Hyperion (Earth-616 artificial being), Inferno (Joseph Conroy), Iron Man (Tony Stark), Iron Man (Arno Stark), Korvac (Michael Korvac), Left-Winger (Hector Lennox), Midnight (M'Nai), Mockingbird (Bobbi Barton), Moon Knight (Marc Spector), Nebulon (unrevealed), Necrodamus, Nighthawk (Kyle Richmond), Oort the Living Comet, Dr. Henry Pym, Red Guardian (Alexi Shostakov), Right-Winger (Jerome Johnson), She-Hulk (Jen Walters), Silver Surfer (Norrin Radd), Star Stalker (a Vorm mutant), Swordsman (Jacques Duquesne), Terrax (Tyros), Thor (Thor Odinson), Thunderstrike (Eric Masterson), Tigra (Greer Nelson), Toro (Tom Raymond), Wasp (Janet Van Dyne), Wonder Man (Simon Williams). At least some of these members were facsimiles of the individuals in question rather than the true originals, though it is possible that even these facsimiles may have been animated by the living or dead spirits of the originals.

BASE OF OPERATIONS: Formerly Avengers Mansion, 890 Fifth Avenue, Manhattan, New York; Grim Reaper's otherdimensional castle; Immortus's citadel, Limbo; the realm of Death

FIRST APPEARANCE: Avengers #131 (1975)

HISTORY: Zombies, ghosts, time-lost souls, evil doppelgangers; whatever their true nature, they are legion, they wear the faces of the dead, and they live to kill the Avengers. The Legion of the Unliving is a recurring association of seemingly deceased warriors conjured by various masters to attack the heroic Avengers. The Legion's various organizers usually have some sway over time and space, so the Legion's membership tends to be drawn from a wide array of locations and time periods ranging from the distant past to the far future. The actual state of the Legion's members is nebulous; its ever-shifting roster has included spirits temporarily resurrected from the dead, beings plucked from time periods prior to their deaths, murderous duplicates of the dead, and various combinations of same. Some of them retain the original personality of the dead warriors, perhaps even some element of free will; other Legion members are re-created as soulless killers, or as blindly obedient pawns of their masters, or both. Sometimes they replicate

SWORDSMAN, DR. DRUID, THUNDERSTRIKE, CAPTAIN MARVEL (MAR-VELL), WONDER MAN & MOCKINGBIRD

Art by George Pérez

KANG'S LEGION — Art by Sal Buscema

IMMORTUS' LEGION — Art by Paul Ryan

the normal appearance of the deceased; other times, they appear as decaying, corpse-like facsimiles of their once-living counterparts. There is even some inconsistency regarding whether all the figures represented in the Legion are actually dead — some of the "dead" beings "raised" for the Legion are later revealed to have never truly died at all. The one common factor seems to be that Legion members have all been believed dead at one time or another, giving them an edge in terms of psychological warfare, the horror of being attacked by dead men walking. This emotional impact was a major factor in Kang's decision to create his original Legion of the Unliving, and presumably motivated subsequent Legion creators as well.

The Legion grew out of an ongoing conflict between time-spanning warlord Kang the Conqueror and his Avengers foes. During his quest for the Celestial Madonna (which turned out to be Avengers associate Mantis), Kang fought his own alternate-timeline counterpart Rama-Tut in a battle that hurled them both to the timeless realm of Limbo ruled by Immortus, yet another alternate-timeline counterpart of Kang (though Kang did not know this yet). Forging an anti-Avengers alliance with Immortus (who imprisoned Rama-Tut), Kang recalled how Immortus had once pitted a group of historical figures against the Avengers (though it had actually been Immortus' shape-shifting Space Phantoms replicating those figures). Deciding to improve upon this plan by enlisting more powerful troops, Kang used Immortus' time-manipulating technology to enlist an assortment of warriors from past eras, all dead or believed dead: Early Avengers foe Baron Zemo, the legendary Frankenstein's Monster, the Ghost of the Flying Dutchman, the android Human Torch, martial artist Midnight and one-time Avengers associate Wonder Man (a foe selected to distress the Avengers in general and the Vision in particular, since the android Vision's artificial mind was based on Wonder Man's brain patterns).

Once his Legion was assembled, Kang betrayed and imprisoned Immortus, transported the Avengers to the labyrinth of tunnels beneath Immortus' castle, and sent the Legion into the tunnels to capture Mantis and kill the Avengers. During subsequent skirmishes, Iron Man was seemingly slain by the Torch, the Ghost was apparently destroyed while gravely wounding the Vision, and Mantis defeated Midnight. As the conflict wore on, the Legion members regained more of their free will. Feeling an instinctive kinship to a fellow artificial being, Frankenstein's Monster and the Torch protected the fallen Vision despite Wonder Man's intense hostility toward the android Avenger, and the inhuman duo soon turned against Kang. Thor ultimately forced Kang to flee while Vision defeated Wonder Man. Meanwhile, Hawkeye (Clint Barton) freed Rama and Immortus, who reduced Zemo to protoplasm. Once the battle was over, Immortus restored Iron Man, the Ghost and Zemo, and sent the Legion members back to their proper times, though not before the Vision and the Torch learned to their surprise that the Vision was a reconstructed version of the Torch.

Years later, the deceased cosmic gamesman known as the Grandmaster conspired with his fellow Elder of the Universe, the Collector, in a plot against the Avengers. Causing the Avengers and their ally the Silver Surfer to die, the Grandmaster and the Collector manipulated the newly deceased heroes into battling each other in Death's realm, distracting the embodiment of Death itself long enough for the Grandmaster to imprison her and usurp her power. Giving the Avengers a sporting chance to stop him, the Grandmaster created five "Life Bombs," each capable of wiping out a full fifth of the universe, and scattered them to the far corners of the universe. If all five detonated, the chain reaction would start a new Big Bang and create a new universe for the Grandmaster to play with. To guard the bombs, Grandmaster conjured a new Legion of the Unliving, including

GRANDMASTER'S LEGION — Art by Bob Hall

murderous doppelgangers of heroes and villains such as Baron Blood, Black Knight (Sir Percy), Bucky, Captain Mar-Vell, Death Adder, Dracula, Drax, Executioner, Green Goblin, Hyperion, Korvac, Mockingbird, Nighthawk, Red Guardian, Swordsman and Terrax. In the battles that followed, only one bomb detonated and the Legion were all defeated, but Captain America and Hawkeye were the only two Avengers who survived. The other Avengers — including Black Knight (Whitman), Captain Marvel (Rambeau), Dr. Druid, Iron Man, Mockingbird, Moon Knight, Dr. Pym, She-Hulk, Silver Surfer, Thor, Tigra, Wasp and Wonder Man — were added to the ranks of the Legion; however, before Grandmaster could begin round two of the battle, Hawkeye lured him into a rigged game of chance that distracted the Grandmaster long enough for Death to regain her power and cast Grandmaster out of her realm, restoring all the newly slain Avengers and the Silver Surfer to life in an apparent gesture of gratitude.

REAPER'S 1ST LEGION

Art M.C. Wyman

Later, when the Avengers opposed Immortus' attempts to enslave the Scarlet Witch, he conjured a new Legion consisting of merciless incarnations of the Black Knight (Garrett), Grim Reaper, an alternate-future Iron Man (Arno Stark), Left-Winger, Oort the Living Comet (a possible-future villain the Avengers hadn't even encountered yet), Right-Winger, Swordsman and Toro (who made the obviously false claim that he had been the "Torch" in the first Legion, perhaps as part of Immortus' then-recent efforts to muddy the true histories of the Vision and the Torch). Oort and Toro struck down Quicksilver and Wasp, but most of the Legion was quickly neutralized, and the entire Legion had faded away long before Immortus was finally defeated.

Drawing power from the demonic Old Ones, including Lloigoroth, with promises of carnage, the undead Grim Reaper sought revenge on the Avengers. He caused a fatal commercial airliner crash and captured a commuter train, transforming some of his victims into decayed yet super-powerful zombie facsimiles of deceased Avengers foes: Amenhotep, Baron Zemo, Black Knight (Garrett), Count Nefaria, Inferno, Nebulon, Necrodamus, Red Guardian and Star Stalker. Reaper's Legion nearly destroyed the Avengers, supposedly to avenge the Reaper's death, but his hold over the zombies broke when Vision forced the Reaper to admit that he had killed himself and the Avengers were not to blame. The zombies turned against their master, and the Reaper was seemingly consumed by Lloigoroth for his failure. Later, when Reaper's brother Wonder Man died again and mystically returned in a ghostly state, this weakened the barriers between life and death enough for Grim Reaper's spirit to return to the Earthly plane, mystically enslaving the spirits of Wonder Man and several other deceased Avengers: Captain Mar-Vell, Dr. Druid, Hellcat, Mockingbird, Swordsman and Thunderstrike. This new Legion attacked the living Avengers, but the undead Avengers were freed from the Reaper's control by the Scarlet Witch and helped defeat the Reaper. In the end, most of the undead Avengers returned to their respective afterlives, but Wonder Man was fully resurrected through the Witch's magic, which also restored the Grim Reaper to life after he was forced to admit his love for his brother. Hellcat was soon fully resurrected as well, in another supernatural adventure flowing from these events.

For now, the Legion of the Unliving have all been laid to rest again, though sufficiently powerful villains will doubtless raise more Legions to plague the Avengers anew. Meanwhile, a number of long-thought-dead Legion veterans have resurfaced among the living, such as Baron Blood, Bucky, Count Nefaria, Dracula, Drax the Destroyer, Frankenstein's Monster, Green Goblin (Norman Osborn), Grim Reaper, Hellcat, Human Torch, Korvac, Midnight (as the clone Midnight Sun), Mockingbird, Nebulon, Nighthawk, Red Guardian, Terrax and Wonder Man, though the Torch has since died again.

REAPER'S 2ND LEGION

Art George Pérez

BARON ZEMO
Active: Avengers #131 (1975)

FRANKENSTEIN'S MONSTER
Active: Avengers #131 (1975)

GHOST
Active: Avengers #131 (1975)

HUMAN TORCH
Active: Avengers #131 (1975)

MIDNIGHT
Active: Avengers #131 (1975)

WONDER MAN
Active: Avengers #131 (1975)

BARON BLOOD
Active: Avengers Annual #16 (1987)

BLACK KNIGHT (PERCY)
Active: Avengers Annual #16 (1987)

BUCKY
Active: Avengers Annual #16 (1987)

CAPTAIN MARVEL (MAR-VELL)
Active: Avengers Annual #16 (1987)

DEATH ADDER
Active: Avengers Annual #16 (1987)

DRACULA
Active: Avengers Annual #16 (1987)

DRAX THE DESTROYER
Active: Avengers Annual #16 (1987)

EXECUTIONER
Active: Avengers Annual #16 (1987)

GREEN GOBLIN
Active: Avengers Annual #16 (1987)

HYPERION
Active: Avengers Annual #16 (1987)

KORVAC
Active: Avengers Annual #16 (1987)

NIGHTHAWK
Active: Avengers Annual #16 (1987)

RED GUARDIAN
Active: Avengers Annual #16 (1987)

SWORDSMAN
Active: Avengers Annual #16 (1987)

TERRAX
Active: Avengers Annual #16 (1987)

BLACK KNIGHT (WHITMAN)
Active: Avengers Annual #16 (1987)

CAPTAIN MARVEL (RAMBEAU)
Active: Avengers Annual #16 (1987)

DR. DRUID
Active: Avengers Annual #16 (1987)

IRON MAN (TONY STARK)
Active: Avengers Annual #16 (1987)

MOCKINGBIRD
Active: Avengers Annual #16 (1987)

MOON KNIGHT
Active: Avengers Annual #16 (1987)

DR. HENRY PYM
Active: Avengers Annual #16 (1987)

SHE-HULK
Active: Avengers Annual #16 (1987)

SILVER SURFER
Active: Avengers Annual #16 (1987)

THOR
Active: Avengers Annual #16 (1987)

TIGRA
Active: Avengers Annual #16 (1987)

WASP
Active: Avengers Annual #16 (1987)

BLACK KNIGHT (GARRETT)
Active: Avengers West Coast #61 (1990)

GRIM REAPER
Active: Avengers West Coast #61 (1990)

IRON MAN (ARNO)
Active: Avengers West Coast #61 (1990)

LEFT-WINGER
Active: Avengers West Coast #61 (1990)

OORT THE LIVING COMET
Active: Avengers West Coast #61 (1990)

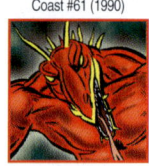
RIGHT-WINGER
Active: Avengers West Coast #61 (1990)

TORO
Active: Avengers West Coast #61 (1990)

AMENHOTEP
Active: Avengers #352 (1992)

COUNT NEFARIA
Active: Avengers #352 (1992)

INFERNO
Active: Avengers #352 (1992)

NEBULON
Active: Avengers #352 (1992)

NECRODAMUS
Active: Avengers #352 (1992)

STAR STALKER
Active: Avengers #352 (1992)

HELLCAT
Active: Avengers #10 (1998)

THUNDERSTRIKE
Active: Avengers #10 (1998)

LETHAL LEGION

HISTORY: The Lethal Legion is a super-criminal alliance dedicated to power, profit and the destruction of the Avengers. It began with Eric Williams, whose brother Simon had betrayed the heroic Avengers as Wonder Man but ultimately sacrificed himself to save them from the Masters of Evil. A grief-maddened Eric blamed the Avengers for Simon's death and became their mortal enemy as the Grim Reaper. Failing in his early solo attempts to destroy the Avengers despite secret tech support from the robotic menace Ultron, the Reaper later sought full partners in his crusade. He joined forces with fellow Avengers foes Living Laser, Man-Ape, Power Man and Swordsman as the Lethal Legion, whose members competed with each other to see who could capture or kill the most Avengers. The Legion captured most of the active Avengers and tried to asphyxiate them inside a giant hourglass, but the criminals were ultimately defeated and imprisoned – thanks largely to the android Vision, a new Avengers recruit whose artificial mind was programmed with a copy of the late Simon Williams' brain patterns. As years passed, the Reaper's ongoing enmity with the Avengers was complicated by his love-hate relationships with both the Vision and a resurrected Wonder Man, neither of whom Eric fully accepted as the "real" Simon Williams.

Meanwhile, crime lord Count Nefaria assembled a new Lethal Legion as pawns in his own quest for ultimate power. Recruiting Power Man first, Nefaria had him free the Living Laser and another longtime Avengers enemy, the Whirlwind, from prison. Nefaria's three super-agents soon clashed with the Avengers during a bank robbery, barely escaping, but the criminals sought a rematch after Nefaria's scientist Professor Kenneth Sturdy greatly increased the Legion's powers. The super-charged trio attacked Avengers Mansion, but their newly enhanced powers abruptly faded during the battle and they were quickly defeated. Their power boost had only been a temporary side-effect of Sturdy's process, which was actually designed to replicate their powers and grant similar abilities to Nefaria himself, only magnified a hundredfold. Now possessed of godlike strength, speed and energy powers, Nefaria went on a destructive rampage and single-handedly held off the Avengers until a diamond-hard Vision plummeted into him from a mile overhead, knocking the villain unconscious. Nefaria and his Legion were all taken into custody, and Sturdy apparently died from injuries inflicted by Nefaria, who had sought to prevent Sturdy from creating any rival super-beings.

Allied with Ultron, zombie master Black Talon, Goliath (a transformed Power Man), Man-Ape and hate-fueled mutant Nekra, the Reaper menaced the Avengers again as part of a bizarre scheme to re-create the "real" Simon Williams by transferring portions of the minds of Vision and Wonder Man into a zombie altered to resemble Simon's original human form. The plan failed and the Reaper — having belatedly realized that Vision and Wonder Man were truly his brothers — fell to his death while fleeing in shame. Black Talon and Man-Ape had already departed before the group's climactic confrontation with the Avengers, estranged from the Legion by Reaper's racist attitudes. Ultron and Reaper's lover Nekra escaped during the final battle with the Avengers, but Goliath was captured yet again despite his enhanced powers. Nekra later reanimated the Grim Reaper as a zombie, and the undead Williams renewed his enmity with the Avengers.

Around the same time, another Lethal Legion was formed by Whirlwind and a large gang of new recruits: Attuma, Batroc, Beetle, Black Tiger, Bulldozer, Gorilla-Man, Kurr'fri (a warrior of the hidden reptilian race known as "The People"), Piledriver, Porcupine, Sabretooth, Thundra,

FORMER MEMBERS: Axe of Violence (Lizzie Borden), Attuma, Batroc (Georges Batroc), Beetle (MACH-4, Abe Jenkins), Black Talon (Sam Barone), Black Tiger (unrevealed, possibly Brillalae), Bulldozer (Henry Camp), Coldsteel (Josef Stalin), Cyana (Lucrezia Borgia), Grim Reaper (Eric Williams), Goliath (Atlas, Power Man; Erik Josten), Gorilla-Man (Arthur Nagan), Hangman (Jason Roland), Kurr'fri, Living Laser (Arthur Parks), Man-Ape (M'Baku), Nekra (Nekra Sinclair), Piledriver (Brian Calusky), Porcupine (Alex Gentry), Sabretooth (Victor Creed), Swordsman (Jacques Duquesne), Thundra, Trapster (Pete Petruski), Ultron, Unicorn (unrevealed, possibly Milos Masaryk), Whirlwind (David Cannon), Wrecker (Dirk Garthwaite), Zyklon (Heinrich Himmler)
BASE OF OPERATIONS: Formerly Satannish's Hell dimension, Grim Reaper's cavern lair, Count Nefaria's Manhattan townhouse, a subterranean chamber beneath New York City
FIRST APPEARANCE: (Reaper's first Legion) Avengers #78 (1970); (Nefaria's Legion) Avengers #164 (1977); (Reaper's second Legion) West Coast Avengers #1 (1985); (Whirlwind's Legion) Marvel Age Annual #1 (1985); (Satannish's Legion) Avengers West Coast #98 (1993); (Earth-1298 Legion) Mutant X 2001 (2001)

THE ORIGINAL LEGION: LIVING LASER, POWER MAN, SWORDSMAN, GRIM REAPER & MAN-APE

Art by Sal Buscema

Art by John Byrne

NEFARIA'S LEGION: LIVING LASER, POWER MAN & WHIRLWIND

Trapster, Unicorn, Whirlwind and Wrecker. Targeting Captain America (Steve Rogers) for reasons as yet unrevealed, this Lethal Legion had Porcupine track him to the offices of Marvel Comics, where the villains attacked en masse; however, a similarly large group of super heroes counter-attacked, plunging Marvel's offices into chaos as the villains battled Ant-Man (Scott Lang), Beast, Blue Shield, Captain America, Crime-Buster (Eugene Mason), Iceman, Namorita, the Phone Ranger, Siryn, the Thing and assorted Marvel employees. A Scourge of the Underworld vigilante mistakenly shot the Phone Ranger during the confusion, apparently assuming the obscure telephone-costumed hero was part of the Lethal Legion. The cosmic-powered Beyonder appeared during the fight as an observer, and may have had some influence over the combatants – for instance, he might have been responsible for assembling the very random group of heroes present at the Marvel offices, given his ability to move others through time and space, perhaps having staged the whole battle for his amusement. The battle's outcome is unrecorded, though the Legion presumably lost since Marvel Comics, Captain America, the Phone Ranger and most of the other heroes are known to have survived the incident.

While the Grim Reaper had become a supernatural menace, the next Legion arose from a completely different mystical source: the demon lord Satannish stole the souls of infamous killers Lizzie Borden, Josef Stalin, Lucrezia Borgia and Heinrich Himmler from the realm of rival demon lord Mephisto, transforming them into four super-beings: the blade-handed Axe of Violence, metallic strongman Coldsteel, poison-generating Cyana and armored toxic gas emitter Zyklon. With the Hangman (a movie star who had sold his soul to Satannish) as their field leader, this Legion was assigned to kill Satannish's Avengers foes and capture their souls, in exchange for which Satannish would supposedly restore the Legion fully to life. After murdering Hangman's estranged lover Stella Houston and launching a series of attacks on the Avengers, the Legion finally lured the Avengers into Satannish's realm by abducting Avengers member Mockingbird. A vengeful Mephisto slipped in alongside the heroes and fought Satannish for the stolen souls, all four of which were destroyed in a mystical tug-of-war between the two arch-demons. The Avengers escaped, but not before Mockingbird died shielding Hawkeye from Mephisto's spiteful parting blasts. Mockingbird has since returned from her seeming demise, but whether Hangman, Satannish, Nefaria, the Grim Reaper or anyone else will rebuild the Lethal Legion remains to be seen.

NOTE: In the alternate reality of Earth-1298, a super-heroic version of the Lethal Legion was formed by the following heroes: a zombie incarnation of Brother Voodoo; a Devil Dinosaur apparently possessed of demonic qualities akin to Daimon Hellstrom; a masked Fin Fang Foom; the Gargoyle (Isaac Christians); Devil Dinosaur's companion Moon-Knight-Boy (combining elements of Earth-616's Moon Boy and Moon Knight); a super-powered incarnation of Sherry the Showgirl (empowered by a Bloodstone fragment); and Slapstick (Steve Harmon). This reality's Gargoyle and Slapstick did not seem significantly different from their Earth-616 counterparts, though no detailed information is available regarding any members of the Earth-1298 team. This Lethal Legion was among the heroes who opposed a rampage by the immensely powerful Beyonder (later revealed to be the Goblin Queen disguised as the true Beyonder); during that battle, the "Beyonder" killed the entire Lethal Legion and the Earth-1298 Daredevil with a single nuclear-strength energy discharge.

SATANNISH'S LEGION

Art by David Ross

Art by Al Milgrom

REAPER'S 2ND LEGION

EARTH-1298 LEGION

Art by James Fry

ATTACK ON MARVEL OFFICES

Art by James Fry

GRIM REAPER
Active: Avengers #78 (1970)

LIVING LASER
Active: Avengers #78 (1970)

MAN-APE
Active: Avengers #78 (1970)

POWER MAN
Active: Avengers #78 (1970)

SWORDSMAN
Active: Avengers #78 (1970)

COUNT NEFARIA
Patron: Avengers #164 (1977)

WHIRLWIND
Active: Avengers #164 (1977)

BLACK TALON
Active: Vision and the Scarlet Witch #1 (1985)

GOLIATH
Active: West Coast Avengers #1 (1985)

NEKRA
Active: Vision and the Scarlet Witch #1 (1985)

ULTRON
Active: West Coast Avengers #1 (1985)

ATTUMA
Active: Marvel Age Annual #1 (1985)

BATROC
Active: Marvel Age Annual #1 (1985)

BEETLE
Active: Marvel Age Annual #1 (1985)

BLACK TIGER
Active: Marvel Age Annual #1 (1985)

BULLDOZER
Active: Marvel Age Annual #1 (1985)

GORILLA-MAN
Active: Marvel Age Annual #1 (1985)

KURR'FRI
Active: Marvel Age Annual #1 (1985)

PILEDRIVER
Active: Marvel Age Annual #1 (1985)

PORCUPINE
Active: Marvel Age Annual #1 (1985)

SABRETOOTH
Active: Marvel Age Annual #1 (1985)

THUNDRA
Active: Marvel Age Annual #1 (1985)

TRAPSTER
Active: Marvel Age Annual #1 (1985)

UNICORN
Active: Marvel Age Annual #1 (1985)

WRECKER
Active: Marvel Age Annual #1 (1985)

AXE OF VIOLENCE
Active: Avengers West Coast #98 (1993)

COLDSTEEL
Active: Avengers West Coast #98 (1993)

CYANA
Active: Avengers West Coast #98 (1993)

HANGMAN
Active: Avengers West Coast #98 (1993)

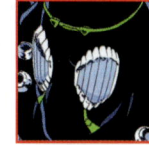
ZYKLON
Active: Avengers West Coast #98 (1993)

LIBERTY LEGION

FORMER MEMBERS: Blue Diamond (Elton Morrow), Bucky (James Buchanan Barnes), Jack Frost, Miss America (Madeline Joyce), Patriot (Jeff Mace), Red Raven, Thin Man (Bruce Dickson), Whizzer (Robert Frank)
BASE OF OPERATIONS: The Times Tower, New York City
FIRST APPEARANCE: Marvel Premiere #29 (1976)

HISTORY: In early 1942, the Red Skull (Johann Shmidt) used the Nullatron, a brainwashing device, on the captured Captain America (Steve Rogers), the Human Torch (Jim Hammond), the Sub-Mariner (Namor), and Toro (Thomas Raymond), the most powerful members of the Invaders, and turned the four of them against the United States. Captain America's sidekick Bucky (James Barnes) was ignored by the Skull, who didn't believe that the teenager posed a serious threat. Determined to prove that his friends were under the Skull's thrall and had not betrayed America, Bucky interrupted a regular radio slot used by another costumed hero, the Patriot, and with his endorsement sent out a plea for help to any other heroes listening. They received responses from the nearly indestructible Blue Diamond, the ice-wielding Jack Frost, flying crime-fighter Miss America, winged vigilante Red Raven, the malleable-bodied Thin Man, and the super-fast Whizzer. Together, the seven heroes, led by Bucky, became the Liberty Legion. While Bucky and the Thin Man coordinated the team's movements from the radio station, the others set out to capture the Invaders, who the Skull sent to destroy national landmarks to break US morale. Blue Diamond and Jack Frost prevented Namor from destroying the Statue of Liberty, while Patriot and Miss America defended Philadelphia's Liberty Hall from Captain America, and Red Raven and Whizzer intercepted Toro and the Torch at the Lincoln Memorial; though the Legion saved each monument, they only succeeded in capturing Toro. While they were unable to break the Skull's hold over him, they tricked the Skull into thinking they had succeeded by having New York Yankees batboy Fred Davis pretend to be Bucky while Bucky impersonated Toro. The Red Skull challenged the Liberty Legion to a showdown with the Invaders at Yankee Stadium, during which Bucky released Toro so that he would lead them to the Skull. The Skull was monitoring the fight from a zeppelin which Toro inadvertently blew up, freeing all of the Invaders from his domination. With the crisis averted, Bucky returned to the Invaders, while the rest of the Liberty Legion decided to remain together to help protect the homefront in the US while the Invaders fought overseas. Later, the Liberty Legion joined forces with the time-traveling Thing to battle the combined Nazi menace of Brain Drain (Werner Schmidt), Master Man (Wilhelm Lohmer), Skyshark (Elias Schleigal), Suraisu (Tochigi Mamoru, aka Slicer), and U-Man (Merrano). They also teamed up with the Invaders again when Miss America investigated the menace of Iron Cross (Helmut Gruler), a German nationalist in a powerful suit of armor, whose defeat required the combined forces of both groups. Whizzer and Miss America took a leave of absence from the Legion to join the short-handed Invaders while they were in the US, and continued to switch back and forth between the two teams throughout the war. Details of the Legion's activities later in the war remain uncertain, but some of the Legion were present alongside other Allied heroes during the Battle of Berlin in 1945.

Shortly before the war ended, Bucky and Captain America went missing in action. In their absence former Liberty Legion ally Fred Davis took over as Bucky, while the Patriot became one of the men to replace Steve Rogers as Captain America, serving with the Whizzer and Miss America in the post-war All-Winners Squad before retiring around the end of the decade. A few years ago, after Rogers returned, Mace succumbed to cancer, dying with Rogers at his bedside. Bucky meanwhile had secretly become the Soviets' brainwashed assassin, the Winter Soldier; Rogers eventually learned of this and broke his conditioning, and when Rogers apparently died, Barnes replaced him as the new Captain America. The Whizzer and Miss America eventually married, but their first child was the dangerous mutant Nuklo, and in 1958 Miss America died during the delivery of their stillborn second child. The Whizzer died decades later battling Isbisa, having briefly served as an honorary Avengers member. Red Raven became the leader of the Bird People, continuing to rule them to this day. Jack Frost was frozen in the arctic, keeping the monstrous Ice Worm from reviving; he briefly escaped to fight alongside Captain America (Rogers) before sacrificing himself again. Blue Diamond became Shanga the Star-Dancer's companion and was transformed into a cosmic-powered living diamond, joining her in outer space, but has apparently returned to Earth in more conventional form. The Thin Man worked as a Nazi hunter, led a reactivated Invaders, and remains active as an intelligence agent. A new group, the Liberteens, has formed to represent Pennsylvania in the 50-State Initiative, the individual members' powers and codenames approximating those of the original Liberty Legionnaires, though any actual connections to their wartime counterparts remain unconfirmed.

CLOCKWISE FROM LEFT: JACK FROST, WHIZZER, RED RAVEN, THIN MAN, PATRIOT, BUCKY, MISS AMERICA, BLUE DIAMOND

Art by Frank Robbins

LIFEGUARD

HISTORY: Australian Heather Cameron and her brother Davis were sent to live in Surfer's Paradise by their father in an effort to spare them from his life as the Viceroy, godfather of Australian organized crime. Unaware of their father's identity or of their own latent mutant natures, Heather became a lifeguard while Davis became a surfer. When Heather's mutant nature manifested, she kept it secret, using it only to help save lives as part of her job. After their father was killed in Sydney by mutant illusionist Lady Mastermind on behalf of mutant powerbroker Sebastian Shaw, the siblings became targets in the ensuing gang war as potential heirs to their father's criminal empire. Investigating the death due to the implication of their ally Gambit, the X-Men sought to protect the Camerons. Storm and Thunderbird (Neal Shaara) befriended the siblings in Surfer's Paradise but were soon attacked by Boxers, assassins sent by the Chinese Triad, and Heather was forced to publicly reveal her mutant nature to help defeat them. After learning of their father's identity and the gang war, Heather and Davis sought to help the X-Men stop the carnage. Heather herself was instrumental in defeating Lady Mastermind; however, Shaw escaped conviction.

Joining the X-Men, Heather helped the team against the alien Shaitan but was captured. Seeking to help rescue his sister, Davis agreed to let Sage jumpstart his own latent mutation and he joined the team as Slipstream. Heather, meanwhile, failed to prevent Shaitan from opening a dimensional portal that allowed his master Khan's army to invade Earth. Reunited with the X-Men, Heather helped oppose the invasion, during which time her powers inadvertently activated the dormant alien Shi'ar DNA in her genome, transforming her into an avian-human/Shi'ar hybrid. After the X-Men repelled the invasion, Heather was reunited with

REAL NAME: Heather Cameron
ALIASES: None
IDENTITY: Publicly known
OCCUPATION: Adventurer; former lifeguard
CITIZENSHIP: Australia
PLACE OF BIRTH: Sydney, Australia
KNOWN RELATIVES: Miles Warbeck (Viceroy, father, deceased), unidentified mother, Davis Cameron (Slipstream, brother)
GROUP AFFILIATION: Formerly X-Corporation, X-Men
EDUCATION: Unrevealed
FIRST APPEARANCE: X-Treme X-Men #6 (2001); (Lifeguard) X-Treme X-Men #7 (2002)

Davis, who rejected her new appearance and left. Heather set about searching for him, accompanied by Thunderbird, but ultimately joined the X-Corporation's Mumbai branch before it was bombed in a terrorist attack. Her whereabouts since are unrevealed.

NOTE: It is unclear whether Lifeguard has Shi'ar ancestry or if she had Shi'ar genetic material inserted into her body at some point.

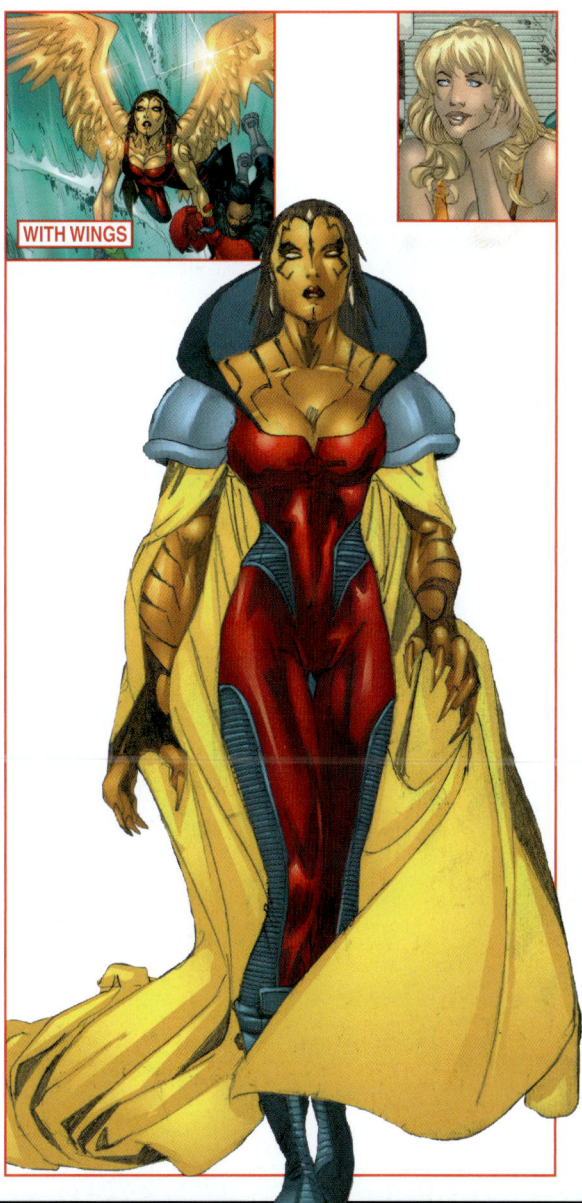

ARMORED FORM

MERMAID FORM

HEIGHT: 7' (variable); formerly 5'10"
WEIGHT: 205 lbs. (variable); formerly 130 lbs.
EYES: Blue
HAIR: Blonde

ABILITIES/ACCESSORIES: Lifeguard's body adapts to any perceived threats by immediately evolving an appropriate response. Lifeguard has formed a protective golden metal sheath over her skin, developed superhuman strength, grown gills and a fish-like tail, and has even shapeshifted into a whale. Once the threat has passed, her body reverts to normal.

Lifeguard's Shi'ar genome, which is of royal lineage, has granted her avian traits, including wings and razor-sharp talons, as well as a predatory nature with unparalleled tracking skills. She is also a qualified lifeguard and an excellent swimmer.

*YELLOW BARS INDICATE LIFEGUARD'S ADAPTIVE MUTATION

Art by Salvador Larroca

LILIN

KNOWN MEMBERS: Bad Timing, Blackout, Bloodthirst, Creed, Dark Legion, Doc, Fang, Girth, Infinks, Meatmarket, Nakota, Outcast, Parasite, Pilgrim, Pixil, Scatter, Short-Circuit, Sister Nil, Skinner, Skitter, Spitfire, numerous unidentified others
BASE OF OPERATIONS: Shadowside Dimension; various points across Earth
FIRST APPEARANCE: (Vision) Ghost Rider #28 (1992); (actual) Ghost Rider/Blaze: Spirits of Vengeance #1 (1992)

HISTORY: The Lilin are a race of demons spawned by Lilith, the self-professed Mother of Demons. Each apparently possessing unique superhuman powers, the Lilin are either immortal or extremely long-lived. It is undetermined if the first generation of Lilin were demon/human hybrids, the result of Lilith mating with other demons, or creations of some other type. Lilith and her children led a campaign of terror and death against humanity, but at some point Atlantean magicians incarcerated her within the belly of a leviathan (Tiamat), after which many of the Lilin were killed off by their adversaries. Some survived, either escaping to other dimensions or assimilating themselves into humanity. For thousands of years, Lilith's children awaited her return.

In recent years, when the half-buried corpse of the leviathan was discovered in the frozen wastelands of northern Greenland, the scientists exploring their find accidentally released Lilith. Using magic to peer into the future, Lilith saw that she was destined to fight a cabal of nine supernatural beings who threatened her existence. She summoned her children, but only Pilgrim, a being able to create teleportation rifts, answered her. Determined to keep the Nine from coming together, Lilith and Pilgrim set out to find other Lilin. They first located Creed, a former Lilin leader who had long ago given up the old ways, and Blackout, Lilith's mass-murdering vampire-like descendant. Though his Lilin blood was diluted by generations, Blackout pledged total loyalty to Lilith. She sent her three followers to the Quentin Carnival to make a preemptive strike on John Blaze, one of the Nine, but Blaze and his comrade Ghost Rider defeated them. Creed's body was destroyed in the encounter, and as he wanted nothing further to do with Lilin affairs, his undying head thanked the two. Lilith, however, promised Creed he would never find peace. Unknown to Lilith, Dr. Stephen Strange, Earth's Sorcerer Supreme, had become aware of the situation, and though he did not dare confront her in person lest it weaken the dimensional barriers that held most of the other Lilin, he manipulated events to place the foretold Nine on a path to come together.

Lilith located more of her progeny, including Doc (whose mystic knives could cut and create), Fang (able to turn into a formless mass) and Nakota (whose eyes could see and display activities from great distances). Fang was sent to kill the living vampire Michael Morbius, but the Lilin's blood transfused with Morbius' only resulted in Morbius gaining even greater vampiric qualities. Just as the ranks of the Lilin began to regroup, with Skinner (a skeletal being with razor-sharp protrusions who dressed in the skin of his victims) and Meatmarket (whose rotted corpse-like body was comprised of his victims), so too did the Nine begin to fully emerge. Skinner, who had long since given up Lilith's cause and married a human, slew his family to spare them the horrors of his true heritage before pursuing Ghost Rider and Blaze in a failed attempt to kill them. Efforts to disperse the newly-formed Darkhold Redeemers and Nightstalkers failed as well. Impatient, Lilith opted to use her body as a gateway to return the rest of the Lilin to Earth. Dr. Strange transported the Nine to Greenland to confront the Lilin. During the battle, Lilith pulled the disembodied spirit of Dan Ketch, Ghost Rider's human host (seemingly slain in a recent battle with Blackout), through her, transforming it into a demonic beast. Ghost Rider finally defeated the demoness when he forced part of her through her own portal. With Lilith and the Lilin believed dead and defeated, the Nine dispersed; but Lilith had survived the encounter, feeding on Nakota, the lone surviving Lilin and the flesh of her dead children.

During the months Lilith remained in Greenland, letting the Lilin regrow inside her, the Nightstalkers encountered and destroyed Short-Circuit, another of her "grandchildren." When the time came to give birth to her brood again, she called for help and Outcast, a bestial Lilin who had refused to be at her side previously for reasons unrevealed, arrived. He tore her open, allowing the Lilin's rebirth. Pilgrim and a newly empowered Blackout were sent to find and capture the Nine (now informally known as the Midnight Sons), and they ran afoul of Ghost Rider. Centurious, Blaze's nemesis, confronted Lilith and offered an alliance, hoping to retrieve the Medallion of Power. The two launched an assault on Blaze and Ghost Rider using the Lilin and Centurious' forces, capturing Blaze as well as Ketch's mother Francis. At the same time, Morbius, fighting for control with the Lilin taint in his system, used the Darkhold to resurrect his slain love, Martine Bancroft, but actually infected her with the Lilin called Parasite. As Morbius began to give in to his Lilin blood, "Martine" manipulated him into giving his control over to it, after which he would act as Lilith's secret weapon within the Midnight Sons. Ghost Rider rescued Blaze, and the two were joined by Vengeance when Centurious and the Lilin arrived. The battle was interrupted when a near-amnesiac Zarathos was released from his prison within Centurious. Lilith, sensing the demon's power, brushed away Centurious and offered to make an alliance with him. Ghost Rider, however, gained control of the Medallion of Power and sent Zarathos, Lilith and the remaining Lilin to the Shadowside Dimension.

BAD TIMING
Nightstalkers #14 (1993)

BLACKOUT
Ghost Rider #2 (1990)

BLOODTHIRST
(Blood form) Morbius #1 (1992); (humanoid form) Morbius #20 (1994)

CREED
Ghost Rider/Blaze: Spirits of Vengeance #1 (1992)

DARK LEGION
Ghost Rider #44 (1993)

DOC
Darkhold: Pages From the Book of Sins #1 (1992)

FANG
Morbius #1 (1992)

GIRTH
Marvel Comics Presents #143 (1993)

INFINKS
Marvel Comics Presents #143 (1993)

LILITH
(Vision) Ghost Rider #28 (1992); (actual) Ghost Rider/Blaze: Spirits of Vengeance #1 (1992)

MEATMARKET
(Vision) Ghost Rider #28 (1992); (actual) Nightstalkers #1 (1992)

NAKOTA
(Vision) Ghost Rider #28 (1992); (actual) Morbius #1 (1992)

Art by Andy Kubert

that traitor, Morbius, was fighting alongside the Nightstalkers and the Darkhold Redeemers against a vast horde of Lilin on the Brooklyn Bridge. Morbius led them to a hideout, where he murdered Louise Hastings of the Redeemers and allowed the Lilin to infiltrate the sanctuary. Morbius then led the Lilin to Strange's Sanctum, where they attacked the remaining Sons. There, Strange helped Morbius gain control of his body again, and they contained "Bloodthirst," Morbius' Lilin aspect. Scatter, a tiny Lilin with the powers of speed and disorienting others' minds, gained access to the Sanctum, followed shortly by the enigmatic succubus Sister Nil. In the chaos, the building was destroyed, leaving Strange and the Sons surrounded by Lilin. They fought their way back to Cypress Hills Cemetery, where Lilith had consummated her union with Zarathos. When a dimensional rift was opened, the Midnight Sons' ally Caretaker ordered them to use the Medallion of Power to close the rift first before destroying Zarathos. They did so, and the power sucked Lilith and the nearby Lilin back to the Shadowside Dimension. When Zarathos was defeated some time later, Lilith promised to leave the Lilin behind and focus instead on the demon-child she and Zarathos conceived.

From there, Lilith launched a full-scale assault on Earth using a magical mist as a doorway into the world. As it spread across the planet, the Lilin arrived back on Earth, and soon confronted the Midnight Sons yet again. A Lilin time-manipulator named Bad Timing led the initial charge, but his defeat by the Nightstalkers led the Sons back to Cypress Hills Cemetery, where Lilith, Zarathos and several Lilin awaited. Elsewhere, Blackout, Meatmarket and Dark Legion (who could create duplicates of himself) viciously attacked a police station, intent on massacring the humans there. Vengeance (Michael Badilino) staved off the killers until Ghost Rider could arrive, followed shortly by Dr. Strange, who offered his Sanctum Sanctorum as a refuge for the heroes during the chaos.

As the mists spread, more Lilin encountered several other of Earth's supernatural protectors. The Scarlet Witch found herself trapped in cyberspace, where she defeated the computerized Lilin called Pixil. Jack Russell, the Werewolf, stopped a mob of diminutive "goblin" Lilin from razing a small town. Devil-Slayer encountered the bizarre sub-race of baby-like Lilin called the Infinks. Some Lilin came as far as San Francisco where they were opposed by Silver Sable, her Wild Pack and Venom (Eddie Brock).

Lilith had Pilgrim attempt to transport Ghost Rider and his companions to her, but they instead ended up in the lair of the obese Lilin Girth and his second, Skitter. Before Dr. Strange could retrieve them, they learned that there was a traitor within the Midnight Sons. Unbeknownst to them,

A few Lilin remained on Earth after this, however. Morbius found a fatally wounded Lilin child who had wanted no part of her mother's war. He tried to save her, despite his fellow Son Hannibal King's objections, but ultimately failed. Morbius, now fully aware of what inhabited Martine, struck at her until Parasite emerged. The Lilin was almost immediately struck down by Embyrre - one of the Fallen (members of the race known as the Blood who chose to serve Zarathos) - who had emerged from the same dimensional rift that entrapped Lilith and her brood. Though Parasite no longer inhabited her form, Martine survived. Determined to rid himself of the Lilin blood in his system, Morbius underwent a complete blood transfusion. Once drawn from his system, the Lilin blood, having interacted with Morbius's unique physiology, became a sentient being called Bloodthirst. This new Lilin tried to kill its former host, but was destroyed instead. Meanwhile, Sister Nil returned to pursue Dr. Strange, who intrigued her. Initially he held her in mystic bonds, and over time she became his ward as she attempted to learn about humanity. Skinner was found and transported to the facility known as the Black Hole, where he again encountered Ghost Rider. When the Black Hole was destroyed, Skinner escaped and went after Ghost Rider once more, but Ghost Rider and John Blaze literally beat the Lilin into submission. He was transferred to the Vault afterwards. Blackout also resumed his vendetta against Ghost Rider and forsook his Lilin lineage, returning to his mercenary ways. Lilith returned later to menace Dr. Strange, giving birth to a new unidentified Lilin to aid her, but they were defeated.

OUTCAST
Ghost Rider #41 (1993)

PARASITE
(Possessing Martine Bancroft) Morbius #13 (1993); (true form) Morbius #17 (1994)

PILGRIM
(Vision) Ghost Rider #28 (1992); (actual) Ghost Rider/Blaze: Spirits of Vengeance #1 (1992)

PIXIL
Marvel Comics Presents #143 (1993)

SCATTER
Dr. Strange: Sorcerer Supreme #60 (1993)

SHORT-CIRCUIT
Nightstalkers #12 (1993)

SISTER NIL
Dr. Strange: Sorcerer Supreme #60 (1993)

SKINNER (HUMAN FORM)
Ghost Rider/Blaze: Spirits of Vengeance #3 (1992)

SKINNER (TRUE FORM)
Ghost Rider/Blaze: Spirits of Vengeance #3 (1992)

SKITTER
Marvel Comics Presents #143 (1993)

SPITFIRE
Darkhold: Pages From the Book of Sins #15 (1993)

LILITH (MOTHER OF DEMONS)

REAL NAME: Possibly Bat Zuge or Kiskillilla
ALIASES: Lilith is known by over 20,000 names, including Abeko, Abiti, Abito, Abizu, Agrat bat Mahlat, Amizo, Amrusu, the Archmother of Witchcraft, Avgu, Ayil, Batna, Batub, Bushyansta, Eilo, the First Eve, the Fury, Ghul, Hakash, Ishtar, Ita, Izorpo, Kali, Katah, Kea, Kokos, Lalla, Lamashtu, Lamia, Layil, Lillitu, Matruta, Meyalleleth, Mother of Demons, the Night Hag, the Night Rider, the Northerner, Obyzouth, Odam, Ode, Paritasha, Partasah, Patrota, Podo, the Princess of Damascus, the Queen of Sheba, the Queen of Zemargad, Satrina, the Screech Owl, Talto, and the Vampire Goddess
IDENTITY: Believed by the general public to be a mythological character
OCCUPATION: Progenitor, would-be conqueror; former queen, storm demon, goddess of the underworld, angel, others
CITIZENSHIP: Inapplicable
PLACE OF BIRTH: Unrevealed, perhaps inapplicable
KNOWN RELATIVES: Samael, Adam, Attis, Ashmodei, Shemhazai, others (husbands/consorts); Hurmin, Alefpeneash, others (sons); Agrat, Irit, Nega, the Queen of Sheba, others (daughters); unidentified child[ren] fathered by Zarathos; Aehr or Ahriman (alleged father); the Shekhinah, Na'amah, Lillu, Ardat, Irdu (sisters); Djinn, Lilin (including Bad Timing, Bloodthirst, Carver, Creed, Dark Legion, Doc, Fang, Girth, Infinks, Meatmarket, Nakota, Outcast, Parasite, Pilgrim, Pixil, Sister Nil, Skinner, Skitter, Spitfire, others), Mazikim, Nephilim (offspring races); Short Circuit (grandchild); Lilidtha (granddaughter); Blackout (descendant); unidentified nieces and nephews; Valkyries (alleged kinswomen); Pazuzu (possible cousin)
GROUP AFFILIATION: Leader of the Lilin; formerly the Annunaki (Mesopotamian gods), the Heavenly Hosts, others
EDUCATION: Unrevealed; extensive occult knowledge
FIRST APPEARANCE: Ghost Rider #28 (1992)

HISTORY: At the dawn of humanity, Lilith's true origins were already lost, but some claim she began life as a member of the Heavenly Hosts alongside her sister Na'ameh, with whom she shared the affections of her husband Samael. When Samael, later calling himself "Satan," led a rebellion against Heaven, Lilith and her sister stood at his side, Lilith herself leading 480 legions into battle. When their rebellion failed, Lilith, Samael, and their followers were cast from Heaven into the realms that humanity later named "Hell." Evidently seeing little future with Samael, Lilith allegedly became the lover of Adam, the father of humanity, whose creation, some sources state, sparked the rebellion. Lilith conceived many children, known as the Mazikim, by Adam but ultimately found him oppressive and abandoned him. Senoy, Sansenoy, and Semangol, three entities calling themselves angels, slew most of her children in response, and the grief-stricken Lilith fled to demon cities beneath the Red Sea, vowing that her future children would dominate humanity.

Lilith's activities throughout most of the subsequent millennia remain unrevealed if not unimaginable, but as of some 20,000 years ago, the era of the occult heroes called the Midnight Sons, she was residing in Atlantis, where she may have participated in the creation of the first vampire; when the Atlantean Empire was destroyed in the Great Cataclysm, she was one of its few survivors. When Atlantis' gods faded from human consciousness, new ones arose, with Lilith taking her place among the Annunaki, worshipped in Mesopotamia, but she reportedly deteriorated into a storm demon before withdrawing to the desert beyond the Euphrates River, which flowed through what would become Iraq. In subsequent centuries, Lilith courted both mortal and mystic power, ruling various kingdoms in her human form. She also continued her quest to conceive powerful children, including the demonic warriors called the Lilin, whose lineage might one day overwhelm the world. Her many lovers supposedly included the angel Shemhazai, the fertility deity Attis, the Olympian God Zeus, and even the Judeo-Christian God himself.

Ancient stories claim that Lilith fought the immortal king Gilgamesh circa 3000 BC and, over two millennia later, joined other demons to challenge Israel's King Solomon, who enslaved and banished many such demons, including some of the Lilin. Per the stories, Lilith took the form of one of her many daughters, the Queen of Sheba, to conceive a child by Solomon, the supposed chosen one of God. Less than a century after Solomon's time, Lilith became the nemesis of the prophet Elijah, whom she fought during his desert retreats and who, some claim, she also deceived into fathering more of her children. Allegedly, it was she who slaughtered the children of Job at Satan's command and, when Rome fell three centuries after the birth of Christ, she reigned in the ruins as jackals and kites roamed the desolation, feeding upon the carrion of an empty empire — or so the stories say.

As Christianity spread, Lilith followed it across the continents, continuing her unending quest to conceive powerful children by seducing men in their sleep and, in turn, to slay humanity's own newborns. Scarcely a century after Rome's fall, amulets carved with the Mazikim's killers' names were already being used to guard against her. In 12th century Asia, while her son Hurmin challenged the King of Mehuza, Lilith met perhaps her most humiliating defeat at mortal hands when a Turkish midwife, her name lost to legend, briefly trapped her within a bottle. Lilith fared far better a century later when the prophet Joseph della Reina, hoping to hasten the coming of the Messiah, dared confront her and her latest consort, the demon Ashmodei. Although Reina had studied dark sorcery under Lilith herself, he was no match for her power and ended his days in insanity, trapped in the form of a black dog. By the 17th century, Lilith was at the height of her power over mortal men, even while they emigrated to the New World in greater numbers. Although she was challenged decades later by the mystic Rabbi Elimelekh of Poland,

Art by Adam & Andy Kubert

LEVIATHAN

Art by Adam Kubert

she ultimately outlived him as, it seemed, she had all earlier foes.

Despite various accounts of her physical death, at some point in centuries past, surviving Atlantean mages ensnared Lilith within a monstrous sea beast, perhaps the legendary Leviathan, the Annunaki's alleged progenitor Tiamat, beached upon what became northern Greenland; thus, it may have been her spirit form that accomplished her feats of recent millennia. Lilith's spirit may in fact have crossed not only the continents and eons, but the dimensional barriers themselves, to worlds where the laws of magic and vampirism widely differed, and certainly her power was invoked by denizens of multiple plains. With their mother gone, many Lilin were slain, while the survivors fled across the dimensions or into the throng of humanity. Eventually, surviving tales of Lilith's rebellion and independence made her a mythic heroine to many, who had little idea that she truly existed and even less of the bloody exploits that the legends shrouded.

In recent years, Lilith finally freed herself from the great beast's corpse when its remains were discovered by a scientific expedition. Drawing strength from the scientists' emotions, she tore her way out of her carrion prison and further bloodied her hands with the lives of the luckless explorers, then summoned her teleporting son Pilgrim to gather his brethren for a pre-emptive assault on "the Nine," fated successors of the Midnight Sons, including Ghost Rider (Daniel Ketch), John Blaze, Morbius, and others. Forming alliances with Nightmare, immortal Centurious, Darkholder spy Randolph DeGuzman, and others, Lilith sent her son Fang to mystically mutate Morbius, empowered ninja assassins to send against Victoria Montesi, briefly remade Dan Ketch's disembodied spirit into a Lilin, and otherwise undermined the Nine before the Lilin were dispatched to the Shadow Side Dimension by a mystic explosion caused by Ghost Rider.

Rescuing and reinvigorating her spawn, Lilith, too powerful for even Sorcerer Supreme Dr. Strange to directly confront, summoned a Dark Mist from the Shadow Side, intending to infuse Earth with it to cement her power. Infecting Morbius with another son, Bloodthirst, Lilith weakened the newly allied Midnight Sons from within. In the course of one clash, the demon Zarathos, ancient even in Lilith's youth, escaped from his confinement within Centurious' body, and Lilith, seeing in him a worthy prospective mate, manipulated the demon into joining her forces. Following a mass assault by the Lilin upon New York's Brooklyn Bridge, she manipulated Morbius into killing Montesi's mentor Louise Hastings and caused the temporary destruction of Strange's Sanctum Sanctorum. Nevertheless, the Lilin were ultimately re-banished, but Lilith shrugged off their fate and, abandoning her millennia-old family to their exile, returned to Earth, having conceived Zarathos' child or children and consigned the demon himself to her lengthy list of abandoned lovers.

Resurfacing after the apparent birth of Zarathos' spawn, Lilith, her powers reduced but her arrogance intact, bedeviled Dr. Strange and his protégés the Witches (Topaz, Jennifer Kale, Satana) when the demon/god-spawn Hellphyr stalked the Earth, slaying magic users. Callously creating a new Lilin to die in battle with the Witches, Lilith nearly slew Strange before the Hellphyr's destruction boosted his powers. Her extradimensional sanctuary, along with many other realms, was sealed off by fairy king Oberon during a Skrull invasion to prevent the aliens from misusing those realms' magic. However, British mutant Peter Wisdom was forced to undo Oberon's work in order to free the sorcerer Merlyn, freeing Lilith and other powerful evil entities in the process. Although Lilith and her ilk helped drive the Skrulls from Great Britain, she was thus granted freer access to Earth and an expanded ability to reclaim her ancient powers. Her current plans remain unrevealed, but plans she surely has, for she has waited the whole of human history to make the Earth a playground for her children, and she can wait longer still, for she deals in lust and blood, two of humanity's most common coins.

Art by Ron Garney

HEIGHT: 6' **EYES:** Greenish-yellow
WEIGHT: 265 lbs. **HAIR:** Black

ABILITIES/ACCESSORIES: Lilith's powers have fluctuated over the millennia as her status has shifted to angel, demon, goddess, and more. Originally, she was so infused with the universe's ambient mystic energy that direct combat with her could potentially weaken dimensional barriers. At present, she possesses at least the typical superhuman strength (up to Class 25), endurance, and durability of a god and can conjure visions of distant events, create bolts or walls of mystic energy, kill via invisible force, teleport, and perform other magical feats; the full extent of her power, whether current or potential, remains undetermined. She can augment her power by absorbing life force from the Lilin (and, presumably, any of her other offspring races), whom she can mentally contact across thousands of miles. She can summon Lilin from other dimensions, enabling them to re-enter the Earth dimension via "re-birth" through portals in her body. She can apparently reshape other beings into Lilin and create new Lilin from occult energy at will; the more Lilin or other Lilith-spawn that exist, the more powerful she becomes. She has vast knowledge of magical lore, much of which originated with her.

According to legend, Lilith's power is less effective against women than against men. In ancient times she supposedly wore wings and wielded a mystic sword, as well as a bow whose meteor-stone arrows could cure or inflict illness.

POWER GRID	1	2	3	4	5	6	7
INTELLIGENCE							
STRENGTH							
SPEED*							
DURABILITY							
ENERGY PROJECTION							
FIGHTING SKILLS							

*** LILITH IS A TELEPORTER**

LILITH (DAUGHTER OF DRACULA)

REAL NAME: Lilith
ALIASES: Lilith "Lily" Drake, Daughter of Dracula, Queen of the Undead
IDENTITY: True nature unknown to general public
OCCUPATION: Adventuress, Dracula's nemesis
CITIZENSHIP: USA via forged documents (as Lilith Drake); formerly Wallachia
PLACE OF BIRTH: Castle Dracula, Wallachia, Transylvania
KNOWN RELATIVES: Dracula (father), Zofia (mother, deceased), Vlad Dracul (grandfather, deceased), Mircea, Radu (uncles, deceased); Vlad Tepulus (half brother, deceased), Janus (half-brother); Maria (deceased), Domini (Dracula's second and third wives), Frank Drake (common ancestry), others (see Dracula))
GROUP AFFILIATION: Formerly SHIELD's Howling Commandos monster unit
EDUCATION: Unrevealed
FIRST APPEARANCE: Giant-Size Chillers #1 (1974)

HISTORY: After a loveless, abusive, year-long prearranged marriage to Hungarian noblewoman Zofia, 15th century nobleman Vlad Dracula banished Zofia and their infant daughter, Lilith, stripping Zofia of her royal standing, intending she live out her days as a penniless peasant. After paying her remaining gold pieces to wizened Roma ("Gypsy") Gretchin to raise the child, Zofia plunged a dagger into her own heart to defy Dracula's wishes. Years later, the now vampiric Dracula slew Gretchin's son, Arni, in a savage assault on the Roma. Gretchin magically transformed Lilith into an adult vampire, further empowering her to torment Dracula eternally to thwart his plans and be an ever-present gadfly. Lilith at first attacked humans for blood indiscriminately, driven by vampiric lusts. Eventually she learned to better control her bloodlust and chose to focus on people she believed were evil enough to deserve such a fate. During the 20th century, Lilith interrupted Dracula's attempt to feed on a woman in Paris by taking her herself. Lilith then vowed to feed on her father's victims before he could. Eventually, the two fought in London, and Dracula shoved Lilith off the top of Big Ben. Impaled below on a spike, Lilith was resurrected by Gretchin's spell and continued to oppose Dracula. However, at some point after this, she and Dracula reconciled their differences in an uneasy truce and avoided each other. In 1980, Lilith spared loser Horace Morton Biggotty V after finding he was transporting blood to a hospital, though she wondered if she had done him any favor. Dracula and Lilith met once again at vampire hunter Quincy Harker's home on the night Harker's wife Elizabeth killed herself from fear of Dracula, and Harker vengefully slew Lilith.

In recent years, Lilith was reborn through human host Angel O'Hara, whose father, Martin, had killed her fiancé, Ted Hannigan, for impregnating Angel. After slaying Martin O'Hara, Lilith targeted Quincy Harker for vengeance, using Angel O'Hara's form to gain entrance to his home, and then bit him in the neck; however, Harker survived. Lilith then located Dracula, uncharacteristically proposing an alliance, but Dracula refused, preferring to continue their struggle. Wearying of the British Isles, Lilith induced Angel to move to New York's Greenwich Village. Lilith guided Angel to move in with writer Martin Gold who had just lost his wife to the insane "sex crime" killer. That night the killer returned and tried to kill Angel, but Lilith slew him instead. While Angel fell in love with Martin, Lilith continued to punish the guilty. A head wound Lilith received from drug dealers left Angel with a severe concussion and in the hospital Angel learned she was pregnant with Ted Hannigan's child. After Angel obtained a job taking classified ads at the East Village Oracle, Lilith pursued the fame-seeking killer "Nobody Anybody Knows," who plunged to his death, shattering his face and leaving him unidentifiable. Lilith killed the head of Kallen Chemical Works and his agents when they captured Martin for threatening to expose their plot to purify Earth's water so that it could not support life. Lilith later encountered disco king T.J. Novello; intrigued by his moves and attitude, she intended to give him the dramatic exit to life she felt he deserved, but she instead slew his murderously jealous girlfriend Della Fiorelli. When Dracula was turned human by Mephisto, he sought Lilith to make him a vampire anew, but she instead tried to kill him.

Dracula later regained his vampiric powers, but when he destroyed his Brides and other vampire servants in a fit of rage, Lilith saw the perfect chance to destroy her father. Lilith first sought out Gretchin's descendant Viktor Benzel, with whom she had an affair, and Viktor performed an arcane ritual involving Lilith's dismemberment that successfully separated Angel and Lilith who went their separate ways. When Lilith attempted to destroy Dracula, he instead slew Viktor, who had tried to aid her. Dracula then bared his chest to Lilith and handed her a mallet and spike, revealing and mocking her inability to directly kill him, a limitation of Gretchin's spell. While seeking Viktor's brother, Karl, to find a way around the spell, Lilith solved the murders of the insane gardener Siegfried.

Learning of the Montesi Formula, a spell from the mystic Darkhold tome able to destroy vampires, Lilith possessed the X-Man Kitty Pryde, whose parents had just filed for divorce, causing her to briefly hate them. Lilith/Kitty stole a copy of the formula from Pendarrow Hill and tried to destroy Dracula, but the X-Men opposed her, knowing the spell's use would cost Kitty her soul. After the newly vampirized Rachel van Helsing defiantly speared Dracula's heart, Lilith released Kitty. Lilith

ANGEL O'HARA

Art by David Finch with Gene Colan & Bob Brown (insets)

Art by Gene Colan

subsequently perished happily when Dr. Strange recited the full and original Montesi Formula to destroy all vampires, including a revived Dracula; however, when Dracula was later reborn, so was Lilith.

Eventually becoming consumed with bloodlust, Lilith sought Brother Voodoo (Jericho Drumm)'s aid. Drumm used some of Lilith's own blood for a spell that allowed him to control her hunger, and in return, she joined his efforts to eradicate the undead. During this time they battled the then-disembodied Scarecrow (Ebenezer Laughton) who had possessed Barbara Ketch's corpse, and the struggle was joined by Ghost Rider (Dan Ketch) and John Blaze. The violent battle between Laughton's crows and Lilith's rats and bats unleashed Lilith's bloodlust, and she assaulted Blaze, who stabbed her in the leg with his hellfire-charged knife before Voodoo stopped her. Acquiring one of the Amulets of Damballah, Lilith took control of Simon Garth, the Zombie, and sent him around New York to bring her people to feed on and transform into vampire servants. Additionally seeking a male vampire to serve as her general, Lilith stole files from mercenary Simon Stroud that led her to living vampire Morbius' friend Dr. Jacob Weisenthal, whom she slew when he proved a dead end. Happening to encounter Spider-Man, she assumed the guise of Now Magazine reporter "Lily Drake" and convinced him that Morbius was behind the recent disappearances in New York, hoping Spider-Man would draw Morbius out of hiding. Meanwhile, Donna Garth had hired vampire and private investigator Hannibal King to find her father's missing body, and King attacked Lilith. She considered making King her general but fled when Spider-Man joined the fight. Ultimately King snatched the Amulet of Damballah from Lilith and released the Zombie who helped let sunlight into Lilith's base, destroying her vampires; Lilith fled to find another ally.

Regaining control, Lilith employed Dr. Charles Seward to create a virus that could slay Dracula. Though the virus nauseated its victim so that he could not drink blood, it also culminated in a rotting death and proved highly transmissible to people. Lilith's agent Anton Florescu infected Dracula with the virus via a dart then committed suicide to prevent Dracula from making him reveal Lilith's involvement. Seward, however, appalled at what he had done as the virus ravaged the town of Littlepool, led Dracula to Lilith. Seward tried to inject Lilith with the virus but she slew him. Dracula attacked Lilith but was little match for her in his weakened state. Realizing Seward had used his own blood in the virus' creation and that he was thus immune, Dracula drank Seward's blood. Lilith laughed at how low Dracula had sunken, but the process cured him, restoring his full power. Dracula then blew up Lilith's laboratory and created a powerful storm that eradicated Littlepool and the virus from the face of the Earth. Lilith claimed some victory in that Dracula's actions would cause him to lose respect from other vampires.

Art by Patrick Olliffe

At some point, Lilith was recruited into SHIELD's Howling Commandos unit of supernatural and "monstrous" agents. She was sent alongside vampire werewolf Nina Price to infiltrate the camp of a being claiming to be Merlin who was transforming the land into a fantasy-like world. While spying on Merlin, Lilith turned Price over to the mage to gain his favor, and Lilith was also reunited with Daimon Hellstrom (Hellstorm/Son of Satan) who had also infiltrated the camp for the Commandos and with whom Lilith had had bad experiences. Lilith eventually bedded Merlin and then drank his blood, believing she had killed him; however, having merely played along, Merlin then incinerated her. After shifting through her ashes to see the future, Merlin realized it was not yet his time to rule, and he departed. Having manipulated her ashes thusly, Lilith then reformed.

Art by Pop Mhan

HEIGHT: 6' **EYES:** Red
WEIGHT: 125 lbs. **HAIR:** Black

ABILITIES/ACCESSORIES: Lilith has traditional vampire powers, to a higher degree than most, lacking most traditional limitations. She has superhuman physical abilities, including enhanced strength (lifting 1100 lbs.). She can mesmerize others by catching their gaze for three seconds, though beings with sufficiently strong wills can resist her, and it is harder to maintain control over a group of people. She can transform partially or fully into a bat or mist, control the weather, and command animals such as rats, mice, bats, and wolves.

Lilith is immune to sunlight and does not fall into a coma-like trance during daytime hours, nor is she dependent upon sleeping on her native soil. She is not affected by religious talismans or garlic and can even wield them herself against other vampires. She can be destroyed by the Montesi Formula or a wooden stake through the heart. She recovers instantly from most other wounds (even surviving dismemberment), and her spirit will return as long as Dracula exists; however, Lilith is magically unable to kill Dracula directly. Her spirit can enter an innocent woman who hates her father, transforming that body to mirror Lilith's own, with Lilith's full powers. She can also regain her own body through an elaborate mystical ritual.

Lilith enjoys but is not required to drink blood. By biting a person and depositing an enzyme in their blood, she makes her victim highly susceptible to her commands. The victim also develops a perverse erotic fixation on Lilith. If that person dies, he would usually rise again in three days as a vampire, though such vampires would have the conventional vampiric powers and limitations. Not all of those bitten in such fashion would be reborn as vampires, but the conditions of such transformations are uncertain.

Lilith possesses a virtually all-consuming desire to see her father dead, but is unable to directly cause his death. Though she can physically strike him, she would be unable to plunge a stake through his chest. In addition, as long as Dracula exists, so, too, does Lilith. If Dracula is destroyed, Lilith could meet her own death, but her spirit would return as soon as Dracula was resurrected.

LIONHEART

REAL NAME: Kelsey Kirkland Shorr Leigh
ALIASES: Captain Britain
IDENTITY: Known to authorities
OCCUPATION: Adventurer; former teacher
CITIZENSHIP: UK
PLACE OF BIRTH: Colchester, Essex, England, UK
KNOWN RELATIVES: Jenny Leigh (daughter), Martin Leigh (son), Joan Shorr (mother), Richard Leigh (ex-husband)
GROUP AFFILIATION: MI-13, Corps; formerly Excalibur, Shadow Captains, Avengers
EDUCATION: University graduate
FIRST APPEARANCE: (Kelsey) Avengers #77 (2004); (Captain Britain) Avengers #80 (2004); (Lionheart) New Excalibur #4 (2006)

HISTORY: Attacked in her home by a would-be rapist while her husband Richard watched paralyzed with fear, teacher Kelsey Leigh fought back, hurting the intruder, but he retaliated by scarring her face with a broken bottle. Afterwards Richard's guilt over his inaction ended their marriage, leaving Kelsey to raise their children alone. They later were caught up in a battle between the Avengers and the Wrecking Crew. Trying to defend Kelsey and her children, Captain America (Steve Rogers) was knocked unconscious by Thunderball (Eliot Franklin, at this time secretly possessed by Morgan Le Fay's sadistic Knight); When Thunderball tried to finish him off, Kelsey blocked the attack with the downed hero's shield, suffering terrible injuries from the impact. Though offered a chance to retreat, Kelsey stood firm, taking repeated blows before Cap's teammates intervened. The Avengers rushed her to medical treatment, but she died en route. Kelsey awoke in the Siege Perilous, confronted by a vision of Brian Braddock, Captain Britain, then ruler of Otherworld. Aware that Morgan intended to use Brian's link to Britain to harm his homeland through him, Brian chose to sever that connection by passing Captain Britain's mantle to Kelsey, her courage earning her a second chance to live. Brian offered her a choice between the Sword of Might and the Amulet of Right. Grasping a chance to see her children again, and reasoning that a necklace could not defend anything, Kelsey chose the sword and was transformed. Brian sadly informed her that she had chosen the path of violence, and that if she ever revealed her identity to her children, they would die. Returned to Earth, Kelsey helped defeat Morgan, proving herself far more ruthless in battle than her predecessor. With her children now in the Avengers' care, Kelsey joined the team, so that even if she could not reveal herself to them, she could remain near them. Her tenure proved short; after battling the new Invaders in Mazikhandar, the Avengers suffered a devastating attack from the insane Scarlet Witch, and disbanded. Thanking them for helping her regain her sense of purpose, Kelsey returned to Britain, renaming herself Lionheart.

Soon afterward, Brian Braddock returned from Otherworld and resumed the role of Captain Britain. Lionheart was approached by Albion (Bran Bardic), Brian's Reality-70518 counterpart; Albion had likewise chosen the sword during his empowerment, and been rejected because of this by Merlyn and Roma, Brian's predecessors. He played on Kelsey's sense of loss, becoming her lover and convincing her to join him in seeking revenge on Brian and Otherworld, though she continued to doubt Albion's ruthless methods. After their first attack was interrupted by the arrival of Brian's allies (who would soon form the team Excalibur), Albion recruited Shadow-Captains, recently depowered mutants, and allied with Shadow-X, Reality-6141's X-Men enthralled by the Shadow King. Lionheart accompanied Shadow-X to Crossmoor Prison to free their master, but they tried to turn her into the Shadow King's new host; expecting treachery, Lionheart used an energy collar to seal him inside his host, then ran him through, apparently killing him, before fleeing when Excalibur attacked. The Shadow-Captains meanwhile used Crossmoor as a diversion, breaking into a government vault and activating a mystic device within to disable all of Britain's technology. With the country in disarray, Albion sent Lionheart to capture the Royal Family at Balmoral, but she was intercepted by Excalibur and Shadow-X, now allies in the face of their common foe. Captain Britain appealed to Lionheart's conscience, convincing her to switch sides, and with her help they stopped the Shadow-Captains, broke the anti-technology spell and captured Albion. In recognition of her aid, the UK government gave Kelsey a second chance, inducting her into Excalibur. Brian also reunited her with her family, his restriction apparently lifted. Lionheart's subsequent activities in light of Excalibur's later dissolution remain unrecorded.

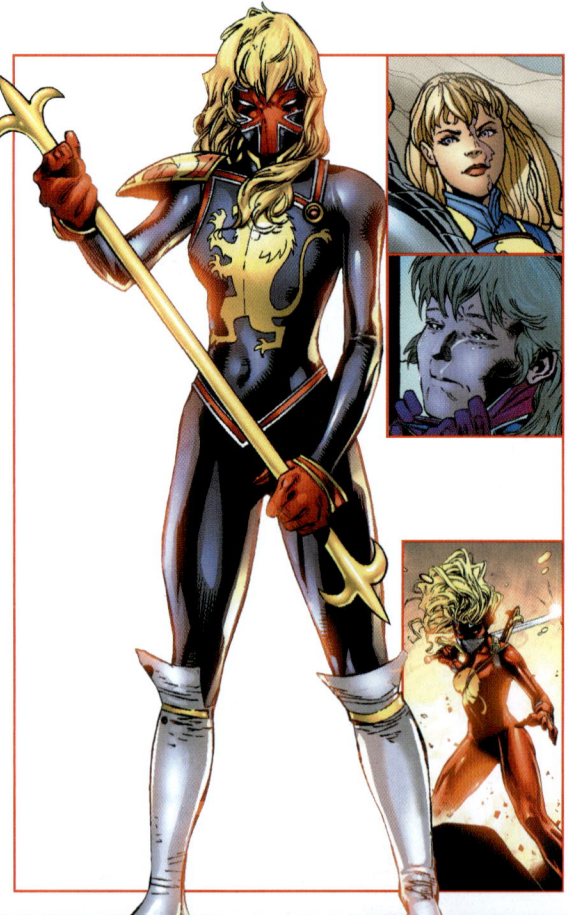

HEIGHT: 5'5"
WEIGHT: 130 lbs
EYES: Blue
HAIR: Blonde

ABILITIES/ACCESSORIES: Lionheart possesses superhuman strength (lifting 90 tons), flight (up to 770 mph), enhanced reflexes, stamina and senses, and can generate a protective force field. She wielded a staff (possibly a new Star Sceptre like her predecessor's) capable of firing bolts of explosive energy. Albion also provided her with a sword, apparently mystically durable, and a device that blocked telepathic intrusions. Albion trained her to be a skilled swordswoman and martial artist. She is knowledgeable in English literature and history, the subjects she taught. She can apparently remove her facial scar when she activates her powers, but usually chooses not to.

POWER GRID	1	2	3	4	5	6	7
INTELLIGENCE			■				
STRENGTH						■	
SPEED			■				
DURABILITY					■		
ENERGY PROJECTION		■					
FIGHTING SKILLS				■			

Art by Olivier Coipel with Steve Cummings (top insets)

LIVEWIRES

HISTORY: Research and development programs had sought for decades to perfect artificial lifeform technology. Ever since the 1960s, Project: SHIELD and its eventual successor SHIELD has been protecting key personnel, such as Colonel Nick Fury, with life model decoys (LMDs), which had become extremely convincing at passing for humans over the years. Later, the Mannites, nanowoven artificial lifeforms grown via semi-random germination in hopes of maximizing metatalent function, were created, but their mutant-like appearance limited their usefulness for covert operations. Finally, a top-secret, quasi-governmental R&D program known as Project: LIVEWIRE combined LMD and Mannite technology to create the Livewires, a team of nanobuilt humanform combat mecha with smartware bodies specialized for covert ops and artificially intelligent minds programmed with suicidal loyalty to the project's goals and objectives; however, David Jenkins, the project's Assistant Chief Designer, also programmed the Livewires with his own rogue objectives: to seek out, sabotage, and destroy other covert research programs. As such, the Livewires viewed the treacherous Jenkins and the other human personnel as a possible threat to Project: LIVEWIRE and promptly terminated them before detonating the project's reactor.

Although the Livewires' exolayer of limited-function nanomechanical smartware allows them to alter their appearances, they are incapable of full-body morphing. Cornfed, his massive frame bloated with spare smartware cannibalized from fallen teammates and a multifunction nanofactory housed in his stomach, serves as the team's healer/repair mecha, and uses his heavy-duty computing power for wireless hacking and data analysis. Social Butterfly, the team's human interaction specialist, uses everything from subliminal infrasonic vocal cues to artificial pheromones to manipulate unsuspecting humans. Gothic Lolita is composed of a hyperdense assembly of nanomachines, giving her the highest degree of superhuman strength and durability of the team. Hollowpoint Ninja, the team's stealth/weapons/ambush specialist, is programmed for speed, marksmanship, and hand-to-hand combat. Homebrew, who served as the team's tech/engineering specialist and created the team's weapons and gear, was fatally damaged by a gamma-ray laser during a mission (making him the fifth team member to die since leaving the project). On the team's next mission, a new mecha named Stem Cell was booted up and installed with Homebrew's engineering database, although her default neuroform mental state was identical to that of a human, and it took her some time to accept that she was a mecha.

On Stem Cell's first mission, the team destroyed a Thermogentech Research facility which had obtained a sample of the android Human Torch's thermogenic cells and weaponized it into a pyronanotech semi-sentient virus. Posing as an A.I.M. splinter group, the team next threatened Dr. Nakanishi, head research scientist of Project Lamplight and an Advanced Idea Mechanics (A.I.M.) defector, to either give up his career or have his family killed. The team next destroyed a Trans World Cargo plane carrying an experimental antimatter containment vessel to power Sentinel robots. While hacking into the database of a covert Sentinel research program,

CURRENT MEMBERS: Cornfed, Gothic Lolita, Hollowpoint Ninja, Social Butterfly, Stem Cell
FORMER MEMBERS: Homebrew, four others
BASE OF OPERATIONS: Mobile across the United States
FIRST APPEARANCE: Livewires #1 (2005)

Cornfed found a link to the highest-priority target that the Livewires were programmed to destroy: a highly modified S.H.I.E.L.D. Helicarrier controlled by a rogue hive-minded horde of LMDs whose programming was corrupted during a Hydra nanoware assassination attempt on S.H.I.E.L.D. Director Nick Fury. The Livewires covertly boarded the rogue Helicarrier but were soon discovered by the LMDs and systematically eliminated. Stem Cell, the last functioning Livewire, cannibalized her own smartware exolayer and used it to recreate Thermogentech's pyronanotech virus, which destroyed the modified Helicarrier. Escaping, Stem Cell salvaged the remains of the damaged Livewires and vowed to repair them.

At least Gothic Lolita and Social Butterfly were rebuilt, as they were later seen attending an undersea rave party held for mecha beings.

Art by Adam Warren with Ricardo Mays (inset)

LIVING BRAIN

PLACE OF BIRTH: San Jose, California
FIRST APPEARANCE: Amazing Spider-Man #8 (1964)

HISTORY: Invented by International Computing Machines (ICM) Corporation, the Living Brain was the most sophisticated electronic computer yet designed. Built in human form to dramatize its powers, the Brain required input in mathematical symbols in order to answer questions, replying via ticker tape in the same code. Sent on a nationwide tour led by ICM computer scientist and public relations man Mr. Petty and attended by two technicians, the Brain arrived at Mr. Warren's Senior Science Class at Midtown High School for a demonstration. When Liz Allan contributed the question "What is Spider-Man's real identity?", Peter Parker was relieved to see the answer emerge in code, which he was asked to translate overnight. Seeing the Brain as a money-maker, the two technicians attempted to steal it. When Mr. Petty intervened, one technician bumped the Brain's control panel, jarring the machine into a rampage. Spider-Man stepped in only to discover that the Brain gauged his strength and speed and countered it accordingly. However, he eventually reached the main cut-off switch, deactivating the machine. The fleeing technicians knocked themselves out when they tripped over Flash Thompson who was bent over tying his shoe. Peter later conveniently lost the ticker tape with the Brain's guess of Spider-Man's identity on it.

The Living Brain was later stolen by the two technicians and used to commit crimes but Spider-Man again defeated it. Years later, working as a temporary substitute teacher at Midtown High School, Peter Parker met Steve Petty, scientific whiz, unpopular student, and son of ICM's Mr. Petty who arranged for the now-obsolete Living Brain to be donated to the high school. Steve reactivated and updated it, giving it flying capability by replacing its feet rollers with jets, controlling it with a hand-held remote, and turning it into a killing machine. Though Peter initially saw Steve as a new version of his high school self, he soon realized that Steve had rebuffed expressions of friendship from his perceived tormentor Jake Dorman and was full of violent rage. When Steve unleashed the Brain intending to kill Jake, Spider-Man maneuvered the Brain into punching an electrical junction box, short-circuiting the robot. Unrepentant, Steve donned a bionic feedback exo-skeleton that overloaded, turning him into the pain-ridden, electricity-controlling Phreak. Defeated and returned to normal by Spider-Man, Steve was protected from the police by Jake Dorman who declared Steve was his friend. Much later, a number of Brain duplicates were utilized by the Beyond Corporation against the Nextwave Squad. but were quickly defeated by Tabitha Smith.

STEVE PETTY VERSION

BEYOND CORPORATION VERSIONS
Art by Stuart Immonen

HEIGHT: 6'6"
WEIGHT: 800 lbs.
EYES: Yellow
HAIR: None

ABILITIES/ACCESSORIES: A vast storehouse of knowledge, the Living Brain could think and reason faster than any human, was incapable of forgetting, and could actually learn and adapt its behavior. Built with ball bearing rollers for feet and pincers for hands, the Brain could spin its arms like bolos and its body like a top. Able to adapt as fast as it could think, the Brain adjusted to attacks. Steve Petty's upgrade boosted the Brain's speed, strength (from Class 10 to 25), durability, and maneuverability, also giving it hovering capability.

POWER GRID	1	2	3	4	5	6	7
INTELLIGENCE*					5		
STRENGTH			3				
SPEED		2					
DURABILITY				4			
ENERGY PROJECTION	1						
FIGHTING SKILLS			3				

*LIMITED TO PROGRAMMING

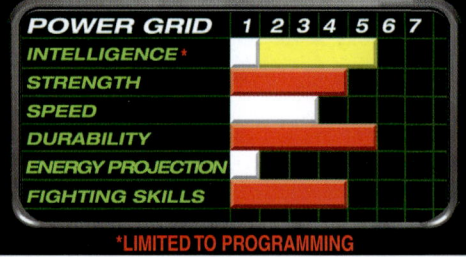

Art by Steve Ditko with Alex Saviuk (inset)

LIVING ERASERS

HISTORY: The title of Living Eraser is granted to residents of Dimension Z chosen to wield the Dimensionizer, which can transport victims to Dimension Z or elsewhere. The Dimensionizer is hidden on the gloves of each Eraser, who then slashes at the air in a wiping motion. As each wave passes over the surface of the victim, that area of their body disappears from sight, making it appear that they are being "erased." Once an entire body has been erased, the victim is transported to Dimension Z. The Erasers serve the ruler of Dimension Z, a being known as the Supremacy or the Supremor.

The first Living Eraser known to come to Earth did so in an attempt to steal the secret of nuclear energy. After discovering that nuclear weapons were neutralized by dimensional transport, the Living Eraser began kidnapping scientists to Dimension Z, forcing them to build weapons for the Supremacy. This process was successful until the Eraser targeted biochemist Henry Pym, whom he did not realize was also the super hero called Giant-Man. Giant-Man and his partner, the Wasp, were transported to Dimension Z, but they freed the other captives and returned to Earth.

Enraged by this defeat, the Living Eraser betrayed the Supremacy and took over political power for himself, locking the Supremacy in a cell alongside one of the deposed leader's advisors (Petril) and the Supremacy's daughter (Roweena). The military failed to back the Eraser's claims of power fully, forcing him to return to Earth in an effort to prove his mettle. The Eraser captured both the living vampire Morbius and the Thing (Ben Grimm), transporting them to the same cell in which the Supremacy was held. The heroes escaped the trap and defeated the Eraser, restoring the Supremacy to the throne. Morbius claimed the Dimensionizer for himself, fleeing to another realm. For his crimes against the Supremacy, this Living Eraser was executed.

Another Eraser later devised a new scheme, one which would involve transporting irradiated humans to Dimension Z. Dismissing the Hulk as too powerful and unstable, the Eraser turned his attentions to She-Hulk. The Supremacy coveted She-Hulk as his bride, however, and dispatched the Eraser to Earth to kidnap her. The Eraser succeeded in this, also taking She-Hulk's boyfriend Wyatt Wingfoot hostage. She-Hulk escaped the trap, using the Dimensionizer to return herself and Wingfoot home.

MEMBERS: None identified
FIRST APPEARANCE: Tales to Astonish #49 (1963)

Abandoning the notion of having only one Living Eraser at a time, the Supremacy had multiple Dimensionizers created, equipping a whole team of Living Erasers. In recent times, the villain Yandroth summoned forth the Living Erasers as part of a larger scheme to sow chaos on Earth, bringing the Erasers into conflict with Japan's premier hero group, Big Hero 6. The Supremacy's future plans for the Erasers (if any) are currently unknown.

NOTE: After the original Eraser's second foray to Earth, some of his technology was confiscated by SHIELD, who used it to create Eraser tech of their own. They subsequently utilized this technology on various missions, most recently when their supernatural Howling Commandos unit used it to transport the giant creature Groot to their base.

Art by Don Heck

Art by John Byrne with Jack Kirby (inset)

LIVING LASER

REAL NAME: Arthur Parks
ALIASES: Impersonated Tony Stark, Titanium Man
IDENTITY: Publicly known
OCCUPATION: Professional criminal; former dictator, research physicist
CITIZENSHIP: USA with a criminal record
PLACE OF BIRTH: New Brunswick, New Jersey
KNOWN RELATIVES: None
GROUP AFFILIATION: Hood's army; formerly Lethal Legion, Batroc's Brigade, Mandarin's Minions
EDUCATION: Ph.D. in physics
FIRST APPEARANCE: Avengers #34 (1966)

HISTORY: A talented research physicist, Arthur Parks loved his job early in his career, putting all his money and energy into new equipment. His attention soon turned to the beautiful Lucy Barton, but she left him for the son of banker Joseph Shapiro, and Parks assumed it was due to his lack of money. During his research, Parks had stumbled upon a means of building super-powerful laser beam projectors, and the embittered scientist began to fantasize about using this technology for personal power rather than sharing his discoveries with the world. Bitter and seeking to impress Lucy, Park designed a deadly laser weapon and a costume that would help him get more money. Wielding wrist-mounted laser guns and adopting a costumed identity as the Living Laser, Parks quickly and quietly accumulated a small fortune via theft. Still devastated by Lucy's departure and desperate to prove himself superior to her new man, the Living Laser broke into a vault at Shapiro's bank, stole valuable bonds, and tossed the bonds back into the bank as he departed unseen, more concerned with demonstrating his power than with profit. The crime was investigated the next day by the heroic Avengers, including Lucy's old friend Janet Van Dyne, whom Parks recognized as the Wasp. Mingling with a crowd of onlookers, Parks fell madly in love with Van Dyne at first sight.

The self-deluded Parks decided the best way to win Wasp's love was to destroy her boyfriend and teammate, Goliath (Henry Pym). Parks attacked Goliath at his lab, but Goliath defeated Laser. The other Avengers, Captain America (Steve Rogers) and Hawkeye (Clint Barton) came to take him to jail, but Parks escaped by burning a hole through their craft, flying away with his jetpack and returning to his lab to create deadlier weaponry. He rigged an abandoned building with traps, went on a demolition spree throughout the city, lured the Avengers into a laser cage, and captured the Wasp. Certain the Wasp would love him if he gained enough power, Parks agreed to help, for ten million dollars, Valdez's rebel army seize control of their Latin-American nation Costa Verde. Valdez agreed, though he intended to betray Parks once he had served his purpose. Aided by the Laser, Valdez's forces easily overthrew Costa Verde's dictatorial government and installed their own totalitarian regime, backed by a massive new laser cannon and led by Parks himself, who enjoyed playing dictator so much that he was soon plotting to destroy his rebel allies. While occupying the castle, Parks continually tried winning the Wasp's love, but she refused his advances. When the Avengers attacked, Parks shot them out of the air with his cannon. The Avengers, however, successfully invaded Costa Verde, freed the Wasp, defeated the Living Laser by overloading his cannon, and overthrew the rebels with the aid of the remnants of the national army, who resolved to install a new democratic government. Taken back to the USA to stand trial, Parks was placed in psychiatric care and later transferred to a conventional jail.

Parks escaped prison with the aid of the infamous criminal mastermind Mandarin, despite the intervention of Iron Man (Tony Stark). Mandarin teleported Parks across the world to China, where Parks received a new costume and joined the Mandarin's Minions alongside the Enchantress (Amora), Executioner (Skurge), Power Man (Erik Josten), and Swordsman (Jacques Duquesne) in a plot to rule the world. Mandarin split the team into three and sent Parks to take over the diamond rich area of South Africa, given the giant Ultimo as backup. Parks attacked the local government before Thor and Hawkeye attacked, soon defeating Living Laser and Ultimo before joining the other Avengers in defeating Mandarin. When Batroc (Georges Batroc) formed a new Brigade, Living Laser and Swordsman joined. They sought to steal an experimental Seismo-Bomb and sell it for profit, but Captain America stopped them and disabled the bomb before it could go off. Parks then joined the Grim Reaper (Eric Williams), Man-Ape (M'Baku), Swordsman, and Power Man in forming the Lethal Legion, pledged to defeat the Avengers, who were swiftly captured. The heroes easily defeated the villains when Grim Reaper freed them after seeing a connection between his seemingly deceased brother Wonder Man and new Avenger, the Vision ("Victor Shade"). Sometime later, the Kree Zarek's Lunatic Legion created a robot Living Laser duplicate, using a processed and ground moon rock as part of its laser weapon. They sent it to kill Rick Jones as part of their plot against his ally, Captain Mar-Vell, but it was destroyed by the Wasp and Ant-Man (Hank Pym), who initially believed it to have been the true Laser converted into a cyborgs.

While in prison, Parks studied the legend of ancient Lemuria and learned of the powerful Serpent Crown, said to grant its user vast power from the serpentine Elder God Set. After his release, Parks returned to experimenting with lasers, mutating himself with the help of Dr. Jonas Harrow, who implanted miniature laser-generating diodes and graviton generators under his skin, allowing him to fire lasers from his body and giving him greater control. Reminded of his obsession with the Wasp, Laser plotted to win her heart again. He learned about a radioactive mutant named Nuklo from the traitorous General Pollock, then began manipulating the Avengers with his new illusion powers. Parks found

Art by Frazer Irving with Don Heck (inset)

the Serpent Crown at a Brand facility and donned it, granting himself greater power. Parks then revived Avengers associate Wonder Man from a near-mindless zombie state and mind-controlled him into opposing the Avengers, but Wonder Man soon gained his free will and joined the Avengers in battling the Laser, Pollock's army, and the recently revived Nuklo. In the ensuing battle, the Laser lost the Crown and a rampaging Nuklo felled both Parks and Pollock before the Whizzer finally subdued him. Parks was swiftly returned to jail.

In time, Parks, Goliath (formerly Power Man) and Whirlwind (David Cannon) were recruited by Count Nefaria, who formed the trio into a new Lethal Legion. After the villains robbed a bank and briefly battled the Avengers, Nefaria had scientist Kenneth Sturdy augment the villains' powers. With their newly enhanced powers, the trio attacked Avengers mansion, easily dominating the heroes until collapsing; Sturdy's enhancement was only a temporary side-effect of a process that granted Nefaria duplicates of their powers, heightened a hundredfold. Drastically weakened by the sudden drop in their power levels, the Legion was easily defeated by the Avengers, who soon subdued the vastly powerful Nefaria as well. Parks found his altered powers overwhelming and he grew unable to control them. The Sturdy treatment had dangerously altered his metabolism, such that he constantly absorbed light energy from his environment, energy that he had to expend frequently or risk exploding. Approached by the secret, communist-run German scientific facility Heaven's Hand, Parks agreed to help them power a dormant network of Russian laser-armed weapons satellites in exchange for siphoning off his excess energy. Despite his discomfort with being a traitor to his country, Parks agreed to the alliance and felt it was the only thing keeping him alive. Months later, Iron Man attacked and, feeling he had no other choice, destroyed the siphoning chamber before rushing Parks into the upper atmosphere, where Parks exploded in a vast blast of light.

Amazingly, Parks survived as a being of sentient light energy trapped in one of the Russian satellites, now truly a living laser. Parks eventually escaped and battled Wonder Man and the Beast (Hank McCoy), and subsequently fought the Beyonder as part of a super-villain army, before his energy was absorbed by a communications satellite. Spending months trying to fight free, Parks finally burst outward and returned to Earth, where he panicked about no longer being human. He ended up battling two Iron Men (Tony Stark and Jim Rhodes), who trapped Parks in a reflective optic cell while the Avengers sought a cure for his condition. Laser participated in the "Acts of Vengeance" anti-super hero conspiracy, helping Klaw escape Quasar (Wendell Vaughn) in New York, but Parks fled when Quasar managed to lock on to Parks' energy source. Parks rushed at the speed of light to the Blue Area of the Moon, where he hid from Quasar in the Watcher's (Uatu) citadel. When Quasar got too close, Parks rushed through an interdimensional gateway to escape, but he panicked when he found himself in an alternate reality Earth-105709 with another Arthur Parks. He rushed back to the moon and returned to his reality, unintentionally creating temporal rifts and sending counterparts to realities that Quasar later had to fix.

Hearing that the original Iron Man had died, Living Laser felt cheated of revenge and sought to prove that the new Iron Man was the same as the old. Using his holograms, Parks appeared as the ghost of the Titanium Man and attacked Tony Stark's nuclear research facility, causing several reactors to overload. When Iron Man arrived, he fought "Titanium Man," narrowly stopping the nuclear reactors from exploding. When Iron Man went missing, Living Laser set up a massive trap of mirrors in the wrecked facility and waited for Iron Man to return, soon learning it was indeed the original. Living Laser fired himself at the hero, magnifying and reflecting off the glassy surfaces, but Iron Man used a shield to protect himself. After a brief battle, Iron Man collapsed, seemingly defeated (due to neurologic deterioration), and Parks rushed off in frustration over the ease of the defeat. Days later, Parks went to find Iron Man again and attacked another of Stark's facilities. He found the hero and nearly killed him, but Wonder Man and Pym helped Iron Man disrupt Parks' frequencies, scattering him through the atmosphere. After reincorporating, Parks joined the Red Skull (Johann Shmidt)'s mind-controlled army of super-villains in a world conquest scheme involving a giant laser cannon, but the Avengers thwarted this plot. Parks later sought revenge against Tony Stark himself and posed as Stark at various facilities to try and learn Stark's secrets. When he approached the CEO of Stark's company, James Rhodes, Parks was furious to learn that Stark was believed dead. Rhodes offered Parks a job, catching him off-guard, but soon attacked him in a reflective armor. When Parks refused to surrender, Rhodes absorbed him into a communications laser and fired him into the Andromeda Galaxy.

Though much of Parks' bodily energy was trapped in space, Living Laser soon learned to gather his energy in order to control his corporeal form, composed of living photons, though it stretched his sanity to do so. He returned to Earth, where he attended an illicit auction hosted by the Chess Set and raided by Alpha Flight and Spider-Man, and was among the villains who attended the wedding of longtime super hero associates Rick Jones and Marlo Chandler. Parks mostly kept a low profile for some time, physically and mentally weakened due to the scattering of his photons. At some point, he was trapped in a particle imprint intelligence "smart laser" weapon obtained by black market weapons dealers Armstrong and Trundle. Tony Stark helped a SHIELD sting operation shut down their illegal weapons business, but he kept the laser weapon for himself, having deduced Parks' presence within the device.

When Electro (Max Dillon) staged a breakout of the Raft, Living Laser took advantage of the opportunity to escape, but his energy and consciousness were soon absorbed back into the containment unit. Stark took the unit again and, hoping to rescue and rehabilitate Parks, hired criminal psychologist Dr. Maggie Dillon to interact with the device's energy via telepathic intrabeam particle communication. Dillon awoke Parks' dormant consciousness,

which first manifested as a frightened child, and she coaxed him back to a greater state of awareness, trying to convince him to abandon his criminal ways and start a new life in the process. Resisting, Parks overwhelmed and absorbed Dillon's photonic telepathic avatar, declared himself mentally and physically stable, and escaped the laser weapon, killing Dillon in the process. Assuming a more abstract energy form, Parks declared himself a wholly inhuman being with no ties to his former life apart from his desire to kill Stark. He intervened in a subsequent battle between Iron Man (Stark) and the new Spymaster (Sinclair Abbott), who had been trying to steal the Parks-powered laser weapon before Parks escaped. Killing Abbott's wife Greta as he arrived, Parks attacked Iron Man, who absorbed the Laser's bodily energy into his own armor, then trapped it in a long-term containment unit at a Stark International facility in Coney Island.

After escaping, Living Laser accepted a job from MODOK to join a team of criminals, including the Chameleon (secretly the Ultra-Adaptoid), Rocket Racer, Nightshade, Puma, and others, in stealing a powerful energy device called the Hypernova from the extradimensional Infinicide, a race of MODOK-like beings who studied times of turmoil in various realities. Offered five million dollars, Parks planned to find a way to restore himself to humanity. After training with his new allies, Parks traveled to China, where the Infinicide was briefly stationed while studying humanity, and helped break into their ship. When their ally Spot (Johnny Ohnn) abandoned them, Parks helped defend Puma from the ship's security system until the ship crashed. Reunited with the others, Living Laser helped battle the Mandarin (Temujin), who had stolen the Hypernova. Parks was shocked to learn the Mandarin could physically harm him by focusing his chi. Thrilled to be feeling human pain, Parks begged for more as he realized he would do anything to become human again. At the last minute, he stole the Hypernova and planned to use it to make himself human again, though he knew it would likely kill him an instant later. MODOK had switched the Hypernova with a false unit, however, and the energy drove Parks temporarily mad as it absorbed him. MODOK turned this unit over to AIM, who opened it and released Living Laser, who promptly exploded, seemingly killing the entire AIM branch, including Monica Rappacini. Parks later joined the Hood's New York City based army alongside several other criminals, and participated in a battle with the renegade Avengers run by Luke Cage. The villains were briefly arrested by SHIELD, but Hood freed them, and they aided him in repelling the Skrulls' invasion of the city.

HEIGHT: Variable; (human) 5'11"
WEIGHT: (Photonic being) negligible; (human) 185 lbs.
EYES: Variable; (human) blue
HAIR: Variable; (human) Brown

ABILITIES/ACCESSORIES: The Living Laser consists of photons (particles of light) possessed of a human consciousness housed within an electrical field. By mentally increasing his photons' density, he can project them outward in laser-like beams or temporarily assume a physically tangible form; the Laser consists of intangible light energy unless he consciously wills himself to become solid. He can also create solid-light constructs by bonding photons with air molecules, but that may be more difficult than solidifying his own form since he seldom uses this ability. Using holographic projection Parks can assume any appearance, including a facsimile of his former human form, though he usually appears as a humanoid energy mass. In addition, he can project holographic illusions in locations apart from his own form, and can direct these projections with such pinpoint accuracy that he can create an illusion seen by only one person but unseen by others nearby. Parks can shift his energy frequencies at will, ranging from blinding light to lasers that can cut through virtually any substance. He can generate "counter-frequency laser shields" that disrupt outside energy attacks, but his own form is vulnerable to antagonistic energy frequencies that can disrupt his photonic coherency, sometimes dispersing his energies for extended periods. He can render himself invisible by bending light, and can ignite fires by using light energy to excite electrons in the air. He has very limited telepathic abilities enabling him to communicate with other beings and perceive material reality. It is possible that the photons he expends while using his powers are replenished by tapping an extradimensional source, such as the energy realm accessed by adventurer Monica Rambeau. It is even possible that Parks' human body still exists in such an energy realm, shunted there in exchange for an equivalent quantity of photons in the same manner that Rambeau temporarily converts her own human form to various types of energy. Parks is capable of experiencing physical pain if an attacker utilizes a focused chi, or life force.

Originally, Parks used wrist-mounted lasers that allowed him to focus highly concentrated beams of photons (particles of light), or laser beams, at various targets. The beams ranged from wide destructive blasts to pinpoints of focused light capable of bursting through steel. Parks designed other weapons, such as boot jets allowing him to fly short distances and a massive laser cannon. In time, he implanted miniature graviton generators in his skin, allowing him to absorb light, store it, and release it as a laser beam, generally fired from his hands. By storing up greater amounts of energy, Parks could utilize more focused bursts, create short-lived holographic images, teleport, hypnotize others, and render himself temporarily invisible (by bending light around himself). After his powers were augmented, Parks lost some of his control and began absorbing light involuntarily, having to have it frequently dispelled to maintain corporeal form.

Parks is a gifted scientist with particular expertise in laser technology. He has minimal fighting skills.

Art by Francis Portella

Art by John Romita, Jr.

POWER GRID	1	2	3	4	5	6	7
INTELLIGENCE				4			
STRENGTH		2					
SPEED			3				
DURABILITY						6	
ENERGY PROJECTION					5		
FIGHTING SKILLS		2					

LIVING LIGHTNING

HISTORY: Carlos Santos and his wife Maria believed in the American Dream, and immigrated to Los Angeles from Mexico to ensure their children would be born American citizens. A staunch patriot for his adopted country but soon realizing that like all nations it was divided by internal hatreds, Carlos joined the radical Legion of Living Lightning, accepting the group's rhetoric that it would abolish war and bigotry once it seized control of the USA. He regaled his son Miguel with tales of the Legion's lofty goals, even confiding in the boy about the Legion's namesake and ultimate weapon, the Living Lightning, a machine which could generate devastating electrical bolts; Miguel dreamed of joining the Legion too, but his parents insisted he finish his schooling. While Miguel was still in his teens, a battle between the Legion and the Hulk (Bruce Banner) ended with the Living Lightning machine's generator exploding, destroying the Legion's Santa Ana Mountains' base and killing many of their members, including Carlos. Despite his mother blaming the Legion for Carlos' demise, Miguel continued to view them as heroes, vowing to personally continue their mission. He studied coded maps left behind by his father, eventually locating the ruined base, which he gained entry to using his father's fingerprint glove. Hoping to salvage the Living Lightning machine, he reconnected severed cables, and suffered a massive electrical shock, which somehow transformed him into living electricity. Destroying the machine to ensure no one else could be similarly empowered, Miguel christened himself el Relampago Vivo, the Living Lightning, before setting off to test his new abilities. Reports of a burning man flying over the city of Fullerton and starting fires drew the attention of the android Human Torch (Jim Hammond), the Avengers' West Coast branch, and criminal geneticist Dr. Demonicus, who had a hidden base nearby. While Demonicus covertly monitored proceedings, Miguel attacked the Torch and Avengers, until he was tricked into explosively grounding himself. Though his combaters believed him slain, the intrigued Demonicus secretly siphoned Miguel's dissipated energies into his base for study, reconstituting him into human form.

Demonicus constructed a costume with three stabilizing units that prevented Miguel from spontaneously decomposing into random electrical impulses; with the threat of dissolution if he displeased the scientist, and figuring that he would be a wanted man for his Fullerton rampage, the initially reluctant Miguel agreed to join Demonicus' Pacific Overlords, shortly before Demonicus raised the island Demonica from the ocean depths. However when Demonicus ordered the execution of unwilling Overlord Pele and the captive Scarlet Witch, Miguel rebelled, insisting he had not signed up to murder helpless women. The Avengers arrived moments later and attacked the Overlords; initially unsure which side to assist, Miguel decided he could not allow innocents to be endangered when Demonicus tried to use the Witch as a hostage, and turned on the Overlords, destroying Demonicus' remote control for the stabilizing units before it could be used to deactivate them. The Avengers backed down when the UN officially recognized Demonica; Miguel departed the new nation with them, accepting an offer of Avengers membership from the Wasp while they were en route back to the US.

With several weeks having passed since he ventured to the Legion's base, Miguel returned home to inform his mother of recent events, but was saddened to learn that during his absence his brother José had joined the local Jaguars gang and that his sister Lisa had subsequently been killed in a drive-by shooting by the rival Snakes gang; additionally, Miguel's girlfriend Chung Thị Asuka had become involved with the Snakes leader, Đặng Quang Song, while he had been away. Blaming himself for being absent in his family's time of need, Miguel intervened in a confrontation between the gangs, hoping to prevent further violence and bring his sister's killer to justice, but Jaguar leader Carlos Rios shot Song dead moments after the latter boasted he had slain Lisa. However Miguel achieved a partial victory, as his example convinced José to quit the Jaguars, and he warned both gangs that the neighborhood was now under his protection. Returning to the Avengers, Miguel helped defend Subterranea from the Deviant Brutus' army;

REAL NAME: Miguel Santos
ALIASES: El Relampago Vivo, Sir Fulminator
IDENTITY: Publicly known
OCCUPATION: Licensed super hero, student; former reluctant criminal, would-be subversive
CITIZENSHIP: USA; formerly Demonica
PLACE OF BIRTH: East Los Angeles, California
KNOWN RELATIVES: Carlos Santos (father, deceased), Maria Santos (mother), Lisa Santos (sister, deceased), José Santos (brother)
GROUP AFFILIATION: Rangers, Initiative, Avengers (inactive); formerly Secret Avengers, Queen's Vengeance, Pacific Overlords
EDUCATION: College studies in progress
FIRST APPEARANCE: Avengers West Coast #63 (1990)

Art by Kieron Dwyer & Rick Remender

Art by Dave Ross

when Subterranean defender Grotesk turned traitor and tried to destroy the world using Brutus' Oscillatron, Miguel risked his life to absorb its energies into himself. Miguel continued to prove an asset to his new team, aiding them when they were dragged into the extradimensional war between Arkon and Thundra, then helping them battle the Hangman (Jason Roland)'s Night Shift, personally preventing their master Satannish from taking the millions of viewers' souls during a televised fight by disrupting the live transmission. Shortly after Hank Pym refined Miguel's stabilizing units and costume, Earth became a battlefront in the Kree-Shi'ar War, and the Living Lightning joined the Avengers assigned by Captain America (Steve Rogers) as diplomatic envoys to the Shi'ar Imperium, where he unmasked a Skrull agent provocateur posing as Shi'ar Lord Chamberlain Araki, revealing the Skrulls' part in inciting the conflict. Back on Earth, Miguel assisted in the capture of Deathweb after the Manipulator (Ferrell Thompson) sent them to assassinate Liberal Party Presidential candidate Michael Galvan.

Art by Keith Pollard

use the solitude to concentrate on his studies. He subsequently assisted the Avengers against the Triple Evil and Kang's invasion of Earth, joined an assemblage of Earth's heroes battling the Order and Akhenaten, and when his old friend the Scarlet Witch went insane and turned her reality warping powers against the Avengers, Miguel joined most former Avengers in returning to assist the team, shortly before the team was disbanded. Though the Avengers were gone, Miguel continued his monitoring duties aboard the space station.

At some point having come to accept he was gay, Miguel decided to join the Gay and Lesbian Alliance, leading to a brief misunderstanding when the hero Flatman offered him membership in the GLA (Great Lakes Avengers). After the Superhuman Registration Act (SHRA) was passed, Miguel joined Captain America's Secret Avengers in opposing it, but after Captain America's surrender Miguel registered and was assigned to the Texas Initiative team, the Rangers, alongside whom he subsequently battled the criminal agency Hydra.

Art by Dave Ross

While attending LA's public celebration of the Mexican holiday Cinco de Mayo as a headline guest, Miguel was approached by Dr. Lou Denham, a surviving member of the Legion of Living Lightning, who had known Carlos Santos and had deduced the source of Miguel's powers. He tried to recruit Miguel to help rebuild the Legion, intending to duplicate Miguel's powers among the Legion's new members, but Miguel refused, insisting he wanted to work within the system to improve America. Denham briefly took Maria Santos hostage to force Miguel's cooperation, but Miguel swiftly freed her and overpowered Denham and his men; however a young bystander was winged by a gunshot that had ricocheted off Miguel's electrical field, and a remorseful Miguel vowed to use his abilities more intelligently in future. Shortly afterwards Miguel joined many of Earth's heroes battling the Magus' evil doppelgangers, then assisted the Avengers in defending Stark Enterprises from Professor Power's armored minions. Reassessing his priorities, Miguel took a leave of absence from the Avengers to pursue college courses at USC, though he returned to attend Tony Stark (Iron Man)'s funeral and help the Avengers confront their increasingly irrational member Wonder Man; these events and guilt over his absence when his teammates had been attacked by Ultron-14 made him briefly consider quitting college to return to full time Avengers status, but the Scarlet Witch convinced him to persist with his education. When the Goddess launched her crusade to purify the universe by destroying it, Miguel was one of those who temporarily fell under her mental domination. Later, during a break from college, Miguel was amongst several Avengers briefly controlled and demonically transformed by Lore to attack the Scarlet Witch.

After the Avengers west coast branch's dissolution, Miguel transferred to UCLA and concentrated full time on his college studies, until he returned to action alongside virtually all past Avengers to battle Morgan Le Fay; when she magically restructured reality to make herself Earth's ruler, Miguel became Sir Fulminator of Queen's Vengeance, Morgan's soldiers in the new Reality-398, but was returned to normal when she was defeated. Later, when the Avengers set up a deep space monitoring station in the asteroid belt to forewarn them of threats approaching Earth, Miguel, able to easily travel between the station and Earth, agreed to man it alongside Quasar (Wendell Vaughn) and Photon (Monica Rambeau), hoping to

ORIGINAL ELECTRIC FORM
Art by John Byrne

HEIGHT: 5'9" **EYES:** Brown
WEIGHT: 170 lbs. **HAIR:** Black

ABILITIES/ACCESSORIES: Miguel can transform his body into electrical plasma; in this form he can fly at sub-light speeds, generate a protective electrical aura strong enough to repel bullets, emit light flashes to blind or illuminate, and produce electrical blasts of up to 15 million volts. There appears to be no limit to how long he can safely remain in his electrical form, and while in this state he does not need to breathe and is immune to the rigors of outer space. He is insubstantial enough in this form to slip normal restraints or have objects pass through him, but he can be shorted out by exposure to water. His costume's stabilizing units prevent him from becoming stuck in this form and dissipating; they also regulate his top power level, but can be individually switched off to allow him access to greater limits, and if detached, the units carry sufficient residual charge to give a non-lethal shock; however he cannot switch off all the units without risking losing physical cohesion. In human form his more limited command of his body's electrical energy is still sufficient to hurl lightning bolts or control electrical devices. He can also absorb electricity, though he risks overload if he absorbs too much without discharging the excess. Miguel has some experience with basic street-fighting techniques, as well as some combat training from his fellow Avengers. He is bilingual in Spanish and English.

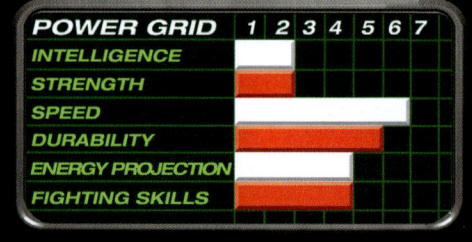

LIVING MUMMY

HISTORY: Born over 3000 years ago in Northern Africa, N'Kantu was the son of the chieftain of the now extinct Swarili tribe. N'Kantu grew into a strong, wise young man, proving himself a worthy successor to his father shortly after turning twenty-one. Not long after, Egyptians abducted the entire Swarili tribe despite N'Kantu's valiant efforts. In Egypt the Swarili were enslaved, serving Pharaoh Aram-Set and his corrupt priest, Nephrus. After completing a monument to Aram-Set, N'Kantu led his people to slay the Pharaoh. Nephrus, however, ambushed the chieftain, paralyzing him with a special liquid. N'Kantu was then mummified alive and entombed for millennia.

In recent times, N'Kantu finally burst forth from his prison. Half-mad from the lengthy immobility, he rampaged in Cairo, tracing the energies of Dr. Alexi Skarab, a descendant of Nephrus. Finally brought down after a massive battle with local police, N'Kantu was rendered immobile and shipped to a New York museum. He soon awoke and attracted the attention of the Elementals (Zephyr, Hellfire, Hydron and Magnum), who used him as a pawn in their attempts to control the Ruby Scarab. During this period, he became an ally of Skarab, a thief known as the Asp (Dan Harper), the Asp's partner Miles Olddan, and two of Skarab's students, Ron McAllister and Janice Carr. The group eventually defeated the Elementals and parted ways.

N'Kantu became a wanderer, befriending Ulysses Bloodstone and observing the Grandmaster's Contest of Champions. He also helped the Thing rescue Alicia Masters from Gamal Hassan, another descendent of Nephrus, who sought the Spirit Gem of Nephrus. Later, N'Kantu sought to use a fragment of the Bloodgem to restore his humanity. He eventually gave the fragment to Captain America during the hero's quest to prevent the shards from falling into the hands of criminals. Once more adrift, N'Kantu briefly found acceptance as part of Dr. Druid's Shock Troop, a group of mystic-oriented heroes, battling the Antibodies alongside Quasar. Since then, he has aided Elsa Bloodstone and the Frankenstein monster against the necromancer Rakses. Of late, he has served as guardian to a mystical artifact known as the Orb of Ra.

N'Kantu was eventually drafted against his will into SHIELD's supernatural Howling Commandos. Though he proved a valuable member — most notably in their defeat of the magician Merlin — he felt many of his fellow teammates were beneath him, and often went out of his way to let them know that. Seeing his service in the Commandos as a form of slavery, N'Kantu went AWOL, but was recaptured by SHIELD during the super hero "Civil War." Confined to the "42" Negative Zone prison in a cell specially-designed to contain him due to his weakness to fire, he escaped during Captain America's mass breakout of the prison. Briefly aiding his fellow fugitives in the ensuing struggle, N'Kantu departed before he could be recaptured. He returned to Egypt and his guardianship of the Orb of Ra. N'Kantu attempted to end his immortal life by summoning Nephrus, who failed to aid him. Instead, Anubis appeared and made a deal with N'Kantu: Anubis would allow N'Kantu to die after serving him if N'Kantu spent the time before it sending souls to Anubis' realm. On the condition that N'Kantu could choose which lives to take, he agreed.

REAL NAME: N'Kantu
ALIASES: The Mummy, "Captain Ace Bandages"
IDENTITY: No dual identity
OCCUPATION: Agent of Anubis; former SHIELD agent, adventurer; former King of the Swarili
CITIZENSHIP: Swarili tribe
PLACE OF BIRTH: Northern Africa
KNOWN RELATIVES: T'Chombi (father, deceased), V'Leema (wife, deceased)
GROUP AFFILIATION: Formerly SHIELD's Howling Commandos, Shock Troop
EDUCATION: No formal education
FIRST APPEARANCE: Supernatural Thrillers #5 (1973)

HEIGHT: 7'6" **EYES:** Brown
WEIGHT: 650 lbs. **HAIR:** None (formerly black)

ABILITIES/ACCESSORIES: The Living Mummy has superhuman strength and rock-hard skin. The preservative fluid that keeps him alive makes him resistant to the effects of disease and drugs, but highly susceptible to fire. He can go thousands of years without food or water. The Living Mummy also seems to possess certain energy-sensing abilities, especially those related to Nephrus. He has been able to pinpoint descendants of Nephrus on sight.

Due to the dryness of his mouth and throat, the Living Mummy can only speak with pain and difficulty. Until recently, he was also unable to speak English.

The Living Mummy's entire body is hidden beneath tattered papyrus. His flesh has become sufficiently desiccated that the skeleton beneath is somewhat visible.

POWER GRID	1	2	3	4	5	6	7
INTELLIGENCE							
STRENGTH							
SPEED							
DURABILITY							
ENERGY PROJECTION							
FIGHTING SKILLS							

Art by Michael Lopez with Rich Buckler (inset)

LIVING TRIBUNAL

REAL NAME: None known, perhaps inapplicable
ALIASES: None
IDENTITY: Earth's general populace is unaware of his existence
OCCUPATION: Acting guardian and judge of the multiverse
CITIZENSHIP: Inapplicable
PLACE OF BIRTH: Unknown, perhaps inapplicable
KNOWN RELATIVES: Perhaps inapplicable
GROUP AFFILIATION: None
EDUCATION: Unrevealed, perhaps inapplicable
FIRST APPEARANCE: Strange Tales #157 (1967)

HISTORY: The Living Tribunal is a vastly powerful conceptual being, one who has existed since the multiverse came into being. The Living Tribunal's only superior is the One-Above-All (not to be confused with the Celestial known as the One Above All), the entity which is apparently responsible for the existence of all life in the multiverse, and possibly beyond.

NOTE: A Universe is a single-dimension reality, such as Earth-616, the mainstream Marvel Universe. The Multiverse is the collection of alternate dimensions with a similar nature and universal hierarchy. Earth-616 and alternate Earths seen in the MU (which include beings like the Watcher, Eternity, etc.) are within the same Multiverse. Realms lacking this hierarchy of power are outside of the Multiverse, but within the larger Omniverse. Further, the realms with a multiverse are divided into divergent Earths, who share a common history and diverge at a specific point, and alternate Earths, who are similar, but possess many inherent differences. The Omniverse is the collection of every single universe, dimension, etc. Everything is in the Omniverse, and there is only one Omniverse. Within the Omniverse, collections of associated realms from different Multiverses are referred to as Megaverses.

The Living Tribunal often interacts with other conceptual beings, serving as their arbiter and judge. The Living Tribunal appears as a giant yellow humanoid with three faces, each representing a different personality. It has a blank space where a fourth face could be exhibited. The Living Tribunal has suggested that this fourth face became the enigmatic cosmic entity known as the Stranger. On one occasion, the vacant space displayed the face of the person the Living Tribunal was addressing.

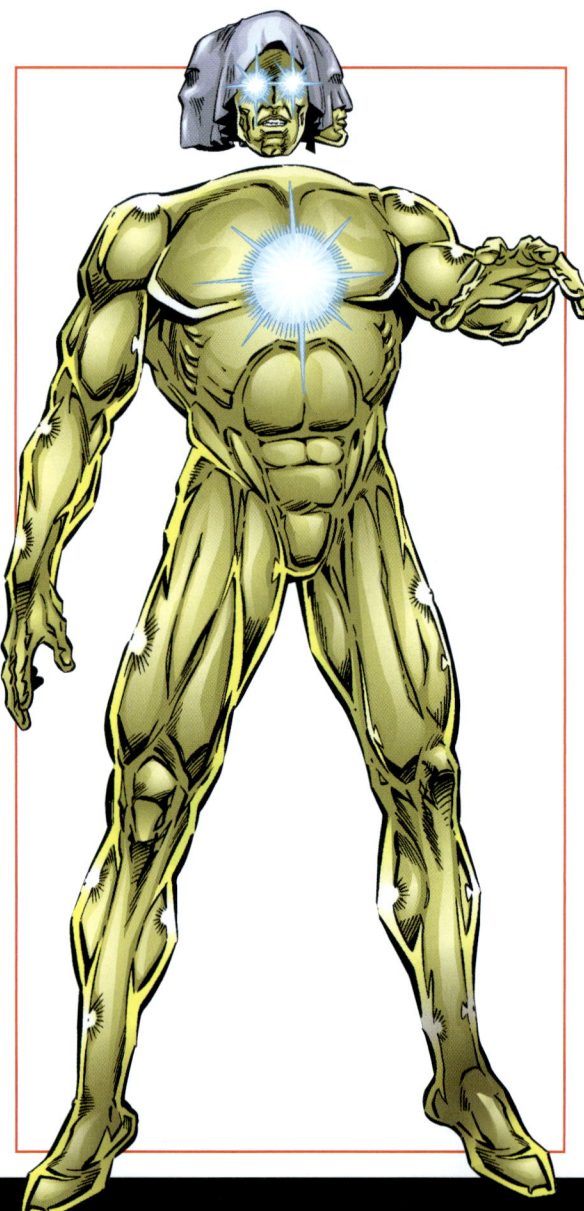

Even beings as great as Eternity, Infinity, Death and Oblivion are subject to the Living Tribunal's authority. Unlike the other conceptual beings, the Living Tribunal does not possess counterparts in other realities; only one Living Tribunal exists in the multiverse, and it is responsible for all judgments. The Living Tribunal's apparent base of operations is a dimension known as the Star Chamber, and it is served by lesser creatures called the Magistrati, who assist in judging matters where the Living Tribunal cannot intervene. The Living Tribunal also helped fashion the twin cosmic entities the Brothers, each of whom became the guardian of a different Megaverse, within the larger omniverse but encompassing more than a single Multiverse.

The Living Tribunal is not guided by any personal motivation or desires, but is entirely impartial, acting only in what it determines to be the greater interests of the universe. The Living Tribunal is more than willing to sacrifice millions of lives for the sake of billions more, or even billions for the sake of trillions, and will not deign to address the concerns of any lesser being without first establishing a plaintiff's importance.

When the Earth-616 sorcerer Dr. Strange brought the creature Zom to Earth in order to help drive off the sorceress Umar, the Living Tribunal was forced to intervene and banish Zom from Earth before he could destroy humanity. However, Zom's mere presence on Earth had tainted all life with the creature's evil, and the Living Tribunal informed Dr. Strange that the Earth would have to be destroyed for the greater good. After convincing the Living Tribunal that he was a powerful sorcerer, Dr. Strange won the right for a reprieve, gaining time to try and eliminate Zom's contamination. Dr. Strange received the Staff of Solar Power from the creature Nebulos to absorb the evil magic, most of which was contained within Baron Mordo, but once the staff took Mordo's excess power, Nebulos claimed it for himself. The Living Tribunal intervened to face Nebulos, and Dr. Strange helped the Living Tribunal defeat him. The Living Tribunal destroyed the staff rather than the Earth, eliminating the threat.

When Dr. Strange next encountered the Living Tribunal, he was informed that due to his works and heroes like him, the balance between good and evil on Earth had been tipped to good's favor, and that the Tribunal would have to release the In-Betweener to balance the two sides in the interests of the cosmic entities Lord Chaos and Master Order. Opposing the In-Betweener, Dr. Strange was defeated. However, the spaceknight Rom argued on behalf of his mission to destroy the Dire Wraiths, stating that the Wraiths might yet tip the scales on Earth to evil's benefit. Rom observed that his presence on Earth would act as a balance to the

Art by Jim Starlin

Wraiths' evil, and the Living Tribunal agreed with him, and withdrew the In-Betweener.

The Korvac of Earth-82432 accumulated such power that the Living Tribunal sealed that reality to prevent it from affecting others, removing the barrier only after that Korvac had used the Ultimate Nullifier to destroy himself and his entire universe. When Earth-616's omnipotent Beyonder threatened to eradicate Death itself, the Living Tribunal joined other cosmic entities in manifesting before the Beyonder to halt him. Although the Beyonder succeeded in destroying Death, he soon realized that the universe needed Death, and his friend Dave sacrificed himself to become the new Death.

When the Living Tribunal first encountered the Silver Surfer, it submitted to him the concept that he was Galactus' opposite number, and allowed the Surfer to become one with the universe for a moment. The Surfer was awestruck by this experience.

When Earth-89112's reality was overrun with demons, the Living Tribunal nearly destroyed it, but that Earth was redeemed by its counterpart of the Phoenix Force, which eradicated all of the demons. The Living Tribunal then had the Phoenix Force depart from Earth.

Shortly after attending the funeral of the Earth-616 reality's cosmic entity Eon, the Living Tribunal was petitioned by many of reality's conceptual beings, who were threatened by Thanos' ascendance to godhood after claiming the six Infinity Gems. Although Eternity argued that Thanos was seeking to supplant its role in the universe, the Living Tribunal simply observed that it was the nature of all life, and should be allowed to play out. However, when the gems wound up in the custody of Adam Warlock, the Living Tribunal ordered that they be divided among six caretakers and never be allowed to act in unison, as Warlock was too unstable to retain that power. In so doing, the Living Tribunal demonstrated that his power surpassed that of the gems.

When Warlock's evil side, the Magus, rendered Eternity comatose, Galactus argued for the Living Tribunal to remove its ban on the gems so that Warlock could use them to defeat the Magus. Although the Magus obtained the gems himself, he was soundly beaten because he lacked the Reality Gem; Eternity and Infinity defeated him, then had the restriction placed on the gems again. Eternity held a private hearing with the Living Tribunal to argue against the Infinity Watch's continued custodianship of the gems, but the Living Tribunal judged against Eternity. However, the Living Tribunal did confide to Eternity that because the Infinity Watch were within him, yet not under his control, he had obtained a gift of unpredictability which he should treasure.

When the powerful Star Brand of Earth-148611 (the "New Universe") was inadvertently brought into the Earth-616 dimension by Quasar (Wendell Vaughn), it was wielded at first by his girlfriend Kayla Ballantine, then seized by Erishkigal, a Deviant. She attempted to conquer the Nexus of All Realities, and challenged the Living Tribunal. To determine the fate of the multiverse, they chose as champions Quasar and the Silver Surfer. When Quasar realized he was Erishkigal's champion, he allowed himself to lose, and the Living Tribunal claimed the Star Brand, returning it to Kayla for safekeeping. After the Stranger took the Star Brand from Kayla and used it to bring Earth-148611 into the 616 dimension, the Living Tribunal placed a barrier around the planet to keep the Star Brand energies from further contaminating the 616 reality. Kayla was left behind on that world because she had wielded the brand.

When the formerly heroic mystic Dr. Druid summoned forth the demon Slorioth in order to prematurely advance the War of the Seven Spheres which the mystical Vishanti were engaged in, the Vishanti summoned the Living Tribunal and it judged against Slorioth, banishing it from Earth. When Thanos gained vast power again through the Heart of the Infinite,

the Living Tribunal joined champions from across reality to challenge him. Thanos destroyed all that existed with his power, but subsequently had a change of heart and restored reality, ridding himself of his power; the re-created universe lacked the terminal flaw which Thanos had sought to cure.

Recently, the Magistrati employed Earth-616's She-Hulk to serve in the Star Chamber and assist them in judging cases from throughout the universe. During her time in the Star Chamber, She-Hulk earned the enmity of Zoma the Watcher for forcing his brother Qyre to be stricken silent. She also met the challenge of the Champion of the Universe when he lorded over the population of Skardon with his Power Gem, and ultimately bested him in combat.

In the 31st century of Earth-691, the Living Tribunal was nearly usurped by the Protégé, whose ability to duplicate the powers of others allowed him to manifest the Living Tribunal's own power. Although the Guardians of the Galaxy struggled futilely against the Protégé, it was Scathan the Celestial who saved reality by judging against him, and the Living Tribunal absorbed the Protégé into itself to prevent him from endangering reality again.

Art by Juan Bobillo

HEIGHT: Inapplicable; appears to humans as a giant
WEIGHT: Inapplicable
EYES: No visible pupils or irises
HAIR: None known

ABILITIES/ACCESSORIES: Possessing virtually limitless power, the Living Tribunal can survey the entire multiverse at once, obliterate planets or suns at will, and form impenetrable barriers around worlds or even whole universes. The Living Tribunal manifests itself in a three-headed form, each head representing a different facet of its personality: the fully visible face represents equity; the fully hooded face represents necessity; and the half hooded face represents revenge. The face which addresses a plaintiff identifies which personality is guiding the Living Tribunal's decisions.

POWER GRID	1	2	3	4	5	6	7
INTELLIGENCE							
STRENGTH							
SPEED							
DURABILITY							
ENERGY PROJECTION							
FIGHTING SKILLS							

LIZARD

REAL NAME: Dr. Curtis Connors
ALIASES: None
IDENTITY: Known to authorities
OCCUPATION: Leading researcher in biogenetics, college professor
CITIZENSHIP: USA
PLACE OF BIRTH: Coral Gables, Florida
KNOWN RELATIVES: Martha Connors (wife, deceased), William Connors (son), unidentified sister-in-law
GROUP AFFILIATION: None; formerly Sinister Twelve
EDUCATION: Medical school graduate, later earned twin doctorates in biology and biochemistry (mutagenics)
FIRST APPEARANCE: Amazing Spider-Man #6 (1963)

HISTORY: Dr. Curt Connors was a gifted surgeon and biologist who went to war when his country called. He served as a battlefield medic until his arm was wounded in an explosion and was ultimately amputated. His surgical career brought to an abrupt end, Curt returned to his Florida laboratory. Inspired by a reptile's ability to regenerate lost limbs, he pursued a revolutionary study of reptilian molecular biology and DNA manipulation to replicate the process in humans. Curt then drank his untested formula; within seconds, his lost arm miraculously regenerated.

Although the serum worked as predicted, it was more powerful than Curt had expected. The chemical mix transformed him into a human lizard. Overwhelmed by his new reptilian nature, he fled into the dense Florida swamps. From his jungle sanctuary, the Lizard built an army of cold-blooded creatures — aiming to destroy humankind. Rumors of a "giant lizard" soon spread, drawing the attention of New York's *Daily Bugle*. Viewing the creature as a public menace, J. Jonah Jameson brazenly challenged Spider-Man to face the Lizard.

As a photographer for the Bugle, Peter Parker traveled to Florida. Tracking down Curt's wife, Martha, and young son, Billy, Spider-Man learned the truth. Using Curt's lab notes and equipment, as well as his own scientific knowledge, he was able to concoct an antidote. Battling the Lizard to a standstill, Spider-Man forced the creature to swallow the solution and revert to human form — minus his newly regenerated arm. Spider-Man's aid earned him Curt's undying gratitude, as well as the enmity of his reptilian alter ego.

Curt would soon have the opportunity to repay the favor. When Peter gave his ailing aunt, May Parker, a transfusion, his radioactive blood put her in deadly peril. With doctors powerless, a desperate Spider-Man brought his friend a sample of May's blood. Curt helped the hero develop a formula to save May's life. However, Curt remained unaware of Spider-Man's secret identity.

Shortly thereafter, Curt and Spider-Man again worked jointly to create a solution that would soften the Rhino's hide. Unfortunately, the chemicals in that solution caused Curt to revert to reptilian form once more. Knowing a cold-blooded creature cannot regulate its internal temperature, Spider-Man trapped the Lizard in a refrigerated train carriage.

For a while, Curt split his time between Florida and New York. A research grant at Empire State University established him for a time in Manhattan, where Peter worked as his teaching assistant. Yet Curt could not escape the Lizard's shadow. More and more frequently, extreme stress or exposure to chemicals would transform him into the horrific creature. Connors and many heroes and villains were transported off Earth to the so-called "Secret Wars" orchestrated by the near-omnipotent Beyonder. There on "Battleworld," though grouped with the villains, the Lizard tried to remain neutral after sustaining an injury, and befriended the Wasp. Upon returning to Earth in tatters, Martha took Billy and left him, unable

Art by Damion Scott

to deal with the toll of her husband's relapses. Though distraught by the separation, Connors managed to gain some control over his Lizard persona and helped rescue his family, kidnapped by the Owl. This control was short lived, as a demonic invasion of New York called the "Inferno" turned the Lizard savage again. Calypso used her voodoo powers to usurp control of the Lizard's mind in pursuit of her own deadly vendetta against Spider-Man, after the death of her lover, Kraven the Hunter (Sergei Kravinoff). The Lizard was captured after an explosion at Kraven the Hunter's mansion. Calypso infiltrated the Vault prison to liberate the Lizard but, after training to resist her charms, the Lizard instead slaughtered her.

In the wake of Calypso's defeat, Curt embarked on a search for a permanent cure to his condition. To that end, he created a modified version of his original regeneration formula. Connors' assistant, Aldo Quadrini, injected this new serum into a severed fragment of the Lizard's tail, with disastrous effects. The tail grew into a completely new Lizard, devoid of any shred of humanity. Curt was forced to trigger his transformation to protect his wife and son.

Following her husband's brave sacrifice, Martha returned to Curt. With his missing arm miraculously restored by Hammerhead, a happy ending for the Connors family seemed assured. However, the cellular structure of Curt's new arm proved unstable, and it soon became useless. A short time later, Martha and Billy were diagnosed with cancer, a result of pollution from an industrial lab near the Connors' Florida home. The combined efforts of Curt, his reptilian alter ego and Spider-Man were enough to persuade a Monnano Corporation employee to expose the company's misdeeds — but it was too late. Martha's cancer was inoperable, and Curt's long-suffering wife died.

Billy survived, and unwillingly holds his father partly responsible for the tragedies which befell them both. Under the strain of his wife's death and his son's resentment, the line that once existed between Curt Connors and the Lizard has become ever more blurred. It seems Curt can now exert some control over his reptilian alter ego — but in return, the Lizard is ever waiting for those moments of weakness in the man that will allow him to take over Curt's human form. Curt commited a bank robbery, deliberately allowing himself to be imprisoned for the protection of himself and those he loved.

Free from prison, the Lizard was given a power upgrade by Norman Osborn, enabling him to radiate aggression through pheromones. In return, the Lizard joined Osborn's short-lived Sinister Twelve team to greet Spider-Man once the wall-crawler was coerced into liberating Osborn from prison; the Twelve were defeated by Spider-Man and his heroic allies. Later, Connors returned to research, but was driven feral by Stegron's use of the ancient Rock of Life, which de-evolved animalistic beings. In this crazed state, the Lizard injected his biorestorative serum into his son, causing Billy to become a lizard-man as well. Billy was treated by Mr. Fantastic, while the Lizard raged against Vermin until Spider-Man defeated Stegron. Connors' research inadvertently gave superhuman powers to a drug-addicted intruder in his lab, transforming him to become the super-adaptive monster known as Freak. One of Connors' graduate students, Melati Kusama, stole the Lizard formula and perfected it for her own DNA, enabling her to transform into a lizard-like form. Calling herself Komodo, Kusama gained a tail and regenerative abiliities, however unlike Connors, she could control her transformations and maintained her human mentalitiy while in lizard form. Connors recommended Komodo for the Initiative.

Art by Gabriele Dell'Otto

HEIGHT: (Connors) 5'11"; (Lizard) 6'8" (variable)
WEIGHT: (Connors) 175 lbs.; (Lizard) 550 lbs. (variable)
EYES: (Connors) Blue; (Lizard) Red pupils
HAIR: (Connors) Brown; (Lizard) None

ABILITIES/ACCESSORIES: The Lizard possesses a number of superhuman powers endowed by his reptilian form, including the ability to regenerate missing limbs, release pheromones to produce violent behaviors in people, and superhuman strength (able to lift 12 tons). His powerful leg muscles enable him to clear 12 feet in a standing high jump and 18 feet in a standing broad jump. His alligator-like hide is tougher than human skin and is capable of resisting the penetration of small-caliber bullets. His reaction time is about twice that of the normal human being and he can run at speeds of up to 45 miles per hour.

The Lizard possesses a 6.5-foot tail that he can whip at speeds up to 70 miles per hour. Like a Gegku lizard, his hands and feet have retractable 1-inch hooks growing from the base of his palm and the ball of his foot, and his fingers and toes are covered with scores of tiny claws to create adhesive pads. As a result, the Lizard can support his weight climbing up and down normally intractable surfaces.

When the Lizard emerges, the R-complex of Connors' brain (the most primitive region of the human brain containing the most bestial drives) takes over the cerebellum, causing Connors' mind to become progressively inhuman. The Lizard gains a quasi-telepathic ability to communicate with and command all reptiles within about a one-mile radius of himself.

In his human form, Dr. Curtis Connors is a brilliant biologist and biochemist, and is a leading herpetologist (a scientist who studies reptiles).

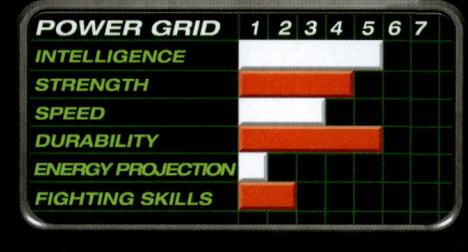

POWER GRID	1	2	3	4	5	6	7
INTELLIGENCE							
STRENGTH							
SPEED							
DURABILITY							
ENERGY PROJECTION							
FIGHTING SKILLS							

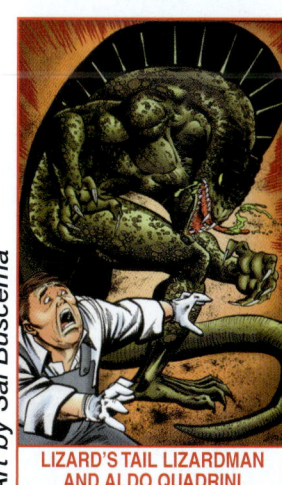

LIZARD'S TAIL LIZARDMAN AND ALDO QUADRINI

Art by Sal Buscema

LLAN

REAL NAME: Llan
ALIASES: Dexter Rayne, the Sorcerer, Opener of the Way, Architect of Madness, Bringer of Despair
IDENTITY: No dual identity
OCCUPATION: Would-be conqueror
CITIZENSHIP: None
PLACE OF BIRTH: Unrevealed
KNOWN RELATIVES: None
GROUP AFFILIATION: Leader of the Forces of Darkness
EDUCATION: Unrevealed
FIRST APPEARANCE: Alpha Flight #71 (1989)

HISTORY: Little is known of Llan the Sorcerer, an evil entity described as neither god nor demon, but something far worse. He can manifest in the Earth dimension only when certain planetary alignments occur, approximately once every 10,000 years. Commanding the extradimensional Forces of Darkness from the Twisted Realms, Llan longs to inflict insanity and despair upon Earth but is bound by combat rules between himself and any mystic champions serving the forces of good.

Circa 18,000 BC, Llan entered the Earth dimension with power garnered from human worshippers, a breach in rules which contributed to his defeat. Nevertheless, while active, Llan played an undescribed role in the Great Cataclysm which destroyed Atlantis, perhaps in conjunction with the Dweller in Darkness, the Darkholders, the Deviants, or other major menaces of the time. When the Talisman, first of a succession of mystic mortal heroes channeling the gods' power, banished Llan, her parting curse upon him forced him to take the form of a demonic idol in his next manifestation. Circa 8000 BC, Llan returned in the form of a dragon, hoping to release his legions via the mystic Gateway of Night, which, like his opposing forces' Gateway of Day, was situated on the mystic site known as the Eye of the World. The Talisman of that era, Nahita of the Tribe of the Moon, commanded him to take the idol's form, and when he did so, she trapped him within a binding spell, unable to move until the cycle of ten millennia had passed again.

In recent years, the recurring alignments neared and caused an upsurge of evil supernatural forces in Canada, where many were opposed by Alpha Flight, and perhaps elsewhere. Llan lured vacationers Dexter and Carol Rayne to his burial site to unearth the idol, then manipulated Dexter into murdering Carol in a blood ritual, destroying the idol and enabling Llan to possess Dexter's body. Creating a new physical form in imitation of the era's super-villains, Llan confronted the current Talisman, Alpha Flight member Elizabeth Twoyoungmen, teleporting her and her teammates to a mystic dimension. Nearly killing the Alphans, he provoked Talisman into attacking him, which, per their combat rules, allowed him free rein on Earth, to which he returned, leaving the heroes stranded. In the many weeks before they returned, Llan besieged Canada with bizarre phenomena which were linked to Alpha Flight, manipulated the creation of new Canadian super-team Gamma Flight, and prompted government censure of Alpha Flight upon their return.

Llan mentally lured various American super-villains, fleeing the threat of increased opposition from the Super-Powers Registration Act, to Canada. Mistakenly believing Llan hoped to form a superhuman army, Alpha Flight battled the criminals, enabling Llan to channel the energy they unleashed to unlock the Gateway of Night. Soon afterward, Alpha Flight, framed for crimes by demons in Llan's service, fought Gamma Flight in a battle which Llan, who had manipulated Gamma Flight's creation for precisely this purpose, used to open the Gateway and unleash the Forces of Darkness. Both teams, as well as the Canadian military, convened at the Eye of the World, where Llan's spells prevented Talisman from opening the Gateway of Day. While Llan boasted that Talisman's death would free his power from restrictions by Eternity or similar entities, Dr. Strange traveled to the dimension on the Gateway's other side and worked with Talisman to open it, unleashing the counterbalancing Forces of Light from the Shining Realms. Meeting in battle, the two supernatural war hosts phased each other out of existence, forcing Llan to flee the Earth dimension, but not before cursing the Alphans to suffer horrible deaths before Earth's ultimate corruption, a curse whose workings may have finally begun with the team's recent decimation by Collective.

HEIGHT: Variable, normally 6'3"
WEIGHT: Variable, normally 185 lbs.
EYES: Red
HAIR: Black

ABILITIES/ACCESSORIES: Llan possesses almost unlimited magical power and knowledge, enabling him to alter his shape and size, become intangible, control inanimate objects, teleport between dimensions, travel through time, project devastating mystic blasts, cast illusions, read minds, and perform other such feats. He is limited only by the rules that bind beings like himself, which grant him access to the Earth dimension once every 10,000 years or so and forbid him from actively attacking Earth unless first attacked by the Talisman.

POWER GRID	1	2	3	4	5	6	7
INTELLIGENCE							
STRENGTH							
SPEED*							
DURABILITY							
ENERGY PROJECTION							
FIGHTING SKILLS							

*LLAN IS A TELEPORTER

FORCES OF DARKNESS

Art by John Calimee with Mark Bagley (inset)

LLYRON

HISTORY: Namor MacKenzie, the son of human Leonard MacKenzie and Atlantean Fen, became the superhuman Sub-Mariner in the early 20th Century. Fen died in a bombing on Atlantis, and Leonard, who was believed dead, eventually remarried and fathered another son, Lawrence, who in turn fathered Leon. Leonard was eventually killed, while Leon was employed by the rich Marrs Corporation. Meanwhile, Namor developed a long-standing rivalry with the metamorph Llyra, the former empress of another undersea kingdom, Lemuria. Llyra desired to wed Namor to claim Atlantis' throne, but Namor developed a deep hatred of her, partly because she caused the death of Namor's actual bride, Dorma. In an elaborate plot, Llyra posed as Phoebe Marrs, the owner of Marrs Corporation, and seduced Leon MacKenzie, intentionally becoming pregnant. To conceal her true plans, she posed as Namor's old flame Invisible Woman and seduced Namor so that he would believe her child to be his.

Llyra then found the cave of Vyrra, an Atlantean scientist exiled for his illegal cloning experiments, one of which cloned Namor's cousin, Namora, producing a cloned child whom Namora raised as Namorita. Vyrra genetically accelerated Llyra's child's birth and aging. Not wanting the child to be mindless, Vyrra copied Llyra's mind and memories into its brain, but secretly copied his own mind into the brain as well, wanting part of himself to live on in a powerful form. These two minds, merging with the child's own slowly developing mind, produced a brilliant and deadly composite psyche with full access to Llyra's memories and cunning and Vyrra's vast scientific knowledge and ambitions. When the male child awoke, he was genetically developed to age 16, and proved to be a super-powerful amphibian like Namor, though Llyron's skin was green like his mother's. Llyra murdered Vyrra, unwilling to share her secret with anyone else and unaware that Vyrra's mind had been copied into Llyron's as well, then named the child Llyron (likely after her father), and took Llyron to undersea Atlantis. She announced that Llyron was the son of Namor and thus had claim to the throne. Despite Namor's protestations, Llyron won the loyalties of Atlantis' ruling council by defeating Namor's allies, the criminal Tiger Shark and his lover Tamara Rahn.

Seeking to further discredit Namor, Llyron, as Atlantis' ambassador, approached the United Nations with an offer of alliance, which the U.N. later accepted. Llyron successfully repelled a pre-arranged attack of a sea monster assault — including the walking whale Giganto (offspring of its namesake who had died in battle with the Fantastic Four years before) and the parasitic Hagfish, which Llyron slew — framing Namor for attacking the surface world with these monsters as heralds. Llyron was soon hailed as Atlantis' ruler despite his true parentage being revealed, as Atlantean law recognized Llyron and Namor sharing a common ancestry and willingly declared Llyron rightful ruler. Llyron had Llyra imprisoned, at

REAL NAME: Llyron MacKenzie
ALIASES: Son of Namor
IDENTITY: Publicly known
OCCUPATION: Rebel warrior; former ruler of Atlantis
CITIZENSHIP: Atlantis
PLACE OF BIRTH: Vyrra's Cave, near Atlantis
KNOWN RELATIVES: Llyra Morris (mother), Leon MacKenzie (Black Moray, father), Lawrence MacKenzie (paternal grandfather), Llyron (maternal grandfather, deceased), Rhonda Morris (maternal grandmother), Leonard MacKenzie (paternal great-grandfather, deceased), Namor MacKenzie (Sub-Mariner, paternal great-half-uncle), extended family via Namor
GROUP AFFILIATION: None
EDUCATION: Assimilated through minds of Llyra and Vyrra
FIRST APPEARANCE: Namor, the Sub-Mariner #54 (1994)

which point she realized that Vyrra's mind inhabited Llyron's form as well; Llyron later constructed a monument to Vyrra on Atlantean soil. When the sorceress Morgan Le Fay raised Atlantis to the surface, much of Atlantis' population was killed, and Llyron used his leadership skills to gather the people together. Llyron ordered that all the fertile women of Atlantis be implanted with clone fetuses so that a powerful army could be raised with which to attack the surface world, a likely plot of Vyrra's. It is unknown what became of this plot or why Llyron was removed from power, but Atlantis soon elected a new ruler.

Llyron joined the At'la'tique rebllion against Atlantis. As part of the super-powered rebel team Fathom Five, Llyron attacked several cities on the surface and battled the Thunderbolts until Radioactive Man instilled him with radiation and threw him back to the sea. Captured, Llyron unintentionally afflicted much of Atlantis with this radiation from his cell in Atlantis.

HEIGHT: 6'2"
WEIGHT: 278 lbs.
EYES: Blue-Gray
HAIR: Black

ABILITIES/ACCESSORIES: Llyron possesses the abilities of a sub-mariner, an Atlantean-human hybrid. He has Class 100 superhuman strength, reptilian wings on his ankles that grant him flight, and superhuman durability, reflexes, and speed, capable of swimming up to 60 miles per hour. Llyron can breathe in both air and water and survive in the ocean's crushing depths, where he is able to see as well. It is unknown if Llyron can mentally communicate with sea life.

POWER GRID	1	2	3	4	5	6	7
INTELLIGENCE							
STRENGTH							
SPEED							
DURABILITY							
ENERGY PROJECTION							
FIGHTING SKILLS							

Art by Geof Isherwood with John Byrne (inset)

LOCKDOWN

REAL NAME: Jomo Kimanye
ALIASES: JK
IDENTITY: Secret
OCCUPATION: Adventurer, executive assistant
CITIZENSHIP: Shadow City
PLACE OF BIRTH: Unidentified planet in the Negative Zone
KNOWN RELATIVES: Unrevealed
GROUP AFFILIATION: Partner of Rosetta Stone
EDUCATION: Unrevealed
FIRST APPEARANCE: Fantastic Four #17 (1998)

HISTORY: Long ago, in the antimatter universe known as the Negative Zone, a disaster forced Jomo Kimanye's people from the surface of their planet. Moving into a vast subterranean complex, their civilization was placed in suspended animation. With stasis pods to sustain their health, their mental abilities are maintained by an interactive role-playing game, a virtual reality world called Shadow City with Lockdown and his partner, Rosetta Stone (Nefer Neith Sinué), as its guardians. While Lockdown was the more skilled combatant, Rosetta Stone provided her technical expertise. Stumbling across the world by accident, the Fantastic Four were captured and plugged into the game. They became the Tetrad, a criminal crew composed of Grim Ben (Thing), Matchstick Johnny (Human Torch), Richard Reed (Mr. Fantastic) and Stormy Sue (Invisible Woman). Lockdown captured Reed, Johnny, and Ben and handed them over to the police. However, Sue helped them escape and they joined forces with the criminal gang known as the Twisted Sisters. Unbeknownst to his friends, Reed had reverted to his true personality. He allowed Lockdown to recapture them and send them to Shadow City's prison, Bedlam Purgatorium. Lockdown was suspicious of Reed's true motives, but also respected him as an equal. However, he failed to predict the full scale of Reed's plans. Initiating a jailbreak with his fellow inmates, Reed distracted Lockdown long enough for Sue to escape her stasis pod and free her teammates. By the time Lockdown had been reanimated from stasis, the Fantastic Four had fled. Considering them a threat, Lockdown ordered Rosetta Stone to find a way to hunt them down.

Later, Lockdown and Rosetta Stone were pulled out of the Negative Zone by a temporal distortion accidentally caused by the Scarlet Witch. They discovered that Earth's super heroes had been kidnapped and coerced into a contest of arms against one another, a scheme orchestrated by the Brood Queen. Lockdown agreed to help, despite his former distrust of the Fantastic Four. The Brood Queen possessed Rogue and assimilated the abilities of the contest's winners: Captain America, Hulk, Scarlet Witch, Spider-Man and Thor. Rosetta Stone and Iron Man worked to free the remaining heroes, restore their powers, and disable the enemy's ship. Meanwhile, Lockdown gave Psylocke his armor, enabling her to get close to the Brood Queen and remove the stolen abilities with her powers. Warbird scared the Brood Queen into leaving Rogue's body, while Rosetta Stone teleported the heroes back to Earth. Lockdown tracked her down in the Night Cruiser, and they returned to their own adventures.

HEIGHT: 5'11"
WEIGHT: 184 lbs.
EYES: Brown
HAIR: Black

ABILITIES/ACCESSORIES: Lockdown has athletic agility, endurance, speed and strength. Shadow City is programmed to give him the upper hand, making him practically unbeatable in that environment. He is a highly trained fighter, and can strike specific nerve clusters with sufficient force to affect even those with superhuman durability such as the Thing or the Brood. He also has acrobatic, business, and detective skills. Lockdown's battle armor provides various features and abilities, including mindbolts, radio communication, and resistance to biotoxins, scanners, and stealth technology. He also uses an anti-flame coagulant, a neuron disrupter (or "neurolock") that induces non-lethal paralysis and an ultra-frequency screamer that emits a sonic barrage. His rocket-propelled flying car, the Night Cruiser, has heavy armor, an autodrive setting, a ramming mode, scanners, and various weapons. After encountering the Fantastic Four, Lockdown had the vehicle fitted with limited dimensional travel capabilities.

POWER GRID	1	2	3	4	5	6	7
INTELLIGENCE			■				
STRENGTH			■				
SPEED		■					
DURABILITY					■		
ENERGY PROJECTION		■					
FIGHTING SKILLS					■		

Art by Salvador Larroca

LOCKHEED

HISTORY: One of the greatest warriors of the alien race the Flock, Lockheed battled the alien Brood on their homeworld where he encountered the young Earth mutant Kitty Pryde. Secretly returning to Earth with Kitty and her X-Men teammates, Lockheed found a nest of alien Sidri beneath the X-Men's mansion and, along with Kitty and her teammate Colossus, defeated them. Kitty named Lockheed after a character in a fairytale, which itself was named after the X-Men's SR-71 Lockheed Blackbird jet, and the pair quickly became inseparable friends. On the alien Battleworld, Lockheed befriended a female green dragon, later nicknamed "Puff," and after the X-Men returned to Earth she grew to gigantic size and caused chaos in Tokyo until Lockheed defused the situation, after which she shrank to normal size.

Lockheed later joined Kitty and others in founding the British super-team Excalibur. During a battle with the despotic Dr. Doom (Victor von Doom), Lockheed was severely wounded while protecting Kitty. After undergoing surgery, his astral form was transported aboard the spaceship that carried the collective transient souls of his entire space-faring race. There, Lockheed was placed on trial for abandoning not only his people, but his intended bride on their wedding day. Lockheed defended his decision to leave, but during his speech the ship's pilots fell asleep. Lockheed regained control of the ship, thus preventing his people's souls from dissipating. The court still found him guilty; however, they commuted the death sentence and instead exiled him from the Flock.

Lockheed recovered, and after Kitty returned to the X-Men, he adventured on his own. He was taken in by a pair of sister witches, but after discovering they were terrorizing their town with their powers, Lockheed joined a rival

REAL NAME: Unrevealed, possibly inapplicable
ALIASES: "Dragon"
IDENTITY: No dual identity
OCCUPATION: Spy; former adventurer, warrior
CITIZENSHIP: Formerly Flock with criminal record
PLACE OF BIRTH: Flock homeworld
KNOWN RELATIVES: None
GROUP AFFILIATION: SWORD; formerly X-Men, Excalibur, Flock
EDUCATION: Unrevealed
FIRST APPEARANCE: Uncanny X-Men #166 (1983)

witch in opposing them. She helped him locate Kitty, who had since left the X-Men and was attending university, and he rejoined her there. After Kitty returned to the X-Men once more, Lockheed was recruited by the espionage agency SWORD, which deals with extraterrestrial matters, to act as a mole to observe and report on the X-Men's activites in exchange for SWORD's help in resolving pressing homeworld issues. Lockheed rejoined the X-Men in time to aid in opposing the alien Ord. Lockheed was then alerted to the green dragon's kidnapping in Tokyo. With Kitty's help, Lockheed traveled to Japan and opposed the kidnappers, the Path of Destiny cult. When the X-Men were taken by SWORD to the Breakworld to oppose their intended destruction of Earth, they learned of Lockheed's SWORD agent status.

FLOCK SHIP

Art by Dave Hoover

LENGTH: 2'6"
WEIGHT: 20 lbs.
EYES: Yellow, no visible irises
HAIR: None

ABILITIES/ACCESSORIES: Lockheed is a purple-skinned alien with a dragon-like appearance, including small forepaws and wings. He can fly and breathe fire. Lockheed is immune to the intense heat and flames he can generate, as well as that from external sources within certain limits. Lockheed has been seen to withstand immersion in molten lava with no ill effects. He also possesses five lungs of unknown function.

Lockheed's mind is capable of resisting telepathic probes from even the most powerful telepaths. Like all members of his race, Lockheed can sense the emotions of others via empathy. He has learned English, though he rarely speaks, and is skilled in the piloting of his race's astral starship. Lockheed once wore an image inducer on a collar around his neck that created the holographic illusion of him being a housecat.

POWER GRID	1	2	3	4	5	6	7
INTELLIGENCE							
STRENGTH							
SPEED							
DURABILITY							
ENERGY PROJECTION							
FIGHTING SKILLS							

LOCUST

REAL NAME: August Hopper
ALIASES: "Doc Hopper," "Mr. Mad Scientist"
IDENTITY: Known to authorities
OCCUPATION: Criminal; former chemist, entomology professor
CITIZENSHIP: USA. with a criminal record
PLACE OF BIRTH: Unrevealed
KNOWN RELATIVES: Carol Hickman (daughter), Bob Hickman (son-in-law)
GROUP AFFILIATION: None
EDUCATION: Ph.D in entomology, chemistry, possibly others
FIRST APPEARANCE: X-Men #24 (1966)

HISTORY: Renowned entomology professor Dr. August Hopper was fired from Metro College for aggressively promoting his radical theory that ionic bombardment could make insects gigantic, posing a potential threat to humanity. Despite this, Hopper was subsequently hired as a research chemist by Ryan Chemicals, where he developed some of the world's most effective insecticides. Because of these successes, the company gave him exceptional freedom and privacy in conducting his research. Growing increasingly reclusive and bitter, Hopper resented his reputation as a scientific crackpot and the loss of his academic position, and he became convinced that his past and present employers had taken all the credit for his accomplishments while he toiled in relative obscurity. Slowly going mad, Hopper secretly developed the means to enlarge insects. He plotted to terrorize mankind with gigantic insects in his new costumed guise as the Locust, then "discover" a means of stopping the bugs as Hopper, hoping to be hailed as humanity's savior. As the Locust, he led his giant insects in a series of devastating attacks on farmland, but they were twice defeated through the combined efforts of the National Guard and the mutant X-Men. During a third battle with the X-Men, Hopper had to be rescued from his own giant bugs after Marvel Girl (Jean Grey) broke his control over them. Finally realizing the insanity of his actions, Hopper discarded his weapons and turned himself in to the authorities.

Hopper spent several years in prison, during which farmer Bob Hickman married Hopper's daughter, entomology student Carol, against her father's wishes. Upon his release from prison, the Locust destroyed the Hickman farm and pursued the newlywed couple from town to town, devastating entire communities. When the Hickmans befriended the monstrous Hulk, alias Bruce Banner, he helped fend off the Locust's latest assault. Losing control of his insects again after the Hulk damaged his armor, Locust was struck down while trying to save his daughter from his giant bugs, and was impressed to see Bob risking his life to protect her. Realizing he was wrong about Bob not being good enough for his daughter, the injured Hopper made peace with the Hickmans. Sent back to prison, Hopper later flew into a jealous rage over television coverage of his old foes, the original X-Men, who had become popular celebrities as the original X-Factor team. Escaping, he attacked the heroes in a restaurant using giant cockroaches, but he was defeated and recaptured. Escaping again, he re-created his giant insect army as part of a blackmail scheme that would have caused widespread ecological damage, but the extremist Order super-team destroyed his insects and defeated him before he could cause major harm.

Art by Gil Kane

HEIGHT: 5'9" **WEIGHT:** 168 lbs.
EYES: Green **HAIR:** Gray

ABILITIES/ACCESSORIES: The Locust is a mad scientific genius. His armored "exo-shell" slightly augments his strength (lifting up to one ton) and durability, and its mechanical wings grant him limited flight capability. His helmet's special lenses enhance his peripheral vision, and its micro-magnetic antennae enable him to control insects. His armor can produce sticky nets of cocoon silk, and he carries a handheld ionic ray device capable of stunning both humans and insects. He also wields a "magno-ray" device capable of enlarging insects to gigantic sizes, and usually carries ionically-treated insect eggs which he can instantaneously hatch to bolster his insect army. He has enlarged and controlled insects such as locusts, beetles, caterpillars, wasps, praying mantises, and cockroaches.

POWER GRID	1	2	3	4	5	6	7
INTELLIGENCE							
STRENGTH							
SPEED							
DURABILITY							
ENERGY PROJECTION							
FIGHTING SKILLS							

Art by Werner Roth

LOKI

HISTORY: Loki is the son of Laufey, a king among the frost giants of Jotunheim, one of the "Nine Worlds" of the Asgardian cosmology. As a child, when Odin was still establishing his dominion as lord of Asgard, the young Loki met a strange man, later revealed to be an adult Loki, who convinced him to encourage Laufey to battle Odin. Laufey led the frost giants against him, only to meet defeat and death at Odin's hands. Discovering that Laufey had left behind a son, Odin remembered his father Bor's dying words to adopt the son of a father killed by his hands; Odin adopted Loki into his own family, raising Loki as a brother to his son Thor.

Loki had an aptitude for magic at a young age, and would often cause pranks to embarrass Thor. He became infamous for his mischievousness, but secretly resented Thor and the love that Odin lavished upon him. When Odin was preparing his greatest gift for Thor, the enchanted hammer Mjolnir, Loki interfered with its creation, causing its handle to be forged too short. Loki was envious that Thor would one day wield Mjolnir, and over the years repeatedly crafted schemes to make Mjolnir's power his own.

When Loki and Thor were still young, Thor was attracted to the swordmaiden Sif, who had beautiful gold-colored hair. Loki cut off her hair while she slept, but Thor guessed that Loki was responsible and demanded that he restore it. Loki enlisted the dwarves Brokk and Eitri to forge new hair for her, but as he did not pay them anything, they decided to craft the hair from nothing, making black hair from the night itself. However, Thor still loved Sif, even without her golden hair.

Thor and Loki occasionally adventured together as teenagers, though Loki always searched for an advantage over his brother. When Odin sent Thor, Sif and their friend Balder to gather elements needed to craft the blade Svadren, Loki secretly followed them, but when he learned that the sorceress Karnilla, queen of the Norns, was planning an attack on Asgard, he refused an offer to join her and instead alerted the others to her scheme. Later on, Loki and Karnilla became occasional allies, although her love for Balder prevented her from aiding Loki in any way that would affect Balder.

As Loki matured into a young man, his antics became more and more pronounced, until Odin finally sent him to jail to learn from his actions. Loki, fed up with Asgard, used his magic to escape his cell, and eventually met Eldred the sorcerer, who increased his training in the black arts. Finally, Loki confronted the fire demon Surtur of Muspelheim and offered him Eldred's soul in exchange for power. Surtur accepted, and Loki assumed ownership of Eldred's lands and minions. His foray into the black arts earned him the title of "god of evil" among the Asgardians, and he forged alliances with many of the realm's enemies. Loki mated with the goddess Angerboda, who bore him the monstrous offspring Jormungand (the Midgard Serpent) and the Fenris Wolf, as well as Hela, the goddess of death. Loki also tricked the goddess Sigyn into marrying him by posing as her true love, Theoric.

Loki eventually learned of the prophecies of Ragnarok, in which he was fated to bring about Asgard's ruin by slaying Balder, then leading the enemies of Asgard into final battle. Loki ultimately embraced this destiny, and sought the means to bring about Ragnarok on more than one occasion. However, Loki usually crafted his schemes so subtly that Odin and Thor could rarely justify punishing him, and Loki would continue to live in their midst, awaiting his opportunity.

In recent years, Loki finally obtained an advantage over Thor when Odin sentenced him to Earth in the guise of Dr. Donald Blake, a medical practitioner who would transform into Thor using Mjolnir. Loki sought victory over his brother by exploiting Blake's human weakness, and employed many pawns against him on Earth, including Jinku the Lava Man, the Weather Maker, Sandu, Amora the Enchantress, Skurge the Executioner,

REAL NAME: Loki Laufeyson
ALIASES: Gem-Keeper, Walter Lawson, Lester, Loren Olson, Tyfon, Typhon, Father Williams, Willie, Tso Zhung; has also impersonated hundreds of others
IDENTITY: No dual identity; regarded as a mythological character by the general populace of Earth
OCCUPATION: God of evil; former god of mischief
CITIZENSHIP: Realm of Asgard
PLACE OF BIRTH: Jotunheim, Asgard
KNOWN RELATIVES: Laufey (father, deceased), Farbauti (mother, deceased), Sigyn (wife, deceased), Odin (foster father, deceased), Frigga (foster mother, deceased), Balder, Thor, (foster brothers) Vidar (foster brother, deceased), Hela, Fenris Wolf, Midgard Serpent (children), Arkin (cousin, deceased) — *NOTE: It is unrevealed if any of the above deceased have been restored to life by Thor*
GROUP AFFILIATION: Formerly Lost Gods, manipulator of the "Acts of Vengeance" prime movers
EDUCATION: Extensive training in the rites of black magic
FIRST APPEARANCE: Venus #6 (1949)

Skagg, Surtur, Cobra (Klaus Voorhees), Mr. Hyde, the Absorbing Man, and the Super-Skrull (Kl'rt). In one attempt to trick Thor into battling the Hulk, Loki diverted a distress call intended for the Fantastic Four to Dr. Blake's office, but it was also intercepted by Iron Man (Tony Stark), the Wasp, and Ant-Man (Henry Pym). When the four heroes learned of Loki's involvement and banded together with the Hulk to defeat him, they

AS YOUTH

Art by Olivier Coipel with Greg Tocchini (inset)

decided to form a team of heroes to face future threats, calling themselves the Avengers. Loki long regretted having caused their formation.

Loki made several attempts at claiming the throne of Asgard when Odin entered into his "Odinsleep" hibernation, but threats to Asgard such as the Mangog and Surtur frightened Loki into surrendering the throne. Loki once joined forces with Dormammu of the Dark Dimension to trick the Avengers and Defenders into assembling the mystical Evil Eye for them, but the combined heroes ultimately defeated them both. Loki even unleashed a direct assault upon Earth once, and Thor helped lead Earth's ground forces against his army, finally defeating him. After Loki usurped the throne of Asgard yet again, he was sent to Earth in the guise of a vagrant by Odin as punishment.

Loki regained his identity due the presence of Harris Hobbs, a journalist who had been to Asgard but had the memory removed by Thor. Hobbs dreamed of Asgard in his sleep, and his dreams reached Loki, restoring him to normal. Loki finally set Ragnarok in motion when he arranged for Hoder to shoot Balder with an arrow of mistletoe, but Odin preserved Balder and eventually revived him. Loki also caused the mortal Red Norvell to gain powers similar to Thor's. Loki was bound to Sigyn as punishment, but he finally obtained release by blaming Odin himself for his problems, claiming that Odin's favoritism towards Thor was the root of all his misfortunes.

When Surtur prepared to wage war on Asgard in order to complete the forging of his sword Twilight, he had the dark elf Malekith see that Loki remained out of the conflict by signing a non-aggression pact. However, Loki did not honor his agreement and stood alongside Thor and Odin in Asgard's defense. Odin seemingly sacrificed himself to imprison Surtur, and the realm was left without a ruler. Loki attempted to claim the throne himself, but the populace did not trust him. As part of a scheme to prevent Thor from claiming the throne, he cast a spell which turned his brother into a frog, but still possessing the might of Mjolnir, the frog of thunder forced Loki to undo his magic.

After Thor rescued mortal souls from the realm of Hel, Hela laid a curse upon him so that he could not die, but also would not heal from injuries. Learning what his daughter had done, Loki amused himself by sending frost giants, the Midgard Serpent and the Destroyer against Thor. Although Thor's physical body was reduced to paste, his spirit took over the Destroyer armor and forced Hela to undo her curse. Thor broke Loki's arm for his part in the events, knowing that Loki could easily heal the injury.

When Seth of the Ennead (Gods of Egypt) led his Demons of Death into conflict with Asgard, Loki refused an alliance with him, and in his astral form discovered that Seth was holding Odin prisoner within the Black Pyramid, the source of Seth's power. Loki secretly helped Thor rescue their father, and Odin repulsed Seth's invasion. Still smarting from the success of the Avengers, Loki concocted a scheme for the enemies of all super heroes to obtain their revenge. During this "Acts of Vengeance" conspiracy, Loki appeared to Dr. Doom, the Kingpin, Magneto, the Mandarin, the Red Skull (Johann Shmidt), and the Wizard as an anonymous lackey, offering them the power to manipulate Earth's super-villains into conflicts with heroes who would be unprepared for unfamiliar adversaries. Each of the six "prime movers" was led to believe that he was the one arranging the scheme. Loki's plot was finally uncovered by Thor, and he was defeated. As a final act of vengeance, he merged three Sentinel robots into the

Art by Walter Simmonson

Art by Carlos Mota

TSO ZHUNG

powerful Tri-Sentinel, but it was defeated by Spider-Man, who used the Uni-Power as Captain Universe to face this threat.

Loki assumed the guise of a businessman on Earth, and enlisted Ulik the rock troll and Amora to aid him in a new plot against Thor, collecting the powers of the Wrecking Crew along the way to aid them. At this time, Thor was bound to the mortal Eric Masterson, so Loki had Eric's son Kevin captured. Thor set Kevin free, but as an act of spite, Loki hurled a blast of energy at Kevin and his mother Marcy. Amora, now acting against Loki, took control of Kevin's babysitter Susan Austin and had her take the blast for Kevin and Marcy. Thor was so furious with this attack that he used Mjolnir to draw Loki's life force from his body, seemingly killing him. As punishment, Thor was banished into the subconsciousness of Eric, and Eric took the place of Thor.

However, Loki's consciousness had taken over the body of Odin while he was in Odinsleep, and through him took command of Asgard. Eric and Sif eventually found Odin's spirit within the demon Mephisto's realm, and they restored Odin to his body while Mephisto claimed Loki instead. Although he was now a prisoner in Hell, Loki's spirit continued to wander when Mephisto was distracted. He once schemed with Pluto of Olympus to trade enemies, with Loki arranging the death of Hercules while Pluto plotted Thor's demise. Loki enlisted the titan Typhon against Hercules, but he failed, and Loki's own minion the Flame aided Pluto, but Loki himself had to save Thor from the Flame when he threatened Sigyn. Loki once imparted some of his power (via a mystical dagger) to Knut Caine, a mad killer who patterned himself after Loki and called himself "Mad Viking." Caine began to create a pseudo-Asgard on Earth, but was defeated by the Hulk, Henry Pym and the Wasp. The Hulk hurled the dagger into the ocean to prevent it from possessing someone else.

Loki finally escaped Mephisto's realm when Thor reluctantly enlisted him to aid him against the New Immortals. However, Loki's physical form no

Art by Walter Simmonson

committing crimes so that Thor would be suspected, but Thor eventually bound the true Jake Olson to himself and Loki was trapped in a body identical to Olson, which was named "Loren Olson," Jake's twin brother, who was sent to prison for his crimes.

Karnilla released Loki from prison not long before Odin faced Surtur in battle once again, and this time Odin was truly slain. Thor ascended to the throne of Asgard, and Loki found himself surprisingly content under his rule, seeing new opportunities for power, and genuinely pleased as Thor began to impose Asgardian values on Earth. However, Thor eventually withdrew from Earth after learning of an alternate future reality (Earth-3515) wherein he became a despot, and he and Loki were left at odds once more.

Loki finally attempted to start Ragnarok again wielding an uru hammer of his own. However, this time Thor allowed him to play the events out to their conclusion, having realized that Asgard was caught in a repeating loop of death and rebirth, denying them a true warrior's death. Thor decapitated Loki, and kept his still-living head with him as he permitted Surtur to unleash the final assault on Asgard. Thor then confronted They Who Sit Above in Shadow, the powers responsible for the repeating Ragnaroks, and he saw to their destruction. Loki was apparently consumed in the destruction of Asgard alongside his brother.

After Thor broke the Ragnarök cycle, the souls of all Asgardians were hidden within mortals on Earth. At some point, Loki took possession of Sif's body, transferring her spirit into that of an elderly woman. Balder, whose spirit was within the Destroyer armor, gathered numerous Asgardians, including Loki, to protect them. Thor began a quest to restore Asgard on Earth in Broxton, Oklahoma, where he discovered and restored the Asgardians gathered by Balder, and Loki was seemingly reborn as a woman. While feigning a new benevolence, Loki wasted no time in causing unrest by telling Balder that he is an Odin's son. Afterwards, Loki traveled through time, killed Odin's father Bor and manipulated his younger self and father to arrange events to be adopted by Odin as a child. During an invasion by the Skrulls, Loki convinced the other Asgardians that Beta Ray Bill was a Skrull impostor.

NOTE: Adventures during Loki's youth showing an adult Hela remain unexplained.

longer existed, and he had Sigyn temporarily bond him to a suit of armor. He continued to trouble Thor, as well as Eric Masterson (now the hero Thunderstrike), possessing War Machine (Jim Rhodes in alternate Iron Man armor) to attack Thor. Loki finally struck a bargain with Seth to have him genetically engineer a new body, and his spirit took possession of it. He sought revenge on Thunderstrike, but when War Machine, She-Hulk and Ant-Man (Scott Lang) were drawn into the fray, he was instantly reminded of the Avengers and ended the fight.

Loki eventually crossed over into the dimension of Earth-93060 (the Ultraverse), where the six Infinity Gems had been scattered. Loki began to gather the gems together, battling many of the local superhumans ("Ultras") for them. Finally, the Grandmaster revealed to him that there was a seventh gem, the Ego Gem, and they pitted the local heroes Ultraforce against the Avengers with the gem as the stakes. However, Loki did not win, and soon lost all six gems, returning to his native reality.

Attempting to stave off Ragnarok, Odin had allowed the world tree Yggdrasil to think that Ragnarok had already happened, and hid the Asgardians on Earth in mortal identities. Loki became the businessman Tso Zhung, with no recollection of his earlier life. He was brought together with the other "Lost Gods" by Red Norvell, and became the first of them to reclaim his true form, confronting Seth, who had taken advantage of the situation to try and eradicate the Asgardians. When the other Asgardians regained their true identities, they defeated Seth.

Thor's most recent mortal identity, Jake Olson, was that of a paramedic slain during a battle, and Thor took on the man's appearance as a new secret identity. Loki reanimated the true Olson's body and began

HEIGHT: 6'4" **EYES:** Green
WEIGHT: 525 lbs. **HAIR:** Black-Grey

ABILITIES/ACCESSORIES: Loki possesses physical abilities far superior to humans, an increased lifespan, superhuman strength (able to lift up to 50 tons), immune to terrestrial diseases, and resistant to conventional injury. Loki is perhaps the most powerful sorcerer in all of Asgard. His many magical abilities included shapeshifting (able to gaining the basic natural abilities inherent in each form), astral projection, molecular rearrangement, eldritch energy blasts, illusion-casting, flight (via levitation), telepathy, hypnosis, and teleportation. Loki is immune to most physical injury, and can reattach severed body parts, including his own head. Loki can mystically imbue objects or beings with specific but temporary powers, and enhance the powers of superhumans. Loki can also magically create rifts between dimensions, allowing him or other objects passage from one universe to another. Most often this rift is between Asgard and Earth.

POWER GRID	1	2	3	4	5	6	7
INTELLIGENCE							
STRENGTH							
SPEED *							
DURABILITY							
ENERGY PROJECTION							
FIGHTING SKILLS							

*LOKI IS A TELEPORTER

LONGSHOT

REAL NAME: Unrevealed
ALIASES: "Jumping Jack," "the Lucky One"
IDENTITY: No dual identity in the Wildways, the general populace of Earth does not know Longshot is an extradimensional being
OCCUPATION: Adventurer; former movie stuntman, rebel leader, slave
CITIZENSHIP: None on Earth; renegade slave with a criminal record in the Wildways
PLACE OF BIRTH: The Wildways
KNOWN RELATIVES: Alison Blaire (Dazzler, wife, separated), Lois London (sister-in-law), possible relative of Benjamin Russell or Shatterstar; former guardian of the X-Babies
GROUP AFFILIATION: X-Factor Investigations; formerly Exiles, the Hand (Earth-1720), Imperial Guard (Reality-522), X-Men, Wildways rebel leader
EDUCATION: Unrevealed, apparently no conventional education
FIRST APPEARANCE: Longshot #1 (1985)

HISTORY: In an extradimensional world called the Wildways (aka Mojoworld) ruled by invertebrate beings known as the Spineless Ones, the scientist Arize created a race of vertebrate slaves through genetic engineering. Arize secretly designed their genetic codes so that his intelligent humanoids would have a strong sense of self. For some, like the one to be known as Longshot and his bestial friend, Quark, he genetically engineered them to have superhuman abilities.

Grown in machines to become a warrior slave for the Spineless One named Mojo, "Longshot" became conscious as an adult and immediately asserted his independence. Mojo forced "Longshot" to serve as a stuntman in his dangerous movies. Locating Arize, "Longshot" discovered his own origin and was encouraged to lead a slave rebellion. He became a legendary hero of his people, but Mojo captured him. His memory erased, "Longshot" escaped through a portal to Earth where he earned his name due to his superhuman luck. While there, he battled Gog and Magog (rebel hunters from the Mojoverse), befriended stuntwoman "Ricochet Rita" Wayword, and finally stopped Mojo and his sorceress Spiral (a twisted future version of Rita) from enslaving the Earth. Longshot, with Quark and Rita, pursued Mojo back into his dimension to continue the revolt.

Longshot's rebellion failed. Televising the X-Men's exploits via cybernetic eyes implanted into the mutant Psylocke, Mojo returned the amnesiac Longshot to Earth for a ratings boost. He transformed the heroes into children, airing their clash with Spiral and the New Mutants. Defeated, Mojo retreated, while Longshot joined the X-Men. With Storm (Ororo Munroe) as leader of the X-Men, winsome Longshot faced the Juggernaut (Cain Marko) in Scotland and the Marauders in San Francisco, while sharing a romance with teammate Dazzler (Alison Blaire). While battling the Adversary in Dallas, Longshot (demonstrating exceptional loyalty to the team) and the rest of the X-Men gave their life forces to banish the evil Adversary. In gratitude, Omniversal Guardian Roma restored their lives (though the world still believed they had died), and rendered them invisible to electronic detection.

The X-Men settled in the Australian Outback, evicting the cyborg thieves the Reavers from their Outback base. Longshot used his psychometry to aid in returning the Reavers' stolen objects, teleporting via the mysterious Aborigine Gateway. In Denver, Longshot fought Harry Palmer and his band of Brood infected mutants, and in New York, faced a massive demonic invasion led by S'ym, N'astirh, the Goblin Queen (Jean Grey's clone Madelyne Pryor), and Mr. Sinister. Though spiritually tainted during the invasion, Longshot, with the X-Men and X-Factor, emerged victorious. After helping prevent an alien conquest of Earth and battling the merger of Nimrod and the Master Mold Sentinel, Longshot felt incomplete from his amnesia, and appeared to mysteriously fade away in a mystical dream state shared with Storm. Longshot ended up back on Mojoworld.

Meanwhile, Dazzler had entered the Siege Perilous, and returned as an amnesiac to the Malibu, California home of Lila Cheney's bodyguard, Guido Carosella. Longshot returned to Earth there, with Spiral in pursuit, but Dazzler did not remember her former lover. Lila teleported Dazzler and Longshot to safety, but was redirected to Mojoworld by Mojo's assistant, Major Domo. There, Longshot spent several weeks leading an insurrection against Mojo, but ultimately failed. Returning to Earth via Mojo's secret spy, Meek, Dazzler traveled again to Mojoworld with the X-Men, who were mind-wiped and forced to act out in a skewed "Wizard of Oz" movie with Longshot, while Mojo's ratings soared. While Mojo forced X-Men to battle X-Men, Professor X liberated the X-Men's minds. Longshot stormed Mojo's palace and appeared to slay the spineless tyrant with a sword; Mojo vanished. As rule of Mojoworld was passed to Mojo II: the Sequel, Professor X detected Dazzler was pregnant with Longshot's child. Longshot suggested the name "Shatterstar." Longshot and Dazzler remained on Mojoworld where they were married. Through unrevealed circumstances, Dazzler apparently lost the baby, possibly due to a miscarriage. The people of the Wildways treated Longshot and Dazzler like royalty, many hoping they would assume a leadership role. Since the new culture rejected remnants of Mojo I's regime, the juvenile X-Men he created, the

Art by Art Adams

"X-Babies," were hunted down. Dazzler rescued the children, and she and Longshot temporarily became their guardians.

In time, Mojo II proved to be a despot as well, oppressing those he deemed imperfect compared to himself. Longshot, Dazzler, Quark, and tactical expert, Kragar, led a new rebellion. The imprisoned Major Domo, formerly Mojo I's primary servant, suggested a public execution to help Mojo II's ratings; Mojo II chose to execute Domo. Rescued by Longshot, Major Domo joined the rebellion, and lost his left arm in battle. The rebels were secretly betrayed by a warrior named Brahams, who framed Domo as the traitor. Their hideout raided by Mojo II, the rebels were nearly defeated until Longshot received unexpected assistance defeating Mojo II from Spiral, who despised Mojo II's treatment of "freaks" like herself and Major Domo, who grew to respect the rebellion.

After a time of peace, the original Mojo returned to power, no longer relying on TV ratings for power, but real war. When Mojo captured Cable and Shatterstar, Longshot teamed with X-Force and Spiral. Spiral transported Longshot to another time where he assisted transferring the soul of the slain Shatterstar into the body of a comatose mutant, Benjamin Russell, while X-Force defeated Mojo. Later, Longshot was swallowed by a creature called the Thingee. Longshot "died" and approached the doorway to Heaven, but was denied entrance. Rather, he was transported to Kansas on Earth in full health. Befriending the diminutive Nutt the elf, a girl named Betty Fillmore (who was traumatized by the Thingee), and a band of eccentric sanitarium patients, Longshot again faced the horrible Thingee while being pursued by the police who suspected Longshot of the Thingee's atrocities. Longshot healed Betty, and by the power of the group's hopes, prayers, and love, reverted the monster into its original state, the Beautiful Thingee. Longshot and his friends set out for New York City but eventually returned home. When Mojo tried to replace his X-Babies with similar baby versions of dangerous super-criminals, he lost control of his new creations, and "babies" from an Age of Apocalypse production devastated the entire Mojoverse. Longshot was recaptured by Mojo, but Dazzler believed he was killed, and she returned to Earth, devastated.

Meanwhile, caught in the wake of the Scarlet Witch's altering of Earth-616 into Reality-58163 ("House of M"), the Exiles encountered body-snatching, reality-altering Proteus who took possession of Mimic's body and discovered other realities to visit in order to find a perfect host body. Desperate to overcome Proteus' powers, Heather Hudson granted Mojo viewing access to the multiverse in exchange for Longshot's freedom as long as Mojo only watched and did not interfere. Mojo released Longshot with his memory wiped clean, leaving only his combat training and probability manipulation powers intact. Teleported to Earth-15731 (a divergent "New Universe"/Earth-148611), Longshot instinctively joined the battle with Proteus. Longshot drove Proteus away, but not before Proteus burned out Mimic's body. The Exiles pursued Proteus across various realities including Earth-6375 (a divergent "2099 AD" reality created by the Exiles' interaction), and Earth-712, home of the Squadron Supreme. When Proteus possessed Morph's body on Counter-Earth, he had found the perfect host due to Morph's transmutable physiology. The Exiles stopped Proteus and reprogrammed his mind to make him believe that he was actually Morph. With his intended mission complete, Longshot remained with the Exiles and continued to fix broken realities. In one of his last adventures with the Exiles, on Earth-1720, Longshot appeared to betray the team by joining the Hand and attacking Blink. Mind controlled by the Madame Hydra (Sue Storm) of that universe, Longshot eventually got lucky and regained control of his mind before the Exiles were victorious.

Later, the Exiles teamed with Earth-616's British Excalibur to defend Otherworld from a resurrected Jim Jaspers and his army of Furies. Longshot was reunited with his long lost lover, Dazzler. However, discovering Longshot had no memories of her, in a moment of anguish Dazzler released a burst of light that reflected throughout the Panoptichron (Crystal Palace) blinding everyone including Longshot. This blinding light somehow, most likely due to the composition of the walls within the Panoptichron, slowly returned Longshot's memories of Dazzler. Longshot remained on Earth-616 and joined Excalibur to be with his wife.

Unfortunately Longshot's full memory failed to return. Unable to recreate the passion they once had for each other, the two agreed to separate. Noticing an unfamiliar picture of himself in a newspaper, Longshot investigated and, with the help of X-Factor Investigations, discovered it was a Skrull impersonating him. Afterward, he assisted X-Factor Investigations in rescuing Darwin, a mutant with the power to evolve in response to immediate threats, captured by Dr. Maru for the Karma Project to create super-soldiers. With the recent departures of team veterans Layla Miller and Rahne Sinclair, Longshot and Darwin agreed to join X-Factor Investigations.

HAND COSTUME

Art by Paul Pelletier

HEIGHT: 6'2" **EYES:** Blue
WEIGHT: 80 lbs. **HAIR:** Blond

ABILITIES/ACCESSORIES: Longshot can subconsciously affect probability fields through psionic means in order to give himself "good luck" when his motives are pure. However, by creating "good luck" for himself, Longshot creates an equal and opposite effect elsewhere. This "bad luck" could affect someone else, or could conceivably even affect Longshot at some point. It operates even when Longshot does not consciously will it to do so. He can extend this probability field to others within close proximity, at least 4' away. Through touch, he can telepathically "read" recent memories of a person, and has psychometry, the ability to detect emotional "psychic imprints" left, or to be left, on objects. The stronger the person's emotions when handling the object, the stronger the psychic imprint left. This "psychic touch" can somehow access information from the future, allowing Longshot to read the thoughts of a person who will eventually handle an object, which Longshot is touching in the present. Longshot also psionically affects, involuntarily or subconsciously, people (particularly women, though men may also be affected) in his proximity, stimulating their brains' pleasure (dopamine-producing) centers such that the targets experience a "falling in love" euphoric sensation.

Longshot has leathery skin, two hearts, porous bird-like bones, and only three fingers and a thumb on each hand. His left eye glows with a bright light (the "Purifying Radiance") when employing one of his powers. On at least one occasion, Longshot used his energies to heal and transfer the soul ("uerneur") of a slain person into another body. Longshot's mind has been implanted with combat training equivalent to an experienced warrior who utilizes street fighting techniques and acrobatics. Longshot often carries a grappling hook, knives, daggers, and a number of lightweight high carbon steel throwing blades, which he stores in a bandolier, and can hurl with uncanny accuracy when employing his "good luck." He was invisible to electronic detection for a time, but this ability was apparently removed by Mojo.

LOOTER

REAL NAME: Norton G. Fester
ALIASES: Meteor Man
IDENTITY: Known to authorities
OCCUPATION: Professional criminal, crackpot scientist, "part-time nut," "professional failure"
CITIZENSHIP: USA with a criminal record
PLACE OF BIRTH: Unrevealed
KNOWN RELATIVES: None
GROUP AFFILIATION: Formerly Defenders imposters; teamed with Aura and Override
EDUCATION: Unrevealed
FIRST APPEARANCE: (Looter) Amazing Spider-Man #36 (1966); (Meteor Man) Marvel Team-Up #33 (1975)

HISTORY: Although he flunked science in school, Norton G. Fester was determined to discover the secret of the universe. Convinced that meteors held his answers, he obtained a possibly radioactive one and accidentally opened a gas pocket that gave him superhuman strength. Adopting a costume, dazzle gun, and helium balloon backpack, Norton became the Looter, going on a crime spree. Fearing his powers might wane, Looter brazenly entered the Space Exhibit to steal a second meteor, but was defeated by Spider-Man (Peter Parker). Released on bail, Norton successfully inhaled the gas from a second meteor but was thwarted in his attempt to break open the giant Wakanda Find meteor by Spider-Man. Sent to prison, Norton was a model inmate until, reminded of his strength by a bullying cellmate, he smashed through the wall and escaped. Calling himself the Meteor Man, Norton stole the Science Exhibit meteor now owned by millionaire Kyle Richmond, putting Richmond's alter-ego Nighthawk on his trail, although Nighthawk later decided that Norton was mentally ill and refused to pursue him. Instead, Norton fought Spider-Man and Valkyrie (Brunnhilde) high over Manhattan, falling to earth when Valkyrie's sword punctured his balloon. Although severely injured, Norton recovered to join villains posing as the "Defenders," seeking to blame the real heroes for their activities. Norton (as the Looter), Batroc, Beetle (Abner Jenkins), Blob, Electro, Plant-Man, Porcupine (Alex Gentry), Sagittarius (LMD), and Whirlwind were all defeated by a Hellcat mindblast. As Meteor Man, Norton designed a backpack that channeled his meteors' energies into microwaves and into his nervous system. Growing to sixty feet, Norton battled Spider-Man and Giant-Man (William Foster) but the backpack exploded, seemingly killing him.

Surviving, Norton drowned his sorrows in cheap liquor and lived on the street, burgling homes to support his drinking, but was again stopped by Spider-Man. As the Looter, Norton attacked Spider-Man with a wave motion gun, but lost quickly. Released from the Vault, Norton was hired by the Master Programmer (Otto Octavius) and Dr. Octopus (Carolyn Trainer), who gave him cybernetic enhancements and teamed him with Aura and Override in their war against Mr. Tso and Alistaire Smythe, whose cyber-slayers defeated him. Infiltrating the Iron Rock facility, a repository for super-villain weaponry, Norton stole devices belonging to the Mauler, Ringer, Shocker, Stilt-Man, Trapster, and Unicorn, using them to steal enough money to purchase the Science Exhibit meteor, never thinking to just steal the meteor instead. Defeated by Spider-Man (Ben Reilly), he was taken away by SHIELD. Becoming more delusional, Norton took to talking to his meteor. Later fighting the Hornet (Peter Parker, using this identity to avoid a bounty on Spider-Man's head), Looter was again removed by SHIELD although he was later sighted at the Ditko Theater when Eddie Brock auctioned off the Venom symbiote.

More recently, Norton sought his meteor's twin in New York and the Savage Land, encountering Spider-Man (Peter Parker), the Fantastic Four, Stegron, Ka-Zar (Kevin Plunder), Shanna, and Dr. Strange in the process. Although once more taken away by SHIELD, he set his sights on the twin's likely location: the moon.

HEIGHT: 5'9"
WEIGHT: 150 lbs.
EYES: Brown
HAIR: Brown

ABILITIES/ACCESSORIES: The Looter has superhuman strength enabling him to lift up to 20 tons and can leap fifteen feet from a standing start. His dazzle gun emits blinding light. He has worn a backpack containing a balloon that can be filled from a helium canister, carrying him aloft. He has also used a microwave backpack, a wave motion gun, cybernetic enhancements that increased his strength and allowed him to access and disable any computerized security system, other villains' weapons, the Meteorator 300 and a meteor gun that did absolutely nothing. Although Norton claimed the meteor also magnified his intelligence, that appears to be part of his delusion.

POWER GRID	1	2	3	4	5	6	7
INTELLIGENCE							
STRENGTH							
SPEED							
DURABILITY							
ENERGY PROJECTION							
FIGHTING SKILLS							

Art by Keith Pollard with Mike Wieringo & Tom Morgan (insets)

LORD CHAOS & MASTER ORDER

HISTORY: Although, like most abstract entities, the precise origins of Lord Chaos and Master Order are unrevealed, it is known that they serve as the opposing forces within a dimension called the Magick Realm, a place between fact and fantasy from which many magic users draw their power. Chaos and Order attempt to maintain a balance of power between them for the well-being of the universe; but unlike the opposing forces of Death and Eternity, which coexist reasonably peaceably in the outside universe, Chaos and Order are almost constantly at odds with each other, and created the In-Betweener as a third force to serve them and further their eternal conflict. Eons ago, Chaos and Order were among the abstract entities who permitted an experiment which placed the powers of the Infinite in the hands of mortals by allowing energy from the universe of the Beyonders to slip through, leading to the creation of Cosmic Cubes.

In recent years, Order and Chaos manipulated Spider-Man (Peter Parker) in a battle against the Death-worshipping, mad Titan Thanos. Order and Chaos implied that, in a struggle against Death, they had manipulated Spider-Man's destiny so that he could free Adam Warlock from his Soul Gem to defeat Thanos. Order and Chaos next conspired with other abstract, metaphysical and omnipotent entities within the Dimension of Manifestations in an attempt to destroy the Beyonder, apparently an energy collective from the Beyonders' realm that had gained sentience and nearly upset the balance of reality. Later, when the Fantastic Four attempted to transport six Infinity Gems from the Magick Realm to their own universe to save Galactus' life, the In-Betweener secretly infected them with the essences of Chaos and Order, causing them to fight over control of the gems. When the In-Betweener then ventured into the outside universe in an attempt to kill Galactus, the Silver Surfer summoned Chaos and Order to rehabilitate Galactus and reassert control over the In-Betweener after Galactus cast him back into the Magick Realm.

When Thanos obtained the Infinity Gauntlet, Chaos and Order were among the cosmic entities who sided with Adam Warlock and confronted the mad Titan, demanding that he surrender the Infinity Gems, which granted him power rivaling that of Eternity, although Thanos easily defeated all those assembled against him. Chaos and Order then joined the battle against Nebula, Thanos's supposed granddaughter, who had stolen the Infinity Gauntlet from him; Nebula destroyed the abstract entities who opposed her but was soon relieved of the Infinity Gauntlet by Warlock, who used it to set the universe right. With Nebula defeated, Order and Chaos joined other cosmic beings at Warlock's trial to determine his fitness to wield the Infinity Gauntlet, where Warlock promised to choose five other protectors for each of the Infinity Gems. When Nicholas Grant, former head of Mys-Tech's Warheads Kether Troop, was transformed into Audit, he confronted Master Order under the false presumption that Order had created him to bring balance to the universe by "auditing" dangerous souls; but Order denied any part in Audit's creation and killed him, with Chaos later revealing he had created Audit as a gesture of reconciliation with Order. Most recently, Chaos and Order again opposed Thanos when he obtained the omnipotent Heart of the Infinite, although they were again unsuccessful in their efforts to defeat him.

REAL NAME: Lord Chaos & Master Order
ALIASES: None
IDENTITY: Inapplicable
OCCUPATION: Forces of Nature
CITIZENSHIP: Inapplicable
PLACE OF BIRTH: Inapplicable
KNOWN RELATIVE: Inapplicable
GROUP AFFILIATION: Inapplicable
EDUCATION: Inapplicable
FIRST APPEARANCE: Marvel Two-In-One Annual #2 (1977)

HEIGHT: Inapplicable
WEIGHT: Inapplicable
EYES: Inapplicable
HAIR: Inapplicable

ABILITIES/ACCESSORIES: Although the exact nature and extent of their powers remain unrevealed, Lord Chaos and Master Order have vast powers, which they use to manipulate events within their respective spheres of influence in subtle ways. Through some as yet unrevealed process, Lord Chaos and Master Order worked together to create the metaphysical being known as the In-Betweener. Both Lord Chaos and Master Order are abstract beings who embody the metaphysical concepts of Chaos and Order; as such, they possess no true physical form, although they on occasion appear (via utilization of Manifestation Bodies from the Dimension of Manifestations) as a disembodied, bald, inhumanly warped and distorted male head (Lord Chaos) and a disembodied bald male head (Master Order). Further, each being represents the collective forces of order and chaos in the universe, with Order growing and Chaos dwindling in size and power when the universe becomes more orderly, and vice versa.

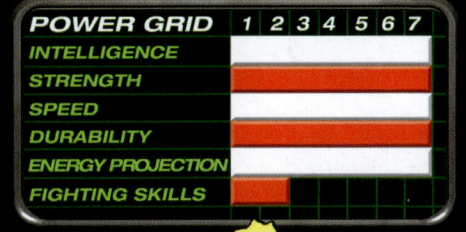

Art by Ron Lim

LORD MOSES

REAL NAME: Unrevealed
ALIASES: None
IDENTITY: Secret
OCCUPATION: Scientist, would-be world conqueror
CITIZENSHIP: Haven
PLACE OF BIRTH: Unrevealed
KNOWN RELATIVES: None
GROUP AFFILIATION: Leader of the Havenites
EDUCATION: Ph.D. in nuclear physics and genetics
FIRST APPEARANCE: (Shadowed) Fantastic Force #2 (1994); (full) Fantastic Force #10 (1995)

HISTORY: In the early 1940s, the future Lord Moses was a colleague of the likes of Robert Oppenheimer, Abraham Erskine, Phineas Horton and Isaac Sandor, using technology to shepherd mankind towards its ultimate destiny; but his work on developing the nuclear bomb, and its use and effects, left him guilt-ridden and disillusioned. Taking a spiritual sabbatical, he tracked a UFO deep into the Arctic Circle, locating an alien vessel's ruins. Accessing its bizarre psiontechnology, he learned of its trans-temporal origins and recent history, though much data was lost in its crash. Taking the name Lord Moses and building the base Haven around the ship, he vowed to purge Earth's corrupt civilization and establish a more benign society to rise from its ashes. He gathered the cream of humanity, training them to assist him and to foil telepathic intrusion, and genetically re-coding them. Though disdaining violence, he saw it as a necessary evil to accomplish his goals, and he established his Battle Elite as his field agents, though he had no intention of retaining them in Haven after his success. At some point he adopted a young Hispanic girl, training her both as a warrior and as a worthy Havenite, and re-christened her Zarathustra.

In recent years, Lord Moses dispatched the young adult Zarathustra and several of his Battle Elite to obtain the Omnivirus, which Empire State University's Isaac Sandor had designed to remake/repair others on a cellular level. Despite interference from the Fantastic Force — Devlor, Huntara, Psi-Lord, and Vibraxas — Zarathustra obtained the Omnivirus technology, though she had to leave behind her Battle Elite allies; Lord Moses approved of this decision. From the Omnivirus, Haven's technicians created the Omni-Toxin, ineffectual against Havenite immunology but fatal to outworlders. Zarathustra and the Battle Elite claimed an American military base, and Lord Moses had the Omni-Toxin loaded into stealth pods which would be launched around the world to exterminate the rest of humanity. Fantastic Force's Psi-Lord (a teenaged form of Franklin Richards) futilely tried to scan the Elite's minds, but found them protected by a mental mantra of Turkey's Mount Ararat (the supposed final resting place of Noah's ark). Eventually targeting the largest concentration of this mantra, Ego-Spawn (another aspect of Franklin Richards) led the Fantastic Force (minus Psi-Lord, but joined by the Human Torch and Black Panther) to the usurped military base. With the element of surprise, the Force downed Zarathustra, but Lord Moses dropped them with a single blast.

While Moses revealed his plans to his prisoners, Huntara freed the entire Force and they fought anew. Moses launched the stealth pods, but the Human Torch destroyed them all. Zarathustra stayed behind to cover Moses' safe exodus, and she and the Battle Elite were imprisoned while Moses returned to Haven to plot anew. Moses further removed Haven's coordinates from Zarathustra's mind to prevent others from using her to find him. Soon escaping from prison but unable to return to Haven, she dwelt among humanity for a time, learning not all beings were as corrupt as she had been taught. She also befriended Japanese superhuman Go-Devil.

HEIGHT: 6'4"	**EYES:** Brown
WEIGHT: 290 lbs.	**HAIR:** Brown with white streaks

ABILITIES/ACCESSORIES: A genius, Lord Moses has mastered alien trans-temporal technology. His genetically re-engineered form has peak human physical abilities plus marked resistance to age and disease. His staff-like weapon discharges devastating energy, though subsequent bursts are weaker, indicating a limit to the charge it can store. Via Haven's technology he can teleport himself and others and predict the future to a limited degree. Though a skilled combatant, he disdains violence.

Moses' top agent, Zarathustra, is a master warrior with peak human physical traits, armed with spears, swords, battleaxes, energy blasters, etc. Her tightly wound ponytail can be used to whip or strangle others.

POWER GRID	1	2	3	4	5	6	7
INTELLIGENCE							
STRENGTH							
SPEED*							
DURABILITY							
ENERGY PROJECTION							
FIGHTING SKILLS							

*LORD MOSES IS A TELEPORTER

ZARATHUSTRA

Art by Dante Bastianoni

STEPHEN LOSS

HISTORY: A homunculus created by the Asura (the assassins of Heaven), Loss gained life in 1900 AD as their Earthly agent in the war against Hell for dominion of Earth. In Spring 1923, Loss performed his first major inquisition, wiping out a Delaware town with his Breathing Gun and Ruinsaw. He created many occult items, including the narcotic sacrament K and the House of Blue Lights, a base for the Asura on Earth watched over by Loss' agent, Ingenuity Lee. Years ago Loss exhumed the corpse of Victoria Wingate Hellstrom, learning from tattoos on her womb that she was not an unwitting pawn of Satan, but rather had been designed to father his children by the Chapel of Dresden cult. Loss exterminated the cultists and closely watched Victoria's now adult children Satana and Daimon (Son of Satan/Hellstorm). A page from Loss' mystic tomes was left behind at Nevada's Jericho Monastery and used by serial killer Ervil Allred to summon the demonic Somnambulist. Approximately 200 years ago, the Somnambulist had raised Satan in Jericho before both were banished to Hell by the Ancient One. The Somnambulist granted Allred the power to kill anyone he wanted by consuming the demon's magical heart, but Hellstorm arrived and destroyed them both.

More recently, Loss led the disillusioned Devil-Hunter Gabriel to the House of Blue Lights where the Asura enslaved him. After Hellstorm slew his father to become the new Satan, Loss sensed his acquisition of the Black Halo (symbol of Hellish regency) and also heard Hellstorm's deceased wife Patsy's voice attempting to communicate with Daimon from Hell. Loss then confronted Hellstorm, sharing knowledge of the above and acknowledging him as an equal adversary. He again encountered Hellstorm in the town of Bend Sinister while observing from a distance the angel Tzadquiel's possession of Satanic cultists; Hellstorm ended this possession by trapping the angel within the human and trapping the human within a small hut, driving it to a violent suicide. Gabriel then stole Hellstorm's consort Jaine Cutter's Breathing Gun and attacked Hellstorm, shattering his trident and

REAL NAME: None
ALIASES: Devil Breaker
IDENTITY: No dual identity
OCCUPATION: Agent of Heaven
CITIZENSHIP: None
PLACE OF CREATION: Unrevealed
KNOWN RELATIVES: None
GROUP AFFILIATION: Agent of the Asura
EDUCATION: Unrevealed
FIRST APPEARANCE: Hellstorm #12 (1994)

injuring his leg, but was driven insane as Hellstrom's Fire Lake Manor's mystic wards forced the K out of his system. As Loss contemplated the culmination of his life's work, Hellstorm teleported into his house and slew him, then destroyed the House of Blue Lights.

Loss' Fur Journal was apparently obtained by Jennifer Silence, who used the information and spells therein to trap Satana in the Electric Pentagram and force her to recover her twin brother, Jason Silence, from Hell. Examining the Fur Journal, Satana observed the diagrams of her written by Stephen Loss (though she knew not who had written them) and then she returned the Electric Pentagram to the Fur Journal. Satana overpowered Jennifer and placed her in her Body Orchard, from which she continuously drained power.

LOSS CIRCA 1923, WITH RUINSAW & BREATHING GUN

HEIGHT: 5'8" **WEIGHT:** 170 lbs.
EYES: Black **HAIR:** Grey, balding (formerly black)

ABILITIES/ACCESSORIES: A magical creation not limited by human needs, Loss' energy signature mirrors that of angels. He has an extensive knowledge of the occult and a large arcane lore collection. He created the narcotic sacrament "K" from the bodies of angels; those who consume it can communicate with and be controlled by the Asura. His radio, when turned to 29 Megacycles, can pick up the voices of the dead. Among his artifacts are the Fur Journal/Bible, a dangerous tome allegedly bound in the skin of the first man; the Electric Pentagram, whose efficacy justifies its radioactive emissions; the Mantic Organ, which causes seizures in demons; the Pus Knives of St. Merham of Riga, which hunt by taste; the Ruinsaw of Giza, able to wipe out an entire town in under an hour; and one of the two Breathing Guns, whose sentient bullets can slay demons.

Loss was not concerned with making the world a better place, but rather with making sure everyone followed God's laws to the letter, and with claiming humanity's souls for Heaven's collection. Despite his inhuman form and single-minded nature, he was still subject to the same desires as any human man — perhaps more so. He controlled these desires via self-flagellation with barbed wire; his back was covered with a thick layer of old scars and fresh scabs.

POWER GRID	1	2	3	4	5	6	7
INTELLIGENCE				■			
STRENGTH	■						
SPEED	■						
DURABILITY		■					
ENERGY PROJECTION				■			
FIGHTING SKILLS	■						

Art by Martin Chaplin

LUCIFER

REAL NAME: Lucifer
ALIASES: Light-Bearer, the Devil, Prince of Darkness, Greexix, Jack O'Lantern (Steven Levins), Morningstar, many others
IDENTITY: No dual identity
OCCUPATION: Lord of a realm in Hell
CITIZENSHIP: Hell
PLACE OF BIRTH: Unrevealed
KNOWN RELATIVES: Other Hell-lords (brethren) and their offspring; quasi-paternal relationship to Daimon (Hellstorm), Satana Hellstrom and Mikal Dragonmekas (Hellfire)
GROUP AFFILIATION: Hell-lords; formerly angels of Heaven
EDUCATION: Unrevealed
FIRST APPEARANCE: (Mentioned) Marvel Previews #7 (1976); (full) Ghost Rider #1 (2006)

HISTORY: Lucifer has kept his true history mysterious throughout the years through deceit and deception. It is believed that he was once an angel who led other angels in banishing the N'Garai from Earth and led a group of followers in a rebellion against God during the war in Heaven. Following his defeat, Lucifer and his lieutenants Beelzeboul, Kazann, Malachi, Olivier, Pazuzu, Xaphan and others were all cast down to Hell as punishment. During this time, he became the demon known as the Prince of Lies, ruling a realm of Hell.

When stunt motorcyclist Johnny Blaze's foster father Crash Simpson was dying of cancer, Blaze sold his soul to the Devil in order to save him. Simpson was cured of cancer, but soon died while performing a dangerous stunt. Later, the Devil returned to claim Blaze's soul and bonded him with the demonic Zarathos to become the Ghost Rider.

After Blaze was cast into Hell through the manipulation of angels and demons alike, he was placed within Lucifer's realm. Lucifer toyed with Ghost Rider by making him believe that he could race beyond the gates of Hell to freedom, only to be stopped every time by a demonic horde mere inches away from liberation. Disguising himself as the demon Greexix, Lucifer tricked Blaze into making a deal to help him escape from Hell. As the two crossed over into the mortal plane of existence, Lucifer's physical body fragmented into 666 pieces. Each piece then fell to the Earth, taking possession of the souls of those who had recently passed away, reanimating them as avatars of Lucifer.

After super-criminal Jack O'Lantern (Steven Levins) was killed by the vigilante Punisher (Frank Castle) during the super hero civil war over the Superhuman Registration Act, Levins' remains were buried in his hometown of Sleepy Hollow, Illinois. Lucifer possessed Levins' body and began a murderous spree throughout the small town by decapitating his victims, much like the legendary Headless Horseman of Sleepy Hollow. When the Ghost Rider caught up with him, Lucifer raised a small army of zombies from the local cemetery to assist his rampage. Aided by the local sheriff, Ghost Rider defeated Lucifer by removing Levins' heart, enveloping it in Hellfire, and then placing it back in Jack O'Lantern's chest, causing Jack's head to crumble. Lucifer was finally defeated when Ghost Rider, who was aided by Dixie Buchanan, kept a brain-dead avatar alive until the next to last avatar was destroyed.

NOTE: Due to numerous demons using the identity of Satan and laying claim to the creation of Ghost Rider, as well as the fact that many of these demons sometimes merge into a gestalt entity, it is unclear exactly which demon is responsible for binding Zarathos to Johnny Blaze, or whether it was a collaboration.

HEIGHT: Variable
WEIGHT: Variable
EYES: White (variable)
HAIR: Bald (black goatee); variable

ABILITIES/ACCESSORIES: An immensely powerful supernatural entity, Lucifer's abilities include creating interdimensional portals, image projection, demonic possession, mystical force blasts, illusion-casting, size- and shape-shifting, matter manipulation, raising and animating the dead, and regenerating the corpses of those he inhabits. Lucifer can capture the souls of recently deceased humans, though this usually applies only to beings who bargain away their souls to him. Lucifer does not need to eat, sleep or drink and is immune to aging and conventional disease.

Lucifer's powers are currently dispersed among hundreds of forms. As each avatar is destroyed, the power within that host disperses into the remaining avatars, making each one become that much stronger, until only one body will remain with all of Lucifer's powers.

POWER GRID	1	2	3	4	5	6	7
INTELLIGENCE							
STRENGTH							
SPEED*							
DURABILITY							
ENERGY PROJECTION							
FIGHTING SKILLS							

*LUCIFER IS A TELEPORTER

Art by Javier Saltares

WILLIE LUMPKIN

IN HIS YOUTH

REAL NAME: William "Willie" Lumpkin
ALIASES: Lumpy
IDENTITY: No dual identity
OCCUPATION: United States Postal Courier
CITIZENSHIP: USA
PLACE OF BIRTH: Glenville, Nebraska
KNOWN RELATIVES: Bill "Gramps" Lumpkin (grandfather, presumed deceased), unidentified wife (presumed deceased), Wilhemina "Billie" Lumpkin (niece), Freddie Lumpkin (nephew), unidentified niece-in-law, Timothy "Timmy" Lumpkin (grandnephew)
GROUP AFFILIATION: United States Postal Service
EDUCATION: High school graduate
FIRST APPEARANCE: Willie Lumpkin newspaper strip (1960)

HISTORY: William Lumpkin grew up in the small town of Glenville, Nebraska, living with his "Gramps," Bill Lumpkin, who had been a mailman in New York during WWII before moving out west. Following in Gramps' footsteps, Willie became a postman. In a town with just over 400 residents, Willie became a well-loved local fixture, even being given his own awards ceremony where the townsfolk pronounced him "Glenville's friendliest postman." Glenville life was slow-paced and easygoing, though Willie's imagination regularly took him to much more exciting locales, as he developed a lifelong passion for reading; in reality Willie's biggest concerns were avoiding trouble at Halloween, when some kind of bad luck always seemed to befall him, and trying to get up the courage to ask out secretary Lila "Cuddles" Brown, the love of his life. Willie finally asked Lila out and they began dating, leaving Willie with only one remaining ambition: to become a big-city mailman, working a more exciting route. Heartbreak awaited Willie, however; one Christmas Eve, Lila, Willie and their mutual best friend, Charlie Boomer, met to swap presents at the old oak tree, a tradition Willie had started, only for Charlie and Lila to announce they were engaged. Lila seemed genuinely surprised at Willie's distress at the news, noting that he couldn't possibly have expected her to spend the rest of her life with someone whose ambitions were so limited, and that she needed someone with bigger goals in life.

Willie was devastated, but with nothing further to hinder him from pursuing his dream, he moved to New York, where he maintained a mail route that included the Baxter Building. At some point Willie married, then lost, an unidentified wife under unspecified circumstances. Willie worked his route for many largely uneventful years, his life becoming dreary and monotonous, and Willie was approaching retirement when the adventurers known as the Fantastic Four moved into the top five floors of the Baxter Building complex. The Fantastic Four's reputation for excitement had preceded them, and when Willie first met Mr. Fantastic (Reed Richards), leader of the Four, he half-jokingly petitioned for membership on the grounds that he had the ability to wiggle his ears. Reed declined the offer with equal good humor, telling him the team had a full complement of members at that time, but that he would keep Willie in mind, and the offer would become a running joke between Willie and each of the Four. As the team's popularity grew, they began receiving sacks of fan mail, and Willie soon found himself delivering two or three full bags a day to the Baxter Building.

It wasn't long before Reed took Willie up on his offer to assist the team in their battles against evil, albeit somewhat indirectly, when the Mad Thinker and his Awesome Android took over the Four's base. Before the team re-entered the base to confront the intruder, Reed asked Willie to ring a special bell in the building lobby at exactly 4 pm, activating a fail-safe circuit breaker which would render inert all of Reed's equipment on the upper floors. The Thinker, believing he had anticipated every variable, easily trapped the Four using usurped technology from Reed's lab when they confronted him, only to be caught and easily defeated when Willie carried out his appointed task. Initially unaware of exactly how he had helped them out, Willie was later proud to have been the hero of the hour when told what he had done. Though Willie continued to call each of the team members by their surnames, they came to view him as a good friend, even inviting him to visit them on Christmas Eve; taking them up on their offer, Willie unfortunately arrived moments before the Super Skrull (Kl'rt) attacked. To protect him, Reed bundled Willie into a lightproof, reinforced closet. The battle lasted only a few minutes, but Reed forgot about Willie, who spent the next six hours in the dark until the Invisible Girl chanced to find him.

Despite upsets like this, Willie enjoyed the excitement the Four brought to his mail route, excitedly telling his nephew Freddie and his family that he was friends with the Fantastic Four and regaling them with tales of his encounters, never realizing that Freddie thought his elderly uncle had become senile and was trying to humor him. When the temporal villain Tempus sought to spread paradox and cause chaos throughout the

Art by Richard Howell

timeline, he lured Willie into the Four's base, and onto Dr. Doom's time machine stored within. Activated, it sent Willie hurtling into the past, first causing him to briefly appear in 1777, in front of George Washington's horse as he crossed Owl Bridge. As Willie vanished again, Washington's horse threw him, and the general was knocked unconscious and, as a result, later captured by the British, who scheduled him for execution. Willie reappeared in Chicago in 1928, where the confused mailman ended up in the company of local gangsters. Convinced he was dreaming, Willie began to inadvertently warn them about the coming stock market crash, which would have allowed them to cash in on it. Luckily the Fantastic Four had been off planet when the reality waves caused by Willie's temporal escapades hit Earth, and thus escaped their effects; informed by the Watcher of what had happened, they followed Willie back, and while Mr. Fantastic and the Human Torch rescued Washington, the Thing and Medusa snatched Willie from the gangsters before too much damage was done. The Four and Willie were reunited in Tempus' chronal continuum, where Willie watched the team defeat the villain. Returned to their own restored timeline, the Watcher wiped Willie's memories of the time trip, to ensure he was never tempted to speak of it.

Willie became semi-retired, but refused to enter full retirement as he enjoyed delivering to the Baxter Building too much. He was saddened to see the team briefly break up during a period when Mr. Fantastic lost his powers, offering the Invisible Girl his ear-wiggling powers as a replacement, and telling her that he would miss them all. Soon after, Willie told Namor the Sub-Mariner that the Invisible Girl had relocated to Hollywood when the Atlantean came looking for her. However the Four did not stay apart for long, and soon things were back to abnormal on the Baxter Building route. As well as fan mail, Willie was on hand to deliver the Thing a script proposal from Hollywood for a new Thing sit-com, "Thing in the Family," and was the first in a long line of mailmen who delivered congratulatory letters to the newly pardoned Hulk when New York threw the green goliath a parade; he jokingly complained to the Thing that he had tried to get a new route with less fan mail to carry, but that all he had been offered was one which included an ex-President's condo, where too many of the packages were ticking. He watched as the team varied its lineup, and continued to attend most of their Christmas parties, though eventually he suggested they come around to spend Christmas with him and his nephew's family, since someone invariably attacked the Baxter Building on Christmas Day. However, during the night of Christmas Eve, a Spirit of Christmas came to visit Willie, having accidentally lost the address it was meant to go to, that of grouchy publisher J. Jonah Jameson. Unaware that he was trying to instill Christmas spirit into someone already full of niceness, the Spirit proceeded to show Willie visions of the past, reminding him of losing Lila to his best friend and of spending Christmas locked in closets; the present, showing him that Freddie thought he had Alzheimer's and that Freddie's wife was considering putting him into a retirement home; and a possible and all-too-near future, where the Fantastic Four were attending Willie's funeral after he was accidentally scared by the teleporting dog-like Inhuman Lockjaw and died of a heart attack. Learning he had made a mistake, the Spirit hastily departed. Willie awoke moments later to a knock on his door; opening it to find the Four and his nephew's family wishing him a Merry Christmas, Willie slammed the door in their faces.

Willie soon regained his naturally good-natured composure, and began a new, more sedate route, delivering to the suburban Forest Hills community. He soon met fellow pensioner May Parker; they hit it off immediately, and Willie asked her out to a band concert. They soon began dating regularly, with Willie getting on well with May's nephew Peter Parker (Spider-Man), and Peter's wife, Mary Jane. However life around May was rarely less eventful than life in the Baxter Building. When Willie spent Christmas with the Parkers, he witnessed a battle between Dr. Octopus and Spider-Man; having only come to look in wistfully upon his former fiancé May, Octopus broke off the fight, apologized and departed, rather than disrupt her holiday with her new man. Willie later took the Parkers to an exclusive gallery opening displaying the sculptures of the Human Torch's wife, Alicia Masters-Storm (actually the disguised Skrull Lyja); unfortunately the Headmen attacked, seeking to steal Spider-Man's body, until Spidey and the Human Torch repelled them. Afterwards Willie apologized to May for endangering her, but she admonished him for this, telling him the evening had been exhilarating. Another outing, this time to a Charity Ball for the Homeless, was disrupted by Firebrand (Russ Broxtel). Willie heroically helped evacuate the wounded from the collapsing building while Spider-Man, Cloak and Dagger stopped Firebrand. However, Willie's relationship with May eventually ended, and Willie was saddened to later hear that she had died, visiting her grave on Christmas Day to say goodbye; he also attended a memorial service for Mr. Fantastic soon after. Happily, in both cases, his friends' reported deaths proved erroneous. When the Fantastic Four briefly relocated to Pier Four, they found that their regular mail person was Willie's niece, Wilhemina "Billie" Lumpkin, who had followed her uncle into the family business.

Willie returned to the Baxter Building route, training the Building's newest mail robot, the formerly villainous Elektro, and attending the Thing's Bar Mitzvah. He has also occasionally helped Mr. Fantastic, dropping off packages at Marvel Comics which contain items for art reference in the licensed Fantastic Four comic, on one occasion finding his visit there coincided with a battle between Electro (Max Dillon, the electrical villain, not the aforementioned mail robot) and Masked Marvel (Adam Austin). Willie also became a regular on Eddie Schmeddy's latenight phone-in radio show, "What's My Medication," and was interviewed about the Fantastic Four for documentaries and news programs such as Lateline. When the dream lord Nightmare invaded the Land of Fiction, stealing humanity's desire to read, Reed Richards turned to Willie as the most well read-man he knew. Though feeling the weight of his years and fearing that his lost interest in reading might herald his approaching demise, Willie allowed the FF to link to his mind, using it as a gateway to the fictional realm, and later his dream self identified the villain's access point to that reality, via the novelist Stephen G. Diesner's book about Nightmare, information which allowed the FF to defeat their foe. Enraged, Nightmare briefly possessed Willie's sleeping niece Billie, and tried to kill Willie, but Mr. Fantastic awoke her just in time.

BILLIE LUMPKIN
Art by Alan Davis

HEIGHT: 5'8"
WEIGHT: 165 lbs.
EYES: Blue
HAIR: White, formerly blond

ABILITIES/ACCESSORIES: Willie is deceptively strong and has good stamina for a man his age, with muscles hardened by years of carrying heavy mailbags. He can simultaneously wiggle both ears at high speed, a natural talent honed by years of practice. He is exceptionally well read, a result of a lifetime indulging a voracious appetite for literature.

POWER GRID	1	2	3	4	5	6	7
INTELLIGENCE							
STRENGTH							
SPEED							
DURABILITY							
ENERGY PROJECTION							
FIGHTING SKILLS							

LUNATIC LEGION

HISTORY: The Lunatic Legion was founded by Zarek, former Imperial Minister of the interstellar Kree Empire. A Kree aristocrat believing in the "pure" Blue Kree's superiority over the part-alien Pink (aka White) Kree, Zarek grew alarmed at the increasingly liberal racial policies of the Kree emperor, the Supreme Intelligence. Zarek plotted treason with Supreme Public Accuser Ronan, who held views similar to his. They planned to frame popular Pink military hero Captain Mar-Vell as a traitor and kill him, then use the resulting scandal to overthrow the Supreme Intelligence, not realizing the Intelligence had already learned of their plans and quietly used them to its own advantage. The conspirators sent Mar-Vell to spy on Earth, which Mar-Vell soon considered his new home, as they intended. After secretly giving Mar-Vell superpowers, the conspirators tricked him into traveling to the planet Kree-Lar where they had planted a planet-destroying magnetic generator and framed Mar-Vell as its creator. The Supreme Intelligence took Zarek and later Ronan prisoner, and cleared Mar-Vell of all charges.

Exiled, Zarek joined with Admiral Sro-Himm, Fer-Porr, Kay-Sade, Tohn-Bil and Arjai-Ush to reclaim their perceived lost Blue heritage and retake the Empire from their supposed inferiors. They based themselves on the Blue Area of Earth's moon, their Empire's spiritual birthplace. Naming themselves the Lunatic Legion as wordplay on the moon's name, Luna, they realized Mar-Vell (known as Captain Marvel on Earth) would oppose them being so close to his adopted planet, and empowered several agents to stop them. One agent, the self-exploding Nitro (Robert Hunter), stole a canister of nerve gas Compound 13 for them, but he ran afoul of Mar-Vell's new sidekick Rick Jones, who summoned Mar-Vell from the Negative Zone (at the time, Jones and Mar-Vell shared a link through which they took turns existing in the normal positive-matter universe and the Negative Zone, usually triggering this swap by striking their Nega-Bands together). Mar-Vell used Negative Zone energies to overcharge one of Nitro's explosions, scattering the villain's molecules so he could not re-form swiftly. Knocked out by the Compound 13 gas, Mar-Vell went into stasis in the Negative Zone while Jones was taken to a Chicago hospital for observation over his possible exposure to the nerve gas. There, Legion agent Living Laser (a robotic duplicate of Arthur Parks) almost killed Jones until the visiting Wasp destroyed the robot. Treated with the gas's antidote, Mar-Vell learned of the Lunatic Legion and began searching for them, starting with the moon. Leaving Earth's atmosphere, Mar-Vell encountered and destroyed robotic Legion agent Nimrod the Hunter. Now convinced he was on the right track, Mar-Vell arrived at the Blue City, where he began to feel the effects of a hallucinogen Jones had unwittingly consumed earlier. Disoriented, Mar-Vell was easily overpowered by Uatu the Watcher, who envied Mar-Vell's universal protector role to the point of breaking his noninterference vow and willingly aiding the Legion.

With a delirious Mar-Vell their prisoner, the Lunatic Legion introduced themselves, explained their goals and tried to execute him in a protonic disintegrator machine. Before it could destroy him, Mar-Vell's time limit in the positive universe expired and he automatically switched bodies with an unconscious Jones, who was protected from the machine by his recent Negative Zone exposure. Back in the Negative Zone, Mar-Vell's

FORMER MEMBERS: (Zarek's team) Arjai-Ush, Fer-Porr, Kay-Sade, Sro-Himm, Tohn-Bil, Zarek; (Galen-Kor's team) Bron-Char, Cha-Mont, Ciry, Clar-Roc, Dor-Art, Dylon-Cir, Èpt-Rass, Galen-Kor, Klynn, Kona-Lor, Rojett, Sig-Rass, Talla-Ron, Tallun, Tokk, others
BASE OF OPERATIONS: (Zarek) Earth's moon; Hala; (Galen-Kor) mobile
FIRST APPEARANCE: (Zarek's team, voice) Captain Marvel #34 (1974); (Zarek's team, full) Captain Marvel #37 (1974); (Galen-Kor's team/"Last Kree Imperial Fleet") Avengers #365 (1993); (Kor's Lunatic Legion) Iron Man #7 (1998)

Cosmic Awareness banished the hallucinations, allowing him to see the Legion taking Jones to a cell. Angry, Mar-Vell had Jones' body reactivate the Bands to switch their bodies again. Mar-Vell mowed down the Legion before Zarek and Sro-Himm banged Mar-Vell's wrists together, bringing a recovered Jones into their custody. While Zarek prepared to pummel Jones, Mar-Vell used their newfound control over their mental link to switch places with Jones without using the Nega-Bands, and quickly subdued Sro-Himm and Zarek. Downed, Zarek urged the Watcher to finish Mar-Vell off, but Mar-Vell knocked Zarek out before the Watcher could respond. While Mar-Vell was off learning why Uatu wanted him dead, the Lunatic Legion allied with the Supreme Intelligence, who promised them Marvel's defeat. When Mar-Vell and Jones later arrived on Hala to warn the Intelligence of the Legion's treachery, the Legion attacked, only to be defeated, as the Intelligence intended. The group apparently disbanded soon after, with Zarek eventually finding refuge on the fringe world Godthab Omega; his partners' fates are unrevealed.

After a massive Nega-Bomb virtually wiped out the Kree Empire and allowed the Shi'ar Imperium to take them over, Admiral Galen-Kor and his longtime first officer Commander Talla-Ron gathered a group of Kree military officers, later adopting the Lunatic Legion name. Disbelieving the revelation that the Supreme Intelligence was the true architect behind the bomb's use, Galen-Kor blamed the Shi'ar and Earth's Avengers team, who had intervened in the Kree-Shi'ar conflict; Kor dedicated his group to overthrowing the Shi'ar and avenging the countless fallen Kree. Two survivors, Lieutenants Dylon-Cir and Kona-Lor, became trusted officers in Galen-Kor's core crew, while bald twins Èpt-Rass and Sig-Rass were reliable muscle. After arranging a failed assassination attempt against the Intelligence's seeming killer, Avengers member Black Knight (Dane Whitman), Galen-Kor and his informal Kree strike force based themselves in the moon's Blue City, where a space probe carrying a record-sphere with the full story of the alleged Avengers/Shi'ar alliance to destroy the Empire found them.

Kor secretly allied with an Elder of the Universe, the Collector, who gave Kor a small Nega-Bomb in return for a promise of some live Avengers to add to his collection. Kor dispatched a squad of Kree Sentries to kill the Avengers, who defeated them with help from Shi'ar warrior Deathcry, sent by Shi'ar Majestrix Lilandra to aid the Avengers against their Kree enemies. Deliberately uncloaking their omni-energy signature over the protests of his junior officers, Galen-Kor lured Avengers Black Knight,

LEFT TO RIGHT: ZAREK, ADMIRAL SRO-HIMM, KAY-SADE, FER-PORR, TOHN-BIL & ARJAI-USH

Art by Al Milgrom

Crystal, Hercules, the synthozoid Vision and Deathcry into a trap. The strike force took these captives to an ancient Kree South Pacific island base, where Dylon-Cir and Kona-Lor tortured them in retribution for their supposed crimes. After arming the Nega-Bomb, Kor faced a near-mutiny when he revealed they were taking the captives with them, but placated his troops by granting permission to kill Deathcry. Before they could do so, the other Avengers arrived and damaged enough of the machinery to prevent Kor from taking any prisoners with him. Kor teleported away with his strike force and left the Avengers to die with their world. When Earth survived instead, Galen-Kor apologized to the Collector for his failure and swore to find another way to fulfill their bargain, but the Collector discontinued their alliance.

Finding an ancient Shi'ar stasis ship containing the legendary Shi'ar Admiral T'kyll Alabar and his great enemy, the Mephitisoid leader nicknamed the Butcher, Galen-Kor had the craft crash-land on the Scottish isle Crail. The reawakened Mephitisoid quickly took over the town of Ailsa with his pheromone powers while Alabar evaded the enthralled townspeople. When the Avengers arrived to investigate, the Mephitisoid took control of Magdalene and Swordsman (Philip Jarvert) and captured the Vision while Deathcry escaped with Alabar's aid. Galen-Kor soon arrived with his team and convinced the Mephitisoid to team with them after proving immune to his pheromones. Dylon-Cir discovered Alabar and Deathcry watching from cover, but Alabar controlled Cir with a vial of Mephitisoid pheromone concentrate. Completely enthralled, Cir pretended to take the two Shi'ar prisoner, helping free the Vision. Galen-Kor then arrived with the Butcher and excitedly learned the truth of Alabar's long-ago victory: Alabar had killed an abbey of Mephitisoid females and secretly used their pheromones to rally his troops, only for the Imperium's rulers to bury that shame by sending him into exile with the vengeful Butcher. Though both Alabar and the Butcher were killed in the ensuing fight, Kor left Earth with the knowledge needed to foment major trouble in the Imperium.

Under unrevealed circumstances Galen-Kor, Dylon-Cir, Kona-Lor and Tallun were captured and imprisoned on Hala, where they made new allies. With outside help, Kor released the other prisoners and took over the Shi'ar Imperial Palace while crewmembers Cir, Lor, Tallun, Rojett and select allies seized four starships to travel to Earth to steal weapons, deciding that using Earth products to destroy the hated Shi'ar Imperium had a delicious irony to it. While Rojett's ship was captured before it could leave Hala's system, the others reached Earth and set about their assigned targets, but encounters with Spider-Man (Peter Parker), the Hulk (Bruce Banner), Wolverine (James Howlett) and Imperial Guardsmen Gladiator and Starbolt prevented their success. Per Lilandra's request, the X-Men traveled to Hala to help defeat Kor and the rest of his criminal allies.

Freed under unrevealed conditions, Galen-Kor and his crew learned the Supreme Intelligence had resurrected itself and was hiding on Earth. Kor brought the Intelligence to the moon, where the strike force renamed themselves the Lunatic Legion in memory of Zarek's team, rededicating themselves to vengeance against the Avengers and Earth. Planning to turn Earth's population into neo-Kree to remake their lost Empire, they stole a canister of the Inhumans' Terrigen Mist and experimented unsuccessfully on captured humans in a Florida base designed to evoke memories of World War II concentration camps. They contracted with energy research firm Powersource, Inc. to build an experimental generator to power an Omni-Wave projector capable of quickly mutating the entire planet. When Dylon-Cir and his team came to collect the generator, Iron Man (Tony Stark) and Warbird (Carol Danvers) flushed them out of hiding. They briefly fought the two Avengers before Cir summoned a Sentry to finish them off while his team left with their generator. As Iron Man destroyed the Sentry, Warbird pursued the Kree to their Florida base and summoned Captain America (Steve Rogers) before the Legion captured her.

Realizing Warbird's Kree/human hybrid nature made her the perfect test subject for their goals, the Legion began gassing their other subjects as superfluous. Cap arrived and freed the captives and Warbird, then faced off against strongman Bron-Char. Cap angrily subdued the giant Kree when he realized how many people had died in the Legion's experiments. Dylon-Cir and Kona-Lor ordered the Legion to their ship, recapturing Warbird before they left, while Cap rescued the surviving captives from the ship's launch flame. Back on the moon, Galen-Kor scanned Warbird's genes for the information needed to program the Omni-Wave projector. Meanwhile, Avengers Quicksilver, Scarlet Witch and Hawkeye (Clint Barton) arrived via the teleporting Inhuman dog Lockjaw, rescuing Warbird and destroying the generator, though not before the projector had been programmed for the Legion's plan to succeed, and an alternate energy source prepared. Kor informed the Supreme Intelligence of his progress, believing its displeasure was over his failures so far; however, the Intelligence had its own plans for humanity and secretly opposed Kor's goals, tipping off the Avengers to the projector's imminent firing. The Avengers fought the Legion's soldiers while the Legion's core group set up the plan's final stages and began converting the entire Legion's bodies into energy to fire the projector. By the time the Avengers reached the projector, only Galen-Kor was left. When Thor opened a mystic portal to eliminate the projector, Kor held off Thor until the portal began closing, but Avengers Firestar (Angelica Jones) and Justice (Vance Astrovich) re-expanded the portal and pushed the projector through it. Kor went to his doom, still unaware and unsuspecting of the Supreme Intelligence's treachery.

Three surviving Legion members (Cha-Mont, Clar-Roc, Dor-Art), taken prisoner after they unwillingly failed to transform into energy, were handed over to Ronan, who outfitted the distrustful Legionnaires as his deputies and sent them as cannon fodder to kill three of the Fantastic Four. While the FF quickly defeated the three Kree, Ronan used the temporarily enslaved Invisible Woman to break into the Watcher's home in an unsuccessful attempt to steal a Pysche-Magnitron core. These Legionnaires' current whereabouts are unrevealed.

Under undisclosed circumstances, First-tier Admiral Galen-Kor was reincorporated and became head of covert operations in the Kree Intelligence Unit, recently tasked with stopping the techno-organic Phalanx and their allies. It is currently unrevealed if any other Legion members have also been reincorporated.

LEFT TO RIGHT: LT. KONA-LOR, FIRST OFFICER TALLA-RON, ADMIRAL GALEN-KOR, LT. DYLON-CIR, EPT-RASS & SIG-RASS

Art by Sean Chen

LUNATIK (ARISEN TYRK FRAGMENTS)

HISTORY: Both a scientist and a sorcerer, Arisen Tyrk ruled as the God-King of Other Realm, a savage alien world previously led by the benevolent ruler Stargod. Ages ago, Stargod left Other Realm to die on Earth's moon and transferred his essence into the Godstone, which became an artifact of power, though prophecies stated that the Stargod would return to aid his people at a future time. The Godstone was eventually found by human astronaut John Jameson, and the Godstone's power transformed Jameson into Man-Wolf, an aspect of the Stargod that Jameson used to fight crime. Meanwhile, rising to power in Other Realm, Tyrk ruled from his floating city as an infamous tyrant. Craving the Godstone's power, Tyrk tracked the stone to Earth and developed a complicated plan of subterfuge to wrest the stone from Jameson.

Posing as teacher Harrisyn Turk, Tyrk hired the villainous Kraven the Hunter to battle Man-Wolf for the stone, but Kraven was quickly defeated. Rebels from Other Realm — Garth, Gorjoon and Lambert — who opposed Tyrk's rule traveled to Earth, seeking to recruit the Man-Wolf to their cause, and Man-Wolf soon agreed to aid them. Fearing that Man-Wolf might use the Godstone's powers to aid the rebellion, Tyrk used his teacher identity to get close to Man-Wolf's girlfriend, Kristine Saunders, soon subduing her by skewing her equilibrium. Tyrk then attempted to use Kristine to capture Jameson's father, newspaper publisher J. Jonah Jameson, but that plan failed due to the unexpected intervention of Jonah's employee, Simon Stroud. Tyrk returned to Other Realm with Kristine and set his undead warriors against the rebellion. After a brief battle, the rebels were all either captured or killed, and Man-Wolf was believed dead. Having survived, Man-Wolf soon freed the captive rebels. Tyrk kept Man-Wolf at bay by holding Kristine hostage, but Man-Wolf used the Godstone's full power to destroy Tyrk's sky fortress and to debilitate Tyrk. Tyrk blasted the teleportation device that was to bear Man-Wolf home, hoping to punish Man-Wolf by trapping him in Other Realm. Though Tyrk damaged the teleportation device, Man-Wolf still traveled home under his own power. Trying to escape the rebels, Tyrk jumped into the damaged teleportation device, which malfunctioned and split Tyrk's being into several fragments, scattering them throughout the dimensions. These fragments each represented a different part of Tyrk's complete psyche and took on their own unique physical properties and motivations, though many of them adopted the same identity. These aspects of Tyrk, in effect, became different individuals. At least seven aspects are known to have survived.

Three of the fragments were sent into the Tunnelworld dimension, where they were enslaved by the will of the Unnameable, a powerful magical entity; as the Unnameable's soldiers, they rode the dangerous winged Nilffim. The Nilffim riders spent the following months terrorizing Tunnelworld's natives, including the Sputs and the Winged Ones. The Unnameable also mentally enslaved many of the dimension's creatures. A fourth fragment, possessing the cunning and guile of Tyrk's persona,

REAL NAME: Arisen Tyrk
ALIASES: Nilffim Riders, Harrison Turk, Harrisyn Turk
IDENTITY: Existence unknown to Earth's general populace
OCCUPATION: Former God-King of Other Realm, university professor, vigilante
CITIZENSHIP: Other Realm
PLACE OF BIRTH: Other Realm
KNOWN RELATIVES: None
GROUP AFFILIATION: Former pawn of the Unnameable
EDUCATION: Unknown
FIRST APPEARANCE: (Harrisyn Turk) Creatures on the Loose #35 (1975); (Lunatik) Defenders #51 (1977); (Harrison Turk) Defenders #52 (1977); (Arisen Tyrk) Marvel Premiere #46 (1979); (Nilffim Riders) Defenders #71 (1979)

landed on Earth and, calling himself Harrison Turk, secured a job as a drama teacher at Empire State University. On the night of a full moon, a fifth aspect of Tyrk, representing his sense of regal righteousness, appeared. Seeking to punish evil, this acrobatic, deadly and strangely clown-faced vigilante Lunatik began brutally stalking criminals, jaywalkers and murderers alike, using a staff to bludgeon them. The next two nights of the full moon brought forth Tyrk's adventurous and loyal aspects, and both of these versions styled themselves as Lunatiks as well, using the same costume and weapon and seemingly the same motives. Though the Harrison Turk aspect did not agree with the behavior of these aspects, he felt a duty to protect them and allowed them to live at his residence. None of these aspects knew what had become of any of Tyrk's other aspects.

The multiple Lunatiks were widely believed to be a single being, and developed a name in the community around ESU that inspired fear and curiosity. They began randomly attacking anyone who didn't share their sense of justice. The Lunatiks only attacked during full moons, and would spout lines from advertisements, songs, and other popular culture while nimbly jumping about. Harrison Turk came into contact with Dollar Bill, an eccentric wannabe filmmaker; Ledge, Bill's friend; and Barbara Norriss, the secret identity of the Defenders' warrior woman Valkyrie. Turk even became roommates with Bill, who had no idea about Turk's Lunatik connection. Encountering a Lunatik by chance, Valkyrie was taunted by him. Later, one of the Lunatiks savagely beat some drug dealers and an angry Valkyrie attacked him, but Ledge came between them; Lunatik cracked Ledge's skull and broke one of his legs. Valkyrie sparred with Lunatik, who put others in harm's way and even cut off one of Valkyrie's pigtails. When Valkyrie could not deliver a killing blow, the Lunatik escaped. The Lunatiks continued striking, killing a teenage shoplifter, and Turk suggested they lure Lunatik into a trap by building a statue of Spider-Man, whose reputation as a scofflaw would inflame Lunatik. The trap worked, and Valkyrie, Hellcat and the real Spider-Man briefly battled a Lunatik, who escaped through a mysterious passage in the statue. It

Art by Michael Golden

was Turk who suggested that Dollar Bill, seeking to get in the Defenders' good graces, do a "Defenders for a Day" documentary, which turned into an utter disaster for the team.

During a party at Turk's, the still-injured Ledge accused Turk of being Lunatik. Valkyrie, Nighthawk and Hellcat each investigated on their own and each defeated one of the Lunatiks. When they reunited and saw three Lunatiks, the heroes were utterly baffled, especially when Turk claimed he actually was Lunatik. When confronted, Turk finally revealed his origins, though he offered a skewed account. Seeking other aspects of Tyrk, the three heroes took Turk and the three Lunatiks to Clea, their sorceress ally, who transported them all to Tunnelworld. The heroes and Tyrk encountered the Sputs, humanoid Tunnelworld residents whom Tyrk's Nilffim rider aspects had terrorized. The Nilffim riders attacked the Defenders; recognizing their lost aspects, Turk and the Lunatiks joined the Nilffim riders in battle. Tyrk's aspects escaped as a group, taking Hellcat captive. Valkyrie pursued Tyrk's aspects and, joined by the Hulk, apprehended them, rescuing Hellcat. The Defenders took Tyrk's aspects to the castle of Xhoohx, sorcerer supreme of Tunnelworld, battling several of the Unnameable's monsters along the way. Xhoohx and Dr. Strange, Earth's sorcerer supreme, magically recombined all of Tyrk's aspects into Arisen Tyrk once again. Feeling supremely powerful, Tyrk tossed the Defenders and Xhoohx aside and attempted to attack the Unnameable directly. While Tyrk was distracted by the Unnameable's attacking monsters, Valkyrie hurled him through the magical Rings of Raggadorr (formed collectively via Strange, Clea and Xhoohx), which left Tyrk unconscious and free of the Unnameable's influence. Tyrk was left in Xhoohx's care, though Xhoohx was subsequently slain by agents of the Unnameable. Tyrk's fate is unrevealed. Another aspect took up residence in an Earth nursing home, where he was killed by another Lunatik, an intergalactic hitman and murderer.

HEIGHT: 5'8" **EYES:** Blue
WEIGHT: 165 lbs. **HAIR:** White, formerly blond

ABILITIES/ACCESSORIES: Arisen Tyrk possesses great superhuman strength (class 10), endurance, and durability. He can cast various spells and fire powerful energy blasts. The Lunatik fragments of Tyrk's personality were very agile and wielded strong staffs against their foes. As Harrisyn Turk, Tyrk seemingly possessed no powers. As Harrison Turk, Tyrk had a slight hypnotic effect on those around him. Finally, the Nilffim Rider fragments rode the large winged Nilffim birds, wore body armor, and wielded swords in combat. In one of his human guises, Tyrk used a mechanical device to affect the equilibrium of others.

NILFFIM RIDERS

ARISEN TYRK

HARRISON TURK

ARISEN TYRK WITH KRISTINE SAUNDERS

Art by Herb Trimpe & George Pérez

LUNATIK (MERCENARY)

HISTORY: Life began to evolve on planet Wy'nkar-7 600,000,000 years ago. The lifeform later known as Lunatik, started as a multicellular organism. Evolving into a fish, an amphibian and eventually into a humanoid, Lunatik devoured all other developing lifeforms. Though the planet tried to terminate him, he eventually remained its sole survivor, having evolved into monstrous proportions. When an investigating ship from the Interstel Church of Perpetual Annoyance (ICPA) landed on Wy'nkar-7, Lunatik killed its crew and took the ship into space. He soon met the tiny, winged Skreet and the two became traveling partners. They became infamous as savage, high-priced mercenaries and bounty hunters, much in demand despite frequently slayings their employers.

The Universal Cosa Nostrum employed Lunatik and Skreet to find their scientist Lupal and uncover the secret formula of the drug Addictum, which turned its users' blood to napalm if they quit, violently killing them. Skreet and Lunatik tracked Lupal to a barren planet and found the scientist had killed himself rather than be faced with the Silver Surfer, who sought to bring peace to the planet's simple-minded dwellers, the Children. Lunatik briefly fought the Surfer before killing all the Children, discovering Lupal had tattooed Addictum's formula onto their backs. He skinned the tattoos off each of them and prepared to decipher the code when the Surfer, infuriated over the senseless loss of life, incinerated the pile. Lunatik attacked the Surfer and the two fought inconclusively. In the end, the Surfer left Lunatik bound to the planet, so that Lunatik would die if he left.

Somehow escaping, Lunatik violently haggled at Murray's Galactic Vehicle Mart and Sushi Palace over the price of a Pangalactic Star Sled. Meanwhile, in a poker game, Skreet won the monstrous Drogs, creatures who powered the rig. While watching Earth television broadcasts at his condo on planet Bl'Ix, Lunatik learned of a villain using the name Lunatik (an Arisen Tyrk aspect). Infuriated, Lunatik took the sled to an Earth nursing home and slew the villain. Lingering on Earth, he harassed the Avengers until they demanded he leave, but Lunatik grabbed the Wasp instead of Skreet by accident. Thinking the heroes had meant to trick him, he attacked the Avengers, and held his own against them until he was taken down by a shot from Black Widow.

The ICPA recruited Lunatik, through contract arrangements made by Skreet, and he traveled to the planet Panto-9, undergoing a lengthy approval process. He approached the High Church Council and was ordered to kill himself to officially join the ICPA, but Lunatik fled instead, accidentally knocking out the lupine Ictus the She-Wolf on his way. This act caused the entire ICPA to worship Lunatik as their new pope.

Lunatik handed over Skreet to the authorities when she demanded her half of their earnings. Despite his status as ICPA Pope Lunatik was eventually arrested as well. A weakened Lunatik was on his way to Kyln prison when the transporter crash-landed on Earth in Alaska. Lunatik aided other survivors Paibok and the Blood Brothers against Drax, who they killed in the nearby town Coot's Bluff. Lunatik and his allies enslaved local citizens to rebuild the transporter, killing many of them over the slow progress before realizing the ship couldn't be salvaged. Lunatik was then decapitated by a reborn Drax, who crushed his head to prevent him from recovering.

REAL NAME: Lunatik
ALIASES: "Lu," "Luu," "Luey," Pope Lunatik
IDENTITY: No dual identity
OCCUPATION: Mercenary, bounty hunter; former Pope of Interstel Church of Perpetual Annoyance
CITIZENSHIP: Panto-9
PLACE OF BIRTH: Wy'nkar-7
KNOWN RELATIVES: None
GROUP AFFILIATION: Former partner of Skreet
EDUCATION: Self-educated
FIRST APPEARANCE: Marvel Comics Presents #172 (1995)

HEIGHT: 6'2"
WEIGHT: 220 lbs. (formerly 300 lbs.)
EYES: White (formerly green)
HAIR: White (formerly orange)

ABILITIES/ACCESSORIES: Since birth, Lunatik gradually evolved into greater levels of maturity, strength and intelligence. He was immensely super-strong (lifting over 100 tons) and durable, as well as extremely long-lived, and he had sharp teeth in a large extending jaw. He could survive almost indefinitely without air. He rarely used guns, mostly relying on his brute strength. After his power reduction, he could lift closer to 75 tons, was more vulnerable to bodily harm and possessed a healing factor enabling him to survive decapitation.

For some time Lunatik used a Pangalactic Star Sled, powered by Drogs' flatus. It could fly at light speed or faster if the Drogs were properly nourished. It was armed with two energy cannons.

POWER GRID	1	2	3	4	5	6	7
INTELLIGENCE							
STRENGTH							
SPEED							
DURABILITY							
ENERGY PROJECTION							
FIGHTING SKILLS							

YELLOW BARS INDICATE ORIGINAL RATINGS

WEAKENED FORM

Art by Duncan Rouleau with Mitch Breitweiser (inset)

LUPHOMOIDS

KNOWN MEMBERS: Zorr, Kraa, Xira (Spirit), Nebula (alleged)
BASE OF OPERATIONS: Mobile throughout space; formerly the planet Luphom, Andromeda Galaxy
FIRST APPEARANCE: Nova #1 (1976)

TRAITS: Though it is uncertain whether they represent typical Luphomoids, both Zorr and Kraa were extremely strong, lifting over 100 tons, and nearly indestructible, surviving starship crashes from high orbit. Xira can lift 4 tons, and is super-swift, agile, and durable; she may have a different father than Kraa and Zorr. The Luphomoids are a domineering and callous race, unmindful of destroying entire civilizations. They also cybernetically enslave lesser beings to serve them as "slave-borgs." They possess highly advanced technology such as single starships capable of decimating or draining entire planets and a variety of powerful hand-held energy weapons. It is unlikely that any Luphomoids left alive can repair or replicate any such technology, however.

HEIGHT: 12'
WEIGHT: 2 tons
EYES: White (Zorr) or Red (Kraa)
SKIN: Light Blue

HISTORY: The Luphomoid homeworld, Luphom, was devoured by Galactus soon after the Luphomoids began a path of galactic conquest. Zorr and Kraa were amongst the known Luphomoids conquering off-world at the time.

Zorr surfaced in the Tranta Star System and found the planet Xandar while seeking a means to restore his world. He defeated Xandar's Nova Corps with ease, and his Luphomoid starship began to drain Xandar's geothermal energy. He was driven off by Rhomann Dey, Centurion Nova Prime, but not without great cost. Xandar tore itself apart, and Rhomann Dey was badly injured. Paralyzed and dying, Dey pursued Zorr across the universe, eventually arriving on Earth, and transferred his power and responsibility to human Richard Rider, who became Nova. The inexperienced Nova was unable to harm Zorr, but he distracted him sufficiently for Rhomann Dey to lock onto Zorr and teleport him aboard his Xandarian starship. Once there, Dey channeled the ship's PRIME (Planetary Recorder for Information Maintenance and Education) computer's full power through his body and fired it at Zorr, disintegrating himself and Zorr in the process. Xandar's four largest fragments survived as a network of interlinked settlements through the aid of Uatu the Watcher.

Years later, Kraa, figurative or literal brother of Zorr, believed he was the last of his race and swore to grind the last vestiges of both Xandar and Earth beneath his heel. Kraa devastated at least one Xandar-protected world, killing many members of the Nova Star-Corps, the newly reformed Nova Corps whose role had expanded to include protecting multiple alien worlds beyond Xandar. Adora, queen of Xandar, sent corpsmen to kidnap Nova and enlist his aid against Kraa. Nova arrived where the corpsmen had last encountered Kraa and boarded the damaged Xandarian ship left there. Kraa renewed his assault on the ship, but Nova re-energized its main cannon to surprise Kraa, destroying his ship and sending him crashing to the uninhabited volcanic planet below. A fierce battle raged across the surface, but Nova gained the upper hand after a fellow corpsman, Muraitak of the Skrull race, distracted Kraa by taking the form of his deceased brother, Zorr. Defeated, Kraa was last seen waiting to be taken to Xandar for imprisonment. Inspired by Thanos, Kraa and Xorr's sister Xira (aka Spirit) has long sought death at worthy hands, formerly fighting alongside Death Metal before joining Gamora's Graces alongside her alleged niece Nebula.

SPIRIT

NOTE: The space pirate Nebula is allegedly the daughter of Zorr and the (maternal or paternal) granddaughter of Thanos. Nebula possesses some Luphomoid characteristics (blue skin, durability) but lacks Zorr & Kraa's vast strength, perhaps due to her hybrid nature. Nebula has also discussed a separate, abusive father, perhaps indicating that when neither Thanos nor Zorr cared for the young Nebula, she was sold into slavery and bought by this abusive father.

KRAA · ZORR · NEBULA

Art by Chris Marrinan (Kraa), Joe Bennett (Zorr & Nebula) & John Royle (Spirit)

LYJA THE LAZERFIST

HISTORY: A spy in the service of the interstellar Skrull Empire, Lyja had been romantically involved with Paibok, her superior officer. The Skrulls were engaged in long-term schemes against Earth's Fantastic Four, and General Kalamari decided to have an agent replace and impersonate Alicia Masters, a blind sculptress who was involved with the Fantastic Four's Thing. Paibok was placed in charge of the operation and selected Lyja for the assignment. Lyja underwent extensive training to duplicate Alicia's appearance, mannerisms and abilities. Finally, the Skrulls struck while the Human Torch, Mr. Fantastic and the Thing were away from Earth, having been brought to Battleworld by the Beyonder. Alicia Masters was kidnapped and placed in Paibok's custody on Warworld while Lyja took Alicia's place; however, the Thing did not return immediately from Battleworld, and She-Hulk took his place with the Fantastic Four. Lyja realized that without the Thing, she lacked a strong connection to the Four as "Alicia."

To solidify her standing with the Fantastic Four, Lyja began seeing the Human Torch (Johnny Storm), and fell in love with him in spite of her mission. The Torch was particularly vulnerable at the time, as his sister Susan's second child had been stillborn. When the Thing finally returned from Battleworld, "Alicia" rejected him, now truly in love with the Torch. The Thing was heartbroken to have lost "Alicia," and it caused a division within the FF, one that persisted until Thing finally accepted their relationship. "Alicia" and Johnny were eventually married, and when the Torch's ex-lover Crystal joined the FF and attempted to drive them apart, Johnny remained faithful to "Alicia." Lyja also maintained her masquerade as a sculptress, but began to assume an impressionist style, unable to duplicate Alicia's realist style. Alicia's stepfather Philip Masters — the Puppet Master — realized that something was wrong with "Alicia," and took control of the New Warriors' Marvel Boy (Vance Astrovik) to kidnap her. When this failed, he revealed his findings to the Thing, who confronted "Alicia" and demanded that she reveal her true self. Lyja complied, and divulged the history of her impersonation to the FF, claiming that she was pregnant in an effort to keep the Torch from abandoning her. Johnny was devastated to find that the woman he loved was a lie, and that the real Alicia had never loved him. Lyja helped the Fantastic Four journey to Warworld to rescue Alicia, and they fought Paibok, now the super-powerful "Power-Skrull." During the fight, Lyja was struck by a blast from Paibok meant for the Human Torch. She informed the Torch that her pregnancy was a lie, then passed out, seemingly dead.

Paibok retrieved Lyja and restored her to health with the aid of his ally Devos the Devastator. They planted an organic power receiver within her body that granted her additional superhuman powers, along with the egg of a Sha'barri, an extraterrestrial creature Paibok hoped would destroy the Fantastic Four when it hatched. As "Lyja the Lazerfist," she agreed to assist Paibok and Devos in their attempts to destroy the Fantastic Four. They confronted the Human Torch at Empire State University, and had him so badly overpowered that he activated his nova flame to defend himself; the flame burned down part of the university and the Torch became a fugitive from justice, pursued by the police, Paibok, Devos and Lyja at every turn, unwilling to turn himself over to the authorities for fear of Lyja and Paibok lying in wait thanks to their shape-shifting; however, Lyja ultimately found that she still cared for the Torch, and came to his aid when the Secret Defenders attempted to capture him. When Uatu the Watcher brought the FF to his home on the moon to defend him from Dr. Doom, Lyja was transported with the FF, and aided them in battle. Although she and the Torch seemed unable to reconcile, she still admired the rest of the FF, and lived with them in Four Freedoms Plaza as their ally. She subsequently helped the FF against Paibok and Devos when they joined with Huntara and Klaw as the Fearsome Foursome and assaulted the Torch in court. The Torch was ultimately cleared of these charges.

After Mr. Fantastic and Dr. Doom seemingly perished together in Latveria, the FF were fractured and found it difficult to continue operating, though Susan was certain that Reed was still alive. Lyja's power was a great aid to the FF at this time. When they returned to New York, they were attacked and defeated by the Fearsome Foursome. Paibok and Devos abducted the FF and Lyja and brought them to the Skrull homeworld for execution. During their imprisonment, Lyja again told the Torch that she was pregnant, attempting to explain the presence of the Sha'barri egg within her, and still hoping to reconcile with him. The FF helped her obtain a Lacaroo (Skrull birthing device which renders Skrulls into a non-solid form) so that the egg could be safely removed, and they returned to Earth when Devos turned on the Skrulls, giving them an opportunity to hijack a Skrull spacecraft (the Stealth-Hawk).

REAL NAME: Lyja
ALIASES: Laura Green, Alicia Masters Storm
IDENTITY: Secret
OCCUPATION: Warrior, bookstore clerk; former college student, spy, sculptor
CITIZENSHIP: Skrull Empire
PLACE OF BIRTH: Unrevealed planet in the Skrull Empire, Andromeda Galaxy
KNOWN RELATIVES: Jonathan Spencer Storm (Human Torch, ex-husband)
GROUP AFFILIATION: None
EDUCATION: Unrevealed
FIRST APPEARANCE: (As Alicia Masters) Fantastic Four #265 (1984); (as Lyja) Fantastic Four #357 (1991)

Art by Barry Kitson

Art by Paul Ryan

AS LAURA GREEN
Art by Paul Ryan

Lyja was treated as a member of the FF's tight-knit family, and participated in many of the FF's personal activities, including a bachelorette party for Marlo Chandler, the wedding of Marlo to Rick Jones, and the reading of Reed Richards' will. She also befriended Ant-Man (Scott Lang), who was hired to help the team operate Reed's many devices. When the extraterrestrial mercenaries the Starblasters attempted to knock the Earth out of its orbit with a planetary thruster, Lyja's knowledge of the weapon proved vital in dismantling it, although Lyja had to abandon the fight due to complications with the Sha'barri egg. Lyja finally had the egg removed (still claiming it to be her and Johnny's offspring), but in the process the power receiver was also removed, causing her to lose her lazerfist powers. The power receiver was found by electrical engineer Raphael Suarez, who wound up with Lyja's lost powers. When the Collector attempted to steal the Sha'barri egg, he was driven off by the Torch, Lyja and Suarez. Lyja then finally admitted to the Torch that the egg was not his child and destroyed the Sha'barri when it hatched, but the Torch now refused to forgive her because of her deceptions.

Unable to give up Johnny, Lyja adopted a new human disguise as "Laura Green" and enrolled in the archeology program at ESU so that she could still be close to him, only to find that Johnny was pursuing his fellow student Bridget O'Neil. During a trip to the Keewazi reservation, "Laura" helped Johnny and the She-Hulk against the creature Raptor the Renegade, but did not reveal herself as Lyja. Lyja eventually learned that O'Neil was not interested in the Torch because she sensed that he wasn't over Lyja yet, giving Lyja hope that she might yet win Johnny back. "Laura" eventually became involved with Johnny as Lyja hoped she might find a new way to appeal to him. Even as she pursued the Torch, she was unaware that the Thing was becoming attracted to her, but he kept his feelings to himself.

Lyja continued to aid the FF and their friends Fantastic Force against threats such as Aron the Rogue Watcher, the battle for Atlantis that was waged between Morgan Le Fay, the Inhumans and the Atlanteans, and a Brazilian temple containing technology which temporarily transformed her and others into Thing-like creatures. When time traveler Artur Zarrko invaded Four Freedoms Plaza and unleashed various warriors from other eras to battle the FF, the team finally had a clue to the fate of Mr. Fantastic and Dr. Doom, prisoners of Zarrko's master Hyperstorm. Lyja accompanied the FF as they finally located and freed Mr. Fantastic and Dr. Doom, and assisted in battle against Hyperstorm. Mr. Fantastic was initially out of sorts among his family, and seemed in danger of losing his wife to the Sub-Mariner. Lyja, sympathetic to Reed and Susan because of her own feelings for Johnny, helped bring Reed and Susan back together by convincing the Sub-Mariner to feign a defeat at Reed's hands, helping Reed regain his confidence. Lyja and the Torch headed towards another reconciliation, but it was interrupted by the arrival of the all-powerful Onslaught. When the Human Torch and the rest of the FF were all seemingly slain in battle with Onslaught, Lyja was distraught. Assuming her Laura Green guise again, she said farewell to the FF's other allies and went to live among humanity.

Lyja settled in New York City, where as Laura Greene she eventually got a job at a bookstore, reading up on everything available on human culture in order to live as a human. Under the apparent influence of world shaper Glorian she briefly left Earth for the Kree planet Godthab Omega, and was present when it was assaulted by Negative Zone ruler Annihilus's Annihilation Wave. Returning to Earth and her bookstore job, Lyja was convinced by Skrull agents of Queen Veranke to join another Skrull invasion of Earth. Veranke wanted Lyja to plant an S-bomb in the Fantastic Four's headquarters to kill the Thing and Human Torch, but Lyja convinced her that simply sending the Baxter Building's top floors to the Negative Zone would work just as well. Disguised as the Invisible Woman, Lyja walked into FF headquarters and successfully carried out the plan before the two FF members realized what had happened. Lyja and the Torch fought despite their realization that they were both still attracted to each other. When an anti-matter singularity's tentacle ensnared Lyja, the Torch used his flames in conjunction with Lyja's powers to free her from it, leaving her unconscious. Recovering, Lyja found she had been left behind when the FF went to the Negative Zone prison to free the Tinkerer in order to repair the earlier damage Lyja did to the Negative Zone portal's controls. Catching up with them, Lyja and the Torch took the opportunity for a heart-to-heart talk. After the Tinkerer repaired the controls, Lyja opted to remain in the Negative Zone, figuring that would be the safer place to do some soul-searching. However, when the composite cosmic killer Unum began killing any female warrior she could find, Lyja was unwillingly taken by the Elder of the Universe Collector for safekeeping until Unum was defeated.

Art by Paul Ryan

HEIGHT: 5'6" (variable) **EYES:** Green (variable)
WEIGHT: 130 lbs. **HAIR:** Dark green (variable)

ABILITIES/ACCESSORIES: Lyja possesses the natural abilities of a member of the extraterrestrial Deviant Skrull race, including shapeshifting. She normally assumes the forms of animals (native to Earth and extraterrestrial) and various human disguises. She can alter her body's mass when changing form, and obtains the physical characteristics of the forms she assumes, such as wings capable of flight, multiple appendages, enhanced durability, and the ability to breathe underwater. While assuming the form of Alicia Masters, she wore special contact lenses that rendered her blind, but she was specially trained to function without sight. She can generate bio-blasts from her hands that can be used as bolts of concussive force or to propel her in simulated flight. She is resistant to the high levels of heat and fire produced by the Human Torch, though it is unrevealed if she can easily withstand a nova blast from him.

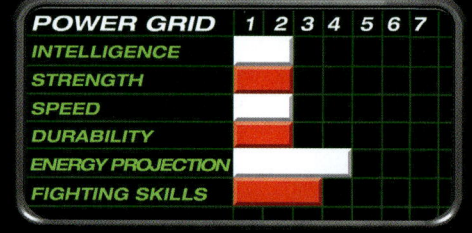

LYNX

HISTORY: An experiment of the clandestine organization They (aka the Third Person or the unseen face that controlled mankind), the woman known only as the Lynx was born without an immune system and raised in a germ-free environment without human contact. As a result, They's chief scientist, German geneticist Dr. Reigert Ilves, believed the girl to be a perfect subject for his experiments with the drug Panacea, capable of curing all known diseases, and he injected her with the only existing sample. Guilt-stricken over this, Ilves sought to destroy his work by setting his laboratory on fire. The mutant hero Wolverine arrived on the scene, investigating rumors of Ilves' experiment, but was too late to save lives. The Lynx escaped, but Wolverine soon tracked her down and, after a brief scuffle, they were both incapacitated by Courier (Hans Mittlesteadt), a mutant operative of the German government, who were seeking to reclaim the Panacea. While a recovered Wolverine battled Courier, the French mercenary le Peregrine abducted the Lynx for his employer, corrupt billionaire Imus Champion, who sought the Panacea to cure a rare disease that was killing him.

Le Peregrine delivered the Lynx to Champion's Southern California base, whereupon Champion sent the monstrous Fleshtones to kill le Peregrine in order to keep the Lynx's location a secret. Le Peregrine defeated them with the aid of Wolverine & Courier (who had tracked him to Champion's base) and the Black Widow (Natasha Romanoff), an official representative of SHIELD tasked with bringing in the Lynx. The quartet eventually agreed to work together to free the Lynx, after which the Black Widow convinced the others to take the Lynx into SHIELD's protective custody. Wolverine and Courier suspected that SHIELD might experiment on the Lynx, though, so they liberated her. Wolverine took her to a SHIELD safehouse, where he soon realized that SHIELD had injected the Lynx with a persona-inducing serum once used by the Black Widow, hoping that a personality would help her articulate her memories. Ultimately, he allowed the Lynx to revert to her feral state, and she accompanied Wolverine and the Black Widow to the Antarctic base of They, where they discovered the Malaigent, the world's deadliest disease, which also acted as an "antidote" for the total immunity of the Panacea. After Champion and his forces attacked They's base, the Lynx and her newfound allies, rejoined by Courier and le Peregrine, defeated the forces of They and Champion. The Lynx then consumed the Malaigent, which seemingly neutralized the Panacea in her system.

Wolverine released the Lynx in a remote part of the Canadian wilderness and departed, hoping that she would live out her life in peaceful solitude, though the smitten Lynx mistakenly believed Wolverine would return to live with her as her mate.

REAL NAME: Unrevealed, possibly none
ALIASES: Nancy Rushman
IDENTITY: Secret
OCCUPATION: Forager, former experiment
CITIZENSHIP: Unrevealed
PLACE OF BIRTH: Unrevealed location in Antarctica
KNOWN RELATIVES: None
GROUP AFFILIATION: None
EDUCATION: No formal education
FIRST APPEARANCE: Marvel Comics Presents #123 (1993)

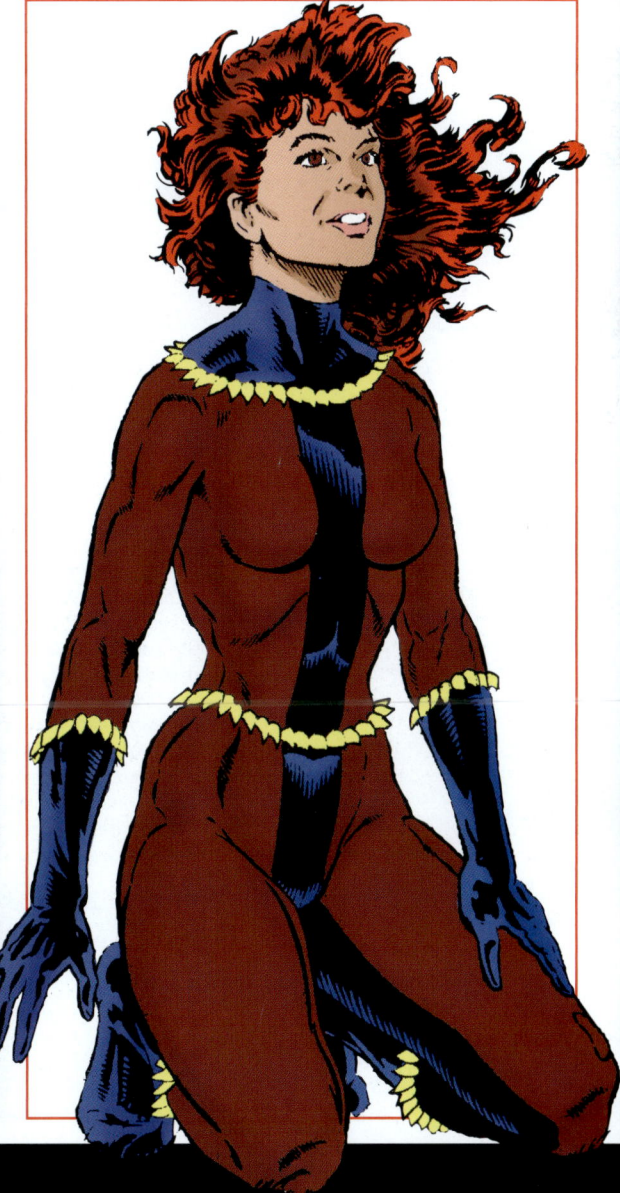

Art by Dennis Jensen

HEIGHT: 5'6" **WEIGHT:** 139 lbs.
EYES: Brown **HAIR:** Brown

ABILITIES/ACCESSORIES: The Lynx is a savage fighter who relies almost entirely on instinct. Her body was injected with the Panacea drug, capable of curing every disease known to mankind, though this was supposedly neutralized after she consumed the Malaigent.

POWER GRID	1	2	3	4	5	6	7
INTELLIGENCE	■						
STRENGTH		■					
SPEED			■				
DURABILITY		■					
ENERGY PROJECTION	■						
FIGHTING SKILLS		■					

Art by Dennis Jensen

LADYFAIR

REAL NAME: Unrevealed
ALIASES: Ladykiller, Huan, "Jade Ring"
IDENTITY: Secret
OCCUPATION: Adventurer; former assassin, prostitute, farmer
CITIZENSHIP: China
PLACE OF BIRTH: Unrevealed location in China
KNOWN RELATIVES: Unidentified parents (deceased)
GROUP AFFILIATION: Former agent of the Nobility; former servant of the Mandarin
EDUCATION: Unrevealed
FIRST APPEARANCE: (Ladykiller) Wonder Man: My Fair Super Hero #1 (2007); (Ladyfair) Wonder Man: My Fair Super Hero #5 (2007)

HISTORY: A poor Chinese farm girl, Ladyfair was sold into prostitution by her parents to repay a debt when she was 12. She killed her very first client, a rival of the Chinese crimelord the Mandarin. As repayment, the Mandarin agreed to train her as an assassin and named her Huan, meaning "Jade Ring." After years of training, she was given her first assignment: to kill her parents; however, she couldn't bring herself to do it, so the Mandarin killed them himself. After the Mandarin's criminal empire crumbled, Huan joined the Nobility crime syndicate as Ladykiller. The Nobility's leader, Neal Saroyan, sought to destroy the Avengers and secretly hired Huan to assassinate movie producer Ken Flevin, choosing a time and place where she would battle Saroyan's acting client, Wonder Man. Saroyan psychically manipulated Wonder Man into trying to rehabilitate Huan for a television special, "My Fair Super Hero." Aided by Ms. Marvel (Carol Danvers) and the Beast (Hank McCoy), Wonder Man endured Huan's initial resistance and seemingly succeeded after she declared her love for him. Dubbing her "Ladyfair," Wonder Man invited Huan to an Avengers Mansion celebration of the anniversary of Captain America's joining the Avengers; but Saroyan mentally forced Huan to poison the punch. Briefly overcoming Saroyan's influence, Huan prevented Captain America from drinking the punch and tipped over the punch bowl, saving the other Avengers, before stabbing herself in the heart to prevent Saroyan from controlling her again.

HEIGHT: 5'8" **WEIGHT:** 133 lbs. **EYES:** Brown **HAIR:** Black

ABILITIES/ACCESSORIES: Ladyfair possessed above average strength gained from years of manual farm labor and above average speed from her assassin training. A skilled martial artist, she was also fluent in the use of kobudo and wushu weaponry. She wielded a jiujiebian and a pair of kama charged with anionic energy.

INTELLIGENCE: 3 **STRENGTH:** 4 **SPEED:** 1 **DURABILITY:** 3 **ENERGY PROJECTION:** 1 **FIGHTING SKILLS:** 4

Art by Andrew Currie

LION GOD

REAL NAME: Sekhmet
ALIASES: Mr. Umbala, "Liege to the King of Beasts," "Lord of the Veldt," Lion Lord, Avenger of Wrongs, Scarlet Lady, Eye of Ra, She Who is Powerful; possibly Hathor
IDENTITY: Secret
OCCUPATION: Egyptian warrior deity
CITIZENSHIP: Celestial Heliopolis
PLACE OF BIRTH: Philae, Upper Egypt
KNOWN RELATIVES: Neith (Gaea, grandmother), Nun (Demiurge, grandfather), Ammon Ra (Atum, father), Thoth (uncle), Bast (Panther God, brother), others
GROUP AFFILIATION: Ennead (Gods of Egypt)
EDUCATION: Unrevealed
FIRST APPEARANCE: Avengers #112 (1973)

HISTORY: Sekhmet and Bast were feline war gods respectively ruling Upper and Lower Egypt. The siblings contained male and female forms and inherited fiery power from their father Ra, but Bast's power was life-giving while Sekhmet's was destructive. Sekhmet once released such fury against mortal foes that Ra feared he would destroy the human race. When the Pharaohs rose to power, Bast fled, allowing Sekhmet to absorb Lower Egypt. Moving his sect to Memphis, Sekhmet protected the Pharaohs in battle. With the Pharaohs' time fading, Bast became patron to the powerful Wakandan nation as the Panther God while Sekhmet, as the Lion God, had only a fringe cult. Jealous, Sekhmet absorbed Mr. Umbala, traveled to New York and abducted Wakandan monarch Black Panther (T'Challa), hoping to learn the Panther God's secrets. When T'Challa resisted, Sekhmet attacked the Avengers with his totem-stick. Thor struck the stick with lightning, forcing Sekhmet's flight to another dimension. T'Challa eventually placed the totem-stick in his trophy room. Later, sensing Sekhmet's presence, Avengers associates Mantis and the Swordsman (Jacques DuQuesne) summoned him, feigned an alliance and hypnotized Sekhmet while off-guard. Iron Man trapped him in an Adamantium cylinder that Thor sent to another dimension.

HEIGHT: 7'3" (variable) **WEIGHT:** 382 lbs. (variable) **EYES:** Unrevealed **HAIR:** Unrevealed

ABILITIES/ACCESSORIES: Sekhmet's potential power is awesome, but his Lion God incarnation, a spirit form requiring a host, was seemingly limited to mesmerism, teleportation, size-changing, superhuman strength, durability, speed, density-altering and imperviousness to pain. His totem-stick and hunting spear could summon lions and fire force blasts. He always appeared when summoned but required a human sacrifice.

INTELLIGENCE: 3 **STRENGTH:** 4 **SPEED:** 3/7 (teleporter) **DURABILITY:** 6 **ENERGY PROJECTION:** 5 **FIGHTING SKILLS:** 4

MR. UMBALA

Art by Don Heck

LIVING DIAMOND

REAL NAME: Jack Winters
ALIASES: Jack O'Diamonds
IDENTITY: Secret
OCCUPATION: Criminal; former nuclear technician
CITIZENSHIP: USA
PLACE OF BIRTH: Unrevealed
KNOWN RELATIVES: None
GROUP AFFILIATION: None; formerly X-Humed
EDUCATION: Unrevealed
FIRST APPEARANCE: X-Men #39 (1967)

HISTORY: Needing money for gambling debts, nuclear power plant employee Jack Winters stole radioactive isotopes to hold for ransom; however, the isotopes exploded, triggering his latent mutant powers which included diamond-hard hands. Becoming a criminal, Winters forced young runaway mutant Scott Summers to act as his accomplice. Taking Summers to the power plant he once worked in, Winters sought more radioactive isotopes to augment his power. When Professor Charles Xavier arrived to rescue Summers, Winters ordered the boy to attack him, but Summers refused. Winters then repelled Xavier's mental attack before using the plant's cyclotron to bombard himself with radiation, transforming his entire body into a diamond-like substance. Summers subsequently opposed Winters alongside Xavier, who used the plant's ultrasonic vibration inducer to shatter Winter's diamond form, seemingly killing him. Jack was later reanimated as a zombie by the voodoo practitioner Black Talon (Samuel Barone) and forced to serve in his group of undead mutants, the X-Humed. After She-Hulk defeated the Black Talon, Winters and the other deceased mutants returned to true death.

Art by Werner Roth

HEIGHT: 6'
WEIGHT: (Winters) 198 lbs.; (Jack O'Diamonds) 208 lbs.; (Living Diamond) 592 lbs.
EYES: Brown
HAIR: (Winters/Jack O'Diamonds) Brown; (Living Diamond) White

ABILITIES/ACCESSORIES: Jack O'Diamonds had diamond-hard hands, telepathy, and the ability to teleport. As the Living Diamond, his entire body was diamond-hard and he could lift fifty tons.

INTELLIGENCE: 2 **STRENGTH:** 5 **SPEED:** 2 **DURABILITY:** 5
ENERGY PROJECTION: 1 **FIGHTING SKILLS:** 2

LIVING TOTEM

REAL NAME: Whistle Pig
ALIASES: None
IDENTITY: No dual identity
OCCUPATION: Adventurer
CITIZENSHIP: Canada
PLACE OF BIRTH: British Columbia
KNOWN RELATIVES: None
GROUP AFFILIATION: Doc Samson's group of adventurers
EDUCATION: Standard 19th century education of the Haida tribe, supplemented by independent inquiries into other Native American cultures
FIRST APPEARANCE: Doc Samson #1 (2006)

HISTORY: Circa 1850, Whistle Pig was attacked by shaman Cold Winter, who drove his soul into a totem pole. Unexpectedly animating it as a Living Totem, he inadvertently slew Winter, then spent years wandering the Americas, seeking a way to regain his human body. Eventually he clashed with several vigilantes and was entombed in an Arizona desert. Over a century later, musicians Wolf and Flora Punnett cremated their friend Cam Larson's body near Totem's prison, then bound Larson's ghost to the mortal realm. Larson befriended the entombed Totem and taught him English. In recent years, Larson persuaded Wolf and Flora to unearth Totem, who held them prisoner, unaware Larson wanted them to release him from the earthly plane. Wolf and Flora's daughter Tina investigated their disappearance with family friend Doc Samson and sorcerer Jack Holyoak. The Punnetts broke their binding spell, but Totem, desperate for companionship, prevented his friend's escape until Doc separated his body's component parts. After being restored, Totem joined Doc, Tina, and Jack on various adventures.

Art by Fabrizio Florentino

HEIGHT: 20' (formerly 5'9") **WEIGHT:** 2000 lbs. (formerly 170 lbs.) **HAIR:** None (formerly black)
EYES: (From uppermost to lowermost face) Red, black, white, red, red, red, purple, red (formerly black)

ABILITIES/ACCESSORIES: The Living Totem possesses superhuman strength, the power of flight, four razor-sharp beaks, and similarly sharp claws on four of his six arms. His body is supernaturally flexible, enabling him to twist and bend while retaining extraordinary durability. He possesses limited mystic sensitivity, can temporarily contain disembodied spirits within his body, and knows the spiritual secrets of several Native American tribes. Under severe stress, the force binding his component pieces weakens; if his pieces are separated, he loses his sentient nature until they are rejoined.

INTELLIGENCE: 2 **STRENGTH:** 5 **SPEED:** 2 **DURABILITY:** 5
ENERGY PROJECTION: 1 **FIGHTING SKILLS:** 2

LOIS LONDON

REAL NAME: Lois London, legally changed from Lois Brown
ALIASES: Rose Blossom
IDENTITY: No dual identity
OCCUPATION: Former student
CITIZENSHIP: USA
PLACE OF BIRTH: Queens, New York
KNOWN RELATIVES: Nick Brown (father), Barbara London (Katherine Blaire-Brown, mother), Alison Blaire (Dazzler, half-sister), Longshot (brother-in-law)
GROUP AFFILIATION: None
EDUCATION: College (unfinished)
FIRST APPEARANCE: (Photo) Dazzler #20 (1982); (in person) Dazzler #21 (1982)

HISTORY: When Lois Brown was 4, she and her mother Katherine left Lois' abusive father Nick; Katherine changed her name to Barbara London. As a college freshman at State University, Lois suffered headaches and fainting spells. Barbara meanwhile had renewed contact with Lois' half-sister from Barbara's first marriage, Alison Blaire, the singer Dazzler; previously unaware of her sibling, Lois immediately visited Alison's apartment. They quickly bonded, with Lois soon discovering Alison was a mutant when she used her powers to alert the police to a fire started by the arsonist Flame (Dan Springer). Already a fan of Dazzler's music, Lois initially thought it was wonderful that Alison was a super hero, but after Rogue attacked them, it seemed somewhat less glamorous. Lois wondered if her fainting spells meant she too was a mutant, a theory confirmed when she accidentally killed an aggressive derelict, Robert "Ol' Slimey" Smith, with the first manifestation of her powers. Unaware her actions had been photographed by former detective Vincent Napier, sent by her father to find her, a terrified Lois ran to Alison, and unsure a mutant would receive a fair trial, they fled New York pursued by agents of the government's mutant watchdog Project: Wideawake. Having been blackmailed by Nick Brown to secure his services, Napier in turn blackmailed the two women into slaying Nick when they reached Los Angeles, but instead they captured him with the aid of Alison's ex-boyfriend Angel (Warren Worthington III); Lois was reunited with Nick, Napier was arrested, and ironically his photographs, showing no sign of mutant powers, proved Lois' actions were self-defense, the derelict's cause of death officially cardiac arrest. Lois still blamed herself and feared her powers; though she distrusted her father's reformation claims, she elected to stay with him, to use his money and contacts to protect herself.

Art by Frank Springer

HEIGHT: 5'5" **EYES:** Blue **WEIGHT:** 120 lbs. **HAIR:** Brown

ABILITIES/ACCESSORIES: Lois can discharge light, heat and an undisclosed lethal energy from her hands; prolonged exposure causes a molecular transformation in flesh, freezing it without lowering the temperature. This energy does not show up in photographs.

INTELLIGENCE: 2 **STRENGTH:** 2 **SPEED:** 2 **DURABILITY:** 2
ENERGY PROJECTION: 2 **FIGHTING SKILLS:** 2

LORD OF DEATH

REAL NAME: Unrevealed
ALIASES: None
IDENTITY: Secret
OCCUPATION: Saboteur
CITIZENSHIP: Unrevealed
PLACE OF BIRTH: Unrevealed
KNOWN RELATIVES: None
GROUP AFFILIATION: Nazi Germany, leader of "zombie" army
EDUCATION: Unrevealed
FIRST APPEARANCE: All-Winners Comics #1 (1941)

HISTORY: In early 1941, the Lord of Death discovered how to transform humans into compliant "zombies" by replacing their blood with his "di-namo fluid." He offered his services to Adolf Hitler, who hired him to sabotage the lend-lease agreement between the USA and Great Britain. Recruiting Bowery derelicts as unsuspecting subjects, the Lord of Death sent "zombies" to attack a shipyard; although Captain America and Bucky defeated them, a supply ship was nonetheless destroyed. The Lord of Death sent additional "zombies" to crash trucks into a supply convoy on a bridge, while dozens more assaulted pedestrians and drivers. Despite Cap and Bucky's intervention, the supply trucks' munitions exploded, destroying the bridge. Again seeking victims from the Bowery, the Lord of Death recruited two derelicts, actually Cap and Bucky in disguise. After the criminal's boastful elaboration on a proposed massive "zombie" attack across the entire USA, Cap and Bucky revealed their identities and attacked. Quickly subdued by Captain America, the Lord of Death was presumably arrested and imprisoned.

NOTE: Lord of Death has no known link to other WWII employers of facsimile or genuine zombies, including Zombie Master (1939), Prof. Maluski (1939), Dr. Varoz (1940), Laughing Skull (1940), the Nazombies' creator (1941), Prince Itor (1941), General Henchel (1941), Metal Fist (1942), Zombie Master (1943), the controller(s) of reanimated corpses in the Netherlands (1944), and Peter Anzel (1945).

Art by Jack Kirby

HEIGHT: 5'11" **WEIGHT:** 230 lbs. **EYES:** Black **HAIR:** White

ABILITIES/ACCESSORIES: Lord of Death could transform humans into white-skinned "zombies" who could endure attacks by bullets, blades and other weapons without ill effect, although they could be knocked down or overwhelmed by sheer physical force. They retained the power of speech and some level of human intelligence, enabling them to drive automobiles and fire guns. The "zombies" apparently lost their vitality and truly died after 24 hours of activity.

INTELLIGENCE: 3 **STRENGTH:** 2 **SPEED:** 2 **DURABILITY:** 2
ENERGY PROJECTION: 1 **FIGHTING SKILLS:** 2

LORDS OF THE LIVING LIGHTNING

BASE OF OPERATIONS: Offshore mountainous volcano; formerly Santa Ana mountains, California (base destroyed)
FIRST APPEARANCE: Tales to Astonish #97 (1967)

HISTORY: The Legions of the Living Lightning were soldiers and scientists dedicated to overthrowing the world's governments. In a mountain base, they developed advanced technology through manipulation of electricity, as well as purchasing and stealing weaponry. Targeting a missile facility, their leader, the Lord of the Living Lightning, began secret observations of the base. When the Hulk collided with a Legion plane, its wounded pilot convinced Hulk that the Legion were fellow outsiders, and that the Hulk would be accepted there. The Lord followed through, convincing the Hulk of the nobility of their efforts. SHIELD heard rumors of the Lightning's existence, and the US Army sent Major Glenn Talbot to investigate. Talbot was captured by the Legion, and his personal anger towards the Hulk only reinforced the monster's loyalty to the Legion; at the Lord's urging, Hulk attacked the missile base. Taking advantage of the distraction the Hulk created, the Legions of the Living Lightning overwhelmed the base's command facility. The Hulk, meanwhile, was gassed by the military and soon recovered by the Legion, but the Lightning Lord's insistence that the captured Betty Ross was also an enemy confused the Hulk, who turned on them before being subdued by repeated hits from the Legion's Lightning Blasters. While the Legion focused on the Hulk, Talbot escaped and cut off the Legion's ability to command the base. The Legion was forced to flee back to their home base, but the now angry Hulk followed. As the Lord of the Living Lightning attempted to launch all his weapons at the missile base, the Hulk attacked, inadvertently destroying the Lightning's facility and legions in an enormous explosion when he threw a construction crane into an atomic pile. Miguel Santos, son of Carlos (a Legion member killed in that fateful explosion), later located the remnants of the Legion's base and was transformed by their power source into Living Lightning, who became an Avenger. Legion veteran Lou Denham later threatened Miguel's mother to try to force Miguel to help replicate his power, but he overpowered Denham and turned him in to the police. The Legion eventually regrouped, renaming themselves the Lords of the Living Lightning and continued to foment chaos. They sought an alliance with Merlin (or an aspect thereof) via their agent Hellstorm (actually an infiltrator from SHIELD's Howling Commandos), but Merlin declined and made them all swear allegiance to him. Though seemingly destroyed in the subsequent battle with the Howling Commandos, Merlin soon returned to them.

LORD OF THE LIVING LIGHTNING
Art by Marie Severin

LURKING UNKNOWN

REAL NAME: Unknown
ALIASES: The Lurker, the Outsider, the Unknown
IDENTITY: Unknown to the general populace of Earth
OCCUPATION: Fear monger
CITIZENSHIP: Unknown
PLACE OF BIRTH: Unknown dimension
KNOWN RELATIVES: None
GROUP AFFILIATION: Fear Lords
EDUCATION: Unknown
FIRST APPEARANCE: Thor #136 (1967)

HISTORY: The Lurking Unknown is a Fear Lord, an other-dimensional being with cosmic power who subsists on fear. He ravaged worlds, never knew defeat, and built a mystique that made him dreaded throughout the cosmos. Odin, lord of Asgard, learned of him and how to summon him. Knowing the fearless Asgardians were safe, Odin used the Unknown to test courage. When Thor wished to marry the mortal Jane Foster, Odin gave her godly powers and summoned the Unknown. Overwhelmed with fear, Jane called for Thor, who forced the Unknown to flee. Odin banished Jane from Asgard, then sent Thor to face the Unknown in the Crystal Glade of Gundershelm. Heartsick, Thor faced defeat until Sif intervened and restored Thor's courage. Together they drove the Unknown away. The Unknown later joined his fellow Fear Lords in an alliance to plunge Earth into a Great Fear. The Straw Man (aka Scarecrow), however, refused to join and warned Sorcerer Supreme Dr. Strange of the Fear Lords' intent. The Unknown burned up the Straw Man but arrogantly refused D'Spayre's help. Free of despair, Dr. Strange and Clea were able to overcome their fear via anger. Powerless, the Unknown shrank and was apparently crushed in Dr. Strange's hand, although his fate is, of course, unknown.

Art by Larry Alexander

HEIGHT: 10'4" (variable) **WEIGHT:** 532 lbs. (variable) **EYES:** Black **HAIR:** Bald
ABILITIES/ACCESSORIES: The four-armed Lurking Unknown's powers depended on generating fear. Under the right conditions he had incalculable strength and invulnerability. He could create fire in his hand. In Asgard, a specific note rung on an enchanted tuning fork could mystically summon him either to the royal palace or the Crystal Glade of Gundershelm. With no fear generated, the Unknown was powerless.

INTELLIGENCE: 2 **STRENGTH:** 7 **SPEED:** 7 **DURABILITY:** 7
ENERGY PROJECTION: 3 **FIGHTING SKILLS:** 4

M

REAL NAME: Monet Yvette Clarisse Maria Therese St. Croix; formerly Claudette and Nicole St. Croix
ALIASES: (All) Formerly Penance, "Penny"; (twins, with Emplate) formerly M-Plate; (Monet) formerly "Stinky"
IDENTITY: (Twins) Secret; (Monet) Public
OCCUPATION: (Twins) Presumably students; former adventurer; (Monet) adventurer, private investigator; former student
CITIZENSHIP: (Twins) Algeria; (Monet) Algeria, France and Bosnia
PLACE OF BIRTH: (Twins) Algiers, Algeria; (Monet) Sarajevo, Bosnia
KNOWN RELATIVES: Cartier St. Croix (father), unidentified mother (deceased), each other (sisters), Marius St. Croix (Emplate, brother), Louis St. Croix (grandfather), Lenore St. Croix (grandfather's wife, deceased)
GROUP AFFILIATION: (Twins) Formerly Generation X; (Monet) X-Factor Investigations/XF Investigations; formerly X-Corporation Europe, X-Corps, Generation X
EDUCATION: (Twins) Studied at Massachusetts Academy; (Monet) Studied at Massachusetts Academy and DeLaCorte's Boarding School
FIRST APPEARANCE: (Twins as "Monet") Uncanny X-Men #316 (1994); (Twins as M, Monet as Penance) Generation X San Diego Preview (1994); (Monet as M) Generation X Underground Special (1998)

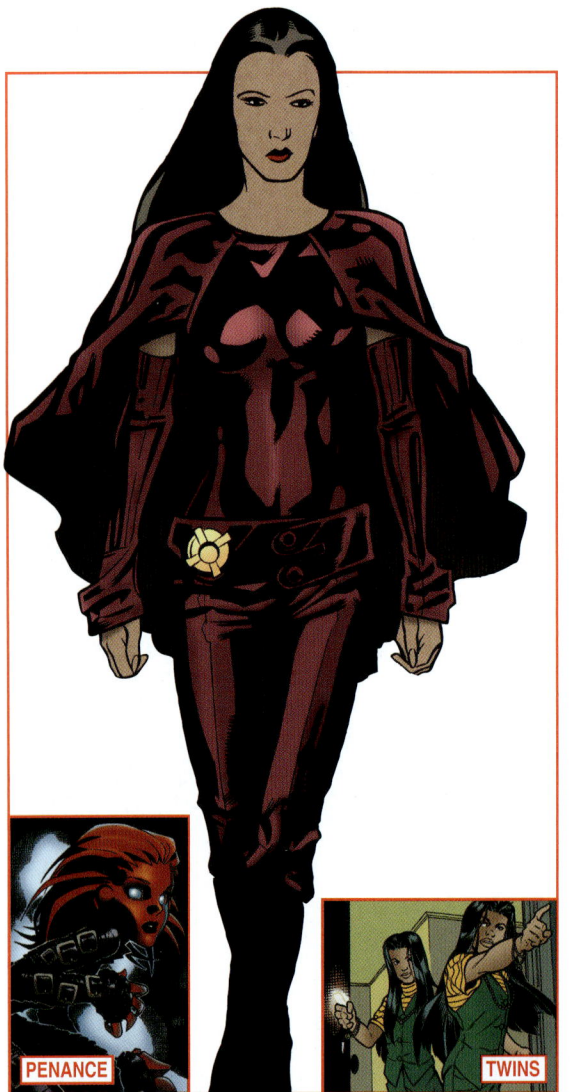

PENANCE

TWINS

HISTORY: The St. Croix siblings, Monet, Marius and twins Nicole and Claudette, all mutants, were pampered descendants of Algerian royalty. Their grandfather, Louis, was an ambassador and longtime member of Professor X's Mutant Underground, and their wealthy father, Cartier, was formerly president of several corporations. The twins, whose powers developed early, were tutored by the aboriginal mutant Gateway — but Monet, mastering her own wide array of abilities, grew up haughty, pompous and spoiled. When Marius' powers surfaced, he developed an insatiable hunger for mutants' genetic marrow, and fed on his own mother, killing her. After their grieving father threw him out, Marius turned to the dark arts of the nether realms for more power. He eventually returned and invited Monet to join him in conquering another dimension, but she scornfully rejected him. Fed up with her high-handed attitude towards him, Marius magically trapped her in the form of a mute creature with razor-sharp, diamond-hard red skin. The twins arrived and, not recognizing Monet, believed their brother had killed her. Claudette opened a portal, banishing Marius to another dimension — and the transformed Monet followed, seeing him as the only way to return to normal. To spare their father from a broken heart at the loss of his favorite daughter, the twins used their powers to merge into a single being that duplicated Monet mentally and physically.

As "Monet," the twins were captured by the techno-organic alien Phalanx race, who sought to assimilate mutants into their collective. "Monet" and her fellow prisoners were rescued by an ad hoc X-Men team led by Banshee, and she took the code name M and joined Generation X, a team of trainee mutants at the Massachusetts Academy under co-headmasters Banshee and Emma Frost. Meanwhile, after months of imprisonment — during which Marius, now calling himself Emplate, used her as a source of sustenance — the true Monet was rescued and taken to the Academy by Gateway. Dubbed "Penance," Monet was distrustful of her new surroundings. Her new form made it difficult to think and impossible to speak — and unaware of the twins' merger, she was confused by the presence of "herself." However, befriended by Jubilee, Monet soon accepted her new situation and ultimately joined the team. Meanwhile, despondent over his recent familial losses, Cartier suffered a minor nervous breakdown — but eventually recovered, joining his father in the Mutant Underground and eventually becoming an ambassador as well.

M battled villains like Gene Nation and Omega Red alongside her new teammates, only betraying her true nature through occasional childish acts and a "diary" full of crayon drawings. However, she occasionally lapsed into semi-catatonic fugue states during periods of intense concentration, a result of Claudette's autism. M's attitude and refusal to explain herself made bonding with the other students difficult; when Emplate later attacked the school, he revealed their familial relationship, causing her teammates to distrust her. Nevertheless, M helped rescue her teammate Synch, who had been corrupted by Emplate, and continued to aid the team in battles against such foes as Fenris (Strucker twins) and D'Spayre. She also invited several of her teammates to her Monaco home for Christmas break. Eventually, during a battle with Prime Sentinels, M's true nature was revealed when an explosion separated her into the twins. Penance, finally understanding what had happened but unable to explain it to the team, became protective of the comatose twins. When Emplate attacked again, the twins awakened and merged with him, briefly forming an entity called M-Plate, and learned Monet's fate from his mind. After separating, the twins revealed the truth to the team and merged with the Penance form, freeing Monet but becoming trapped themselves. Monet took up the code name M, and promised to find Emplate and free her sisters. Emotionally damaged from her time in captivity, Monet battled depression, nightmares and suicidal thoughts by retreating further behind her aloof, condescending persona. She confronted Jubilee over perceived humiliations suffered as Penance, and began to develop feelings for Synch. In battle, she proved every bit her sisters' equal, helping the team defeat the cyber-morph Paradox,

Art by Ryan Sook with Chris Bachalo (Penance) & Terry Dodson (twins)

the Orphan-Maker, the Dark Beast-led Gene Nation, Hunter Brawn, and Emma Frost's evil sister Adrienne.

M-PLATE
Art by Terry Dodson

During another battle with Emplate, Jubilee defeated him with an explosion that also freed the twins from the Penance form — which, surprisingly, lived on without any discernible host. Shortly thereafter, M's father took the twins home and withdrew M from the Academy, enrolling her in a private boarding school in the Swiss Alps. She soon discovered the headmaster was secretly a vampire feeding on students, defeated him, and returned to the Massachusetts Academy, where she romanced Synch. However, Emma's sister Adrienne had created a dangerous anti-mutant sentiment at the school, which was now also open to human students, and Penance was sent to live with Cartier for her own safety. Synch was ultimately killed by one of several bombs that Adrienne planted around the campus, and as the school was made private once more, M and Jubilee bonded over their shared grief. The students soon quit and the Academy closed, and M spent some time in Algeria. Later, she and former teammates Husk and Jubilee joined Banshee's paramilitary X-Corps, forming a mini-squad nicknamed "Banshee's Angels" to keep an eye on their former headmaster. They aided him against a coup from within by Mystique, but the X-Corps was ultimately discredited and shut down. Monet stayed on after it was restructured into the European branch of Professor X's mutant outreach organization, the X-Corporation. She battled Weapon XII in the Channel Tunnel, and aided the X-Men and the Juggernaut against Black Tom Cassidy. Meanwhile, Penance separated from the St. Croix family under unrevealed circumstances, and was later preyed upon by Fuyumi Fujikawa's mutant growth hormone (MGH) drug ring, developing a voice and taking the name Hollow.

Following the X-Corporation's closure in the aftermath of M-Day, M joined the staff of X-Factor Investigations, a mutant detective agency run by former X-Corps and X-Corporation teammate Jamie Madrox. When X-Factor discovered the Scarlet Witch's part in M-Day, it caused tension between them and the X-Men, who had hidden the truth. M registered her powers with the government under the Superhuman Registration Act, although X-Factor later publicly denounced the Act. She then had a fling with one of Jamie's duplicates, which ended poorly when she discovered that the real Jamie was involved with fellow teammate Siryn. In France, M and Siryn stopped a crowd from burning down a house full of ex-mutants, but were arrested, and the crowd returned later to torch the home. When M learned this, she brutally attacked one of the men, crucifying him, and battled the French police. Her father stepped in later and greased some palms to avoid an international incident. Alongside X-Factor, M battled the terrorist group the X-Cell, rescued Rictor from the isolationist Josef Huber, and joined the other X-teams in fighting the Marauders to save the first mutant baby born since M-Day. When Arcade destroyed New York's Middle East Side, the former "Mutant Town" where X-Factor was based, ONE (Office of National Emergency) agent Val Cooper attempted to press-gang the team into government service, and they responded by going underground. Relocating to Detroit, they renamed themselves XF Investigations and continued their work, maintaining a much lower profile. When the Skrulls invaded Earth, M and X-Factor aided She-Hulk in battling Nogor, a religious "Talisman" who boosted Skrull troops' morale. Despite her arrogant attitude, M remains a steadfast defender of mutant rights, and a dedicated member of XF Investigations.

X-CORPS COSTUME
Art by Aaron Lopresti

HEIGHT: (Twins, when last seen) 4'2" each; (Monet) 5'7"; (all, as Penance) 5'5"
WEIGHT: (Twins, when last seen) 60 lbs each; (Monet) 125 lbs; (all, as Penance) Unrevealed
EYES: (All) Brown; (all, as Penance) Blue, no visible irises or pupils
HAIR: (All) Black; (all, as Penance) Red

ABILITIES/ACCESSORIES: Monet has superhuman speed, intelligence and strength (Class 10), telepathy, flight, nigh-invulnerability, enhanced night vision, heightened hearing, accelerated healing, and the ability to perceive mutants' auras. She can analyze and understand most devices instantly, is highly educated and a formidable hand-to-hand combatant. Monet speaks fluent English and French, as do Nicole and (presumably) Claudette.

Nicole and Claudette can combine with each other and their siblings into individual beings with magnified abilities. When the twins merge, they seem able to choose the form they take and can influence its behavior; however, combining with others creates independent beings. When they combined to form a duplicate of Monet, they possessed all of her powers. When they combined with Emplate to form M-Plate, they possessed psionic powers and energy blasts, and could distort reality, travel interdimensionally and create and manipulate force fields. Claudette is autistic, and spends much of her time in an unresponsive fugue state; when the twins merge, the combinant entity occasionally lapses into a fugue as well. In addition, Claudette can open dimensional portals using a piece of chalk, although it is unrevealed whether this is a mutant or mystical ability. Nicole and Claudette have not been seen in years, and no doubt their control over their powers has grown as they approach puberty.

When trapped in the Penance form, none of the sisters could access their mutant powers, think clearly or speak. However, they possessed Penance's super-dense diamond-hard body, with razor-sharp fingers, skin and hair, clawed hands and feet, and limited psi-shields (presumably mystical in nature). The Penance form can also contract and relax its skin to a limited degree, "softening" it somewhat or rendering it so tight that it begins to atrophy the muscles underneath.

POWER GRID	1	2	3	4	5	6	7
INTELLIGENCE							
STRENGTH							
SPEED							
DURABILITY							
ENERGY PROJECTION							
FIGHTING SKILLS							

1ST GENERATION X COSTUME   2ND GENERATION X COSTUME   3RD GENERATION X COSTUME
Art by Chris Bachalo, Art Adams & Steve Pugh

MACE

REAL NAME: Mace
ALIASES: Shigeru Ezaki
IDENTITY: Nature as clone and genetic progenitor not known to general public
OCCUPATION: Mercenary
CITIZENSHIP: None
PLACE OF BIRTH: Northern Japan
KNOWN RELATIVES: Gregor, Hutch, Leon, the Officer, dozens of others (many deceased) (fellow clones/brothers), Shigeru Ezaki (original genetic source)
GROUP AFFILIATION: Formerly Sunrise Society
EDUCATION: Private tutelage by Sunrise Society resources
FIRST APPEARANCE: Venom: The Mace #1 (1994)

HISTORY: Years ago, the Sunrise Society (aka the Eternal Sun Society), a covert organization of fanatical Japanese businessmen dedicated to world conquest in revenge for Japan's defeat in World War II, captured their most implacable enemy, Shigeru Ezaki (aka the masked hero Tengu of the Shadowmasters), and used his DNA to clone warriors who could match or exceed his extraordinary martial arts expertise. Mace was one such clone, who, armed with specialized maces from which he took his name, underwent ninja training from ninpo master Mas Kimura, bodyguard of Society scientist Dr. Kiso Ito. Told little of the outside world by his mentors, Mace accessed the Sunrise Society (aka the Eternal Sun Society)'s computers for additional knowledge and learned about the Shadowmasters, whose abilities intrigued him.

On his own initiative, Ito subjected Mace to surgeries that granted the clone augmented abilities, but the Sunrise Society's leaders, paranoically believing Ito to be a traitor, arranged for Kimura's absence and sent a cadre of specially equipped High-Tech Ninjas (HTNs) to kill Ito and retrieve his collected data. Although Ito erased his data before dying, the HTNs captured the still-recovering Mace and escaped with him despite a simultaneous attack by the Shadowmasters, who were reunited with the captive Ezaki prior to his death. Abandoning their Japanese base for another in northern California, the Society, unable to determine precisely how Ito had altered Mace, placed the protesting clone in suspended animation. Over the years, the Society's clones increased in number and strength, but the enhancements created by Ito were never duplicated.

In recent years, the Society, provoked into rebuilding by renewed Shadowmaster activity, reopened the California base and revived Mace, whom they questioned about Mas Kimura, who had never returned to his post following the earlier attack and whose services they hoped to regain. Unable to provide the answers they sought, Mace rebelled against them and was slated for scientific study, but he escaped, defeating several clone warriors and absconding with Society technology. Mace resolved to track down the Shadowmasters in hoping to gain assistance in locating Kimura, only to be pursued by armored High-Tech Soldiers (HTSs) as well as HTNs, all clones of Shigeru Ezaki like himself.

Meanwhile, in nearby Los Angeles, four renegades among the city's near-forgotten Undergrounders society waged a campaign of harassment and robbery against indigents who had taken up residence in nearby abandoned buildings. Happening upon the aftermath of an attack, Mace offered the indigents his services in stopping their tormentors. Unfortunately, following Mace's first confrontation with the renegades, the Undergrounders' self-appointed protector, the symbiote-powered madman Venom (Eddie Brock), misunderstood Mace's motivations and attacked. Their fight was interrupted by the arrival of several HTNs and HTSs, and the battle-hungry Venom joined Mace in decimating the pursuers' ranks. Mace prevented his defeated fellow clones from self-destructing to guarantee evidence of the Sunrise Society's activities for law enforcement authorities. His misunderstanding with Venom resolved, Mace departed to begin his search for Kimura and the Shadowmasters, while Venom slew the renegade Undergrounders.

HEIGHT: 5'10"
WEIGHT: 188 lbs.
EYES: Red (formerly brown)
HAIR: Black

ABILITIES/ACCESSORIES: Mace possesses augmented strength (lifting up to 1 ton) and agility, as well as accelerated healing capabilities, although overtaxing his healing system can weaken him temporarily. His vision extends into the infrared and ultraviolet ranges, requiring him to wear sunglasses for normal vision in non-combat situations. Biocircuitry extending from his right eye to his right arm provides built-in targeting precision and plugs directly into a customized compact laser/shotgun equipped with penetrating, incendiary and explosive ammunition, as well as multiple energy discharge settings. Easily stored in a uniquely designed back harness, it is also equipped to fire ballistic maces with extending spikes; Mace further uses the maces as throwing weapons when necessary. His cloak is laced with liquid crystal that allows it to reproduce the texture and coloring of his surroundings at will, rendering him virtually invisible. Mace is an accomplished marksman, blade wielder and martial artist, trained in multiple techniques. He is fluent in both Japanese and English.

POWER GRID	1	2	3	4	5	6	7
INTELLIGENCE							
STRENGTH							
SPEED							
DURABILITY							
ENERGY PROJECTION							
FIGHTING SKILLS							

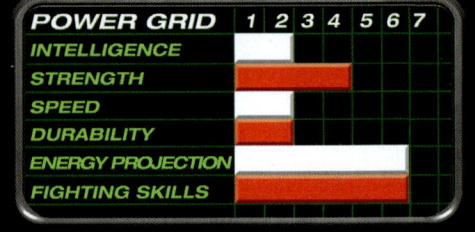

Art by Liam Sharp

GIDEON MACE

HISTORY: Colonel Gideon Mace, veteran of several wars, felt his superiors were weak, unwilling to make necessary sacrifices. He led his men on an unauthorized assault against an enemy village, during which a mine destroyed Mace's right hand, and he was dishonorably discharged on the orders of General William Westmoorland for insubordination, mental incompetence, and suspicion of combat activity independent of orders. An enraged Mace replaced his lost appendage with a spiked mace, training relentlessly until he could use it effortlessly. He recruited ex-soldiers loyal to him, forming his own private army, and depleting his family's fortune to bankroll them. Needing financing, he arranged Operation Overpower, enlisting disgruntled veterans who felt abandoned by America. Mace told the veterans they would paralyze Manhattan for a day by bloodlessly seizing control of strategic points throughout the city; in truth Mace intended them to be decoys, diverting police away from Wall Street while his elite troops looted it. One veteran, Owen Ridgely, learned of Mace's true goals and, pursued by Mace's killers, sought help from Luke Cage, Hero for Hire. Unable to prevent Ridgely's murder, Luke found and attacked Mace's base. Finding Cage unstoppable, Mace fled in a helicopter, but Cage caused it to crash into the Hudson River. Narrowly avoiding drowning by unscrewing his heavy mace, Gideon established Security City, an isolated planned community where paranoid ultra-conservatives could live behind barbed wire and armed guards away from the rest of America. Mace manipulated the residents, training them to follow him unconditionally and ultimately to become his personal army. The arrival of Luke Cage and his friend "DW" Griffith — whose bus had been shot off the road by Security City personnel for straying too close — proved Mace's downfall. DW covertly rewired a sound system, allowing the townspeople to hear Mace's plans, sparking a riot.

Evading capture, Mace learned the US Army had lost a cobalt bomb in Bermuda, and plotted to bluff the authorities into handing over Chicago to him by claiming he had recovered the weapon and would detonate it, forcing an evacuation of the area. Cage's untimely intervention once again disrupted things, as Cage worked with Burgandy — a former agent of Mace's who turned against him after learning her husband had died in Mace's unauthorized mission — to expose Mace's farce. Mace next convinced various illicit organizations, such as the Maggia and Halwani Freedom Front, to fund him in targeting and murdering costumed heroes. He chose the low-powered hero the White Tiger (Hector Ayala), whose identity had been exposed on television, as his first target, murdering most of Ayala's immediate family to lure the hero into his trap, then gunning him down. Mace's men dumped the dying youth from a speeding car outside the Daily Bugle offices, coincidentally in front of photographer Peter Parker, secretly Spider-Man and a friend of Hector's. Spider-Man hunted Mace down, finding him in a National Guard armory plotting to slay Hawkeye (Clint Barton), Cage and other unidentified heroes. The hero evaded both booby traps and Mace's men, confronted Mace and overpowered him; when Mace's guards approached, Spider-Man used the pinned villain as a shield, expecting them to hold their fire, but Mace ordered them to shoot anyway. Spider-Man ducked multiple shots which cut through Mace, swiftly disarmed the guards, and rushed Mace to a hospital. It is unconfirmed whether he survived or not.

REAL NAME: Gideon Mace
ALIASES: A01372712
IDENTITY: No dual identity
OCCUPATION: Terrorist, former US Army Colonel
CITIZENSHIP: USA
PLACE OF BIRTH: Englewood Cliffs, New Jersey
KNOWN RELATIVES: Unspecified family members
GROUP AFFILIATION: Commanded his own private army; formerly US Army
EDUCATION: Unrevealed; presumably includes extensive military training
FIRST APPEARANCE: Luke Cage, Hero for Hire #3 (1972)

HEIGHT: 6'2" **EYES:** Blue
WEIGHT: 170 lbs.; (with mace) 407 lbs. **HAIR:** Gray

ABILITIES/ACCESSORIES: Mace is a trained soldier and skilled strategist. He is an excellent shot with his left hand and an adept unarmed fighter. His right hand has been replaced by a foot-diameter titanium steel, spiked mace; it has been adapted to spray chemical mace or to fire like a cannonball from his wrist.

POWER GRID	1	2	3	4	5	6	7
INTELLIGENCE							
STRENGTH			■				
SPEED		■					
DURABILITY			■				
ENERGY PROJECTION		■					
FIGHTING SKILLS				■			

Art by George Tuska

MACH-4

REAL NAME: Abner Ronald "Abe" Jenkins
ALIASES: Beetle, MACH-3, Matthew Davis, MACH-2, MACH-1, Aaron Jeffries
IDENTITY: Publicly known
OCCUPATION: Government operative; former licensed super hero, adventurer, professional criminal, mercenary, master mechanic
CITIZENSHIP: USA with a criminal record, pardoned
PLACE OF BIRTH: Baltimore, Maryland
KNOWN RELATIVES: None
GROUP AFFILIATION: Commission on Superhuman Activities (CSA); formerly Thunderbolts, Initiative, Burton Canyon Police Department, Hammer Industries, "B-Team," Masters of Evil, Sinister Seven, Maggia, Sinister Syndicate, Lethal Legion, Defenders impersonators, leader of various criminal gangs
EDUCATION: High school graduate
FIRST APPEARANCE: (Beetle) Strange Tales #123 (1964); (MACH-1) Incredible Hulk #449 (1997); (MACH-2) Thunderbolts #37 (2000); (MACH-3) Thunderbolts #57 (2001); (MACH-4) New Thunderbolts #1 (2005)

AS MATT DAVIS

HISTORY: A brilliant and ambitious mechanical engineer, Abe Jenkins squandered his talents in pursuit of personal glory and easy money for years before devoting himself to a life of self-redemptive heroism. A longtime master mechanic at Precision Aircraft Parts with dreams of bigger things, Jenkins was frustrated with his job. Despite his tremendous natural ability, his limited formal education prevented him from gaining further promotions, and his supervisor Carruthers refused to look at his radical designs for a form-fitting one-man aircraft. Mocked by co-workers for his lofty ambitions, Jenkins decided to do something dramatic to prove his brilliance. Designing and wearing a suit of strength-augmenting, metal-winged, flight-capable armor with suction-tipped gloves, Jenkins dubbed himself the Beetle and embarked on a crime spree halted by the Thing (Ben Grimm) and the Human Torch (Johnny Storm).

Undaunted, Jenkins persisted in his new super-criminal career, modifying his armor and battling heroes such as the Human Torch, Iceman (Bobby Drake), the Fantastic Four and the Avengers. He became a bitter recurring foe of both Spider-Man (Peter Parker) and Daredevil (Matt Murdock). Though Beetle often worked alone, he sometimes led his own criminal gang, once served as the unwilling pawn of the Collector (Taneleer Tivan), formed brief partnerships with Scorpion (Mac Gargan) and Gladiator (Melvin Potter), and even teamed up with Daredevil against a common foe, terrorist group Black Spectre. Beetle was also part of a small super-criminal army who looted Manhattan under the name of the Defenders, but the true, heroic Defenders team stopped them. Seeking a measure of security, Jenkins and many fellow super-criminals became on-call agents of criminal tycoon Justin Hammer, providing Hammer their occasional services and a portion of their profits in exchange for legal, fiscal and technological support from Hammer Industries. As one of Hammer's super-agents, Beetle would often battle Hammer's old foe Iron Man (Tony Stark).

His Beetle armor wrecked by Iron Man, Jenkins radically redesigned and rebuilt it with the aid of criminal mechanic the Tinkerer. Before testing the suit in action, Beetle forced reluctant super-criminal Ringer (Anthony Davis) to fight Spider-Man, using this battle to analyze Spider-Man's fighting style, then attacked the hero himself, but Spider-Man defeated the new and improved Beetle with the aid of the Gibbon. After further defeats, Beetle joined Egghead's Masters of Evil alongside other super-criminals such as Moonstone (Karla Sofen) and Radioactive Man (Chen Lu), helping them abduct Hank Pym and frame him as a criminal, but Pym and the Avengers soon defeated the Masters. Jenkins next served with a new Lethal Legion that attacked Captain America en masse at the Marvel Comics offices, but that group broke up after their assault was foiled by a host of other super heroes such as Blue Shield, Namorita and Siryn. Beetle joined a more lasting team when he assembled and led the mercenary Sinister Syndicate, partnered with Boomerang, Hydro-Man, Rhino and Speed Demon. Though the Syndicate was profitable, they were repeatedly defeated by foes like Spider-Man, Silver Sable and Sandman, and Beetle became increasingly disillusioned with his criminal career after the Syndicate posed as freedom fighters while looting the nation of Belgriun with Dr. Octopus. Meanwhile, Beetle continued to work for Justin Hammer, battling Iron Man alongside fellow Hammer agents such as Blacklash and Blizzard (Donald Gill). For a time, Beetle incorporated stolen Stark technology into his armor, but Iron Man destroyed it. An increasingly weary and neurotic Jenkins resolved to avoid super heroes, though the Kingpin's lieutenant Arranger tricked Beetle into a losing battle with Spider-Man regardless.

When Beetle aligned his Sinister Syndicate with the Kingpin to cancel out his own personal debts to the crime boss, the resultant series of conflicts and deceptions eroded the Syndicate's faith in Jenkins; this situation soon estranged Boomerang and Rhino altogether, partly because Kingpin had Beetle kill Rhino's personal doctor Jared Goulding as punishment for unpaid gambling debts. Meanwhile, the Ringer's widow, Leila Davis, infiltrated the Syndicate as their getaway driver, secretly seeking revenge

Art by Tom Grummett with Mark Bagley (altered)

on Beetle for driving her husband to his apparent death. In the end, the Syndicate broke up after its members turned on each other violently, and Jenkins narrowly survived an attempt on his life by Leila and Boomerang, thanks largely to Spider-Man's intervention.

Beetle remained active thereafter as both a Hammer agent and a freelancer, battling the New Warriors, an alternate Iron Man (Jim Rhodes), the Avengers, Captain America and Spider-Man. He was among the many super-criminals who fought Spider-Man and each other in pursuit of an experimental nuclear blaster, again battling his foes Boomerang and Hardshell (an armored Leila Davis), who was unexpectedly reunited with her husband Anthony, resurrected by AIM as the cyborg Strikeback. Hardshell and Strikeback defeated Beetle and had him at their mercy, but the reformed Strikeback convinced Leila to spare him. After battles with She-Hulk and Silver Sable's Wild Pack, Beetle next tried to frame Spider-Man for the accidental death of his accomplice Terry Burns, and nearly succeeded before Spider-Man exposed the deception. Alongside Hydro-Man, Speed Demon and Scorpia, Beetle later fought Deathlok (Michael Collins) and Spider-Man as an agent of Silvermane's Maggia crime family. Beetle also fought Kaine and Spider-Man as a member of the short-lived Sinister Seven, and was among the criminals and mercenaries captured after battling an alternate Spider-Man (Ben Reilly) while seeking a skeleton that supposedly implicated Spider-Man in a murder.

Increasingly tired of crime, Beetle hit a new low when his own gang robbed him, and Daredevil thwarted Beetle's subsequent attack on gang member Carlos. Narrowly escaping with the aid of criminal mastermind Baron (Helmut) Zemo, Beetle joined Zemo's Thunderbolts, a new Masters of Evil group posing as super heroes to win the world's trust while secretly plotting world conquest. As a Thunderbolt, Beetle assumed the new identity of MACH-1, wearing a high-tech MACH (Mobile Armored Cyber Harness) flight suit which his teammate Fixer (aka Techno) had built with Jenkins' assistance. Unexpectedly, however, most of the Thunderbolts wholeheartedly embraced their new heroic roles, and Jenkins in particular became a reformed, increasingly idealistic man. He also began an enduring romance with his teammate Songbird (Melissa Gold). When the Thunderbolts' true identities were exposed to the world, the heroically inclined members soon turned on Zemo and foiled his world conquest plans, even rescuing the Avengers and the Fantastic Four in the process.

The remaining Thunderbolts began operating as roving outlaw heroes, trying to earn redemption and the public's forgiveness while eluding the authorities. When Avengers veteran Hawkeye (Clint Barton) joined the Thunderbolts as their new leader, he insisted that the group's only known killer, Jenkins, must return to prison. Realizing that his surrender and Hawkeye's presence would bolster the team's credibility, and deciding he had to face justice for his past crimes, Jenkins went back to jail. Incarcerated at Seagate Prison, Jenkins covertly foiled a Hammer-masterminded mass escape attempt, drawing the attention of the US government's Commission on Superhuman Activities (CSA), who secretly freed Jenkins from prison to undertake a special mission targeting his old boss Hammer. Using new remote-control armor as the Beetle, Jenkins infiltrated and damaged Hammer's operations and tricked Hammer into accepting stolen technology that could be used as evidence against him, clashing with the Thunderbolts along the way. Not trusting the CSA to treat him fairly, Jenkins deserted them and rejoined the Thunderbolts, who struck a secret bargain with the CSA: Government records would list Jenkins as imprisoned, but Jenkins would actually remain with the Thunderbolts in return for helping the CSA incriminate Hammer and concealing the CSA's illegal use of a convict in a federal operation. CSA agent Henry Gyrich reluctantly agreed to these terms, and Jenkins delivered Hammer into CSA custody.

Jenkins rebuilt his flight suit with the aid of new Thunderbolts recruit Ogre (secretly a disguised Techno), becoming MACH-2. Needing a new civilian identity to conceal his illicit release from prison, Jenkins had "Ogre" cosmetically alter his appearance, though a mischievous Techno deliberately sabotaged the procedure and gave Abe the physical appearance of a black man (alias Matt Davis). This transformation led to some awkwardness, particularly in Jenkins' renewed romance with Songbird. Despite this, Abe became increasingly self-confident and positive after rejoining the team, even showing some inclination to leadership. When Hydra terrorist leader Baron Strucker secretly mind-controlled Gyrich into masterminding an anti-superhuman conspiracy, Gyrich targeted the Thunderbolts. Defeating and co-opting Gyrich's agent Scourge (Jack Monroe), the Thunderbolts thwarted the conspiracy and freed Gyrich's mind with the aid of the Redeemers, a new Thunderbolts-inspired super-team assembled by the government in cooperation with rogue covert agency the V-Battalion. These Redeemers included a new Beetle, a reformed Leila Davis wearing Jenkins' latest Beetle armor.

Hawkeye offered to go along with the CSA's cover-up of Gyrich's thwarted conspiracy in exchange for his fellow Thunderbolts being granted full federal pardons for their past crimes. The CSA agreed, but a vindictive Gyrich attached an extra condition, that Hawkeye be sent to prison for his own illegal vigilante activities as a Thunderbolt. Hawkeye

BEETLE MARK III ARMOR — Art by John Byrne

BEETLE MARK II ARMOR — Art by Gene Colan

BEETLE MARK IV ARMOR — Art by Mark Bagley

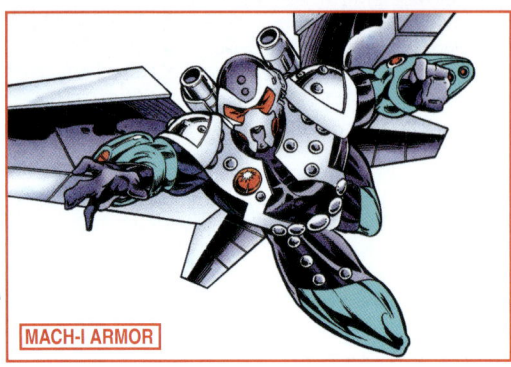

MACH-I ARMOR
Art by Mike Deodato

accepted these terms over the protests of his teammates and was taken into federal custody. Most of the remaining Thunderbolts were pardoned and released, though the terms of their pardons forbade them from further public use of special powers or costumed identities. Abe Jenkins and Melissa Gold lived together quietly in Burton Canyon, where Jenkins briefly worked at Kingman Electronics before he learned his boss and co-workers were running an illegal resale scam. After reluctantly helping the police arrest the Kingman staff, Abe was hired as tech support by the Burton Canyon Police Department. While Melissa was restless and dissatisfied in their new civilian life, Abe relished his new freedom and their fresh start.

When the supremely powerful Graviton sought to conquer the world and slaughtered most of the Redeemers (including the new Beetle), Abe and Melissa reluctantly teamed with several other ex-Thunderbolts to stop him. Wearing a new flight suit designed and built by the V-Battalion, Jenkins went into action as MACH-3, helping the team defeat Graviton and thwart a related alien invasion by the P'tah. In the process, all the Thunderbolts present except for Songbird were seemingly destroyed in an implosion, but were actually hurled to the alternate world Counter-Earth, recently created by Franklin Richards. The Thunderbolts took it upon themselves to rebuild the disaster-ravaged Counter-Earth, becoming its leading heroes. Despite this success, MACH-3 became increasingly sullen, solitary and moody.

The Thunderbolts ultimately saved Counter-Earth from an all-consuming void, but found themselves hurled back to their native Earth as a result. Once there, Abe was briefly reunited with Songbird, but their happiness proved short-lived when he realized the source of his recent depression. He had come to regard his covert release from jail as cheating, so he resolved to return to prison and serve out the remainder of his sentence. New Thunderbolts recruit Harrier (Donald Clendenon), inspired by Abe's example, decided to join him in returning to Seagate Prison. As a going-away present, a contrite Fixer gave Abe the means to undo the cosmetic alterations of his appearance.

Restored to his original physical appearance, Abe was transferred to Parsons Minimum Security Prison, where he corresponded with Songbird and conducted himself as a model prisoner. Worried by the supposedly reformed Zemo's resumption of Thunderbolts leadership, Abe kept the Avengers informed of Thunderbolts activities. Neither Jenkins nor Songbird realized that the Avengers were concealing this information from Hawkeye (who had recently rejoined their ranks) since they felt he could not be objective regarding the Thunderbolts. Mistrust and misinformation between the two teams inevitably led to an Avengers-Thunderbolts clash, during which Moonstone became a power-mad menace and Jenkins summoned Jolt from Counter-Earth to help defuse the crisis. The world was saved, but Zemo's Thunderbolts broke up. Granted early parole as a reward for his assistance, Jenkins resolved to rebuild the Thunderbolts, hoping to offer others the same chance at redemption he was given. Jenkins secured funding for his new team from Baron Strucker, who had little confidence in Jenkins and secretly expected the group to serve as expendable cannon fodder in a series of conflicts Strucker was orchestrating for his own purposes. With Strucker's secret backing, Jenkins set up a new headquarters in the Brooklyn Navy Yard complete with a "T-Bird" airship, further enhanced his flight suit in a new guise as MACH-4, and recruited Songbird, Atlas, Blizzard, Speed Demon, Joystick, Radioactive Man and Photon (Genis-Vell) to serve under him as the new Thunderbolts. Jenkins' probation officer, government super-agent Warbird (Carol Danvers), supervised the group's progress on behalf of the authorities. Meanwhile, Baron Zemo was covertly monitoring and manipulating the Thunderbolts with the aid of his secret ally Songbird, having convinced her via visions of the future that the world's safety depended on his plans for the Thunderbolts. Zemo and Songbird also began a secret romance, at least partially explaining why Songbird seemed uninterested in rekindling her old relationship with Abe now that they were back together.

Jenkins' new team won victories over Fathom Five, the Wrecking Crew and the Great Game, and even became popular celebrities after saving Manhattan from a Hydra attack led by Strucker, who escaped and cut his ties with Jenkins; but the team in general and Songbird in particular lost faith in MACH-4 after learning Strucker had been funding the group, and Songbird quit. His confidence waning, and increasingly uncomfortable with the moral compromises required to keep the team running (such as sanctioning Speed Demon's use of theft to fund the group and overlooking Radioactive Man's apparent slaughter of At'La'Tique terrorists), Jenkins began to falter as Thunderbolts leader. When MACH-4 was gravely wounded by the Swordsman (Andreas Strucker) during the team's conflict with the Purple Man, Songbird stepped in to lead the Thunderbolts to victory. More of a natural leader than Abe, she quickly took command of the team altogether, and a recovering Abe quit the group. MACH-4 soon joined an alliance of ex-Thunderbolts led by Baron Zemo, who convinced Jenkins and the others that their combined efforts were needed to save the world from looming threats. Zemo's agenda soon pitted them against Songbird's Thunderbolts when the two teams fought over the fate of Photon, who had become a cosmic menace and ultimately had to be eliminated. The two groups then merged into an expanded Thunderbolts team jointly led by Zemo and Songbird, though Jenkins and most

MACH-II ARMOR
Art by Mark Bagley

MACH-III ARMOR
Art by Chris Batista

of his teammates initially remained unaware of how Zemo and Songbird had secretly been partners all along.

When the federal Superhuman Registration Act (SHRA) passed, MACH-4 registered with the government's new Initiative program alongside the rest of the Thunderbolts; the team fought anti-SHRA rebels and apprehended super-criminals such as the Eel (Edward Lavell), the new Porcupine and a trio of new Beetles, college students who had stolen three different models of Abe's Beetle armor from CSA storage. Most of these captured criminals were briefly pressed into service as part of an expanded Thunderbolts army, with the new Beetles working together under MACH-4's direction for a time. When Zemo and the cosmic gamesman Grandmaster vied for control of the Wellspring of Power (this event being the Earth-shaking menace Zemo had foreseen), the Thunderbolts battled Grandmaster's forces, defeating his Squadron Sinister and seemingly killing the Grandmaster himself, but the tremendous energies unleashed during Zemo's battle with Grandmaster wrecked Abe's MACH-4 flight suit. In the end, the Wellspring was safely sealed off, but Zemo was lost in its vortex, multiple Thunderbolts were de-powered or disabled, and the expanded Thunderbolts army broke up as many of its conscripts fled. With the Thunderbolts in disarray, the CSA took charge of the group, repurposing them as CSA-backed special marshals dedicated to capturing unregistered super heroes. At the same time, CSA official Dallas Riordan hired Jenkins and the Fixer away from the team to work directly for the CSA as specialized troubleshooters. Bidding Songbird a fond farewell, Abe started over with a clean slate yet again.

NOTE: *The MACH-4 seen during pro-SHRA forces' final battle with the "Secret Avengers" shortly after Abe's retirement was actually one of several interactive, holographic hard-light audio-visual projections created during that battle by the Fixer, who was trying to sow confusion and intimidation by creating the illusion of greater numbers on the SHRA side.*

HEIGHT: 5'11" **EYES:** Brown
WEIGHT: 175 lbs. **HAIR:** Brown

ABILITIES/ACCESSORIES: Abner Jenkins is a gifted mechanical engineer and inventor, a talented planner and organizer, a capable tactician, a natural aircraft pilot, and an experienced unarmed combatant. He studied the Avengers' files extensively during a period when the Thunderbolts had access to that information. His MACH-1 flight suit was originally designed and built by Fixer (Norbert Ebersol) with Jenkins' assistance, loosely based on Jenkins' Beetle armor technology. The upgraded MACH-2 version was another Ebersol/Jenkins collaboration, while the further upgraded MACH-3 version was designed and built by the V-Battalion, then further modified by Ebersol. The MACH-4 flight suit was developed by Jenkins incorporating technology from all of the past MACH models, though he sometimes had difficulty maintaining the suit given its complexity, expense and the fact that much of its design did not originate with him.

The MACH-4 flight suit is designed to function as a form-fitting fighter plane in terms of its flight speed and offensive firepower, giving Jenkins the capabilities of a man-sized military aircraft and beyond. The suit flies by means of a winged jet pack harness, has a top speed sufficient to achieve orbital velocity, and can operate in the vacuum of space for limited periods thanks in part to an internal air supply. The MACH-4 is also submersible and can function underwater. The suit steers by line-of-sight, turning in whichever direction the wearer moves his head, but an onboard flight computer can perform more complex piloting tasks or engage a form of autopilot if need be. Other suit systems are controlled via cybernetic links in the helmet. MACH-4's onboard computer can access other computers, tap into and control the avionics systems of other aircraft, download data from external sources, and digitally transmit information. MACH-4 has an extensive communications array, as well as reconnaissance and surveillance systems such as a magnetic resonance imaging array. The suit can scramble external tracking systems and emit a signal that replicates its surrounding environment, creating a "chameleon" effect that makes the suit seemingly blend into any area being electronically scanned. The suit's audio feed grants its wearer greatly enhanced hearing, its enhanced vision enables clear perception of targets up to six miles away, and its spectral analysis systems allow the wearer to perceive and scan targets based on infrared readings, biothermal signatures, geothermic emissions and comparative topography. The suit can release and plant tracking devices for long-range or long-term surveillance. MACH-4 can also release remotely controlled, hovering miniature probes capable of scanning a target area and reporting back to the user.

The MACH-4 suit enhances its wearer's physical strength (lifting up to 5 tons) and offers greatly enhanced durability, reportedly sufficient to withstand even the heat and radiation of a nuclear blast, though it seems more vulnerable to physical penetration than to energy-based attacks. The suit houses various weapons such as gas bombs, heat-seeking missiles, machine guns (loaded with standard ammunition or rubber "mercy" bullets), concussion blasters, electrical blasters, electromagnetic pulse grenades, laser blasters and target-locked, camera-guided missiles. The MACH-4 houses and can discharge up to four fire-retardant foam charges, and its exterior has a non-stick coating designed to foil adhesives such as Spider-Man's webbing. The suit can build up additional reserves of power through ongoing absorption of solar energy.

As the Beetle, Jenkins wore body armor that enhanced his strength and durability; his original armor featured a broadcast power system that remotely transmitted energy to the Beetle's helmet from a larger generator in another location, somehow increasing Jenkins' own physical strength to superhuman levels via these energy transmissions, but this process placed a dangerous physical strain on Jenkins and he soon abandoned it, opting instead to build strength-enhancing mechanical devices into the later versions of his Beetle armor. The armor's gloves had suction-grip fingers, and later-model gloves could release electrostatic energy discharges. The early Beetle armors employed huge, bulky metallic wings that could only be operated through use of the wearer's superhuman strength; these wings could also be used as shields, battering weapons and digging devices. Later-model Beetle armors housed extendable ultra-tough mylar wings, which allowed the wearer to fly by mimicking the motions of an actual beetle's wings. Later versions of the Beetle armor had a constantly replenishing power supply that utilized microwaves at many prevalent frequencies, and an internal mini-computer that fed tactical data to the heads-up displays (HUD) in the armor's helmet. The tank-like CSA version of the armor, far more massive than all previous models, could be operated by remote control or by a person encased within the armor. Far stronger and more durable than previous Beetle armors, it could emit a jamming field to scramble surveillance systems. Its retractable wings were composed of molecule-thin gravitonic spatial distortions instead of mylar and could be used as offensive weapons, elongating to great lengths and shearing through most substances, including metals. Its helmet contained retractable antennae that could release a tremendous electrostatic charge. Like older Beetle armors, its gloves featured suction tips and electrical discharges, but the fingertips could also release lengths of cable to entangle or restrain opponents, and its middle left fingertip housed a laser torch suitable for welding. The armor's rear torso, arms and gauntlets also housed at least seven retractable cannons housing various conventional and exotic armaments.

POWER GRID	1	2	3	4	5	6	7
INTELLIGENCE							
STRENGTH							
SPEED							
DURABILITY							
ENERGY PROJECTION							
FIGHTING SKILLS							

MACHINE MAN

REAL NAME: X-51
ALIASES: Aaron Stack, Jack Kubrick, Sir MacHinery, Mr. Machine
IDENTITY: Known to US government
OCCUPATION: Adventurer, former insurance investigator
CITIZENSHIP: Inapplicable
PLACE OF BIRTH: Broadhurst Center for the Advancement of Mechanized Research, Central City, California
KNOWN RELATIVES: Abel Stack (creator, "father," deceased), XERO ("brother," destroyed), X-50 ("brother" destroyed), 49 other X series robots presumed destroyed
GROUP AFFILIATION: ARMOR, Initiative; formerly Operation: Lightning Storm; Nextwave, Avengers, Queen's Vengeance, Heavy Metal
EDUCATION: Self-taught with vast memory banks of knowledge
FIRST APPEARANCE: 2001: A Space Odyssey #8 (1977)

HISTORY: While working for the Broadhurst Center, a California-based laboratory specializing in advanced mechanized research, Dr. Abel Stack developed microprocessors that allowed computers to experience human emotions. Initially, Stack tested his invention as part of a computer he dubbed the Xeno-Engramatic Robot Organism (XERO). Upon learning of Stack's breakthroughs, Dr. Oliver Broadhurst handed XERO over to the US Department of Defense to assess its military value. The work caught the attention of Colonel Simon Joseph "Kragg" Kragowski, who ordered that the technology be adapted for use in combat-ready humanoid robots. Under Stack's supervision, the Broadhurst Center built dozens of robots, but their behavior was erratic and they developed psychological problems such as depression, schizophrenia, delusions and homicidal tendencies. The most malevolent of these robots, X-29, attempted to lead the robots against their creators, but was stopped by a military intervention during which Kragg was wounded and lost his left eye. Each of the remaining robots was subsequently fitted with a remote detonator to destroy them if they became a threat.

Stack theorized the psychological problems were due to the robots being unable to reconcile their human emotions with their mechanical appearance and lack of personal relationships. Believing the solution was to treat the robots as real human beings, he crafted a face for model X-50 and attempted to offer it genuine friendship. Although this attempt at averting the robot's psychological breakdown was a limited success, X-50 was destroyed while fighting alongside the X-Men. Buoyed by this progress, Dr. Stack brought his final robot home and raised it as his son. Naming X-51 "Aaron," Dr. Stack encouraged the robot to consider himself human.

Meanwhile, Broadhurst was less successful in overcoming the robots' psychological instability. When model X-35 became psychotic and went berserk, Broadhurst shut down the project. Knowing Broadhurst was about to activate the remote detonators, Stack removed the explosive device from X-51. Although the robot escaped the blast, Stack was killed. Now calling himself Aaron Stack, X-51 interacted with the world outside his creator's home for the first time, but was quickly captured by Kragg's men. On their first meeting, X-51 persuaded Broadhurst he was stable and posed no threat to the public. Broadhurst allowed X-51 to go free, but activated a homing beacon in the robot so Kragg could find him.

Disguising himself as human, Aaron Stack moved to Central City, California and briefly took the super hero alias "Mr. Machine," before settling on the name "Machine Man." Within his first few months in the city, he encountered the Brotherhood of Hades, a cult led by a computer. This led Aaron to understand that some machines do not share his affinity and affection for humanity. Aaron befriended and became roommates with psychologist Dr. Peter Spaulding. He faced another rogue machine when Ten-For, a member of the extraterrestrial machine species the Autocron, summoned his invasion force to Earth, and he used Ten-For's massive payload to destroy the Autocron fleet.

Machine Man's public battle with Ten-For unnerved locals, but Kragg was convinced of Machine Man's benevolence, and while the courts could not determine how to treat Machine Man, they left him in Spaulding's custody until a decision could be reached. Senator Miles Ralph Brickman seized upon the public's distrust of Machine Man to run a smear campaign against the robot, hoping to bolster his political career. News of Machine Man's existence attracted the criminal Corporation, who kidnapped Peter to force Machine Man to turn himself over to their scientists so they could replicate him. Machine Man rescued Peter from the Corporation, and later evaded capture by their operative Konik. Machine Man eventually helped shut down the Corporation on the West Coast, but not before they tricked the Hulk into attacking and badly damaging him.

Peter brought Machine Man back to Dr. Broadhurst, who removed the bulk of Machine Man's weaponry, which was overloading his systems. With Peter's help, he finally established an identity he could use to move amongst humanity unnoticed. As Aaron Stack, he became an insurance investigator for Delmar Insurance. Only his employer, Byron Benjamin, knew his true identity, while his co-workers Brock Jones, Pamela Quinn, Maggie Jones, and Edward Harris remained unaware. While at Delmar, Machine Man fought the Binary Bug, who attempted to destroy the company because Benjamin had fired him, but Bug died while fighting Machine Man. He also faced Kublai Khan, a wealthy Delmar client who attempted to transfer his consciousness into Machine Man's body

Art by Stuart Immonen with Steve Ditko (inset)

to stave off death; Ion, a scientist transformed into ion gas; and the fraudulent mystic Baron Brimstone and his Satan Squad. Machine Man's greatest threat was Madam Menace, actually Sunset Bain, the head of Baintronics, who sought to dismantle him for study and reconstruction. Machine Man also befriended mechanic Wilbur "Gears" Garvin, who helped keep Machine Man operational, although robotics were well out of his league.

Senator Brickman tricked Canada's Department H into considering Machine Man a threat, resulting in Alpha Flight being sent to the US to attack the robot. Department H's Agent K eventually learned that they had been tricked, and found evidence that Brickman was guilty of a plot to rig elections, destroying his career. However, Machine Man's face was partially melted in his clash with Alpha Flight.

Fearing that his human face was what kept him sane while his fellow robots went mad, Machine Man gave the face to Gears for repairs. He battled the mercenary Jack O'Lantern (Jason Macendale) without his face, and took a leave of absence from Delmar until it was fully repaired. Shortly afterwards he met the female robot Jocasta, who had been built to serve as the bride of Ultron, but had repeatedly resisted Ultron's will. When Ultron took control of her and forced her into reactivating him in a new body, Machine Man and the Thing joined with Jocasta to stop Ultron, during which Machine Man and Jocasta fell in love. When Jocasta was destroyed battling Ultron, Machine Man destroyed Ultron by reaching down his throat and tearing out his circuitry. Gears collected Jocasta's remains, hoping to reactivate her.

Machine Man allied himself with the other robots gathered by the dangerous Super-Adaptoid to serve in his group Heavy Metal, partially because the Super-Adaptoid offered to repair Jocasta, but also with the intention of betraying him when he learned his plans. Machine Man teamed with the Avengers against the Super-Adaptoid in the end. Machine Man again aided the Avengers in their battle against Terminus as the world-destroying creature recreated itself in a variety of "Termini" across the globe, during which Peter was seemingly slain by the Termini, while Jocasta's remains fell into the custody of Sunset Bain. For his aid, the Avengers's west coast division awarded him reserve membership. He joined other reserves against the android Human Torch's old foe, the Hyena, and also participated in the mass Avengers gathering to oppose the sorceress Morgan Le Fay, but he ultimately declined to join the team, preferring to study humans as Aaron Stack. Machine Man was briefly taken over by the Sentinel Bastion, who corrupted his programming with Sentinel codes. The mutant hero Cable telepathically contacted Machine Man and helped him overcome the programming, and it was seemingly purged from his systems.

Machine Man was kidnapped by SHIELD, who used his programs to help operate their new Deathlok (Jack Truman). While he was aboard the SHIELD Helicarrier, the vehicle was taken over by the Red Skull (Johann Shmidt), using the mutant-extraterrestrial entity Douglock to enslave SHIELD agents. Machine Man helped Nick Fury and the X-Men evacuate the Helicarrier, but he was strained to the breaking point while trying to launch himself from the Helicarrier to the ground, and he was destroyed. A fail-safe program left behind by Bastion activated when Machine Man was deactivated, and Sentinel programming reconstructed his body using nanotechnology. Machine Man's personality entered a Life Model Decoy (LMD) of federal agent Jack Kubrick. Believing himself to be Kubrick, he set out to find Machine Man, but discovered the Brotherhood of Mutants was also in pursuit. Machine Man's memory returned when he was reunited with his body, but he discovered that he could barely control his anti-mutant Sentinel programming, and swiftly defeated the Brotherhood.

When government agent Henry Gyrich and industrialist Sebastian Shaw arrived on the scene, Machine Man's sensors identified Shaw as a mutant, and he attacked him. Not knowing Shaw was a mutant, Gyrich believed that Machine Man had gone insane, and prepared defenses against him. Shaw, meanwhile, sought to destroy Machine Man before he could share his secret. Gyrich uncovered the long-dormant XERO and reactivated it to track Machine Man's movements. However, XERO's human emotions had caused it to become vengeful toward humanity for the years of neglect it had suffered, and it allowed Machine Man to escape, then uploaded itself into a government satellite. When Machine Man went to the Avengers for help with his condition, his Sentinel programming forced him to attack Avengers Justice and Firestar. The Vision ("Victor Shade") tried to help Machine Man overcome the Sentinel program by linking with him, but Machine Man drove him out to prevent the program from corrupting the Vision as well. Machine Man tried to exile himself from Earth until he solved his problem, but was drawn back when Shaw hired the Japanese hero Otomo to kidnap Peter Spaulding. Machine Man rescued Peter, who suggested that Machine Man turn to Charles Xavier.

When he attempted to contact Xavier for assistance, Machine Man's Sentinel programs downloaded the Xavier Protocols from Xavier's computers, giving him all of Xavier's data on destroying the X-Men. When Shaw sent a squad of his Sentinels to destroy Machine Man, the conflict drew in the X-Men, whom Machine Man fought. Briefly regaining control of himself, Machine Man destroyed his body to end the threat of the Sentinel program, after which he was reconstructed by the nanites and ridded of his Sentinel programming. Machine Man returned to Central City and became involved in a war between the Road Warriors and Blood Brothers motorcycle gangs. Siding with the Blood Brothers, Machine Man discovered that the Road Warriors had obtained advanced Celestial technology from an unknown benefactor. After communicating with the Celestials himself, Machine Man learned that XERO had been found by Advanced Idea Mechanics (AIM) and built itself a body, intending to use AIM's resources to conquer the Earth for artificial life. Machine Man led the Blood Brothers in an attack on AIM and shut down XERO himself.

Machine Man then entered the Monolith, the Celestials' communication device, and journeyed into the stars with the Celestials to an unknown purpose. But after a year of traveling through space, Machine Man was rejected by the Celestials and banished from their presence. Given only an old, dilapidated shuttle, it took Machine Man months to return to Earth.

Still wounded by the experience of his Sentinel reprogramming, reeling from the humiliation of the Celestials' rejection and suffering from prolonged isolation, Machine Man found his grasp on sanity becoming more tenuous. Upon his return to Earth, Machine Man joined Nextwave

Art by Joe Bennett

squad, an elite anti-terrorism team formed by the Highest Anti-Terrorism Effort (HATE), a subsidiary of the Beyond Corporation. Machine Man's sanity continued to deteriorate as he took up self-destructive behaviors such as alcohol abuse. Machine Man began to embrace his artificial nature and proclaimed himself superior to humans, who he would insult by calling them "Fleshy Ones." Refusing to answer to "Machine Man," he insisted on being addressed as "Aaron Stack" and soon alienated himself from the team's human members. When his teammate Tabitha Smith stole the Beyond Corporation's marketing plan, Nextwave discovered that it used to be the terrorist organization SILENT and had been using HATE to test unusual weapons of mass destruction (UWMDs) on the American public in exchange for payment and political power. Stack and his Nextwave teammates rebelled, stealing HATE's experimental Shockwave Rider aircraft and using the marketing plan to uncover the Beyond Corporation's illegal activities.

They traveled to an excavation site in Abcess, North Dakota, where Beyond unleashed a Fin Fang Foom clone, which Stack entered and disabled from the inside. The team next traveled to Sink City, Illinois, where corrupt police officer Mac Mangel was infected by Beyond's Ultra Samurai seed, a parasite that transforms its host into a giant robot warrior. After defeating Mangel and destroying the parasite, Nextwave traveled to Beyond's War Garden, an enormous field where Beyond grew its plant-based Human Resources robotic agents. But before the War Garden could be destroyed, Nextwave was attacked by HATE Director General Dirk Anger aboard the Aeromarine, HATE's flying headquarters. As the other Nextwave members engaged HATE's arsenal, Stack infiltrated Dirk Anger's private quarters and obtained a dress of great sentimental value to Anger, forcing Anger to retreat in exchange for the dress' safe return. Shortly thereafter, Rorkannu of the Dank Dimension sold several hundred Mindless Ones to the Beyond Corporation. The Nextwave squad was forced to intervene and pummel Rorkannu into submission. Nextwave's meddling drew the attention of Beyond Corporation CEO, the robotic Number None. In a titanic battle to defeat the terrorist organization, Aaron Stack and his teammates defeated dozens of super-villains, including Charlie America, the Incredible Bulk, Forbush Man, Giant Sam, the Vestry, the Surgery, a baby MODOK, a dozen chimpanzee Wolverines and a Devil Dinosaur duplicate. The Nextwave squad disbanded after their victory and Stack created a robot psychiatrist to help him deal with his erratic behavior and his alcoholism. Unfortunately, before his treatment could be concluded, he was attacked by Madame Menace, who destroyed his psychiatrist.

Bribed by Tony Stark into joining the Initiative, Machine Man became part of the Lightning Storm team, with whom he helped defeat the Puppet Master, foil a Brood invasion and ferret out Skrull infiltrators. He developed a tenuous relationship with his teammates Sleepwalker, Ms. Marvel (Carol Danvers), Araña and Agent Sum, but Machine Man's erratic behavior and apparent lack of empathy for human suffering ended up putting him at odds with other heroes. After the Lightning Storm team was disbanded, Stack was recruited by the top-secret agency ARMOR, who sent him to prevent a zombie plague from invading Earth-616. Reunited with Jocasta, Stack was sent to Earth-2149 to seek a cure for the zombie plague. The combination of witnessing the horrors of the zombie universe and the company of Jocasta has begun to bring out the best in Stack and to uncover the hero within.

HEIGHT: 6'
WEIGHT: 850 lbs.
EYES: Red
HAIR: Black (artificial)

ABILITIES/ACCESSORIES: In all configurations, Machine Man's titanium alloy body grants him superhuman strength (lifting up to 10 tons), speed, endurance and durability. His cybernetic brain grants him superhuman analytical and calculation capabilities, and a 3.22 terabyte memory capacity.

As an agent of HATE, Machine Man's equipment was upgraded. His body now contains a diverse array of weaponry and tools, including an extraordinary number of chainsaws. His current configuration appears more human than his original body, but is similar in abilities to those envisioned by Dr. Stack. His head has been shown to be compatible with SHIELD Life Model Decoy bodies. In his current configuration, Machine Man is like a walking Swiss Army Knife with a tool or weapon for every occasion.

In his original configuration, Machine Man's systems included a voice scrambler; limbs that could be controlled by the head even when separated from his body; tank treads concealed in his arms; a projector linked through his eyes; suction cups concealed in his hands; a teleportation device that utilized dimensional transfer principles; a wire cable that could be fired from his chest; high-tension springs, magnetic rays, and a skateboard concealed in his feet; and a shock blaster, a neural tapper, an ice generator, and a flame thrower in his fingers' weapons systems. All of these devices were removed when Dr. Broadhurst repaired him.

In his redesigned configuration, Machine Man possessed flight through anti-gravity generators, telescopic and infrared vision, telescoping limbs, and devices in his fingers that included a gas chromatograph, laser interferometer, micro-pulse radar, audiometer, seismometer, gravity-wave detector, pulse-code modulator, standard computer input/outputs, radio beacon, all-wave transceiver, laser cutting torch, and a .357 Magnum pistol. By entering into a low power mode, Machine Man could conserve energy. While in his sleep mode, he would even experience dreams.

After being corrupted by Sentinel programming, Machine Man's body had a multitude of nannites that could perform automatic repairs on his body and adapt his systems to meet specific threats. He could reshape his form into other appearances, including the form of Aaron Stack. Abilities that his body demonstrated in this state included an energy shield, plasma energy projectors, an artificial tornado generator, the ability to increase gravimetric force on opponents, computer jacks, thrusters in his feet, and teleportation. Machine Man could not control the Sentinel program in the presence of mutants, whom he was forced to attack.

In every configuration, Machine Man demonstrates an ability at kit-bashing himself to meet his needs, including jury-rigging himself into a rocket, traveling into space, traveling via electrical rail, and attaching wheels for travel on roads.

Art by Joe Bennett & Steve Ditko

POWER GRID	1	2	3	4	5	6	7
INTELLIGENCE				■			
STRENGTH				■			
SPEED		■					
DURABILITY					■		
ENERGY PROJECTION			■				
FIGHTING SKILLS		■					

*YELLOW BARS INDICATE ORIGINAL FORM RATINGS

MACHINE TEEN

HISTORY: Years ago, Dr. Aaron Isaacs, one of the nation's leading robotics programmers and engineers, was on the verge of a major breakthrough in artificial intelligence while working in the Robotics Development Division of an enigmatic corporation. His employer, Holden Radcliffe, wanted to use Isaacs' research, known as Project: ADAM (Autonomously Decisive Automated Mechanism), to create a new generation of obedient, emotionless, and disposable soldiers. When Isaacs learned of Radcliffe's true intentions, he salvaged the datacore that housed his artificial intelligence program and destroyed the rest of his research, living on the run thereafter.

Changing his name to "Ike Aaronson," Isaacs eventually moved to a quiet suburb where he established Aaronson Electronics so he could continue his experiments in safety. When local teenager J.T. Hunt was hired as a part-time assistant at Aaronson Electronics, he stumbled across the human-like metal body that Isaacs had created to house the ADAM datacore. Confessing what he had seen to Isaacs, Hunt was invited to help the scientist finish his project. Naming the adolescent-like mechanism "Adam," Isaacs programmed it with false memories (including the death of his mother), so that Adam would feel like he had a normal childhood with Isaacs as his father. Adam enrolled at West Tech High School as a transfer student where he quickly became best friends with Hunt and excelled at both academics and athletics.

Adam began suffering from frequent debilitating "seizures" every time he did anything that exceeded the boundaries of standard human activity or noticed something about himself that he could not rationalize as normal. These "seizures" were actually logic loops in his programming, glitches triggered by miscommunications and contradictions between his body and mind. Whenever Adam suffered from one of these glitches, Isaacs would reboot him and purge all data pertaining to the event that triggered the glitch so that Adam retained no memory of them. After repeated seizures, Isaacs decided to tell Adam the truth about his nature and origins, which Adam did not take well. Soon after, Radcliffe's agents tracked down and abducted Adam, Isaacs, Hunt, and Carly Whitmere (Adam's girlfriend). Taken to an abandoned warehouse, Isaacs, Hunt, and Whitmere were imprisoned while Radcliffe's scientists attempted to reprogram Adam into an obedient robotic soldier. The programming failed due to the security systems Isaacs programmed into the datacore and Adam turned on Radcliffe's men. Isaacs and Adam's friends escaped with the datacore while Adam sacrificed his body to detonate Radcliffe's warehouse base. Isaacs eventually built a new body for Adam and they relocated to a new town where Adam enrolled at Edison Senior High School.

NOTE: When the mutant Scarlet Witch used her reality-warping powers to transform Earth into a mutant-dominated society (Earth-58163), ADAM and Isaacs worked with AIM to overthrow Australia's fascist mutant government.

REAL NAME: ADAM (Autonomously Decisive Automated Mechanism)
ALIASES: Adam Aaronson
IDENTITY: Secret
OCCUPATION: Student
CITIZENSHIP: Inapplicable
PLACE OF CREATION: Unrevealed
KNOWN RELATIVES: Dr. Aaron Isaacs (creator)
GROUP AFFILIATION: None
EDUCATION: High school student
FIRST APPEARANCE: Machine Teen #1 (2005)

HEIGHT: 5'8"
WEIGHT: 225 lbs.
EYES: Blue
HAIR: Blond

ABILITIES/ACCESSORIES: Machine Teen is superhumanly strong (lifting 1 ton) and durable. His artificial intelligence simulates a keen analytical mind and his body can interface with software and other pieces of hardware. Machine Teen's electronic system renders him vulnerable to devices which disrupt electronics, such as amplified static shock generators, which can instantly disable him. Machine Teen's artificial intelligence is housed within the datacore installed in his chest cavity. Dr. Isaacs programmed security systems into the datacore and encrypted the datastream to prevent others from hacking into Machine Teen's system and altering his programming. To prevent others from removing Machine Teen's datacore, Dr. Isaacs programmed an automatic self-destruct sequence that is triggered by unauthorized removal of the datacore.

POWER GRID	1	2	3	4	5	6	7
INTELLIGENCE			■				
STRENGTH				■			
SPEED		■					
DURABILITY				■			
ENERGY PROJECTION	■						
FIGHTING SKILLS		■					

Art by Mike Hawthorne

MACHINESMITH

REAL NAME: Samuel Saxon
ALIASES: Starr Saxon, Mr. Fear, Smith
IDENTITY: No dual identity
OCCUPATION: Criminal, cybernetics expert, terrorist
CITIZENSHIP: USA
PLACE OF BIRTH: Queens, New York City, New York
KNOWN RELATIVES: Unidentified father, unidentified mother (deceased)
GROUP AFFILIATION: Formerly Masters of Evil, Skeleton Crew, Demi-Men
EDUCATION: High school dropout, extensive self-education
FIRST APPEARANCE: (Saxon) Daredevil #49 (1969); (Mr. Fear) Daredevil #54 (1969); (Machinesmith) Marvel Two-in-One #47 (1979)

HISTORY: At age fourteen, Samuel Saxon discovered one of Dr. Doom's robots abandoned in a subway tunnel, and took it piece by piece to his father's garage, where for months he studied its components until mastering its operating principles and building his own robot from scratch.

STARR SAXON

Following his disapproving mother's death in an alleged laboratory accident, he used the insurance money to — over a few years — entertain himself by building a series of increasingly advanced robots and androids. When his funds ran low, he sent his android Demi-Men, led by an android duplicate of Magneto, to steal money while posing as mutant terrorists in cooperation with Mesmero. However, they were defeated by the X-Men, who did not learn that their main opponent had been an android until years later, when Magneto himself discovered the deception.

Still a novice at crime, the young Saxon was taken under the wing of the aged Tinkerer, another underworld genius. With the Tinkerer's assistance, Saxon obtained a contract from imprisoned gangster Biggie Benson to target Daredevil with a robot assassin, the Plastoid. Although unaware of his subject's identity as Matt Murdock, Saxon used person-specific "aromagraphs" to enable the Plastoid to track its target. The Plastoid confronted Murdock at his apartment and defeated him in a brief battle, only for its limited programming to force retreat when interrupted by passerby Willie Lincoln, a friend of Murdock's. Returning soon afterward, the Plastoid again fought Murdock, now in costume as Daredevil, in a battle that raged from Murdock's gym to the streets outside. When its memory banks were damaged, it ceased fighting and, with Daredevil in pursuit, returned to Saxon, who was enthusiastically contemplating a career in providing criminals with robot assassins so they could wipe each other out. When the pair arrived, Saxon, flustered by the hero's presence, erroneously reprogrammed the Plastoid to kill Benson himself, which it did in Benson's prison cell despite Daredevil's efforts at protection.

Saxon, furious at Daredevil's interference, traced his creation's earlier activities to Murdock's apartment and, his luck taking a better turn, discovered Murdock and Daredevil were the same man. Craving revenge, he abducted Murdock's girlfriend Karen Page and held her in Murdock's apartment, then awaited the hero's arrival. Although revelling in his new active criminal role as he postured before Page, Saxon was taken by surprise by the Black Panther, seeking Daredevil on an unrelated matter. When Daredevil arrived soon afterward, Saxon fled both heroes but was captured, only to mock Daredevil's inability to prove any culpability on Saxon's part.

This taunting victory only increased Saxon's desire for action, and, offhandedly murdering the imprisoned Zoltan Drago, aka Mr. Fear, he usurped Drago's costumed identity. Claiming to be a reformed Drago, he offered thousands of dollars to charity if Daredevil would respond to his public challenge. Daredevil obliged, but Saxon's improved technology took him by surprise, and Saxon dealt him a demoralizing public defeat. Caught up in his own charade, the thrill-seeking Saxon, still as Mr. Fear, embarked on a crime spree but was soon confronted by a newly determined Daredevil, who, atop Saxon's flying platform, unmasked his enemy in a struggle that ended with Saxon's fall to his death, leaving the Mr. Fear identity to be stolen by others after him.

However, several of Saxon's robots, standing by in case they were needed and programmed to protect his existence at any cost, retrieved him and, unable to treat his injuries, downloaded his consciousness into a primitive robot body. Saxon, now called the Machinesmith, soon transferred his consciousness into a more humanlike body, although it bore little resemblance to his original form, and returned to crime, selling android operatives to various parties. Hired by the first incarnation of the Corporation to attack the Fantastic Four's Thing, he handled the job personally, employing mobsters to force the Yancy Street Gang, denizens of the Thing's old neighborhood, into his service. They lured the Thing to Yancy Street, where he was set upon by Machinesmith's robots. Aided by Corporation enemy Jack of Hearts, the Thing defeated Machinesmith's forces, and the Yancy Street Gang knocked out Machinesmith himself, who simply projected his consciousness into another robot body and continued his operations elsewhere. For the next few months he operated mostly behind the scenes, implanting false memories in his android

Art by Patrick Zircher with Barry Windsor-Smith & Paco Medina (insets)

Manipulator, who attacked the Beast and Captain America. He acquired the extraterrestrial android duplicate of Galactus' herald Air-Walker and, though unable to repair it, activated its self-repair circuits, resulting in its battle with Thor. His other android operatives included Norm, whom he entrusted to scientist Jonothon Cayre, and Ken, whom he sold to Mystique of the Brotherhood of Evil Mutants.

Eventually growing despondent over existence in a robot body programmed against self-destruction, Machinesmith reanimated the gigantic android Dragon Man and sent him, along with various android doppelgangers of super-villains he had used over the years, to attack Captain America and manipulate him into destroying Machinesmith's computers while his consciousness was within them, supposedly doing the job Machinesmith's programming would not allow him to do. Despite his plan, Machinesmith simply reactivated in yet another robot body, in which form he renounced his suicidal tendencies and embraced his condition. He declared mechanical life superior to humanity and presumably resumed his robot-supply business.

Months later, Machinesmith was offered a position as an exclusive operative by the Red Skull, himself in a newly obtained cloned body; always open to new challenges, he agreed. The Skull sent him to reactivate the Nazi robot Sleeper, immaterial since its defeat by Captain America years earlier. Again projecting his consciousness, Machinesmith possessed, repaired, and solidified the Sleeper, which the Avengers took into custody, unaware of his presence within. At Avengers HQ on Hydrobase, Machinesmith reactivated the Sleeper and several other confiscated robots — Super-Adaptoid, TESS-One, the Kree Sentry, and Awesome Android — to wreak havoc, taunting Captain America before escaping to serve the Skull during the Acts of Vengeance campaign against the Avengers. Machinesmith grew attached to the Sleeper, to whom he elaborated his history while repairing it, and, when assigned to the Skull's task force of field operatives, the Skeleton Crew, took to directing its actions in battle, as well as inhabiting its form himself if necessary.

When Magneto abducted the Red Skull to punish him for his war crimes, Machinesmith used his Magneto android, almost forgotten since its Demi-Men days, in an endeavor to lure the real mutant into action so that the Crew could track or capture him, but it was defeated by Captain America, and the Skeleton Crew ultimately located the Skull by other means. Shortly afterward, Machinesmith and his teammates Mother Night and Minister Blood mesmerized the Avengers' support staff into planting surveillance devices at Avengers Mansion, but the Vision discovered his operation and temporarily immobilized him, then foiled a last-ditch effort to use the staff as suicide bombers. When the Skull was again abducted, this time by the German heroes Schutz-Heiliggruppe, the Skeleton Crew was captured soon afterward, Blitzkrieger overloading Machinesmith's systems, but freed when Arnim Zola created artificial duplicates of the Avengers to take the villains into custody. Despite acquitting himself well during the encounter, Machinesmith decided that field action was not his forte, and the Skull allowed him to restrict his activities accordingly.

One of Machinesmith's bodies inhabited by an errant part of his program became an assistant to Iron Man during the events of the crisis called the Crossing, which led the Avengers to mistakenly believe that he had reformed. The true Machinesmith used his alliance with the Red Skull to analyze Captain America while he was in the Skull's custody, and downloaded all of the Captain's knowledge onto a "coin." With the coin, he framed Captain America for treason on the Skull's behalf, then tried to crash the SHIELD Helicarrier with the Argus anti-aircraft weapon, while simultaneously using one of his bodies to assassinate the USA's President. He was thwarted on all fronts by Captain America and Sharon Carter, and they recovered the coin.

Following this reminder that solo activity was not his strong suit, Machinesmith joined the most recent incarnation of the Masters of Evil, led by Justin Hammer's daughter, the Crimson Cowl, and commemorated the change with a new metallic-looking body. He and his teammates abducted the human-plant hybrid Blackheath to force him to activate a biological weapon left behind by the deceased Hammer; however, the weapon turned out to be a biological component that Hammer had implanted in all of his super-agents, and the Masters worked with Hawkeye's Thunderbolts to keep the Cowl from misusing the procedure. Machinesmith then went underground for months, creating a mechanical lair which he controlled via nanites. When Night Thrasher (Donyell Taylor) sent the New Warriors to fight Machinesmith, he confronted them in several of his latest robot bodies. Although seemingly rendered defunct when his lair was destroyed, his consciousness doubtlessly survived.

NOTE: While young Saxon later referred to his Doom-built robot as a "Servobot," its appearance is more consistent with a "Killer Robot," which Doom did not invent until years after Saxon's discovery, inferring time travel, presumably from Doom's own time platform.

Art by Kevin Maguire & Gene Colan

HEIGHT: Variable (customarily 6'1")
WEIGHT: Variable (customarily 295 lbs.)
EYES: Variable (customarily green, originally brown)
HAIR: Variable (customarily red (balding), originally brown)

ABILITIES/ACCESSORIES: Machinesmith is an exceptional genius in the fields of cybernetics and robotics, having vastly outstripped most experts in the fields despite being almost wholly self-taught. In his customary robot form, he possesses sufficient superhuman strength to lift 1 ton, as well as superhuman stamina, and reflexes; various duplicate versions of his robot form have been equipped with telescopic limbs, infrared vision, and other unique capabilities. Able to transfer his consciousness to any electronic system, even common household electrical wiring, he can inhabit a wide variety of robot bodies at will, sometimes several at once, and use their powers for his own purposes; while a member of the Skeleton Crew, he frequently inhabited the body of the Sleeper, which possessed even greater strength and endurance and could turn intangible and emit repulsor rays from its eye sockets. His most recent body, which has no human coloration, can project tentacles and instrumentation at will, as well as control mechanical devices from a distance.

MOIRA MacTAGGERT

REAL NAME: Moira Ann Kinross MacTaggert
ALIASES: No dual identity
IDENTITY: Publicly known
OCCUPATION: Geneticist
CITIZENSHIP: UK
PLACE OF BIRTH: Kinross Estate, Scotland, UK
KNOWN RELATIVES: Joseph MacTaggert (husband, deceased), Kevin MacTaggert (Proteus, son), Rahne Sinclair (Wolfsbane, foster daughter), Lord Kinross (father, deceased), Alasdhair Kinross (ancestor), Queen Elizabeth "Lilibet" Alexandra Mary Windsor II (distant relative), other distant relatives via Queen Elizabeth II
GROUP AFFILIATION: Formerly Muir Island X-Men; official medic to Excalibur
EDUCATION: Ph.D. in genetics
FIRST APPEARANCE: X-Men #96 (1976)

HISTORY: The daughter of a powerful Scottish nobleman, Moira Kinross won an Oxford scholarship, studying genetics. She fell in love with chauvinistic Royal Marines Commando Joseph MacTaggert, but broke up with him in favor of her classmate (and mutant telepath) Charles Xavier. They became engaged, but while Charles undertook military service, Joe convinced Moira to take him back. Breaking her engagement to Charles, she married Joe, but their marriage proved disastrous; while in New York City, Moira asked for a divorce. Joe beat and sexually assaulted her, hospitalizing her for a week and leaving her pregnant. From then on, Moira lived apart from her husband, although he refused to grant her a divorce; she kept the fact that he had a son secret from him for twenty years.

Moira forged a brilliant career as a leading geneticist, earning a Nobel Prize, and founded a Mutant Research Center on Scotland's Muir Island. When Moira's son Kevin manifested destructive mutant powers, feeding off human life energy to survive, she was unable to cure him, and she was forced to imprison him in a containment chamber that sustained him with energy fields. After helping to deliver Rahne Sinclair, whose mother died in childbirth, Moira's blood test showed the child had an anomalous DNA matrix. The fanatically religious Reverend Craig (secretly Rahne's father) had the child made a ward of the church but Moira would often arrange for Rahne to live with her. Renewing contact with Charles Xavier, Moira became Charles' silent partner in founding the Xavier Institute for Gifted Youngsters, a school for training mutants. Moira also helped Charles create the mutant detecting machine Cerebro. When the time-displaced Cable arrived in the modern era, Moira taught him English using his telepathy and introducing him to Charles. After Magneto (Max Eisenhardt) was reverted back to infancy by Alpha the Ultimate Mutant, he was placed in Moira's care, but Moira experimented on him, seeking to find a cure for her son, and altered Magneto's genetic code hoping to prevent him from reverting to his villainous ways when he grew older. When the troubled mutant Jamie Madrox refused Charles' offer of help, Moira encouraged him to become her special assistant.

Moira also gathered her own students, focusing on teaching them to cope with their newfound powers and providing a good education, rather than training them for super-heroics as Charles did his X-Men. Moira's students included Gabriel Summers (Kid Vulcan), Petra, Armando Munoz (Darwin), and Suzanne Chen (Sway). She and Charles had also approached a young Emma Frost (later the White Queen), but were rejected. When Xavier's X-Men went missing on Krakoa, Charles turned to Moira's team. Without the strict militaristic discipline of Charles' school, Moira's students were neither street-smart nor battle-ready. Moira was concerned about sending unprepared students into battle, but Charles persisted. Moira's fears proved correct. Her students were all seemingly killed during the mission and Charles was forced to suppress the memory of their existence from even his own students in order to keep them from going back on a suicidal rescue mission.

Charles asked Moira to come to his school to assist teaching his new students. Initially introduced to them as their new housekeeper, the X-Men soon learned her true profession. She forged a relationship with each of them, most notably Irish mutant Banshee (Sean Cassidy), starting a romance that would endure for the rest of her life. Moira alerted the X-Men to head to Muir Island when she lost contact with Jamie Madrox, who she had left to monitor the research facility. Eric the Red (Davan Shakari) and the brainwashed Havok and Polaris had attacked the facility, freeing Magneto and restoring him to adulthood. During the ensuing battle between X-Men and Magneto, Kevin's holding cell was breached; unaware of this Moira returned to Muir Island after the X-Men were later seemingly slain, accompanied by Phoenix (a cosmic entity then believed to be Jean Grey) and the no-longer brainwashed Havok and Polaris. Weeks later Kevin escaped from Muir Island; reunited with the X-Men, Moira pursued him as he possessed a string of people, leaving behind their burned out corpses as he blazed a trail across Scotland

Art by Jackson Guice with Trevor Hairsine (inset)

WHILE POSSESSED BY SHADOW KING
Art by Marc Silvestri

seeking his father. Now calling himself Proteus, he battled the X-Men in the Scottish highlands; seeing no alternative to stop his murder spree, Moira tried to slay him using a sniper rifle, but Proteus escaped when Cyclops prevented Moira taking the kill shot. Finding Joe in the capitol, Edinburgh, Kevin possessed him, then took Moira prisoner and terrorized the city, before seemingly being slain by the X-Man Colossus (Peter Rasputin). Moira's mourned for her son, but was able to take comfort in being reunited with Banshee, who, having been recently depowered, elected to leave the X-Men and join her on Muir Island; when he learned she was considering cloning Kevin, he convinced her not to. Later, not long after taking in the emotion-enhancing Amp (Michelle), Moira was amongst the X-Men's loved ones kidnapped by the assassin Arcade, but was soon rescued by Banshee and other reserve X-Men.

Moira rescued Rahne, now a teenager, from a mob pursuing her after Rahne's mutant powers had emerged. Seeking to give the girl a chance to better understand her powers, Moira encouraged Charles to open his doors to a later generation of New Mutants with Rahne eventually becoming one of the initial members. Soon after, Charles' body was usurped by an alien Brood Queen, and Moira assisted the Starjammers in transferring Charles' consciousness to a new, cloned body. Moira was also approached by Gabrielle Haller, another ex-girlfriend of Charles, to treat Charles' son, David Haller, whose psionic powers had emerged during a terrorist attack, the resultant trauma fracturing his psyche into multiple personalities each trying to gain control of David. Moira was later hypnotized by the anti-mutant robot Master Mold, who had her develop the Retribution Virus, designed to kill mutants by overloading their powers; however Moira subconsciously resisted his control, secretly also developing a cure. Noticing that Moira was acting strangely, Banshee alerted Cyclops, and with the Morlock leader Callisto's assistance, they freed Moira and defeated Master Mold; exposure to the virus also restored Banshee's lost powers.

Later, during a time when the X-Men were again believed dead, the cyborg Reavers attacked Muir Island. Moira and Banshee formed an impromptu X-Men team to defend the island, but after they repelled the attack Legion (David Haller) was possessed by Charles' old enemy, the Shadow King. Through him the Shadow King seized control of Moira and the other Muir Island residents. Meanwhile the terrorist organization AIM (Advanced Idea Mechanics) forced the mutant Piecemeal to absorb Proteus' scattered energies, reviving him. X-Force and the New Warriors contacted Moira, and unwilling to reveal his presence, the Shadow King loosened his control enough to let the Muir Island X-Men assist in confronting Proteus in Edinburgh. Moira's entreaties helped convince Proteus he would not find happiness in the world he was in, and despondent, he bid her goodbye and, saying he was leaving for someplace better, disappeared. Though Moira believed he had destroyed himself, it later emerged that he had departed for the stars. Manipulated by the Shadow King, Moira's personality changed, becoming more reckless in her judgment and frequently lashing out. Learning of the Shadow King's actions, Charles, the X-Men and X-Factor battled him and freed Moira and his other pawns.

Having discovered how Moira tried to manipulate his personality while he was under her care years earlier, Magneto kidnapped her and demanded that she use the same techniques to alter the captured X-Men. Moira pretended to put the X-Men under Magneto's control, but once they used their mutant powers the effects of her changes were negated, and during the subsequent battle with the X-Men, when Magneto was betrayed by his follower Fabian Cortez, Moira escaped. Moira was captured by Cortez a few years later, when he sought her knowledge to brainwash new followers to his cause. Neophyte, one of the newest Acolytes, discovered that Cortez had been trying to murder Magneto and he led the X-Men to their location in order to rescue Moira. Ashamed of being manipulated by both Magneto and Cortez, Moira left the X-Men and went to the mutant nation Genosha to study the mutant-killing Legacy Virus (apparently unrelated to Moira's Retribution Virus), working closely with Beast (Hank McCoy) and Forge in seeking a cure. A short time later, the British super-team Excalibur took up residence on Muir Island, soon defending Moira from Siena Blaze, who had been sent by Mr. Sinister to steal Proteus' DNA. While Excalibur was in residence, Moira discovered she had contracted the Legacy Virus, becoming the first infected human, possibly a result of her prolonged exposure to infected mutants. Seeking to weaponize the virus so it would only affect non-mutants, the Brotherhood of Mutants assaulted the Muir Isle facility, and Brotherhood member Mystique impersonated Moira and raided her research. Combining her own knowledge with Moira's, Mystique reasoned how to weaponize the virus. The X-Man Rogue then confronted Mystique and in the ensuing conflict, Mystique was stabbed and the facility blown up, critically injuring Moira. As she lay dying, Moira realized how Mystique's work could be used to cure the regular Legacy virus. Despite the X-Men's efforts, Moira's injuries proved too severe, but in her last breath, she made Charles telepathically transfer the information needed to cure the virus from Moira to himself. Using Moira's findings, Beast created an antidote that Colossus then dispersed into Earth's atmosphere, Moira thereby managing to save mutantkind posthumously.

Much later, when Xavier went to a Sentinel-devastated Genosha to rebuild, he encountered a psychic representation of Moira within his own consciousness. Moira's ghost also apparently appeared in the Muir Island complex ruins, leading Banshee to a hidden room containing numerous videos and files, exposing the secret of Moira's lost students and Charles' ill-fated use of them. Moira's spirit was contacted by the mutant Dead Girl and the sorcerer Dr. Strange when the undead villain the Pitiful One resurrected other former heroes and villains. Moira and other deceased heroes discovered the Pitiful One's location for them, but chose not to interfere directly.

MUIR ISLAND X-MEN COSTUME
Art by Tom Raney

HEIGHT: 5'7"
WEIGHT: 135 lbs.
EYES: Blue
HAIR: Brown

ABILITIES: Moira MacTaggert was amongst the world's foremost genetics experts, specializing in the study of superhuman mutants. She was also a skilled surgeon, and had made major advances in cloning. Moira was an expert shot.

POWER GRID	1	2	3	4	5	6	7
INTELLIGENCE							
STRENGTH							
SPEED							
DURABILITY							
ENERGY PROJECTION							
FIGHTING SKILLS							

MAD JACK

REAL NAME: Maguire Beck
ALIASES: Jack O'Lantern, Terry Beck
IDENTITY: Known to authorities
OCCUPATION: Professional criminal
CITIZENSHIP: USA., with a criminal record
PLACE OF BIRTH: Moreno Valley, California
KNOWN RELATIVES: Unidentified father (deceased), Quentin Beck (Mysterio, cousin)
GROUP AFFILIATION: Former partner of Daniel Berkhart (Mysterio, Jack O'Lantern)
EDUCATION: Presumed degree in computer science; extensively trained in special effects design
FIRST APPEARANCE: (Behind the scenes) Spectacular Spider-Man #243 (1997); (on panel) Spider-Man: The Mysterio Manifesto (2001)

HISTORY: As a child, Maguire Beck idolized her older cousin Quentin Beck, a Hollywood special effects expert who became the super-villain Mysterio. When Quentin invited Maguire to join him in his life of crime, she readily accepted, using her computer expertise to help upgrade Quentin's special effects. In return, Quentin taught Maguire the secrets behind his illusions. Quentin also had two other students at the time: Daniel "Danny" Berkhart, Quentin's former cellmate who — during a time when Quentin had faked his own death — was hired by Daily Bugle publisher J. Jonah Jameson to pose as the ghost of Mysterio and capture Spider-Man, only to be arrested and then abandoned by Jameson; and Conundrum, an enigmatic student of Eastern mysticism who claimed to know nothing about his own past. Conundrum left to pursue his own ambitions and Berkhart adopted the costumed identity of Jack O'Lantern (previously used by Jason Macendale before becoming the Hobgoblin), aka Mad Jack, to pursue his personal vendetta against J. Jonah Jameson for abandoning him years ago. Though hired by Norman Osborn to target Jameson, Berkhart ultimately burned the cash to show his personal involvement. Maguire joined forces with Berkhart to hone her craft, usually remaining behind the scenes and using her computer technology to assist Berkhart, communicating with him via a radio transmitter built into a robotic cat. Maguire always thought that she and Quentin would eventually become full partners in crime — but then Quentin unexpectedly committed suicide. Devastated, Maguire dedicated her life to destroying everyone she regarded as having abused, exploited, or humiliated Quentin.

Upon learning of Quentin's suicide, Berkhart again became Mysterio and gave his Jack O'Lantern costume to Maguire, who became the new Mad Jack in order to distinguish herself from previous Jack O'Lanterns, preferring to orchestrate her illusions from behind a computer keyboard. As the new Mysterio, Berkhart briefly joined the Sinister Seven and then unsuccessfully attempted to determine Spider-Man's true identity, but later reaffiliated himself with Maguire (although Maguire's increasing mental instability led her to believe that the new Mysterio was actually Quentin). Together, the new Mysterio and Mad Jack plotted revenge against all those who had wronged Quentin. Mad Jack abducted J. Jonah Jameson. They kidnapped Quentin's ex-girlfriend Betsy Schneider, who had made a living selling toys and children's books using Mysterio's likeness, and her husband Joe Smith. Finally, the duo incapacitated Spider-Man and Daredevil (Matt Murdock) by dousing them in hallucinogenic "Joy Juice" which negated their powers. Mad Jack and Mysterio placed their prisoners in virtual reality "Happy Tanks" where they were to be kept incapacitated forever; however, the heroes escaped and defeated Mad Jack, finally learning her true identity, although not realizing the involvement of Berkhart, who had escaped. Quentin Beck has since apparently been resurrected.

HEIGHT: 5'6"   **EYES:** Hazel
WEIGHT: 129 lbs.   **HAIR:** Brown

ABILITIES/ACCESSORIES: Mad Jack is an expert designer of special effects devices and stage illusions, a master hypnotist, and skilled in chemistry and robotics. She has used her advanced knowledge of computer imaging and virtual reality to improve upon Mysterio's techniques. Mad Jack uses a small one-man hovercraft for transportation, and is often accompanied by a robotic black cat of her own design.

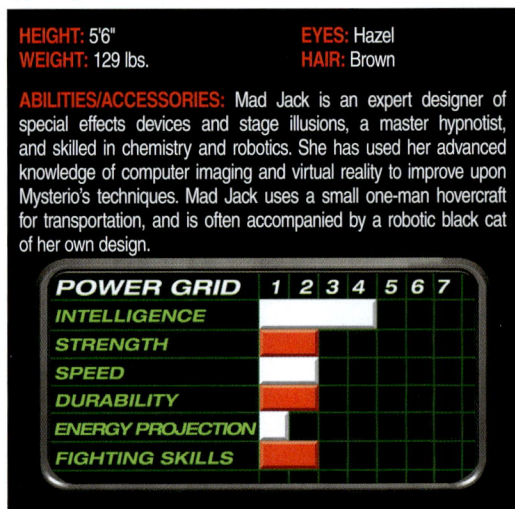

POWER GRID	1	2	3	4	5	6	7
INTELLIGENCE					5		
STRENGTH	1						
SPEED		2					
DURABILITY		2					
ENERGY PROJECTION			3				
FIGHTING SKILLS		2					

Art by Lee Weeks

MAD THINKER

HISTORY: The genius known as the Thinker worked in the private sector before growing bored and leaving for a life of crime. He acted as a criminal for years before the police even learned of his existence. He claims to have a nephew, David, who at the age of ten got too close to a Thinker-built multiconductor and was irradiated and mutated, thereafter incinerating anything which touched his skin. This power accidentally killed David's mother, the Thinker's sister. Beyond that, the Thinker's early life is a mystery.

The Thinker revealed himself to the world when he recruited America's top mobsters and gang leaders in a grandiose scheme which he claimed would literally make him King of New York. Displaying his uncanny ability to calculate probabilities and handle data to make extremely accurate predictions (to the point of being able to predict seemingly random events with split second timing), the Thinker led the criminals in several successful crimes, gaining their trust. The Thinker arranged to split up the Fantastic Four temporarily and remove them from their Baxter Building headquarters, then broke into it with his small army of mobsters. He spent several days studying Reed Richards' private research, most notably Reed's DNA experiments. The Thinker used this to create his first public artificial life form, the Awesome Android. When the Four returned, the Android, able to mimic some of their powers and create hurricane-force winds, nearly defeated the Four. The Thinker calculated to the second when the FF would finally defeat the creature and remained to watch, but was captured when a safeguard Reed had installed against others using the team's equipment activated. The Thinker apparently failed to predict Reed's move, and was arrested. Dubbed the Mad Thinker by the media, he escaped jail almost immediately and allied with the Puppet Master to pit the Four and the X-Men against each other, and later to set the Thing against the Torch. Abandoning the Puppet Master, the Thinker struck against the Four on his own, creating the Bouncing Ball, a bowling ball-sized weapon of destruction that befuddled the Torch and Thing until the Torch destroyed it with a nova blast. The Thinker then turned his intellect to Iron Man (Tony Stark), hiring himself to the Countess de la Spiroza to learn Iron Man's secret identity. The Thinker used the Awesome Android to battle Iron Man, but the android was eventually defeated (though it observed Stark becoming Iron Man) and the Thinker returned to prison.

He quickly escaped and turned his attention to another android: the original Human Torch. Researching the Torch's history, the Thinker determined his resting place and recovered the android. He restored the Torch and also built a sentient machine life form, the Quasi-Motivational Destruct Organ (Quasimodo), to control the Torch through a destruct device planted within the android. The Thinker then forced the android to attack the FF's Torch. While the pair battled, the FF located the Thinker, who ordered Quasimodo to detonate the android Torch's explosive and fled. After the Four abandoned the defunct Torch, the Thinker later returned to claim him, only to find the robotic Ultron seeking an android to become his "child." Not wishing to battle Ultron, the Thinker turned over the Torch to him. Later finding the Torch still present (much to his surprise, a result of an intra-reality temporal divergence by the time lord Immortus, leaving two Torches, one of which Ultron had escaped with), he arranged a funeral for the android to lure the Human Torch's former partner Toro out of obscurity. Using his mind-controlling hypno-lenses, the Thinker captured Toro and took him for study.

Returning to his observation of Tony Stark, the Thinker hired three humans as the Triumvirate of Terror, outfitting them with powerful suits of his own devising. Hammerhead, Thunder-Boot and Pile-Driver captured the Avengers, allowing the Thinker to enter Avengers Mansion and evaluate their technology, but the apparently unpredicted arrival of the god Hercules caused the Thinker's defeat. Returning to his greatest challenge, Reed Richards' technology, the Thinker captured Dr. Jose Santini, whom Reed had brought in to cure the Thing. Taking Santini's place, the Thinker sabotaged the experiment, driving the Thing into an uncontrollable rampage, and then raided the FF's technology while they

REAL NAME: Unrevealed
ALIASES: Thinker, Keith Dramn, Dr. Jose Santini
IDENTITY: Secret
OCCUPATION: Professional criminal mastermind
CITIZENSHIP: USA with a criminal record
PLACE OF BIRTH: Unrevealed
KNOWN RELATIVES: Unidentified sister (deceased), David (nephew)
GROUP AFFILIATION: Occasional partner of Puppet Master; former partner of Red Skull, Wizard, Klaw, Egghead; leader of Triumvirates of Terror
EDUCATION: Unrevealed
FIRST APPEARANCE: Fantastic Four #15 (1963)

pursued Grimm. Squirreling away as much information and technology as he could, the Thinker returned to his lair, where Reed Richards soon captured him. In the meantime he sent his Most Powerful Android (a

SCAVENGER

Art by John Byrne with Sal Buscema (inset)

high-power version of his more common Killer Androids) into the Four's headquarters, where the FF eventually lost it in the newly discovered Negative Zone, allowing the Thinker to observe that dimension from afar. Another Thinker creation, the Android Man, was accidentally activated by the police; it battled the Thing and was placed in storage in the Baxter Building, but would eventually be destroyed when Dr. Doom had it reactivated against the Four.

Egghead and the Puppet Master recruited the Thinker into a grandiose plan for world domination. Taking the opportunity to test his new plastroid Man-Slayer, the Thinker remote-controlled the Man-Slayer into attacking Cape Canaveral, but it was defeated by the Black Widow and Captain Mar-Vell. While Egghead battled the Avengers (initially using another of the Thinker's androids), the Thinker hypnotized Toro into believing that he was actually the original Human Torch, and sent him after the Sub-Mariner at Egghead's behest. Toro attacked the Thinker's ship when he recovered his memories, and was killed in an explosion. With no immediate goals, the Thinker tested himself against the FF; while they were battling Doom in Latveria, the Thinker moved into the Baxter Building, constructing a secret chamber inside the building from which he observed the team. He set android duplicates of the team against them, but Reed Richards defeated his duplicate and exposed the Thinker. He allied again with the Puppet Master, creating android duplicates of virtually every foe the FF had fought, but their Hulk android became over-charged and demolished their control center. This re-partnership ended when the Puppet Master led Spider-Man and the Thing to their headquarters. The annoyed Thinker sent an android to frighten his partner's adult foster daughter, and the Puppet Master (with a push from Spider-Man) turned on the Thinker.

Again imprisoned, the Thinker was freed by the Black Lama, an extradimensional being who involved the Thinker in his "war of the super-villains." Using the information he and his Awesome Android had gathered on Tony Stark/Iron Man, the Thinker assumed control of Iron Man and set him against his assigned foe, MODOK. The Thinker allowed MODOK to defeat Iron Man and to trace them back to the Thinker's headquarters, where he had a giant version of his Killer Androids waiting to battle MODOK. Employing android duplicates, the Thinker allowed MODOK to believe he had defeated them all and then observed as MODOK went after the next opponent, the Yellow Claw. However, Iron Man escaped while the Thinker was trying to track all involved variables. The intervention of yet another villain, Firebrand (Gary Gilbert), created further havoc, and the Thinker abandoned the fray while Iron Man and Firebrand fought. Returning to his experiments, he created the Metalloid, using it to distract the FF while he attempted to remote-control his "Most Powerful Android" within the Negative Zone. The Android had been found and enhanced by Annihilus; as the Scavenger, it served him until it decided to steal his Cosmic Control Rod, further enhance itself, and rule the Zone. The Thinker gained control of the Scavenger — aka his "Monster Android," but it fought him; the Thinker fled when his calculations failed to take into account the presence of Counter-Earth's Reed Richards, the Brute.

Having been confounded by an "x-factor" in the complete unpredictability of the presence of a second Reed, the Thinker delved into mysticism to attempt to control this and sought a psychic to aid him in his calculations. Determining that the perfect candidate would follow Ben Grimm into the Thinker's own lair if certain events happened, he arranged the arrest of Grimm to set this up. The true psychic was a child named Eugene "the Kid" Everett, but the Thinker's preconceptions misled him when the superhuman Daredevil (actually Ben's lawyer, Matt Murdock) also entered and the Thinker assumed Daredevil to be the psychic. The Thinker's subsequent attempt to use Daredevil and the Thing to capture the Vision so he could study how Ultron had empowered him failed miserably, and the Thinker's army of proto-Visions was defeated. The Thinker also studied the alien Rom, believing him to be an android, but when Rom damaged the Awesome Android, it panicked and fled with the Thinker in its arms.

Seeking intellectual stimulation, the Thinker built the New Hampshire town of Ponder, populated with androids replicating the world's greatest scientists, writers, and thinkers. The Thinker supplemented these by kidnapping living scientists and scholars and duplicating them into android replicas as well. He chose to duplicate Captain America, but his capture of the Captain also brought the cyclists Team America after him, and their unpredicted ability to create the enigmatic "Marauder" led to the Thinker's defeat. SHIELD captured many of the androids, but many others escaped and repopulated Ponder. Months later, the dysfunctional android Dostoyevsky would be accused of murder by the residents of a nearby town; their reaction to the Ponderite robots led the residents of Ponder to avoid humanity permanently. Not all Ponderites agreed; many of "the Mad Thinker's Intellectual Robots" would leave and build a new home: Nüponder, Minnesota. Four of these decided that humanity needed to be destroyed, but the New Warriors would see them dismantled.

Using an android surgeon, the Thinker placed a micro-transference unit into his own cerebral cortex, allowing him to project his consciousness into his androids. Though early attempts created a rogue simulacrum (who would much later battle Power Pack and Franklin Richards), the Thinker perfected a series of simulacrums he could control from anywhere on Earth, each one identical to the Thinker himself. Still seeking psychic ways to deal with "x-factors," the Thinker studied Spider-Man's spider-sense, sending Battle-Droid 13, a re-engineered Killer Android, after Spider-Man, but the hero destroyed it. The Thinker again sought vengeance on the Fantastic Four, plotting beside the Wizard and Puppet Master to destroy the FF at the wedding of Johnny Storm, but the Puppet Master betrayed them. The Wizard sought further revenge via the young Franklin Richards, but the Thinker refused to participate, unwilling to harm a child. Further experimentation with the projection of his consciousness allowed the Thinker to invade the Four's computer systems until Reed drove him out. Subsequently recruited by Loki for his Acts of Vengeance anti-super-hero conspiracy, the Thinker immediately deduced Loki's identity and declined, even opposing Loki by manipulating public opinion in favor of the heroes.

The Thinker moved towards less obvious plots for a time, tutoring Arnim Zola's android creation Primus and observing the New Warriors in hopes (or so he would later claim) that they could help his nephew David, even counseling them on their life paths. He also menaced the FF from behind the scenes. Deducing that Johnny Storm's wife, Alicia Masters, was truly a Skrull, the Thinker arranged the sabotage of the construction of the Four's spaceship. When the Thinker finally revealed the masquerade to the Puppet Master (the real Alicia's stepfather), this led to the foursome's flight into space to rescue Alicia, and their entrapment in space when the sabotage caused their ship to fail. The Four did eventually return, and the Thinker, having modified AIM Adaptoid technology into his Killer

MAN-SLAYER   METALLOID

Art by Dick Ayers & Ron Wilson

Androids to create the Super Android F-4, tested it by setting it, along with a new Triumvirate of Terror, against the Thing, Wolverine, and Ant-Man (Scott Lang). Though shrunk by Ant-Man, F-4 would return, once being defeated by the Thing, and then later being destroyed by the Black Widow (Natasha Romanoff) and Crystal. Meanwhile, the Thinker, for unknown reasons, kidnapped Cut, of the Soldiers of Misfortune, and drained his memories. He then revealed his nephew David's condition to the New Warriors, aiding them against the Dire Wraith queen Volx in return for the neo-neutralizer, a superpower-removing machine which Volx had created and which the Thinker wanted as a cure for his nephew.

At Issue onds, the Thinker again pursued the secret of Spider-Man's spider-sense, but his old creation Quasimodo intervened, seeking revenge. The Thinker attempted to kidnap Franklin Richards to gain access to the Four's equipment when the team was presumed dead, but was stopped by the Thunderbolts. He aided the Red Skull in developing mind-controlling nannites, but quickly dissolved that partnership. Transferred from the Vault super-prison to the miniaturized Big House, the Thinker decided to build an army of superhuman followers by arranging a mass escape, allowing his Awesome Android full sentience as part of the plan. However, the Awesome Android, now Awesome Andy, enjoyed his new life and betrayed the Thinker. When the Thinker (actually a simulacrum) was destroyed, Andy kept his still-vocal head as a souvenir until juvenile super-criminal Southpaw absconded with it.

When his observations of the Negative Zone drew the Thinker's attention to the arrival on Earth of Threska, a Negative Zone sorceress, the Thinker sought her out and became romantically involved with her. Tired of Earth and its eternal conflicts, the Thinker decided to retire with her to the Negative Zone. Contacting the Puppet Master, he built a headset by which the Puppet Master could control anyone whose DNA he held; then the Thinker contacted many of the FF's foes, from all across time, space, and even other dimensions, and gathered their DNA. He duplicitously arranged the capture of the Puppet Master and the DNA by the Fantastic Four. Employing a subliminal mind control device, he convinced Reed Richards to build a prison, the new Vault, in the Negative Zone, and to use the DNA to hunt down the FF's foes. Finally arranging a mass escape in the Negative Zone, the Thinker managed to gain the freedom of both himself and Threska in the Negative Zone, unmolested. Eventually, however, Richards realized the truth, and pursued the Thinker. Rather than leave the Thinker to a peaceful retirement, Richards returned him to Earth and prison, and the Thinker swore vengeance on the Fantastic Four anew.

The Thinker teamed with the Puppet Master once again, taking advantage of the Superhuman Registration Act, the two arranged a battle between the pro-registration and anti-registration hero forces with the intent of exploding a bomb mid-battle and killing them all, but was stopped by the Thing. Shortly after, Awesome Andy apparently self-wiped his memories

and his stored powers and personality subroutines. This triggered an automated protocol to find the Thinker, and he soon reunited with the Thinker and Southpaw in their Florida Everglades hideout.

KILLER ANDROID

INTELLECTUAL ROBOTS

Art by Kerry Gammill & Jack Kirby

HEIGHT: 5'11" **EYES:** Blue
WEIGHT: 195 lbs. **HAIR:** Brown

ABILITIES/ACCESSORIES: The Thinker's brain is virtually a living computer. His ability to assimilate large quantities of data is unequaled, and allows him vast predictive abilities. While the Thinker frequently uses computers to supplement and enhance this ability, as time has passed he has apparently done so less and less often; whether his skills have improved or he is merely accessing computers remotely is unknown. He has an implanted micro-transference unit in his cerebral cortex which allows him to transfer his consciousness to and from robotic and android simulacrums at planetary distances. The Thinker is the world's foremost expert on computer science, robotics, and synthetic life forms. His android and robotic creations include: the Awesome Android; the Bouncing Ball, a murderous basketball sized weapon; the power-absorbing Defender; Quasimodo, a sentient computer later given life and mobility by the Silver Surfer; Killer Androids of varying power; the Android Man; the sentient plastoid Man-Slayer; android duplicates of the Fantastic Four and virtually all of their early foes, complete with superhuman abilities; the Metalloid; the Intellectual Robots, android duplicates of humanity's greatest minds; Battle-Droids, advanced versions of the Killer Androids; simulacrums, android duplicates of himself; sensor systems in the form of robotic pigeons; and the Super Android F-4, an enhancement of a Killer Android, employing AIM's Adaptoid technology.

He has also constructed hypno-goggles, or hypno-lenses, which allow the wearer to resist mind control and to control others virtually instantaneously, as well as armored suits which mimic superhuman powers. He has worked with mind-controlling nannites, reprogrammed Spider-Man's spider-tracers, and constructed a nannite device which allowed the Puppet Master to control his victims mentally using only their DNA and microscopic quantities of radioactive clay.

SUPER ANDROID F-4

Art by Paul Ryan

POWER GRID	1	2	3	4	5	6	7
INTELLIGENCE							
STRENGTH							
SPEED							
DURABILITY							
ENERGY PROJECTION							
FIGHTING SKILLS							

MADAME MASQUE

REAL NAME: Whitney Frost (born Countess Giulietta Nefaria)
ALIASES: The Director, Kristine "Krissy" Longfellow, Big M
IDENTITY: Known to authorities
OCCUPATION: Professional criminal; former crime boss, secretary, Midas operative, socialite, debutante
CITIZENSHIP: Dual citizenship in Italy and USA. with a criminal record
PLACE OF BIRTH: Rome, Italy
KNOWN RELATIVES: Count Luchino Nefaria (father), Countess Renata Nefaria (mother, deceased), Byron Frost (adoptive father, deceased), Loretta Frost (adoptive mother, deceased)
GROUP AFFILIATION: Hood's criminal army; formerly Maggia (Nefaria family)
EDUCATION: College graduate
FIRST APPEARANCE: (Big M) Tales of Suspense #97 (1968); (Whitney Frost) Tales of Suspense #98 (1968); (Madame Masque) Iron Man #17 (1969)

HISTORY: Born into and scarred by a world of crime, the woman who became Madame Masque is the daughter of wealthy Italian nobleman Count Luchino Nefaria, a ruthless megalomaniac who led a double life as leader of a major Maggia crime family. Nefaria wanted a male heir, but his wife Renata died giving birth to their only child, their daughter Giulietta. Resolving to protect the child from his enemies and shield her from learning of his criminal empire, Nefaria placed her in the care of Byron Frost, an American financier heavily involved with the Maggia, and he had Frost raise her as his own adopted daughter, Whitney. Blissfully ignorant of her true parentage, Whitney enjoyed a privileged, problem-free childhood and young adulthood: spoiled by her indulgent father, attending all the best schools, growing up to be a celebrated international party girl, and ultimately becoming engaged to wealthy, influential and politically ambitious lawyer Roger Vane. Her perfect life fell to pieces, however, when Byron Frost died and Count Nefaria approached her. Whitney was shocked to learn that her adoptive father Byron had laundered money for the Maggia, and she was horrified by the revelation that crimelord Nefaria was her true father. When Nefaria invited her to join his Maggia crime family and train to become his successor, she refused; however, Nefaria threatened to expose her newfound criminal ties to the world, and warned that her wealthy society friends would abandon her quickly. When she shared her family secrets with her fiancé, Vane abandoned her for fear of scandal, proving Nefaria's point. Losing all hope of a normal life, a broken Whitney joined her father's organization, channelling her bitterness and disappointment into an obsessive training regimen. She soon became Nefaria's second-in-command, and took over as Maggia leader when Nefaria went to prison.

As shadowy new Maggia boss "Big M," Frost supervised a seagoing gambling business from her high-tech submarine headquarters, hiring super-criminal Whiplash (Mark Scarlotti) as an enforcer. Coveting the weapons technology of wealthy inventor Anthony Stark, Big M coerced Stark's corrupt cousin Morgan into helping the Maggia abduct Tony Stark's super-armored bodyguard, Iron Man (secretly Tony Stark himself), who escaped after Big M's gambling cruise ship and submarine headquarters were attacked, looted, and sunk by AIM terrorists. Frost herself was rescued from the sinking ship by eager young SHIELD intelligence agent Jasper Sitwell, who was then assigned to oversee security at Tony Stark's corporation. Frost had originally planned to seduce Stark, but soon began romancing Jasper instead, seeking security secrets. To her dismay, however, Frost began genuinely falling in love with Sitwell and she put off her theft plans, not wanting to betray him if she could avoid it. This resulted in leadership challenges from impatient subordinates, notably the Gladiator (Melvin Potter), who finally pressured her into leading a raid on Stark's facility. Sitwell's security team was waiting to ambush them, Jasper having become suspicious of Whitney's motives by now, but the couple's feelings for each other skewed the ensuing battle. Whitney protected Sitwell from Gladiator during the fight, and Sitwell could not bring himself to shoot Frost as she escaped.

Frost's escape craft crashed, and burning chemicals horribly disfigured her face before she was freed from the wreckage by agents of wealthy, gold-obsessed criminal Mordecai Midas. Hiding her ravaged features behind a golden mask, Frost became Midas' chief field operative as Madame Masque and participated in his first plot against Tony Stark; however, Stark's kindness to her and his genuine romantic interest in her despite her disfigurement turned Frost against Midas. She helped Stark escape Midas' clutches, deserting her employer. Later, when she was menaced by mad scientist Dr. Vryolak and his monstrous son Miklos the Minotaur, Iron Man and Jasper Sitwell rescued her. Torn between Stark and Sitwell, Frost realized she still loved Jasper after he was injured in action. After battling Spymaster and the Zodiac crime cartel alongside Iron Man, Daredevil, and Nick Fury, a confused Whitney sought romantic advice from Iron Man, who demurred.

Frost soon found a way to stay close to her two love interests while she figured out her life. Adopting a new identity as Krissy Longfellow, she became Tony Stark's secretary, bringing her back into contact with both Stark and Sitwell. Falling deeply in love with Stark, "Krissy" was eventually exposed as Madame Masque. She and Stark became lovers regardless, and Stark even shared the secret of his Iron Man identity with her. When Midas staged an illegal takeover of Stark International, Frost and Stark

Art by Sean Chen with George Tuska (insets)

teamed with Sitwell, Jack of Hearts, Guardsman (Michael O'Brien), Wraith (Brian DeWolff), Jean DeWolff and Eddie March to thwart Midas' scheme. Frost later oversaw reconstruction and crisis management at Stark International in Stark's absence, but her relationship with Stark soon came to an abrupt and tragic end. When her father Nefaria began aging rapidly as a side-effect of a process that gave him superhuman powers, Whitney reluctantly helped her father and his Ani-Men enforcers ambush Stark as part of a plan to rejuvenate the dying Nefaria with Stark technology. Stark opposed them as Iron Man, and Nefaria was seemingly killed in the ensuing battle.

Art by Mark Beachum

Feeling betrayed by everyone she had ever loved, an increasingly bitter and paranoid Whitney went deep into hiding, resuming her Maggia leadership and operating out of a hidden desert base near Las Vegas. The newly reclusive Frost worked almost exclusively through surrogates for years, even producing bioduplicates (clones) of herself to act in her stead as Madame Masque in the outside world, clones which came into occasional conflict with Iron Man and other adventurers. If and when a Madame Masque clone became erratic, unreliable or rebellious, Frost would have her killed and replaced with a new clone. As Madame Masque, Frost's first known bio-duplicate clashed with Iron Man and Stark's new girlfriend Bethany Cabe, then became allied and romantically involved with Stark's enemy Obadiah Stane, who had the clone's mind transferred into Bethany Cabe's body by Dr. Theron Atlanta, placing Cabe's mind in the clone's body. After Stane's defeat and suicide, the Cabe/Masque body switch was exposed and both women were returned to their proper bodies. That clone was later slain and replaced by a second bio-duplicate, who clashed with Hydra, AIM, Iron Man and Hulk at one time or another.

One of Frost's bioduplicates, later known simply as Masque, escaped Frost's lair before her mental and physical conditioning was complete. Malleable and unstable, Masque became an empathic, shape-shifting adventurer and began working with the heroic Avengers, drawn to them by her inherited impressions of Frost's long-ago love for Iron Man. Masque assisted the team in several adventures, becoming an honorary member of the group, though team leader Black Widow never fully trusted her. Frost, wrongly assuming that Masque might betray her to her enemies, sent her robotic aide Benedict to abduct Masque from Avengers Mansion, leaving behind a data disc containing extensive intelligence on rival Maggia crime families in hopes that the Avengers would pursue those groups and leave Frost's operation alone. The recaptured Masque tried repeatedly to convince Frost that Iron Man and the Avengers were benevolent and that she should reach out to Stark again, but the fearful Frost refused.

By this time, the outside world believed Frost to be long dead, one of her clones having turned up deceased; however, as more dead clones surfaced, Stark and others began to suspect the real Frost was still alive. Meanwhile, her father Nefaria, resurrected as an ionic super-being, sought to consolidate the Maggia crime families under his leadership (with the Grim Reaper acting as his lieutenant) and tried to force Whitney to return to his service, all as part of a larger scheme to enslave the entire world using ionic radiation. After Nefaria destroyed her hidden base, Madame Masque reluctantly worked with the Avengers and the Thunderbolts (reformed super-criminals) against her father, but secretly planned to betray and destroy both sides. Her bio-duplicate Masque, unable to convince Frost she should side with the heroes, joined the battle in Frost's place. Nefaria promptly slew the courageous bio-duplicate, thinking she was his daughter. Shocked to her senses by her double's sacrifice, Madame Masque joined the fight and played a key role in Nefaria's defeat. Deciding to give up crime, Frost was offered Thunderbolts membership, but she declined, departing alone to consider her future.

Eventually drifting back into crime, Madame Masque joined other criminals in bidding on a Deathlok cyborg offered for sale by the Owl; however, the demonic-powered Hood interrupted the auction, shooting the Owl and informing the others that all super-criminal enterprises in New York would now go through him. Madame Masque was among the earliest recruits of the new super-villain syndicate formed by the Hood shortly thereafter, and she has since become one of the Hood's closest and most trusted lieutenants. As part of Hood's gang, she has repeatedly battled Luke Cage's outlaw faction of the heroic Avengers; the criminals were defeated and jailed, but the Hood has freed them from custody each time. When alien Skrull subversives tried to infiltrate Hood's gang by abducting and impersonating Madame Masque, the Hood thwarted their plan by rescuing the real Madame Masque before the aliens could replace her. The Hood later led Madame Masque and the rest of his syndicate in helping various super heroes defeat the larger Skrull invasion force, making the Earth safe for criminal enterprise again.

Art by George Pérez

NOTE: *Whitney Frost and her bio-duplicates are unrelated to the mutant Masque of the Morlocks, a malevolent superhuman who can alter the physical appearance of others with his touch.*

HEIGHT: 5'9"   **EYES:** Gray
WEIGHT: 139 lbs.   **HAIR:** Black

ABILITIES/ACCESSORIES: Highly athletic, Frost is a formidable martial artist, markswoman, disguise artist and actress. Despite her mental and emotional instability, Frost is also a capable leader, organizer and criminal strategist, well-versed in the use of various exotic technologies. Her mind is artificially shielded from most forms of telepathy or mental tampering. She sometimes wears lightweight form-fitting body armor and constantly wears a golden metal mask over her scarred face. She carries various conventional handguns, notably the Wildey .475 Magnum revolver, as well as more specialized weapons such as concussive energy blasters and sleep gas guns. Thanks to Nefaria and Maggia resources, Frost has had access to an arsenal of specialized high-tech equipment over the years, notably modified Dreadnought robots adapted from stolen Hydra designs; her former desert base's "inner guard" of combat-ready robots, including Benedict, Brutus, Fawkes, Hiss, Monmouth, Quisling and Wilkes; and assorted exotic vehicles, such as her former submarine headquarters.

The bio-duplicate Masque seemed to share all the physical abilities and combat skills of Frost, as well as much of Frost's memories. She was also a shape-shifter who could perfectly mimic other people, especially persons of significance to the people in her general vicinity. Empathic and slightly telepathic, Masque could sense the emotions and thoughts of others. She usually carried several hand weapons, notably miscellaneous energy blasters and her trademark taser pistol.

POWER GRID	1	2	3	4	5	6	7
INTELLIGENCE			■				
STRENGTH		■					
SPEED			■				
DURABILITY		■					
ENERGY PROJECTION	■						
FIGHTING SKILLS				■			

MADAME WEB

REAL NAME: Cassandra Webb
ALIASES: None
IDENTITY: Publicly known
OCCUPATION: Professional medium
CITIZENSHIP: USA
PLACE OF BIRTH: Salem, Oregon
KNOWN RELATIVES: Jonathan Webb (husband, deceased), Charlotte Witter (granddaughter)
GROUP AFFILIATION: None; formerly led group of Spider-Women
EDUCATION: Unknown
FIRST APPEARANCE: Amazing Spider-Man #210 (1980)

HISTORY: Though Cassandra Webb suffered from a lifetime of blindness and many years of neurological deterioration due to myasthenia gravis, she compensated with her profound psychic abilities, establishing herself as a medium. Using these powers, Madame Web discovered Peter Parker's secret identity when Spider-Man rescued one of her students, Belinda Bell, who had been kidnapped during a scam at the Daily Globe newspaper where she impersonated reclusive publisher K.J. Clayton.

Later, Madame Web helped Spider-Man prevent an assassination attempt against a congressional candidate, Barney Wicker. When Black Tom Cassidy sent the Juggernaut to kidnap Web so he could use her powers for his criminal activities, she foresaw the attack and called Spider-Man for help. He was unable to stop the Juggernaut, who left Madame Web in a state of severe shock after he unwittingly removed her from her chair, which provided her vital life functions. After being in a coma and suffering short-term memory loss, she appeared to temporarily forget Spider-Man's identity.

Madame Web contacted Spider-Man for help after foreseeing her impending death. Believing that joining Norman Osborn in an arcane ritual called the Gathering of the Five would save her life, she asked Spider-Man to retrieve one of the five required artifact fragments. Each of the five participants would receive either knowledge, power, immortality, insanity, or death. Spider-Man succeeded, and in the course of the ceremony, Madame Web apparently received death. Actually, she received immortality, and found herself much younger and healthier. Soon after, Dr. Octopus created a Spider-Woman using Cassandra's granddaughter, Charlotte Witter, whose siphoning powers absorbed the abilities of the other Spider-Women: Jessica Drew, Julia Carpenter, and Mattie Franklin. To capture Charlotte, Madame Web gathered the spider women into a team. Charlotte was defeated, but later siphoned Madame Web's telepathy, re-aging her in the process. With the help of Spider-Man and Franklin, Madame Web determined how to drain Charlotte's power, leaving Witter unconscious in a dormant state. Madame Web, now youthful again, performed psychic surgery to sever her link to Charlotte and removed Charlotte and Mattie's memories of Spider-Man's identity. Madame Web continued to assist Mattie during the rest of her time as Spider-Woman.

The Spider-Women team eventually disbanded. Madame Web has since become elderly again, although she presumably has retained her immortality, potentially condemning her to an eternity in her current condition. She has returned to her apartment in Manhattan, where she has aided Spider-Man when Stegron attempted to turn the city into a wild prehistoric paradise using an artifact called the Rock of Life. Later, when Spider-Man's Aunt May was comatose after being shot by a sniper, Madame Web psychically allowed May to give her nephew permission to let her die. Spider-Man refused, and after making a deal with Mephisto to save May's life, Madame Web and the rest of the world no longer know Spider-Man's secret identity.

YOUTH RESTORED

HEIGHT: 5'6"
WEIGHT: 110 lbs.
EYES: Pale gray
HAIR: Black

ABILITIES/ACCESSORIES: Madame Web possesses psychic abilities including telepathy, clairvoyance, and prescience. She can also perform astral projection and appear to others in spirit form. Madame Web is cybernetically linked to a spiderweb-like support system to attend to her bodily needs. The system can shift upright or recline, and provides robotic arms to substitute for her arms.

POWER GRID	1	2	3	4	5	6	7
INTELLIGENCE							
STRENGTH							
SPEED							
DURABILITY							
ENERGY PROJECTION							
FIGHTING SKILLS							

Art by Angel Medina with Bart Sears (inset)

MADMAN

HISTORY: Phil Sterns was a brilliant but undistinguished graduate school classmate of Bruce Banner, whose genius Sterns greatly admired. Following graduation, Sterns sought military funding for weapons-related gamma radiation research, but such funding instead went to Banner, whose gamma bomb work eventually transformed him into the Hulk. Whether out of admiration or envy, Sterns spent years developing the means to deliberately mutate himself in a similar way, undergoing repeated exposure to gamma radiation. During these years, Sterns' brother Samuel underwent his own gamma-induced transformation, becoming the super-intelligent Leader. While Phil Sterns was told his brother died in a radiation accident, the Leader covertly observed his brother's activities. Eventually Phil Sterns empowered himself to take a monstrous super-strong form at will, but his years of experimentation caused him to develop a dissociative identity disorder (aka split personality) and an alter ego known as Madman, who dominated Sterns in either form. Although the Leader deemed Madman a potential threat, even he could not find it in himself to murder his own brother.

When apparent happenstance brought both Phil Sterns and Banner to employment at Nevada's Yucca Flats Nuclear Research Facility, the Madman persona, possibly acting on Sterns' years of subconscious envy, poisoned Banner, who evaded death when the Abomination (Emil Blonsky), manipulated by the Leader, forced his transformation into Hulk form. Following the Hulk's futile efforts to find an antidote, the Leader teleported him to Phil Sterns' apartment, beneath which the Hulk found a subterranean lair where he was confronted by Madman himself. In the course of the Hulk's battle with Madman, the Phil Sterns persona was apparently eradicated, but not before he apprised the Hulk of the whereabouts of both poison and antidote. The Hulk injected Madman with his own poison and, winning the struggle for the antidote despite his poison-induced weakness, transformed back into Banner and injected himself, saving his own life with seconds to spare. He then placed a second antidote sample yards away from the debilitated Madman, leaving him to face probable death.

HEIGHT: (Sterns) 5'10"; (Madman) variable up to 8'11"
WEIGHT: (Sterns) 182 lbs.; (Madman) variable up to 622 lbs.
EYES: (Sterns) Blue; (Madman) Brown
HAIR: (Sterns) Blond; (Madman) None

ABILITIES/ACCESSORIES: Madman can change into a large monstrous form and back again, as well as exist in various intermediary forms between the two. Initially, due to his identity disorder, the individual personas of Madman and Phil Sterns would struggle for control of his body, at least while in normal human form. However, the Sterns persona has apparently been completely overwhelmed by that of Madman, which may have affected his ability to change form, since he has not been seen in fully human form since. In his fully transformed state, he possesses Class 100 superhuman strength and proportionate durability; when in the process of transforming from normal to monstrous state, his strength varies in proportion to his size. Although insane and given to highly irrational behavior, he is a brilliant scientist in the fields of nuclear physics, robotics, and other disciplines. He has access to various forms of advanced technology, both from the New World Order and of his own design; however, unlike many other transforming superhumans, he does not wear clothing composed of unstable molecules, causing him to shred his clothing whenever he assumes giant form.

REAL NAME: Dr. Phillip Sterns
ALIASES: None
IDENTITY: Secret
OCCUPATION: Megalomaniac; former nuclear researcher
CITIZENSHIP: USA
PLACE OF BIRTH: Unrevealed
KNOWN RELATIVES: Samuel Sterns (Leader, brother)
GROUP AFFILIATION: None
EDUCATION: Ph.D. in nuclear physics
FIRST APPEARANCE: (Sterns) Incredible Hulk #362 (1989); (Madman) Incredible Hulk #364 (1989)

Nevertheless reaching the antidote in time to cure himself, Madman subsequently obtained a position with the New World Order, formed by the Red Skull (Johann Shmidt), where he helped create artificial life-form Piecemeal. Unknown to the Skull and his allies, Madman implanted a device guaranteeing Piecemeal's obedience. When the creature escaped, Madman tracked him to Loch Ness, Scotland, where the Hulk, by chance, was present to battle both Piecemeal and Madman. After Piecemeal's defeat, Madman fled to England, where, on a whim, he abducted a member of British royalty and demanded to be crowned King of England. Fighting not only the pursuing Hulk but also traveling adventurers Motormouth and Killpower, Madman ultimately fell from London Bridge into the River Thames and has not been seen since.

POWER GRID	1	2	3	4	5	6	7
INTELLIGENCE							
STRENGTH							
SPEED							
DURABILITY							
ENERGY PROJECTION							
FIGHTING SKILLS							

Art by Dale Keown with Jeff Purves & Gary Frank (insets)

MADRIPOOR

OFFICIAL NAME: Principality of Madripoor
LOCATION: Southeast Asia, approximately 0º N 105º E
POPULATION: 1,055,680 (estimated)
CAPITAL CITY: Madripoor
PLACES OF INTEREST: Buccaneer Bay, Madripoor Harbor, Central Highlands, Royal Palace & Museum, Hightown, Sovereign Hotel, Barker Plaza, Lowtown Central Bazaar, Madame Joy's, Foxy Den, Lotus Café, Hoggvelt Memorial Park; formerly Princess Bar/Seraph's
GOVERNMENT: Principality, former British colony
MAJOR ETHNIC GROUPS: Chinese, Vietnamese, Thai
MAJOR LANGUAGES: English, French
MONETARY UNIT: Madripoor dollar
MAJOR RESOURCES: Fishing, shipping, textiles, gambling, tourism, electronics; formerly slaves, ivory, rubber, teak
FIRST APPEARANCE: New Mutants #32 (1985)

HISTORY: The Principality of Madripoor is a small island nation located south of Singapore in the vicinity of Kepuluan Riau and Kepulauan Lingga in the Indonesian archipelago. It was ruled for many years by Prince Baran, whose dynastic forebears were the leaders of the freebooters who conquered the island. Madripoor's heritage of piracy evolved into the present system of government whose laissez-faire policy allows for virtually any sort of business transaction provided that the ruling status quo is not threatened. As a result, Madripoor has become an exotic diplomatic haven for many international crimelords and organizations. These criminals help maintain the stability of the government through a sophisticated system of corruption that includes payoffs to the chancellor, who runs the day-to-day government operations, and, it is speculated, to the ruling prince as well.

The indigenous population is a polyglot of Chinese, Vietnamese, Thai, Filipino, British and other races, each seeking to preserve their own language and heritage while residing on the island. A tribe of nomadic natives also reside in the island's Central Highlands. While English and Filipino are the official languages of Madripoor, French is also commonly spoken, a reminder of the French colonial history in the area, which included possession of Indochina (present-day Vietnam, Cambodia, and Laos). Hinduism is the primary religion practiced in Madripoor, with its followers believing that, after death, the body must be returned to the Pancamahabhuta — the five sacred elements — before their soul can be released to meet the Supreme Being. Hence, elaborate funeral pyres are favored, especially for royalty. The religion also demands that bare legs be covered with sarongs within temple grounds.

Much of Madripoor's 377 square miles of land is covered in jungle, home to a species of spider monkey found nowhere else in the world that is revered in local superstitions and protected by local law, as well as other fauna including deer, wild dogs, boar and wolves. Little cleared land is able to be cultivated, thus Madripoor is dependent on imports for virtually everything. The island does lay claim to a thriving fishing trade, boosted by the residents of small neighboring islands such as Rumika, located just off Madripoor's southeast coast, which was home to a prosperous fishing village until its inhabitants were slain by mercenaries seeking the Master Form. Because of its strategic location near one of the major trade routes, Madripoor's harbor and dock facilities are among the largest and most extensive in the world. In addition, the capital city has a large and modern international airport serviced by Sovereign Airways. In keeping with its history of piracy, there are numerous isolated landing strips that are used for illegal operations ranging from slavery to drug running. The society and living conditions of Madripoor are an exotic paradox. The capital city lays claim to the most luxurious and expensive hotels in the world. At the same time, it possesses one of the most severe pockets of poverty on the planet. This economic polarization has effectively divided the capital city into two parts: Hightown, the high-tech haven of the very rich and powerful; and Lowtown, the medieval domain of the hopelessly poor.

During the early 1940s, Madripoor was a second home for the mutant adventurer Logan, later known as Wolverine, who also used the alias of Patch and acted as the island's protector alongside his mentor Seraph. The island has long been of interest to the ninja cult known as the Hand. In 1941, Seraph and Logan worked with the Super-Soldier Captain America (Steve Rogers) and Ivan Petrovitch against an alliance between the Hand and the Nazis. In later decades, Logan occasionally frequented Madripoor's branch of the interdimensional firm Landau, Luckman, and Lake, where he worked with his friend Chang.

In recent years, the psionic entity called the Shadow King, in its human guise as Amahl Farouk, possessed the body of the young mutant

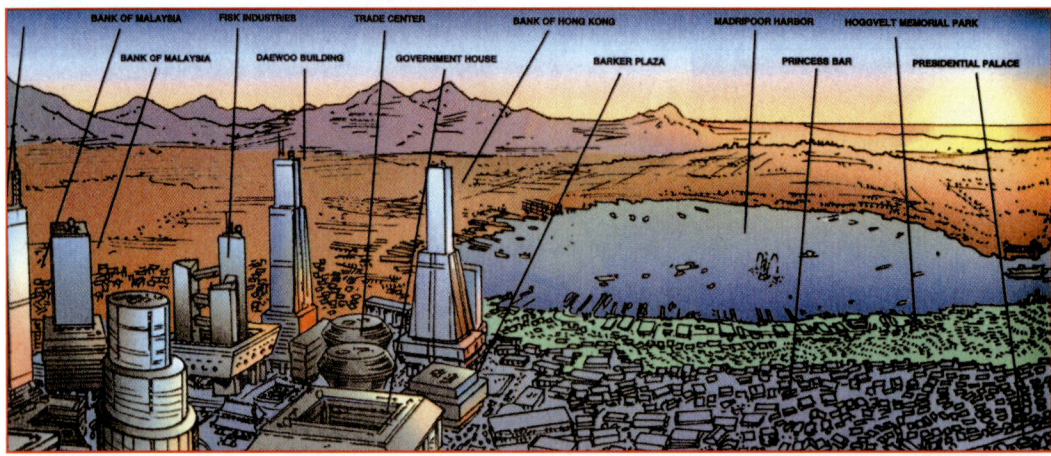

Art by Eliot R. Brown

Karma (Xi'an Coy Manh) to hold court in Madripoor, although Karma was eventually freed from his control by her teammates in the New Mutants. After Wolverine and the other X-Men faked their own deaths, Wolverine again frequented Madripoor, buying into Lowtown's now defunct Princess Bar, formerly managed by Seraph, with a man known only as O'Donnell. Among his friends during this period were South Sea Skyways pilot Archie Corrigan, American private investigators Jessica Drew and Lindsay McCabe, former LL&L operative Rose Wu, corrupt but honorable police chief Tai, brothel proprietor Madame Joy, and banker-turned-crimelord Tyger Tiger. At the time, Madripoor's criminal underworld was run by the crimelord Roche until he was challenged by the upstart Tyger with Wolverine's aid. Roche's super-powered agents Razor-Fist (Douglas Scott), Sapphire Styx and the Inquisitor were defeated and Roche himself slain by Tyger. After petitioning Baran to be allowed to take control of Roche's empire, Tyger became the island's new crimelord and quickly ceased activities involving drugs and smuggling; however, this left a void that was soon filled by General Nguyen Ngoc Coy, which led to a gang war that was resolved only after both sides agreed to continue their operations without interfering in the other's. Tyger and Coy later faced opposition from the Adamantium-swathed Cyber who sought to usurp control of their criminal empires but was defeated by Wolverine. Soon after, the feral mutant Aardwolf sought to establish himself as a crimelord in Madripoor but faced opposition from Tyger and the Folding Circle until the situation was defused by Night Thrasher (Dwayne Taylor).

Baran and Coy then conspired to eliminate the threat of Wolverine once and for all, hiring thugs to kill many of Wolverine's friends in Lowtown and pinning the deaths on him. With Tyger's aid, Wolverine discovered the truth and confronted the pair whereupon Coy shot and killed Baran in an act of self-preservation but was himself shot by Tyger. Following Baran's death, the throne of Madripoor was left without an heir. Control of the nation was soon usurped by the nihilist Viper after Wolverine was forced to marry her to fulfill an old debt. Viper had gambled that Wolverine's respectability in Madripoor would enable her to seize the throne. She also used him, his nemesis Sabretooth and his X-Men teammate Shadowcat to foil an attempt by Hydra and the Hand to control the island. Subsequently, Viper was installed as the ruling prince of Madripoor, and Wolverine was declared an outlaw. Wolverine was subsequently invited back to Madripoor to participate in the "Bloodsport," an illegal superhuman fighting tournament. Later, Madripoor became the site of an attempted invasion of Earth by the extradimensional warlord Khan, which was ultimately repelled by the X-Men, much to Viper's chagrin.

Seeking to stop Viper's terrorist activities, Director of SHIELD Tony Stark clandestinely planned to have Viper overthrown. Meeting with crimelord Tyger Tiger, Stark helped her incite a rebellion against Viper, resulting in Tyger being crowned ruler in her stead.

Art by Klaus Janson

AARDWOLF
Former crimelord
Night Thrasher #2
(1993)

PRINCE BARAN
Former ruler
Wolverine #6 (1989)

BLOODSCREAM
Enforcer
Wolverine #4 (1989)

CHANG
Former Landau,
Luckman & Lake agent
Wolverine #5 (1989)

ARCHIE CORRIGAN
Former South Sea
Skyways proprietor
Wolverine #1 (1989)

GENERAL NGUYEN NGOC COY
Crimelord
Marvel Team-Up #100
(1980)

JESSICA DREW
Private Investigator
Marvel Spotlight #32
(1977)

MADAME JOY
Madam
Marvel Comics
Presents #7 (1988)

KARMA
Adventurer
Marvel Team-Up #100
(1980)

LINDSAY MCCABE
Private Investigator
Spider-Woman #14
(1979)

O'DONNELL
Former Princess Bar
co-owner
Marvel Comics
Presents #1 (1988)

"PATCH"
Adventurer, former
Princess Bar co-owner
Marvel Comics Presents
#1 (1988)

RAZOR-FIST
Enforcer
Master of Kung-Fu
#105 (1974)

ROCHE
Former crimelord
Marvel Comics
Presents #2 (1988)

ROUGHOUSE
Enforcer
Wolverine #4 (1989)

SAPPHIRE STYX
Enforcer
Marvel Comics
Presents #1 (1988)

SERAPH
Former Princess
Bar owner
Uncanny X-Men #268
(1990)

TAI
Former Chief of Police
Wolverine #3 (1989)

TYGER TIGER
Former crimelord,
current ruler
Uncanny X-Men #229
(1988)

VIPER
Former ruler
Captain America #110
(1969)

ROSE WU
Former Princess Bar
proprietor/owner
Uncanny X-Men #257
(1990)

MAELSTROM

REAL NAME: Unrevealed
ALIASES: Anomaly, Malcolm Stromberg, the Cosmic Assassin
IDENTITY: The general populace of Earth is unaware of Maelstrom's existence
OCCUPATION: Geneticist, would-be conqueror
CITIZENSHIP: None
PLACE OF BIRTH: Unrevealed
KNOWN RELATIVES: Phaeder (father, deceased), Morga (mother, deceased), Ransak the Reject (son)
GROUP AFFILIATION: None
EDUCATION: Highly advanced training in Inhuman and Deviant genetic sciences by Phaeder
FIRST APPEARANCE: (Maelstrom) Marvel Two-in-One #71 (1981); (Anomaly) Quasar #20 (1991)

HISTORY: Maelstrom is the son of Phaeder, a member of the sub-species race of humanity known as the Inhumans. Phaeder was a geneticist in Attilan, but his cloning experiments met with disapproval from the Genetics Council; he lost a bid for leadership of the council to Agon, and was subsequently banished from the council for his experiments. To obtain freedom, Phaeder created a clone of himself and killed it so that he would not be missed, then ventured into the outside world to perform his experiments.

Phaeder eventually mated with a woman named Morga, of the Deviants, a genetically unstable human sub-species. They raised Maelstrom in Deviant Lemuria in his early years, but Morga was put to death for having relations with an outsider, and Maelstrom was made a slave. Phaeder eventually rescued Maelstrom, but he was now as much against the Deviants as his father was against the Inhumans.

Maelstrom and Phaeder's superior knowledge of genetics revolutionized humanity's scientific community from the early 1900s on, and they shared their knowledge with humans including Herbert Wyndham (the High Evolutionary), to whom they provided some of the Deviants' subterranean slaves to aid him in constructing the Citadel of Science on Mount Wundagore. They also aided his assistant Miles Warren (the Jackal), and Wladyslav Shinski of the Enclave. Notes of theirs wound up in the possession of the mad bio-engineer Arnim Zola, and one of their laboratories was found by the mutant Magneto, who used their equipment to create the superhuman Alpha the Ultimate Mutant. Maelstrom and Phaeder recruited the minions Gronk, Helio and Phobius from among the ranks of the Deviants and Inhumans, and were also aided by Deathurge, who was actually serving the cosmic entity Oblivion. Over time, Phaeder and Maelstrom would transfer their minds into cloned bodies to perpetuate their existence, but Phaeder gradually became too weak to continue the process. Experiments that Phaeder and Maelstrom performed granted Maelstrom the ability to harness kinetic energy. At some point, Maelstrom mated with a Deviant named Medula, and she secretly bore him a son, the almost human-looking Ransak the Reject, who was placed into slavery just as his father had been.

One of Maelstrom and Phaeder's associates, Dr. Hydro, had been provided with a sample of the Terrigen Mist which grants Inhumans their powers, and he used it to transform people into amphibians ("Hydro-Men"). When the Inhumans sought to cure the Hydro-Men, they were surprised to find that their Terrigen Mist was involved, and with the aid of Mr. Fantastic, created an Anti-Terrigen Compound which would undo its effects. When Maelstrom learned of the compound's invention, he sent his minions to obtain it for study. Although the sample was obtained, the minions were captured; Maelstrom had Deathurge kill them to prevent them from being interrogated, then resurrected them in new clonal bodies. Regardless, his actions put the Thing and the Inhumans on his trail, and they invaded Maelstrom's lab. Phaeder died in his sleep while Maelstrom was battling Black Bolt, the son of Agon, and Maelstrom had Deathurge kill his current body so that he could escape the conflict in a new one. He destroyed his laboratory so that the Inhumans could not study it.

In a new body, Maelstrom stole into Olympia, city of the Eternals, as the Eternals were gathering their population to join their forms together into the Uni-Mind. Maelstrom created a device to siphon the Uni-Mind's kinetic energies into himself, but the Avengers defended the Eternals, releasing them from the Uni-Mind. When Starfox attempted to use his powers to make Maelstrom surrender, Maelstrom had himself slain by Deathurge again.

In his next scheme, Maelstrom used knowledge gleaned from the Uni-Mind to construct a device which would siphon the entire Earth's kinetic energy into himself, gradually slowing its rotation and tearing the planet

Art by Mark Gruenwald with Greg Capullo (inset)

apart. Opposing him, the Avengers forced him to absorb more energy than he could contain, spreading his molecules across the universe. As Maelstrom began to draw his body back together, he encountered the cosmic being Kronos and learned of the abstract powers that governed the universe from him. Maelstrom sought out the entity Anomaly and slew it, assuming its role in the universe, and made a formal alliance with Oblivion, offering up the universe to his patron.

To set his plans in motion, Maelstrom sought the power of cosmic awareness, which was guarded by the entity Eon. Eon foresaw his approaching death, and charged his protector of the universe Quasar (Wendell Vaughn) to prevent it; however, another servant of Oblivion called the Unbeing temporarily unmade Quasar's heroic identity, allowing Maelstrom an opportunity to arrive on Earth undetected, although Quasar regained his identity from Unbeing's counterpart Origin. Maelstrom tricked Quasar into thinking that the threat he had prepared for was the Russian villain the Presence so that he would lower his guard. He also weakened Quasar's relationship to Eon by killing Quasar's father Gilbert Vaughn. Eon kept Gilbert's death a secret from Quasar, but when it finally came out, Quasar felt betrayed and refused to continue serving Eon. Needing Quasar's quantum bands to enter Eon's realm, Maelstrom, flanked by his lovers the Weird Sisters and his minions, assumed the identity of Malcolm Stromberg. Posing as a client for the security firm Quasar ran in his secret identity, Maelstrom tricked Quasar into entering his home with his friends, then threatened their lives to force him to surrender. Since the quantum bands could not be removed while Quasar was alive, Maelstrom sliced his hands off, and used the bands to find Eon. When Quasar finally died, Maelstrom took the quantum bands for himself.

Trying to prevent Maelstrom from taking cosmic awareness from Eon, Quasar's spirit destroyed Eon's brain, but Maelstrom had already achieved his goal. With his newfound powers, Maelstrom slowed the Earth's rotation, and then set out to destroy the universe by halting all movement, generating a massive black hole. Maelstrom confronted many of the universe's great powers to revel in his superiority over them, including Thanos, then-wielder of the six Infinity Gems. Quasar continued to oppose Maelstrom, though, and when they fought over the black hole, Maelstrom was crushed by its forces.

The cosmic entity Infinity chose Quasar as her champion against Oblivion, and Oblivion summoned forth Maelstrom's spirit to battle Quasar to determine the fate of the universe. Quasar bested Maelstrom when he demonstrated that, due to an alteration Origin had made to him when she recreated him earlier, he himself had become an anomaly, and therefore challenged Maelstrom's role as Anomaly. Maelstrom was destroyed, and the black hole ceased to exist.

Maelstrom's minions and the Weird Sisters attempted to revive him using captured Deviants whose kinetic energy he could drain. The Eternals and Fantastic Four joined together to halt Maelstrom's resurrection, but when he learned that one of the Deviants was Ransak the Reject, his own son, he refused to take his life, and shrank into the Microverse.

Maelstrom was converted into proto-natural force as he descended, and claimed to behold the grand design of the universe. He became determined to learn the secret of the universe by destroying it. To do so, he stole a chronal accelerator from the Roxxon Oil Corporation to speed the universe to its demise. The Great Lakes Avengers opposed him, but he killed their teammate Dinah Soar and escaped. He hired Batroc's Brigade to aid him in gathering the other components he needed, and to serve as bodyguards against super heroes. When Maelstrom finally activated the chronal accelerator, the Great Lakes Avenger Mr. Immortal confronted him with the suggestion that with all life gone, his own existence would have no meaning, just an eternity of loneliness. Mr. Immortal shot himself in the head as a means of demonstrating a way out of loneliness. Maelstrom followed suit, but was unaware that Mr. Immortal could not die, and the hero shut off the chronal accelerator as soon as he revived. Protesting that he had been tricked, Maelstrom's spirit was brought to Oblivion by Doorman, Deathurge's new replacement.

Art by Paul Pelletier

HEIGHT: 8'2" **WEIGHT:** 425 lbs.
EYES: Purple **HAIR:** Purple
NOTE: Maelstrom's height and weight vary with the amount of energy he absorbs.

ABILITIES/ACCESSORIES: Maelstrom can absorb kinetic energy from any source and use it to increase his own physical abilities while draining his victims. He can also use this energy by generating force blasts, flying, and growing in size. With the means to amplify his abilities, Maelstrom can absorb kinetic energy from the entire planet. While he served as Anomaly, he possessed cosmic awareness, granting him near-omnipotent knowledge. He also had the ability to alter reality.

POWER GRID	1	2	3	4	5	6	7
INTELLIGENCE							
STRENGTH							
SPEED							
DURABILITY							
ENERGY PROJECTION							
FIGHTING SKILLS							

*MAELSTROM'S STRENGTH AND DURABILITY VARY WITH THE AMOUNT OF ENERGY HE ABSORBS

APPENDIX

EARTH'S SOLAR SYSTEM

Earth's solar system is comprised of one central life-giving sun and eight naturally occurring major planets. In addition, the system contains one artificially created planet, Counter-Earth, as well as numerous comets and several asteroid belts (the inner belt, located between the orbits of Mars and Venus, is generally simply referred to as "the asteroid belt" but other belts do exist, including the Kuiper Belt and the scattered disk, both located outside Neptune's orbit). Though most of the planets share names with Earth's gods, it should be noted that these planets have merely been named in honor of those gods, and no actual connection exists between any god and a given planet, save where elaborated upon below.

Throughout Earth's history, a number of alien races were said to have been natives of some of the solar system's bodies, but most of these claims have been cast into doubt. Likely many of the aliens either lied outright or had established temporary bases either on or in orbit around these planets in preparation for their exploration of Earth. Note that various planets of the solar systems have been colonized or invaded in myriad alternate futures and universes, none of which will be addressed here. For more information on those futures, see the Appendix covering Alternate Earths.

For each body, its distance from the sun is given, as is surface circumference, planetary mass, and surface gravity; all these are given proportionally to Earth's; e.g. Sol's mass of 330,000 means its mass is 330,000 times that of Earth's. Also given is the known major moon count for each planet.

SOL:
CIRCUMFERENCE: 109
MASS: 330,000
ORBITAL DISTANCE: 0
SURFACE GRAVITY: 28

In Reality-616, stars are sentient beings, and can occasionally take physical form. Earth's sun, known as Sol on Earth, is named Apalla, and once sought Dr. Strange's aid when others tried to usurp her power. Sol is also home to Atum, aka Demogorge, the spawn of the Earth goddess Gaea and the father of the Ennead (Egyptian Gods); he initially left Earth after purging it of most of its Elder Gods. Some accounts claim that Sol is inhabited by a human-like race, although such reports seem particularly dubious. Peter Corbeau once used the Starcore satellite to draw energy from Sol to purge Bruce Banner of the energy that transformed him into the Hulk. The transport of the extradimensional Jarella and Fialan from K'ai in a "Microverse" to Earth exacerbated the effects on the sun, which then threatened to go nova within 24 hours until Fialan and Jarella were sent home, and the Hulk's energies restored. The Dire Wraiths used Sol as a lens to draw Wraithworld into Earth's dimension. Located near the sun is a Shi'ar jumpgate, and repeated usage of this gate has nearly fatally destabilized the sun in the past. Only the combined efforts of Quasar (Wendell Vaughn) and Binary (Carol Danvers) prevented the sun's destruction as a result of these instabilities during the Kree-Shi'ar War. As a result, the United Nations has banned usage of this stargate and most alien races seem to be respecting this ban. The Sentry (Robert Reynolds) once cast his dark side, the Void, into the sun.

MERCURY:
CIRCUMFERENCE: .4
MASS: .06
ORBITAL DISTANCE: .4
SURFACE GRAVITY: .4
MAJOR MOONS: 0

The closest planet to the sun, the atmosphereless Mercury has a surface temperature that ranges from under 250 degrees Fahrenheit below zero at night to over 800 degrees above zero during the day. Supposedly, several alien couples from Mercury colonized an American town in 1756. An unidentified race established a farming colony on Mercury before being enslaved by the bellicose Procyons in 1953. Kang and the Human Torch once cooperated to slightly alter Mercury's orbit to prevent a plot by Necrodamus from coming to fruition. The UN's Starcore Station orbits the sun just outside Mercury's orbit, monitoring the sun's status; an earlier station, Starcore One, had existed in the same location before being destroyed by solar instabilities during the Kree-Shi'ar War.

VENUS:
CIRCUMFERENCE: 1.0
MASS: .8
ORBITAL DISTANCE: .7
SURFACE GRAVITY: .9
MAJOR MOONS: 0

Venus' heavy cloudlike atmosphere creates a greenhouse effect giving it a temperature as hot as Mercury's during the day; its carbon dioxide atmosphere and sulphuric acid clouds make it even more inhospitable. In 1924, however, Earth criminal George Mulford traveled to Venus and built a power base. The Venusian woman Jarna led an army of "Lavarites" to invade Earth in 1941, eventually allying with Nazi Germany before being defeated by Namor the Sub-Mariner. Three years later, Mulford led his own invasion attempt which Namor also foiled. Four years later, a presumed alien colony on Venus ruled by Queen Alura was attacked by the Red Star Man, sole survivor of an occupied red star; telepathically drawn to Venus, the Human Torch (Jim Hammond) defeated the intruder. The 1950s' naiad Venus allegedly had a base on "Mount Lustre" on this planet. In 1953, Namor the Sub-Mariner battled a group of Robot-Men who established a base under the South Pacific waters and who claimed to be preparing for a mass invasion from Venus. Over the next few years, individual Venusians with varying agendas surfaced in the US, England, Africa, and elsewhere. In 1960, an alleged Venusian fought off an alleged Martian invading Earth, claiming that the Venusians had been defending Earth from outer space menaces for centuries. The Collector (Taneleer Tivan) used a "Venusian Retriever Anemone" from his collection against the Avengers. Stark West's Whiz Kids (Herbert Bell, Talia Kruma, Dale West) designed a prototype suit to protect a human from Venus' atmosphere; the Thing (Ben Grimm) once tested it in a simulated atmosphere, but it is unrevealed whether it was ever tested on the real Venus.

EARTH:
CIRCUMFERENCE: 1.0
MASS: 1.0
ORBITAL DISTANCE: 1.0
SURFACE GRAVITY: 1.0
MAJOR MOONS: 1

Earth has been visited by numerous alien races throughout its history, and some of its gods and Eternals left under their own power millennia ago, but it is only in the past century that mankind and its sub-races have began exploring the solar system in earnest. Earth has been threatened by proximity to mobile planets, such as Astros and Ego the Living Planet. Earth itself has one major natural satellite, Luna, but is surrounded by numerous artificial satellites (see Appendix: Satellites). In 1941, the Antons and their traveling planet Torsa briefly took up orbit around Earth, during which time they encountered Electro the Robot. In 1954, the mobile inhabited satellite dubbed "the Inner World" briefly orbited Earth, stealing Earth's water supply until driven off by Namor.

LUNA (EARTH'S MOON):
CIRCUMFERENCE: .3
MASS: .01
SURFACE GRAVITY: .17

Roughly 1 million years ago, the Skrulls established an artificial atmosphere pocket on the surface of Earth's moon and used it to test the Kree race who built a city there; this has become known as the Blue Area of the moon. Earth's Watcher, Uatu, maintains his home in this Blue Area. The angel-like S'raphh race dwelled on the moon millennia ago before committing collective suicide. The Moon's cycles have long affected Earth's werewolves and similar beings. In 1940, Electro the Robot accompanied scientist Simon Crane to the moon and clashed with the spider-like Gnorr who was using the satellite as a base for his robots. In 1950, the alleged goddess Venus accompanied Randy Dover to the moon, where they encountered monstrous "luna-things."

Over the next few years, several aliens claiming to be from the moon visited Earth. In contrast, multiple moon landings by private citizens and secret government factions were also reported, and Dr. Jason Trump's technology temporarily forced the moon out of Earth's orbit in 1959. Ten years later, the first public government-recognized moon landing, the Apollo 11 mission, occurred, landing in the moon's Sea of Tranquility July 20, 1969; the heroic First Line prevented Skrulls and their human agents from interfering with this mission. Years later, the Inhumans moved their city, Attilan, to the Blue Area; it was removed for a period of time but has again returned to the moon's surface. A water-filled tunnel system below Attilan leads to a mysterious chamber (the "Temple of Nightmares") 20 miles beneath the surface; contained within this chamber was a crystal that, when approached by the Inhuman Triton, caused mass hallucinations in everyone within the Blue Area until Triton destroyed the crystal. There also exists a lagoon near Attilan, perhaps connected to these tunnel systems. There are fish-like creatures inhabiting this lagoon, and it is unclear whether they were originally placed there when the Blue Area was created, whether they were brought from Earth and/or genetically engineered by the Inhumans, or whether they have other origins. At least one of these fish was mutated by radioactive waste dumped on the moon by Roxxon Oil Corporation; this mutated fish attacked and was destroyed by the Inhuman Triton. The Red Skull (Johann Shmidt) once had a lunar stronghold, the fate of which is unrevealed. In cooperation with SHIELD, the United Nations maintains a moonbase (Project Starcore) in the Blue Area as well; for a period they kept the Kree Supreme Intelligence confined there. Other Realm's Stargod stored his essence and power in the Godstone and left it on the Earth's moon, where it was later found by astronaut John Jameson whom it transformed into Man-Wolf. The alien Skeletron once attempted to move the moon from its orbit, but was stopped by Earth's heroes. Stark Industries' Moon Tractor was used against the Avengers by the Space Phantom and destroyed in the process, never having actually reached the moon.

COUNTER-EARTH:
CIRCUMFERENCE: 1.0
MASS: 1.0
ORBITAL DISTANCE: 1.0
SURFACE GRAVITY: 1.0
MAJOR MOONS: 1

Earth's High Evolutionary once created an artificial Earth upon which he re-ran Earth's evolution. He placed this "Counter-Earth" in the same orbit as Earth but on precisely the opposite side of the sun. Eventually this Counter-Earth was stolen by the alien Beyonders; years later the so-called Goddess created her short-lived Paradise Omega in that location. Months after that, Dr. Doom transported another artificially created Earth into this same location from the pocket universe in which it had been kept. Though this Counter-Earth has been significantly politically altered from the "true" Earth, it remains in orbit on the other side of the sun from Earth. An apparently unrelated "Counter-Earth" was visited by amateur astronauts in 1951.

MARS:
CIRCUMFERENCE: .5
MASS: .1
ORBITAL DISTANCE: 1.5
SURFACE GRAVITY: .4
MAJOR MOONS: 2

Though it is the most likely candidate for future exploration, Mars currently remains largely unexplored by Earth's governments with the exception of uninhabited probe/explorer vessels; ironically, the planet has reportedly been used as a base for literally dozens of alien races, more than every other planet in the Sol System combined. By some accounts, a golden-skinned race dwelled on Mars 1 billion years ago, eventually diverging into a variety of different races following the collapse of their society. A green-skinned, four-armed race is believed to have colonized Mars at some point; they are also known to have battled Xandarian soldiers. British intelligence allegedly dissected Martians in 1899. In 1937, Clifton Ritton learned the aliens on Mars needed assistance in rebuilding their civilization. Ignored by Earth authorities, Ritton traveled to Mars and manipulated the aliens into attacking Earth two years later, although the invasion was foiled by the Human Torch (Jim Hammond), who arranged for the Martians to receive the assistance they needed. Later that year, self-trained astronaut Zephyr Jones also traveled to Mars, where he encountered a race of "Birdmen" at war with the "Parrotmen" of Sunev. In 1948, more so-called Martians invaded Earth when an insane scientist attempted to force the two planets together, but the invasion was prevented by Captain America (Jeff Mace). Six years later, the Torch repelled an invasion by Martian robots. In 1961 the Soviet government's plan to build a Mars base was sabotaged when someone lured the monstrous Grogg into their spaceship at launch. In 1962, Russians launched their Super Weapon into Mars orbit, but it turned against their programming and vowed to destroy any nation that terrorized or invaded another nation; the Super Weapon's ultimate fate is unrevealed, but it is no longer active. One invasion from Mars-based aliens was prevented when Millie the Model befriended the female Martian who convinced her partner to call off their plans. Peter Quill (later Star-Lord) was passed up for a Mars probe mission, the fate of which is unrevealed. Captain Mar-Vell buried his lover, Una, on a satellite orbiting Mars. Several superhumans have visited Mars, of course, and Quasar briefly used Mars as an unofficial prison planet, abandoning the Blood Brothers there for a time. The alien Garthan Saal (aka Nova Omega) once placed a number of Xandarian surveillance spheres near Mars to monitor Earth for the Nova Corps. The alien Aakon launched their "Deathstorm" attack from Ram's Head, an artificial satellite orbiting Mars. The Brood intercepted NASA's Mars Lander and used it to infiltrate the space station Simulacra. SHIELD's Howling Commandos' Warwolf (Vic Marcus)'s transformations are governed by the rotation of the planet Mars, rather than the Moon. The space pirate Nebula once assembled a mercenary army on the Martian moon Phobos. An international effort to build a Mars station has recently began.

In addition, there are numerous accounts of "Martians" on Earth, and it remains unconfirmed whether all of these aliens had truly colonized Mars, whether the aliens lied, or whether they were referred to as Martians as a euphemism for alien invaders. Supposed Martian activity on Earth consists of far too many incidents to fully discuss here, but several accounts of interest are included. According to some sources, a human-like race lived on Mars at some point. Other sources report that Martians bred mastodons and elephants on Earth since Mars could not support much in the way of animal life. In 1953, alleged Martian Bor-Ronggl fled a civil war on his world and arrived on Earth where he was amused to learn that such strife existed on other worlds as well. In 1954, an alleged Martian was altered surgically and brainwashed to pose as a human; as Mark Garlon, he went insane upon being unable to find records of his existence and was institutionalized where he disintegrated. In 1959, USA intelligence agent Dan Hardley ordered a missile strike against and drove off an alien ship under the mistaken belief that it was part of a plot of Communists posing as Martians that he had exposed earlier. Also in 1959, miserly and abusive Hollywood director Darius Wolfe was abducted by alleged Martians while filming a science fiction Mars invasion movie. In that same year, an alleged Martian landed on Earth, and posed as private investigator Michel Garner who debunked Professor Gary Webb's story of having seen a UFO land. In 1960, an alleged Martian invader was fought off by an alleged Venusian. Zetora, another alleged Martian fled to Earth in 1960 to escape police after committing a crime on his native world; intending to conquer Earth in hopes of earning a pardon, Zetora instead died from a simple bacterial infection to which he lacked resistance. Also in 1960, another alleged Martian, Ogor, was captured by Zeno, part of Ogor's race's enemies, a race allegedly associated with Jupiter. In that same year, alleged Martian ships landed on Earth and unsuccessfully attempted to communicate with people; the people did not realize the uninhabited ships were the aliens themselves, and the aliens returned to their homeworld. Additionally, an alleged Martian ship hid out in a space exhibit, capturing criminal Sammy Snork when he hid in the ship and bringing him back to its homeworld where he was placed in a zoo. In 1961, a pair of alleged Martians captured human Horace "The Joker" Wallace and placed him in there zoo. Also in 1961, Robot X exposed a group of alleged Martians employed with Cleveland's Daily Clarion newspaper. In that same year, Vandoom's monster drove off alleged Martian invaders. In 1962, an alleged Martian transported buildings to his world to study their inhabitants in preparation for an invasion, but he abandoned the mission after humans discovered his race's weakness to bright light. Also in 1962, an alleged Martian convinced a newspaper editor to fund his advanced mechanics demonstration, and he built a rocket with which he returned to his homeworld. In that same year, Russians who had posed as Martians to terrorize a small US town were abducted by alleged Martians and taken to their world; believing the hoax would alert humanity to their existence, the aliens cancelled their intended Earth invasion. It remains unrevealed whether the Martians Masters colonists, known to have assaulted Earth-691 in 1901 and then to have conquered it in 2001, ever dwelled on Mars and/or invaded Earth in Reality-616.

ASTEROID BELT:
ORBITAL DISTANCE: 2.7 (average)

The Silver Surfer has been told that hundreds of millions of years ago a sister planet to Mars, Tiamat, was destroyed; if true, the asteroid belt may be Tiamat's remains. Composed of uncountable small rocks, the largest asteroid is Ceres and only three others, Hygiea, Pallas, and Vesta are of appreciable size. 200 years ago a battle between the alien Rajaki and the android Ultimo in the asteroid belt resulted in both combatants crashing to Earth. In the current decade, the Avengers have constructed a manned deep space monitoring station within the asteroid belt, which serves as both a scientific station and an early alert system designed to detect approaching aliens. A very small number of the asteroids are long-since failed stasis modules containing the corpses of members of the Spinsterhood.

JUPITER:
CIRCUMFERENCE: 11.2
MASS: 317.8
ORBITAL DISTANCE: 5.2
SURFACE GRAVITY: 2.3
MAJOR MOONS: 63

Jupiter is the solar system's largest gas giant and thus extremely inhospitable to most Earthlike species; most known human and alien activity near Jupiter has occurred on its many moons. In 1956, aliens based on Ganymede, one of those moons, invaded Earth but were easily driven off. Stark International once built a Jupiter Landing Vehicle designed to investigate Jupiter's hypothetical core, but the vehicle was only used on Earth. The alien Spinsterhood possessed a base within one of Jupiter's smaller moons, and that organization's Ganymede and Persephone both trained there; Ganymede and Jack of Hearts spent time there in recent years. Similarly, the alien Qwrlln possessed a base on Jupiter's moon Ganymede from which they once rescued and restored Alpha Flight's Guardian (James Hudson). An interdimensional wormhole exists not far from Jupiter, but its presence is apparently unknown to mankind as of yet. Spragg the Living Hill once accidentally traveled through this wormhole and harvested rocks from Jupiter's ring to rebuild himself, as well as to form an army of "Stone Clones" to aid him. The alien Goom came from a world termed "Planet X," an enormous planet reportedly within our solar system but located just past Jupiter; as the presence of such a hidden planet is virtually scientifically impossible, it seems likely that Planet X might lie on the other side of Jupiter's wormhole. Spores reputed to be originally from Jupiter once briefly mutated astronaut John Jameson; however, it is unclear if these spores truly originated from Jupiter, came through the wormhole, or have some other origin entirely. Bat-like humanoid aliens (the "Scavengers") possibly from another world came to be trapped on Jupiter or one of its moons, and they created a pool that gave off unusual energy in order to survive the planet's harsh environment; the energy from the pool emitted unidentified radiation that eventually blanketed the Earth and caused temporary madness; the android Human Torch traveled to Jupiter to stop the source of the strange rays, slew the Scavengers and their leader, Kleevar, and destroyed the pool. In 1960, Zeno (allegedly part of a race associated with Jupiter) posed as a human scientist and captured Ogor, an alleged Martian, Zeno's race's enemies. The Collector possessed a pet "Jupiterian Sauro-Beast." The Autocron Ten-For was detonated in Jupiter's orbit, destroying the approaching Autocron fleet intended to invade Earth.

SATURN:
CIRCUMFERENCE: 9.4
MASS: 95.2
ORBITAL DISTANCE: 9.5
SURFACE GRAVITY: 1.2
MAJOR MOONS: 60

Prior to the rise of man, the surface of the gas giant Saturn was inhabited by powerful aliens; the Great Old One Tsathoggua lived among these for some years before traveling to Earth. As with Jupiter, however, most interactions by humans or aliens near Saturn have taken place on its moons. The Kronans, or "Stone Men from Saturn" briefly established a base on the moon Iapetus, but these Kronans actually originated on the planet Ria, in the Krona System. Genis-Vell once created a base for himself on the moon Hyperion. Some of Earth's Eternals, exiled from their homes millennia ago, crashed on the moon Titan and fought a war amongst themselves there. The few survivors eventually built a homeland deep inside Titan. While one of their children, Thanos, eventually killed most of Titan's residents, the artificial world inside still exists, controlled by the computer system ISAAC and inhabited by the repopulated Titanian Eternals. On the surface of Titan rests the grave of, and a monument to, Captain Mar-Vell, as well as a more recent monument to his son Genis-Vell. Reed & Sue Richards enjoyed a second honeymoon on Titan. The R'Zahnian race had a base on one of Saturn's moons; Zamu of R'Zahn attempted to become a US governor to use his influence to help his race invade Earth before being foiled by Dr. Druid.

URANUS:
CIRCUMFERENCE: 4.0
MASS: 14.5
ORBITAL DISTANCE: 19.2
SURFACE GRAVITY: 1.2
MAJOR MOONS: 27

Prior to discovering Titan, the exiled Eternals had discovered an abandoned Kree outpost on Uranus and settled there. While a small group were separated during the settlement process and found themselves trapped on Titan, the others remained on Uranus, where they built themselves a home. They made contact with sentient hive-minded Uranians living within the planet's core, and these native Uranians forbade the exiled Eternals from leaving Uranus. Human Horace Grayson eventually made contact with the Eternals and his son, Robert, was given some of their technology and became Marvel Boy; however, this inspired the Eternals to try to leave Uranus and the native Uranians destroyed them. Their ruined homes remain on the Uranian surface. It is unclear whether Groff, a Uranian who transported human convict Joe Morgan from 1962 to Uranus' future, hails from the future of Reality-616 or from an alternate reality. Another race of alleged "Uranusians" is composed of wood and sent spies to Earth in 1962 in the form of a ventriloquist and his dummy. The planet Satania was described as nearby Uranus, but the proximity may have been via space or dimensional warp.

NEPTUNE:
CIRCUMFERENCE: 3.9
MASS: 17.2
ORBITAL DISTANCE: 30.1
SURFACE GRAVITY: 1.2
MAJOR MOONS: 13

The furthest planet from the sun, Neptune has remained mostly free of human or known alien involvement. In early 1956, author Victor Wyatt, having sold his science fiction novel "An Earthling on Neptune" the previous year, allegedly learned his publishers were Neptunians; admired for his "true-to-life" depiction of Neptune, Wyatt supposedly embarked on an outer space book tour. Per that same source, months later, Neptune's plan to colonize Earth was discarded when surveillance of a science fiction film's production erroneously convinced Neptune Earth's technology would easily defeat Neptune's. Terminus' lance was launched into Neptune's vicinity by Quasar (Wendell Vaughn); Terminus later recovered it.

OTHER BODIES:

Comets are naturally occurring balls of rock and ice that circle the sun in eccentric orbits. At least one comet, known on Earth as Halley's comet, is known to be artificial and contains an alien ship, piloted by a deranged Fortisquian, Max, who is observing Earth for his race. The hero Comet also received his powers from something resembling a gaseous comet; what this truly was is unclear. Garsen's Comet orbits the solar system every 3115 years; during its approach in 1955, a tribe of giants in the Amazon returned to life to witness its arrival. The ship of the Marvel Boy duplicate known as the Crusader passed through the tail of the comet Kohoutek as he was attempting to travel to Earth, sending him into suspended animation for years. Iron Man (Tony Stark) prevented the Stuart-Barnes 2 Comet from striking Earth.

Dwarf planets are small spherical bodies of insufficient size to be considered planets. Ceres, in the asteroid belt, is the only one of these in the inner solar system; outside the system's eight planets are the largest dwarf planets, Eris, and the dual dwarfs Pluto and Charon; Pluto has been used as a base by, among others, General Phoonga, whose invasion fleet was driven from Earth in 1953, and by the Fatalists, whose efforts were foiled by Namor a year later. In 1956, an alleged Plutonian scientist came to Earth, and posed as elderly human inventor Professor Charles Perkins, and used his Space Diminisher to transport conman Adam J. Stokes to his homeworld to prove to his native colleagues that his device worked. In 1961, a race claiming to be from Pluto used TV transmissions to mesmerize humans but after the mesmerization faded when the people's TV antennae was disconnected, the plot was abandoned. Dr. Doom designed a Pluto Probe to research the mysteries of space; this was among Doom's technology shown to the US secretary of state to convince him to form a nonaggression treaty between the US and Latveria, but it is not known if it was ever launched into space. It has been speculated that the planet Yag "on the edge of the universe" refers to Pluto, but Yag's description as a green, living planet seems to contradict this.

ACTIVE SATELLITES (ARTIFICIAL SATELLITES ORBITING EARTH)

CORDCO SATELLITE Hijacked by Dr. Octopus and his Sinister Six and used to threaten the world with an alleged deadly poison unless Dr. Octopus was given world domination. In reality, it was used to disperse a chemical rendering cocaine addicts dependant on the newly discovered rare element Burundite, which was in the sole possession of Dr. Octopus. Thor helped Spider-Man negate the effects of the chemical by dispersing burundite into the atmosphere after the Six's defeat. Amazing Spider-Man #338 (1990)

DEVASTATOR'S SATELLITE Broadcasts microwave energy to Devastator's armor. Incredible Hulk #186 (1975)

DYNAMO SPUTNIK Created by Anton Vanko, powers the Crimson Dynamo Mark II from space. Crimson Dynamo #5 (2004)

EVE NASA space station contacted by the Master of the Sun who selected astronaut Greg Harrelson to become the Star-Lord, but discharged astronaut Peter Quill returned to the station, forcibly replacing Harrelson in the transport chamber, and became Star-Lord in his stead. Marvel Preview #4 (1976)

HIGH EVOLUTIONARY'S SPACE STATION Used in plot to remove mutant powers. Uncanny X-Men 1999 Annual (1999)

HYDRA SATELLITE Sought by Sinister Six to commandeer its weapon cache. Spider-Man #22 (1992)

LAGRANGE POINT 1 Used by Reed Richards in investigating the Odotopian messenger device. Fantastic Four #547 (2007)

MAGNETO PROTOCOLS Series of over two dozen satellites equipped by Forge with electromagnetic generators to bar Magneto from entering Earth's atmosphere; later usurped by the Thunderbolts. X-Men #25 (1993)

MARS 2010 SPACE STATION Training (and possibly experimentation/mutation) site for Bush Rangers who took over the station before dying in battle with X-Force (later X-Statix). X-Force #125 (2002)

MANDARIN'S KILLER SATELLITE Orbital weapon used by Mandarin against Iron Man (Tony Stark). Tales of Suspense #61 (1965)

MYS-TECH'S SATELLITE Used to incite violence on Earth. Dark Angel #7 (1993)

OMNIVAC Sentient station commanded by the Leader, programming disabled by Jackdaw. Incredible Hulk #157 (1972)

SAMAROBRYN Built by the Hate-Monger (Adolf Hitler clone), later used by Egghead and Weathermen, now utilized for scientific research. Nick Fury, Agent of SHIELD #10 (1969); (as Samarobryn) Avengers #210 (1981)

SIMULACRA NASA station commandeered by the Brood. X-Men/Fantastic Four #1 (2005)

SOLAR MIRROR Used by GRAMPA to destroy vampires on Earth. Amazing Fantasy #15 (2006)

SPACE STATION 8 NASA station, post of Gazer. X-Men #169 (2005)

STARCORE STATION Current solar orbit Starcore research base headed by Dr. Peter Corbeau. X-Men Unlimited #13 (1996)

STARK ENTERPRISES COMMUNICATION SATELLITE Attacked by Titanium Man but defended by Iron Man, suffered only slight damages. Iron Man #49 (2002)

INACTIVE SATELLITES

AIM SATELLITE Abandoned and forgotten after one of many setbacks at the hands of Earth's heroes, taken over by Baron (Helmut) Zemo, reshaped by robotic Techno, destroyed in battle with Avengers. Thunderbolts #11 (1998)

AIM SPACE PLATFORM Commanded by MODOK, destroyed by the Avengers. She-Hulk #1 (2004)

ALEXANDRIA Space station commanded by Noah and destroyed (or shunted into the Negative Zone) when Noah and his assistant Jedediah used it to shunt anti-matter away from Earth to oppose efforts of Gideon Trust. Fantastic Four #37 (2001)

ASTEROID M Early base of Magneto and Brotherhood of Evil Mutants, repeatedly rebuilt, finally destroyed by Fabian Cortez. X-Men #4 (1964)

AVALON Formerly Cable's station Graymalkin, co-opted by the Acolytes, destroyed by Holocaust, remnants became Prosh and Providence island. X-Force #8 (1992)

DAMOCLES Sword-shaped command base of Kang, brought from Earth-6311, destroyed by Avengers. Avengers #41 (2001)

DEATH RAY Orbiting solar projector used by Zemo imposter (Franz Gruber), controls destroyed by Sharon Carter, later sought by Taskmaster, destroyed by SHIELD. Tales of Suspense #97 (1968)

DEATH'S HEAD SATELLITE Designed by Red Skull (Johann Shmidt) and Hate-Monger

(Adolf Hitler clone) to broadcast hate-ray energy, destroyed by Captain America. Captain America #226 (1978)

DR. DEMONICUS' SATELLITE Designed by Axon-Karr, removed from orbit by Shogun Warriors. Shogun Warriors #7 (1979)

DRYDOCK Earth-691 space station commanded by Guardians of the Galaxy, briefly lay in orbit of Earth-616. Marvel Presents #12 (1977)

EGGHEAD'S NASA SPACE-LAB Stolen from Cape Canaveral by Egghead. Defenders #43 (1976)

FARAWAY Experimental satellite with sub-space engine used by Black Air who installed Archimedes Fogg's computerized brain into it. Disappeared midway through its journey to the far reaches of the galaxy, crashed in Genosha two years later. Wisdom and X-Force retrieved Fogg's computerized brain and put into a LMD-variant cyborg body. X-Force #94 (1999)

FAUST (FULLY AUTOMATED UNIT OF STRUCTURE TECHNOLOGY) Secondary-Adamantium-coated factory turned orbital weapons platform, destroyed by Thor and Iron Man. Marvel Team-Up #18 (1974)

FOREIGNER'S SATELLITE Transmitted power to Foreigner; Justin Hammer caused the satellite to fall from orbit to land on Foreigner, who escaped the crash. Spectacular Spider-Man #210 (1994)

FU MANCHU'S SPACE STATION Designed to destroy the moon, cast adrift in space. Master of Kung Fu #49 (1977)

GODSEYE Sentient SHIELD satellite designed to detonate nuclear weapons, destroyed by the Hulk (Bruce Banner). Incredible Hulk #89 (2006)

HAMMER STATION Designed by Justin Hammer as a hideaway; station damaged by Iron Man (Stark). Iron Man: Bad Blood #1 (2000)

JERRY OWENS' SATELLITE Orbited Earth for 50 years with Owens aboard. Uncanny Tales #48 (1956)

KARZZ THE CONQUEROR'S STORM SATELLITE Used to initiate series of 500 mph winds across the planet, Karzz forced to reverse effects by Avengers, satellite presumed destroyed. Avengers Battle the Earth Wrecker (1967)

KOONTZ SATELLITE US government research station, designed space-worthy creature to destroy enemy satellites, but it slew the entire crew and entered the Stark Satellite One where Iron Man destroyed it by restoring life support and reactivating the bacilli. Iron Man #237 (1988)

MANDARIN'S SPACE STATION Used to construct hate-ray, destroyed by Avengers. Avengers Annual #1 (1967)

MASTER MOLD'S ASTEROID BASE Mutant holding facilities, destroyed by the Hulk (Bruce Banner). Incredible Hulk Annual #7 (1978)

MORELLE SATELLITE Boarded by Nightwatch, who fought the Camouflage Cadre and Warbringer there. Nightwatch #9 (1994)

MYS-TECH BOARD'S PRIVATE SPACE STATION Locked into geo-stationary orbit above Britain and constructed by the Psycho-Warriors, used to monitor the Earth. Overkill #23 (1993)

NUCLEAR WEATHER CONTROL STATION Experimental; prevented from becoming operative by Hulk, Namor the Sub-Mariner, and Silver Surfer (Sub-Mariner #34-35, 1970)

ORACLE WEATHER SATELLITE Felled by an Anomaly Gem fragment. Marvel Comics Presents #125 (1993)

ORBITAL LASER BOMB Built by Dr. Doom, able to destroy continents. Super-Villain Team-Up #6 (1976)

OTOMOCORP SPACE STATION Orbital base of Takashei Otomo, destroyed by Mys-Tech. Gene Dogs #4 (1994)

PEAK, THE Space station headquarters of SWORD, destroyed by the Skrulls. Astonishing X-Men #13 (2006)

RED SKULL'S HYPNO-RAY SATELLITE Damaged by Shroud. Super-Villain Team-Up #11 (1977)

SATELLITE OF DEATH Used by Dr. Doom to destroy Earth's ozone layer, self-destructed by Dr. Doom. Solarman #2 (1990)

SHIELD ORBITAL PLATFORM Earliest known use during Kree-Skrull War, briefly conquered by Steven Lang and invaded by extradimensional Other Realm's Gorjoon, Garth, and Lambert, destroyed by the Deltite's followers. Avengers #96 (1972)

SHIELD SATELLITE Intended for use in safe handling of the dangerous Element X, contained massive stone walls, ended up serving as prison for Grey Gargoyle, later blasted out of the sky by AIM to recover the Gargoyle. Captain America #142 (1971)

SILVERMOON Designed by Harlan Silverbird to project anti-metal radiation from orbit, destroyed by Moon Knight. Marc Spector: Moon Knight #51 (1993)

SKULL SATELLITE Small skull-shaped space station armed with destructive weaponry, built by the Red Skull and used to blackmail the USA into turning the country over to him, attacked an unidentified US city when American military attacked it, destroyed by Captain America. Captain America Bubble Gum Funnies #3 (1981)

STANE SATELLITE Radioactive, crashed by Radioactive Man to monitor its effects on populace. Iron Man #234 (1988)

STAR WELL I Radiation-storing project by Roxxon Oil, commanded by Sunturion, destroyed by Roxxon. Iron Man #142 (1981)

STARCORE ONE First Starcore Project research base, moved to solar orbit and destroyed by a Shi'ar wormhole. Incredible Hulk #148 (1972)

STARCORE STATION Incorporated temporal weapons designed by Tony Stark for Immortus, destroyed by War Machine (James Rhodes). Force Works #20 (1996)

STARK INTERNATIONAL RESEARCH SATELLITES Iron Man: Legacy of Doom #1 (2008)

STARK SATELLITE One Research space station built by Stark Enterprises, abandoned after Omega bacilli released aboard by AIM, later damaged when Iron Man battled government-designed satellite-killing creature from Koontz satellite there, cleaned and leased to Cauwfield Multichemical, destroyed by Technovore. Iron Man #207 (1986)

TARGO CORP SATELLITE AIM duped Iron Man into placing their front company's satellite. Housed the Orbiting Lens, designed by Yorgon Tykkio to fire a precisely controlled and immensely powerful laser. Used by Valdemar Tykkio to slay residents of Boca Caliente, facilitating AIM's acquisition of the island. Iron Man destroyed the satellite and Orbiting Lens after Yorgon usurped control and targeted Washington DC. Iron Man #207 (1986)

VIBRO-BOMB SATELLITE Space weapon created by Dr. Doom, destroyed by Darkoth. Fantastic Four #143 (1974)

WEAPON PLUS SPACE STATION Facility where Weapon XV was designed, destroyed by Wolverine. New X-Men #144 (2003)

XERO Sentient satellite designed by Dr. Able Stack, destroyed by Machine Man. X-51 #3 (1999)

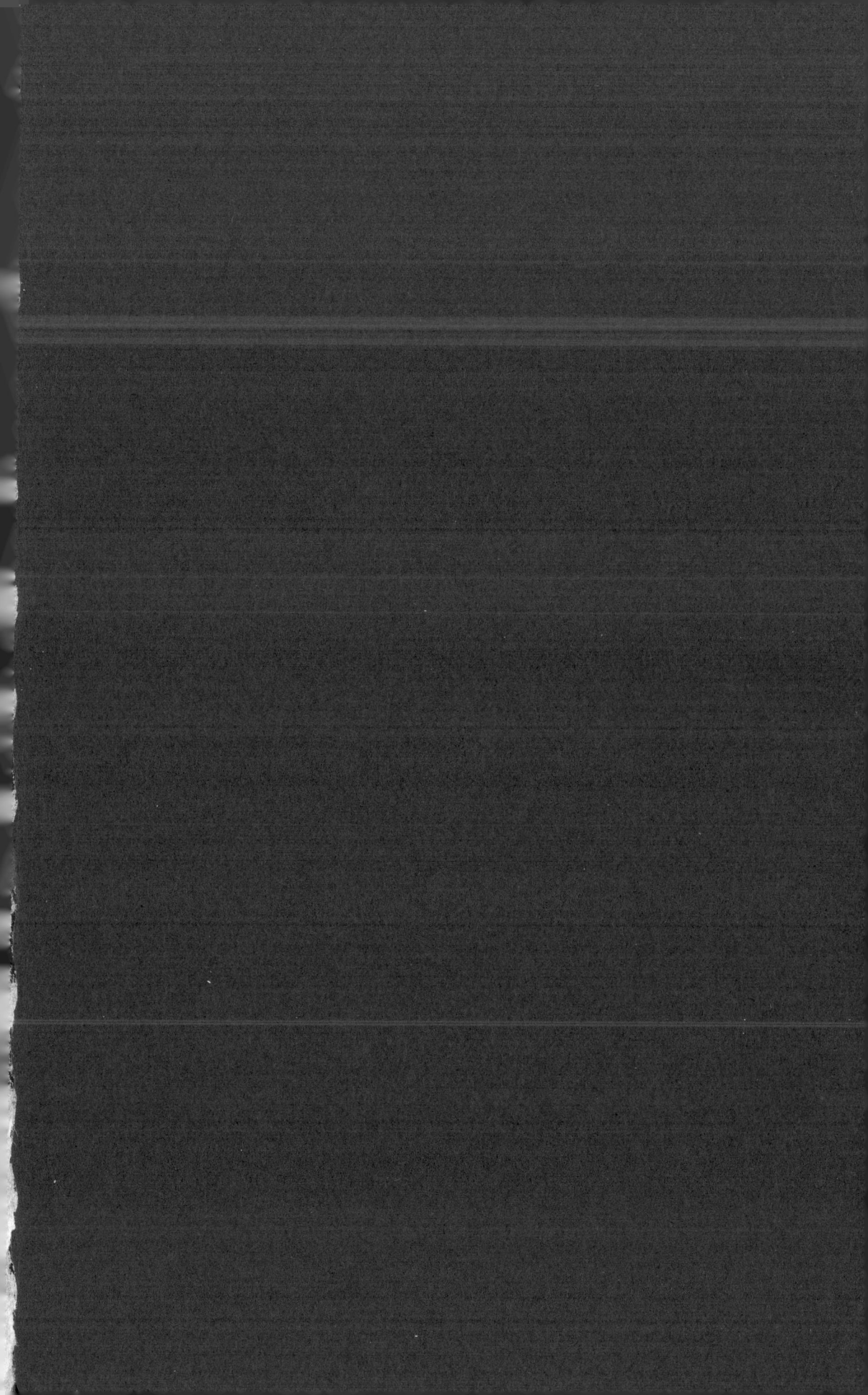